The Institute of Chartered Accountants in England and Wales

CERTIFICATE IN INSOLVENCY

Study Manual

ICAEW Certificate in Insolvency

Seventh edition January 2016
First edition April 2010

ISBN: 9781 4727 4003 8
Previous ISBN: 9781 4727 2640 7

British Library Cataloguing-in-Publication Data
A catalogue record for this book is available from the British Library

Published by

BPP Learning Media Ltd
BPP House, Aldine Place
142–144 Uxbridge Road
London W12 8AA

www.bpp.com/learningmedia

Printed in the United Kingdom by

Ricoh UK Limited
Unit 2
Wells Place
Merstham
RH1 3LG

Your learning materials, published by BPP Learning Media Ltd, are printed on paper obtained from traceable sustainable sources.

All rights reserved. No part of this publication may be reproduced, stored in a retrieval system or transmitted in any form or by any means, electronic, mechanical, photocopying, recording or otherwise, without the prior written permission of BPP Learning Media.

The contents of this book are intended as a guide and not professional advice. Although every effort has been made to ensure that the contents of this book are correct at the time of going to press, BPP Learning Media makes no warranty that the information in this book is accurate or complete and accept no liability for any loss or damage suffered by any person acting or refraining from acting as a result of the material in this book.

We are grateful to the Insolvency Practitioners Association for permission to reproduce past examination questions.

©
BPP Learning Media Ltd
2016

A note about copyright

Dear Customer

What does the little © mean and why does it matter?

Your market-leading BPP books, course materials and e-learning materials do not write and update themselves. People write them: on their own behalf or as employees of an organisation that invests in this activity. Copyright law protects their livelihoods. It does so by creating rights over the use of the content.

Breach of copyright is a form of theft – as well as being a criminal offence in some jurisdictions, it is potentially a serious breach of professional ethics.

With current technology, things might seem a bit hazy but, basically, without the express permission of BPP Learning Media:

- Photocopying our materials is a breach of copyright

- Scanning, ripcasting or conversion of our digital materials into different file formats, uploading them to facebook or emailing them to your friends is a breach of copyright

You can, of course, sell your books, in the form in which you have bought them – once you have finished with them. (Is this fair to your fellow students? We update for a reason.) But the e-products are sold on a single user licence basis: we do not supply 'unlock' codes to people who have bought them second-hand.

And what about outside the UK? BPP Learning Media strives to make our materials available at prices students can afford by local printing arrangements, pricing policies and partnerships which are clearly listed on our website. A tiny minority ignore this and indulge in criminal activity by illegally photocopying our material or supporting organisations that do. If they act illegally and unethically in one area, can you really trust them?

Contents

•	Introduction	v
•	Syllabus and learning outcomes	vii

SECTION A : The legal and regulatory framework for insolvency

1	The legal and regulatory framework	3
2	Business turnaround and restructuring	15
3	The Insolvency Practitioner: key professional issues	27
4	Key ethical issues	49
5	Insolvency computations	65
6	Position of directors in insolvency situations	91

SECTION B: Corporate insolvency

7	Voluntary liquidation	107
8	Compulsory liquidation	123
9	Liquidators' investigations and antecedent transactions	139
10	Asset protection regime in liquidation	153
11	Proofs of debt in liquidation	167
12	Vacation of office	185
13	Company Voluntary Arrangements	195
14	Introduction to administrations	215
15	Procedure for administration	227
16	Implementation of administration	245
17	Introduction to receivership	265
18	Effect of administrative receivership and duties of receivers	275
19	Administrative receivership: practical aspects and closure	293

SECTION C: Personal insolvency

20	Bankruptcy	315
21	Post bankruptcy order procedure	337
22	Meetings of creditors	355
23	Bankruptcy estate	369
24	Bankrupt's home	385
25	Powers of the trustee	401
26	Proofs of debt	417
27	Discharge and annulment	431
28	Vacation of office	441
29	Individual voluntary arrangements	451
30	Voluntary arrangement procedures	477
31	Post approval matters	495
32	Insolvent partnerships	507
33	Administration of the estates of deceased insolvents	525

•	Index	533

Introduction

This is the seventh edition of BPP Learning Media's Study Manual for the ICAEW Certificate in Insolvency.

Features include:

- Full syllabus coverage
- Fully up-to-date reflecting changes introduced in March to October 2015
- A user-friendly style for easy navigation
- Chapter introductions to put the topic into context and explain its significance for the assessment.
- Section overviews and chapter summaries
- Self test questions and answers

As well as this Study Manual, BPP Learning Media publishes a suite of additional products for the ICAEW assessment, including:

- Question Bank
- Distance Learning Programme

ICAEW Certificate of Insolvency

The syllabus covers all types of insolvency in England and Wales.

The detailed syllabus is set out below.

Module aim

To ensure that students have a good grounding in the fundamentals of insolvency work to enable them to work effectively in an insolvency at a junior level and to provide a basis for further qualifications in this area.

On completion of this module, students will be able to:

- Understand the legal and regulatory environment within which insolvency practitioners work in England and Wales

- Understand the basic principles of the work of an insolvency practitioner and appreciate the impact of an insolvency appointment on the affected parties

- Understand the detailed characteristics of the full range of insolvency possibilities open to individuals

- Understand the detailed characteristics of the full range of types of corporate insolvency

Specification grid

This grid shows the relative weightings of subjects within this module and should guide the relative study time spent on each. Over time the marks available in the assessment will equate to the weightings below, while slight variations may occur in individual assessments to enable suitable questions to be set.

	Weighting (%)
The legal and regulatory framework for insolvency	15
Concepts and principles of insolvency	25
Personal insolvency	20
Corporate insolvency	40
	100

Syllabus and learning outcomes

1 The legal and regulatory framework for insolvency

Candidates will be able to describe the legal and regulatory environment within which insolvency practitioners work.

In the assessment, candidates may be required to:

(a) Explain briefly the provisions of the laws and other rules relevant to insolvency, their purposes and the interactions between them:

   (i) Insolvency Act 1986 as amended
   (ii) Insolvency Act 2000
   (iii) Insolvency Rules 1986 as amended
   (iv) Deregulation Act 2015
   (v) Small Business Enterprise and Education Act 2015
   (vi) Company Directors Disqualification Act 1986
   (vii) Enterprise Act 2002
   (viii) Law of Property Act 1925
   (ix) Part 26 Companies Act 2006

(b) Describe the role of the courts in insolvency

(c) Describe the impact of EU regulation and cross-border issues upon the work of the insolvency practitioner

(d) Describe the membership and the role of the Joint Insolvency Committee

(e) Explain the purpose and contents of the Statements of Insolvency Practice (SIPs)

(f) State the names of the Recognised Professional Bodies relating to insolvency in England and Wales and how and by whom they become recognised

(g) State and describe the qualification and licensing requirements of a licensed insolvency practitioner

(h) State the key ethical and professional issues for an insolvency practitioner undertaking insolvency work and explain the reasons for the existence of ethical and professional rules relating to the undertaking of insolvency work

(i) State which government departments require information and returns from those undertaking insolvency work, and the nature of the information required

2 Concepts and principles of insolvency

Candidates will be able to explain the fundamentals of the work of an insolvency practitioner and describe the impact of an insolvency appointment on the affected parties.

In the assessment, candidates may be required to:

(a) Define insolvency according to the definitions in the Insolvency Act 1986 (s123, s268 and s272) and explain the meaning of these definitions

(b) Explain the effect of an unchallenged statutory demand

(c) State the different types of insolvency that can be entered into and their purposes, and describe the characteristics of each type

(d) Describe and explain the roles of the following in the different types of insolvency:

   (i) The insolvency practitioner
   (ii) The Official Receiver
   (iii) The Law of Property Act receiver
   (iv) The Insolvency Service

(e) In a given scenario, select the appropriate form of insolvency and give reasons for the selection

The insolvency practitioner

(a) Explain the distinctions between an insolvency practitioner and other business professionals

(b) Describe the processes involved in appointing an insolvency practitioner in an insolvency

(c) Explain the actions to be taken by the insolvency practitioner immediately on appointment, in a given scenario

(d) Explain the powers, rights and ongoing obligations of an insolvency practitioner in an insolvency

(e) Describe the processes involved in concluding an insolvency

Impact of insolvency on affected parties

(a) Describe the impact of an insolvency upon employees, creditors and other affected parties in a given scenario, with reference to:

   (i) Employment law, Employment Rights Act and the Transfer of Undertakings (Protection of Employment) Regulations (TUPE)

   (ii) The Sale of Goods Act 1979

   (iii) The Landlord and Tenant Acts

(b) Define 'retention of title' and explain how it can affect an insolvency and the parties affected by the insolvency

Assets and transactions

(a) State the classes of assets that arise in insolvencies and describe the characteristics of each

(b) Calculate the value of individual assets or a group of assets in an insolvency, using information given, and explain how the value is arrived at

(c) State the general procedures to be taken in investigation and asset recovery

(d) Explain the purpose of bonding and how the amount of the bond is calculated in an insolvency

(e) Define security and quasi-security and explain the effect of fixed and floating charges

(f) Explain the antecedent transaction rules and identify such transactions from information given

Statement of affairs, other reports and estate accounting

(a) Calculate figures to be included in the

   (i) Statement of affairs
   (ii) Estimated outcome statement
   (iii) Deficiency account
   (iv) Receipts and payments account

   (including the quantum of the bond, dividends and distributions, insolvency practitioner remuneration and other fees) in a given scenario and using information given, taking account of:

   - The order of application of assets
   - Priority
   - The prescribed part

(b) Explain the circumstances when estate accounting and the insolvency service account (ISA) would be used by the insolvency practitioner

3 Personal insolvency

Candidates will be able to describe and explain the detailed characteristics of the full range of insolvency possibilities open to individuals

In the assessment, candidates may be required to:

General concepts for personal insolvency

(a) Compare the characteristics of the different types of personal insolvency, including statutory and non-statutory types

(b) State the classes of creditors and their rights in personal insolvency

(c) Describe who controls the progress of a personal insolvency and how this is achieved

(d) Describe the powers, rights and duties of the insolvency practitioner in a personal insolvency

Individual voluntary arrangements (IVAs)

(a) Describe the processes undergone in the creation of an individual voluntary arrangement

(b) State the contents of the IVA proposal and explain how the contents are prepared

(c) Describe the processes undergone in order to obtain an interim order

(d) Describe the ongoing obligations upon the insolvency practitioner in an IVA with regard to

   (i) Meetings
   (ii) Record keeping
   (iii) Reporting
   (vi) Time limits
   (v) Creditors

(e) State the criteria for completion of an IVA and describe the processes of completion

(f) Describe the characteristics of a trading IVA and a consumer IVA, and compare the two types of arrangement

(g) Explain the role of the insolvency practitioner as nominee and supervisor in an IVA

(h) Describe the obligations of debtors in an IVA and explain the effects of the default of a debtor

(i) Describe the circumstances that might bring about a failure of the arrangement, the impact that the failure has upon parties related to the arrangement and the procedures that should be followed by the insolvency practitioner on the failure of the arrangement

Insolvent partnerships

(a) Describe briefly the characteristics of a partnership voluntary arrangement

(b) Describe the processes undergone in the creation of a partnership voluntary arrangement and compare these with the processes followed in the creation of an IVA

(c) State the other types of partnership insolvency

Bankruptcy

(a) Explain the processes involved in the creation of a bankruptcy order, including the grounds for debtors' and creditors' bankruptcy petitions

(b) State the effects of the bankruptcy order

(c) State the roles of the trustee in bankruptcy and the Official Receiver

(d) State the position of creditors in bankruptcy and the role of the creditors' committee

Introduction

(e) Describe the consequences of bankruptcy for the bankrupt, including

  (i) Impact on employment or business
  (ii) Income payments agreements and orders
  (iii) Bankruptcy restrictions orders
  (iv) Bankruptcy offences
  (v) The bankrupt's estate
  (vi) Impact on the bankrupt's (and family's) right to occupy the family home
  (vii) Antecedent recoveries

(f) Describe the ongoing obligations upon the insolvency practitioner in a bankruptcy with regard to

  (i) Meetings
  (ii) Record keeping
  (iii) Reporting
  (iv) Time limits

(g) Describe the grounds for annulment of the bankruptcy order and the processes involved in annulment

(h) Describe the processes involved in discharge from bankruptcy

(i) Describe the reasons for suspension of discharge and the processes involved in suspension

Other solutions to personal insolvency problems

(a) Describe the characteristics of statutory solutions:

  (i) Debt relief orders
  (ii) County Court administration orders

(b) Describe the characteristics of non-statutory solutions:

  (i) Informal arrangements with creditors
  (ii) Debt management plans, including consolidation and re-scheduling
  (iii) Mortgage and re-mortgage

4 Corporate insolvency

Candidates will be able to describe and explain the detailed characteristics of the full range of types of corporate insolvency.

In the assessment, candidates may be required to:

General concepts for corporate insolvency

(a) Compare the characteristics of the different types of corporate insolvency and explain the difference between solvent and insolvent liquidations

(b) Explain the following aspects of corporate insolvency, their origins, characteristics and effects:

  (i) The winding-up resolution
  (ii) The role of the liquidator
  (iii) Enforcing co-operation
  (iv) Antecedent recoveries
  (v) The role of the liquidation committee
  (vi) Undertakings to distraining creditors
  (vii) Conclusion of the winding up

(c) Identify the potential civil and criminal liabilities of directors of insolvent companies in a given scenario

(d) Explain how disqualification of company directors might arise and the processes involved in disqualification

(e) State the classes of creditors and their rights in corporate insolvency

(f) Explain the advantages and disadvantages of trading on by the insolvency practitioner as compared with selling the business

Member's voluntary liquidations

(a) Explain the processes involved in the commencement of a members' voluntary liquidation, including the declaration of solvency and other formalities

(b) Describe the ongoing obligations upon the insolvency practitioner in a members' voluntary liquidation with regard to

    (i) Meetings
    (ii) Record keeping
    (iii) Reporting
    (iv) Time limits

(c) State the criteria for closure of a members' voluntary liquidation and describe the processes of closure

(d) Explain how distributions to shareholders are decided upon and made, and calculate distributions in a given scenario and from information provided

(e) Describe the processes undergone to convert a members' voluntary liquidation into a creditors' voluntary liquidation

Creditors' voluntary liquidations

(a) Explain the processes involved in the commencement of a creditors' voluntary liquidation, including meetings held under the provisions of s98 Insolvency Act 1986 ('Section 98 meetings')

(b) Describe the ongoing obligations upon the insolvency practitioner in a creditors' voluntary liquidation with regard to

    (i) Meetings
    (ii) Record keeping
    (iii) Reporting
    (iv) Time limits

(c) State the criteria for closure of a creditors' voluntary liquidation and describe the processes of closure

(d) Describe the powers of the liquidator in a creditors' voluntary liquidation

(e) Describe how ongoing receiverships might affect a creditors' voluntary liquidation

(f) Describe voidable transactions (including re-use of name under s216 Insolvency Act), explain how they impact upon the insolvency, and describe the powers of the insolvency practitioner relating to them

(g) Identify voidable transactions from information provided and in a given scenario

Compulsory liquidations

(a) Explain the processes involved in the commencement of a compulsory liquidation, including

    (i) The petition
    (ii) Petitioning creditors and substitution
    (iii) The winding-up order
    (iv) Statutory advertisement

(b) Describe the ongoing obligations upon the insolvency practitioner in a compulsory liquidation with regard to

    (i) Meetings
    (ii) Record keeping
    (iii) Reporting
    (iv) Time limits

(c) State the criteria for closure of a compulsory liquidation and describe the processes of closure

(d) Explain the processes needed to appoint the following, their roles, and the effects of their appointment upon the liquidation:

Introduction

- (i) Provisional liquidator
- (ii) Special manager
- (iii) Liquidator
- (iv) The liquidation committee

(e) Compare the respective roles of liquidator and Official Receiver

(f) Describe voidable transactions (including re-use of name under s216 Insolvency Act), explain how they impact upon the insolvency, and describe the powers of the insolvency practitioner relating to them

(g) Identify voidable transactions from information provided and in a given scenario

(h) Explain the methods open to a liquidator to enforce co-operation from parties affected by the liquidation

Company voluntary arrangements (CVAs) and Part 26 Companies Act 2006 arrangements

(a) Describe the processes undergone in the creation of a company voluntary arrangement and an arrangement under Part 26 Companies Act 2006

(b) State the contents of the CVA proposal and explain how the contents are prepared

(c) Explain the use and the effects of the moratorium procedure

(d) Describe the ongoing obligations upon the insolvency practitioner in a CVA with regard to

- (i) Meetings
- (ii) Record keeping
- (iii) Reporting
- (iv) Time limits
- (v) Creditors

(e) State the criteria for completion of a CVA and describe the processes of completion

(f) Explain the role of the insolvency practitioner as nominee and supervisor in a CVA

(g) Describe the circumstances that might bring about a failure of the arrangement, the impact that the failure has upon parties related to the arrangement and the procedures that should be followed by the insolvency practitioner on the failure of the arrangement

Administrations

(a) Explain the purposes and effects of administration

(b) Explain the processes involved in the commencement of an administration

(c) Describe the ongoing obligations upon the insolvency practitioner in an administration with regard to

- (i) Meetings
- (ii) Record keeping
- (iii) Reporting
- (iv) Time limits

(d) Describe and explain the following aspects of administration

- (i) The moratorium
- (ii) The role and remuneration of the administrator
- (iii) Notice and advertising requirements
- (iv) Proposals
- (v) Meetings

(e) Describe how an individual ceases to be an administrator, through discharge, release or other exit routes

(f) Define 'pre-packs' and explain the relative requirements of SIP 16

Receiverships

(a) Explain the effect of the Law of Property Act 1925 and its relation to fixed charge receiverships

(b) Explain the effect of the Enterprise Act 2002 in relation to administrative receivership

(c) Explain the purposes and effects of administrative receivership

(d) State the different types of receiver and describe their roles

(e) In relation to the appointment of an administrative receiver, describe
   (i) Who has the power to appoint the receiver and the source of that power
   (ii) The indemnities possessed by the appointer of the receiver and by the eventual liquidator

(f) Describe the ongoing obligations upon the insolvency practitioner in an administrative receivership with regard to
   (i) Meetings
   (ii) Record keeping
   (iii) Reporting
   (iv) Time limits

(g) State the criteria for completion of an administrative receivership and describe the processes of completion

Business turnaround and restructuring

(a) Explain the ways in which companies are legally able to try to avoid formal insolvency

(b) Explain the work of turnaround specialists and the methods that they might employ

(c) Explain how stakeholders in a business turnaround or restructuring are identified and managed by the turnaround specialist

(d) Describe briefly how companies may reorganise their businesses and legal structure

The ICAEW assessment

The assessment

- 2 ½ hours
- Pass mark 55% (44 marks)

There are 80 questions in the assessment and each question is worth one mark. Some questions are in two parts and both parts must be correct to gain the mark.

Some questions are grouped around scenarios. Each scenario has between two and five questions (each worth one mark).

How to use this Study Manual

To pass the assessment you need a thorough understanding in all areas covered by the syllabus.

Recommended approach

(a) To pass you need to be able to answer questions on **everything** specified by the syllabus. Read the Study Manual very carefully and do not skip any of it.

(b) Learning is an **active** process. Do **all** the activities as you work through the manual so you can be sure you really understand what you have read.

(c) After you have covered the material in the Study Manual, work through the questions in the Question Bank.

(d) Before you take the assessment, check that you still remember the material using the following quick revision plan:

   (i) Read through the chapter learning objectives. Are there any gaps in your knowledge? If so, study the section again.

   (ii) Read and annotate the diagrammatic summary of each chapter.

   (iv) Do all the questions again. If you know what you're doing, they shouldn't take long.

This approach is only a suggestion. You or your college may well adapt it to suit your needs.

Remember this is a **practical** course. Try to relate the material to your experience in the workplace or any other work experience you may have had.

Section A:

The legal and regulatory framework for insolvency

CHAPTER 1

The legal and regulatory framework

Introduction
Topic List
　　1　The legal framework
Summary and Self-test
Answers to Self-test

Introduction

Learning objectives

- Describe the legal and regulatory framework within which insolvency practitioners work
- Explain briefly the provisions of the laws and other rules relevant to insolvency and the interactions between them
- Describe the role of the courts in insolvency
- Describe the impact of the EC regulation and cross border issues on the work of the insolvency practitioner
- Describe the membership and role of the Joint Insolvency Committee

Stop and think

The world of insolvency is dominated by rules and regulations. Who creates these rules, what is the relationship between them? What happens when they are not complied with?

Working context

All those working in insolvency must understand, comply with and apply the regulatory rules that govern this area. They must understand what the rules are, where they can be found and how they should be applied. To be able to do this properly an understanding of the relationship between the various rules and regulations is very important.

1 The legal framework

Section overview

- In this section we are going to look at all of the bodies involved in the administration of insolvency and the various rules both legal and non-legal that regulate the work of the insolvency practitioner. We also consider what we mean by insolvent.

1.1 The legal framework

To understand fully the legal and regulatory framework that governs insolvency situations it is necessary to first appreciate the distinction and relationship between legal and non-legal rules and the nature of the legal rules that govern this area.

1.2 Distinction between legal and non-legal rules

Essentially legal rules are rules that can be enforced by the courts. There may be penalties for breaching legal rules which may be criminal and/or civil in nature. For example if a director breaches the rules on fraudulent trading he may be guilty of a criminal offence which can be punished by imprisonment, he may also have civil liability as the court can order him to make a monetary contribution to help pay the debts of the company.

Although non-legal rules cannot be enforced by the courts that does not mean to say that there are no consequences for failing to comply with them. For example if an Insolvency Practitioner (IP) is accused of acting negligently by failing to comply with a statement of insolvency practice (SIP) it may constitute grounds for disciplinary action to be taken against him. Also if a court is asked to decide whether or not an IP is liable for damages arising from his negligence, whether or not he has complied with the relevant SIP(s) will be taken into account by the court when it makes its determination.

1.3 Sources of insolvency regulation

The area of insolvency is regulated by a mixture of legal and non-legal rules.

Legal rules

There are three sources of law of which you need to be aware.

- **Statute law**

    Statute law (or legislation) is created by Parliament. It is made up of both Acts of Parliament eg Insolvency Act 1986 and statutory instruments eg Insolvency Rules 1986. Acts of Parliament are often referred to as primary legislation whereas statutory instruments are often referred to as secondary legislation. This is because a statutory instrument can only be created if an Act of Parliament allows it.

    Generally speaking Acts of Parliament are statements of principle ie they set out the purpose of the legislation and what it is trying to achieve, whereas the statutory instruments set out the detail of how the law works in practice. Although this distinction is not always adhered to strictly, generally speaking you are more likely to find information on things like filing requirements and time limits in the Insolvency Rules (or other relevant statutory instruments) than the Act.

- **EC Law**

    EC law is created by the institutions of the European Union for example the EC Regulation on Insolvency Proceedings 2000, which seeks to harmonise the ways in which member states of the EU deal with insolvency proceedings. The Regulation takes effect in the UK as if it were an Act of Parliament.

- **Case law/precedent**

    Case law is created by judges. The role of judges is to administer the insolvency regime and apply the law to disputes that are brought before the court. However if a question arises in insolvency proceedings about the interpretation of insolvency legislation the judge hearing the case will have to make a decision on how the statute should be interpreted. Depending upon the seniority of the

judge that decision may become a legal precedent that has to be followed in subsequent cases. Likewise if the insolvency statutes don't deal with a particular issue any decision that the judge makes about what the law is may also become a precedent.

- **Supremacy of law**

    Generally speaking European law has supremacy over statute and case law. Consequently in the event of a conflict (rare) the European law would have to be followed. In turn statute law is superior to case law. So for example if Parliament does not approve of the way that the courts have interpreted a statutory provision it can overturn that legal rule by amending the legislation.

1.4 Table of key statutes and statutory instruments

Title	Amended by	Key changes
Insolvency Act 1986 ('IA 86') This Act sought to consolidate the provisions in relation to bankruptcies and corporate insolvency procedures that were found in the Companies Act 1985 and Insolvency Act 1985 into one single Act of Parliament. The Act has been amended on a number of occasions.	Insolvency Act 2000	Introduced the small company moratorium in voluntary arrangements for companies.
	Enterprise Act 2002	Abolished HMRC/Crown preference. Changed the administration procedure. Curtailed the availability of administrative receivership. Sought to encourage a culture of corporate rescue. Provided for administration to be commenced out of court. Introduced restrictions orders and early discharge into the bankruptcy process.
Company Directors Disqualification Act 1986 ('CDDA 86') Deals with disqualification of directors where their conduct in relation to insolvent companies makes them unfit to be involved in the management of the company.	Various	
Companies Act 2006 ('CA 2006') Part 26 of the Act deals with schemes of arrangement. There are also provisions relevant to the work of insolvency practitioners relating to: the duties of directors; payment of debts from the proceeds of a floating charge and fraudulent trading.	This Act replaces the Companies Act 1985 and is fully in force.	
Law of Property Act 1925 (LPA 25) This statute contains important information about the enforcement of fixed charge security and the powers of LPA Receivers.		

Insolvency Rules 1986 The main statutory instrument relating to insolvency law and practice.	Various (most recently Insolvency Amendment Rules 2010) Insolvency Rules 2015	
Administration of Insolvent Estates of Deceased Persons Order 1986. The purpose of DPO 1986 is to modify the IA 1986 in respect of insolvent estates. In the event of any conflict between the two the DPO 1986 prevails.		
Insolvent Partnerships Order 1994 Revoked the Insolvent Partnerships Order 1986. Together with Insolvency Act 1986 sets out options available to insolvent partnerships.	Insolvent Partnerships (Amendment) No 2 Order 2002	Amended rules on partnership voluntary arrangements.

EC Regulation on Insolvency Proceedings 2000

Gives guidance on what types of insolvency proceedings the UK courts have jurisdiction to hear. The EC Regulation applies to all EU member states with the exception of Denmark. It governs when insolvency proceedings can be opened in a member state and which national laws should apply to those proceedings.

Practice directions/statements

A new Practice Direction on Insolvency Proceedings was issued in July 2014. This replaces all previous Practice Directions, Practice Statements and Practice Notes relating to insolvency proceedings. It seeks to guide the parties on the court procedure, practice and approach to various issues.

Deregulation Act 2015

- The main relevance is the reduction of RPBs including the Law Society and Secretary of State.

Small Business Enterprise and Employment Act 2015

- Simplifies a number of procedures and increases powers of the administrator, liquidator and trustee, including those exercisable without sanction.

1.5 Non-legal rules

Type	Key features
Statements of Insolvency Practice 'SIPs'	These are prepared by the Association of Business Recovery Professionals 'R3' and approved by the Joint Insolvency Committee. They give guidance to insolvency practitioners and set out standards that they are expected to adhere to. Compliance is monitored by the recognised professional bodies that authorise IPs to act. Failure to comply with a SIP may result in disciplinary action against an IP.
Technical releases	SIPs 5 and 6 were replaced in 1999 by technical releases which apply as if they were SIPs.
Insolvency guidance papers	Unlike SIPs they are purely for guidance, they do not set out required practice. They are authorised by the Joint Insolvency Committee.
Joint Insolvency Code of Ethics	The Code governs the conduct of practitioners who should be guided by the fundamental principles.

1.6 List of SIPs

SIP	Name
1	An introduction to the SIPs
2	Investigations by officeholders in administrations and insolvent liquidations
3	3.1 – Individual voluntary arrangements (for England and Wales and Northern Ireland)
	3.2 – Company voluntary arrangements (for England and Wales, Scotland and Northern Ireland)
	3.3 – Trust deeds (Scotland only)
4	Disqualification of directors
5	Non preferential claims by employees dismissed without proper notice by insolvent employers (replaced by Technical Release 5)
6	Treatment of directors' claims as employees in insolvencies (replaced by Technical Release 6)
7	Presentation of financial information in insolvency proceedings (effective 2 May 2011)
8	Summoning and holding meetings of creditors convened pursuant to s98
9	Payments to insolvency office holders and their associates (effective November 2011)
10	Proxy forms
11	The handling of funds in formal insolvency appointments
12	Records of meetings in formal insolvency proceedings
13	Acquisition of assets of insolvent companies by directors
14	A receiver's responsibility to preferential creditors
15	Reporting and providing information on IPs functions to committees in formal insolvencies
16	Pre-packaged sales in administrations (effective 1 November 2013)
17	An administrative receiver's responsibility for the company's records

1.7 EC regulation and cross-border issues

The EC Regulation on Insolvency Proceedings 2000

The single market created by the EU together with an increasingly globalised market place means that a company (or individual) may operate (or live) in more than one country. Hence in an insolvency situation dispute or confusion may arise as to where any insolvency proceedings should be heard and what laws should apply. The EC regulation seeks to address this problem within the EU.

The EC regulation applies to all EU member states with the exception of Denmark. It seeks to govern when insolvency proceedings can be opened in a member state and which national laws should apply to those proceedings. It also compels all member states to recognise proceedings that have been opened properly. So for example the acts of an administrator appointed by an English court will be recognised as lawful by the French courts.

The regulation makes a distinction between main proceedings and secondary proceedings.

The member state in which a company or individual's 'centre of main interest' ('COMI') is situated has jurisdiction to open main insolvency proceedings. If a company's COMI is outside the EU the EC Regulation will not apply.

Main proceedings are: compulsory liquidation; creditor's voluntary liquidation; administration; voluntary arrangements and bankruptcy. The EC regulation does not apply to administrative receivership and fixed charge/LPA receivership.

The COMI will correspond to the place where the company or individual conducts the administration of its business on a regular basis (which may not correspond to the location of a company's registered office). However as a starting point in determining the COMI of a company it will be presumed that the

COMI is in the same location as the registered office unless there is evidence to the contrary. It is important when determining a COMI that attention is paid to what is 'ascertainable to third parties'. This is necessary because creditors need to be able to calculate what may happen in the event of insolvency. That in turn, will be determined by the laws of the COMI country. No presumption as to the location of the COMI applies in personal insolvency.

In the legal case of *Re Daisytek* the court was called upon to decide the COMI of a group of companies. The parent was located in the UK and had its registered office here but other subsidiaries were located in and had their registered offices in France and Germany. Although the subsidiaries traded in their respective countries most of the administration of the companies and their finance was organised through a subsidiary company located in the UK. Key creditors were located in the UK and the creditor's contracts with the non-UK subsidiaries were organised through the UK companies. On balance therefore the court took the view that the COMI for the whole group was the UK and proceedings could be opened in England.

It is possible for a company's or individual's COMI to change though the court will need to be satisfied that any change is a genuine migration and not just an attempt to take advantage of more relaxed insolvency laws that may apply in a particular member state.

Secondary proceedings may be opened in other member states in parallel to the main proceedings. This is provided that the company or individual has an establishment in the member state and carries out non-transitory economic activity. Secondary proceedings are limited to those that qualify as winding up proceedings in member states.

Cross-Border Insolvency Regulations 2006

The Cross-Border Regulations adopt the UNCITRAL Model Law on cross-border insolvency into domestic law. It is designed to assist those states that have signed up to it deal with cross border insolvency effectively. Its overriding aim is to help ensure that where the assistance of foreign courts is needed to deal with an insolvency, that assistance can be given more easily. In Great Britain it is not however essential that the country which seeks help from a British court has signed up to the UNITRAL model law. Assistance can still be given.

1.8 Bodies involved in the administration of the insolvency regime

- **The Secretary of State**
    - The political head of the Department of Business, Innovation and Skills (**DBIS**)
    - Appoints the Official Receivers
    - Responsible for amendment of the Insolvency Rules and other statutory instruments and the creation of new rules and regulations
    - Exercises the function of a creditors' committee where none exists
    - Applies for disqualification of directors under CDDA 1986.

- **The Insolvency Service**

    Is an executive agency within DBIS. Its primary role is to supervise those involved in the administration of bankruptcies and compulsory liquidations.

- **The Official Receiver ('OR')**

    Is an officeholder (appointed by the Secretary of State) who is part of the Insolvency Service dealing with bankruptcies and compulsory liquidations. All ORs are officers of the court and will be allocated to all bankruptcies and compulsory liquidations arising within the jurisdiction of their allocated court. In bankruptcies and liquidations with few assets the OR will usually act as trustee and liquidator for the duration of the insolvency, in others only until a private insolvency practitioner ('IP') is appointed.

- **Companies House**

    Companies House is an Executive Agency of DBIS headed up by the Registrar of Companies. All forms of company in Great Britain (England, Wales and Scotland) are incorporated and registered with Companies House and file specific details at Companies House as required by the Companies Act 2006 and Insolvency Act 1986. When the legislation requires something to be served on the Registrar of Companies it will be sent to Companies House.

- *The London Gazette*

    The London Gazette (or *Gazette* as it is often referred to) is one of the official journals of record of the British government. It is in this newspaper that certain statutory notices, including those relating to insolvency situations are required to be published.

- **The courts**

    The courts have exclusive jurisdiction over the making of orders for the bankruptcy of individuals and the compulsory liquidation of companies. The courts do not automatically get involved in other procedures though they may if the legislation so provides or they are requested to do so because a dispute has arisen.

- **Insolvency practitioners (IPs)**

    IPs are people who are authorised and licensed to act in relation to insolvency matters and accept appointments as: liquidators; provisional liquidators; administrators; administrative receivers, nominees and supervisors of voluntary arrangements; and trustees in bankruptcy. (Law of Property Act receivers 'LPA receivers' do not have to be IPs.)

- **Recognised professional bodies (RPBs)**

    In Great Britain (England, Wales and Scotland) most IPs are authorised to act through their membership of one of the RPBs set out in a statutory instrument the Insolvency Practitioner (Recognised Professional Body) Order 1986. They are:

    – The Association of Chartered Certified Accountants
    – The Insolvency Practitioners Association
    – The Institute of Chartered Accountants in England and Wales
    – The Institute of Chartered Accountants in Ireland
    – The Institute of Chartered Accountants of Scotland

    Those who are not able to obtain authorisation through an RPB may apply direct to the Secretary of State. They must establish that they are 'fit and proper' persons. (The requirements for the education, training and experience of IPs are found in the Insolvency Practitioner Regulations 2005.) The Secretary of State is no longer able to deal with this licensing as a consequence of the Deregulation Act 2015.

    All IPs must:

    – Provide security
    – Not be bankrupt or subject to other restriction (see Chapter 3)
    – Not be disqualified under the CDDA 1986.

    Any IP that acts without proper authorisation commits a criminal offence.

- **R3**

    The Association of Business Recovery Professionals is the professional body for Insolvency Practitioners and together with the JIC and RPBs plays a key role in the production and implementation of SIPs. (See para 1.5.) R3 is not an RPB.

- **Joint Insolvency Committee (JIC)**

    Made up of representatives from each of the RPBs, Insolvency service, and R3. They are concerned primarily with the setting of professional and ethical standards and achieving consistency across the profession.

Summary and Self-test

Summary

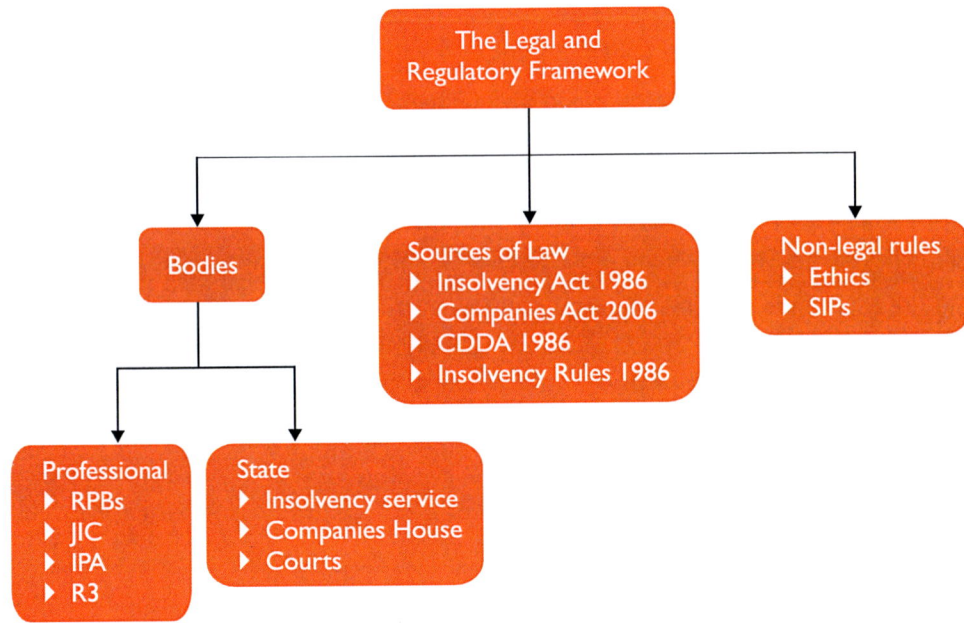

Self-test

1. What RPBs are listed in the Insolvency Practitioner (Recognised Professional Body) Order 1986?

2. Pursuant to the EC Regulation on Insolvency Proceedings 2000 to commence a main insolvency proceeding in England where must the company have its centre of main interest ('COMI')?

3. If a company's registered office is located in Jersey but its head office administrative functions are carried out in London, will this be sufficient to override any presumption that a company's COMI is located in its place of registration?

4. Who commissions SIPs; who produces SIPs; and who is responsible for their adoption?

5. Are the following statements about SIPs true or false?

    (i) They set out required practice and thereby seek to maintain the professional standards of the insolvency profession.

    (ii) They seek to ensure that the insolvency profession takes a similar approach to the conduct and administration of insolvency cases.

    (iii) They set out standards and procedures with which an IP is expected to comply.

    (iv) They have the same legal force as statutory instruments.

Answers to Self-test

1 Most IPs are authorised to act through their membership of one of the RPBs set out in a statutory instrument the Insolvency Practitioner (Recognised Professional Body) Order 1986. They are:

- The Association of Chartered Certified Accountants
- The Insolvency Practitioners Association
- The Institute of Chartered Accountants in England and Wales
- The Institute of Chartered Accountants in Ireland
- The Institute of Chartered Accountants of Scotland

2 Its COMI must be in the UK.

3 Yes, the courts will look to see where a company actually conducts the administration of its business on a regular basis and what would be ascertainable to third parties.

4 Joint Insolvency Committee; R3 (the Association of Business Recovery Professionals); RPBs (recognised professional bodies).

5 (i) True
  (ii) True
  (iii) True
  (iv) False

CHAPTER 2

Business turnaround and restructuring

Introduction
Topic List
1 Business turnaround and restructuring
2 The role of the turnaround practitioner
3 Formal insolvency procedures
4 Considerations for directors of distressed companies

Summary and Self-test
Answers to Self-test

Introduction

Learning objectives

- Explain the ways in which companies are legally able to avoid formal insolvency
- Explain the work of turnaround specialists and the methods they might employ
- Explain how the stakeholders in a business turnaround are identified and managed by the turnaround specialist
- Describe how companies may reorganise their businesses and legal structure

Stop and think

What does restructuring mean, what are its aims and objectives, what stands in the way of a successful restructure?

How might formal insolvency proceedings help to achieve a restructure?

Who are the stakeholders in a restructuring situation, what are their particular interests likely to be?

Working context

Since the changes brought about by the Enterprise Act and the corresponding demise of administrative receivership and rise of administration, insolvency professionals are increasingly looking to advise businesses on how they can best avoid formal insolvency proceedings or use the administration or CVA procedures to achieve the long term survival of the business. Those working in this area need to understand how best to: identify the problem and the relevant stakeholders; stabilise the business; and assess the restructuring options in order to implement an appropriate solution.

1 Business turnaround and restructuring

Section overview

- When a business finds itself in financial difficulties there may be steps that the owners and managers can take to try to avoid a formal insolvency situation. Even if some form of formal insolvency procedure is necessary it is worth noting that of all the insolvency procedures open to a business some are primarily designed to help rescue the business or part of it. Procedures such as administration or voluntary arrangements are primarily hoping to save the business (although there is likely to be a significant restructure). These procedures are therefore often referred to as 'non-terminal' insolvency procedures as opposed to liquidation and bankruptcy (which as they will almost certainly result in the closure of the business) are referred to as 'terminal' procedures.

- Before considering in more detail what steps can be taken to rescue a business or what formal insolvency procedures are available it is useful to take a step back and consider how a business may be structured and who exactly is insolvent.

  The basic distinction in law is between incorporated and non-incorporated businesses.

  Incorporated businesses

  An incorporated business has its own identity which is recognised in law and as such it is wholly responsible for its own debts. Incorporated businesses are companies (public or private) and limited liability partnerships (LLPs). The owners and/or managers of incorporated businesses do not have liability for the debts of the business unless they have voluntarily taken on liability, for example by the giving of a personal guarantee or because the law imposes liability for the business debts, for example where company directors are guilty of wrongful trading. Directors of companies and members of LLPs may invest monies into the business and just like other investors should the business fail they may lose any monies that they have invested. [Note that LLPs are not part of the syllabus.]

  Unincorporated businesses

  By contrast the owners of an unincorporated business: sole traders; or partners in what are often referred to as simple partnerships; are wholly responsible for the debts of the business. That is because the business does not have a separate legal identity and as such the law makes no distinction between the personal or business debts of the owner(s).

- It is also useful to consider – what is insolvency? There are two tests to determine whether or not a company is unable to pay its debts and is hence insolvent: the cash-flow test and the balance sheet test.

  Cash-flow test

  A company (or individual) will be deemed insolvent if it is proved to the satisfaction of the court that it cannot pay its debts as they fall due. Debt means a liquidated sum not, for example, damages. The level of debt must be in line with the prescribed limit, currently £750 or more for individuals and in excess of £750 for companies.

  The balance sheet test

  This test does not apply to individuals.

  Despite the name of this test one cannot simply look at the most recent accounts of a company and come to a decision about whether its liabilities exceed its assets. When valuing assets for the purpose of the test it is necessary to look at the realisable value of the assets not simply their book value. In addition, liabilities must include both contingent and prospective liabilities. In a recent case the Supreme Court said the test is not simply an assets versus liabilities test. It is about whether a company has, and will have sufficient assets to meet its liabilities when they are due (*BNY Corporate Trustee Services v Eurosail*). In the recent case of Re Casa Estates, the Court of Appeal held that the cash flow and balance sheet tests are part of a single exercise to determine whether a company is unable to pay its debts.

  [The application of these tests are considered more fully in later chapters – Chapter 8 for companies and Chapter 20 for individuals.]

1.1 Different types of creditor and their rights

When a business is in distress the creditors become its most important stakeholder. Their support will be crucial to the success of any restructure or rescue and ultimately the creditors have the power to bring insolvency proceedings.

Understanding the different types of creditor and their rights is important as this will impact significantly on the bargaining position of the parties.

- **Fixed charge holders**

    Fixed charge holders are secured creditors/lenders who have a charge over specific asset(s). The business cannot dispose of the asset without the charge holders consent. Consequently there are limited assets that are suitable for being offered as fixed charge security. The most likely assets subject to a fixed charge are land and buildings, fixed plant and machinery and intellectual property rights. Both incorporated and non-incorporated businesses can offer security by way of fixed charge.

- **Floating charge holders**

    Floating charges can only be granted by companies. Floating charge holders are secured creditors who have a charge over a general pool of assets that may change from time to time eg stock. It is common for a charge to be created over all the assets of the company. Unlike with a fixed charge, where there is a floating charge the company remains free to deal with the assets.

    On default, depending upon the date of creation of the charge, the company may appoint either an administrative receiver and/or an administrator to take control of the company assets and dispose of them.

    [See Chapter 5 for further detail on secured creditors.]

- **Suppliers with the benefit of a retention of title clause (also known as reservation of title)**

    When goods are supplied the contract may specify that legal title (ownership) of the goods will not pass to the buyer until goods are paid for. Provided that: the clause is actually incorporated into the contract; it is properly drafted; and the goods are still identifiable, the creditor may have the right to repossess the goods if payment is not made. If those goods are vital to the business a retention of title clause puts a supplier in a strong negotiating position.

- **Landlords of commercial premises**

    Landlords enjoy two rights that are not generally available to other creditors, that of distraint (or distress) and forfeiture. *Distraint allows a landlord to seize goods on the tenant's premises and sell them to satisfy claims for unpaid rent. Certain goods are protected against distraint these are called 'privileged goods'. Such goods include, for example, perishable goods eg food, livestock, gas, water, electricity, and tools of the tenant's trade. (Note that others such as HMRC and local authorities also have the right to distrain but for assessment purposes we focus on the rights of a landlord.)

    Forfeiture will allow landlords to terminate any lease agreement and repossess the premises. If the premises are vital to the business this puts the landlord in a very strong negotiating position. Note that distraint and forfeiture are **not** statutory rights and in normal circumstances landlords do not require the permission of the court to exercise these rights. However once a formal insolvency procedure has commenced the landlords rights may be modified. We will consider this more fully in later chapters.

    *Note that from 6 April 2014, the remedy of distress is no longer available to landlords of commercial premises for recovery of rent. Commercial landlords instead have recourse to Commercial Rent Arrears Recovery or CRAR which sets out a new procedure for recovery of rent by seizure of goods. See Chapter 10 for further details.

- **Preferential creditors**

    In an insolvency situation some debts enjoy preferential status giving the creditors priority over the ordinary unsecured creditors. We will look at the various categories of preferential debt in later chapters but essentially it includes monies due in respect of unpaid wages, holiday pay and unpaid contributions to occupational pension schemes. Any plan to rescue a business must take into account the enhanced rights that these creditors hold in formal insolvency proceedings as they are highly unlikely to support any plans that put them in a worse position than formal insolvency.

[See Chapter 5 for further detail on preferential creditors.]

- **Execution creditors**

    Provided that an unsecured creditor has obtained judgment against the debtor he may take steps to enforce (or 'execute') that judgment and by doing so may improve his prospects in the insolvency.

- **Ordinary unsecured creditors**

    The bulk of any creditors in an insolvency are likely to be unsecured and hence they will have the most to lose on the failure of a business. Such creditors are only likely to support any plans to rescue the business if it will result in a better return for them. Unsecured creditors cannot be ignored as they may still have the right to petition for the winding up of a company or the bankruptcy of an individual.

2 The role of the turnaround practitioner

Section overview

- Any attempt to turnaround the fortunes of a business will usually involve professional advisers. 'Turnaround' practitioners are often accountants who specialise in investigating the affairs of a business and making recommendations as to how a business can best move forward. They do not have to be insolvency practitioners (though some are) as they are working with businesses before any formal insolvency procedures come into play.

- This pre-insolvency period is sometimes referred to as the 'twilight' zone and it may be that during this period a business will dip in and out of insolvency. Directors of companies must be especially careful during this period to ensure that they are aware of their duties to the company and to the creditors of the company as breach of these duties could constitute a criminal offence and may also make a director liable for the debts of the company. Directors must be especially careful to keep a good record of all their dealings with the company and the rationale behind any decisions that they make [see para 4 below].

Appointment of a turnaround practitioner may be instigated by the owners or managers of the business or by one of its creditors, usually the bank.

Once appointed the turnaround practitioner will look to:

- Stabilise the finances of the business and ensure access to funds to pay immediate debts
- Diagnose the business' fundamental problems and identify key stakeholders
- Implement an appropriate rescue plan for the medium/long term

2.1 Stabilisation

In order to stabilise a business in crisis robust action will be needed to ensure the short term future of the business and to create an opportunity to implement a longer term rescue plan. Success is likely to depend upon the business having sufficient finance in place to keep trading and avoid enforcement action by creditors. Action will be needed to ensure:

- Financial data is reliable and up to date (preparation of cashflow forecasts will be crucial)

- Steps are taken to conserve cash and put short term cash generation to the top of the agenda eg improve debt collection and stretch creditor terms

- If not already in place the factoring of book debts may be considered (see para 2.7)

- Initial steps are taken to realise assets (eg liquidate surplus stock) and reduce costs

- Key stakeholders are identified and communicated with

2.2 Key stakeholders

A typical feature of many distressed businesses is that they have poor communication and relationships with their stakeholders who might include:

Business turnaround and restructuring

- The bank and other creditors
- Shareholders and other investors
- Employees
- Customers

Key to obtaining stakeholder support is clear communication. Should formal insolvency procedures be necessary that support will be crucial.

2.3 Long term survival

If a business survives the critical period and is successfully stabilised, changes will have to be made to ensure the longer term survival of the business. There are likely to be changes in all or some of the following areas:

- Change in the leadership of the business

- The restructure of the business eg closure of branches; or outsourcing certain operations such as payroll and technical support that might be done more cheaply and efficiently by a third party

- Refinancing by way of an injection of new capital or a debt restructure

- Cost reduction eg cutbacks on staffing and overheads

- Look to divest the company of businesses that are not part of its core assets so that it can concentrate on what it does best. One way that this could be achieved would be by a de-merger of a subsidiary company. The management of that subsidiary may be willing to become the new owners (a management buy-out 'MBO'). Alternatively where the non-core business is not packaged so conveniently in a subsidiary company it may hive down the non-core business into a new company, and seek a buyer for that company

- Raise funds through a sale and leaseback of freehold property

- Consider whether a joint venture might save costs and reduce risk and/or give access to new markets

- Sell the business, this could be to a third party who will probably install their own management team (a management buy-in 'MBI') or alternatively the company could seek a MBO

- Consider a new business model for example, franchising

2.4 Role of the banks

Banks play a key role in determining whether or not a business in distress can be turned around as usually the bank is the key source of funding and quite often also a helpful source of advice for a beleaguered business.

The objectives of a financial restructuring are to restore the business to solvency. The business will need to satisfy the criteria for solvency applying both the cash flow and balance sheet tests. Steps will need to be taken to align the business capital structure with the level of projected cash flow. If the long term survival of the company is to be achieved it will require both new money to implement a turnaround plan and the restructuring of existing debt. New money may come from existing or new lenders or from existing shareholders for example by way of a rights issue. Debt may convert into other negotiable instruments eg a debt to equity swap.

A restructure of existing debt is simply not possible without the consent of the lenders involved. Any restructure will almost certainly result in lenders compromising their contractual rights and so a restructure cannot be forced on lenders without their consent. Things can be kept relatively simple if only one or two lenders are involved but in larger groups of companies the debt arrangements can be very complex with a number of lenders involved. Often the debt will be tiered and in turn that debt may have been syndicated. In such cases negotiations are likely to be complex and protracted. Consequently the lenders may apply the London Rules/Approach to give a framework/structure to the negotiations.

2.5 The London Rules/Approach

The approach of the main banks to distressed business situations has to some extent become formalised into what is referred to as the London Rules/Approach 'The Approach'. The Approach is a set of principles developed by the Bank of England which determine how financial creditors should deal with companies in financial difficulties.

Its overriding aim is to give the distressed company breathing space whilst the banks work together to see if the distressed company can survive and to collectively support the company during this period.

It has two stages. Stage one is often referred to as the workout stage. The banks will appoint investigative accountants (turnaround practitioners) to report on the viability of the company and will not, during the period of the workout, take enforcement action against the company. The banks will also allow the company access to funding during this period. If new money is made available this is granted priority over existing debt. Although this may be done informally it is often in the interests of both the company and the bank(s) involved to negotiate a formal standstill or moratorium agreement and so regulate the terms of their agreement.

What happens in stage two will depend upon the recommendation of the investigators and much will depend upon the valuation that the investigators place on the company. If the view is that the company cannot be saved some form of formal insolvency procedure will be very likely to follow. Even if the findings are that the company is viable restructuring of the company debt and very probably the company's business will be necessary.

2.6 Financial restructuring

The investigator will have given his finding on the level of debt that the company can sustain (relative to its value) and that will drive the terms of the financial restructure.

Usually the bank with the largest exposure will take on the role of co-ordinator and will provide much of the momentum needed to push the restructure through. The role is not advisory it is more akin to that of an administrator or project manager.

The terms of any financial restructure may include:

- Writing off some debt
- Converting debt to equity
- A new injection of equity funds or subordinated debt
- Changes to existing agreements eg payment dates may be rescheduled, interest rates changed

To be legally enforceable and workable all of the lenders will have to agree to the financial restructure.

2.7 Factoring of book debts

One of the most crucial things for a distressed business is to maintain its cash flow so that it continues to be able to pay its debts as they fall due. Some businesses may consider factoring their book debts (unpaid invoices) to maintain good cash flow.

Definition

Factoring: Factoring is a financial transaction whereby a business will sell the right to collect its book debts to a third party ('the factor'). The factor will pay a proportion of the debt in advance of collection to the business, with the balance being paid on receipt of the debt by the factor, but subject to the deduction of agreed charges.

There are two types of factoring agreements, recourse factoring where the business continues to carry the risk of the bad debt, and non-recourse factoring where the risk passes to the factor.

In a recourse factoring agreement if the business, whose debt has been factored, fails to pay the factor, the business will usually have to repay the sums advanced by the factor together with certain fees and charges that would have been payable had the debt been paid in full. The business will then decide whether or not to take further action to enforce the debt. However where debts have been factored on a non-recourse basis, the factor becomes the legal owner of the debt and hence assumes the risk of bad debts and responsibility for them. As a consequence non-recourse factoring attracts higher fees than recourse factoring.

3 Formal insolvency procedures

Section overview

- In some cases a business may be so distressed that it cannot be turned around without the aid of a formal rescue procedure. Some formal insolvency procedures are designed to try to help rescue the business whereas procedures such as liquidation recognise that the business has failed and cannot be saved.

Whilst it may be advantageous for a business to avoid formal insolvency it may not be possible as a number of factors may make avoiding formal insolvency difficult.

For example:

- A creditor cannot be forced to agree to any changes to its agreement with the business without its consent

- The business will not get any breathing space from the pressures of its creditors' claims whilst it seeks to reach agreement with them

- The creditors are only likely to be supportive if they have confidence in the management team and the viability of the business. Keeping that confidence will be crucial

- The business will have to have sufficient cash flow to continue to trade.

What formal rescue procedures are available to a business depend upon whether or not it is an incorporated or unincorporated business. Here we deal with limited companies, sole traders and simple partnerships. (Other trading entities are not part of the syllabus.)

Trading entity	Procedure	Key features
Limited company	Administration	Moratorium on debt enforcement available
		Proposals put to creditors
		Approval by >50% in value
	Company voluntary arrangement	Moratorium only available for small companies
		Proposals put to creditors
		Approval requires at least 75% (in value) of the creditors to support it
	Administrative receivership	Less common than administration
		No moratorium
		Administrative receiver acts for the appointing bank
		Unsecured creditors are not involved
	Scheme of arrangement under Part 26 of Companies Act 2006	No moratorium
		Of use generally in complex cases and practically where a CVA is inappropriate for example where a company is seeking to bind dissenting secured creditors to a restructure
		Complicated voting structure but can bind unsupportive creditors
		Court approval needed both to call the meeting(s) to approve the scheme and to sanction the decisions of the meeting(s). The court must be satisfied that the procedural requirements of the CA 2006 have been complied with and that the scheme is fair to creditors generally
		Can be initiated by the company

Certificate in Insolvency

Trading entity	Procedure	Key features
Sole trader	Individual voluntary arrangement	Moratorium (interim order) available Proposals put to creditors Approval requires at least 75% (in value) of the creditors to support it
Partnership	Partnership voluntary arrangement or individual voluntary arrangement	Moratorium only available if the partnership qualifies as a small company (see Chapter 32) Proposals put to creditors Approval requires at least 75% (in value) of the creditors to support

In circumstances where a company cannot be saved liquidation (winding up) will follow. Sole traders and partners may enter into bankruptcy.

We will look at all of these procedures in more detail in the chapters that follow.

4 Considerations for directors of distressed companies

Section overview

The directors of a company have duties which, if they breach may have serious consequences. It's important that directors fully understand their obligations and what happens if they breach their duties.

While a company is solvent directors owe a duty of care to the company as represented by the company shareholders/members. They owe no duty of care to the company's creditors. Once a company is insolvent however that position changes and they owe a duty to creditors to take the necessary steps to minimise the losses that they may suffer. A breach of this duty may have significant consequences for any director. He may be held liable to make a financial contribution to the company to assist in paying its debts; he may have criminal liability; he may face disqualification as a director. Consequently directors must proceed with caution when seeking to turnaround a company that is technically insolvent. (See Chapter 6 for further discussion of this area.)

Summary and Self-test

Summary

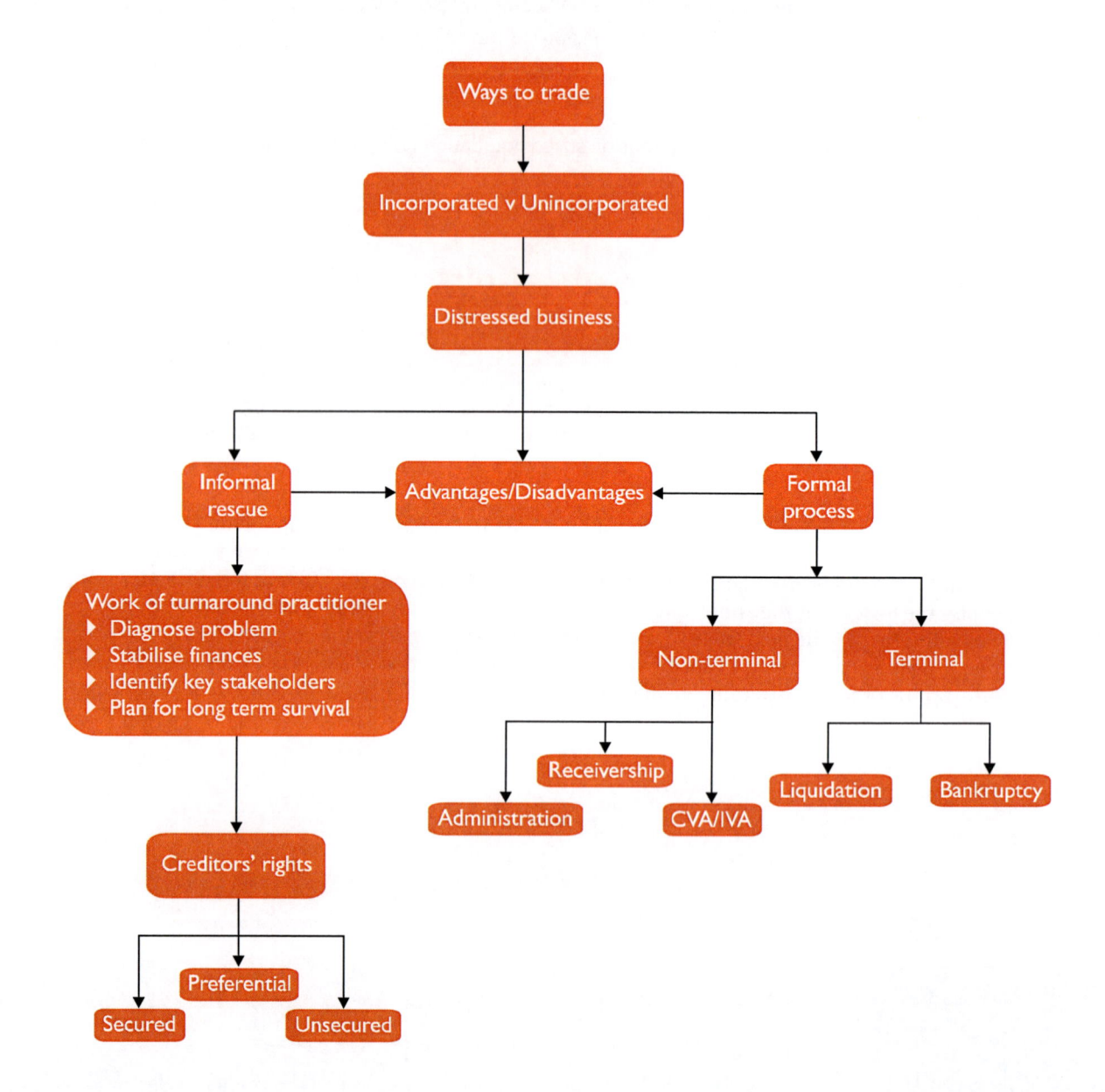

```
                    Ways to trade
                          │
                          ▼
              Incorporated v Unincorporated
                          │
                          ▼
                  Distressed business
                          │
        ┌─────────────────┼─────────────────┐
        ▼                 ▼                 ▼
    Informal      Advantages/Disadvantages   Formal
    rescue                                  process
        │                                      │
        ▼                              ┌───────┴───────┐
  Work of turnaround practitioner      ▼               ▼
  ▸ Diagnose problem              Non-terminal      Terminal
  ▸ Stabilise finances                 │               │
  ▸ Identify key stakeholders      ┌───┼───┐       ┌───┴───┐
  ▸ Plan for long term survival    ▼   ▼   ▼       ▼       ▼
        │                    Admin. Receiv. CVA/IVA Liquid. Bankruptcy
        ▼
  Creditors' rights
        │
   ┌────┼────┐
   ▼    ▼    ▼
Secured Preferential Unsecured
```

24 Certificate in Insolvency

Self-test

1 Which **one** of the following is most likely to have had a significant negative impact on the position of a distressed company?

    A   High levels of customer dissatisfaction
    B   The company factoring its debts
    C   Poor retention rates for junior employees
    D   Failure to deal with the renewal of a lease in a timely manner

2 What are the two types of security that a company can offer over its assets?

3 If a company is in financial difficulty what is the most crucial matter that will require attention?

4 Who are the key stakeholders in any turnaround?

5 List the so called non-terminal insolvency procedures open to a company.

Now, go back to the Learning Objectives in the Introduction. If you are satisfied that you have achieved these objectives, please tick them off.

Answers to Self-test

1. A – this can be a subjective area but on the basis of the information and options here A is the best available option.

2. A company can offer both fixed and floating charges.

3. A business cannot survive without ready money with which to fund its trade. Therefore it needs to sort out its cash flow and access to short term funding.

4. The creditors.

5. Administration and CVA. (Receivership is only available to secured creditors.)

CHAPTER 3

The Insolvency Practitioner: key professional issues

Introduction
Topic List
1 Insolvency Practitioners (IPs)
2 The offices an IP can hold
3 IP progress reports and records
4 Remuneration and expenses
5 Expenses and disbursements

Summary and Self-test
Answers to Self-test
Answers to Interactive questions

Introduction

Learning objectives

Tick off

- State the names of the recognised professional bodies relating to insolvency in England and Wales and how and by whom they become recognised ☐
- State and describe the qualification and licensing requirements of a licensed insolvency practitioner ☐
- Explain the practical uses of bonding and how bonding arises in an insolvency ☐
- Calculate figures including the quantum of the bond and insolvency practitioner remuneration ☐

Stop and think

What requirements apply to those who want to seek a licence to act as an IP? What reporting requirements apply to IPs? What rules govern the remuneration of an IP – what rights do creditors have to challenge an IPs remuneration and expenses?

Working context

You may be asked to prepare progress reports for distribution to creditors and ensure that relevant time limits are complied with. You may need to deal with creditor queries, ensure that SIP 9 is complied with and prepare time statements.

1 Insolvency Practitioners (IPs)

> **Section overview**
>
> - Insolvency Practitioners (IPs) are subject to significant regulation through legislation, their professional bodies, SIPs and the insolvency code of ethics. Breaches of the rules that IPs are subject to can have very serious consequences, they may face financial liability, disciplinary proceedings and even criminal proceedings.

1.1 Who may act as an IP?

Under the provisions of the Insolvency Act 1986 it is a criminal offence to act as a liquidator, administrator, administrative receiver, supervisor of a voluntary arrangement, trustee in bankruptcy, or administrator of the estate of a deceased insolvent unless qualified to do so.

To be 'qualified' an individual must satisfy a number of criteria. First, an individual cannot qualify to act if 'disqualified' eg bankrupt or subject to a debt relief order, subject to a bankruptcy (or debt relief) restrictions order or undertaking, subject to disqualification under the Company Directors Disqualification Act 1986, or is a company, or mental health patient. Second the individual must be authorised to act by either one of the recognised professional bodies 'RPB' or the Secretary of State. (See Chapter 1.) Those that can regulate were changed by virtue of the Deregulation Act 2015. Finally, the individual must have in place proper security for the performance of his functions.

1.2 IP Bonding

The means by which an IP can satisfy the requirement to provide security is through putting in place a fidelity bond. The surety under the bond will assume liabilities for both general and specific penalties in respect of the individual IP. The level of bond that must be in place is set out in the IP Regulations 2005.

- General Penalty Sum – set at £250,000

- Specific Penalty Sum – is calculated by reference to the estimated assets in each insolvency case. The specific penalty sum must be kept under review and increased as necessary. The maximum sum is £5m; the minimum sum is £5,000

- The purpose of the bond is to compensate creditors for any breaches of duty by an IP that may result in financial loss

1.3 The Bordereau

This is the form on which the IP enters details of his appointments and increases in specific penalties. This must be sent to his insurers and RPB monthly.

Interactive question 1: IP bonding

Max has been appointed supervisor in the voluntary arrangement of Harry Schmidt. Under the terms of the arrangement Harry will make a voluntary contribution of £500 per month for 5 years and pay over the proceeds from the sale of his house. His house is valued at £350,000 but subject to a mortgage of £125,000. What is the value of the specific penalty bond that Max needs to put in place?

See **Answer** at the end of this chapter.

2 The offices an IP can hold

The role and duties of an IP will vary depending upon the office that he/she is holding. Although we will consider these roles and duties in more detail in subsequent chapters a quick summary appears below.

Name	Definition	Purpose/main duties
Trustee in bankruptcy	Either the Official Receiver 'OR' or IP who takes control of a bankrupt's assets following the making of a bankruptcy order.	The purpose of the trustee is to realise the bankrupt's estate assets and distribute to creditors (s305 IA86).
		The trustee is an officer of the court and must act with honour and integrity in the carrying on of his duties (*Ex parte James*).
		A private IP must give assistance to the OR if required.
Liquidator	An IP appointed by creditors following either a winding up order or resolution to wind up the company.	The function of the liquidator is to realise the company's assets and distribute to creditors in accordance with the statute.
	In a compulsory liquidation the OR sometimes acts as liquidator.	The liquidator is the agent of the company and hence usually acts without personal liability. Any liabilities that arise from the acts/contracts of the liquidator are therefore payable as an expense of the liquidation in priority to both creditors' claims and the liquidator's own remuneration.
		Despite the fact that the liquidator usually acts without personal liability he has a fiduciary duty to the company and the creditors generally and must always act in their best interests. He must also act with reasonable care ie not be negligent. If any breach of these duties results in a loss to the company, and hence the creditors generally, legal proceedings to recover the loss may be taken against the liquidator under the misfeasance provisions in s212 IA86. [Note however that these duties are not owed to individual creditors who may not take action against the liquidator for personal losses.]
		A liquidator in a compulsory liquidation is an officer of the court, a liquidator in a voluntary liquidation is not. However both types of liquidator are subject to the rule in *Ex parte James* (see above).
Nominee	An IP who assists a debtor (individual or company) to put forward a voluntary arrangement to creditors.	Statutory duty to make an initial assessment of the proposal and if acting as chairman of the approval meetings to ensure that they are summoned and held in accordance with the rules.
		Creditors unhappy with the acts of the nominee can seek to enforce these statutory duties under s6 or s262 IA86.

Name	Definition	Purpose/main duties
Supervisor	An IP who is appointed under the terms of an approved voluntary arrangement and assists in implementing its terms and taking steps necessary to enforce the debtor's compliance with the proposal.	To supervise the arrangement in accordance with the Act and terms of the arrangement. Creditors can take action against a supervisor for breach of duty under the provisions in s7 or s263 IA86.
Provisional Liquidator (PL)	Either the OR or an IP appointed by the court to protect and preserve the assets of a company pending the hearing of a petition.	The PL has a fiduciary duty to the company and the creditors generally and must always act in their best interests. Acts as the agent of the company and hence usually acts without personal liability. Is an officer of the court and is therefore subject to the rule in *Ex parte James*.
Interim Receiver (IR)	Either the OR or an IP appointed between the presentation of a bankruptcy petition and the making of a bankruptcy order to safeguard and protect the debtor's assets where there is concern that they may be dissipated.	The IR has a fiduciary duty to the individual and the creditors generally and must always act in their best interests. Acts as the agent of the individual and hence usually acts without personal liability. Is an officer of the court and is therefore subject to the rule in *Ex parte James*.
Administrator	IP appointed by either the court or (using the out of court method) the company directors or holders of a qualifying floating charge. An administrator is given wide statutory powers to manage the company in accordance with the administration proposals.	Owes duties to all the company's creditors para 3(2) schedule B1 IA86 and *Kyrris v Oldham*. Owes fiduciary duties to the company. Acts as an officer of the court and is therefore subject to the rule in *Ex parte James*. [See Chapter 14 for more detail on the administrators function and duties.]
Administrative Receiver (AR)	IP appointed under the terms of a floating charge dated pre 15 September 2003. He is both receiver and manager of the floating charge assets. (See s29(2) IA86.)	On appointment he takes control of the secured assets. Acts as agent of the company (s44 IA86). However it is an unusual agency in that the AR's primary duty is to the debenture holder not the company.
Fixed charge receiver	An individual (not necessarily an IP) appointed by a fixed charge holder under the express terms of a fixed charge to realise fixed charge assets. The powers of such a receiver are contained in the Law of Property Act 1925 but usually these are supplemented and modified by the terms of the charge.	An agent of the company. Owes duties to the fixed charge holder.

Name	Definition	Purpose/main duties
Law of Property Act Receiver (LPA Receiver)	An individual (not necessarily an IP) appointed by a fixed charge holder under the power contained in the Law Of Property Act 1925. This is usually because there is no express power in the security documentation to appoint a fixed charge holder (rare). An LPA receiver will have only those powers specified in the LPA 1925.	An agent of the company. Owes duties to the fixed charge holder.

Note that officers of the court have a 'right of audience' before the courts ie an automatic right to address the court, they need not ask the court for its permission to be heard.

3 IP progress reports and records

Section overview

- Once an IP has accepted an appointment he or she must ensure that his/her conduct cannot be criticised. It is essential if IPs are going to achieve the required standard that they maintain proper records and returns and ensure that they are served at the relevant times on the relevant persons (as required by the legislation).

3.1 Progress reports

- **In compulsory liquidation** the liquidator must produce a progress report for the first year from the date of his appointment and thereafter every year until he ceases to act (Rule 4.49B). No progress report is required for any period after the liquidator has sent a draft final report to creditors.

    The content of progress reports is prescribed by Rule 4.49B of the amended rules and must include:

    - A statement of the creditors' rights to request further information about remuneration and/or expenses and the right to challenge the same (Rules 4.49E and 4.131)
    - A statement of the liquidator's receipts and payments for that period

    The progress report must be sent to the Registrar of Companies, members and creditors, within two months of the end of the period to which the report relates (subject to an extension of time granted by the court). The liquidator's draft final report must be sent to each creditor at least eight weeks before a final meeting. The final meeting cannot be held until any challenge to the liquidator's remuneration has been dealt with. Rule 4.49B does not apply where the liquidator is the official receiver.

- **In CVL and MVL** the liquidator must produce a progress report for each year commencing on the date of his appointment and thereafter every year until he ceases to act (Rule 4.49C). If he ceases to act, the period for which a liquidator must produce a report ends on the date that he ceases to act. Any new liquidator must produce a report for the period starting immediately after that date and every 12 months thereafter. No progress report is required for any period after the liquidator has sent a draft final report to creditors.

    The content of progress reports is prescribed by Rule 4.49B of the rules and must include:

    - A statement of the creditors' rights to request further information about remuneration and/or expenses and the right to challenge the same
    - A statement of the liquidator's receipts and payments for that period

    The progress report must be sent to the Registrar of Companies; members and creditors within two months of the end of the period to which the report relates (subject to an extension of time granted by the court). The liquidator's draft final report must be sent to each creditor at least eight weeks before a final meeting.

- **In administration** the administrator must produce a progress report for the period of six months commencing on the date that the company entered administration and every subsequent period of six months or until he ceases to act.

    The report must provide full details of the progress of the administration to date, including
    - A statement of the creditors' rights to request further information about remuneration and/or expenses and the right to challenge the same
    - A statement of the administrator's receipts and payments for that period

    Where a creditors' resolution has been passed, fixing the basis of an administrator's remuneration, he should notify the creditors of that resolution in his next report to creditors as 'relevant information' for creditors within Rule 2.47.

    In all subsequent progress reports to creditors, an administrator should specify the amount of remuneration drawn down and provide the same level of information as when seeking remuneration approval.

    The progress report must be sent to the creditors and Registrar of Companies within one month of the end of the period to which the report relates. This period can be extended by the court. Any administrator failing to comply with Rule 2.47 is liable to a fine and for continued contravention a daily default fine.

    The final report together with a notice of the automatic end of the administration must be filed with the court within five business days of the end of the administration (Rule 2.111). Copies must also be sent to the Registrar of Companies and all other persons who received a copy of the administrator's proposals as soon as is reasonably practicable.

- **In bankruptcy** the trustee (not OR) must produce a progress report for the first year from the date of his appointment and thereafter every year until he ceases to act (Rule 6.78A). No progress report is required for any period after the trustee has sent a draft final report to creditors.

    The content of progress reports is prescribed by Rule 6.78A and must include:
    - A statement of the creditors' rights to request further information about remuneration and/or expenses and the right to challenge the same (Rules 6.78C and 6.142(I))
    - A statement of the trustee's receipts and payments for that period

    The progress report must be sent to the creditors within two months of the end of the period to which the report relates. The trustee's draft final report must be sent to each creditor and the bankrupt at least eight weeks before a final meeting. The final meeting cannot be held until any challenge to the trustee's remuneration has been dealt with.

- **In CVA** the supervisor of a CVA must circulate an annual report setting out progress (from the date of commencement) and the prospects of success (Rule 1.26A(4)). The annual report must include an abstract of receipts and payments (or where there are no receipts and payments a statement to that effect). The report must be sent within two months of the end of the period to which the report relates to:
    - The Registrar of Companies
    - The company
    - The bound creditors (of whose addresses the supervisor is aware)
    - The members of the company (unless the court gives permission not to circulate the report or permits the availability of the report to be advertised and sent to those who request a copy)
    - The company auditors unless the company is in liquidation

    If within the two month period the supervisor becomes obliged to circulate a final report (Rule 1.29) the obligation to send the final report negates the need to send the annual report.

- **In IVA** the supervisor of a IVA must circulate an annual report setting out progress from the date of commencement and prospects of success (Rule 5.31A(4)). The annual report must include an abstract of receipts and payments (or where there are no receipts and payments a statement to that effect). The report must be sent within two months of the end of the period to which the report relates to:

- The bound creditors (of whose addresses the supervisor is aware)
- The debtor

If within the two month period the supervisor becomes obliged to circulate a final report (Rule 5.34) the obligation to send the final report negates the need to send the annual report.

- **In administrative receivership** the receiver must, within three months of his appointment, send out an initial report (s48 report) on the company to the creditors and the Registrar of Companies. Thereafter he must send an account of his receipts and payments to each member of the creditor's committee, the Registrar of Companies, the company and his appointer within two months after the end of 12 months from the date of appointment and every subsequent period of 12 months. If he ceases to act the account must be sent within two months after he ceases to act (Rule 3.32).

- **In fixed charge receivership** the receiver must, within one month after the end of the 12 months from the date of his appointment, and every subsequent period of six months, deliver an account of his receipts and payments to the Registrar of Companies, s38 IA86.

3.2 Electronic delivery of documents

Subject to a particular form of delivery being required by the Act, Rules or court order, notices and documents can be given, delivered, or sent, electronically, provided that the intended recipient has consented and has provided an electronic address for delivery. (R12A.10).

Any notice or document sent electronically by an office holder must either contain or be accompanied by a statement that the recipient may request a hard copy of the notice or document and give details of how the hard copy can be requested. Where so requested, the hard copy must be sent within five business days of receipt of the request by the office holder. No fee can be charged Rule 12A.11.

3.3 Use of websites

Except where personal service is required office holders may give, deliver, or send a document to any person by sending notice that it is available for viewing on a website. Information about the right to request a hard copy must also be given and it must be sent within five business days of any request. No fee can be charged.

3.4 Keeping records

An IP must comply with the statutory requirements to keep proper accounting records and (as required by the legislation) serve them at the relevant times on the relevant persons. Schedule 3 Insolvency Practitioners Regulations 2005 requires a specific record to be kept in relation to each appointment. These records can be inspected by the relevant RPB or the Secretary of State. They must be kept for at least six years after the IP obtains his release from office or if later the date on which his bond ceases to have effect.

With the implementation of SBEEA2015, the minimum requirements for the contents of the records to be maintained under schedule 3 were:

- Details of IP acting in the case:

    Name, IP number, principal business address, authorising body (including competent authority)

- Details of the insolvent:

    Name of person in relation to whom the practitioner is acting, type of insolvency proceedings

- Progress of administration:

    Date of commencement of the proceedings, date of appointment of the IP, date on which the appointment was notified to the Registrar of Companies

- Bonding arrangements in the case:

    Amount of specific penalty sum, name of surety or cautioner

- Matters relating to remuneration:

    Basis on which the IP is to be remunerated, date and content of any resolution of creditors in relation to the remuneration of the IP

- Meetings (other than final meetings of creditors):
    - Dates of members meeting, date of first meeting of creditors to consider administrator's proposals/administrative receiver's report/in liquidation or bankruptcy/to consider VA proposal/according to trust deed for creditors
    - The dates and purposes of any subsequent meetings
- Disqualification of directors:

    Dates returns/reports due and submitted
- Vacation of office:
    - Dates of final notice to, or meeting of, creditors
    - Date IP vacates office
    - Date of release or discharge of IP
- Distributions to creditors:

    Name of person to whom payment made, date of the payment, amount of the payment
- Statutory returns:

    Date return is due, date return filed
- Time recording:

    Records of the amount of time spent on the case by the IP and any persons assigned to assist in the administration of the case

The SBEEA2015 states that it is no longer necessary to hold this information in a prescribed form, and it is a common misconception that the IP record has been revoked. This is not the case, in fact the new act suggests that you add matters of materiality to the case records.

In addition, IPs need to comply with the relevant SIPs to ensure that their record keeping and reporting follows best practice. Departure from the standards set out in the SIPs is a matter for consideration in respect of disciplinary proceedings.

3.5 Records of meetings – SIP 12

- SIP 12 ('Records of Meetings in Formal Insolvency Proceedings') provides that it is best practice that records should be kept of all meetings of creditors and members.
- The record should include as a minimum the following information:
    - Title of the proceedings
    - Date, time and venue of meeting
    - Name and description of chairman and any others involved in conduct of meeting
    - A list of attendees (either in the report or appended to it). This should include creditors, members, debtor and if a company the officers and former officers of the company
    - The exercise of any discretion by the chairman in relation to the admissibility or value of any claim for voting purposes
    - The resolutions taken and the decision on each one and in the event of a poll being taken the value or number of votes for and against each resolution
    - Where a committee is established the names and addresses of the members
    - Such other matters as are required by statute or, in the case of a voluntary arrangement, the proposal
    - When the meeting ended
- The record should be authenticated by the chairman and be either retained with the record, or entered in the company's minute book and a copy retained with the record of the proceedings (whichever is appropriate). If the meeting has approved the setting up of a committee then copy records of committee meetings should be sent to attendees of those committee meetings

- Forms of proxy and poll cards should also be retained. This is in any event a requirement of Rule 8.4. It will be particularly important in VAs if any appeal on the basis of a material irregularity is later made
- Information provided at a meeting in support of a request that the meeting approve the IP's remuneration should also be retained
- If the nominee/supervisor has not chaired the meeting he or she should ensure that the record complies with the above principles
- If the meeting is chaired by anyone other than the IP, an authority to chair must be granted

4 Remuneration and expenses

Section overview

- There are a number of statutory provisions that govern this area. The relevant Insolvency Rules are:

    R4.127(1) CVLs and compulsory liquidations
    R4.148A(1) MVLs
    R6.138(1) bankruptcies
    R2.106(1) administrations
    R1.28 company voluntary arrangements
    R5.33 individual voluntary arrangements

- SIP 9 ensures that office holders are familiar with the statutory provisions and covers, amongst others: on what basis remuneration is to be calculated; what criteria should be used to judge the reasonableness of fees; who should authorise the drawing of fees; and what an office holder can do if he is dissatisfied with the level of fees.

- The IR2015 imposed that from 1 October 2015, any trustee, liquidator or administrator seeking fees on a time costs basis must provide significantly more information that must be given prior to consideration of the same.

- Office holders obtain payment of their fees out of assets which would otherwise be available to creditors. It is imperative therefore that those with a direct financial interest in the level of the office holders fees (ie creditors) feel confident that the rules relating to the charging of remuneration have been properly complied with.

4.1 Basis of calculation of remuneration

- **In liquidation (compulsory and voluntary) and bankruptcy** remuneration may be calculated in three ways:

    (i) As a % value of assets distributed or realised or both

    (ii) By reference to the time properly given by the office holder and his staff in attending to matters arising

    (iii) As a fixed fee/set amount

Different bases for calculating remuneration can be adopted in respect of different actions by the office holder and different percentages (where applied) can be set.

- **In administration** the same rule applies save that the percentage value is calculated as a percentage of the assets dealt with.

    The rules (R2.67(1)(h)) allow recovery of fees charges and expenses incurred by an IP before appointment provided that they meet the following criteria: they are unpaid pre-appointment costs; and the IP incurred the costs with 'a view' to administration (likely to be interpreted as work done once the decision to place the company into administration has been taken).

    [The expenses of a pre-pack sale will not fall into the above exception see Chapter 16.]

- **In receiverships** remuneration is a contractual matter between receiver and charge holder. There is no statutory criteria to be applied and no provision for a dissatisfied IP to appeal to creditors or the court. (However, the liquidator may apply to court for receiver's fees to be fixed (s36).)

- **In voluntary arrangement** the IP's remuneration is set out in the terms of the arrangement which will also cover the criteria to be applied when fixing fees and how to deal with any dissatisfaction.

4.2 Criteria

Guidance is given to IPs on what they should consider when determining the level of their remuneration and what (in the event a dispute) they will be allowed to recover. The following criteria give guidance on how to judge the reasonableness of the fees being requested:

- The 2014 Practice Direction on Insolvency
- SIP 9: The fixing and approval of the remuneration of appointees
- Insolvency Rules

Remuneration should be proportionate to:

- The complexity (or otherwise) of the case
- Any responsibility of an exceptional kind or degree which falls on the office holder
- The effectiveness with which the office holder appears to be carrying out, or has carried out, his duties
- The value and nature of the property with which the office holder has to deal

It is for the IP to justify the level of his or her fees with any doubt being resolved **against** the practitioner. Furthermore, an IP cannot expect to be rewarded for time spent (however well documented) if that time spent achieved no value for the creditors. The practice direction specifically seeks to reward the value of the service rendered rather than simply recognising the time spent by the office holder and his staff.

As detailed above, where fees are sought by a trustee, liquidator or administrator on a time cost basis the advisor must also provide the following information:

- The anticipated time costs in an estimate detailing what is to be done, by whom and at what rate
- The period to which the fees relate
- What disbursements are likely to be incurred by the IP
- The overall outcome to creditors

Where such time is exceeded, the IP must seek further sanction form creditors prior to drawing more fees. There is no resultant entitlement to draw fees exceeding the amount agreed by the creditors on a time costs basis.

4.3 Who authorises remuneration?

- **In compulsory liquidation** the liquidation committee (if there is one) or a meeting of creditors, however if remuneration has not been fixed within 18 months of appointment the Schedule 6 scale rate applies (see paragraph 4.4).
  In the event of liquidator dissatisfaction and on application by the liquidator the court can fix his remuneration.

  If the company was in administration immediately prior to going into liquidation then the basis of remuneration fixed in the administration applies to the liquidation.

  If a liquidator realises assets for a secured creditor holding a fixed charge the liquidator takes his remuneration from the proceeds of sale.

- **In CVL** the liquidation committee (if there is one); or a meeting of creditors, however if remuneration has not been fixed by the committee or creditors (and not later than 18 months from the date of appointment) the court will fix the remuneration.

  If the company was in administration immediately prior to going into liquidation then the basis of remuneration fixed in the administration applies to the liquidation.

If a liquidator realises assets for a secured creditor holding a fixed charge the liquidator takes his remuneration from the proceeds of sale.

- **In MVL** the company in general meeting. In default the court can fix the liquidator's remuneration provided that he has made application to the general meeting and applies within 18 months of appointment.

- **In administration** if there is a creditors' committee the committee fixes the remuneration. If there is no committee or the committee fails to reach agreement on his remuneration or the administrator is dissatisfied he can apply to:
    - The secured creditors (if no distribution to preferential creditors)
    - The secured creditors and more than 50% in value of the preferential creditors (if distribution to preferential creditors)
    - The unsecured creditors in a general meeting

  In the event of administrator dissatisfaction and on application by the administrator the court can fix his remuneration (within 18 months of appointment).

- **In bankruptcy** the creditors' committee (if there is one); or a meeting of creditors, however if remuneration has not been fixed within 18 months of appointment the Schedule 6 scale rate applies.

  In the event of trustee dissatisfaction and on application by the trustee the court can fix his remuneration.

- **Joint appointments.** Joint liquidators (R4.128(2)), joint trustees (R6.139(2)) and joint administrators (R2.106(7)) must decide an apportionment of remuneration amongst themselves failing which the court, committee or creditors can decide. In an MVL the same rule applies (R4.148A(5)) except that the court or company in general meeting settle any disputes.

4.4 Schedule 6 scale

Where neither the creditors' committee nor a general meeting of creditors has determined the basis of fees for a trustee in bankruptcy or a compulsory liquidator, the Schedule 6 scale (as set out in Schedule 6 of Insolvency Rules 1986) provides a fallback position. In the assessment you may be given the realisation and distribution figures upon which the scale rate will be applied. If you have to calculate the figures yourself note that the realisation scale is applied to sums paid into the Insolvency Services account (ISA) less any amount paid to redeem any charges on the sale of the property and the costs of any trading, and the distribution scale is applied to the amount otherwise available to distribute by way of dividend.

The scale rate is as follows:

Band		Realisation scale %	Distribution scale %
First	£5,000	20	10.0
Next	£5,000	15	7.5
Next	£90,000	10	5.0
All further sums		5	2.5

4.5 What can IP do if he is dissatisfied?

- **In compulsory liquidation and CVL** where remuneration has been set by the liquidation committee (or by the creditors' committee where liquidation follows on from administration) the liquidator can apply to a meeting of creditors under Rule 4.129A. In addition, the court has jurisdiction to hear any application under Rule 4.130. The application is made on 14 days' notice to the committee or where there is not one, the creditors.

- **In MVL** a liquidator unhappy with the level or basis of remuneration set by the company in general meeting he may apply to the court (Rule 4.148A) on giving 14 days' notice to the contributories of the company.

- **In administration** where remuneration has been set by the creditors' committee the administrator can apply to a meeting of creditors under Rule 2.107. If no dividend to unsecured or preferential creditors is anticipated application can be made to the secured creditors. If a dividend to preferential creditors is anticipated, application is to each secured and preferential creditor whose debts amount to more than 50% of the value of preferential debts, ignoring those that creditors who do not respond to any invitation to give or withhold approval. In addition, the court has jurisdiction to hear an application under Rule 2.108. The application is made on 14 days' notice to the committee or where there is not one, the creditors.

- **In bankruptcy** where remuneration has been set by the creditors' committee the trustee can apply to a meeting of creditors under Rule 6.140. In addition, the court has jurisdiction to hear any application under Rule 6.141. The application is made on 14 days' notice to the committee or where there is not one, the creditors.

4.6 Is variation possible?

- In all cases if after fixing the remuneration there is a 'material and substantial' change in circumstances the office holder may request that the basis be changed. The request is made to the body that first fixed the remuneration and it will not apply retrospectively.

4.7 Creditors' rights to request further information about remuneration and expenses

A liquidator (but not the OR) an administrator or a trustee in bankruptcy may be requested to provide further information about the level of remuneration and/or expenses set out in any progress report. A request may be made by: a secured creditor; an unsecured creditor with the support of at least 5% in value of the creditors (or members in an MVL); and any unsecured creditor (or member) with the permission of the court.

The rules set out the timetable for any application.

- Request to be made within 21 days of receiving the progress report unless the report is in anticipation of a liquidator or trustee's resignation in which case the time limit is seven business days.
- Office holder then has 14 days to either respond or justify why he will not do so. Justification includes: that the office holder considers the time or cost of preparing a response to the request excessive; disclosure may prejudice the liquidation/administration/bankruptcy or lead to violence against any person; the office holder is subject to an obligation of confidentiality in respect of the information.
- Any creditor/member (not just the creditor/member making the request) may then apply to court within 21 days of either the expiry of the 14 days or receipt of any justification by the office holder as to why he will not provide the information.

4.8 Right to request time statements

Under Regulation 36A of Insolvency Regulations 1994 an IP is required to provide certain information about the time spent on a case, free of charge, upon request. The persons who are entitled to ask for this information are:

- Any creditor in the case
- Where the case relates to a company, any director or contributory, of that company
- Where the case relates to an individual, that individual

The information to be provided is:

- The total number of hours spent on the case by the office holder or staff assigned to the case
- For each grade of staff, the average hourly rate at which they are charged out
- The number of hours spent by each grade of staff in the relevant period

The information must be provided within 28 days of receipt of the request by the office holder.

[In respect of VAs this regulation has now been incorporated into the rules – R1.55 and 5.66.]

4.9 Creditors' dissatisfaction with level of remuneration

Creditors claiming that remuneration (or expenses) is excessive in CVLs and compulsories (R4.131), bankruptcy (R6.142) and administration (R2.109) may apply to the court. In all cases:

- At least 10% of creditors in value (including applicant) must concur
- An application must be made within 8 weeks of receipt of the account or report in which the remuneration or expenses were set out

If the court considers the application to be well-founded, it must make one or more of the following orders:

(a) An order reducing the amount of remuneration which the officeholder was entitled to charge

(b) An order fixing the basis of remuneration at a reduced rate or amount

(c) An order changing the basis of remuneration

(d) An order that some or all of the remuneration or expenses in question be treated as not being expenses

(e) An order that the officeholder pay to such person as the court may specify the amount of the excess of remuneration or expenses or such part of the excess as the court may specify

Unless the court orders otherwise, the costs of the application shall be paid by the applicant, and do not fall on the estate.

[Note that in bankruptcy Rule 6.207A extends the right to challenge a trustee's remuneration to bankrupts but only where the bankrupt is seeking annulment.]

Interactive question 2: Remuneration

In a creditors' voluntary liquidation, who is charged with approving the drawing of the liquidator's remuneration, upon what basis may it be calculated and what matters should be taken into account by those determining the reasonableness of the fees being requested?

See **Answer** at the end of the chapter.

4.10 SIP 9

SIP 9 has been reviewed and the new version SIP applies from 1 December 2015. The SIP sets out best practice with regard to the provision of information to those responsible for the approval of fees and reminds IPs of their responsibilities under the Act and Rules.

There remains some ambiguity about the applications of the 2015 guide and the guide.

The office holder must ensure that those charged with approving his fees have access to sufficient information about the basis of fees to be able to make an informed judgment as to the reasonableness of the proposed fees when seeking agreement to the terms of remuneration and seeking approval of fees to be taken.

In previous versions of the SIP there were produced guidance notes for creditors which it was intended that office holders make available to them.

If the fees are drawn on a number of bases, the IP must disclose all such bases in the report.

He must also disclose whether a fee estimate has been exceeded and what, if anything he intends to do about this.

4.11 Key features of the SIP

4.11.1 Seeking agreement to the bases of remuneration

When seeking approval for the basis or bases of remuneration, an office holder should provide sufficient supporting information to enable the approving body, having regard to all the circumstances of the case, to make an informed judgment as to whether the basis or bases sought is/are appropriate. The nature and extent of the information provided will depend on the stage during the conduct of the case at which approval is being sought.

If any part of the remuneration is sought on a time cost basis, an office holder should provide details of the minimum time units used and current charge-out rates, split by grades of staff, of those people who have been or who are likely to be involved in the time costs aspects of the case.

An office holder should also provide details and the cost of any work that has been or is intended to be sub-contracted out that could otherwise be carried out by the office holder or his or her staff.

If work has already been carried out, an office holder should state the proposed charge for the period to date and provide an explanation of what has been achieved in the period and how it was achieved. The explanation should be sufficient to enable the progress of the case to be assessed and assessment to be made as to whether the proposed charge is reasonable given the circumstances of the case. Where the proposed charge is calculated on a time cost basis, the office holder should disclose the time spent and the average charge-out rates, in larger cases this should be split by grades of staff and analysed by appropriate activity.

4.11.2 Seeking agreement to fees once the bases have been fixed during the course of an assignment

The requirements in this section are in addition to the reporting requirements under the insolvency legislation.

When reporting periodically to creditors, an office holder should provide an explanation of what has been achieved in the period under review and how it was achieved. This explanation should be sufficient to enable the progress of the case to be assessed. Creditors should be able to understand whether the remuneration charged is reasonable in the circumstances of the case (whilst recognising that the office holder must fulfil certain statutory obligations and regulatory requirements that might be perceived as bringing no added value for the estate).

Where any remuneration is on a time costs basis, an office holder should disclose the charge in respect of the period, the time spent and the average charge-out rates, in cases where fees exceed £10,000, the cases should be split by grades of staff and analysed by appropriate activity.

If there have been any changes to the charge-out rates during the period under review, rates should be disclosed by grades of staff, split by the periods applicable.

When agreement to fees is sought the office holder should provide an up to date receipts and payments account.

Where fees are based on a time cost basis, the office holder should disclose details of time spent and charge out values and such additional information as may reasonably be required having regard to the size and complexity of the case. This would include an analysis of time spent on the case by activity and grade of staff.

The Appendix of SIP 9 sets out a suggested format for producing the information required. This suggested format classifies work functions as follows:

- Administration and planning
- Investigations
- Realisation of assets
- Trading
- Creditors
- Case specific matters

The table classifies the hours spent on those functions by grade of staff as follows:

- Partner
- Manager
- Other senior professional
- Assistants and support staff

The level of disclosure should be proportionate to the circumstances of the case.

4.11.3 Sub contracted work

Where fees are based on a % basis, the office holder must provide details of any work which has or is to be sub-contracted out which would normally be carried out by the office holder.

4.11.4 Payments received by secured creditors

Where the office holder realises an asset on behalf of a secured creditor and receives remuneration out of the proceeds, he should disclose the amount of that remuneration to: the committee; to any meeting of creditors convened for the purposes of determining his fees; and in his report to creditors.

4.11.5 Pre-appointment costs

When approval is sought for the payment of outstanding costs incurred prior to an office holder's appointment, disclosure should follow the principles and standards contained in this statement.

4.11.6 Payments to associates

Where services are provided from within the practice or by a party with whom the practice, or an individual within the practice, has a business or personal relationship, an office holder should take particular care to ensure that the best value and service is being provided. An office holder should also have regard to relationships where the practice is held out to be part of a national or international association.

Payments that could reasonably be perceived as presenting a threat to the office holder's objectivity by virtue of a professional or personal relationship should not be made unless approved in the same manner as an office holder's remuneration or category 2 disbursements.

4.11.7 Provision of information to successive officeholders

When an office holder's appointment is followed by the appointment of another insolvency practitioner, whether or not in the same proceedings, the prior office holder should provide the successor with information in accordance with the principles and standards contained in SIP 9.

5 Expenses and disbursements

Section overview

SIP 9 sets out best practice with regard to the disclosure and drawing of expenses and disbursements.

- All disbursements should be disclosed
- Category 1 disbursements do not require approval
- Category 2 disbursements require prior approval

5.1 Priority of expenses and disbursements

Liquidation R4.218	All remuneration and expenses are payable from 'free' assets (assets not specifically pledged) in priority to all unsecured creditors and preferential claims (s115 IA86). If insufficient they are paid before floating charges. (Free assets do not include the prescribed part.)
Administration R2.67	Para 99 Sch.B1 IA86 provides that remuneration and expenses are payable in priority to any floating charge.
Receivership ss37 and 45 IA86	Remuneration expenses and sums due under an indemnity are paid out of the charged assets in priority to the charge holder.
Bankruptcy expenses R6.224	The priority of the trustee's remuneration and expenses is set out in Rule 6.224.

In liquidation, administration and bankruptcy there is a prescribed list of expenses and the order in which they should be paid out. There is no prescribed list in receivership.

5.2 Disbursements

Office holders should disclose and explain how charges are made up and the basis upon which they have been calculated. They should be disclosed to those responsible for approving remuneration, that is, the creditors' committee or the general body of creditors.

Costs met by and reimbursed to an office holder in connection with an insolvency appointment should be appropriate and reasonable. Such costs will fall into two categories.

Category 1 disbursements

These are costs where there is specific, ascertainable expenditure directly referable both to the appointment in question and a payment to an independent third party. These may include, for example, advertising, room hire, storage, postage, telephone charges, specific travel expenses, and equivalent costs reimbursed to the office holder or his or her staff.

Category 2 disbursements

These are costs that are directly referable to the appointment in question but may not be a payment to an independent third party, or are incapable of calculation at a precise cost. They may include shared or allocated costs that can be allocated to the appointment on a proper and reasonable basis, for example, business mileage.

Category 1 disbursements can be drawn without prior approval, although an office holder should be prepared to disclose information about them in the same way as any other expenses.

Category 2 disbursements may be drawn if they have been approved in the same manner as an office holder's remuneration. When seeking approval, an office holder should explain, for each category of expense, the basis on which the charge is being made.

The following are not permissible:

(a) A charge calculated as a percentage of remuneration

(b) An administration fee or charge additional to an office holder's remuneration

(c) Recovery of basic overhead costs such as office and equipment rental, depreciation and finance charges

If an office holder has obtained approval for the basis of category 2 disbursements, that basis may continue to be used in a sequential appointment where further approval of the basis of remuneration is not required, or where the office holder is replaced.

Further, where any payment is made to a business that is defined as a legal associate in accordance with CA2006, this should automatically be disclosed as a category 2 disbursement, irrespective of the level or basis of fees drawn.

5.3 Litigation expenses in liquidation

Special rules are in place with regard to litigation expenses (incurred for the purpose of either swelling the assets available for creditors or for protecting or realising the estate assets). No consent is needed to deduct litigation expenses of up to £5,000 but if the expense is in excess of that sum and deduction from the floating charge pool will reduce the sums available to a floating charge holder the prior consent of the affected charge holder(s)/preferential creditors will be required before the deduction can be made. Alternatively, approval must be sought from the court.

Summary and Self-test

Summary

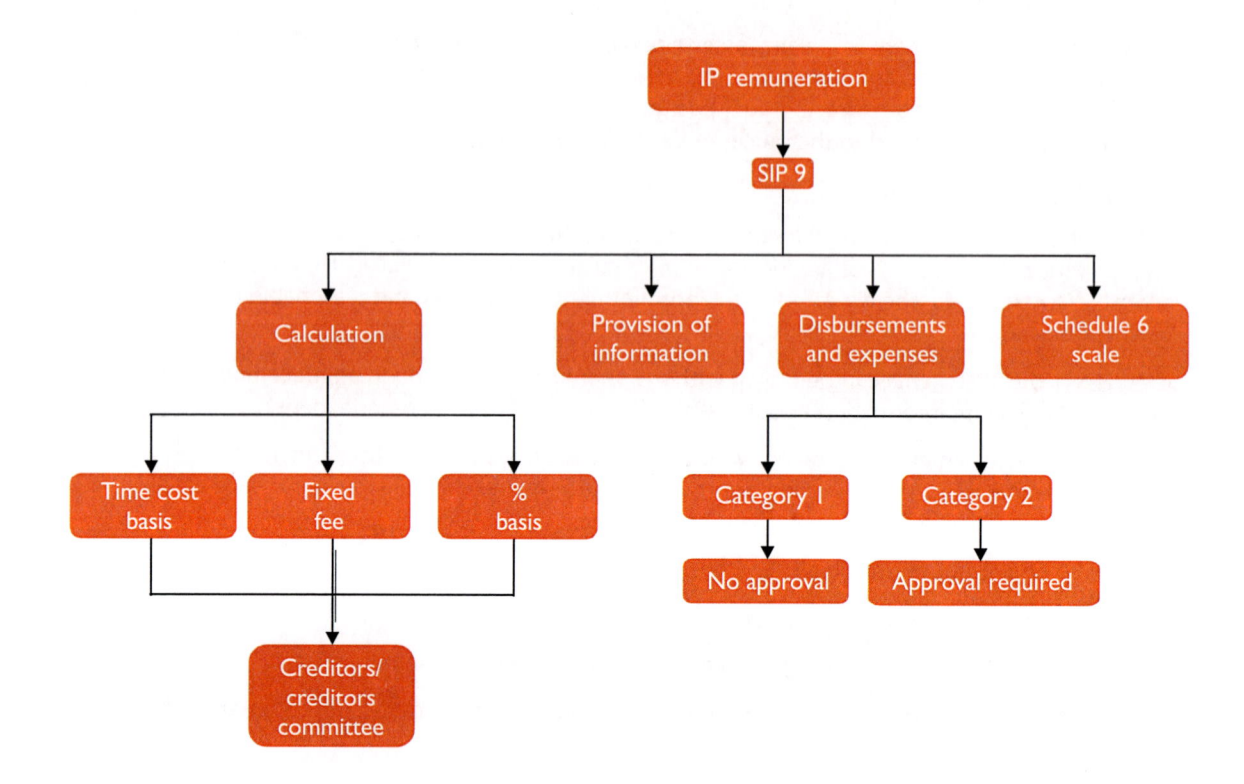

```
                        IP remuneration
                              │
                            SIP 9
         ┌──────────────┬─────┴────────┬──────────────┐
     Calculation    Provision of   Disbursements   Schedule 6
                    information    and expenses      scale
         │                               │
   ┌─────┼─────┐                   ┌─────┴─────┐
Time cost  Fixed   %            Category 1   Category 2
 basis      fee   basis              │            │
         │                       No approval  Approval required
   Creditors/
   creditors
   committee
```

Certificate in Insolvency

Self-test

Answer the following questions.

1   Which of the following criteria are not required to be taken into account by R4.127(4) when determining the level of a liquidator's remuneration?

   A   The complexity of the case
   B   The value of assets with which the liquidator has to deal
   C   The expected dividend to creditors
   D   The effectiveness with which the liquidator has carried out his duties
   E   Responsibilities of an exceptional kind or degree.

2   State whether a liquidator is allowed to recover the following costs in a liquidation with which he is dealing. Where you state that he can recover such costs state whether or not the basis of the cost recovery must be disclosed and authorised by those who approve the liquidator's remuneration.

   (i)   Specialist copying carried out on the liquidator's firm's photocopier for a circular to creditors

   (ii)   Case advertising

   (iii) The liquidator's office and equipment rental costs

   (iv)   Room hire for a creditors meeting at the liquidator's business premises

   (v)   Reimbursement of a member of the liquidator's staff in respect of an invoice which the staff member has paid for international air travel incurred in connection with a contract debt owed to the company in liquidation

   (vi)   Document storage costs in respect of records of the company in liquidation which are stored in the liquidator's basement

   (vii) Mileage to and from the client or as otherwise connected to the case

3   Fred Baker was appointed trustee in bankruptcy of Jane Swallow. Assets have been realised totalling £93,420 and dividends totalling £73,000 have been distributed to the preferential and unsecured creditors. Calculate the trustee's remuneration using the scale laid down in Schedule 6 Insolvency Rules 1986.

4   Is the following statement true or false?

   The expenses of a pre-pack administration can be recovered as pre appointment costs under Rule 2.67.

   A   True
   B   False

5   What % of creditors (in value) must concur to apply to court for an order that the office holders' remuneration is excessive?

   A   5%
   B   10%
   C   25%
   D   50%

Now, go back to the Learning Objectives in the Introduction. If you are satisfied that you have achieved these objectives, please tick them off.

Answers to Self-test

1   C

2   (i)   Specialist copying – recovered, approval required
       (ii)   Case advertising – recovered, no approval required
       (iii)   Office and equipment costs – not recoverable
       (iv)   Room hire – recoverable, approval required
       (v)   Reimbursement of air fares – recoverable, no approval required
       (vi)   Document storage – recoverable, approval required.
       (vii)   Mileage – recoverable, approval required (even if within the HMRC guidelines)

Costs recovered should have been directly incurred in respect of the liquidation. There should be a reasonable method of calculation of the cost and the resultant charge should be in line with the cost of external provision.

3   **Realisation fee**

	£
5,000 × 20%	1,000
5,000 × 15%	750
83,420 × 10%	8,342
£93,420	10,092

Distribution fee

	£
5,000 × 10%	500
5,000 × 7.5%	375
63,000 × 5%	3,150
£73,000	4,025

Total fees = £14,117

4   B (False)

5   B

Answers to Interactive questions

Answer to Interactive question 1: IP bonding

Max will have to have a specific penalty bond of £255,000 in place

Proceeds of house	£350,000
Less mortgage	(£125,000)
Add contributions	
(£500 × 12 × 5)	£30,000
	£255,000

Answer to Interactive question 2: Remuneration

The liquidator is entitled to receive remuneration for his services as liquidator. The basis of such remuneration shall be fixed as:

(a) A percentage of the value of assets realised or distributed or of the one value and the other in combination; or

(b) By reference to the time taken by the Insolvency Practitioner; or

(c) As a fixed amount.

Different tasks undertaken by the liquidator may be remunerated on different bases.

It is for the liquidation committee to determine which of the bases to be used and percentages or fixed amounts as appropriate. If there is no committee or they make no determinations, then the remuneration may be fixed by a resolution of a meeting of creditors. If still not fixed, then the basis of remuneration shall be fixed by the court. The application must be made within 18 months of the liquidator's appointment. The matters to be considered in determining the remuneration are:

(i) The complexity of the case
(ii) Any exceptional responsibility or costs by the liquidator
(iii) The effectiveness of carrying out the role of the liquidator
(iv) The value and nature of assets dealt with

Different obligations are required of the IA where fees are sought on a time costs basis.

CHAPTER 4

Key ethical issues

Introduction

Topic List
1. Fundamental principles
2. Threats
3. Safeguards
4. Specific considerations before accepting appointments - Receiverships, CVAs and administrations
5. Specific considerations before accepting appointments - Liquidations
6. Specific considerations before accepting appointments - Bankruptcy and voluntary arrangements

Summary and Self-test

Answers to Self-test

Answer to Interactive question

Introduction

Learning objectives

Tick off

- Identify the fundamental principles ☐
- Identify self review threats and self interest threats and how they affect the office holder's ability to accept insolvency appointments ☐

Stop and think

Why shouldn't an office holder with a close personal relationship with a director of a company act as liquidator in respect of that company? Why should an office holder not act as liquidator of a company when he has previously acted as administrative receiver of the company? Why shouldn't an office holder be allowed to purchase assets of an insolvent company in respect of which he is acting as liquidator?

Working context

When deciding whether to accept an insolvency appointment, all office holders must adhere to the Code of Ethics for insolvency practitioners. Office holders are appointed at a time when companies and individuals are insolvent. Creditors and others involved are in a vulnerable position often having lost sums of money. The Code of Ethics provide a framework within which office holders work so that anyone dealing with an office holder can be certain that their needs are being dealt with fairly, honestly and with integrity at all times. All aspects of insolvency work are governed by the Code of Ethics so a practical understanding of them is a necessity.

1 Fundamental principles

> **Section overview**
> - The practice of insolvency is principally governed by statute and secondary legislation. The Insolvency Code of Ethics gives guidance to office holders in relation to the application of the Code and also in matters not directly covered by legislation. In all aspects of his work the office holder will be governed by the fundamental principles outlined in the Code.

1.1 Fundamental principles

An IP should not engage in any business, occupation or activity that impairs or might impair integrity, objectivity or the good reputation of the profession and as a result would be incompatible with the fundamental principles.

The fundamental principles are as follows:

- **Integrity** – an IP should be straightforward and honest in all professional and business relationships
- **Objectivity** – an IP should not allow bias, conflict of interest or undue influence of others to override professional or business judgments
- **Professional competence and due care** – an IP has a continuing duty to maintain professional knowledge and skill at the level required to ensure that a client or employer receives competent professional service based on current developments in practice
- **Confidentiality** – an IP should respect the confidentiality of information acquired as a result of professional and business relationships and should not disclose any such information to third parties without proper and specific authority unless there is a legal or professional duty to disclose. Confidential information acquired as a result of professional or business relationships should not be used for the personal advantage of the IP or third parties
- **Professional behaviour** – an IP should comply with relevant laws and regulations and should avoid any action that discredits the profession

1.2 Records

IPs should document their consideration of the fundamental principles and the reasons behind their agreement or otherwise to accept an insolvency appointment. Evidence of a properly carried out conflicts check and associated discussion (if applicable) should also be retained.

2 Threats

> **Section overview**
> - The IP must identify actual or potential threats to the fundamental principles and determine whether there are any safeguards that might be available to offset them.

Threats to the fundamental principles may fall into five categories:

- Self-review threat
- Self-interest threat
- Advocacy threats
- Familiarity threats
- Intimidation threats

2.1 Self-review threat

A self-review threat may occur when a previous judgement made by an individual within the practice needs to be re-evaluated by the IP.

Key ethical issues

Examples of circumstances that may create self-review threats include:

- The acceptance of an insolvency appointment for an entity where an individual within the practice has recently been employed by that entity and is now in a position to exert significant influence over the conduct of the insolvency appointment
- The acceptance of an appointment for an entity where the IP or the practice has carried out professional work of any description, including sequential insolvency appointments, for that entity

However, such self-review threats may diminish over the passage of time.

Definition

Entity: An individual, partnership or corporate body.

2.2 Self-interest threat

A self-interest threat may occur as a result of the financial or other interests of a practice or an IP or of an immediate or close family member of an individual within the practice.

Examples of circumstances that may create self-interest threats for an IP include:

- An interest in a major creditor which could influence the level of fees paid to the IP
- Concern about the possibility of damaging a business relationship
- Concerns about potential future employment
- A personal connection with an entity or a principal of an entity
- The acquisition of assets of the entity

2.3 Advocacy threats

Advocacy threats may occur when an individual within the practice promotes a position or opinion to the point that subsequent objectivity may be compromised.

Examples of circumstances that may create advocacy threats include:

- Acting in an advisory capacity for a creditor (or a group of creditors) of an entity prior to an insolvency appointment in respect of that entity
- Acting as an advocate for a client in litigation, or disputes with third parties, prior to an insolvency appointment in respect of that client

2.4 Familiarity threats

Familiarity threats may occur when, because of a close relationship, an individual within the practice becomes too sympathetic to the interests of others.

Examples of circumstances that may create familiarity threats include:

- An individual within the practice having a close or immediate family relationship with an entity or principal of an entity
- An individual within the practice having a close or immediate family relationship with an employee of the entity who is in a position to exert direct and significant influence over the conduct of an insolvency appointment
- A principal or employee of an entity who was or is an individual within the practice

Familiarity threats can arise if services are provided by a regular source. Safeguards to mitigate such threats should ensure that a proper business relationship is maintained between the parties and such relationships should be reviewed periodically to ensure that best value is being obtained.

Safeguards may include clear guidelines and policies within the practice on such appointments, particularly concerning disclosure of relevant information to creditors' committees.

IPs may build relationships with firms of agents where a regular flow of work is beneficial for both parties. Such relationships should be reviewed at regular periods to ensure that best value is being obtained for creditors.

2.5 Intimidation threats

Intimidation threats may occur where an IP is deterred from acting objectively by threats, actual or perceived.

Examples of circumstances that may create intimidation threats include:

- Being threatened with dismissal or replacement in relation to a professional service, whether by a creditor or any other person
- Being threatened with litigation
- Being pressured not to follow regulations, the Code of Ethics, technical or professional standards
- Where the IP is an employee rather than a principal of the practice and has insufficient control, as an officeholder, over the insolvency appointment

3 Safeguards

> **Section overview**
>
> - Before agreeing to accept any insolvency appointment an IP should consider whether acceptance would create any threats to compliance with the fundamental principles. The significance of threats should be evaluated. If identified threats are other than trivial, safeguards should be considered and applied as necessary to eliminate them or reduce them to an acceptable level.

Appropriate safeguards (amongst others) may include:

- Leadership that stresses the importance of compliance with the fundamental principles
- Policies and procedures to implement and monitor quality control of engagements
- Documented policies regarding the identification of threats which should extend to AML and anti-bribery legislation
- Documented internal policies and procedures requiring compliance with the fundamental principles
- A disciplinary mechanism to promote compliance with the principles
- Consulting an independent third party, such as a committee of creditors, a licensing or professional body or another IP
- Seeking directions from the court
- Obtaining knowledge and understanding of the entity, its owners, managers and those responsible for its governance and business activities
- Acquiring an appropriate understanding of the nature of the entity's business
- Assigning staff with the necessary competencies
- Using experts where necessary

If the IP is of the opinion that there are no safeguards which can mitigate a particular threat he should not accept the insolvency appointment.

3.1 Perceived conflicts

IPs must be mindful of how they will be perceived by others. A perception of conflict will undermine public confidence in an IP's ability to carry out the engagement and the appointment should therefore be declined.

3.2 Maintaining professional competence

IPs are required to maintain their professional competence. This requires a continuing awareness and understanding of relevant technical and professional developments including:

- Developments in insolvency legislation
- The regulations of their licensing body
- Technical issues being discussed within the profession
- Guidance issued by their licensing body or the Insolvency Service
- Statements of Insolvency Practice

3.3 Conflicts of interest

An IP should take reasonable steps to identify circumstances that could pose a conflict of interest which might give rise to threats to compliance with the fundamental principles.

Examples of where a conflict of interest may arise are where:

- An IP has to deal with claims between the separate and conflicting interests of entities over whom he is appointed
- There are succession appointments
- A significant relationship has existed with the entity or someone connected with the entity

Where a conflict of interest is identified that cannot be eliminated or reduced to an acceptable level, the insolvency appointment should not be accepted.

The following specific safeguards should be considered:

- The use of separate IPs and/or staff
- Procedures to prevent access to information
- Clear guidelines for individuals within the practice on issues of security and confidentiality
- The use of confidentiality agreements signed by individuals within the practice
- Seeking directions from the court
- Regular reviews of the application of safeguards by a senior individual within the practice not involved with the insolvency appointment

3.4 Fees

The special nature of insolvency appointments makes the payment or offer of any commission for, or the furnishing of any valuable consideration towards, the introduction of insolvency appointments inappropriate. This does not, however, preclude an arrangement between an IP and a bona fide employee whereby the employee's remuneration is based in whole or in part on introductions obtained for the practitioner through the efforts of the employee.

The acceptance of referral fees or commissions should not be accepted.

It is acceptable to make payment to an introducing source that has assisted in giving advice and/or providing documentation in relation to the client. Such intentions and fee should be formally recorded as required by SIPs/legislation.

3.5 Marketing

When insolvency appointments are sought through marketing, a self interest threat to the compliance with the principle of professional behaviour might arise if services, achievements or products are marketed in a way that is inconsistent with that principle.

Advertisements and other forms of marketing should be clearly distinguishable as such and have regard to principles of legality, decency, honesty and truthfulness.

An IP should never promote or seek to promote his services in such a way, or to such an extent as to amount to harassment.

3.6 Gifts and hospitality

An IP should not offer or provide gifts or hospitality where this would give rise to threats to compliance with the fundamental principles.

3.7 Significant professional and personal relationships

The most common threat to an IP's independence and integrity is from ongoing and previous relationships.

The IP should ensure that all business and professional relationships are conducted in a fair and transparent manner.

An IP should not accept an insolvency appointment in relation to an entity where any personal, professional or business connection with a principal is such as to impair or reasonably appear to impair the IP's objectivity.

In considering whether objectivity may be threatened an IP should identify and analyse the significance of any professional or personal relationship which may affect compliance with the fundamental principles.

Consideration should be given to whether any relationships exist between any individual within the practice or the practice itself and a principal or employee of an entity for which an insolvency appointment is being considered. In deciding whether a relationship is significant the IP should consider how others would regard the relationship.

A professional relationship would arise where:

- An individual within the practice is carrying out, or has carried out, audit work or any other professional work
- An individual in the practice has an interest in the entity

Issues to consider may include:

- The perception of the relationship - what a reasonable and informed third party, having knowledge of all of the relevant information, would reasonably conclude to be acceptable
- How recently the work was carried out – audit work carried out for an entity in the previous **three years will** be considered significant. However there may be instances where in respect of non-audit work, any threat is still at an acceptable level even though it was within the three year period. Conversely there may be situations which require a much longer period to have elapsed before any threat posed can be reduced to an acceptable level
- Whether the fee received for the work by the practice is or was significant to the practice itself
- The impact of the work conducted by the practice on the financial state / stability of the entity
- The nature of the previous duties undertaken by a practice, or an individual within the practice, during an earlier relationship with an entity
- Whether the insolvency appointment to be conducted involves any consideration of any work previously undertaken by the practice for that entity
- The extent of the insolvency team's familiarity with the individuals connected with the insolvency appointment

Where a threat arises from a significant relationship and the threat cannot be overcome by safeguards, the professional work should not be undertaken.

Safeguards to consider include:

- Withdrawing from the insolvency team
- Supervisory procedures
- Terminating (where possible) the financial or business relationship giving rise to the threat
- Discussing the issue with hissgher levels of management within the practice

3.8 Purchase of assets of an insolvent company or debtor

Under no circumstances is at acceptable that, an office holder, or his staff to acquire, directly or indirectly, any assets of a company or debtor in relation to which he holds an insolvency appointment.

3.9 Accepting appointments

Before accepting any appointment the Insolvency Practitioner should ensure that he is qualified to act (s390). To be qualified, the office holder must:

- Be an individual
- Be authorised by a Responsible Professional Body / 'competent authority'
- Have security in force, that is a general penalty bond of £250,000 and a specific penalty bond up to £5,000,000
- Not be disqualified from being an IP as a bankrupt, a patient under Mental Health Act 1963 or under the Company Directors (Disqualification) Act 1986 (CDDA 86) or while subject to a bankruptcy restrictions order or a debt relief restrictions order/undertaking

3.10 Joint appointments

Joint appointees are guided by similar principles to sole appointees.

4 Specific considerations before accepting appointments – Receiverships, CVAs and administrations

Section overview

- Appointments should not be accepted where there has been a significant professional relationship or the IP or practice has carried out audit work within the previous three years.
- Appointment as an investigating accountant does not usually preclude a later appointment as an administrative receiver.
- A receiver should not accept an appointment as liquidator of a company.
- Supervisors of CVAs and administrators can usually accept appointment as liquidator of an insolvent company.
- Holders of insolvency appointments should not also act as an auditor of a company/business.

Note. In every case the IP must consider the Code of Ethics before accepting an appointment

4.1 Significant professional relationship

Where there has been a significant professional relationship with a company no principal or employee of the practice should accept an appointment as:

- Administrative Receiver (AR)
- Receiver (LPA receiver/appointed under a fixed charge)
- Nominee or supervisor of a voluntary arrangement
- Administrator

4.2 Investigating accountants

The fact that his firm has acted previously as investigating accountants does not usually preclude an IP from accepting an appointment as AR. This is subject to the condition that the firm's main client relationship is with the appointing bank and that the company is aware of that fact. Also that there has been no direct involvement in the company's management by the firm.

4.3 Receivers

Where a principal or employee of a practice is, or has recently been, AR of a company or LPA receiver or appointed under a fixed charge, he should not usually accept an appointment as liquidator of the company in an insolvent liquidation. This does not apply to court appointed receivers – though the office holder should give careful consideration as to whether his objectivity might, or might appear, to be impaired.

There is no objection to an IP being made AR in relation to a group of companies providing that on the balance of convenience the advantages of a single appointment outweigh the disadvantages of any potential conflict of interests *(Re Arrows Ltd No.2)*.

4.4 Supervisors of CVAs and administrators

Supervisors of CVAs and administrators can generally accept appointment as liquidators of insolvent companies. However, where administration is followed by compulsory winding up, the administrator should only accept an appointment as liquidator with the formal or informal agreement of the creditors.

4.5 Auditors

Supervisors of CVAs, administrators, ARs and receivers should not accept appointment as auditor of a company for any accounting period during which they acted.

5 Specific considerations before accepting appointments – Liquidations

Section overview

- Appointments should not be accepted where there is/has been a significant professional or personal relationship (SPR), or audit work has been carried out in the previous three years.
- However appointment as liquidator in a members' voluntary liquidation may be accepted where there exists a significant professional relationship 'SPR'. However an office holder must review his position as liquidator where the MVL is likely to be converted into a CVL.
- An office holder should not usually accept an appointment as liquidator if he acted previously as AR or LPA receiver.
- Appointment as liquidator following a court appointed receivership is usually acceptable.
- Appointment as liquidator in a compulsory winding up is usually acceptable even though he has previously acted as administrator or supervisor of a creditors' voluntary arrangement (CVA).
- Agreement of the creditors is required prior to accepting an appointment as liquidator which follows on from an appointment as administrator.
- Payments should not be made to secure an appointment as liquidator.

Note. In every case the IP must consider the Code of Ethics before accepting an appointment and document any issue which he think may trigger a concern in that regard

5.1 Significant professional relationship

An office holder should not accept appointment as liquidator of an insolvent company where there is or has been a significant professional relationship (which includes audit work within the previous three years).

5.2 Members' voluntary liquidation

An office holder can usually accept appointment as liquidator in a members' voluntary liquidation, despite there having been a significant professional relationship.

This is usually as the case is solvent and therefore the distribution of assets/shares and the creditors have less control in the matter, largely due to the fact that they shall be paid in full.

He must give careful consideration to all the implications of acceptance and must consider whether the director's statutory declaration of solvency is likely to be substantiated by events.

5.3 Insolvent members' voluntary liquidation

Where an office holder has been acting as liquidator in a members' voluntary liquidation and he calls a s95 meeting (because he is of the opinion that the company is unable to pay its debts) and there has been a significant professional relationship, there are two situations to be considered:

- If the liquidator is of the opinion that, despite the calling of the s95 meeting, the company will eventually return to solvency, he may accept appointment as liquidator at the s95 meeting. (If it subsequently appears that he was mistaken in his belief he should resign.)

- If the liquidator does not believe that the company will return to solvency he should not accept appointment as liquidator at the s95 meeting.

There is an assumed merit in continuing in office, but the IP must be mindful to the above.

5.4 Receivers

An office holder should not accept appointment as liquidator of an insolvent company where he, or a partner or employee in the same firm, has acted as administrative receiver or LPA receiver of that company.

5.5 Court appointed receiver

An office holder could, after due consideration, accept appointment as liquidator following a court appointed receivership.

5.6 Compulsory liquidation

An office holder may usually accept appointment as liquidator in a compulsory winding up where he, or a partner or employee in the same firm, has acted as administrator or supervisor of a CVA in relation to the company.

5.7 Liquidation following administration

Where the winding up follows on from administration the administrator should only accept the nomination if:

- The creditors' committee (if any) in the administration agree

- The administrator has the support of a general meeting of creditors (either called informally or under the Act) of which all known creditors have been given notice

The administrator should not therefore simply accept a s137 Secretary of State appointment without creditor support, even though there is an assumed merit in continuing in office, but the IP must be mindful to the above.

5.8 Financial inducements

s164 – It is an offence to give, agree or offer to give any member or creditor of a company any valuable consideration with a view to:

- Securing appointment or nomination as liquidator; or
- Securing or preventing the appointment or nomination of someone else as liquidator.

Contravention of s164 will lead to a fine.

R4.150 – the court may order remuneration to be disallowed where any improper solicitation has been used by or on behalf of the liquidator to obtain proxies or procure appointment.

Interactive question 1: Barry Engineering Limited

The directors of Barry Engineering Limited, an audit client of your firm, have approached your partner for advice.

Barry Engineering Limited is owed the sum of £175,000 by Jones & Sons Limited, a supplier of scrap metals. The directors of Barry Engineering Limited are considering presenting a petition for the compulsory winding up of Jones & Sons Limited.

Requirement

Outline the ethical considerations of accepting any appointment in respect of Jones & Sons Limited.

See **Answer** at the end of this chapter.

6 Specific considerations before accepting appointments – Bankruptcy and voluntary arrangements

Section overview

- Appointment should not be accepted where there has been a significant professional or personal relationship with an individual.
- A supervisor of a voluntary arrangement may usually act as trustee in relation to the debtor.
- Appointment should not be accepted where there is a close personal connection with an individual.
- Appointment may be accepted in relation to a company which has a close connection to an individual in respect of whom the office holder is acting.

Note. In every case the IP must consider the Code of Ethics before accepting the appointment.

6.1 Significant professional relationship

An office holder should not accept appointment as nominee or supervisor of a voluntary arrangement, or trustee in bankruptcy where he has had a significant professional or personal relationship with the individual.

6.2 Trustee in bankruptcy

There is no objection to an office holder being made trustee in bankruptcy of a debtor where he has previously acted as supervisor of a voluntary arrangement in relation to that debtor. However that does not mean that the IP need not consider the application of the Code of Ethics before accepting the appointment.

6.3 Personal connection

Where there has been a personal connection with an individual, (that falls short of a significant personal relationship) the office holder should not accept an insolvency appointment in relation to that individual, where the connection is such as to impair, or reasonably appear to impair, the office holder's objectivity.

6.4 Company connection

If an office holder is already acting as an IP in relation to an individual, he may usually accept an insolvency appointment in relation to a company of which the debtor is a major shareholder or creditor, or where the company is a creditor of the debtor. He must however, take steps to minimise any potential conflicts of interest and ensure that his integrity and objectivity are, and are seen to be, maintained. If they cannot be he must refuse the appointment.

Summary and Self-test

Summary

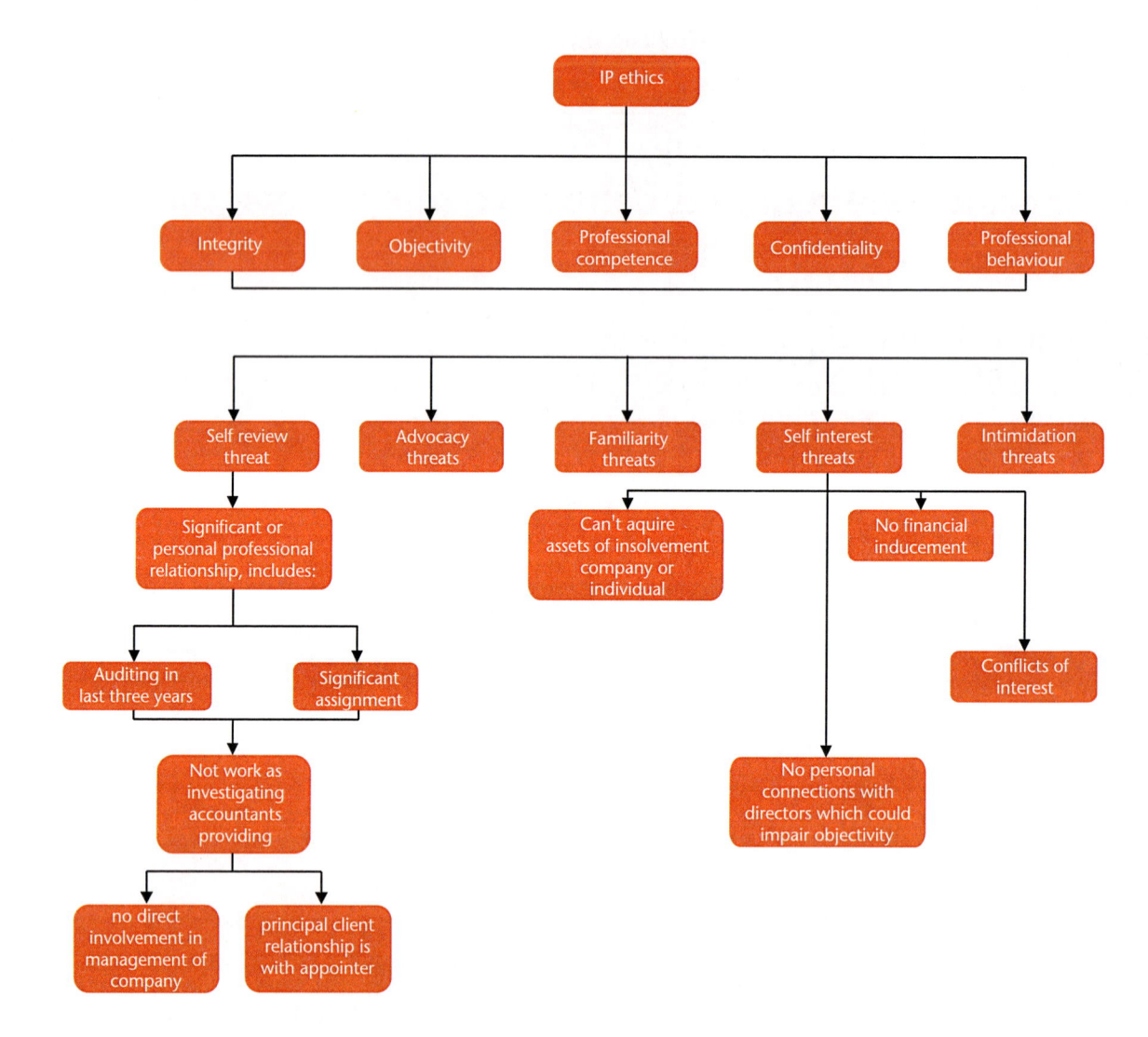

```
                                    IP ethics
                                        |
   ┌────────────────┬──────────────────┼──────────────────┬────────────────┐
   ▼                ▼                  ▼                  ▼                ▼
Integrity      Objectivity       Professional       Confidentiality   Professional
                                  competence                            behaviour

   ┌────────────────┬──────────────────┬──────────────────┬────────────────┐
   ▼                ▼                  ▼                  ▼                ▼
Self review     Advocacy          Familiarity        Self interest    Intimidation
  threat         threats            threats             threats          threats
   │                                   │                  │                │
   ▼                               ┌───┴────┐         ┌───┴────┐           │
Significant or                  Can't aquire       No financial            │
personal professional        assets of insolvement  inducement             │
relationship, includes:         company or                                 ▼
   │                             individual                         Conflicts of
   ├──────────────┐                                                   interest
   ▼              ▼
Auditing in    Significant
last three    assignment
  years           │
   └──────┬───────┘
          ▼
     Not work as
     investigating
     accountants
      providing
          │
    ┌─────┴─────┐
    ▼           ▼
no direct    principal client
involvement in  relationship is
management of   with appointer
  company
```

No personal connections with directors which could impair objectivity

60   Certificate in Insolvency

Self-test

Answer the following questions.

1 A trustee in bankruptcy must immediately resign his office in which of the following circumstances?

　A　If he is disqualified from acting as an insolvency practitioner
　B　If he resigns from a firm in which he was a partner when he was appointed to the estate
　C　If the firm in which he is a partner merges with a firm who were tax advisers to the debtor
　D　If he is convicted of an offence involving dishonesty
　E　If a joint trustee resigns his office

2 Which of the following appointments may usually be accepted where there has previously existed a significant professional relationship between the entity and the proposed office holder?

　A　Administrator
　B　Supervisor of a company voluntary arrangement
　C　Liquidator in a members' voluntary liquidation
　D　Liquidator in a creditors' voluntary liquidation
　E　Fixed charge receiver

3 An insolvency practitioner should not accept appointment where either a practice, a partner, or a person who, at the time of the appointment is employed by the practice, has acted as auditor in he previous:

　A　One year
　B　Two years
　C　Three years
　D　Four years
　E　Five years

4 Which of the following appointments may usually be accepted?

　A　Trustee in bankruptcy of a debtor following appointment as a supervisor of a voluntary arrangement in respect of that debtor
　B　Liquidator of an insolvent company following acting as administrative receiver of that company
　C　Liquidator of an insolvent company following acting as an LPA receiver
　D　Liquidator in a compulsory winding up having previously acted as administrator
　E　Liquidator in a compulsory winding up having previously acted as supervisor of a company voluntary arrangement in relation to that company

5 List the five fundamental principles to which office holders should adhere.

6 s390 lists the requirements for an individual to act as an insolvency practitioner. What are these requirements?

Now, go back to the Learning Objectives in the Introduction. If you are satisfied that you have achieved these objectives, please tick them off.

Answers to Self-test

1. A   Answer C is also tempting but resignation is only necessary if the tax advice constituted significant professional work.

2. C

3. C

4. A, D, E

5.
   (i) Integrity
   (ii) Objectivity
   (iii) Professional competence
   (iv) Confidentiality
   (v) Professional behaviour

6.
   (a) Must be an individual

   (b) Must be authorised by RPB/ competent authority

   (c) Must have security in force

   (d) Not be disqualified from being IP as a bankrupt, patient under MHA 83 or disqualified under CDDA 86 or while subject to a bankruptcy restrictions order or a debt relief restrictions order

Answer to Interactive question

Answer to Interactive question 1: Barry Engineering Limited

Before agreeing to accept any insolvency appointment the partner should consider whether acceptance would create any threats to compliance with the fundamental principles.

The fundamental issues regarding the ethical consideration in accepting any appointment are the importance of integrity and objectivity.

The ethical guidelines state that it is not only a question of whether the individual member is satisfied as to their independence but also how they are perceived by others.

The partner should not accept an appointment as liquidator if there has been a significant professional or personal relationship with the company. Any relationship with the petitioner (eg as an audit client) is irrelevant unless there are likely to be contentious issues between it and the liquidator.

Additionally the partner should consider whether there is any personal or professional connection with individual directors involved in Jones & Sons Limited which could possibly impair, or appear to impair, their objectivity.

There are no specific guidelines regarding the acceptance of an appointment as a special manager, however similar considerations should be borne in mind when accepting such an appointment.

Before accepting the appointment the partner should ensure that he is qualified to act.

CHAPTER 5

Insolvency computations

Introduction
Topic List
1. Order of payment in insolvency
2. Secured and preferential creditors
3. The prescribed part
4. Office holders' accounting records and Secretary of State fees
5. Statement of Affairs
6. The Deficiency Account
7. Estimated Outcome Statements
8. Receipts and Payments Accounts
9. Bank reconciliations

Self-test
Answers to Self-test
Answers to Interactive questions

Introduction

Learning objectives

- Calculate figures to be included in the:

    Statement of Affairs
    Estimated outcome statement
    Deficiency account
    Receipts and payments account
    Dividends and distributions
    The prescribed part

- Explain the circumstances when estate accounting would be used by the insolvency practitioner

Tick off

Stop and think

Why do office holders prepare financial statements? What do they show? Who uses them? Why is the Statement of Affairs an important document? What are the statutory requirements regarding the preparation of financial statements?

Working context

It is a statutory requirement for office holders to produce Statements of Affairs and Receipts and Payments accounts. You will be asked to assist in preparing these statements for inclusion in reports to creditors and other interested parties and to fulfil the office holder's statutory duties.

1 Order of payment in insolvency

> **Section overview**
>
> - The overriding aim of the main insolvency procedures is to treat creditors equally – the pari passu principle. However that principle applies only to ordinary unsecured creditors – there are other creditors who enjoy priority rights. For the purpose of estate accounting particular attention must be paid to the rights of secured and preferential creditors.
>
> - The payment order in insolvency is important as it decides where in the order of priority a creditor will be paid out by an office holder and consequently how likely it is for a creditor to be paid out. We look at the position in both corporate and personal insolvency.

1.1 Order of payment in corporate insolvency

1. Pool of fixed charge assets
   (a) Costs of realisation/preservation
   (b) Fixed charge holders in order of registration at Land Registry
   (c) Fixed charge surplus (if any) to free asset pool (unless the surplus is caught by any floating charge)

2. Pool of floating charge assets
   (a) Expenses of the insolvent estate and costs to the extent that there are insufficient free assets to meet them
   (b) Preferential creditors (see below)
   (c) The prescribed part (15.9.2003 onwards)
   (d) Floating charge holders in order of creation
   (e) Surplus to free asset pool

3. Free asset pool
   (a) Costs and expenses of liquidation
   (b) Floating charge holders re payment to preferential creditors
   (c) Ordinary unsecured creditors
   (d) Deferred creditors
   (e) Subordinated debt
   (f) Shareholders (see articles) – usually:
      – Preference shareholders
      – Ordinary shareholders
   (g) Surplus to ordinary shareholders

1.2 Order of payment in bankruptcy

- Costs and expenses of bankruptcy
- Preferential debts
- Ordinary debts
- Post-commencement interest on debts
- Deferred debts (spouses/civil partners)
- Surplus to bankrupt

2 Secured and preferential creditors

> **Section overview**
> - Secured and preferential creditors enjoy enhanced rights on insolvency. Secured creditors hold either fixed or floating charges (or both). Preferential creditors are primarily employees with claims for unpaid wages and holiday pay.
> - A fixed charge holder has a charge over specific ascertainable assets which will attach to the asset(s) at the moment of creation whereas a floating charge holder will have a charge over a class of assets which will change from time to time.
> - A floating charge does not affect the company's ability to deal with the asset(s) until crystallisation occurs. [Note. Only companies can create floating charges.]
> - Secured creditors are paid out in accordance with the order of priority (see para 1). This assumes that the charge(s) is valid eg properly registered at Companies House in accordance with the Companies Act 2006 and not overturned as a voidable transaction under Insolvency Act 1986. [The validity of charges is considered fully in later chapters.]

2.1 Fixed/floating charges

- **Fixed charge holders**

    A fixed charge holder is a secured creditor with a charge over assets such as freehold and leasehold land and buildings; fixed plant and machinery (which may include ships and aircraft); intellectual property (which may included patents, copyright and domain names) and goodwill.

    [Note. Reference to 'fixed assets' in the balance sheet means assets used long term in the business and does not imply that they are covered by a fixed charge.]

    Following the decision by the House of Lords in *Spectrum v National Westminster Bank* it will be unusual for fixed charges to be created over book debts and such a charge will only be possible with very careful drafting. Most charges purporting to be fixed charges on book debts in fact operate as floating charges. In the assessment unless you are expressly told that there is a valid fixed charge over book debts you should assume that book debts will (if appropriate in the context of the question) be caught by a floating charge.

    Both incorporated and non-incorporated businesses can offer security by way of fixed charge. Assuming that it is validly created and registered, a fixed charge attaches to the charged property on creation. The effect of this is that the company is no longer free to dispose of the charged property and will need to seek authorisation of the charge holder before realising the charged property.

    In the event of default on a secured loan fixed charge holders will have the right to repossess and sell the charged asset(s) and appoint a fixed charge receiver.

    In the event of more than one charge being registered against an asset they will be paid out in accordance with the rules on priority.

- **Floating charge holders**

    A floating charge holder is a secured creditor with a charge over assets such as cash, stock (inventories), non-fixed plant and machinery and usually non-factored book debts. Be aware that the floating charge assets may be subject to prior claims, for example stock may be subject to retention of title claims which will reduce what is available to the floating charge holder and plant and machinery may be subject to HP or other financing agreements. Also the amount available to a floating charge holder in respect of book debts may be reduced because of bad or doubtful debts and creditors claiming set off.

    Although factored book debts will not be subject to a floating charge any surplus will be. [See Chapter 2 for further information about factored book debts.]

Unlike with a fixed charge, where there is a floating charge the company remains free to deal with the assets. That freedom remains until 'crystallisation' occurs. Crystallisation occurs automatically when:

- A winding up order is made
- The company ceases to trade
- A secured creditor takes steps to enforce its security
- On the happening of any other event specified in the security documentation

The effect of crystallisation is that the company is now prevented from disposing of assets without the consent of the floating charge holder. In the event of more than one charge being registered against an asset they will be paid out in accordance with the rules on priority.

- **Rules on priority of charges**

Where there is more than one secured creditor they may always agree between themselves as to the order in which they will rank should the company default on its loans.

Similarly a bank may always make it a condition of granting a loan that a company does not create charges ranking in priority to its own security. It may require, for instance, that no subsequent fixed charges are created ranking in priority to its own floating charge (a negative pledge).

Where there is no agreement the following rules apply:

- Fixed charges over land are paid in order of registration at the Land Registry
- Fixed charges over other assets are paid in order of creation

Charge holders will receive realisations after deduction of costs, expenses and remuneration properly attributed to the fixed charge assets.

Where there is more than one floating charge the charges are paid out in the order of creation unless the lenders have entered into a deed of priority in which case they are paid out in the order set out in the deed.

2.2 Preferential creditors

In an insolvency situation some debts enjoy preferential status giving those creditors priority in the order of payment over the ordinary unsecured creditors.

Preferential creditors are:

- Arrears of employee pay* for 4 months pre the 'relevant date' restricted to £800
- All accrued holiday pay to a maximum of six weeks within a twelve month period of the relevant date
- The Redundancy Payments Office ('RPO') to the extent that it settles employees' preferential claims out of the National Insurance Fund [the RPO are subrogated to the position of employees in the order of payment]
- Unpaid contributions to an occupational pension scheme (4 months for employee contributions, 12 months for employer contributions)
- Various European coal and steel levies (rare)

[*Pay includes unpaid wages (but not expenses).]

The 'relevant date' for calculation of preferential claims is set out in s387.

- For CVAs this is the date of approval of the proposal unless the directors have applied for a small company moratorium in which case the date of filing for that moratorium is the relevant date. If the CVA takes effect within administration, the date that the company entered administration is taken.
- In administration the relevant date is the date on which the company enters administration.
- In compulsory liquidation it is the date of the winding up order (or if appointed) the date of appointment of a provisional liquidator. Where compulsory liquidation follows administration the relevant date is the date on which the company enters administration.

- In voluntary liquidation it is the date of the passing of the resolution to wind up the company.
- Where administration is followed by either a voluntary or compulsory liquidation, the relevant date is the date on which the company entered administration.
- In receivership, the relevant date is the appointment of the receiver.
- In bankruptcy it is the date of the order.

3 The prescribed part

Section overview

- Part of the ethos of the Enterprise Act 2002 was to treat unsecured creditors more fairly. The legislature wanted to ensure that unsecured creditors felt the benefit of the Crown giving up its status as a preferential creditor. To achieve that the legislation introduced the idea of a prescribed part. Consequently pursuant to s176A IA86 where a floating charge is created on or after 15 September 2003, a prescribed amount must be set aside from floating charge realisations to be paid over to unsecured creditors.

3.1 When does it apply?

The rules on the prescribed part apply to all floating charges created on or after 15 September 2003 when the company is in either liquidation or administration or there is a receiver or provisional liquidator in office. (Note the date as questions may test whether or not you understand its significance.)

The effect of the rule is to ensure that the office holder makes a prescribed part of the company's net property available for unsecured creditors and does not distribute it to the floating charge holder(s).

3.2 When does it not apply?

There are three situations where no prescribed part distributions need be made:

- The net property is under £10,000 in value and the liquidator, administrator or receiver believes that the costs of making the distribution would outweigh the benefits.
- The net property is £10,000 or more and the liquidator, administrator or receiver applies to court for an order that the prescribed part rules should not apply. The ground of the application is that the costs of making the distribution would outweigh the benefits. This would be useful where, for instance, there are a large number of unsecured creditors each owed a relatively small amount of money.
- Where the liquidator or administrator proposes a CVA or a CA06 Scheme of Arrangement the terms of the CVA or the Scheme can disapply the prescribed part rules. Obviously unsecured creditors will only vote in favour or such a proposal if they believe it to be in their best interests to do so.

3.3 Calculation of the prescribed part

The office holder must make a prescribed part of the net property available to unsecured creditors. Unsecured creditors will not include floating charge holders with a deficit as s176A states that the office holder 'shall not distribute that (prescribed) part to the proprietor of a floating charge'.

The 'net property' is what would have been available for floating charge holders, that is, floating charge realisations less costs and preferential creditors.

The prescribed part is calculated as follows:

- 50% of the first £10,000 of the net property
- Plus 20% of the balance
- Up to a maximum prescribed part of £600,000

In practice, the ordinary unsecured creditors will never get £600,000 through the prescribed part mechanism because the rules provide that the costs of making the distribution must be deducted from the prescribed part itself (R12.2(2)).

Interactive question 1: Bowring Limited

Your principal was appointed liquidator of Bowring Limited at a s98 meeting of creditors. The following information has come to light during the course of the liquidation:

- The company owes Satwest Bank plc the sum of £345,000 which is secured by way of fixed and floating charges over the company's assets, created on 26 June 2006
- The company's trading premises have been sold and the sum of £168,000 paid to Satwest Bank plc under their fixed charge
- To date, floating charge realisations amount to £240,000, the costs of realising those assets total £18,700
- Preferential creditor claims total £65,000
- Unsecured creditor claims total £278,000
- You estimate that the costs of making a prescribed part distribution will amount to £5,000

Requirement

Calculate the prescribed part to be made available to the unsecured creditors.

See **Answer** at the end of this chapter.

4 Office holders' accounting records and Secretary of State fees

Section overview

- When preparing accounting records it is usual for office holders to maintain a record of just the cash and banking elements of transactions. In insolvency cases accounts take the form of a receipts and payments accounts rather than profit and loss accounts and balance sheets.
- SIP 7 gives guidance on the contents of office holder accounts.
- Use of the Insolvency Services Account (ISA) is regulated by part 2 of the Insolvency Regulations 1994.

4.1 Who pays into the ISA?

Liquidators in compulsory liquidation and trustees in bankruptcy must pay into the ISA. Payments must be made (without deduction) once every 14 days or immediately without deduction if £5,000 or more has been received. Voluntary liquidators cannot use the ISA. It is possible however, for compulsory liquidators and trustees to make application to the Secretary of State for permission to open a local bank account.

4.1.1 Secretary of State Fees

A case administration fee is charged by the Insolvency Service on chargeable receipts paid into the ISA. 'Chargeable receipts' are amounts paid into the ISA after deducting sums paid to secured creditors and the cost of carrying on the business.

Rates for petitions presented on or after 6 April 2010 and bankruptcy or winding up orders made on or after 6 April 2010:

Bankruptcy	Liquidation
0% charge on first £2,000	0% charge on first £2,500
100% charge on next £1,700	100% charge on next £1,700
75% charge on next £1,500	75% charge on next £1,500
15% charge on next £396,000	15% charge on next £396,000
1% charge on balance	1% charge on balance
Capped at £80,000	Capped at £80,000

For orders made pre 6th April 2010 the charge is the same for both bankruptcy and liquidation – the first £2,000 at 0% thereafter at 17% capped at £80,000.

5 Statement of Affairs

Section overview

- It is a statutory requirement under the IA 86 to produce a Statement of Affairs in a prescribed format.

Definition

Statement of Affairs: A picture of the company's financial position as at the date of:

- Receivership
- Administration
- Liquidation
- Company voluntary arrangement

5.1 Contents

When a Statement of Affairs is produced under any insolvency procedure, it must contain details of the following information:

- The debtor's assets, debts and liabilities (book value and estimated to realise values of assets)
- The names and addresses of the debtor's creditors
- What securities are held by any creditors eg a fixed charge over property
- Dates upon which the securities were given
- Such further or other information as may be prescribed

Definitions

Book value: the value of the assets shown in the accounts at the date of insolvency.

Estimated realisable value: what the assets are likely to realise when sold.

5.2 Summary of rules re Statement of Affairs

	Date prepared	Produced by	Form
Administration	As at date of administration	Those who are or have been officers of the company	2.14B
Administrative receivership	As at date of appointment	Those who are or have been officers of the company Those in employment deemed able to give information	3.2
Compulsory liquidation	At date of commencement	Officers of the company	4.17
Creditors voluntary liquidation	Not more than 14 days before date resolution to wind up	Directors	4.19
Company voluntary arrangement	Not more than 14 days before date of notice to nominee under R1.4	Directors	1.6

5.3 Format

The format for a Statement of Affairs is shown below.

Estimated Statement of Affairs for ABC Limited as at X.X.1X

	Notes	Book Value	Realisable Value
ASSETS SPECIFICALLY PLEDGED	1		
Assets		X	X
Less amounts due to charge holder			(X)
			X/(X)
ASSETS NOT SPECIFICALLY PLEDGED	2		
Assets		X	X
Total assets available for Preferential Creditors			X
SUMMARY OF LIABILITIES			
PREFERENTIAL CREDITORS	3		(X)
Surplus/deficiency as regards preferential creditors			X
PRESCRIBED PART	4		(X)
Assets available for floating charge holder			X
FLOATING CHARGE HOLDER	5		(X)
Surplus/deficiency			X/(X)
Prescribed part carried down			X
UNSECURED CREDITORS	6		(X)
Total surplus/deficiency as regards creditors			X/(X)
ISSUED AND CALLED UP SHARE CAPITAL			(X)
Estimated deficiency as regards members			X

5.4 Notes to Statement of Affairs:

1 **Assets Specifically Pledged**

   This is where the company has given some form of security to a creditor for the advance of funds or purchase of an asset. This will include:

   - Assets pledged as fixed charge assets ie freehold property, goodwill
   - Assets subject to HP agreements
   - Debts subject to a factoring agreement

   The sums owed to the charge holder should appear under this heading and the net deficiency or surplus carried down. Any surplus usually goes to the free asset pool unless it is caught by the floating charge.

2 **Assets Not Specifically Pledged**

   These are all other assets of the company not dealt with above. This will include:

   - Book debts
   - Motor vehicles
   - Stock
   - Plant and machinery
   - Office equipment

   It may be necessary to adjust asset realisable values to take into account bad debt provisions, obsolete assets etc.

3 **Preferential Creditors**

   These creditors are paid in priority to other creditors. They include:

   - All holiday pay owed to employees (to a maximum of 6 weeks accrued in any 12 month period prior to relevant date)
   - Any wages due at the date of insolvency (accruing in four months prior to insolvency) to a maximum claim per employee of £800

4 **Prescribed Part**

   Where the floating charge is created on or after 15 September 2003 a prescribed part of the net property must be paid to ordinary unsecured creditors (see earlier in this chapter for details).

5 **Floating Charge Holders**

   A bank may hold a floating charge over the assets of the company. The floating charge ranks after the claims of the preferential creditors but before the ordinary unsecured creditors.

6 **Unsecured Creditors**

   These are the normal creditors' claims. It will also include employee claims for redundancy and notice pay and any shortfall owed to charge holders. Any claims above preferential limits will also rank as unsecured.

Interactive question 2: Estimated Statement of Affairs

Your principal, Anne Jones, has been approached by the directors of Modern Printing Limited with a view to obtaining assistance to put the company into creditors' voluntary liquidation.

They provide her with the following information:

1 The company's share capital consists of 100,000 £1 ordinary shares which are fully paid.

2 The company trades from freehold premises in Plymouth. They are shown in the books with a value of £150,000 however they have recently been professionally valued in the sum of £285,000. The property is subject to an outstanding mortgage with Hull Property Services in the sum of £95,000 which is secured by way of a fixed charge over the property.

3 The company has a trading overdraft with Satby Bank plc which currently stands at £79,000. The overdraft is secured by way of a floating charge over the company's other assets which was created on 2 March 2002.

4   The directors have obtained professional valuations of the company's other assets:

	Book Value £	Estimated to realise £
Plant and machinery	64,000	21,000
Fixtures and fittings	19,000	11,000
Motor vehicles	43,000	20,000

5   The sales ledger balances currently total £156,000. The directors advise you that a debt of £60,000 is unlikely to be realised due to the liquidation of the company. The directors feel that a further provision for bad debts of 20% would be prudent.

6   The company is holding stocks valued at £42,000 (book value £71,000). It is understood that £16,000 worth of stock is subject to ROT claims.

7   VAT is owed for the last two quarters in the sum of £12,000.

8   PAYE is also outstanding for the last six months in the sum of £23,000.

9   Employee claims are as follows:

	£
Holiday pay	22,000
Wage arrears (two weeks owed, less than £800 per employee)	12,000
Redundancy	15,000
Pay in lieu	15,000

10   Trade creditors are owed £213,000.

Requirements

(a)   Prepare a Statement of Affairs for Modern Printing Limited as at today's date from the information available. You should show all of your workings.

(b)   How would your figures in the Statement differ if the floating charge to Satby Bank plc had been granted on 1 December 2003?

See **Answer** at the end of this chapter.

6 The Deficiency Account

Section overview

- The deficiency account reconciles the last set of accounts with the position shown in the Statement of Affairs. It explains why a once profitable company now appears insolvent, or why an insolvent company has now become more insolvent.

6.1 Format

A pro forma for a deficiency account is shown below:

ABC Limited in Liquidation – Deficiency Account for the period X.X.X0 to X.X.X1

Balance on Profit and Loss account	1	X
Less assets written down in Statement of Affairs	2	(X)
Less items arising on insolvency	3	(X)
Balancing figure attributable to loss in the period	4	(X)
Deficit to creditors per Statement of Affairs	5	(X)
Share capital write off	5	(X)
Deficit to members per Statement of Affairs	5	(X)

6.2 Notes to Deficiency Account

1 Balance on Profit and Loss account

- This is taken from the last audited balance sheet (if available) or management accounts
- If a credit (positive) balance, begin with a positive figure
- If a debit (negative) balance, begin with a negative figure
- If this figure is not available, use net assets instead

2 Assets written down in Statement of Affairs

- This section details the difference between the book values and estimated to realise values of all assets shown in the Statement of Affairs
- If assets have increased in value, add this figure instead

3 Items arising on insolvency

- These represent known items which have arisen as a result of the insolvency only and have added to the liabilities of the company
- These will include:
    - Pay in lieu of notice
    - Redundancy
    - Damages for breach of contract
    - Termination payments on a lease

4 Balancing figure attributable to the loss in the period:

- This will be the balancing figure on the statement

5 These figures are taken straight from the Statement of Affairs.

Interactive question 3: Deficiency account

You have been asked to prepare a Deficiency account for a s.98 meeting of creditors to be held on 1 September 20X0. The last statutory accounts relate to the year ended 31 January 20X0 and these show accumulated profits at this date of £8,500.

The company's books and records are up to date but do not show the following claims which will arise on the liquidation of the company:

- Breach of contract £52,000
- Redundancy pay, pay in lieu of notice £36,700

Extracts from the Statement of Affairs are as follows.

	Book value £	Estimated to realise £
Freehold property	185,000	240,000
Book debts	98,000	40,000
Plant and machinery	72,000	21,000
Fixtures and fittings	24,000	8,500
Stocks	63,000	29,000
Motor vehicles	80,000	32,000

The estimated total deficiency to creditors as at 1 September 20X0 is £280,200 and the estimated total deficiency to members is £330,200.

Requirement

Prepare a Deficiency account for the period 1 February 20X0 to 1 September 20X0 Show all workings and assumptions.

See **Answer** at the end of this chapter.

7 Estimated Outcome Statements

Section overview

The Statement quantifies the outcome of a particular course of action for one or more interested parties. It can be used to:

- Make a comparison of alternative offers for the sale of a business
- Calculate the return to creditors of pursuing a voluntary arrangement rather than opting for bankruptcy (or comparing a company voluntary arrangement with liquidation)
- Enable an office holder to decide whether to continue trading by comparing outcomes of ceasing to trade with continuing.

7.1 Format

There is no standard layout for an Estimated Outcome Statement, this will be determined by the information available and the purpose for which it is prepared.

When estimating returns to creditors it is useful to follow the format of the Statement of Affairs as a guide, with comparative Statement of Affairs figures shown wherever possible.

When comparing offers/comparable outcomes, always try to show the relevant figures side by side. This makes comparisons easier.

Worked example: Estimated outcome statement (1)

You were approached on 26 March 20X0 by Mr Gill, the managing director of Anvill Garden Machinery Limited (AGM Ltd). The company has been experiencing cash flow problems for some time however, the directors are confident that they are about to sign a substantial contract which will return the company to profitability.

Mr Gill provides you with the following information:

	Book value £	Forced sale value £
Assets		
Freehold property	125,000	180,000
Fixtures and fittings	75,000	25,000
Plant and machinery	110,000	40,000
Stock	45,000	17,000
Debtors	98,000	60,000
Liabilities		
Pay in lieu (estimated)		24,000
Redundancy (estimated)		29,000
Trade and expense creditors		271,000

Mr Gill is keen for AGM Ltd to avoid liquidation and enter into a company voluntary arrangement. He anticipates that the company will be able to make monthly contributions from profits into the arrangement in the sum of £3,500 per month for the next four years.

In addition, the company has successfully bid for an innovation award in respect of the new contract, which means that the company will receive the sum of £30,000 in eight months time when Phase 1 of the new contract is successfully completed.

The following information is also relevant:

Your partner estimates that if the company is placed into liquidation the liquidator's fees would be £20,000 in addition to a fee of £3,500 for convening the necessary meetings of the company's members and creditors.

Under a company voluntary arrangement, nominee's fees would be £4,500 and supervisor's fees would be £4,000 per annum.

Estate agent's fees of 1.5% would be incurred in selling the property along with legal fees of £5,000. Auction costs of £12,000 would be incurred disposing of the remaining assets.

Debtors are expected to be realised in full if trade continues.

Requirement

Prepare an estimated outcome statement for AGM Ltd comparing the outcome for creditors under a company voluntary arrangement (CVA) with a creditors voluntary liquidation (CVL).

Solution

Estimated Outcome Statement – Anvill Garden Machinery Limited as at X.X.X0

	Notes	CVL	CVA
Realisations			
Freehold property	1	172,300	–
Fixtures and fittings			
Plant and machinery	2	70,000	–
Stock			
Debtors		60,000	98,000
Contributions from trading	3		168,000
Innovation award			30,000
		302,300	296,000
Less costs			
liquidator's remuneration		(20,000)	–
meetings fees		(3,500)	
nominee's fees			4,500
supervisor's fees	4		16,000
Available for creditors		278,800	275,500
Less creditors			
pay in lieu of notice		24,000	–
Redundancy		29,000	–
trade and expense		271,000	271,000
		(324,000)	(271,000)
Shortfall/surplus to creditors		(45,200)	4,500
Creditors will receive		86p in £	100p in £

Workings

1 *Freehold property*

	£
Realised	180,000
Less estate agents fees @ 1.5%	(2,700)
Legal fees	(5,000)
	172,300

2 *Fixtures and fittings, plant and stock*

	£
Realisations (25,000 + 40,000 + 17,000) =	82,000
Less auction costs	(12,000)
	70,000

3 *Contributions from trading*

£3,500 x 12 x 4 = £168,000

4 Supervisor's fees:

£4,000 per annum for 4 years = £16,000

Interactive question 4: Estimated Outcome Statement (2)

Bill Norris has made an appointment to see you. The catering business which he ran with his brother has recently ceased trading following his brother's involvement in a car accident which has left him unable to work. The business was run on an informal partnership basis and Bill has found himself liable for all of the business debts as well as his ongoing personal liabilities. He has heard of a voluntary arrangement and considers that this may be a more acceptable alternative than bankruptcy.

He provides you with the following information.

1. The business operated from a former bakery in Kettering. Bill owns the property and lives in a flat above the premises. The property has recently been put up for sale on the open market in the sum of £295,000. There is an outstanding mortgage with Freeby Bank plc in the sum of £195,000 which is secured by way of a fixed charge over the property.

2. The kitchen equipment used by the business has already been sold and the money used to pay pressing creditors.

3. Business debtors are outstanding in the sum of £55,000. Bill estimates that only 30% of this sum is now realisable.

4. Bill currently uses the catering van to get around in. The vehicle has been valued in the sum of £9,000. Bill is of the opinion that a vehicle is a necessity however he agrees that it need not be a specialist catering van. A replacement van can be purchased for £4,000.

5. Bill has found employment with another catering firm and estimates that he will have surplus monthly income in the sum of £500.

6. He has a personal bank account which has a credit balance of £5,000 and a business account with Satby Bank plc which has an overdrawn balance of £28,250.

7. Bill has no other assets apart from the usual household effects. He advises you that none of these items are new.

8. The outstanding business liabilities total £128,000.

9. Bill has credit card debts totalling £12,000 and an unsecured personal loan with Easy Debt Limited in the sum of £8,000.

10. Bill owes £16,500 in respect of tax and £8,500 re VAT due in the last two quarters.

11. You anticipate that nominee's fees to set up an arrangement will be £3,500 and supervisor's fees would be £1,000 per annum.

Requirement

Prepare an estimated outcome statement showing how much will be received by Bill's creditors if he enters into a voluntary arrangement lasting three years.

See **Answer** at the end of this chapter.

8 Receipts and Payments Accounts

Section overview

A receipts and payments account is prepared by office holders to:

- Provide information to creditors and other interested parties
- Fulfil statutory requirements under IA 86 re submission of progress reports (see Chapter 3)

SIP 7 sets out recommended practice with regard to the preparation of receipts and payments accounts.

8.1 Format

Reports to members, creditors, committees and other interested parties should include in the body of the report, or by way of an annexe, details of the office holder's receipts and payments.

The receipts and payments account is a summary of all receipts and payments made by the office holder during the relevant period.

The procedure for preparing a receipts and payments account is the same for whatever purpose the account is being prepared.

The layout will be determined to some extent by the requirements on individual cases. SIP 7 provides guidance to office holders when preparing receipts and payments accounts.

8.2 Additional considerations

The following points are made in SIP 7.

- **Payments to office holders and associates.** Office holders must disclose all their remuneration and expenses and set out:
    - The amount received for work done while in office
    - Any pre-appointment costs recovered from the insolvent estate
    - Amounts paid to the office holder for work done supervising the trade of a business
    - Amounts paid to agents for work that the office holder or his staff could have done
    - Remuneration for work done in connection with the insolvency that was recovered from a source other than the insolvent estate

- **Form and general presentation of accounts.** As far as possible receipts and payments should be classified under the headings used in the statement of affairs or estimated outcome statement so as to facilitate comparison. The *Estimated to Realise* figures on the statement of affairs should be shown so that the comparisons with the actual realisations made to date may be made.

- **Receipts.** Asset realisations should be shown gross. The cost of realising assets should be shown under payments. When assets subject to charges are sold, by (or on the instructions of) the charge holder, or other person(s) with a legal right to do so, the net amount should be shown in the account (even if nil) with the gross realisation(s), costs of realisation and the amount retained by the charge holder shown separately by way of a note. In other words the office holder will in these circumstances only account for his actual receipt(s).

- **Payments.** Any payments should be stated separately by category and specifically details should be given of any:
    - Amounts paid under duress, for example to a creditor threatening repossession of goods, or payments to landlords to avoid distraint and/or forfeiture
    - Dividend payments to secured creditors, preferential creditors and unsecured creditors. The dates and amount of any dividend (pence in the £) should also be stated

- **Third party funds.** Other amounts received and banked which are not part of the estate and are due to be paid to third parties should be noted. Any agreed charge to the person entitled to the monies should be disclosed.

- **Trading accounts.** Must be prepared specifying: the assets used in the course of a trade; any uncollected debts and liabilities in respect of the trade and any assets such as stock that remain to be realised in further trading.

- **VAT.** It is acceptable to show amounts net of VAT with the total net VAT being shown separately or show all amounts inclusive of VAT. It is important that the treatment of VAT adopted within an account should be consistent and the implications of that treatment made clear.

- **Statement of funds held.** There should be a statement of funds showing where the balance of the funds shown in the account are being held, distinguishing between: those funds held in interest bearing accounts; those held in non-interest bearing accounts; amounts held in the Insolvency Services Account; and amounts held in Treasury Bills and other forms of investment. An office holder may present multiple R&P accounts in more than one currency where bank accounts are held in more than one currency, but should explain:

- Why funds have been held in currencies other than sterling
- The impact of currency holdings on the estate
- An indication of the sterling value as at the date of the account

Worked example: Receipts and payments account

You were appointed liquidator of DOT Limited following a s98 meeting of creditors 12 months ago. The following information is available:

1. The company's freehold property was sold for a sum of £285,000. The property was subject to a fixed charge held by Satby Bank plc in the sum of £115,000. Agent's and solicitor's fees paid in relation to the sale totalled £21,500. The property was shown in the Statement of Affairs in the sum of £240,000.

2. The company's other assets (machinery, fixtures and stock with a Statement of Affairs value of £55,000) were sold at public auction. The liquidator received the sum of £49,000 after the auctioneer deducted the sum of £5,750 in relation to his costs.

3. Book debts with an estimated to realise value of £93,000 have to date been realised in the sum of £72,000. Legal costs of £6,500 have been incurred in realising debtors to date.

4. Liquidator's remuneration has been drawn in the sum of £12,500 on a time cost basis.

5. Expenses totalling £2,500 have also been drawn relating to case advertising, copying etc.

6. Insurance costs of £1,800 have been paid.

7. A dividend has been paid to preferential creditors totalling £55,000. No dividend has yet been paid to the unsecured creditors.

Requirements

Prepare a Receipts and Payments account for DOT Limited for the period from your appointment to date.

Solution

DOT Limited in Liquidation – Receipts and Payments account for the period X.X.X0 to X.X.X1

	Per Sof A £	Realised to date £
Receipts		
Freehold property	240,000	285,000
Machinery, fixtures, stock	55,000	54,750
Book debts	93,000	72,000
		411,750
Payments		
Satby Bank PLC		115,000
Agents and solicitors fees		21,500
Auctioneer's costs		5,750
Insurance		1,800
Legal fees re debt collection		6,500
Liquidator's remuneration		12,500
Liquidator's expenses		2,500
Payments to creditors		
Preferential creditors 100p in £		55,000
Balance in hand		191,200
		411,750

8.3 Handling of funds in formal insolvency appointments

SIP 11 provides guidance to office holders on the handling of funds in the administration of insolvency cases (it is not limited to liquidations).

It recommends that members should ensure that funds (including and interest earned thereon) and other assets of each case are maintained separately and cannot be intermingled with those of any other case or those of the office holder or his firm. Separate bank accounts should be operated for each case to ensure that these principles are adhered to.

Where funds relating to a case are received by cheque payable to the office holder or his firm which cannot be endorsed to the insolvent estate, such cheques may be cleared through an account maintained in the name of the office holder or his firm. Such accounts should be operated on a trust basis and should be maintained separately from the practitioner's office accounts. Funds paid into such accounts should be paid out to the case to which they relate as soon as possible.

Money coming into the hands of practitioners which is the property of individuals or companies for which they are acting (otherwise than in the capacity of insolvency office holder) must be held in an account operated on trust principles and subject to any applicable client money rules.

There is also an overriding requirement to assess the level of bank charges and interest accruable on the estate funds.

9 Bank reconciliations

> **Section overview**
>
> - At the end of an accounting period when a trial balance has been drawn up, a number of control (checking) procedures are carried out to ensure the completeness, accuracy and validity of the figures.
> - A bank reconciliation is used to reconcile the balance on the company's cash book with the balance shown on the company's bank statement.

The company's cash book is used to record the detailed transactions of receipts and payments into and out of the bank account.

Bank statements provide an independent record of the balance on the bank account.

These are unlikely to exactly agree to the company's cash book for a number of reasons:

- Timing differences:
    - Unpresented cheques (cheques paid out by the company which don't yet appear on the bank statement)
    - Unrecorded lodgements (money paid into the bank account by the business but not yet appearing as a receipt on the statement)
    - Date of issue of the bank statement (these are usually issued monthly and are therefore always out of date when compared to the cash book)
- Errors by the business:
    - Omissions, ie standing orders, bank charges, interest
    - Transposition errors
    - Casting errors
- Errors by the bank:

    Crediting the wrong account

You should note that the bank uses debits and credits the opposite way round, in particular on the bank statement.

In the books of the business:

- POSITIVE bank balance = ASSET = DEBIT
- NEGATIVE (overdrawn) bank balance = LIABILITY = CREDIT

From the bank's point of view:

- POSITIVE balance = LIABILITY = CREDIT
- NEGATIVE (overdrawn) balance = ASSET = DEBIT

9.1 Preparation

When preparing a bank reconciliation:

1. Compare bank statements to the cash book and tick off items which agree.
2. Remaining items must represent timing differences or errors.
3. Amend all errors found.
4. Adjust cash book balance for all unticked items on the bank statements:

    Interest, bank charges, standing orders. (These represent items which have gone through the bank account but haven't been recorded in the cash book.)

5. Reconcile balance on the bank statement to adjusted cash book figure using pro forma shown below:

Balance per bank statement	X
Less unpresented cheques (those in cash book which remain unticked)	(X)
Add outstanding lodgements (those in cash book which remain unticked)	X
Balance per adjusted cash book	X

Self-test

Answer the following questions:

1 Jean was made bankrupt on her own petition. Her property was repossessed by the mortgage company. The amount due to the mortgage company was £105,000 and the costs of sale were 3% of the sale price of £340,000. What figure will the trustee show in his receipts and payments account in respect of the property?

2 The statement of affairs of Freshen Up Ltd shows the following:

Assets

Fixed charge assets	500,000
Fixed charge holder	450,000

Liabilities

Preferential creditors	50,000
Unsecured creditors	300,000

For what amount should the liquidator set the specific penalty bond?

3 Which of the following is not required to be shown in a Statement of Affairs prepared for a company in liquidation? Is it?

A Book value and estimated to realise values of assets
B Securities held by creditors
C Names and addresses of the creditors
D Names and addresses of the directors

4 You were appointed liquidator of Goody Limited on 2 November 20X0 following a s98 meeting of creditors. It is now over six months since your appointment and all of the company's assets have now been realised. You have paid a first dividend to the unsecured creditors.

Below are copies of your receipts and payments along with a copy of your bank statements for the period of liquidation to date.

Cash book receipts

			£
2/11/X9	A Debtor Ltd		750
10/11/X9	Sale of assets at auction		11,500
12/11/X9	B Debtor Ltd		1,800
20/11/X9	C Debtor Ltd		2,500
1/12/X9	D Debtor Ltd		180
18/02/X0	Sale freehold property		140,000
1/06/X0	E Debtor Ltd		5,000

Cash book payments

10/11/X9	Auctioneer's costs	10012	1,500
15/12/X9	Liquidator's remuneration	10013	5,000
15/12/X9	Liquidator's disbursements	10014	900
18/02/X0	Estate agents fees	n/a	3,500
18/02/X0	Fixed charge holder	n/a	7,000
18/02/X0	Solicitor's fees	n/a	2,100
10/05/X0	u/sec div Abbot Ltd	10015	20,300
20/05/X0	u/sec div Freeway Ltd	10016	11,700
20/05/X0	u/sec div Barnes Ltd	10017	19,200
20/05/X0	u/sec div Potts Ltd	10018	36,750
20/05/X0	u/sec div Parkway Ltd	10019	18,600
04/06/X0	Liquidator's remuneration	10020	5,000

Bank statement

Date	Description	Debits £	Credits £	Balance £
2/11/X9	Bank giro credit		750	750
10/11/X9	Bank giro credit		11,500	12,250
10/11/X9	10012	1,500		10,750
12/11/X9	Bank giro credit		1,800	12,550
20/11/X9	Bank giro credit		2,500	15,050
01/12/X9	Bank giro credit		180	15,230
10/12/X9	Bank charges	35		15,195
15/12/X9	10013	5,000		10,195
15/12/X09	10014	900		9,295
18/02/X0	Bank giro credit		127,400	136,695
27/05/X0	10016	11,700		124,995
28/05/X0	10017	19,200		105,795
01/06/X0	10019	18,600		87,195

Requirement

Prepare a bank reconciliation as at 04 June 20X0.

5 What is the order of priority of payment for creditors in a creditors' voluntary liquidation?

Now, go back to the Learning Objectives in the Introduction. If you are satisfied that you have achieved these objectives, please tick them off.

Answers to Self-test

1. SIP 7 states that when assets subject to charges are sold by or on the instructions of the charge holder (or other person with a legal right to do so), the net amount should be shown in the account (even if nil) with the gross realisation(s), costs of realisation and the amount retained by the charge holder shown separately by way of a note.

    Therefore show £224,800 [340,000 less 3% less 105,000].

2. £50,000 – the amount available for preferential and ordinary unsecured creditors.

3. D

4. Bank reconciliation as at 04 June 20X0.

	£	£
Balance at bank 01/06/X0		87,195
Add: outstanding lodgements		5,000
Less: unpresented cheques 10015	(20,300)	
10018	(36,750)	
10020	(5,000)	
		(62,050)
Balance per adjusted cash book		30,145
Balance at cash book 04/06/X0		30,180
Less: bank charges		(35)
Adjusted cash book balance		30,145

5. (i) Fixed charge creditors
   (ii) Costs of liquidation (including liquidator's remuneration)
   (iii) Preferential creditors
   (iv) Prescribed part if applicable
   (v) Floating charge creditors
   (vi) Unsecured creditors
   (vii) Interest on creditors' claims
   (viii) Return of capital

Answers to Interactive questions

Answer to Interactive question 1: Bowring Limited

Net property available to the floating charge holder

	£
Realisations	240,000
Less costs	(18,700)
preferential creditors	(65,000)
	156,300
Prescribed part	
£10,000 @ 50%	5,000
£146,300 @ 20%	29,260
£156,300	34,260
Less costs	(5,000)
Prescribed part	29,260

Answer to Interactive question 2: Estimated Statement of Affairs

(a) Estimated Statement of Affairs for Modern Printing Limited as at X.X.X0

	Working	Book value £	Estimated to realise £
ASSETS SUBJECT TO FIXED CHARGE			
Freehold property		150,000	285,000
Less charge holder			(95,000)
			190,000
ASSETS SUBJECT TO FLOATING CHARGE			
Plant and machinery		64,000	21,000
Fixtures and fittings		19,000	11,000
Motor vehicles		43,000	20,000
Book debts	1	156,000	76,800
Stocks	2	71,000	42,000
			170,800
PREFERENTIAL CREDITORS			
Holiday pay		22,000	
Wage arrears	3	12,000	
			(34,000)
Assets available for floating charge holder			136,800
Satby Bank plc			(79,000)
Assets available for unsecured creditors			247,800
UNSECURED CREDITORS			
HM Revenue and Customs		35,000	
Redundancy		15,000	
Pay in lieu		15,000	
Trade creditors		213,000	
			(278,000)
DEFICIT AS REGARDS CREDITORS			(30,200)
Share capital			(100,000)
DEFICIT AS REGARDS MEMBERS			(130,200)

Notes

1   This statement does not include the costs of liquidation.

2   ROT creditor claims have been received totalling £16,000. These claims have yet to be verified and are therefore not reflected in the Statement of Affairs.

Workings

1   *Book Debts*

	£
Total	156,000
Less bad debt	(60,000)
	96,000
Less 20% provision	(19,200)
Realisable	76,800

2   *Stocks*

ROT claims have not yet been verified so no account has been taken of ROT claims at this stage.

3   *Wages – preferential claims*

Wage arrears arising in the four months prior to liquidation may be claimed preferentially subject to a maximum preferential claim per employee of £800.

(b) If the charge had been created on 1 December 2003 a 'prescribed part' would have had to have been made available for the unsecured creditors.

This is calculated as follows:

50% of first £10,000 of the net property, plus 20% of the balance to a maximum prescribed part of £600,000.

Net property is the property which would have been available to the floating charge holder.

Here:

	£
Net property	136,800
50% x 10,000	5,000
20% x 126,800	25,360
136,800	30,360

The floating charge receiver would therefore receive up to £106,440.

Answer to Interactive question 3: Deficiency Account

Deficiency account

	£	£
Balance per Profit and Loss account		8,500
Less amounts written off assets per Statement of Affairs		
freehold property		
(negative figure because property has increased in value)	(55,000)	
book debts	58,000	
plant and machinery	51,000	
fixtures and fittings	15,500	
stocks	34,000	
motor vehicles	48,000	
		(151,500)
Less amounts arising on liquidation		
breach of contract	52,000	
redundancy, pay in lieu of notice	36,700	
		(88,700)
Est trading loss 01/02/X0 to 01/09/X0*		(48,500)
Total deficiency to creditors		(280,200)
Share capital		(50,000)
Total deficiency to members		(330,200)

*Balancing figure

Answer to Interactive question 4: Estimated Outcome Statement (2)

Estimated Outcome Statement – Bill Norris – Individual Voluntary Arrangement as at X.X.X0

	Workings	£	£
ASSETS SPECIFICALLY PLEDGED			
Freehold property	1		100,000
OTHER ASSETS			
Book debts	2	16,500	
Catering van	3	5,000	
Voluntary contributions	4	18,000	
Bank account		5,000	
			44,500
			144,500
Less costs			
nominee's fees		(3,500)	
supervisor's fees	5	(3,000)	
			(6,500)
ASSETS AVAILABLE FOR CREDITORS			138,000
UNSECURED CREDITORS			
Satby Bank plc		28,250	
Business debts		128,000	
HM Revenue and Customs		25,000	
Credit cards		12,000	
Easy Debt Limited		8,000	
			(201,250)

Creditors will receive 69p in £ (138,000/201,250)

Workings

1. *Freehold property*

	£
Realisation	295,000
Less Freeby Bank PLC	(195,000)
	100,000

2. *Book debts*

    £55,000 @ 30% = £16,500 realisable.

3. *Catering van*

	£
Realisable value	9,000
Less cost of reasonable replacement	(4,000)
	5,000

4. *Voluntary contributions*

    36 months @ £500 per month = £18,000

5. *Supervisor's fees*

    £1,000 x 3 years = £3,000

CHAPTER 6

Position of directors in insolvency situations

Introduction
Topic List
1   Directors: duties, effect and risks of insolvency
2   Disqualification of directors
3   SIP 13 – Acquisition of assets of insolvent companies by directors
Summary and Self-test
Answers to Self-test
Answer to Interactive question

Introduction

Learning objectives

- Identify the potential civil and criminal liabilities of directors in a given scenario
- Explain how the disqualification of a director might arise and the processes involved in disqualification
- Explain briefly the provisions of Company Directors Disqualification Act 1986

Stop and think

Why should a director's conduct be investigated? What constitutes undesirable conduct? Who should be notified of the results of investigations carried out?

Working context

Liquidators have a duty to investigate the conduct of directors of insolvent companies. You may be required to review the company's books and records to identify matters which require further detailed investigation. You may also be asked to assist in the completion of the director's conduct report.

1 Directors: duties, effect and risks of insolvency

> **Section overview**
> - While a company is solvent directors owe a duty of care to the company as represented by the company shareholders/members. They owe no duty of care to the company's creditors. Once a company is insolvent however that position changes and they owe a duty to creditors to take the necessary steps to minimise the losses that they may suffer. A breach of this duty may have significant consequences for any director. He may be held liable to make a financial contribution to the company to assist in paying its debts; he may have criminal liability; he may face disqualification as a director.

1.1 Types of director

The Insolvency Act 1986 (s251) defines a director as 'any person occupying the position of director, by whatever name called'. This definition includes:

- **De jure directors**. Anyone properly appointed in compliance with the company's internal rules (Articles of Association). The appointment should be detailed at Companies House. Directors divide into executive and non-executive directors. Executive directors are usually employees of the company (even if they are also shareholders) and have responsibility for the day to day management of the company. Non-executive directors are usually retained to attend board meetings, their role is to bring objectivity to the decisions of the main board. They are not usually employees.

- **De facto directors**. Anyone who acts as a director and is treated as a director by the board despite a lack of formal appointment.

- **Shadow directors**. Defined in the Insolvency Act as 'a person in accordance with whose instruction the directors of the company are accustomed to act'. Professional advisers are not usually shadow directors. The legislation is designed to ensure that those who tell the directors what to do don't evade responsibility for breaches of duty by the simple fact that they have not been formally appointed. It must however be the case that the appointed directors actually follow the direction of the shadow director(s).

1.2 Effect of insolvency procedures on the position of directors

- **Liquidation**

    A director's powers cease on the appointment of the liquidator unless he is sanctioned to continue by the liquidator or members in an MVL (s91(2)) or by the liquidation committee or creditors in a CVL (s103).

    In any period between the commencement of liquidation and the appointment of the liquidator pursuant to s114(2) IA86 the directors can only act with the sanction of the court.

    There are two exceptions to this rule:

    (i) To act in connection with the calling of a s98 meeting and preparation of a statement of affairs in a CVL

    (ii) To dispose of perishable goods or to take action necessary to protect the company's assets

    In a compulsory liquidation the winding-up order operates to terminate a director's powers and dismiss him/her from office.

- **Administration**

    In administration the directors remain in office unless removed, but can only act with the administrator's consent. The administrator has the power to appoint and remove directors.

- **Receivership**

    Except in relation to the management and realisation of assets subject to the fixed charge the directors retain their usual powers.

- **Administrative Receivership**

    The administrative receiver takes on the management of the company and the realisation of assets subject to the charge. However, the directors remain in office and they continue to exercise their powers to the extent that to do so does not interfere with the administrative receivership.

- **CVA**

    The directors carry on as normal subject to the supervision of the supervisor.

1.3 Directors' general duties to the company

In brief the general duties of a director are set out in Companies Act 2006. A director has a duty to:

- Act in accordance with the company's constitution and exercise powers for the purpose for which they were given
- Act in good faith to promote the success of the company for the benefit of the shareholders as a whole
- Exercise independent judgment
- Exercise reasonable care, skill and diligence
- Avoid conflicts of interest
- Not accept benefits from third parties given by reason of his directorship or for him to do/not do something as a director
- Declare to the other directors the nature and extent of any direct or indirect interest that he may have in any proposed transaction or arrangement with the company.

1.4 Directors' specific duties to the office holder (not CVAs or fixed charged receiverships)

For the purpose of the legislation directors are 'relevant persons', which definition also includes:

- Those who are or have been officers of the company.
- Those who in the 12 months prior to commencement took part in the company's formation or were employed by the company.
- Those who in the 12 months prior to commencement were officers or employees of a company which is (has been) an officer of the company. (For example, an employee of the company's auditors.)

The duties owed include:

- Providing statement of affairs
- Co-operating with the office holder
- Attending on the office holder at such times as he may reasonably require

Directors must also attend an initial meeting of creditors if required to do so by either a liquidator or administrator.

1.5 Risks to directors in winding up

- **Breach of duty or misfeasance (s212 IA86)**

    A liquidator, creditor or contributory can apply to court for an order compelling a director to pay compensation for any breach of duty or misfeasance or to make good any loss suffered by the company because of the misapplication of company funds or assets. This provision is commonly used where a liquidator finds evidence that a director has caused loss to the company through allowing it to enter into a preference or transaction at an undervalue, or through negligence.

An action can be brought against directors, former directors and also against a former liquidator or administrative receiver. Administrators are not subject to s212 but can be subject to an action for misfeasance pursuant to para 75 schedule B1 IA 86.

Misfeasance is a civil matter. Liability for misfeasance may support an application for disqualification (see later in the chapter.)

- **Wrongful trading (s214 IA86)**

Directors may be liable to contribute to the assets of a company if the company is allowed to continue trading at a time when a director knew or ought to have known that there was no reasonable prospect of the company avoiding insolvent liquidation ('the relevant time').

Actions for wrongful trading are brought by the liquidator of an insolvent company or an administrator under the extended rights imposed by SBEEA 2015. It will be for the liquidator/administrator to ascertain the point at which the director knew or ought to have known that the company could not avoid insolvency and that he continued to trade on in circumstances where a reasonable director of his level of skill and experience would not have done so. No dishonesty on the part of the director need be shown. The defence available to the director is that he took every step that he ought to have taken to minimise the loss to creditors.

It is for the court to decide what the level of contribution from the director should be. In practice, it is likely to be equal to the increase in creditor losses after the relevant time. As well as facing liability for wrongful trading a director may also be disqualified from acting as a director (see para 2).

- **Fraudulent trading (s213 IA86)**

Where there is an element of dishonesty in the director's actions the liquidator/administrator may consider bringing an action for fraudulent trading against the director concerned. The consequences of fraudulent trading are as per wrongful trading with the additional possibility of criminal proceedings being brought under the Companies Act 2006. If convicted of fraudulent trading a director could face up to 10 years imprisonment. Dishonest conduct may include things like: deliberately allowing the company to incur further debt where it is clear that the debt cannot be repaid; making misleading statements to creditors; or taking very definite steps to avoid paying creditors. Note that s213 is not limited in scope to insolvent liquidations (unlike misfeasance). Evidence of fraudulent trading will be relevant in disqualification proceedings.

- **Re-use of company name (s216-217 IA86)**

General Rule

- s216 provides that a director/shadow director of a company in insolvent liquidation is prohibited from being a director of a company known by a prohibited name for a period of five years.

- The individual concerned must have been a director/shadow director of the insolvent company in the 12 months ending with the day before it went into insolvent liquidation.

- The individual may not act as a director in the new company and also not be in any way concerned, directly or indirectly in the promotion, formation or management of the company. It also applies to the carrying on of a business under a prohibited name.

- If the provision is breached, the individual may be subject to a fine and/or imprisonment.

- In addition, the person in breach becomes liable for 'relevant debts'. These are all liabilities for the period during which they were involved in the management of the **new** company or acting on instructions.

Definition

Prohibited name: any name by which the liquidating company was known in the last 12 months or which is so similar that it suggests an association with the liquidating company.

Exceptions

Various exceptions to the provisions in s216 exist. These are:

- **Sanction of court** – permission of the court may be obtained by application under s216(3) and R4.227A.

- **Rule 4.228** – this is where the IP has arranged for the transfer of the whole, or substantially the whole, of the business to a successor company. Notice must be given to creditors of the insolvent company by the successor company within 28 days of the completion of the arrangement. The notice must give details of the prohibited name, name and registered number of the insolvent company and circumstances of the acquisition.

- **Rule 4.229** – this applies while applicants are awaiting court sanction under s216(3) within seven business days from the date that the company went into liquidation. The applicant can use the name until the earlier of six weeks or the day the court disposes of the application.

- **Rule 4.230** – this applies when the successor company has been known by the name for 12 consecutive months prior to the date the insolvent company went into liquidation and that it was not dormant at any time in those 12 months.

- **Key criminal offences**

Criminal offence	Section number
Fraud in anticipation of winding up	s206
Transactions in fraud of creditors	s207
Misconduct in case of winding up	s208
Falsification of company books	s209
Material omissions from statement of affairs	s210
Fraudulent representations to creditors	s211
Restriction on re-use of company name	s216

2 Disqualification of directors

Section overview

- The OR, liquidators, administrators and administrative receivers are all required to report to the Secretary of State on the conduct of past or present directors (and shadow directors) where it appears to him that the conduct of the director makes him unfit to be concerned in the management of a company, s7(3) Company Directors Disqualification Act 1986 (CDDA 86). SIP 4 provides guidance to office holders re disqualification of directors. The law is contained in CDDA 86 and the Insolvent Companies (Reports on Conduct of Directors) Rules 1996.

2.1 Statutory requirements

The following office holders are required to report on the director's conduct:

- Compulsory liquidation – the OR
- Insolvent voluntary liquidation – the liquidator
- Administration – the administrator
- Administrative Receivership – the administrative receiver

The office holder should make the necessary returns within six months of the relevant date.

The relevant dates are:

- Creditors' voluntary liquidation – date of the resolution to wind up

- Members' voluntary liquidation – date when the liquidator formed the opinion that the company was unable to meet its liabilities

- Administrative receivership – date of appointment of the receiver
- Administration – date administration order made by the court

The office holder is required to file a D1 report for those directors with unfit conduct and a D2 return for those directors whose conduct is deemed to be fit. The returns should include all directors and shadow directors who were in office in the three years preceding the relevant date.

The Secretary of State must make an application for a disqualification order within three years from the relevant date.

The court shall make a disqualification order when it is satisfied that an individual:

- Is or has been a director of a company which has at any time become insolvent
- His conduct as a director of that company or with other companies makes him unfit to be concerned in the management of a company

The minimum period for a disqualification order is two years with the maximum being 15 years.

2.2 Terms of a disqualification order

A person shall not, without the permission of the court:

- Be a director of a company, act as a receiver of a company's property or in any way, whether directly or indirectly, be concerned or take part in the promotion, formation or management of a company; or
- Act as an insolvency practitioner.

Acting in contravention of a disqualification order is an offence (s13 CDDA 86) and such a person will become jointly and severally liable for the company's debts (s15 CDDA 86).

2.3 SIP 4 Guidance

SIP 4 – Disqualification of directors

- SIP 4 provides further guidance to IPs on the submission of disqualification reports to the Secretary of State and the work they are required to undertake.
- SIP 4 states that if an IP has not found any 'unfitted' conduct within three months (SBEEA2105, or whatever period the Secretary of State deems fit) or if the information is insufficient to make a decision, they should make an interim return. If they later find any evidence of adverse conduct then an adverse report can be submitted.
- Liquidators do not have to carry out any specific investigations into director conduct – they can base the return on information coming to light in the ordinary course of their investigations.
- The liquidator should be aware that the matters of unfitness set out in Schedule 1 to the CDDA 86 are not exhaustive and other matters considered relevant should be included in the return.
- IPs shouldn't take a pedantic view of isolated technical failures but should form an overall view of a director's conduct.

  The IP may become a witness in future proceedings against the director and should back up all opinions with documentation. As such the IP should meet with and interview the directors to gain a full understanding of relevant matters.

- In the report itself an IP should:
  - Avoid defamation
  - Include copies of accounts and reports to creditors' meetings where relevant
  - Give specific examples of instances of unfitted conduct where possible
  - Avoid disclosure of the contents of the report to outsiders

- Matters that disqualification unit look at include:

  Directors' misconduct

  - Loans to directors to purchase shares in the company
  - Personal benefits obtained by the directors
  - Director's criminal convictions

- Misfeasance/breach of duty
- Misapplication of funds
- Voidable transactions
- Attempted concealment of assets
- Misconduct overseas

Prejudicing creditors

- Dishonoured cheques
- Deposits accepted for goods/services not supplied
- Delaying tactics
- Retention of crown monies to finance trading
- Transactions at an undervalue
- Preferences
- Phoenix operations (s216)

Interactive question 1: Fred Ginger

Your principal, Fred Ginger, has been asked to address a training day for insolvency staff regarding the area of directors' disqualification. He has been asked to give a short presentation on when a directors report should be submitted.

Requirement

What points should be made in the presentation?

See **Answer** at the end of this chapter.

2.4 Disqualification undertakings

Insolvency Act 2000

- Insolvency Act 2000 introduced a regime of disqualification undertakings into the CDDA 86.

- A disqualification undertaking is where the Secretary of State accepts an undertaking by any person that for a period of time (specified in the undertaking document) they will not be a director etc of any company and will not act as an insolvency practitioner.

- The minimum and maximum periods for undertakings are as per a normal disqualification order (s1A(2) CDDA 86).

- The Secretary of State may accept an undertaking from a person instead of applying for, or proceeding with an application for, a disqualification order.

- Following the giving of a disqualification undertaking the court may vary the undertaking by reducing the period for which the undertaking is to be in force, or by discharging it.

- An application for variation must be made to the court by the person subject to the disqualification undertaking (s8A(1) CDDA 86).

3 SIP 13 – Acquisition of assets of insolvent companies by directors

Section overview

- The SIP ensures that office holders are familiar with the legal obligations of directors in relation to the acquisition of assets of companies and the statutory provisions relating to such acquisitions. It sets out best practice with regard to the disposal of assets to and their acquisition by, directors (and other connected parties eg shareholders) and the disclosure of such transactions.

3.1 Concerns regarding sales to directors/connected parties

There are three basic concerns regarding the acquisition of assets by directors/connected parties:

(i) Assets are disposed of for less than market value

(ii) Creditors prejudiced by the insolvency of the disposing company are exposed to further risk by the continued trading of the responsible directors

(iii) Such transactions are conducted with propriety and are fully disclosed

3.2 Directors' duties with regard to the purchase of assets

Under CA 2006 the overriding duty of directors is to promote the success of the company. Failure to do so exposes directors to risks of claims for breach of duty or misfeasance. Consequently they must refrain from entering into transactions which may be set aside as transactions at an undervalue or preferences.

Where an asset sale between directors and the company amounts to 'a substantial property transaction' it will require prior approval of the members (shareholders) in general meeting (s190 CA 2006). A substantial property transaction is one where the transaction exceeds the lower of:

- £100,000; or
- 10% of the company's net asset value (subject to a minimum of £5,000).

If a company is in insolvent liquidation or in administration, approval of the members is not required. under s190 CA 2006 (s193 CA 2006). However, if the company is in administrative receivership or MVL, approval of substantial property transactions is still required. (ss190, 193 CA 2006.)

3.3 Sales to directors prior to liquidation

The SIP acknowledges that it can be in the creditors best interests for a sale of assets to directors prior to the winding-up, but places an obligation on the IP to conduct a thorough appraisal of the propriety of the sale and the benefits expected to accrue to creditors, and to consider whether it is appropriate for the advising IP to seek appointment as liquidator.

Such sale must be fully disclosed to creditors.

3.4 Post appointment transactions

The duty to maximise realisations does not prevent directors and IPs making disposals to directors (or other connected parties eg shareholders). However the office holder should advertise or circularise sales particulars to all potentially interested parties.

The office holder should ensure that transactions with directors/connected parties are at arm's length and assets subject to a professional valuation.

If the sale to directors is via a pre-pack sale in administration the office holder should comply with SIP 16, but in a CVL, it should comply with SIP13

Connected party transactions should be disclosed as follows:

1. Administrations – the administrator should include in his proposals reference to any connected party transactions undertaken in the period since the making of the administration order. If a creditors' committee is appointed, the members of the committee should be advised of any such transaction undertaken after the meeting of creditors to consider the proposals.

2. Administrative receivership – the AR should include in his report to creditors at the s48 meeting information regarding any connected party transaction if this has taken place prior to the meeting and if it takes place after the meeting, report it to any creditors' committee appointed at that meeting.

3. Creditors voluntary liquidation – the liquidator should include in his report to creditors at the s98 meeting his intention to accept such an offer from the connected party. Such information should be issued to all creditors with conformation of whether sale has been effected as soon as practicable, or if this is after notice of the liquidation has been issued, at the next available statutory report.

Any disclosure should include the following information:

- The date of the transaction
- Details of the assets involved and the nature of the transaction
- The consideration for the transaction and when it was paid
- The name of the counterparty
- The nature of the counterparty's connected party relationship with the seller
- If the transaction took place before the appointment of the member as office holder, the name of any adviser to the seller
- Whether the purchaser and (if the transaction took place before the appointment of the member as office holder) the seller were independently advised
- Where the transaction took place before the commencement of liquidation or administration, the scope of the office holder's investigation and the conclusion reached
- Where the disclosure is to a liquidation committee and the committee has not been consulted prior to contract, the reason why such consultation did not take place
- Where, in a liquidation, the disclosure is to creditors, whether the liquidation committee (if there is one) has been consulted and the outcome of such consultation

Summary and Self-test

Summary

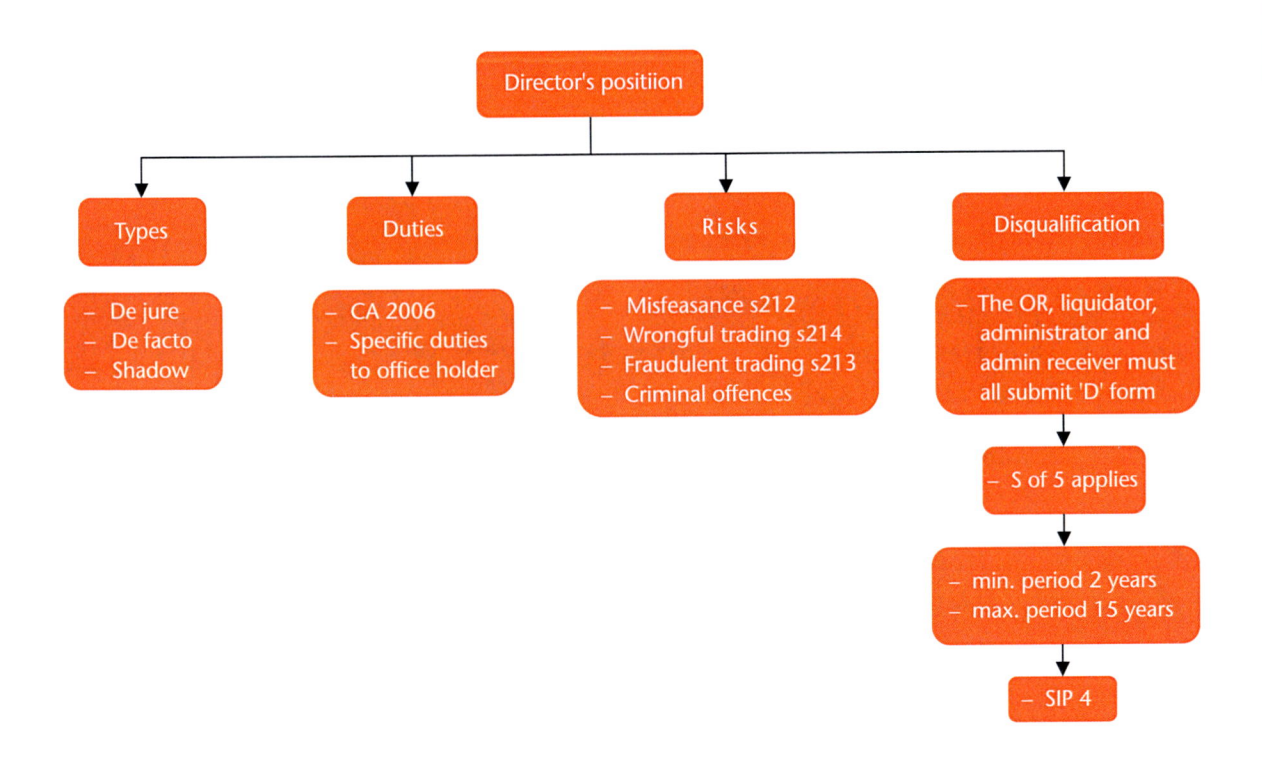

```
                        Director's positiion
        ┌───────────────┬──────────────┬───────────────┐
      Types           Duties          Risks       Disqualification
    - De jure       - CA 2006    - Misfeasance s212   - The OR, liquidator,
    - De facto      - Specific duties - Wrongful trading s214  administrator and
    - Shadow          to office holder - Fraudulent trading s213  admin receiver must
                                   - Criminal offences    all submit 'D' form
                                                              │
                                                        - S of 5 applies
                                                              │
                                                        - min. period 2 years
                                                        - max. period 15 years
                                                              │
                                                            - SIP 4
```

Self-test

Answer the following questions.

1   In which of the following cases is the office holder not required to report on the conduct of the directors?

    A   Members' voluntary liquidation
    B   Creditors' voluntary liquidation
    C   Compulsory liquidation
    D   Administration

2   In a CVL, the Secretary of State must make an application for a disqualification order within what period from the date of the resolution to wind up?

    A   12 months
    B   2 years
    C   3 years
    D   There is no time limit

3   What is the definition of a shadow director?

4   For which of the following periods may a director be disqualified?

    A   1 year
    B   Minimum period of 1 year, maximum period of 5 years
    C   5 years
    D   2 years
    E   Minimum period of 2 years, maximum period of 15 years

5   Within what period from the relevant date should the responsible office holder submit a return on the directors of a company?

    A   3 months (or whatever time deemed fit by SoS)
    B   6 months
    C   12 months
    D   18 months
    E   As soon as practically possible

Now, go back to the Learning Objectives in the Introduction. If you are satisfied that you have achieved these objectives, please tick them off.

Answers to Self-test

1. A
2. C – Changed by SBEEA 2015
3. A person in accordance with whose instructions the directors are accustomed to act
4. E
5. A

Answer to Interactive question

Answer to Interactive question 1: Fred Ginger

An office holder is required to report on the directors' conduct in the following cases:

(i) Compulsory liquidation
(ii) Insolvent voluntary liquidation
(iii) Administration
(iv) Administrative receivership

The conduct of all directors and shadow directors who were in office in the three years preceding the relevant date should be reported on.

A D1 report should be filed for those directors with unfit conduct.

A D2 return should be submitted for those directors whose conduct is deemed to be fit.

All reports should be submitted with three months given that the application for a disqualification order must be made with three years.

Section B:

Corporate insolvency

CHAPTER 7

Voluntary liquidation

Introduction
Topic List
1 Introduction to voluntary liquidation
2 Members' voluntary liquidation
3 Declaration of solvency
4 Procedure to follow where company becomes insolvent
5 Creditors' voluntary liquidation
6 Liquidation committee

Summary and Self-test
Answers to Self-test
Answers to Interactive questions

Introduction

Learning objectives

Tick off

- Explain the process involved in the commencement of a creditors' voluntary liquidation including s98 meetings ☐

- Explain the difference between solvent and insolvent liquidations ☐

- Explain the processes involved in the commencement of a members' voluntary liquidation including the declaration of solvency and other formalities ☐

- Describe the on-going obligations upon the insolvency practitioner in a members' voluntary liquidation and a creditors' voluntary liquidation with regard to:
  - Meetings
  - Record keeping
  - Reporting
  - Time limits ☐

- Explain the following aspects of corporate insolvency, their origins, characteristics and effects:
  - The role of the liquidator
  - The role of the liquidation committee ☐

Stop and think

Why are there two forms of voluntary liquidation? How does a members' voluntary liquidation differ from a creditors' voluntary liquidation? Why are creditors not involved in a members' voluntary liquidation? What is the role of a creditors' committee?

Working context

A large number of companies enter into voluntary liquidation each year. It is likely therefore that you will be involved in working on liquidation cases. You may be asked to assist the office holder in preparing the relevant notices to convene a s98 meeting of creditors, or in putting together the relevant information to be provided at that meeting.

You may also be asked to attend a s98 meeting on behalf of a client and sit on a creditors' committee on their behalf.

1 Introduction to voluntary liquidation

> **Section overview**
>
> - A voluntary liquidation commences with a resolution to wind up passed by the members of a company. Voluntary liquidations must be contrasted with compulsory liquidations which commence with a court order. The legislation makes a distinction between the different types of liquidation proceeding so take care to note what type of liquidation is referred to in any question that you may face in the assessment.

1.1 Types of voluntary liquidation

There are two types of voluntary liquidation:

- **Members' Voluntary Liquidation (MVL)** – solvent liquidation where directors swear a declaration of solvency, the members (shareholders) choose the liquidator.
- **Creditors' Voluntary Liquidation (CVL)** – insolvent liquidation, creditors have an opportunity to appoint a liquidator of their choice.

The law relating to liquidations is contained mainly in Part IV (Sections 73 – 205) IA 86 and the rules are set out in Part 4 of the Insolvency Rules 86. [We cover compulsory liquidation in the following chapter.]

1.2 Powers of the liquidator

The powers of the liquidator are detailed in Schedule 4 IA 86. Historically some of these powers required sanction but the requirement for sanction was removed by SBEEA2015 to mean prior sanction was not required. By s165(1), in a voluntary liquidation historically sanction was obtained as follows:

- In MVL, by the passing of a special resolution by the company in general meeting
- In CVL, either from the liquidation committee (or if there is none) a creditors' meeting or the court

[In practice, the Secretary of State would give sanction to liquidators in situations where there was no liquidation committee. Where the liquidator was unable to obtain sanction he would still be able to apply for sanction from the court.]

1.3 Powers exercisable with sanction (Part I) *now no longer required*

The following powers require sanction in any type of liquidation.

- To make compromises or arrangements with creditors or claimants against the company
- To bring legal proceedings under ss213, 214, 238, 239, 242, 243 or 423

1.4 Powers exercisable without sanction in a voluntary winding up (Part II)

The following powers are exercisable without sanction in a voluntary winding up, however they would require sanction in a compulsory winding up.

- To bring or defend any action or other legal proceedings in the name and on behalf of the company
- To carry on the business of the company so far as may be necessary for its beneficial winding up
- To pay any class of creditor in full

1.5 Powers exercisable without sanction in any type of liquidation (Part III)

- Sell company property
- Execute all documents
- Claim in the insolvency of debtor individuals and companies
- Draw/make (etc) bills of exchange and promissory notes
- Raise money on the security of company assets
- Take out letters of administration in the name of deceased contributories
- Appoint an agent

- Do all such other things as may be necessary for winding up the company's affairs
- Compromise claims by the company against debtors, potential debtors and contributories

1.6 Powers which require notice to be given to the liquidation committee

If the liquidator disposes of any company property to a party connected with the company, he must give notice of it to the liquidation committee.

1.7 Powers between members' and creditors' meetings

Usually the General Meeting (GM) and the s98 creditors' meeting will be held on the same day. However, if the members agree to calling the GM at short notice a liquidator may be appointed and the company placed into liquidation. The s98 meeting of creditors may be held at any time within the following 14 days. This is called a 'centrebind' procedure.

In the period between the GM and the s98 creditors' meeting, the members' liquidator's powers are limited to the following (s166).

- To take into custody or control all of the company's property
- To dispose of perishable/wasting goods
- To do all things necessary for the protection of the company's assets

The exercise of any other powers requires the sanction of the court.

The members' liquidator must attend the s98 creditors' meeting and expressly report to it on the exercise of his powers.

Definition

Contributory: An individual who is liable to contribute to the assets of a company when it is wound up. For example shareholders/members who have not paid for their shares.

2 Members' voluntary liquidation

Section overview

- A members' voluntary liquidation (MVL) is a solvent liquidation which is initiated by the members of the company. A MVL is deemed to commence on the date that the special resolution is passed by the members to wind up the company. A declaration of solvency must be sworn by the directors. Because the creditors will be paid in full they have no interest in the winding up.

2.1 Procedure to initiate members' voluntary liquidation

The procedure to follow to initiate a members' voluntary liquidation is as follows:

1   Meeting of Board of Directors:

    The directors are required to pass the following resolutions:

    - Recommend MVL to the members
    - Authorise the calling of an General Meeting (GM)
    - Select a director to chair the GM
    - Authorise the swearing of a statutory declaration of solvency (see para 3 below for details)
    - To provide the liquidator with an indemnity for early distribution to shareholders

2   Hold General Meeting (GM):

    - Notice:

        14 days' notice of the GM must be sent to all members of the company unless the company's Articles of Association (ie the company's constitution/internal rules) specify a longer period of notice or a higher threshold. The members can waive the notice period however, provided

that at least 95% of those entitled to attend and vote are in favour of this proposal (90% if private company).

The notice sent to members must contain the date, time and place of the meeting. The resolution to wind up the company should be stated in full. The notice should also include a proxy form.

There is no requirement to pre-advertise the GM.

- Conduct at meeting:

The quorum required for the meeting will be stated in the company's Articles of Association. It is often two, unless it is a single member company when the quorum will be reduced to one.

One of the directors will chair the meeting.

At the GM, the following resolutions need to be passed:

- A special resolution to wind up the company (s84(1)(b)). This will require a 75% majority or more of the votes cast at the meeting
- An ordinary resolution to appoint a liquidator. This requires a simple majority (**over** 50%) of the votes cast at the meeting

The special resolution to wind up the company must be filed with the Registrar of Companies within 15 days and advertised in the *Gazette* within 14 days, accompanied by Form 600.

Following his appointment, the liquidator must give notice of his appointment to:

- All creditors within 28 days
- In the *Gazette* within 14 days
- To Registrar of Companies within 14 days

The company can avoid holding a meeting if it passes the special resolution by asking members to sign the resolution to signify their consent to it – a written resolution. It must be agreed to by at least 75% of the total voting rights of eligible members.

- The members may decide to pass other resolutions at the meeting, including:

    - An ordinary resolution regarding the basis of the liquidator's remuneration
    - A special resolution sanctioning the exercise of the liquidator's powers contained in Schedule 4 Part 1 (see paragraph 1.3). These were extended by SBEEA 2015
    - A special resolution sanctioning the distribution of assets in specie

3 Declaration of solvency

Section overview

- In order for the liquidation to proceed as a MVL the directors must swear a declaration of solvency. If no such declaration is sworn, the liquidation must proceed as a CVL.

3.1 Statutory requirements

The declaration of solvency must be made within five weeks preceding the date of the passing of the resolution to wind up.

It must be sworn by all of the directors of the company, or where there are more than two directors, a majority of them.

The declaration must include details of the company's assets and liabilities as at the latest practicable date before its making.

The declaration must be filed with Registrar of Companies within 15 days of the passing of the resolution to wind up.

3.2 Content of Declaration of Solvency

s89 provides that the declaration must state that the directors have:

- Made a full enquiry into the company's affairs
- Formed the opinion that the company will be able to pay its debts in full, together with interest at the official rate
- Within such period, not exceeding 12 months from the date of commencement of the winding up, as may be specified in the declaration

This includes detailing statutory interest for known creditors ad a provision for the costs of winding up.

4 Procedure to follow where company becomes insolvent

Section overview

- A members' voluntary liquidation is a solvent liquidation. If the company subsequently becomes insolvent the liquidation cannot continue as a MVL and the liquidator must take the necessary steps to convert the liquidation to a CVL.

4.1 Duties of a liquidator where a company becomes insolvent

- On becoming aware that the company will be unable to pay its debts within the specified period, the liquidator must:
    - Hold a meeting of creditors within 28 days of discovering the company is insolvent (s95(2A)(a))
    - Send notices of the meeting to creditors not less than 7 days before the date of the meeting(s95(2A)(b))
    - Advertise the meeting in the *Gazette* and additionally advertise the meeting in other newspapers if thought appropriate
    - Prior to the date of the meeting provide creditors with such information concerning the affairs of the company as they may require (s95(2A)(e))
- This meeting will be deemed to be the creditors' meeting required to be held for a creditors' voluntary liquidation.
- The liquidator must also (s95(3)):
    - Make out a statement in the prescribed form as to the affairs of the company
    - Lay that statement before the creditors meeting
    - Attend and chair the meeting
- If the liquidator fails to comply with these requirements he is liable to a fine.

4.2 Conversion to a creditors' voluntary liquidation

s96 provides that, as from the date on which the creditors' meeting is held under s95, it has the effect as if the directors declaration had not been made. The creditors' meeting and the company meeting (when the resolution to wind up was passed) are now treated as if they were the meetings required for a creditors' voluntary liquidation under s98. Consequently the members' voluntary liquidation is duly converted into a creditors' voluntary liquidation.

If a company becomes insolvent after the resolution to wind up the company is passed, it is presumed that the statutory declaration was not made on reasonable grounds s89(5). As a result, the directors who swore the declaration will be liable to imprisonment and/or a fine.

4.3 Acceptance of appointment as liquidator

Where an IP has been acting as liquidator in a MVL and he calls a s95 meeting he must consider whether the Insolvency Code of Ethics permits him to take up the appointment of liquidator in the CVL.

If there has been no significant professional relationship and provided due consideration is paid to the requirements of the Code the IP can usually accept the appointment.

If there has been a significant professional relationship and the IP is of the opinion that, despite the calling of the s95 meeting, the company will eventually return to solvency, he may usually accept appointment as liquidator at the s95 meeting. If it subsequently appears that he was mistaken in his belief he should resign. If the IP does not believe the company will return to solvency he should not accept appointment as liquidator at the s95 meeting.

The liquidator should also reconsider the aspect of risk under AML and anti-bribery under a continuing obligation.

Interactive question 1: Declaration of Solvency

What matters are required to be stated in a Declaration of Solvency?

See **Answer** at the end of this chapter.

5 Creditors' voluntary liquidation

Section overview

- A creditors' voluntary liquidation (CVL) is an insolvent liquidation. It is deemed to commence on the date that the special resolution is passed by the members to wind up the company. A creditors meeting is also held at which the creditors are given the opportunity to appoint their choice of liquidator.

5.1 Procedure to initiate creditors' voluntary liquidation

The procedure to initiate a creditors' voluntary liquidation is as follows:

1 **Meeting of Board of Directors**

   The directors are required to pass the following resolutions:
   - Recommend CVL to the members on the basis that the company is unable to pay its debts
   - Authorise and facilitate the calling of a General Meeting
   - Authorise and facilitate the calling of a meeting of the company's creditors under s98
   - Select a director to chair both meetings
   - Arrange for the drawing up of a Statement of Affairs
   - The instruction of the IA and any fees payable in regard to that instruction

2 **General Meeting**
   - Notice

   14 days' notice of the GM must be sent to all members. The members can waive the notice period provided that at least 95% of those entitled to attend and vote are in favour of this proposal (90% if a private company). Both the notice period and the threshold are subject to contrary provisions in the company's articles.

   (Resolution to wind up could be passed at the company's Annual General Meeting, 21 days' notice to members would be required. Notice may be waived if 100% of members agree.)

   Notice must be given to any qualifying charge holder. This gives the charge holder the opportunity to appoint an administrator if they wish. If an administrator is appointed, no winding up resolution may then be passed (s84).

   Note also that the passing of a resolution to wind up the company voluntarily does not prevent creditors from presenting a winding up petition.

The notice sent to the members must contain the following information:
- Date, time and place of the meeting
- The resolution to wind up must be set out in full

- Conduct at the meeting

    The GM
    - The quorum required for the meeting will be defined in the company's Articles. It is often two, unless it is a single member company where it is reduced to one
    - One of the directors will chair the meeting
    - At the GM, the following resolutions will be passed:
        (i) A special resolution to wind up the company (s84(1)(b)). This will require a 75% majority or more of the votes cast at the meeting.
        (ii) An ordinary resolution to appoint a members' liquidator. This requires a simple majority (**over** 50%) of the votes cast at the meeting. If there is a delay before the creditors' meeting s166 1A86 limits the powers of the liquidator. Essentially a liquidator will only be able to take necessary action to protect the company's assets.
        (iii) The special resolution to wind up the company must be advertised in the *Gazette* within 14 days (s85(1)), and a copy must be forwarded to the Registrar of Companies within 15 days (s84(3)), accompanied by the Form 600.

3 **Meeting of creditors**

SIP 8 is concerned with the convening of the s98 creditors' meeting. The advising member (ie retained insolvency practitioner) (AM) must ensure that the directors are aware of all of their responsibilities including giving clear instructions.

If there is any question of the directors asking the AM to act contrary to the SIP he should refuse the instruction. In particular the AM should be convinced that, having passed the special resolution to wind-up the company, the directors will make an appointment of a liquidator.

The AM should not accept work without giving proper consideration to the Insolvency Code of Ethics.

- Convening the s98 creditors meeting
    - The meeting must be held within a maximum of 14 days from the members meeting (s98(1A)(a)), but is usually held on the same day
    - Creditors must be given at least seven days notice of the meeting (s98(1A)(b))
    - The notice must state:
        (i) Venue of meeting
        (ii) Name of IP who will furnish creditors with information regarding the company's affairs (s98(2)(a)) and associated contact details
        (iii) A place in the relevant locality where a list of names and addresses of the company's creditors will be available for inspection on the two business days prior to the meeting (s98(2)(b))
        (iv) Whether any resolutions are to be considered in the drawing of fees
    - The meeting must also be advertised in the *Gazette* and may be advertised in such other manner as the directors think fit
    - Relevant locality means the company's principal place of business in Great Britain. If there is more than one then the meeting must be advertised in **all** relevant localities (s98(3))

- Venue for the s98 meeting should:
    - Be convenient for creditors
    - Offer adequate accommodation for the attending creditors
    - Be of a convenient date and time as well as being reasonably geographically located

Remote attendance is possible by telephone, video conferencing or on-line meeting.

- Information to be provided to creditors:
  - If directors provide a list of creditors it should be in a reasonable location
  - Include names and addresses in alphabetical order (but not the amounts owed)
  - Be available between 10.00am and 4.00pm on the two business days before the date of the s98 meeting
  - Include copies for representatives
- Information to provide at the meeting should include:
  - Sufficient copies of a full or summarised statement of affairs
  - Details of any prior involvement between the AM and the directors
  - A detailed report of the members' GM
  - Details of costs paid eg for preparation of the statement of affairs
  - A report of the company's relevant trading history to include, for example, date of incorporation and the nature of the business
  - If a receiver was previously appointed his report (including receipts and payments)
  - Details of any transactions between the company and its directors
  - Fee and disbursement policy where sanction for remuneration is sought
- Conduct of the s98 creditors meeting:
  - The quorum required for the meeting is at least one creditor entitled to vote
  - One of the directors will chair the meeting (s99(1)(c))
  - Creditors or their representatives should be asked to sign an attendance list
  - The directors must also prepare a statement of the company's affairs in the prescribed form and lay this before the meeting (s99(1)(a) and (b))
  - Creditors should be given the opportunity to ask questions

  The resolutions to be passed include:
  - The appointment of a liquidator or liquidators
  - To consider the establishment of a liquidation committee
  - If no liquidation committee is formed, to confirm how the liquidator(s) should be remunerated
  - If joint liquidators appointed, to confirm whether acts are to be done by one of them or both
  - If necessary, to adjourn the meeting for up to 14 days
  - Any other resolution which the chair sees fit to allow
- Appointment of the liquidator:
  - Although the members will have already passed an ordinary resolution to appoint a liquidator, the creditors are also given the opportunity to appoint a liquidator(s) (s100(1))
  - If there is any conflict between the choice of liquidator, then the creditor's liquidator is appointed (s100(2))
  - If no liquidator is appointed by the creditors, then the members' choice will be appointed liquidator (s100(2))
  - If either group is unhappy with the liquidator appointed, an application can be made to the court within seven days for their replacement (s100(3))

- The nominated IP must provide the chair with completed Form 4.27 (that he is an IP, duly qualified to act as liquidator and that he consents to act)
- The chair will certify the appointment and send a copy to the liquidator. The appointment is deemed to be retrospective to the date of the resolution
- The liquidator must keep this certificate as part of his record of the liquidation. This is proof of the IP's authority to exercise the powers of a liquidator (R4.105)
- The liquidator must then:
    (i) Advertise his appointment in the *Gazette* and send notice to Registrar of Companies, accompanied by Form 600 within 14 days (s109(1))
    (ii) Notice may also be advertised in such other manner as the liquidator thinks fit (R4.106)
    (iii) File Statement of Affairs with Registrar of Companies within five business days (R 4.34 CVL (2)(3)).

Interactive question 2: s98 meeting

What resolutions will be passed at the s98 meeting of creditors?

See **Answer** at the end of this chapter.

Interactive question 3: Voluntary liquidations

Outline the main differences between a creditors' voluntary liquidation and a members' voluntary liquidation.

See **Answer** at the end of this chapter.

6 Liquidation committee

Section overview

- A creditors' liquidation committee may be formed at the s98 meeting of creditors or any subsequent meeting of creditors in order to assist the liquidator in the carrying out of his duties. The liquidation committee acts on behalf of the creditors as a whole. In voluntary liquidation where no liquidation committee is in place the powers of the committee are vested in the general body of creditors. Additionally the liquidator may apply to the court under s112 IA 86.

    SIP 15 is concerned with the principles and procedures for convening and holding committee meetings across all types of insolvency. The SIP replicates the rules for each type of insolvency procedure.

6.1 Membership of the committee

The committee consists of at least three, but not more than five, creditors.

R4.152(3) any creditor is eligible for membership provided:

- The debt is not fully secured over any assets
- They have lodged a proof of debt
- The proof has neither been wholly disallowed for voting purposes, nor wholly rejected for purposes of distribution or dividend

Companies are eligible to become a member of the committee but must act through a representative, who holds a letter of authority signed on behalf of the company. A representative can only act for one member of the committee and cannot be a member of the committee in their own right as well.

All creditors must agree to act as committee members.

The liquidator must issue a certificate of due constitution (Form 4.47), but not until the minimum number of creditors have agreed to act.

The certificate must be sent to the Registrar of Companies.

Any subsequent changes to the membership of the committee must be notified to the court and the Registrar of Companies.

The acts of the liquidation committee are valid notwithstanding any defect in the appointment or in the formalities of the establishment of the committee (R4.172A).

6.2 Meetings of the committee

- The first meeting of the committee must take place within six weeks of the later of the appointment of the liquidator and the formation of the committee (R4.156(2)).
- Subsequent meetings must be held:
    - Within 21 days of a request being received from a committee member (R4.156(2)(a))
    - On the date previously resolved by the committee (R4.156(2)(b))
- The liquidator must give the members of the committee written notice of the venue of the meeting at least five business days prior to the meeting (R4.156(3)) (If the attendance is remote the notice period is seven business days)
- The chair of any meetings must be the liquidator or a person appointed by him in writing (R4.157(1)).
- The quorum for a committee meeting is at least two members present or represented

6.3 Liquidator's duties to the committee

- The liquidator must report to the members of committee on all matters which appear to be, or have been indicated as being, of concern with regard to the winding-up (R4.155(1)).
- On matters indicated to be of concern no report is required if the request is unreasonable or the cost of complying would be excessive or there are not sufficient assets to enable him to comply (R4.155(2)).
- If the committee was originally formed more than 28 days after the liquidator was appointed, then a report, in summary form, must be provided on all actions taken since appointment (R4.155(3)).
- In addition the liquidator must provide a written report to every member of the committee on the progress of winding up. This must be done when directed by the committee (but not more often than once in any period of two months) or at least once every six months (R4.168.

6.4 Dealings by committee members

- Rule 4.170 states the committee members (including their associates and representatives) or those who have been a member in the previous 12 months may not:
    - Receive as an expense of the liquidation any payment for services given or goods supplied in connection with the liquidation
    - Obtain any profit from the liquidation
    - Acquire any asset forming part of the estate
- However, such contracts may be entered into, with prior permission or subsequent ratification by the court or with prior sanction of the committee (affected members must abstain).

6.5 Duties of the committee

The committee have the following duties:

- Represent the interests of the creditors as a whole
- Assist the liquidator generally and act as a sounding board for him to obtain views on matters pertaining to the liquidation

- Attend meetings of the committee – the appointment will be automatically terminated if they fail to attend three consecutive meetings of the committee
- Not to enter into any transaction whereby they:
  - Receive out of the company's assets any payment for services given or goods supplied in connection with the liquidation
  - Acquire any asset forming part of the estate
  - Obtain a profit from the liquidation
- To resign from the committee a member must give notice to the liquidator R4.160

6.6 Powers of the committee

The following powers are vested in the committee.

- Sanction the continuance of the directors' powers
- Sanction the exercise of certain powers of the liquidator [see paragraph 1]
- The committee can insist that the liquidator report to it on all matters which concern it R4.155
- Require the liquidator to convene a meeting of the committee within 21 days of the request being made
- Vote on resolutions – one vote per member. (Resolutions are passed when a simple majority of the committee votes in favour)
- Require the liquidator to hold a committee meeting to discuss postal resolutions
- Agree liquidator's remuneration
- Allow the liquidator to divide, in its existing form among the creditors, any property which, because of its peculiar nature or other special circumstances, cannot be sold readily or advantageously (an 'in specie' distribution)
- Resolve that any costs, charges or expenses payable out of assets be determined by the court
- Request access to the liquidator's records and seek an explanation of any matter within the committee's responsibility R4.155
- Request that the liquidator submit to them the financial records of the liquidation

Interactive question 4: Liquidator's duties

What are the liquidator's duties to the liquidation committee?

See **Answer** at the end of this chapter.

Summary and Self-test

Summary

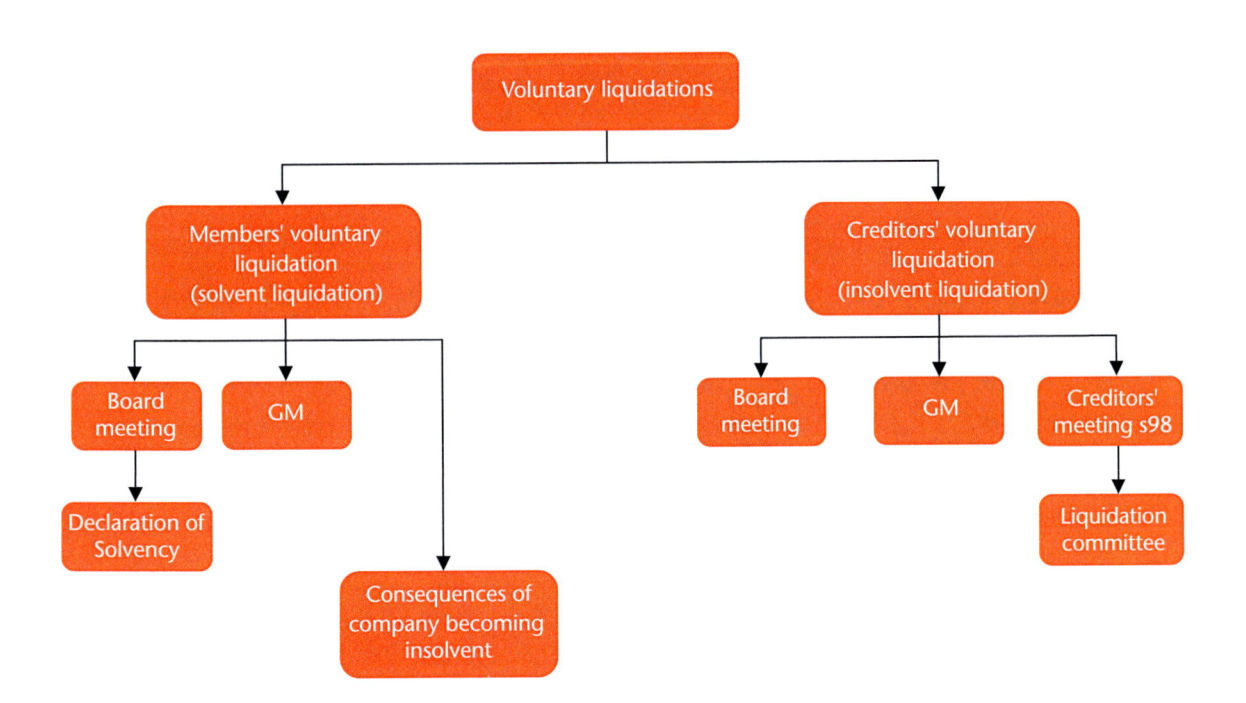

```
                        Voluntary liquidations
                       /                      \
          Members' voluntary            Creditors' voluntary
             liquidation                    liquidation
          (solvent liquidation)          (insolvent liquidation)
          /        |         \            /       |        \
       Board      GM                   Board     GM     Creditors'
      meeting      |                  meeting              meeting s98
         |         |                                           |
    Declaration    |                                      Liquidation
    of Solvency    |                                       committee
                   ↓
            Consequences of
         company becoming
              insolvent
```

Voluntary liquidation   119

Self-test

Answer the following questions.

1. A company went into members voluntary liquidation on 24 March 20X1. By which date must the liquidator have given notice of his appointment to the creditors of the company?

    A   7 April 20X1
    B   14 April 20X1
    C   21 April 20X1
    D   24 April 20X1

2. What constitutes a quorum at a meeting of a liquidation committee in a CVL?

    A   Two members present or represented
    B   Three members present or represented
    C   One member present or represented
    D   A majority of members present or represented
    E   All members present or represented

3. When is a creditors' voluntary liquidation deemed to commence?

    A   Date resolution for winding up is passed by the creditors of the company
    B   Date Board of Directors pass a resolution recommending CVL to the members
    C   Date resolution for winding up is passed by the members
    D   Date resolution for winding up is advertised in the *London Gazette*

4. The s98 meeting of creditors must be held within how many days of the general meeting at which a resolution to wind up the company is passed?

    A   7 days
    B   14 days
    C   21 days
    D   28 days

5. How many days' notice of a general meeting must be given to members of a company?

    A   7 days
    B   14 days
    C   21 days
    D   28 days

Now, go back to the Learning Objectives in the Introduction. If you are satisfied that you have achieved these, please tick them off.

Answers to Self-test

1 C liquidator must give notice to creditors within 28 days
2 A
3 C
4 B
5 B subject to the provisions of the company's articles of association

Answers to Interactive questions

Answer to Interactive question 1: Declaration of Solvency

s89 – the directors have made a full enquiry into the company's affairs, and

- They have formed the opinion that the company will be able to pay its debts, in full, together with interest at the official rate
- Within a period not exceeding 12 months

Answer to Interactive question 2: s98 meeting

The following resolutions may be passed at the s98 meeting of creditors:

- To appoint a liquidator(s)
- To establish a creditors committee
- If no committee, to establish the basis of the liquidator's remuneration
- If joint liquidators appointed, whether acts are to be done by one of them or both
- To adjourn the meeting for up to 14 days
- Any other resolution which the chair sees fit to allow

Answer to Interactive question 3: Voluntary liquidations

Members' voluntary liquidation	*Creditors' voluntary liquidation*
Solvent liquidation	Insolvent liquidation
Declaration of solvency	Statement of Affairs
No creditor involvement	s98 meeting of creditors

Note that both procedures are initiated by a special resolution in GM.

Answer to Interactive question 4: Liquidator's duties

Liquidator's duties are as follows:

- Must report to the members of the committee on all matters which appear to be, or have been indicated as being, of concern with regard to the winding up.
- If the committee is formed more than 28 days after the liquidator was appointed, he must report, in summary form, on all actions taken since his appointment.
- He must provide a written report, at least once every six months, to every member of the committee on the progress of the winding up.

CHAPTER 8

Compulsory liquidation

Introduction
Topic List
1 Introduction to compulsory liquidations
2 Grounds for presenting a winding up petition
3 Provisional liquidator
4 Procedure for obtaining a winding up order
5 First meetings of creditors and contributories
6 Powers of the liquidator in compulsory liquidation

Summary and Self-test
Answers to Self-test
Answers to Interactive questions

Introduction

Learning objectives

- Explain the following aspects of corporate insolvency, their origins, characteristics and effects:
    - The winding up resolution
    - The role of the liquidator

- Explain the processes involved in the commencement of a compulsory liquidation including:
    - The petition
    - Petitioning creditors and substitution
    - The winding up order
    - Statutory advertisement

- Describe the on-going obligations upon the insolvency practitioner in a compulsory liquidation with regards to:
    - Meetings
    - Record keeping
    - Reporting
    - Time limits

- Explain the processes needed to appoint the following, their roles, and the effects of their appointment upon the liquidation:
    - Provisional liquidator
    - Special manager
    - Liquidator
    - The liquidation committee

- Compare the respective roles of the liquidator and Official Receiver

Stop and think

What is a compulsory liquidation? Why would a creditor wish to put a company into compulsory liquidation? Who is the Official Receiver?

Working context

You may be asked to give advice to a client on how to seek recovery of a debt, this may include the presentation of a petition to wind up a company.

1 Introduction to compulsory liquidations

Section overview

- Unlike voluntary liquidation compulsory liquidation is a court process. It commences with the presentation of a petition to wind up the company compulsorily. The Official Receiver is appointed liquidator. He will act as such until a private IP is appointed liquidator (if any). The law is contained mainly in s117 to 160 IA 86 and Part IV of the Rules.

- A compulsory liquidation is deemed to commence at the date of the presentation of the petition rather than the date of the winding up order.

2 Grounds for presenting a winding up petition

Section overview

- A compulsory liquidation commences with the presentation of a petition to wind up the company.

2.1 Grounds

s122(1) sets out the grounds for the winding up of a company by the court. These are:

- The company resolves by special resolution to wind up compulsorily
- A plc has not been issued with a trading certificate and 12 months have passed since incorporation
- The company is an old public company
- The company has not commenced business within a year from incorporation or, suspends its business for a whole year
- The company is unable to pay its debts
- At the time at which a moratorium for the company under s1A comes to an end, no voluntary arrangement has been approved under Part 1 in relation to the company
- The court is of the opinion that it is **just and equitable** that the company should be wound up

  The court will make an order on **just and equitable** grounds in the following circumstances:

  - Where the main purpose of the company has failed
  - Where there is a deadlock in management
  - Where a person has been excluded from management
  - Where the company was formed to carry out a fraud or to carry on an illegitimate business.

2.2 Inability to pay debts

The most common ground for a creditor's petition is **inability to pay debts** – s122(f). This can be shown in four ways:

1. Unsatisfied statutory demand – the debt must:

   - Exceed £750 and this must be due to a single creditor.
   - Be for a liquidated sum which is due and payable at once.
   - Not disputed on substantial grounds.
   - Not extinguished or reduced below the prescribed level by a genuine cross-claim or set-off.
   - The statutory demand must have been personally served at the registered office of the company rather than just being posted. Defective service can have significant consequences. Unless the debtor company acknowledges receipt, service of the demand cannot be proven, and therefore any winding up petition based upon an unsatisfied statutory demand, will be bound to fail.

For the statutory demand to be satisfied, payment must have been made or secured to the reasonable satisfaction of the creditor in the 21 days following service.

Note that unlike the position in personal insolvency there is no mechanism to set aside a statutory demand served on a company. If the debt is disputed and the creditor cannot be persuaded to withdraw it voluntarily, the debtor must apply to court to either restrain the presentation of a winding up petition, or, if it has already been presented and issued, restrain its advertisement. An order will only be granted if the court is satisfied that there are good grounds for believing that the debt is genuinely disputed.

2 Unsatisfied judgment execution – this is where the company has been found liable in court proceedings to pay compensation. The successful party becomes known as the judgment creditor.

If the judgment creditor has tried to enforce the judgment through court proceedings and has been unsuccessful he will be entitled to issue a winding up petition based on the unsatisfied judgment execution.

3 Where it is proved to the satisfaction of the court that the company is unable to pay its debts as they fall due a winding up order may follow. This is the '**commercial insolvency test**' eg it is usually based on evidence of an unpaid, undisputed invoice. Practically this means that in corporate insolvency (unlike personal insolvency) there is no legal need to serve a statutory demand before issuing a winding up petition (although it would be sensible to do so in circumstances where liability and/or quantum might be disputed).

4 Where the court is satisfied that the value of the company's assets is less than the amount of its liabilities, taking into account its contingent and prospective liabilities –'**balance sheet test**'. (See Chapter 2 for more detail.)

2.3 Who may present a winding up petition?

The following persons may present a winding up petition to the court:

- The company itself

- The director(s) of the company – the petition is in the director(s) own names

- A creditor or group of creditors

- Contributories (members) of the company – the petition should only be presented if the contributories have an interest in the winding up

- The Secretary of State – the petition can only be presented on the following grounds:
    - s122 (1) (b) or (c) ie where a plc has no trading certificate or it is an old public company
    - s72 Financial Services Act – where an authorised person/appointed representative is unable to pay its debts or it is just and equitable to do so
    - s124A – where it is expedient in the public interest

- The Official Receiver (OR) – this is where the company is already being wound up voluntarily

- Attorney General – this petition can only be presented against a charitable company under s30 of the Charities Act

- Clerk of the Magistrates Court – in respect of unpaid fines levied on the company

- Supervisor of a CVA (s7(4)(b)). The petition is presented in the name of the company and will be treated by the court as though it has been presented by the contributories

- Administrator (Sch 1 para 21) – Rule 4.7(7) states that the petition must be presented in the name of the company and must give details of the administrator, the court case number and the date the company entered administration together with an application under para 79 Sch B1 for the appointment of the administrator to cease to have effect

- Administrative receiver (Sch 1 para 21) – case law suggests that the courts will accept petitions in the same way as for administrators

The most common petitioners for compulsory winding up orders are creditors. It is usually the unsecured creditors who present petitions as secured creditors will rely on their security for repayment of debts.

3 Provisional liquidator

Section overview

- The court may, under s135, appoint a provisional liquidator (PL) at any time after the presentation of a winding up petition and before the making of a winding up order.

3.1 Appointment of provisional liquidator (PL)

Either the Official Receiver or any other fit person (for example an IP) may be appointed as PL.

The petitioner, the company, a creditor, a contributory or the Secretary of State may apply for a PL to be appointed – R4.25.

The applicant will have to show that, the assets of the company are in jeopardy and that unless a PL is appointed there is a real fear that the assets of the company will not be available for distribution amongst creditors in the proper way.

The application must be supported by a witness statement stating:

- The grounds on which it is proposed that a PL should be appointed
- If some other person other than the Official Receiver is to act as PL, that that person has consented to act and is a qualified insolvency practitioner
- Whether or not the Official Receiver has been informed of the application
- The applicant's estimate of the value of the assets in respect of which the PL is to be appointed
- Whether to the applicant's knowledge:
    - There has been proposed or is in force a Company Voluntary Arrangement
    - An administrator or administrative receiver is acting in relation to the company
    - A liquidator has been appointed for its voluntary winding up

Copies of the application and witness statement must be sent to the Official Receiver (who may attend the hearing) and the PL.

3.2 Functions and powers of the provisional liquidator

The order of appointment will specify the functions to be carried out by him. The normal function of a PL is to preserve assets and records of the company until the hearing of the petition.

The powers of the PL will be limited by the court order appointing him. If greater powers are required, the PL will have to apply to court.

3.3 Effect of appointment

On appointment of a PL:

- No proceedings can be commenced or continued with against the company except with the permission of the court
- Where any persons are required to furnish the OR with a statement of affairs they shall do so within 21 days

3.4 Termination of appointment

The appointment will end automatically upon the making of a winding up order.

It may also be terminated by the court upon his application or on that of any of the persons entitled to appoint a PL. He must notify (as soon as reasonably practicable) the Register of Companies and publish notice in the *Gazette*.

Interactive question 1: JB & Sons Limited

JB & Sons Limited are owed £22,000 by Barnaby Limited. The directors of JB & Sons Limited are concerned that assets are being removed from the company's premises and therefore they intend to apply for the appointment of a partner in your firm as provisional liquidator of Barnaby Limited immediately following the presentation of a winding up petition.

Requirements

(a) Who may be appointed as provisional liquidator and what grounds are commonly stated in the application as the reason for appointment?

(b) What are the duties of the provisional liquidator?

(c) Who should be notified of the application for the appointment of a provisional liquidator?

See **Answer** at the end of this chapter.

4 Procedure for obtaining a winding up order

Section overview

- The Insolvency Act 86 (s117 – s140) and Rules (R4.1 – R4.24) specify the procedure to be followed when seeking to have a company wound up by the court.

Before presenting a winding up petition the creditor must conduct a search to ensure that no petition is already outstanding (para 11 of Practice Direction on Insolvency Proceedings 2014). A second petition should not be presented whilst a prior petition is pending save in exceptional circumstances.

The procedure is as follows:

1 Issue a petition

- The following items must be delivered to the court office:
    - Petition
    - Three copies of the petition
    - Additional copies, if necessary, for any voluntary liquidators, administrators or supervisors of CVA
    - Court fee
    - Witness statement verifying that the statements made in the petition are true [this must be made within 10 business days of the petition being issued]
    - The receipt of the deposit (which is payable on the presentation of the petition)
    - A SAE if the petition is posted to the court
- The court endorses the petition with the date, time and place of the hearing.
- The petition itself should include the following details (save where by reason of the nature of the company or its place of incorporation the information cannot be stated, in which case as much similar information as is available should be given):
    - The full name and address of the petitioner;
    - The name and registered number of the company
    - The date of incorporation of the company
    - The address of its registered office
    - Share capital of the company
    - The principal objects of the company

- The grounds on which the petition is presented including where applicable, particulars of the debt
- A statement that the company is insolvent and unable to pay its debts
- Whether the EC Regulation on Insolvency Proceedings applies and if it does, whether the proceedings will be main, territorial or secondary proceedings
- The statement that "in the circumstances it is just and equitable that the company be wound up under the provisions of IA 1986"

2 Service of the petition

- The petition must be served at the company's registered office last notified to the Registrar of Companies. It may be handed (at the registered office) to any person acknowledging that they are a director, officer or employee of the company or a person authorised to accept service. If no-one is at the registered office then the petition can be left at the office in such a way that it is likely to come to someone's attention. If there is no registered office then the petition should be served at the company's principal or last known place of business.

- The petition must also be served on any voluntary liquidator, administrator or supervisor of a CVA.

- Unless the court so directs, the petition must be advertised in the *Gazette* not less than seven business days after it has been served on the company and not less than seven business days before the day fixed for the hearing under Rule 4.11. Consequently service of the petition must be at least 14 business days before the hearing.

- Any creditor may give notice to the petitioning creditor, or its solicitors, that it intends to appear at the hearing of the petition.

- At least five business days before the hearing a certificate of compliance must be filed in court Rule 4.14.

3 Hearing of the petition

- At the hearing of the petition, the court has the following options available to it:
    - Dismiss the petition
    - Adjourn the hearing conditionally or unconditionally
    - Make an interim order
    - Make a winding up order
    - Make any other order it sees fit

- If an order for winding up is made by the court, the Official Receiver attached to the court, by virtue of their position, is appointed liquidator of the company (s136(2)) unless the winding up follows an administration or voluntary arrangement (s140(3)). In those circumstances the administrator or supervisor is usually appointed liquidator.

- The petitioning creditor may withdraw the petition with the consent of the court up to five business days before the hearing. Permission to withdraw will **not** be given if the petition has been advertised or a creditor has submitted an intention to either support or oppose the application. In circumstances where there is a supporting creditor, even if at the hearing the petitioning creditor does not want to proceed, that supporting creditor may take over the conduct of the petition (ie be substituted) and hence a winding up order may still be made.

- If the debtor company wishes to oppose the petition it must file the relevant evidence in support of its opposition not less than five business days before the hearing R4.18.

- The winding up of the company is deemed to commence on the date of presentation of the petition **not** the making of the order (s129(2)). However if the order is made when hearing an administration application (Para 13 (1) (e) of Sch B1) commencement occurs on the date the order is made.

- Note that the court cannot refuse to grant a winding up order because the company has no assets or all of its assets are secured. Consequently an order may be granted even though the company is already in administration or administrative receivership. However to the extent that the company's assets are in the hands of the administrator or receiver the liquidator must wait until the administration/receivership is complete before he can take steps to distribute any assets that remain.

4.1 Following the making of a winding up order

The effect of the **winding up order** being made is that no court action or proceedings may be continued with or commenced against the company or its property except with the permission of the court.

The Official Receiver will be appointed liquidator of the company. He will receive notice of the making of the order and copies of the order from the court.

Copies of the order must be served by the Official Receiver on the company at its registered office and the Registrar of Companies.

The Official Receiver must also advertise the order, as soon as reasonably practicable, in the *Gazette* and additionally he may advertise in such manner as he thinks fit.

In addition, the Official Receiver should notify the following, where appropriate, of the making of the order:

- Directors and other officers of the company
- Court Enforcement Officer
- Utility companies
- Bank
- Any professional advisers of the company
- Landlords
- Mortgage companies
- Debtors of the company
- Any IP in office

4.2 Duty of OR to investigate

Under s132(1), the Official Receiver has a duty to investigate if the company has failed, the causes of the failure and generally, the promotion, formation, business dealings and affairs of the company.

If thought necessary, the Official Receiver will report the outcome to the court.

In the course of these investigations, the Official Receiver may

- Carry out an inspection of the company's premises

- Take custody of deeds, books, records and the company's seal

- Call the principal directors for interview

- Require a statement of affairs to be submitted by one, or more, of the officers of the company (s131 (1))

4.3 Public examination

s133 (1) – If the Official Receiver wishes to obtain further information he has the power to apply to the court for the public examination of:

- Past and present officers of the company
- Any liquidator, administrator, receiver or manager of the company
- Any person who has taken part in the promotion, formation or management of the company

One half, in value, of the company's creditors or three-quarters, in value, of the company's contributories may require the OR to apply for a public examination.

A public examination takes place in court. The following people may attend and ask questions:

- Official Receiver
- Liquidator of the company (if any)
- Special manager (if any)
- Any creditor who has tendered a proof
- Any contributory

If a person fails to attend a public examination without a reasonable excuse they will be in contempt of court. The punishment for non-attendance may be the issue of a warrant for their arrest, and/or seizure of the person's books, papers, records, money, or goods in their possession.

4.4 Appointment of a special manager

s177 – where a company has gone into liquidation or a provisional liquidator has been appointed, the court may appoint any person (need not be an IP) to be the special manager of the business or property of the company.

Application for the appointment may be made by the liquidator or provisional liquidator where it appears that the nature of the business or property of the company, or the interests of the company's creditors or contributories or members generally, require the appointment of another person to manage the company's business or property.

The application must be supported by a report:

- Setting out the reasons for the application
- Including an estimate of the value of the assets in respect of which the special manager is to be appointed

The special manager will have such powers as may be given by the court.

The court order will specify the duration of the appointment.

The special manager must:

- Give security – based on the value of the assets in respect of which he is appointed
- Prepare and keep accounts showing details of his receipts and payments – these must be prepared for each three month period since appointment and produced to the liquidator for approval

The remuneration of the special manager will be fixed from time to time by the court.

Acts of the special manager are valid notwithstanding any defect in his appointment or qualifications.

The appointment of the special manager will terminate if:

- The winding up petition is dismissed
- The provisional liquidator is discharged with no winding up order being made
- The liquidator is no longer of the opinion that the employment of a special manager is necessary
- Creditors request the liquidator to apply to court for the dismissal of the special manager

Interactive question 2: Find Us Maps Limited

The directors of Shiny Limited have approached you for some advice. Shiny Limited are owed the sum of £58,700 by Find Us Maps Limited. The directors of Shiny Limited advise you that the sum has been outstanding for a number of months and the company have ignored repeated requests for repayment of the debt.

Requirement

What is the procedure that should be followed to place Find Us Maps Limited into liquidation.

See **Answer** at the end of this chapter.

5 First meetings of creditors and contributories

> **Section overview**
> - s136 – the Official Receiver has a duty to decide whether to call separate meetings of the company's creditors and contributories in order to choose an insolvency practitioner to become liquidator of the company in place of the Official Receiver.
> - The Official Receiver has 12 weeks following the date of the granting of the winding up order to decide whether to call such meetings. If he decides to do so he must call the meetings within four months of the winding up order.
> - If he decides not to call such meetings he must give notice of this to the court, the company's creditors and contributories (s136(5)(b)).
> - One quarter, in value, of the company's creditors can require the Official Receiver to call such a meeting (s136(5)(c)). The meeting must be called within three months of the requisition R4.50(6).

5.1 Procedure for calling the first meeting - R4.50

- Notice of the meetings must be given to every:
    - Creditor known to the Official Receiver in respect of the creditors' meeting.
    - Person appearing to be a contributory of the company, in respect of the contributories' meeting.
- Creditors and contributories must be given at least 14 days' notice of the meetings.
- The notices issued should contain details of the time and date by which proofs and proxies must be lodged in order for individuals to be entitled to vote at the meeting. This should not be later than 12.00 hours on the business day before the date fixed for the meeting.
- Notice of the meetings shall be Gazetted and in addition, details of the meeting may be advertised in such other manner as the Official Receiver thinks fit.
- Remote attendance at the meetings is permissible.

5.2 Matters to be dealt with at meetings

- The business of the meetings is, in the main, the same as that to be dealt with at a s98 meeting of creditors (see the voluntary liquidation chapter).
- Both meetings may nominate a liquidator.
- If the creditors' meeting nominates a liquidator – then this person is appointed as such.
- If the creditors' meeting does not nominate a liquidator, then the contributories' choice will become liquidator.
- If both meetings nominate different people then the creditors' choice will be appointed as liquidator subject to the right of objection to the court.
- Any creditor or contributory can object to the appointment but such an objection must be made within seven days of the liquidator's appointment. The court can make such an order as it sees fit.
- If neither meeting nominates a liquidator, the Official Receiver **must** consider making an application to the Secretary of State for a liquidator to be appointed in their place (s137(2)). In such a circumstance the Secretary of State has the discretion whether to appoint a liquidator or not.

5.3 Reports by Official Receiver

At least once in the period after the making of a winding up order, the Official Receiver must report to creditors and contributories with respect to the proceedings and the state of the company's affairs (Rule 4.43). If a Statement of Affairs has been lodged in the proceedings, a summary of this must be included within the report to creditors and contributories R4.45(1).

6 Powers of the liquidator in compulsory liquidation

Section overview

- The powers of the liquidator are detailed in Schedule 4 IA 86. Certain of these powers were only exercisable with sanction but this requirement for sanction has now been removed.

- Historically, by s167, in a compulsory liquidation sanction was obtained from either the liquidation committee or the court. In practice, the Secretary of State would give sanction in situations where there was no liquidation committee. [In voluntary liquidation where no liquidation committee was in place the powers of the committee were vested in the general body of creditors.] Additionally the liquidator could apply to the court under s112 IA 86.

6.1 Powers exercisable with sanction (Part I) *now no longer required*

The following powers require sanction in any type of liquidation.

- Make compromises or arrangements with creditors or claimants against the company
- Bring legal proceedings under ss213, 214, 238, 239, 242, 243 or 423

6.2 Powers exercisable with sanction in a compulsory winding up (Part II) *now no longer required*

The following powers are exercisable with sanction (but note that they would not require sanction in a voluntary winding up).

- Bring or defend any action or other legal proceedings in the name and on behalf of the company
- Carry on the business of the company so far as may be necessary for its beneficial winding up
- Pay any class of creditor in full

6.3 Powers exercisable without sanction in any type of liquidation (Part III)

- Sell company property
- Execute all documents
- Claim in the insolvency of debtor individuals and companies
- Draw/make etc bills of exchange and promissory notes
- Compromise claims by the company against debtors, potential debtors and contributories
- Raise money on the security of company assets
- Take out letters of administration in the name of deceased contributories
- Appoint an agent
- Do all such other things as may be necessary for winding up the company's affairs

6.4 Powers which require notice to be given to the liquidation committee

In a compulsory liquidation the liquidator must notify the liquidation committee if he disposes of any property to a party connected with the company, or employs a solicitor.

Summary and Self-test

Summary

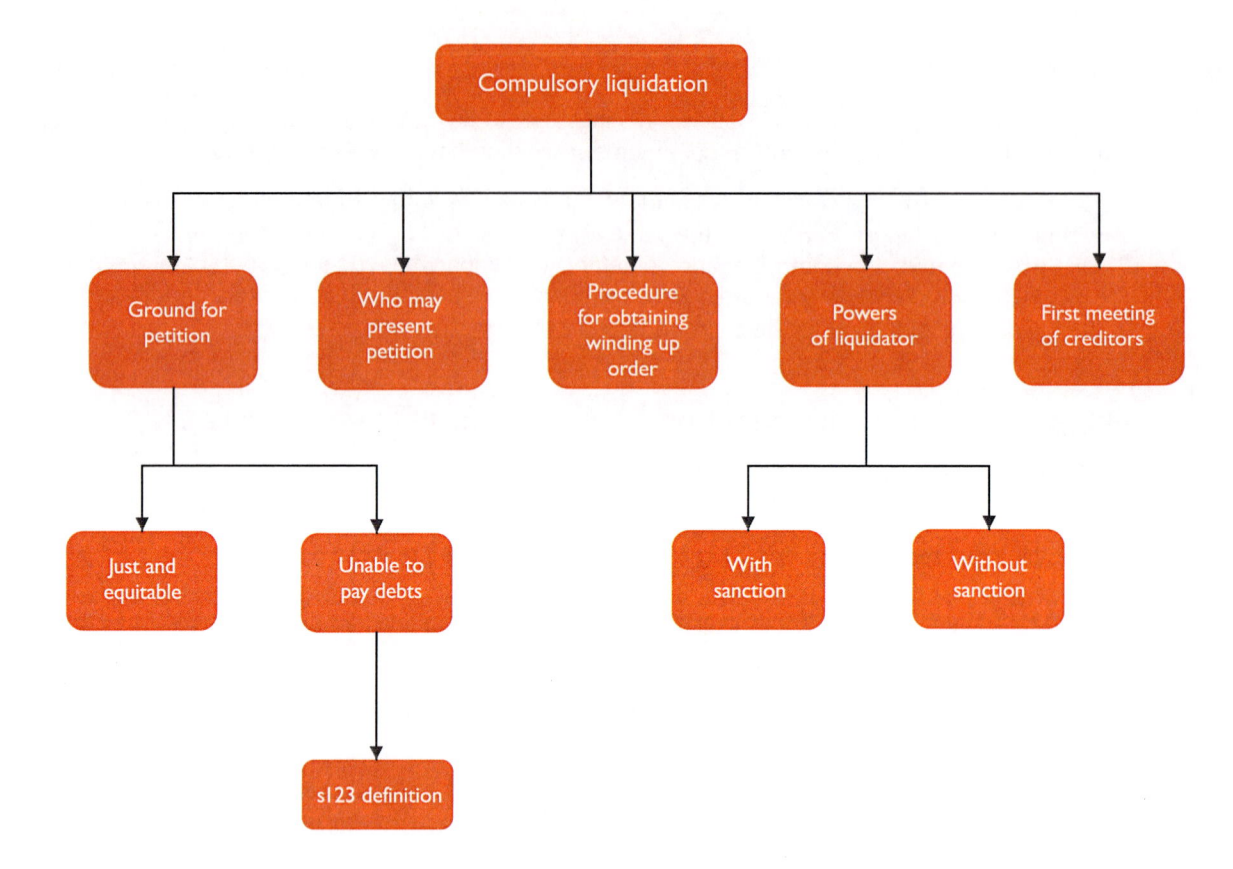

```
                        Compulsory liquidation
        ┌──────────┬──────────┬──────────┬──────────┐
   Ground for   Who may    Procedure    Powers    First meeting
    petition    present   for obtaining of liquidator of creditors
                petition  winding up
                          order
     ┌────┴────┐                      ┌────┴────┐
  Just and  Unable to                  With      Without
 equitable  pay debts                sanction   sanction
              │
         s123 definition
```

Self-test

Answer the following questions.

1. In order for a creditor to issue a statutory demand the debt owed must exceed a certain level. What is this level?

    A   £200
    B   £500
    C   £750
    D   £900

2. Which of the following office holders (if not the Official Receiver) does not have to be a qualified IP?

    A   Liquidator in a MVL
    B   Special manager
    C   Provisional liquidator
    D   Administrator

3. (i) X plc is a company in distress and has not paid its employees for a number of weeks. Is this failure to pay of itself a ground for a winding up order to be made under s123 IA 86?

    A   Yes
    B   No

   (ii) If a statutory demand is served on a director of X plc whilst at the company's head office, will this be sufficient service for the purpose of obtaining a winding up order against the company on the basis of an unsatisfied statutory demand?

    A   Yes
    B   No

4. What value of creditors may require the Official Receiver to convene a meeting of the company's creditors?

    A   One third in value
    B   One quarter in value
    C   Majority in number
    D   Majority in value
    E   Three quarters in value

5. Within what time period must the OR decide whether or not to call a first meeting of creditors in liquidation?

    A   5 weeks
    B   7 weeks
    C   9 weeks
    D   12 weeks

Now, go back to the Learning Objectives in the Introduction. If you are satisfied that you have achieved these, please tick them off.

Answers to Self-test

1   C

    Note that in corporate insolvency the prescribed limit is **in excess** of £750 unlike personal insolvency where the prescribed limit is £750 or more.

2   B

3   (i)   B

    s123 specifically states that the following circumstances are grounds for the presentation of a winding up petition.

    - Unsatisfied statutory demand
    - Unsatisfied judgement execution
    - Proved to the satisfaction of the court that the company is unable to pay its debts as they fall due – 'commercial insolvency test'
    - Value of the company's assets is less than the amount of its liabilities –'balance sheet test'

    (ii) B

    Service must be at the company's registered office which will not necessarily be the same as the company's head office address. The requirement for the statutory demand to be 'unsatisfied' will not be satisfied if service of the demand was defective.

4   B

5   D

Answers to Interactive questions

Answer to Interactive question 1: JB & Sons Limited

(a) The OR or any other fit person, qualified to act as a licensed IP, in relation to the company, may be appointed provisional liquidator (PL).

The grounds of appointment are:

(i) Preservation of the company's assets
(ii) Public interest or other reasonable grounds

(b) The duties of the PL are stated in the order of appointment. The principal duty is to safeguard the property of the company.

As an officer of the court, the PL also has a duty to act with the utmost good faith and he acts in the interests of the company, not the creditors who petitioned for his appointment.

(c) The following persons should be notified of the PL's appointment:

(i) The proposed PL, if not the OR
(ii) The OR (R4.25(3))

Answer to Interactive question 2: Find Us Maps Limited

It is likely that the only way that Find Us Maps could be forced into liquidation by Shiny Limited is by petitioning for the compulsory winding up of the company. As a creditor, Shiny Limited can petition to wind up Find Us Maps Limited, on the grounds that the company is unable to pay its debts (s122(f)).

In order to establish inability to pay debts Shiny Limited should:

- Serve a statutory demand as the debt is for more than £750
- It must be served at the company's registered office
- It should specify the amount of the debt and any consideration

If the statutory demand is not complied with within three weeks, and if the debt is not disputed on any substantial grounds, then Shiny Limited can petition for the winding up.

Shiny Limited could also petition if they had a judgment debt or some other form of execution which wasn't satisfied or if they could prove to the satisfaction of the court that the company is unable to pay its debts as they fall due or the assets of the company are less than the amount of its liabilities.

The petition (and copies for service) must be presented to the appropriate court with the court fee and a deposit.

In addition, the creditor must file a witness statement verifying the position.

The petition must be served at the company's registered office at least 14 business' days prior to the date of the hearing.

Not less than seven business days after serving the petition on the company nor less than seven days before the hearing date, the petition must be advertised (unless the court directs otherwise) in the *London Gazette*.

At least five business days before the hearing the petitioner is required to file in court a certificate of compliance verifying the advertisement.

At any time after a winding up petition is presented the court may make an interim order to protect any interests.

At the hearing the court has the following options:

- Dismiss the petition
- Adjourn the hearing conditionally or unconditionally
- Make an interim order
- Make a winding up order
- Make any other order it sees fit

On the making of the winding up order the OR is appointed liquidator of the company.

The winding up is deemed to commence on the presentation of the petition.

CHAPTER 9

Liquidators' investigations and antecedent transactions

Introduction

Topic List

1 Liquidator's investigations
2 SIP 2
3 Actions which a liquidator can take to recover funds
4 Relevant time periods

Summary and Self-test

Answers to Self-test

Answer to Interactive question

Introduction

Learning objectives

- Explain the following aspects of corporate insolvency, their origins, characteristics and effects:
  - The role of the liquidator
  - Enforcing co-operation

- Explain the methods open to a liquidator to enforce co-operation from parties affected by the liquidation

- Explain briefly the provisions of Company Directors Disqualification Act 1986

- State the general procedures to be taken in investigation and asset recovery

- Describe voidable/antecedent transactions (including re-use of name under s216 IA86), explain how they impact upon the insolvency, and describe the powers of the insolvency practitioner relating to them

- Identify voidable transactions from information provided and in a given scenario

- State the general procedures to be taken in investigation and asset recovery

Stop and think

Why should the director's conduct be investigated? What constitutes undesirable conduct? Who should be notified of the results of investigations carried out? Why should a liquidator identify whether any voidable transactions have taken place? How does this benefit the creditors?

Working context

Officeholders have a duty to investigate the conduct of directors of insolvent companies. You may be required to review the company's books and records to identify matters which require further detailed investigation or to find evidence to support a claim against the directors of a company or third parties. You may be asked to assist in the completion of the director's conduct report.

1 Liquidators' investigations

> **Section overview**
> - The function of a liquidator is to get in the company's assets and distribute them to the creditors. To this end he has a duty to investigate what assets can be realised and whether any further recoveries can be made.

1.1 Statutory duties

Under s132(1) an Official Receiver (OR) in a compulsory liquidation has a duty to investigate the causes of the company's failure, and generally the promotion, formation, business dealings and affairs of the company.

The OR must make a report to court on the outcome of his investigations if he sees fit.

In a voluntary liquidation there is no specific duty laid down in the legislation that a liquidator must investigate the affairs of a company. He must however carry out an investigation in order to:

- Determine the assets and liabilities of the company
- Review the conduct, decisions and actions of the directors
- Determine, if necessary with the benefit of legal advice, whether any transactions may be set aside
- Identify any rights of action which the company or the liquidator may have against third parties

The liquidator will always try to get assistance voluntarily from the directors and other third parties (usually officers of the company, employees and previous office holders) who have a duty to assist him. This avoids the costs and time involved in the liquidator having to seek sanction to bring court proceedings to enforce co-operation. However if necessary the liquidator may exercise one or more of the following powers:

(a) s234 IA 86 – an order for delivery up of a company's property, books, papers or records. Where the liquidator seizes and/or disposes of any property which is not property of the company but has reasonable belief/grounds for believing that the company is entitled to the property etc (whether or not he had a court order) he has no liability for losses incurred (except in negligence). [Note that this power is also enjoyed by administrators, administrative receivers and provisional liquidators.]

(b) Enforce the duty under s235 which obliges the directors, officers, employees and other specified persons to co-operate with the office holder. Failure to comply with s235 renders the person liable to a fine and daily default fine. [Note that this power is also enjoyed by administrators, administrative receivers and provisional liquidators.]

(c) Submit to examination under s236. Failure to submit to examination may result in a warrant for the arrest of the person in default and seizure of any property, books, records etc in that person's possession. Following any examination the court may order delivery up of property etc under s237. [Note that this power is also enjoyed by administrators, administrative receivers and provisional liquidators.]

2 SIP 2

> **Section overview**
> - The objective of SIP 2 is to set out basic principles and essential procedures with which office holders are required to comply when conducting an investigation into the affairs of an insolvent company. The SIP applies to both liquidators and administrators.

2.1 Seeking information

SIP 2 recommends that the following investigations are carried out regardless of whether there are assets available.

The general principles with which the office holder should comply are to: ensure that investigations are proportionate to the circumstances of each case and report clearly on the steps taken and relevant outcomes.

As a priority the office holder should ascertain the location and safeguard and list the company's books, records and other accounting information. Other steps to be taken under the SIP to ascertain information and make an initial assessment as to how to proceed include:

1 Inviting the creditors' committee and creditors of the company to bring to his attention any matters of concern about the operation of the business in the run up to the insolvency and identify potential recoveries that the office holder might pursue. This invitation should be extended in the office holder's first communication with creditors, at the first meeting of creditors and the first meeting of any committee.

    Thereafter creditors should be kept informed of progress/developments in every progress report unless circumstances demand a more frequent correspondence. Even where there are no funds to pay for an investigation the office holder is still required to demonstrate that he has determined if any matters require further investigation. He will do this by considering the information acquired in the conduct of the case and by questioning directors/senior employees of the company as to the company's affairs, including the reasons for the company's failure and the location of the company's books and records.

2 An office holder must always bear in mind the need to ascertain and investigate what assets can be realised. Enquiries should include identifying possible rights of action against third parties and others under antecedent transaction legislation. The office holder should also investigate the conduct of others involved with the company.

Other practical steps to obtain information

1 Compare the statement of affairs with the last audited, filed or management accounts in order to identify material movements in fixed and current assets.

2 Review the books, records and minutes for the last six months to identify unusual and exceptional transactions.

It is not the duty of the officeholder to investigate criminal conduct, but if it should come to his notice that any past or present officer (or member) of the company may have been guilty of an offence in relation to the company for which he is criminally liable, then the liquidator should report the matter. In a compulsory winding up it should be reported to the OR and in a voluntary winding up to the Secretary of State.

SIP 2 reminds an office holder that he should keep contemporaneous records of initial assessments, investigations and conclusions including any conclusion that further investigation is neither required or feasible. He should also record any decision to restrict the content of reports to creditors.

3 Actions which a liquidator can take to recover funds

Section overview

- While investigating the affairs of an insolvent company, a liquidator must consider whether any voidable transactions have taken place. Such transactions can be attacked by a liquidator if they fall within certain time limits and may result in funds being recovered for the benefit of creditors.

- The liquidator can take action under the Insolvency Act 1986 against directors and others in order to recover funds for the benefit of the creditors of the company.

- Actions which the liquidator may take are as follows:
    - s238   Transaction at an Undervalue
    - s239   Preference
    - s244   Extortionate credit transaction
    - s245   Avoidance of floating charges
    - s213   Fraudulent trading
    - s214   Wrongful trading
    - s212   Misfeasance
    - s216   Re-use of company name
    - s423   Transactions defrauding creditors

3.1 Transaction at an undervalue s238

- A transaction at an undervalue is where there has been a gift (or other transaction with no consideration) or the value received by the company is significantly less in money or money's worth than that given.
- The company must have been insolvent at the time of, or become insolvent as a result of, the transaction taking place.
- The transaction must have taken place within the relevant time (see below).
- There is a defence where the transaction was entered into in good faith and there were reasonable grounds for believing it would benefit the company.
- Either a liquidator or administrator can apply to court for the position of the company to be restored to what it was prior to the transaction.

Definition

Transaction: includes a gift, agreement or arrangement (s436).

3.2 Preferences s239

- A preference is a transaction where:
    - The person preferred is a creditor, guarantor or surety.
    - The company 'must do anything' or 'suffer anything' to be done which puts that creditor, guarantor or surety in a better position in the event of insolvent liquidation than they would otherwise have been in.
    - The company must have been influenced by a desire to prefer (ie the company must actually wish to improve the position of the creditor etc). Desire is assumed if the parties are connected (see below).
- The company must have been insolvent at the time of, or become insolvent as a result of, the preference taking place.
- The preference must have taken place within the relevant time (see below).
- Either a liquidator or administrator can apply to the court for the position of the company to be restored to what it was prior to the transaction.

Definitions

Connected person: (s249) A person is connected with a company if he is:

- A director or shadow director of the company or an associate of such a director or shadow director
- An associate of the company

Associate: (s435) A person is an associate of an individual if that person is the individual's husband or wife or civil partner, or former or reputed spouse/civil partner or is a relative of the individual or the individual's husband or wife or civil partner. Relatives are brothers, sisters, uncles, aunts, nephews, nieces, lineal ancestors eg parents and lineal descendants eg children.

A person is also an associate of any person with whom he is in partnership, and of the husband or wife, civil partner or relative of any individual with whom he is in partnership.

A person is an associate of any person whom he employs or by whom he is employed.

A person in his capacity as trustee of a trust is an associate of another person if the beneficiaries of the trust include, or the terms of the trust confer a power that may be exercised for the benefit of, that other person or an associate of that other person.

A company is an associate of another company if:

- The same person has control of both, or a person has control of one and persons who are his associates, or he and persons who are his associates, have control of the other; or

- A group of two or more persons has control of each company, and the groups either consist of the same persons or could be regarded as consisting of the same persons by treating (in one or more cases) a member of either group as replaced by a person of whom he is an associate.

A company is an associate of another person if that person has control of it or if that person and persons who are his associates together have control of it.

3.3 Extortionate credit transaction s244

- An extortionate credit transaction is where:
    - The company is or has been a party to a transaction involving the provision of credit to the company, and having regard to the risk undertaken by the giver of the credit the terms of agreement require grossly exorbitant payments to be made, or otherwise grossly contravene the ordinary principles of fair dealing.
- It is assumed by the court that transactions are extortionate and it is therefore left to the defence to prove that this is not the case.
- The provision of credit must have taken place within the relevant time (see para 4 below).
- The liquidator or administrator can apply to the court to have the whole or part of the obligation set aside or for the variation of the agreement.

3.4 Avoidance of floating charges s245

- A floating charge on the company's undertaking or property is invalid except to the extent of the aggregate of any fresh consideration given for it.
- The creation of the floating charge must have been within the relevant time period (see below).
- If a liquidator, or administrator, is able to prove that a floating charge is invalid, the assets covered by the charge can be claimed, security free, for the benefit of the estate. (See Chapter 5 for more detail.)

3.5 Fraudulent trading, wrongful trading and misfeasance

Both a liquidator and administrator (as extended by SBEEA 2015) may be able to swell the assets of the company by bringing actions for fraudulent trading, wrongful trading and/or misfeasance. Where proven the court may order those liable to make a contribution towards the payment of the debts of the company. [This area was covered more fully and Chapter 6 and you may wish to refer back to that chapter to refresh your knowledge of this area.]

3.6 Transactions defrauding creditors s423

Actions under s423 can be brought by a liquidator, administrator, trustee, supervisor and creditors. The aim of the provision is to prevent debtors from disposing of assets to the detriment of creditors. Unlike a transaction at an undervalue the legislation does not specify a relevant time limit, therefore it is a useful tool where a transaction at an undervalue claim would fail because it took place outside of the relevant time period. Such actions are however still subject to the usual rules on limitation and **may** be statute barred after 6 or 12 years depending upon the type of claim. (See Chapter 11 for further detail on statute barred debts.) Assuming that any applicant for an order under s423 can establish that a transaction at an undervalue has occurred, to be successful he must further show that the intent of the debtor in entering into that transaction was to put assets beyond the reach of creditors, or to prejudice their interests.

The purpose of any court order will be, as far as possible, to restore the position to what it would have been had the transaction not taken place.

[Remember wrongdoing by directors may give rise to disqualification proceedings as discussed in Chapter 6.]

3.7 Re-use of company name (ss216-217 IA86)

s216 provides that a director/shadow director of a company in insolvent liquidation is prohibited from being a director of a company known by a prohibited name for a period of five years. The individual concerned must have been a director/shadow director of the insolvent company in the 12 months ending with the day before it went into insolvent liquidation. If the liquidator is acting in relation to a company where the directors are in breach of the provisions of s216, he can take action to make those directors liable for 'relevant debts'. These are all liabilities for the period during which they were involved in the management of the **new** company or acting on instructions. [See Chapter 6 for a fuller explanation of s216.]

3.8 Protection for third parties

Although the court has wide powers to restore assets to the estate where there has been a transaction at an undervalue, preference, transaction defrauding creditors, or other void disposition, those third parties who have dealt with the debtor in good faith (ie for value and without notice of the insolvency/petition/order) are generally protected. They will not be ordered to restore assets to the estate. When considering value in this context the courts look for valuable consideration which is not necessarily the same as market value. In other words the courts recognise that a debtor in financial distress may be forced to sell assets quickly and that a forced sale may impact negatively on the price. Such third parties as sometimes referred to as '**bona fide** purchasers for value without notice'.

4 Relevant time periods

Section overview

- Action may only be taken if the transactions have occurred within a relevant time period.

4.1 Summary

- A summary of the relevant time periods is provided below:

Provision	Relevant Time	Is insolvency required at transaction date?	Is insolvency presumed?
Transactions at an undervalue – unconnected person	Two years	Yes	No
Transactions at an undervalue – connected person	Two years	Yes	Yes
Preference – unconnected person	Six months	Yes	No
Preference – connected person	Two years	Yes	No (but 'desire to prefer' will be)
Extortionate credit transaction – unconnected or connected person	Three years	No	N/A
Transactions defrauding creditors	Any time	No	No
s245 – unconnected person	12 months	Yes	No
s245 – connected person	Two years	No	N/A

- In the case of transactions at an undervalue, preferences and s245 the time periods are calculated back from the 'onset of insolvency' (s240(1)(a)).

- The onset of insolvency in liquidation is the date of **commencement** (s240(3)):
    - Compulsory liquidation, the presentation of the petition
    - CVL, the date of the resolution to wind-up the company

Note. You should ensure that you do not confuse these rules with the rules in personal insolvency.

Interactive question: Bassets Limited

You have recently been appointed liquidator of Bassets Limited at a s98 meeting of creditors.

Your initial review of the company's books and records has revealed the following:

1   The company's fixed asset register listed a widget cutting machine with a book value of £32,000. This machine does not appear on the company's Statement of Affairs. The directors advise you that the machine was sold to Another Company Limited three months prior to the company entering liquidation. The cash book shows a receipt from Another Company Limited in the sum of £12,000. You can see no other receipt of monies from this company.

2   Mr Brown, the sales director, has personally guaranteed amounts due to a major supplier, Wells Wood Limited. The company has submitted a proof of debt form in the sum of £1,500, however a review of the company's aged creditor ledger shows that as little as four months prior to the liquidation there were sums in excess of £19,500 due to the company.

3   Six months prior to the company entering into liquidation the company had granted a floating charge to Wellsby Bank plc to secure the company's trading overdraft which stood at £48,000.

Requirement

Detail why, as liquidator, you would be concerned with any of these transactions. What further steps would you take to substantiate any action which you may wish to take in respect of these matters.

See **Answer** at the end of this chapter.

Summary and Self-test

Summary

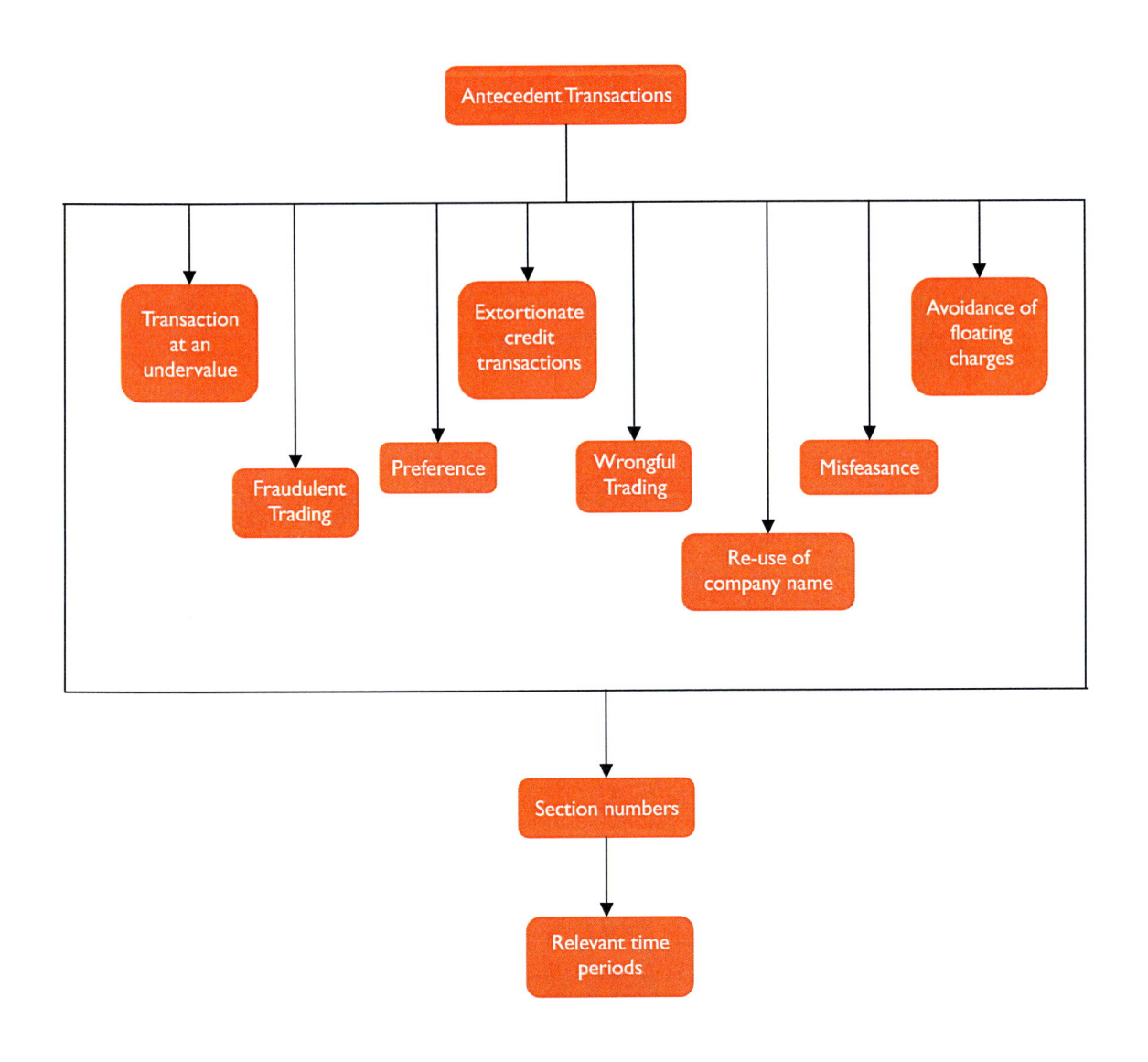

```
                    ┌─────────────────────────┐
                    │  Antecedent Transactions │
                    └─────────────────────────┘
                                │
   ┌────────────┬───────────┬───┴───┬───────────┬────────────┐
   │            │           │       │           │            │
Transaction  Fraudulent  Extortionate  Wrongful  Re-use of  Misfeasance  Avoidance of
at an        Trading     credit        Trading   company                 floating
undervalue               transactions            name                    charges
```

- Transaction at an undervalue
- Fraudulent Trading
- Preference
- Extortionate credit transactions
- Wrongful Trading
- Re-use of company name
- Misfeasance
- Avoidance of floating charges

↓

Section numbers

↓

Relevant time periods

Self-test

Answer the following questions.

1. What of the following does not have to be proven for a liquidator to take action for a preference given to a connected party?

    A   Person preferred must be a creditor, guarantor or surety
    B   The company must have been insolvent at the time of or as a result of the preference
    C   There must have been a desire to prefer
    D   The preference must have taken place at a relevant time

2. What is a relevant time for the purposes of an extortionate credit transaction under s244?

    A   One year
    B   Two years
    C   Three years
    D   There is no time limit

3. An action for misfeasance under s212 cannot be taken against which of the following persons?

    A   A former officer of the company
    B   A supervisor of the company's voluntary arrangement
    C   A liquidator of the company
    D   An administrative receiver of the company

4. Which of the following office holders has no power to challenge a transaction at an undervalue under s238?

    A   An administrative receiver
    B   A liquidator in a creditors' voluntary liquidation
    C   A liquidator in a compulsory liquidation
    D   An administrator

5. What is the relevant time period for a transaction at an undervalue to a connected person?

    A   Six months
    B   One year
    C   Two years
    D   There is no time limit

6. What must a liquidator prove in order to bring a claim for wrongful trading?

Now, go back to the Learning Objectives in the Introduction. If you are satisfied that you have achieved these objectives, please tick them off.

Answers to Self-test

1. C It is presumed where the transaction is with a connected party
2. C
3. B It is worth noting that although s212 does not apply to administrators, administrators can be subject to a misfeasance application brought under para 75 Sch B1.
4. A
5. C
6. The liquidator must show:

    - That the company is in insolvent liquidation
    - At some time before the commencement of the winding up of the company, the person knew or ought to have concluded that there was no reasonable prospect that the company could avoid going into insolvent liquidation
    - The person was a director of the company at that time

    Defence – that the director took every step to minimise the loss to creditors.

Answer to Interactive question

Answer to Interactive question: Bassets Limited

1 **Sale of machine**:

This could be challenged as a possible transaction at an undervalue – s238.

This is where there has been:

- A gift or no consideration
- The value received by the company is significantly less in money or monies worth

To be proven the transaction must have taken place at a relevant time, which is within two years of the onset of insolvency (the date of the resolution to wind up the company).

The company must have been insolvent at the time of the transaction (this is assumed if the transaction is with a connected party).

There is a defence that the transaction was entered into in good faith and there were reasonable grounds for believing that it would benefit the company.

If proven the court may make such order as it thinks fit for restoring the position to what it would have been if the company had not entered into that transaction.

Here:

The machine appears to have been sold for £12,000 which is significantly less than its book value.

Further steps required:

(i) No details of timing of transaction – must show that it took place within previous two years.

(ii) Need to obtain a company search to establish whether the companies are connected. If not, need to establish that company was insolvent at the date of the transaction.

(iii) Obtain copies of the sale agreement – are further sums due?

(iv) Obtain professional valuation of machine.

(v) Obtain legal advice re costs of action, likelihood of success etc.

2 **Reduction of debt due to Wells Wood Limited**:

This could be challenged as a possible preference – s239.

The liquidator must show the following:

(i) The person preferred must be a creditor, guarantor or surety.

(ii) The company must do anything or suffer anything to be done which puts that person in a better position, in the event of insolvent liquidation than they otherwise would have been in.

(iii) The company must have been influenced by a desire to prefer (assumed if the transaction was with a connected person).

(iv) The transaction must have taken place at a relevant time.

(v) The company must have been insolvent at the time of the transaction.

Relevant time: within six months of onset of insolvency (or two years if parties are connected)

If proven, the court may make such order as it thinks fit for restoring the position to what it would have been if the company had not entered into that transaction.

Here:

Creditor's claim appears to have substantially reduced within four months of liquidation of the company, transaction took place at a relevant time.

Further steps required:

(i) Discuss with directors why creditor was paid (refute desire to prefer)
(ii) Determine whether parties are connected
(iii) Establish insolvency of company at date of transaction
(iv) Look at books and records of the company, were other creditors being paid?

3 **Creation of charge to Wellsby Bank plc**:

This could be challenged under s245 – avoidance of floating charges.

A floating charge created at a relevant time is invalid except to the extent of any fresh consideration given for it.

The liquidator must show that the charge was created at a relevant time:

(i) Where parties are unconnected, within 12 months from the onset of the insolvency and the company must have been insolvent at the time of the creation of the charge.

(ii) If parties are connected, within two years from the onset of insolvency and insolvency is assumed.

If the charge is invalidated, the bank will rank as an ordinary unsecured creditor in the liquidation and the liquidator will be free to deal with the charged assets.

Further steps required:

- Determine whether parties are connected, if not, need to prove insolvency at date of creation of the charge.
- Have any new monies been provided since the creation of the charge?
- Was the charge created at a relevant time?

CHAPTER 10

Asset protection regime in liquidation

Introduction

Topic List

1. Introduction to the asset protection regime
2. Actions or proceedings (litigation) against the insolvent company
3. Execution
4. Commercial Rent Arrears Recovery (CRAR)
5. Post commencement dispositions
6. Retention of title
7. Disclaimer in liquidation

Summary and Self-test

Answers to Self-test

Answers to Interactive questions

Introduction

Learning objectives

- Explain the following aspects of corporate insolvency, their origins, characteristics and effects:
    - Enforcing co-operation
    - Undertakings to distraining creditors (now Commercial Rent Arrears Recovery) creditors
- Describe the impact of an insolvency upon creditors and other affected parties in a given scenario
- Define 'retention of title' and explain how it can affect an insolvency and the parties affected by the insolvency

Stop and think

Why should creditors be prevented from taking action to recover their debts once a company is in liquidation? How would the presentation of a petition for the winding up of a company affect a creditor who is seeking to take action to recover a debt?

Working context

When a company is insolvent it is likely that a number of creditors will be seeking to recover their debts. Upon appointment therefore, the liquidator may be required to deal with creditors taking action such as a commercial landlord seeking to use CRAR for unpaid rent. It is important therefore to understand the rights of the liquidator in such circumstances and also the rights which creditors have to continue with an action against the company.

1 Introduction to the asset protection regime

Section overview

The assets of a company are at risk of being dissipated by:

- Third parties exercising rights of action against the company
- The company making voluntary dispositions of its assets

The objective of the statutory provisions is to ensure that assets of the company are available for all of the creditors of the company, to be distributed equally amongst creditors of the same class (the *pari passu* principle).

The asset protection regime is stricter and the rules more complex in the case of compulsory winding up.

1.1 Rights of action by third parties

Third parties may exercise rights of action against the company in the following ways:

- A creditor may take legal action against the company.

- A creditor who has obtained judgment against the company may levy execution against the assets of the company.

- Previously a landlord could distrain for unpaid rent over the assets of a tenant situated at the let property. Since April 2014 the remedy of distress has been abolished. A landlord of commercial premises may exercise CRAR for unpaid rent.

- Retention of title, HP and/or leasing agreement creditors may try to recover their goods.

The extent to which a third party may exercise these rights once a company is in a formal insolvency process depends largely upon the type of insolvency procedure to which a company is subject. The following paragraphs consider limitations on the rights of creditors to take legal action, execute judgments, exercise CRAR and recover goods against companies in liquidation.

2 Actions or proceedings (litigation) against the insolvent company

Section overview

- A creditor may seek to bring or continue with legal proceedings against a company. The creditor's right to do so will depend upon the type of liquidation that the company is subject to and whether the creditor is looking to enforce rights post petition or post order.

2.1 The position in compulsory liquidation

- Between the presentation of the petition and the granting of the winding up order:

    There is no automatic stay of legal proceedings so creditors can continue with any action against the company. However, s126(1) allows the company, any creditor or contributory to apply to the court for an order to stay or restrain the proceedings.

- Post winding up order:

    s130 (2) provides that once a winding up order has been made then no action or proceedings may be proceeded with or commenced against the company or its property (this section is also triggered by the appointment of a provisional liquidator).

    The creditor can however apply to the court for permission to continue.

Asset protection regime in liquidation

- Settlement:

    Settlement of any debts should be with the liquidator not the company. If the liquidator wants to enter into a compromise with a creditor the sanction of the creditors' committee will be required.

2.2 The position in voluntary liquidation

s126(1) and s130(2) do not apply in a voluntary liquidation. Actions may be commenced or continued with (including petitions for a winding up order). However the liquidator (or any creditor or contributory) may apply to the court under s112 for the proceedings to be stayed.

As in compulsory liquidation settlement of any debts should be with the liquidator not the company. If the liquidator wants to enter into a compromise with a creditor the sanction of the creditors' committee will be required.

3 Execution

Section overview

- Execution or attachment refers to the situation where a creditor of a company is seeking to use the enforcement mechanism of the court to obtain repayment of a debt in respect of which judgment has been obtained. There are different ways to enforce (or execute) a judgment debt. The main types of execution are: third party debt orders (historically known as garnishee orders); a writ of fi.fa. (often referred to as 'sending in the bailiffs') and charging orders.
- A third party debt order compels third parties that are holding funds for the debtor (eg bank) to pay them over to the judgment creditor.
- A writ of fi.fa. (High Court) or warrant of execution (County Court) is an execution against goods. The court enforcement officer is instructed to seize and sell the debtor's goods to satisfy the judgment debt.
- A charging order is a method of securing a judgment debt by imposing a charge over the debtor's beneficial interest in land (usual) or other securities. To realise the charge the creditor must obtain an order for sale.

Whether or not a creditor can keep the benefit of any execution depends upon whether or not the execution is completed before commencement of the liquidation. s183(3) states that execution or attachment are completed on the happening of one of the following events:

- Against goods, by seizure and sale or by the making of a charging order
- Attachment of a debt, by receipt of that debt
- Against land, by seizure or appointment of a receiver or the making of a charging order

3.1 The position in compulsory liquidation

- Execution pre-commencement of liquidation:

    s183 provides that if the creditor completes execution prior to the commencement of liquidation, he may retain the benefit of that execution.

    If the execution is not completed, he is not entitled to retain any assets seized and the liquidator may require him to hand over such assets.

    The court has the power to set aside the provisions of s183 in favour of the creditor. A third party buying goods through a court enforcement officer's (CEO) sale will always acquire good title providing they acted in good faith.

    s184 imposes a number of duties on the CEO:

1 Where notice is served on the CEO that a provisional liquidator has been appointed or a winding up order has been made, the CEO (on being required to do so) must deliver any goods and money seized or received in satisfaction, to the liquidator. The costs of execution are a first charge on the goods/moneys handed to the liquidator.

2 Whenever execution is levied in respect of a judgment exceeding £500, the CEO must retain the proceeds for 14 days. If within this period the CEO is notified of the presentation of a petition to wind up the company, he must pay the proceeds (less his costs) to the liquidator on the making of the winding up order.

- Execution post commencement of liquidation:

Under s128(1), any attachment or execution put in force against the company after commencement is void.

Definition

Commencement: A compulsory liquidation is deemed to commence on the date of the petition to wind up the company (s129). A voluntary liquidation is deemed to commence on the date of the passing of the resolution to wind up the company (s86).

3.2 The position in voluntary liquidation

s183 and s184 do apply in a creditors' voluntary liquidation. A creditor must complete the execution by the date of the winding up resolution in order to retain the benefit of it.

SIP 8 recommends circulating the notice of the GM with the notice of the s98 meeting, since this brings forward the date by which the execution must be completed to the date on which the creditor had notice of the GM at which the resolution to wind up will be passed.

s128 does not apply in a creditors' voluntary liquidation. Execution could be continued with, however the liquidator does have the power under s112 to apply to court for the action to be stayed.

Interactive question 1: Peet and Blue Limited

You have recently been appointed liquidator of Peet and Blue Limited at a s98 meeting of creditors held on 8 May.

Having been appointed you carry out an initial investigation into the company and soon discover that one of the company's creditors, Smith Limited, received judgment against Peet and Blue Limited for the non-payment of a debt to the value of £16,000. Smith Limited entered into litigation in respect of this debt and received court judgment on 24 April.

The CEO issued execution against the property of Peet and Blue Limited on 28 April and sold the goods at public auction on 29 April, receiving a reasonable market value for the goods. As of 8 May the proceeds of sale have not been passed by the CEO to Smith Limited.

Requirement

What, if anything, can you do in respect of this action by the CEO? Include in your answer any reference to statutory action you can take and the reasons for taking it.

See **Answer** at the end of this chapter.

4 Commercial Rent Arrears Recovery (CRAR)

Section overview

- The Tribunals, Courts and Enforcement Act 2007 and the Taking Control of Goods Regulations 2013 which came into force in April 2014, have abolished the common law right for a landlord of commercial premises to distrain for rent. Landlords now have recourse to CRAR which is a new procedure for recovery of unpaid rent by seizure of goods. This is a remedy available to landlords which does not require a court order. However once a company is in liquidation the IA 86 operates to place restrictions upon a landlord's rights.

4.1 The position in compulsory liquidation

Two rules need to be considered when looking at the position of the landlord in a compulsory winding up.

1. s128 provides that where a winding up order is made CRAR put in force after commencement is void. Landlords cannot therefore validly exercise CRAR for arrears of rent after the date of the petition.

2. s176 provides that where any person has exercised CRAR against the goods or effects of the company in the three months prior to the winding up order, the goods/effects/sale proceeds are charged for the benefit of the company with the preferential debts of the company but only to the extent that the company's property is for the time being insufficient for meeting those preferential debts.

The practical effect of this rule is that landlords and others (eg HMRC) who have used CRAR during the three month period may be required to surrender the benefit of the procedure to the liquidator.

The creditor would then rank as preferential to the extent of their surrender or payment to the liquidator.

Worked example: Two rules

A landlord exercised CRAR over some machinery at his tenant's factory on 1 February. A petition was presented against the tenant on 7 February and a winding up order was made on 1 March.

To what extent is the landlord's use of CRAR valid?

Answer:

s128 does not apply as CRAR was put in force prior to commencement on 7 February.

s176 however will apply as the action is within three months of the date of the order. If the assets of the company are insufficient for the time being to meet preferential claims, the liquidator will be able to claw back the proceeds of sale for the benefit of the preferential creditors. So if the goods seized against are valued at £100,000 and the shortfall to the preferential creditors is £80,000 the liquidator can require the landlord to surrender £80,000 of the proceeds of CRAR for which he will prove in the liquidation. He will keep the other £20,000. The landlord will be paid a dividend in respect of the surrendered proceeds before any dividends are paid out in respect of unsecured claims.

The purpose of the overlap of the two rules is to therefore catch CRAR commenced pre-petition but not completed until post-petition.

4.2 The position in voluntary liquidation

s128 and s176 do not apply in a voluntary liquidation. There is no restriction on the use of CRAR in a voluntary winding up, however the liquidator may be able to persuade the landlord to hold off with his action or he could apply to court under s112 to restrain the action.

5 Post commencement dispositions

> **Section overview**
> - A disposition will include:
>   - Payments out of the company's bank account
>   - Payments into an overdrawn account
>   - Payment to a creditor
>   - Sale of assets for less than their market value

5.1 The position in compulsory liquidation

s127 states that dispositions of the company's property made after the date of the presentation of the petition are void unless the court orders otherwise.

Post petition transfers of shares or alterations in a members' status are also void.

This rule creates a potentially serious practical problem for the directors of a company, since at the time of presentation of the petition it will not be certain whether a winding up order will be made or not. If it is made however, s127 will operate retrospectively to avoid all post petition dispositions.

The company or any interested party (eg the creditor) may apply to court for sanction to exempt a transaction from the effect of s127. The application should be made prior to the winding up order being made.

Transactions will only be validated if they are not likely to reduce the assets available for the creditors.

5.2 The position in voluntary liquidation

s127 does not apply in voluntary liquidations.

Interactive question 2: Glaxow Limited

Following the presentation of a winding up petition on 8 May against Glaxow Limited, the company paid £20,000 to a key supplier in respect of goods supplied to the company two months earlier in March. It was argued that this payment was essential in order to obtain further goods so as to enable a contract to be completed that would yield a net profit of £15,000.

Requirement

Set out the main section of the Act that you consider applies and give a brief summary of the content of the relevant section.

See **Answer** at the end of this chapter.

6 Retention of title

> **Section overview**
>
> - Under the Sale of Goods Act 1979, title (or ownership) of goods passes when the parties intend it to. It is not uncommon for suppliers of goods to retain ownership of goods supplied until payment has been received. Such clauses are termed retention of title (or reservation of title) clauses 'ROT'. Provided that a supplier can establish a valid claim the clause will permit the supplier to repossess his goods leaving him in a very strong negotiating position. A liquidator will therefore be anxious to determine whether or not the clause is legally binding and if so the effect of the IA 86 on the enforcement of the clause. If the liquidator sells goods subject to a valid ROT clause the ROT creditor will be able to take action against him/her.

6.1 Is the ROT clause legally binding?

For the clause to be legally binding it must be incorporated into the contract and be validly worded.

To be incorporated into the contract both supplier and buyer must have known of its existence at the time the contract was made. It cannot, for example, be incorporated if it is simply included in post contractual documents such as invoices or delivery notes.

To be validly drafted it must be clear from the wording of the clause that title to goods will not pass until payment is received. There are two main types of ROT clause – a simple clause and an all-monies clause.

A simple clause operates to prevent ownership of specific goods passing until payment is received for those specific goods.

An all-monies clause retains ownership of goods until all outstanding sums due to the supplier are paid. Both can be valid.

However if a clause seeks to not only retain ownership of goods until monies are paid but also create a right to the proceeds arising on sale, the clause may be considered a registerable charge and void for want of registration under CA06.

It is normal for retention of title clauses to give the supplier of goods the right to go onto the buyer's premises to recover goods subject to the clause.

6.2 Are the goods sufficiently identifiable?

Assuming that the clause is validly incorporated and worded, to be recoverable goods must still be identifiable as belonging to the supplier. So if goods have been delivered and placed in a warehouse with similar goods, to the extent that the supplier cannot recognise his goods, the claim will fail. Following the case of *Blue Monkey Gaming (2014)*, the onus is on retention of title claimants to locate and identify retention of title goods.

Problems will also arise where goods have lost their identity after being incorporated into other goods for example once leather has been used to make leather bags it has lost its identity and an ROT claim will fail. However items that can be removed easily from goods will not have become incorporated. For example if luggage tags have been supplied subject to an ROT clause and then attached to suitcases, an ROT claim will not fail on the ground of incorporation provided that the tags can be removed easily without damage to the suitcase.

It is important therefore that a supplier imposes a duty upon buyers to segregate goods and to keep the products distinct.

The onus is on the claimaint to identify the goods, not the IP.

6.3 Effect of liquidation on the suppliers right to enforce an ROT clause

If the clause gives the ROT creditor the right to enter onto the premises and repossess the goods the creditor can proceed to exercise that right in respect of a valid clause regardless of the type of liquidation. If there is no right of entry the creditor cannot repossess his goods unless the court so orders. In a compulsory liquidation proceedings by the creditor will be prevented pursuant to s130.

In voluntary liquidation there is no automatic prevention, it will be for the liquidator to take steps to restrain the proceedings.

[In administration the moratorium will prevent repossession without the permission of the court.]

7 Disclaimer in liquidation

Section overview

- The liquidator can disclaim any onerous property s178. Usually questions will concern a lease. The key rules are R4.187 and R4.188.

Definition

Onerous property: Any unprofitable contract or any other property comprised in the debtor's estate which is unsaleable, or not readily saleable, or such that it may give rise to a liability to pay money or perform any onerous act.

The liquidator can disclaim property even if he has:

- Taken possession of the property
- Endeavoured to sell the property
- Exercised rights of ownership in relation to it

Effect of disclaimer

- A disclaimer discharges an insolvent company from all further liability in respect of the property concerned.

Procedure for disclaimer Rules 4.187/4.188

The liquidator prepares a notice of disclaimer, authenticates and dates it. The notice is effective from that date. The liquidator must include enough detail on the relevant form to enable ready identification of the property being disclaimed.

- Within seven business days of the notice the liquidator must send a copy to:

    - Anyone who claims an interest in the property

    - Anyone who is under any liability in respect of the property eg a guarantor of a lease (unless the liability will be discharged by the disclaimer).

    A copy must be sent to the Registrar of Companies (Rule 4.187) and also the Land Registry if the disclaimer relates to registered land.

Rights of third parties/notice to elect

Disclaimers affect third parties only to the extent necessary to release the company from its obligations. So for example, the disclaimer will not release the guarantor of a lease from his obligations under the lease.

A third party suffering a loss as a result of a disclaimer can claim in the liquidation s178(6).

s178 allows any person interested in property of the company (eg a landlord of leasehold property) to apply in writing to the liquidator requiring him to decide whether or not to disclaim.

- The liquidator must be served with notice (notice to elect) by such method as is necessary to prove service, so personal service is preferable. [Electronic service is possible if the liquidator has provided an address.]

- The liquidator has 28 days from receipt of the notice to disclaim the property. If he fails to disclaim, he can no longer do so (s316(1)) and is deemed to have adopted any contract. Any sums due in respect of the adopted contract eg rent under a lease agreement are now payable as an expense in the liquidation.

Summary and Self-test

Summary

Asset protection	Compulsory Winding-up	CVL
Litigation against the company	s126 – between petition and order – company/creditor/contributory can apply for a stay. s130 – from the winding-up order/appointment of a provisional liquidator – 'no action/proceeding shall be proceeded with/commenced', subject to permission of the court.	s126 and s130 do not apply – ie actions/proceedings can continue/commence though: • Liquidator can compromise claims (with sanction of the liquidation committee). • s112 applies – the liquidator (or creditor or contributory) can apply to court to request exercise of the powers the court has in compulsory winding-up.
Execution	s128 – execution put in force post commencement (petition) is VOID. s183 – Creditor can retain the benefit of execution completed prior to commencement. s184 – the CEO has various duties re handing over monies to a liquidator.	s128 doesn't apply though liquidator can apply under s112 as above. s183 and s184 do apply though 'commencement' is the date of the resolution, unless the date of notice of the GM is substituted.
CRAR	s128 – CRAR put in force post commencement (petition) is VOID. s176 – Proceeds of CRAR from an action completed within three months prior to the order are subject to the preferential claims to the extent that the estate is insufficient.	s128 and s176 do not apply – ie no restriction on using CRAR though if court involvement is required – s183 and s184 and s112 apply as above.
Post commencement dispositions	s127 – dispositions of assets post commencement (petition) are void as is any transfer of shares or alteration in the status of the company's members.	s127 does not apply. In CVL the members'/creditors' liquidator is in place already s88 contains similar provisions re shares/alteration of status. These are void without the sanction of liquidator
Retention of Title	Liquidator requires the permission of a valid ROT creditor to sell goods. Valid ROT creditor can repossess goods (permission needed to issue proceedings).	The liquidator requires the permission of an ROT creditor to sell goods. A valid ROT creditor can still repossess goods. However s112 is available if the liquidator wants to restrain legal proceedings by the creditor.

Self-test

Answer the following questions.

1   If execution is levied in respect of a judgment for more than £500 the CEO must retain the proceeds for how many days?

   A   7 days
   B   14 days
   C   28 days
   D   1 month

2   Any disposition of property is void under s127 (unless ratified by the court) if it takes place between what dates?

   A   The date of the presentation of the petition and the date of the appointment of the liquidator
   B   The date of the winding up order and the appointment of the Official Receiver
   C   The date of the winding up order and the appointment of the liquidator
   D   The date of the presentation of the petition and the date of the winding up order

3   When a liquidator is served with 'notice to elect' he must decide whether or not to disclaim within what time period?

   A   7 days
   B   14 days
   C   21 days
   D   28 days

4   What is the 'three month' rule under s176?

5   (i)   To be valid a retention of title clause must be incorporated into a contract for the sale of goods.

      A   True
      B   False

   (ii) A retention of title clause will be ineffective where goods have lost their identity

      C   True
      D   False

Now, go back to the Learning Objectives in the Introduction. If you are satisfied that you have achieved these objectives, please tick them off.

Answers to Self-test

1. B
2. D
3. D
4. Where a person has exercised CRAR against the goods or effects of the company in the three months prior to the winding up order, the goods/effects/sale proceeds are charged for the benefit of the company with the preferential debts of the company, to the extent that the company's property is for the time being, insufficient for meeting the claims of the preferential creditors.

    The creditor will rank as preferential to the extent of any surrender or payment to the liquidator.

5. (i) A
   (ii) C

Answers to Interactive questions

Answer to Interactive question 1: Peet and Blue Limited

This is a voluntary winding up (we know this because a s98 meeting of creditors is referred to in the question). s128 will therefore not apply and the execution can continue.

The liquidator could make an application to court under s112 to void the execution from the commencement of the liquidation. The court can decide, on the balance of the facts, to stay the execution or allow it to continue. However the court is likely to allow the action to continue as it is in respect of a debt validly owed to Smith Limited and to allow them to continue with the execution would not unduly prejudice the preferential creditors.

s183 and s184 will apply however.

The liquidator should have served the creditors and the CEO with a notice of the GM of the company at which the resolution to wind up the company was going to take place. If the action is not complete (ie goods sold and sale proceeds passed to the creditor) by the date of receipt of the notice, then the creditor is not entitled to receive the benefit of it.

Under s184 as the judgment is for more than £500 the CEO is under a legal duty to retain any proceeds of sale for a minimum of 14 days from the date of sale. If, within this time, notice is passed to the CEO that the company is in voluntary liquidation, the CEO must pass the proceeds of sale to the liquidator, less any reasonable costs of sale.

Here, the liquidator must check whether notice was sent to the creditors and the CEO. As the execution is not complete (as of 8 May the sale proceeds had not been passed to the judgment creditor) notice should be served immediately on the CEO. He will be holding the proceeds for 14 days under s184 and will pass them to the liquidator (net of his reasonable costs).

Answer to Interactive question 2: Glaxow Limited

s127 provides that in a compulsory liquidation any disposition of the company's property after the commencement of winding up is void, unless the court orders otherwise. Commencement is the date of the presentation of the petition to wind up the company.

In this situation, the creditor could apply to the court for the payment to be validated. The court is likely to sanction the payment because the supplies were obtained in order to continue trading in the general interests of creditors and the contract should generate a profit which will benefit all creditors.

CHAPTER 11

Proofs of debt in liquidation

Introduction
Topic List
1 Provable debts
2 Proof of debt
3 Voting rights and proxies
4 Proving for a dividend – special cases
5 Payment of dividends
6 Rules of priority

Summary and Self-test
Answers to Self-test
Answers to Interactive questions

Introduction

Learning objectives

- State the classes of creditor and their rights in corporate insolvency
- Describe the impact of an insolvency upon creditors
- Describe the on-going obligations upon a insolvency practitioner in a liquidation with regard to meetings
- State the criteria for closure in a liquidation
- Understand the rules re payment of dividends, notices required, timetables, priority of payments

Tick off
☐ ☐ ☐ ☐ ☐

Stop and think

Why do creditors have to formally submit a claim to the liquidator? Why aren't the amounts due to creditors taken from the books and records of the company? Why are there statutory rules governing the payment of dividends?

Working context

Dealing with creditors' claims is an important part of the role of an insolvency office holder. Creditors have to submit claims in order to vote at the s98 meeting of creditors and to rank for dividend payments. It is therefore important to understand the statutory requirements when dealing with creditors' claims.

1 Provable debts

> **Section overview**
> - A creditor establishes his right to vote at meetings of creditors and his right to a dividend by submitting a proof of debt form. It is for the liquidator to decide whether or not the creditor has established his right to be treated as a creditor within the provisions of the Act and Rules.

1.1 Debts for which a creditor may prove

- Any debt or liability to which the company is subject at the date on which it goes into liquidation
- Any debt or liability to which the company may become subject after that date by reason of any obligation incurred before that date.
- Any provable interest as mentioned in R4.93(1) (see para 4.1).
- R13.12(2) makes it clear that liabilities in tort are provable providing the cause of action accrued prior to the company going into liquidation.
- R13.12(3) states that it is immaterial whether the debt is:
    - Present or future
    - Certain or contingent
    - Fixed or liquidated or is capable of being ascertained by fixed rules or as a matter of opinion
- R12.3 re-iterates R13.12 and states that all claims by creditors are provable whether they are present or future, certain or contingent, ascertained or sounding only in damages.

> **Definitions**
>
> **Liability**: A liability to pay money or monies worth.
>
> **Debt**: The money the company owes.

1.2 Debts which are not provable

- R12.3(2)(b) states that any obligation arising under a confiscation order made under: s1 of the Drug Trafficking Offences Act 1986; s71 of the Criminal Justice Act 1988; or the Proceeds of Crime Act (Parts 2-4) are not provable.
- In addition, certain claims under the Financial Services and Markets Act 2000 and other postponed debts are only provable once all other creditors have been paid in full (R12.3(2A)(c). [See also paragraph 4.]

2 Proof of debt

> **Section overview**
> - In a compulsory winding up the liquidator must send a proof of debt form to every creditor. In a voluntary liquidation, the creditor's proof may be in any form.

> **Definitions**
>
> **Prove**: A creditor who claims (whether or not in writing) is referred to as 'proving' for his debt (R4.73).
>
> **Proof**: A document by which a creditor seeks to establish his claim.

2.1 Contents of a proof of debt

R4.75 provides for the contents of a proof of debt. The contents are:

- The creditor's name and address, and if a company, its company registration number
- The total amount of his claim as at the date when the company went into liquidation
- Whether or not that amount includes outstanding uncapitalised interest
- Whether or not the claim includes VAT
- Whether the whole or any part of the debt is preferential and if so which part
- Particulars of how and when the debt was incurred by the company
- Particulars of any security held, the date when it was given and the value which the creditor puts upon it, which should include details of any reservation of title **(retention of title)** in respect of goods to which the debt refers
- The name, address and authority of the person signing the proof if other than the creditor himself

3 Voting rights and proxies

Section overview

- Under R4.67 a creditor is only entitled to vote at a meeting of creditors if there has been duly lodged a proof of debt by the time and date stated in the notice of the meeting and any proxy requisite for that requirement.

3.1 Proving for voting and dividend purposes

A creditor's proof will usually be admitted for the same amount for both voting and dividend purposes. However proofs can be admitted for different amounts. This is most commonly seen where creditors are seeking to prove for either future or unascertained debts.

- Future debts
  - These must be discounted in accordance with R11.13 for dividend, but not for voting, purposes.
- Unspecified debts
  - R4.67(3) provides that a creditor shall not vote on such debts unless the chair agrees to put upon the debt an estimated minimum value.
  - R4.86 provides that for dividend purpose the liquidator shall estimate the value of any debt which by reason of its being subject to a contingency or any other reason does not bear a certain value.

3.2 Entitlement to vote – creditors

R4.67 states that at a meeting of creditors, a person is only entitled to vote as a creditor if:

- There has been duly lodged a proof of debt
- There has been lodged, by the time and date stated in the notice of the meeting, any proxy requisite for that entitlement
- A creditor shall not vote in respect of a debt for an unliquidated amount except where the chairman agrees to put upon the debt an estimated minimum value for the purpose of entitlement to vote and admits his proof for that purpose
- A secured creditor is entitled to vote only in respect of the balance of his debt after deducting the value of his security as estimated by him

In both a voluntary and compulsory liquidation R4.68 gives the chairman a discretion to allow a creditor to vote notwithstanding that the proof has not been lodged in accordance with R4.67(1)(a) provided that he is satisfied that the failure to comply was due to circumstances beyond the creditor's control.

Votes are calculated according to the value of a creditor's debt at the date of the meeting.

3.3 Proxy forms

Rules governing the use of proxies are found in R8.1 onwards. Additional guidance is given to IPs in SIP 10. A proxy is 'the authority given by one person to another to attend, speak and vote as his representative at a meeting'.

All notices convening meetings must enclose a form of proxy. No proxy form can be sent out with the name or description of any person already endorsed on it.

To be valid a proxy must comply with the following rules:

- The proxy must be received by the time and date specified in the notice.

- A proxy can be signed by either the principal or on his behalf by an authorised person. The relationship of the authorised person to the principal must be stated on the proxy form eg director of the company.

- A proxy issued for a specific meeting can be used at any adjournment of that meeting.

- The principal may revoke a proxy at will.

- A faxed proxy is valid for voting purposes *IRC Conbeer v Anor*. (Following the changes introduced by the 2010 Amendment Rules electronic delivery is also possible if the rules relating to such delivery are complied with.)

- Although the chairman of a meeting has discretion to admit a proof due to circumstances beyond his control there is no such discretion in respect of failure to lodge a proxy.

- If a proxy represents a corporation (eg a company or an LLP) at a meeting he must produce to the chairman of the meeting a copy of the resolution (letter of authority) from which he derives his authority.

3.4 Admission and rejection of proofs for voting purposes

R4.70 gives the chairman the power to admit or reject a creditors' proof of debt for the purposes of his entitlement to vote. This decision is subject to appeal to the court by any creditor or contributory.

If the chairman is in doubt whether a proof should be admitted or rejected, he shall mark it as objected to and allow the creditor to vote, subject to his vote subsequently being declared invalid if the objection to the proof is sustained.

3.5 Entitlement to vote – contributories

At a meeting of contributories, voting rights are as at a general meeting of the company, subject to any provision in the company's Articles of Association affecting entitlement to vote, either generally or at a time when the company is in liquidation R4.69.

4 Proving for a dividend – special cases

Section overview

- It is often necessary for creditor's proofs to be amended for the purposes of paying a dividend.

4.1 Interest

Pre-commencement interest:

- R4.93 applies to interest arising before the company went into liquidation or if preceded by administration, the date on which it went into administration.

- R4.93(1) states that where a debt proved in the liquidation bears interest, the interest is provable as part of the debt except any due for the period after the company went into liquidation.
- If the debt is due because of a written instrument and payable at a certain time, interest can be claimed from that time to the date of liquidation.
- If the debt is due for another reason interest can only be claimed if the creditor served a written demand for the payment of the interest and stated that the interest would be payable from the date of the demand to the date of payment.
- The rate of interest payable in both the circumstances above is that specified in s17 of the Judgments Act 1838 on the date the company went into liquidation. This is currently 8%.
- If the debt is due by virtue of a contract, the contractual rate of interest will apply unless it is deemed to be extortionate.

Post-commencement interest:

- s189 provides that interest is payable on any debt proved in the winding up.
- s189(2) requires any surplus remaining after the payment of debts proved in the winding up to be applied in the paying of interest on those debts in respect of the period that they have been outstanding since the company went into liquidation.
- The interest payable under s189 ranks equally even if the debts on which it is payable do not rank equally.
- The rate of interest that is payable is the greater of the rate:
    - Specified in s17 of the Judgments Act on the day the company went into liquidation.
    - Applicable to that debt apart from the winding up.

Late payment of commercial debts:

- The Late Payment of Commercial Debts (Interest) Act 1998 (LPCD) gives businesses (and individuals) a statutory right to claim interest on the late payment of commercial debts by making the entitlement to interest an implied contractual term.
- The LPCD applies to contracts for the supply of goods and services where both parties are acting in the course of business. It does not apply to consumer credit agreements, mortgages and charges.
- Interest under the LPCD runs from the day following the agreed date of payment, or if no agreed date, from 30 days after the supplier performs its obligation under the contract.
- The rate of interest is 8% over the base rate in force on 30 June or 31 December immediately before the day on which the interest starts to run.
- The interest will be provable up until the date the company goes into liquidation and the same rules for proving apply.
- Parties cannot contract out of the LPCD unless there is a substantial contractual remedy for late payment of the debt.

4.2 Foreign currency debts

R4.91 states that the debt must be converted into sterling at the official rate as at the end of the day on which the company went into liquidation.

The official rate is the Bank of England mid-market rate. If there is no rate then the court will determine a rate.

4.3 Discounts

R4.89 states that all discounts available to the company but for its liquidation must be deducted (eg trade discounts).

Early settlement discounts should not be deducted.

4.4 Payments of a periodical nature

Payments due to creditors of a periodical nature (eg under a leasing agreement) can be proved for. The creditor will prove for amounts due and unpaid up to the date the company went into liquidation. This will include all payments due in advance that fell due before liquidation and remain unpaid.

Where, on the date of the liquidation, any payment was accruing the creditor claims for the amount that would have fallen due on that date, if accruing from day to day. (See R4.92.)

4.5 Secured creditors

R4.88 states that when a secured creditor realises his security he may prove for the balance owing.

If the secured creditor voluntarily surrenders the security he may prove for the whole debt.

Alternatively, the secured creditor can estimate the value of the security and prove for any shortfall as an unsecured creditor. As this amount is unliquidated/contingent the estimate is subject to the agreement of the liquidator R4.86.

The creditor can revalue the security in the proof with either the court's or liquidator's permission.

4.6 Negotiable instruments

R4.87 states the proofs in relation to money owed on a negotiable instrument (eg cheque) must be accompanied by the original instrument or a certified copy.

4.7 Future debts

R4.94 refers to debts which are payable at a future time.

These debts can be proved for but are subject to R11.13 in relation to discounting the amount due for the purposes of paying a dividend.

R11.13 provides a formula to calculate the percentage discount as follows:

$$\frac{x}{1.05^n}$$

Where x = the value of the admitted proof
n = decimalised amount of time from relevant date to the date the debt is due expressed in years and months.

Relevant date = commencement of liquidation or in the case of a winding up which was preceded by an administration, the date the company entered administration.

4.8 Double proof

Where a debt has been guaranteed the creditor and the guarantor may not both prove in the liquidation of the company for the same debt.

The general rule is that the primary creditor should prove in the proceedings.

4.9 Foreign tax

Government of India v Taylor provided that foreign tax claims are not enforceable in the UK courts. Therefore they are not provable in a liquidation.

Article 39 of the EC Regulation on Insolvency Proceedings 2000 provides that any creditor who has habitual residence, domicile or registered office in a Member State other than the State opening the proceedings, including the tax authorities, shall have the right to lodge claims in insolvency proceedings.

As a result EU tax is provable in liquidation (with the exception of Denmark which is not subject to the EC Regulation).

4.10 Set-off

R4.90 applies where, before the company goes into liquidation, there have been mutual credits, debits or other dealings between the company and a creditor.

R4.90(3) states that account should be taken of what is due from each party to the other in mutual dealings and the sums due from one party shall be set-off against the sums due from the other.

R4.90(2) states that set-off should not occur where at the time the debt was incurred, one of the parties was aware that a petition has been presented or that a s98 meeting had been called.

Only the balance is provable in the liquidation (or paid over to the liquidator if due to the company).

4.11 Rent and other claims by landlords

Landlords may have claims for arrears of rent and loss of future rent, service charge and dilapidations.

4.11.1 Rent

Claims for arrears of rent and/or service charge may be admitted in full.

A claim for rent payable in advance which straddles the date the company went into liquidation should also be admitted in full. So, for example, if the quarterly rent was due on 30 June and was unpaid when the company went into liquidation on 31 July, all of the rent due for the quarter is considered to be in arrears and the claim will be admitted in full.

To the extent that the liquidator occupies the premises for the purpose of the beneficial winding-up of the company the rent due will be an expense of the liquidation.

4.11.2 Dilapidations

The position in relation to dilapidations will depend upon whether or not the landlord has carried out the work required to make the premises good (ie has liquidated his claim) or whether the works have not been carried out (ie the landlord has an unliquidated claim). If the claim has been liquidated the landlord will prove in full for the amount spent which (provided the liquidator is satisfied that the sum spent is justified under the terms of the lease) will be admitted in full. If the works have not been carried out and the claim is still unliquidated the liquidator will have to value the debt and the normal rules relating to unliquidated claims will apply.

4.11.3 Future rent

On the liquidation of a tenant company, it is usual for the lease to be terminated either through forfeiture by the landlord (usually for non-payment of rent), a surrender agreed between the landlord and liquidator, or a disclaimer by the liquidator.

If the landlord chooses to forfeit the lease any right to future rent due under the lease will terminate (he may however still have a claim for dilapidations).

If the lease is surrendered the landlord and liquidator will usually agree the total amount for which the landlord can prove and this will be recorded in the surrender agreement.

If the liquidator disclaims the lease the landlord will have a right to claim arrears (and dilapidations if due) and additionally statutory compensation for the losses caused by the disclaimer which, are usually the loss of future rent and a claim for dilapidations. In *Re Park Air Services plc* it was held that the landlord's compensation following a disclaimer is measured by reference to the difference between the rents and other payments which the landlord would have received in the future, but for any disclaimer, and the rents and other sums which the disclaimer would enable the landlord to receive by re-letting. Allowance should also be made for early receipt using the yield on gilt-edged securities for an equivalent term from the date of the disclaimer. This measure of discount should be used rather than the early payment provision in Rule 11.13 as the court held that a landlord's entitlement is a present right to immediate payment rather than a future payment. (See Chapter 10 for further details on disclaimer.)

The landlord has a duty to mitigate his loss. For example he must take steps to find a new tenant.

4.12 Preferential creditors

Preferential creditors are paid in priority to other creditors out of floating charge assets.

Preferential debts mainly comprise, all holiday pay without limit and wages arrears arising in the four months prior to the winding up, subject to a maximum preferential claim of £800 per employee. (See Chapter 5 for further detail on preferential claims.)

4.13 Statute – barred debts

The effect of the Limitation Act is that after a set period debts and legal claims become statute barred meaning that they cannot be sued upon. The law in this area can be very complex but generally speaking claims arising from contractual disputes are statute barred after six years (unless the contract was made under seal/by deed in which case the period is extended to 12 years). Mortgages are made under seal so a 12 year limitation period applies for any shortfall due to a mortgage lender. Personal injury claims are statute barred after three years. Consequently if a debt can not be enforced in court it cannot be proved for an insolvency proceeding either.

In principle, it is often difficult to establish details of all communication between the parties to establish whether the provisions of the Limitations Act can be applied.

Interactive question 1: Proofs of debt

Your principal, Karyn Jones, was appointed liquidator of City Bags Limited on 2 March 20X9 at a s98 meeting of creditors.

All assets have been realised and sufficient funds are now in hand to enable a dividend to be paid to both preferential and unsecured creditors.

You have been asked to review the creditors claims received to date.

1. One of the company's major suppliers, J Gunter Ltd is based in Austria. They have submitted a claim in the sum of 8,560 euros. Exchange rate details are as follows:

Date of invoice	£1 : 1.50 euros
Date of resolution to wind up	£1 : 2.50 euros
Date of submission of the claim	£1 : 3.00 euros
Today's date	£1 : 2.75 euros

2. Hamlyn Ltd have submitted an unsecured claim in the sum of £15,000. You note from the accompanying paperwork that the debt is not actually due to be paid for 2 years.

3. The company traded regularly with Green Leather Ltd and enjoyed a 5% prompt payment discount and a 10% regular customer discount. Green Leather Ltd have not taken any discounts into account when submitting their claim for £940.

4. Accessories Limited have submitted a claim in the sum of £420. This debt was personally guaranteed by a director, Mr Gardener, who has also submitted a claim in respect of the same debt.

5. Wayne Ltd have submitted an unsecured claim in the sum of £5,672. This includes a sum of £380 which is claimed in respect of interest for the period from the date of liquidation to the date the claim was submitted.

6. HM Revenue and Customs have submitted a claim in the sum of £5,600 in respect of VAT due from the last three quarters' trading.

7. Barwest Bank plc are owed the sum of £575,000. This debt was secured by way of a fixed charge over the company's trading premises which have since been realised for the sum of £390,000.

8. The company traded regularly with Floral Designs Ltd, purchasing fabrics from them and selling completed bags back to them. At the date of liquidation, Floral Designs Ltd were shown in the company's books as a creditor in the sum of £18,000 and as a debtor in the sum of £7,200.

9   Fred Blogs, a former employee of the company has submitted the following claim:

	£
Holiday pay (five weeks holiday outstanding)	2,300
Wage arrears (eight weeks wage arrears)	3,400
Redundancy and pay in lieu of notice	15,800

Requirement

Advise for what amounts, if any, you would admit these claims for dividend in the liquidation. Support your answers with any necessary workings or assumptions.

See **Answer** at the end of this chapter.

5 Payment of dividends

Section overview

- Under R4.180 whenever a liquidator has sufficient funds in hand for the purpose he shall, subject to the retention of such sums as may be necessary for the expenses of the winding up, declare and distribute a dividend among the creditors in respect of the debts which they have respectively proved. The rules relating to the payment of dividends are found in Part 11 of the Rules.

5.1 Notice of intended dividend

R11.2 – before declaring a dividend the liquidator must give notice of his intention to declare and distribute a dividend to all creditors whose addresses are known to him and who have not proved their debts.

The notice must state a last date for proving (not less than 21 days from that of the notice) and that the liquidator shall declare a dividend within two months from the last date for proving.

5.2 Final admission/rejection of proofs

The liquidator must, within five business days from the last date of proving, deal with every creditors' proof.

If the liquidator wishes to reject a creditor's proof he should:

- Prepare a written statement detailing the reasons for rejecting the creditor's claim and send it to the creditor as soon as reasonably practicable (R4.82(2))

- If the creditor is dissatisfied with the liquidator's decision he may appeal to the court within 21 days from receiving the statement (R4.83)

- The court will fix a venue for the application to be heard and notice must be sent by the applicant to the creditor who lodged the proof (if it is not himself) and to the liquidator

- On receipt of the notice the liquidator must file in court the relevant proof and his statement under R4.83(4)

- After the application has been heard and determined the proof will be returned to the liquidator by the court, unless it has been wholly disallowed

5.3 Declaration of dividend

Within the two month period the liquidator must proceed to declare the dividend, (in cases which are pre the 2010 changes, this remains 4 months.)

Under R11.6 the liquidator must give notice of the dividend to all creditors who have proved their debt.

The notice should contain such information to enable creditors to comprehend the calculation of the amount of the dividend and the manner of its distribution.

R11.6(2) provides a list of details which should be included:

- Amounts realised from the sale of assets, indicating (so far as practicable) amounts realised from the sale of particular assets
- Payments made by the IP in the administration of the insolvent estate
- Provision (if any) made for unsettled claims, and funds (if any) retained for particular purposes
- The total amount to be distributed, and the rate of dividend
- Whether and if so when, any further dividend is to be expected

R4.182 states that when calculating and distributing dividends a liquidator should make provision for:

- Any debts due to persons who, by reason of the distance of their place of residence, may not have had sufficient time to establish and tender their proofs
- Any debts which are the subject of claims not yet determined
- Disputed proofs and claims

5.4 Rights of creditors

The Rules provide that any creditor who has not proved for his debt before the declaration of any dividend, is not entitled to disturb the distribution of either that dividend or other dividends declared before the date on which he actually submits his proof. Instead any further monies available for the payment of future dividends shall be used to pay that creditor his outstanding dividends before any further dividends are paid. (R4.182(2).)

If a liquidator refuses to pay a dividend rightly due the court may intervene and order him to pay it if it sees fit. Also the court may order him to pay, out of his own money, any interest on the dividend and the costs of the proceedings. (R4.182 (3).)

The SBEEA 2015 states that a discretional provision may be applied in both personal and corporate insolvency for creditors that are deemed to be owed less than £1,000 in the debtor's affairs. This does not preclude the right of the IP to exclude such a claim if the creditor has reasonably failed to prove in the estate or indeed evidence their claim.

5.5 Unclaimed dividends

The liquidator must pay any unclaimed dividends into the Insolvency Services Account.

Interactive question 2: Barley Limited

Your principal has been acting as the liquidator of Barley Limited for the last 18 months. All assets have now been realised and the liquidator is keen to close the case.

Requirement

Prepare a memo for your principal, outlining the procedures to be followed to ensure that dividend payments are made in accordance with the requirements of the Insolvency Act 1986.

See **Answer** at the end of this chapter.

6 Rules of priority

Section overview

- The Insolvency Act lays down the order of priority of payments from monies coming into the hands of the liquidator.

6.1 Order of payment

The order for payment of debts is as follows:

- The expenses of the winding up, including the liquidator's remuneration (s115)
- The preferential debts, as defined by ss386-7 and Schedule 6 (s175)
- Any preferential charge on goods seized under the CRAR process that arises under s176(3)
- The company's general creditors
- Interest on debts outstanding for the period after the company went into liquidation (s189(3))
- Any debts or other sums due from the company to its members as members eg dividends or profits (s74(2)(f))
- The members generally, in accordance with their respective rights and interests (s107)

Secured creditors are, in principle, entitled to be paid out of the proceeds of their security ahead of all other claims.

Remember that if the security is by way of a floating charge then the preferential debts must be paid first under s175(2)(b), also, as appropriate, the prescribed part must be set aside for unsecured creditors. (See Chapter 5 for further details about the prescribed part.)

An administrative receiver appointed after the commencement of the winding up will be liable to pay the liquidation expenses out of any assets subject to a floating charge. This is in preference to the payment of any preferential creditors or the charge holder.

Interactive question 3: Belkis Limited

You were appointed liquidator of Belkis Limited on 1 September 20X8. All assets have now been realised and the case is ready for closure.

Relevant information is as follows:

1. The company's freehold property was sold for £490,000. Satby Bank plc hold a fixed charge over the property to secure borrowing in the sum of £390,000.
2. Floating charge assets realised the sum of £70,000.
3. Agents and solicitors fees have been incurred in the sum of £9,500.
4. The liquidator's remuneration has been agreed in the sum of £10,000 and expenses and disbursements totalling £3,500 have been incurred.
5. Barwest Bank plc hold a floating charge over the company's assets which was created on 1 January 2002. The banks indebtedness under the charge is £62,000.
6. Preferential claims have been received totalling £21,000 and unsecured creditor claims total £218,000.
7. The fixed charge surplus is not caught by the floating charge.

Requirement

Calculate the estimated dividend to be paid to the creditors of Belkis Limited.

See **Answer** at the end of this chapter.

Summary and Self-test

Summary

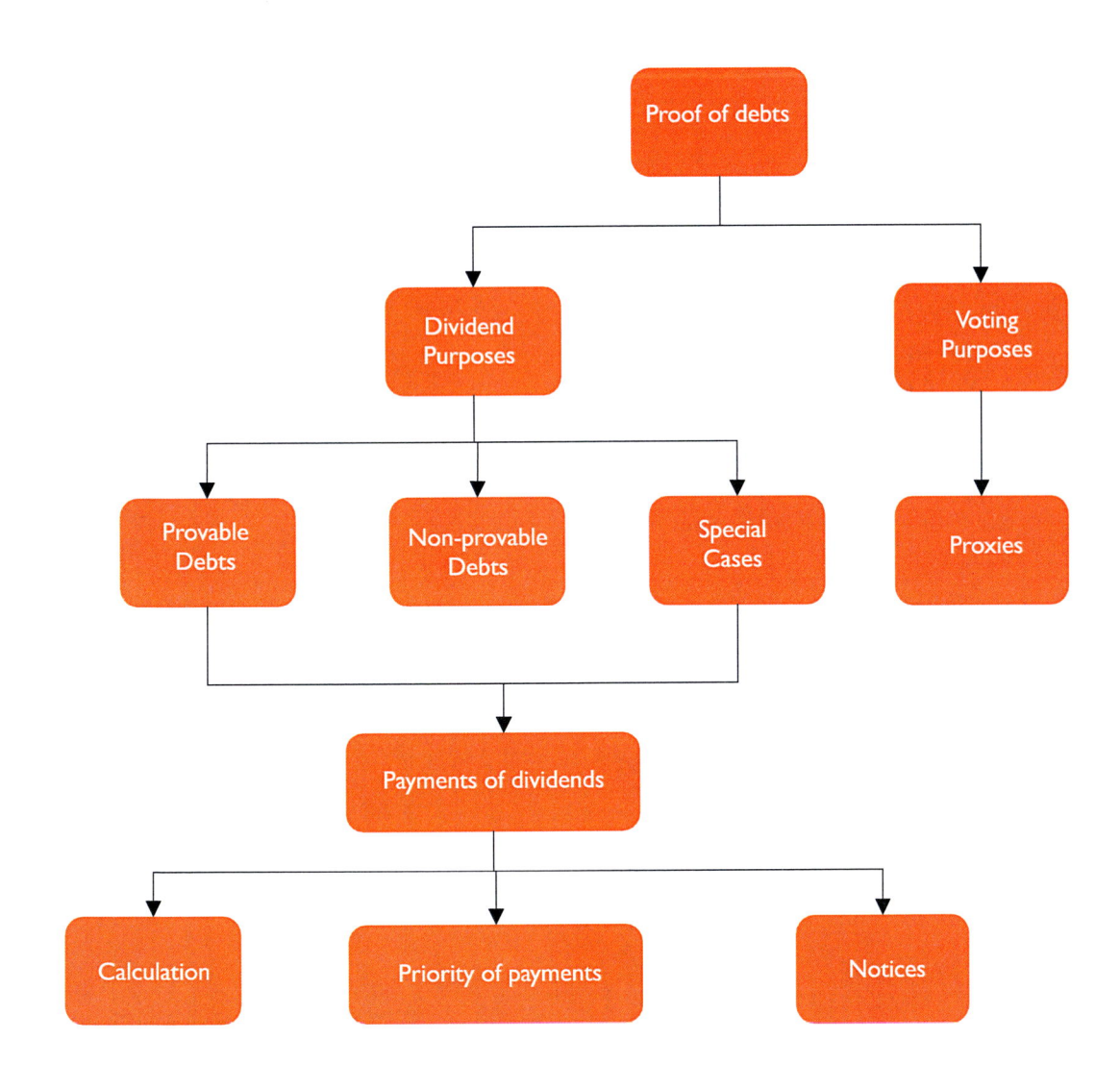

```
                    ┌─────────────────┐
                    │  Proof of debts │
                    └────────┬────────┘
                 ┌───────────┴───────────┐
                 ▼                       ▼
         ┌──────────────┐         ┌──────────────┐
         │   Dividend   │         │    Voting    │
         │   Purposes   │         │   Purposes   │
         └──────┬───────┘         └──────┬───────┘
      ┌────────┼────────┐                │
      ▼        ▼        ▼                ▼
  ┌────────┐ ┌────────┐ ┌────────┐   ┌────────┐
  │Provable│ │  Non-  │ │Special │   │Proxies │
  │ Debts  │ │provable│ │ Cases  │   │        │
  │        │ │ Debts  │ │        │   │        │
  └───┬────┘ └────────┘ └───┬────┘   └────────┘
      └──────────┬──────────┘
                 ▼
       ┌───────────────────┐
       │Payments of dividends│
       └─────────┬─────────┘
      ┌──────────┼──────────┐
      ▼          ▼          ▼
  ┌────────┐ ┌──────────┐ ┌────────┐
  │Calcu-  │ │Priority  │ │Notices │
  │lation  │ │of        │ │        │
  │        │ │payments  │ │        │
  └────────┘ └──────────┘ └────────┘
```

Self-test

Now answer the following questions.

1. A debt incurred in a foreign currency must be converted into sterling using the official rate as at what date?

    A   Date the company entered liquidation
    B   Date the debt was incurred
    C   Date of payment of the dividend
    D   Date creditor proved his debt

2. What is the maximum amount of wage arrears which may be claimed by an employee as a preferential claim?

    A   £350
    B   £800
    C   Four weeks' wage arrears
    D   Six months' wage arrears

3. Within what time period from the last date for proving must the liquidator declare the dividend?

    A   Within 7 days
    B   Within 28 days
    C   Within 2 months
    D   Within 6 months

4. If a creditor is dissatisfied with the liquidator's decision regarding his proof he may appeal to the court within how many days of receiving the liquidator's statement?

    A   7 days
    B   14 days
    C   21 days
    D   28 days

5. What should the liquidator do with any unclaimed dividends?

    A   Redistribute the monies amongst the remaining creditors
    B   Pay the money to the directors
    C   Retain it to cover the liquidation expenses
    D   Pay it in to the Insolvency Services Account

Now, go back to the Learning Objectives in the Introduction. If you are satisfied that you have achieved these, please tick them off.

Answers to Self-test

1 A

Note. We take the Bank Of England mid-market rate applicable at the end of the day on which the company entered liquidation]

2 B

3 C

4 C

5 D

Answers to Interactive questions

Answer to Interactive question 1: Proofs of debt

1 J Gunter Ltd:

 The amount of the debt must be converted into sterling at the official exchange rate on the date when the company went into liquidation.

 Date of the resolution to wind up £1 : 2.5 euros

 Admit claim £3,424

2 Hamlyn Limited:

 Rule 11.13 provides that for dividend purposes only, the amount of the claim must be reduced as follows:

 $$\frac{x}{1.05^n}$$

 Where x = the amount of the debt
 n = the period beginning with the relevant date and ending with the date on which the payment of the creditor's debt would otherwise be due, expressed in years and months in a decimalised form

 $$\frac{£15,000}{1.05^2} = £13,605$$

3 Green Leather Limited:

 The creditor must deduct any discounts that would have been available to the company but for its liquidation, however discounts for early payment do not have to be deducted.

 £940 less 10% regular customer discount = £846 unsecured claim.

4 Accessories Limited:

 Two claims may not be made in respect of the same debt. It is usual to accept the claim of the principal creditor ie Accessories Limited and reject the claim of the director.

 If the director has settled the debt under the guarantee, the creditor would have to pay him the dividend or you could seek to get Accessories Limited to retract their claim (on the grounds that it had been paid by the director), in which case the director could then submit a claim.

5 Wayne Limited:

 Interest is not provable in respect of interest claimed for the period after the company went into liquidation. Post liquidation interest will only be paid if all creditors have been paid in full and further monies are available.

 Admit unsecured claim £5,672 – £380 = £5,292

6 HM Revenue and Customs:

 Admit unsecured claim £5,600.

7 Barwest Bank plc:

 Secured creditors can claim for any shortfall.

 Admit unsecured claim £575,000 – £390,000 = £185,000

8   Floral Designs Ltd:

   Where, before the company goes into liquidation, there has been mutual credits, mutual debits or other mutual dealings, the sums due from one party should be set off against the sums due from the other party and only the balance claimed for.

   £18,000 – £7,200 = £10,800 unsecured claim.

9   Fred Bloggs:

   Wage arrears may be claimed preferentially in respect of four months arrears of wages, to a maximum preferential claim of £800. The remainder of the claim will be unsecured.

   Holiday pay may be claimed preferentially without limit.

   Redundancy and pay in lieu are unsecured claims.

	Preferential £	Unsecured £
Wage arrears	800	2,600
Holiday pay	2,300	
Redundancy and pay in lieu of notice		15,800

Answer to Interactive question 2: Barley Limited

R4.180 – the liquidator must declare and distribute dividends amongst the creditors who have proved their debts whenever he has sufficient funds in hand.

R11.2 – he must give notice to all creditors who are known not to have proved their debts of his intention to declare and distribute a dividend.

- Notice must be given by public advertisement (unless the liquidator has previously invited creditors to prove their debts by public advertisement). The notice should be Gazetted and the IP may also advertise the notice in such other manner as he thinks fit.
- The notice must specify a last date for proving (not less than 21 days from that of the notice).
- The dividend must be declared within the period of two months from the last date for proving.
- R11.3 – within five business days from the last date for proving, the liquidator must deal with every creditors' proof, by admitting or rejecting in whole or in part. He is not obliged to deal with proofs after the last date for proving

The liquidator must declare the dividend, giving notice to all creditors who have proved their debts.

The notice must include:

- Amounts realised from the sale of assets
- Payments made by the IP in the administration of the estate
- Provision (if any) made for unsettled claims and funds (if any) retained for a particular purpose
- The total amount to be distributed and the rate of dividend
- Whether, and if so when, any further dividend is to be expected

In the calculation and distribution of a dividend the liquidator shall make provision for:

- Any debts which appear to him to be due to persons who, by reason of the distance of their place of residence, may not have had sufficient time to tender and establish their proofs
- For any debts which are the subject of claims which have not yet been determined
- For disputed proofs and claims

The dividend may be distributed simultaneously with the notice declaring it.

The payment of dividend may be made by post or arrangements may be made with any creditor for it to be paid to him in another way.

R4.186 – where all assets have been realised the liquidator shall give notice either:

- Of his intention to declare a final return
- That no dividend or further dividend will be declared.

Answer to Interactive question 3: Belkis Limited

	£
Fixed charge realisations	490,000
Less: Fixed charge holder Satby Bank plc	(390,000)
Surplus available to unsecured creditors	100,000
Floating charge realisations;	70,000
Less: Agents and solicitor's fees	(9,500)
Liquidator's remuneration	(10,000)
Expenses and disbursements	(3,500)
Assets available for preferential creditors	47,000
Less: Preferential creditors	(21,000)
Assets available for floating charge holder Barwest Bank plc	26,000
Fixed charge surplus b/d	100,000
Less: Unsecured creditors;	
Trade creditors	(218,000)
Shortfall Barwest Bank plc	(36,000)
	(254,000)
Shortfall to unsecured creditors	(154,000)
Creditors will receive:	
Satby Bank plc, fixed charge holder	100p in £
Preferential creditors	100p in £
Barwest Bank plc, floating charge holder	64.80p in £
Unsecured creditors	39.37p in £

CHAPTER 12

Vacation of office

Introduction
Topic List
1 Vacating office
2 Duties on vacating office
3 Final meetings and release
4 Closure checklist
Summary and Self-test
Answers to Self-test
Answer to Interactive question

Introduction

Learning objectives

- State the criteria for closure in a liquidation and describe the processes of closure.
- Explain the following aspect of corporate insolvency:
    - Conclusion of the winding up

Tick off
☐
☐

Stop and think

Why is it important for cases to be closed properly? What information should be given to creditors by a liquidator when he vacates office?

Working context

As part of your role you may be asked to review cases ready for closure. It is important therefore to know the relevant statutory provisions when finalising a liquidation.

1 Vacating office

> **Section overview**
> - The liquidator may vacate office in three ways:
>   1. Removal
>   2. Resignation
>   3. By operation of law.

1.1 Removal

- In a compulsory liquidation s172(2) provides that a liquidator may be removed by:
    - An order of the court
    - A meeting of creditors called specifically for that purpose in accordance with R4.113
- In a voluntary winding up, a liquidator may be removed from office by (s171(2)):
    - An order of the court
    - A meeting of creditors (CVL) or a meeting of members (MVL) summoned specifically for that purpose

    At least 25% in value of creditors can force the liquidator to call a meeting to consider his removal.

    A majority of creditors in value must agree for him to be removed.

- If the liquidator was appointed by the Secretary of State then he may be removed by a direction of the Secretary of State.

1.2 Resignation

R4.108 provides that the grounds upon which a liquidator may resign from office are:

- Ill-health
- Intends ceasing to be an insolvency practitioner
- A conflict of interest or change in personal circumstances which make it impossible or impracticable to continue
- Where joint liquidators are appointed and it is no longer expedient to continue with that number of joint liquidators

A meeting of creditors must be called for the purpose of receiving the liquidator's resignation.

The liquidator will have his release from the date on which he gives notice of his resignation to the Registrar of Companies.

1.3 By operation of law

A liquidator will also cease to be in office in the following situations:

- Death (R4.132 and 4.133)
- Ceasing to be an IP (R4.134 and R4.135)
- Following the final meeting of creditors (ss171(6), 172(8))
- In a CVL on the making of a compulsory winding-up order (R4.136)

2 Duties on vacating office

> **Section overview**
> - The liquidator has a number of statutory duties to comply with upon vacating office.

2.1 Statutory duties

The liquidator must deliver up to any successor the:

- Assets, after deducting any properly incurred expenses and distributions made
- Records of the liquidation including any correspondence and proofs
- Company's books, papers and other records

In a compulsory liquidation, the liquidator must give notice of his intention to vacate office to the Official Receiver, together with the notice of any meeting of creditors to be held.

If the liquidator vacates office after a final meeting in a compulsory winding up, all records not already disposed of must be delivered up to the Official Receiver.

3 Final meetings and release

> **Section overview**
> - The liquidator must summon a final meeting of creditors (in both voluntary and compulsory liquidation) in order to receive his account of the winding up and for the purpose of receiving his resignation.

3.1 The position in compulsory liquidation – R4.125

When a company which is being wound up by the court and for practical purposes the liquidation appears complete, the liquidator must summon a final meeting of creditors to:

- Receive the liquidator's report of the winding up
- Determine whether the liquidator should have his release

Creditors must be given at least 28 days' notice of the meeting. In addition, notice of the meeting must be advertised in the *Gazette* at least one month before the meeting. At least eight weeks before the meeting a draft final report of the liquidator's conduct of the liquidation must be sent to creditors in accordance with Rule 4.49D. However the report should not be sent before giving notice of the intention to declare a dividend under Rule 4.186.

The liquidator's report to be laid before the meeting should include (R4.125(2)):

- An account of the liquidator's administration of the winding up
- A summary of receipts and payments including details of remuneration charged and expenses incurred
- The basis on which liquidator's remuneration was fixed
- A statement that he has reconciled his account with that held by the Secretary of State
- A statement of the amount paid to unsecured creditors by virtue of the prescribed part of the company's net property (s176A)
- A statement of the creditors' right to request information under Rule 4.49E and challenge the liquidator's remuneration and expenses under Rule 4.131

Once the meeting has been held the liquidator must give notice to that effect to the court together with a copy of the report laid before the meeting and whether he has been granted his release. A copy should also be sent to the Official Receiver.

If there is no quorum at the meeting the liquidator must report this fact to the court together with the fact that the meeting was summoned in accordance with the rules. The meeting will then be deemed to have been held and the creditors not to have resolved against the liquidator having his release.

Provided that the creditors have not resolved otherwise, the liquidator will be deemed to get his release on the date the notice of the final meeting is filed at court.

If the creditors resolved that the liquidator should not have his release then it must be obtained from the Secretary of State. The date of release will be the date specified in the certificate issued by the Secretary of State.

3.2 The position in creditors' voluntary liquidation – R4.126

As soon as the company's affairs are all wound up the liquidator is required to call a general meeting of the company and a meeting of creditors for the purpose of laying before it an account of the winding-up.

The meeting must be advertised in the *Gazette* at least one month before being held. Creditors should receive at least 28 days' notice. At least eight weeks before the final meeting a draft report of the liquidator's conduct of the liquidation must be sent to creditors.

Within a week after the meeting has been held the liquidator must send a copy of the account to the Registrar of Companies, together with a return of the holding of the meeting. Failure to file these documents will render the liquidator liable to a fine (s106).

If a quorum is not present at the meeting the liquidator makes the return stating that the meeting was convened but that no quorum was present. In these circumstances it is deemed that the requirements have been complied with, and the creditors are deemed not to have resolved against the liquidator having his release.

If the liquidator fails to call the meeting as required he will be liable to a fine.

At the final meeting, the creditors may question the liquidator with respect to any matter contained in the account, and may resolve against the liquidator having his release.

If the creditors resolve against his release, the liquidator may apply to the Secretary of State (R4.126). The date of release will be the date specified in the certificate issued by the Secretary of State.

3.3 Final progress reports in CVL

The content of the final progress report in CVL is prescribed in R4.126. It must be accompanied by a statement of the creditors' right to challenge the liquidator's remuneration and expenses under R4.131. The draft report cannot be sent out before the liquidator has given notice under R4.186 of his intention to declare a final dividend.

3.4 The position in members' voluntary liquidation

The rules regarding the final meeting in an MVL are the same as in a CVL (s94).

The liquidator is deemed to be released from office from the date of giving notice to the Registrar of Companies of his ceasing to act.

Interactive question: T Wylde Limited

Your principal, Nigel Taylor, was appointed liquidator of T Wylde Limited at a s98 meeting of creditors. All assets have now been realised and Nigel is keen to close the case.

Requirement

Outline the procedure for calling the final meetings to close the case and obtain release.

See **Answer** at the end of this chapter.

4 Closure checklist

> **Section overview**
> - There are a number of practical steps to be taken by the liquidator when closing a case.

4.1 Checklist

1. Review files
2. Ensure all creditor claims have been admitted or rejected
3. Ensure all assets have been realised
4. Ensure all expenses of the winding up have been settled
5. Ensure liquidator's remuneration approved and drawn
6. Obtain written confirmation from agents and solicitors that their remuneration has been settled
7. Withdraw any undertakings given
8. Ensure all employee claims dealt with
9. Ensure D returns submitted and all necessary proceedings against officers and others have been disposed of
10. Obtain HM Revenue and Customs clearance that all tax and VAT matters have been completed
    input tax for up to three years can be reclaimed from HMRC on form VAT 426
11. Check final dividend has been paid:
    - Calculate final dividend
    - Send notice of intention to declare dividend
    - Pay dividend
12. Ensure all uncashed dividend cheques are returned to ISA
13. Close all bank accounts
14. Notify insurers of ceasing to act and cancel bordereau
15. Notify PPF of intention to cease to act issuing appropriate s122 PA2004 statement
16. Call final meetings of members and creditors
17. Prepare final account of winding up
18. Send return of final meetings to Registrar of Companies
19. Do not dispose of company's books and records until at least one year after dissolution
20. Retain financial and administrative records for at least six years

Summary and Self-test

Summary

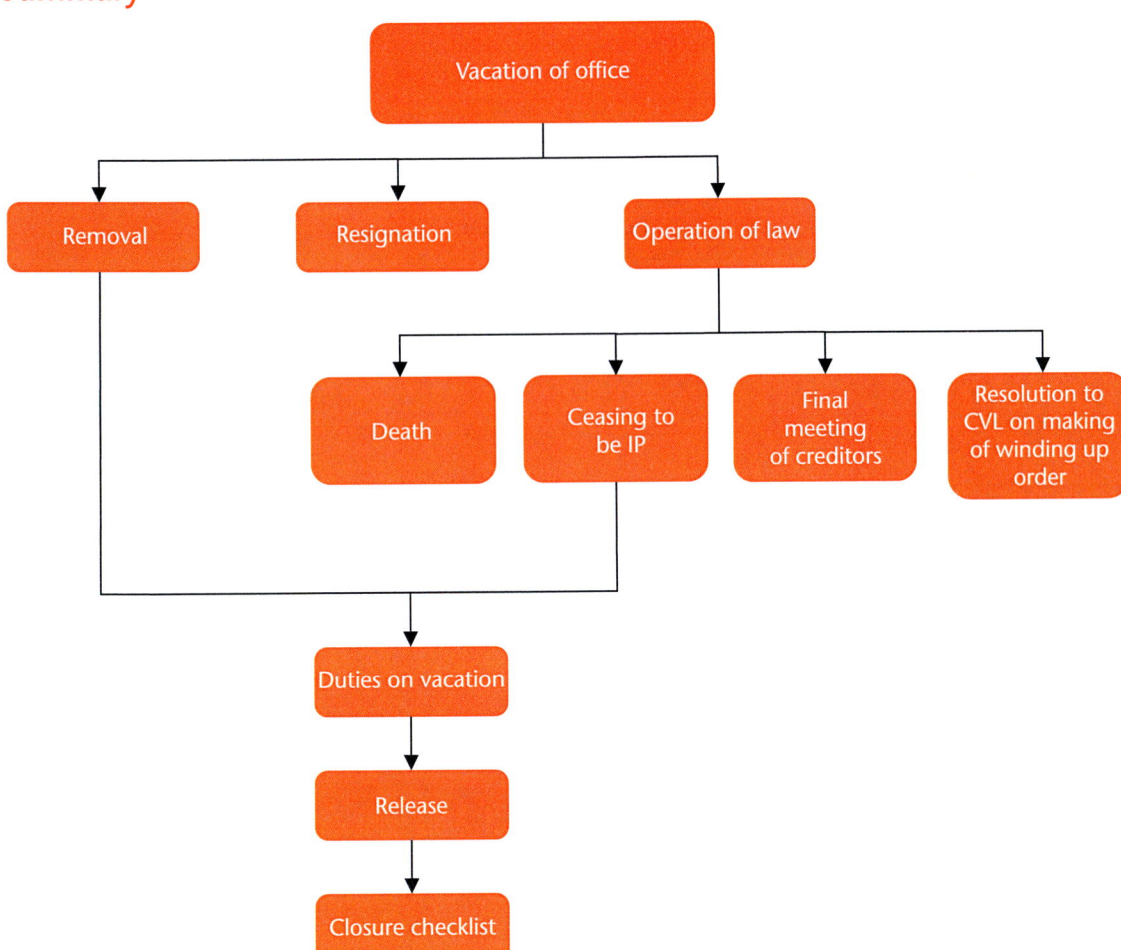

```
Vacation of office
├── Removal
├── Resignation
└── Operation of law
    ├── Death
    ├── Ceasing to be IP
    ├── Final meeting of creditors
    └── Resolution to CVL on making of winding up order

Removal & Ceasing to be IP → Duties on vacation → Release → Closure checklist
```

Self-test

Answer the following questions.

1. How many days' notice must creditors be given of a final meeting in a compulsory liquidation?

    A   7 days
    B   14 days
    C   21 days
    D   28 days

2. In a compulsory liquidation where must notice of the final meeting be advertised?

    A   *The Gazette*
    B   *The Gazette* and one newspaper in the relevant locality
    C   *The Gazette* and in one other national newspaper
    D   There is no requirement to advertise.

3. Within what period from the final meeting must a liquidator in a creditors' voluntary liquidation submit a return of the meeting to the Registrar of Companies?

    A   7 days
    B   14 days
    C   21 days
    D   28 days

4. After what period may the books and records in a creditors' voluntary liquidation be destroyed?

    A   At the liquidator's discretion
    B   One year after the final meetings
    C   One year after the company has been dissolved
    D   Immediately following the final meetings

5. What are the grounds per R4.108 upon which a liquidator may resign from office?

Now, go back to the Learning Objectives in the Introduction. If you are satisfied that you have achieved these, please tick them off.

Answers to Self-test

1. D
2. A
3. A
4. C
5. (a) Ill health
   (b) Intend ceasing to act as an IP
   (c) A conflict of interest or change in personal circumstances which make it impossible or impractical to continue
   (d) Where joint liquidators are appointed and it is no longer expedient to continue with that number of joint liquidators

Answer to Interactive question

Answer to Interactive question: T Wylde Limited

- Liquidator must convene a general meeting of the company and a meeting of the creditors
- 28 days' notice must be given to all creditors who have proved their debts
- The meeting must be advertised in the *London Gazette* at least one month before being held
- At the meeting:
    - Lay before it an account of the winding up showing how it has been conducted and the company's property disposed of
    - The creditors may question the liquidator with respect to any matter contained in the account
    - Creditors may resolve against the liquidator having his release
- Within a week after the meeting, the liquidator must send a copy of the account to the Registrar of Companies, together with a return of the holding of the meeting
- If a quorum is not present at the meeting the liquidator makes a return stating that the meeting was convened but that no quorum was present. It is deemed that the requirements have been complied with and the creditors are deemed to have not resolved against the liquidators release
- If the creditors resolve against his release, the liquidator may apply to the Secretary of State. The date of release will be the date specified in the certificate issued by the Secretary of State
- If creditors have not resolved against his release, the liquidator will have his release from when he gives notice of the final meeting to the Registrar of Companies.

CHAPTER 13

Company Voluntary Arrangements

Introduction
Topic List
1 Introduction to Company Voluntary Arrangements
2 The proposal and statement of affairs
3 Procedure for Company Voluntary Arrangements
4 Post approval matters

Summary and Self-test
Answers to Self-test
Answers to Interactive questions

Introduction

Learning objectives

- Describe the processes undergone in the creation of a CVA
- Explain the role of an IP as advisor, nominee and supervisor in a CVA
- State the contents of the CVA proposal and explain how the contents are prepared
- Explain the use and effects of the moratorium procedure
- Describe the on-going obligations upon the IP in a CVA with regard to meetings, record keeping, reporting, time limits
- State the criteria for completion of a CVA and the process of completion and the circumstances that might bring about failure and the effect of failure

Tick off
☐ ☐ ☐ ☐ ☐ ☐

Stop and think

What is a company voluntary arrangement? How does it differ from an individual voluntary arrangement? Why should a company choose a voluntary arrangement rather than liquidation or administration?

Working context

You may be asked to assist in putting together proposals for a company voluntary arrangement or advising directors of a company on the options available to them. It is therefore important to understand the procedure for a company voluntary arrangement and have an understanding of when a voluntary arrangement may be appropriate for a company.

1 Introduction to Company Voluntary Arrangements

> **Section overview**
>
> - Company Voluntary Arrangements (CVA) were introduced by the IA 86 as an alternative to liquidation for companies experiencing difficulties in paying their debts as and when due. A good working knowledge of IVAs makes the CVA procedure easier to learn as there are so many similarities between the two types of arrangement. Legislation regarding CVAs is found in Part 1 of the Act (s1 – 7B) and Part 1 of the Rules (R1.1 – 1.54) and SIP 3.2.

1.1 Advantages of CVA

- Possible survival of the company as a going concern.
- Higher returns to creditors due to:
  - Sale as a going concern/profitable trading
  - Lower costs – no Secretary of State fees, possibility of lower costs as directors (rather than IP's staff) remain responsible for managing the business.
- Capital gains tax advantages – gains on asset disposals may be set against losses.
- Floating charges will not be invalidated under s245.
- Binds all creditors who had notice of and were entitled to vote at the creditors' meeting.
- Small companies moratorium available.
- No D return completed by supervisor.
- Supervisor may not bring proceedings for wrongful trading.
- No notice on letterhead helps to preserve goodwill.
- No application to court required.
- Directors retain control of the company (albeit under supervision).

1.2 Disadvantages of CVA

- Supervisor has no power to claw back assets under s238, s239 and s244.
- If arrangement fails, liquidation is likely to be the only remaining course of action.
- Unlike an IVA, a CVA does not have moratorium as an intrinsic part of the procedure and it is only available to small companies.
- Act of notifying creditors of the CVA may precipitate a run on the assets.
- Secured and preferential creditors must consent to any modification of their rights.

1.3 Who may make a proposal for a CVA?

A proposal may be made by:

- A liquidator or administrator (where the company is in liquidation or administration s1(3)
- The directors s1(1)

1.4 The role of the advisor, nominee and supervisor

- SIP3.2 extended that prior to engagement, the IP must discuss all opportunities available to the company explain in full the advantages, disadvantages and costs of each. The IP must ensure that the board have fully understood the alternates and the obligations on them as a consequence of the CVA. He must also advise the effect of rejection of the arrangement.

- Prior to the acceptance of the arrangement by the creditors the IP will act as nominee. He has a duty to balance the interests of the creditors and the company. The nominee is required to report to the court and has a duty to perform an independent objective review and assessment of the proposal.

- Upon acceptance of the arrangement by the creditors, the IP will become the supervisor of the arrangement. His responsibilities will be governed by the terms of the arrangement. His role is to ensure that the arrangement proceeds as anticipated by the terms of the proposal and to report on its progress to creditors.

1.5 Initial meeting with the directors

The following matters need to be considered by the IP and the directors when evaluating whether or not a CVA will be appropriate.

IP matters

Can the IP act for the directors in the light of the code of ethics, including consideration of his policy of anti-bribery and AML?

Are arrangements in place for the IP to be remunerated for advice given to the directors before the advising IP agrees to become the nominee? The proposal itself can only set out the remuneration of the nominee and the supervisor.

The overriding duty of the IP is to balance the interests of creditors, the company and others who may be affected by the CVA.

Directors must be advised of the IPs duty to maintain independence and his duties generally. The duties of the IP when acting as nominee cannot be fettered by the instructions of the directors.

The nominee needs to be satisfied that any proposal is:

- Fit to be put to the creditors
- Fair
- Feasible ie has a real prospect of implementation
- An acceptable alternative to liquidation or other formal insolvency process

Protection from creditors

There is no statutory protection from creditors unless the company qualifies for a small company moratorium. Therefore the directors need to identify creditors who may be able to take enforcement action against the company and devise a strategy to deal with:

- Landlords who may be able to exercise CRAR or forfeit leases
- The company's bank who may be entitled to appoint a receiver and whose support will be needed for continued trading
- Overseas creditors who may, notwithstanding the CVA, be able to take enforcement action in foreign jurisdictions
- Judgment creditors
- HM Revenue and Customs and local authorities who may be able to levy distress
- Any creditor(s) petitioning for winding up
- Creditors with proprietary rights eg ROT suppliers or creditors under HP agreements or equipment leases

Protection could be obtained by entering administration first, or by applying for a small company moratorium (see para 3.3 for more detail) or by petitioning for a winding up order and applying for the appointment of a provisional liquidator (SIP 3).

[The lack of an automatic moratorium is the main reason why CVAs have not proved very popular.]

Identification of creditors

Need to ensure that all creditors have been correctly identified.

Creditors who were not notified of the creditors' meeting to vote on the proposal are still bound by the CVA providing they would have been entitled to vote at the meeting had they been notified.

Nonetheless non-notified bound creditors may be able to appeal to the court to overturn the decision of the meeting on the basis of material irregularity – so it makes sense to take every precaution to notify all creditors.

Directors should identify all contingent creditors.

Addresses of creditors should be accurate to ensure that actual notice can be given.

Are creditors (and members) likely to vote in favour of the proposals?

Third party funds

Directors or third parties who are intending to inject funds into the company should be advised to seek their own independent professional advice to avoid any subsequent allegations of conflict of interests.

The Nominee should seek confirmation of their intention on writing and make enquiries as to whether such intention is indeed in relation to the arrangement.

Warnings to directors

Directors should be warned of the consequences of not making full and accurate disclosure in the statement of affairs, in the proposal, or at the creditors' meeting, as:

- Creditors may find out and vote against the proposal or require adjournments and/or modifications
- Creditors may appeal on the basis of a material irregularity
- The inducing of a CVA through fraud constitutes a criminal offence (s6A) which carries a potential term of imprisonment

The directors must establish that trading on will be viable and should be warned of the risks of wrongful trading. Consequently they should take the following steps.

- Ensure adequate funding available
- Prepare cash flow forecasts, a business plan and projections. Must show that both ongoing trading is viable and that dividends to creditors shown in the proposal are likely to be paid
- Independent confirmation from the bank that it will support the proposal and continue to provide funding
- Consider other sources of funds
- Investigate whether the directors have the support of management, staff, key suppliers and customers
- Consider whether any major contracts with customers give the right to terminate if the company is in an insolvency procedure

Engagement letter and next steps

Once the alternate options (including non-insolvency options) have been considered and the board are satisfied with the CVA as a process, the IA should agree such terms in writing.

The engagement letter should be issued to the directors confirming the IP's advice in writing. It will then be for the directors to submit their proposal and statement of affairs to the nominee. Note that one director has capacity to do this though historically two directors were required to act and in practice are likely to continue to do so. The notice of proposal endorsed with the IP's consent to act should be returned as soon as reasonably practicable (Rule 1.4).

2 The proposal and statement of affairs

> **Section overview**
> - The required contents of the proposal are set out in Rule 1.3 (and SIP 3.2) and are virtually identical to those for an IVA.

2.1 Content of proposal

The proposal should deal with the following:

- **The nature of the arrangement.** Is it a composition for the full and final settlement of debts or a scheme of arrangement?
- **Background** to the proposal
- **Comparison of the estimated outcomes** of the CVA and liquidation (including costs)
- **The financial proposal being put to creditors**

    Include details of what assets are being realised or excluded with respective values. Sums to be paid to the supervisor during the arrangement period. Availability of third party sums.

- **Claims or potential claims under ss238, 239, 244 and 245**

    The proposal must detail whether any transactions amount to a transaction at an undervalue, preference, or extortionate credit transaction. Additionally any floating charges which may fall foul of s245 (invalid floating charge) must also be detailed.

- **Proposed duration**

    As in an IVA there is no set duration but remember that with a CVA the issue of automatic discharge from bankruptcy after one year does not arise. The alternative for a company may well be liquidation. Creditors are in a strong position in a CVA to press for lengthy duration if that is in their best interests.

- **Provision of guarantees**

    The rule specifically mentions directors as possible providers of guarantees. If they are to provide guarantees this must be disclosed.

- **The conduct of the business of the company**

    - Supervisor to supervise not manage the business, but may be given additional powers (as deemed necessary)
    - Supervisor to avoid personal liability
    - Duties on company management to provide supervisor with regular information and accounts
    - A provision detailing which firm of accountants will be responsible for the preparation of accounts and provision for payment of their costs
    - Supervisor to have general power to implement terms of CVA

    Proposal will need to deal with the usual factors an IP needs to consider when contemplating continuing to trade for example:

    - Grounds for director's belief that the company can return to profitable trading
    - Whether the company can rely on the continued support of the bank, major customers and suppliers as well as the work force
    - From where working capital is to be derived

- **Creditors' claims**

    The rules contain no details on how unliquidated and contingent claims are to be dealt with for dividend purposes. Therefore for unliquidated claims the proposal may provide for the creditor to submit proof and evidence as to quantum and for the supervisor to estimate the amount due and provide the creditor with written notice of that estimate. In the event that creditor does not agree the claim provision can be made for arbitration or appeal to the court (under s7(3)).

For contingent claims the proposal may provide for retention by the supervisor of funds pending crystallisation of the claim, perhaps for a limited period after which the sum retained would be paid out to creditors generally.

- **Prescribed part**

    The proposal now has to set out how much unsecured creditors would get if the company went into liquidation. This is so that creditors can make a meaningful comparison between what they are promised in the proposal versus what they might get in a voluntary liquidation.

    This is relevant for comparison purposes as the prescribed part is not applicable in a CVA procedure.

2.2 Statement of Affairs

The directors must also provide a statement of affairs to comply with Rule 1.5. It will need to give details of the company's assets, estimated values, security over the assets and the names and addresses of creditors and members with the details of their claims and shareholdings. It must be made up within 14 days of the notice of proposal given to the nominee and verified by statement of truth by at least one director.

Under Rule 1.56 the nominee, directors or other interested person may apply to court for an order omitting specified information from any statement of affairs to be sent to creditors. This is on the ground that disclosure would prejudice conduct of the CVA or might reasonably be expected to lead to violence against any person.

2.3 Nominee's comments on proposal – [SIP 3.2 applies]

Within 28 days of endorsing a notice of the proposal with consent to act, the nominee is required to file in court his comments on the proposal.

The nominee should normally comment on the following matters:

- Whether in his opinion the proposed voluntary arrangement has a reasonable prospect of being approved and implemented

- Whether a meeting of the company and its creditors should be summoned to consider the proposal and if so details of the time(s) place(s) and date(s) at which meetings should be held

- Whether the company's financial position is materially different from that contained in the proposal, explaining the extent to which the information has been verified

- Whether the CVA is manifestly unfair

- Whether the CVA has a reasonable prospect of being approved and implemented

The nominee should take care to ensure that his report is as comprehensive and accurate as it can be.

In *Greystoke v Hamilton-Smith and others*, the court set out three tests which the nominee should apply before concluding that a meeting of creditors should or should not be summoned. They are:

- That the debtor's true position as to assets and liabilities is not materially different from that which it is represented to the creditors to be

- That the debtor's proposal has a real prospect of being implemented in the way it is represented to be

- That there is no already manifest yet unavoidable prospective unfairness in the proposal

Interactive question 1: Fine Foods Limited

You have been approached by Mrs Cook, the managing director of Fine Foods Limited. Fine Foods Limited has been experiencing cash flow problems for some time, but Mrs Cook is confident that a new contract, which they are on the brink of signing, will restore the company to profitability.

Mrs Cook provides you with the following information.

	Book Value £	Forced sale Value £
Assets		
Machinery	65,000	30,000
Fixtures and fittings	27,000	14,000
Stock	45,000	10,000
Vehicles	15,000	5,000
Debtors	150,000	95,000
Freehold property	250,000	300,000
Liabilities		
Pay in lieu of notice		51,000
Redundancy		47,000
Trade and expense creditors		475,000

Mrs Cook anticipates that should the new contract be signed the company would have surplus monthly income of £5,000. She is keen for the company to avoid liquidation and enter into a company voluntary arrangement, with the company making contributions of £5,000 per month into the arrangement for four years.

She states that if a voluntary arrangement is approved Cook Limited, a company which she also controls, will subordinate its unsecured claim of £100,000 to those of other unsecured creditors.

The following information is also relevant:

- Debt collection fees are 10% of recoveries. Debtors are expected to realise £120,000 if trading is continued due to the ongoing provision of after-sales services and guarantees

- Estate agent fees of 1.5% would be incurred in disposing of the property and legal fees of 2%. Chattel agent fees would be 5% of realisations on the company's remaining assets

- The company will need to retain all of its assets if trading continues under a voluntary arrangement

- Your partner estimates that if the company is placed into liquidation, liquidator's remuneration would be £25,000. This is in addition to a fee of £5,000 for convening meetings of members and creditors to place the company into liquidation

- Under a voluntary arrangement the nominee's fees would be £4,000 and the supervisor's fees would be £3,500 per year

- The property is subject to an outstanding mortgage with Satby Bank PLC in the sum of £85,000

Requirement

Prepare an Estimated Outcome Statement for Fine Foods Limited comparing the estimated outcome in a creditors' voluntary liquidation with that in a company voluntary arrangement.

Show all workings and assumptions.

See **Answer** at the end of this chapter.

3 Procedure for Company Voluntary Arrangements

Section overview

- Proposals for a CVA can be made by the directors, liquidator or administrator and may or may not include an application for a small company moratorium. Meetings of both creditors and the company members will be held to approve the CVA. However although the members vote on the proposal in the event of a conflict the creditors' wishes take priority.

3.1 Procedure for CVA – directors' proposals – no application for moratorium

s1(1) provides that in situations where the company is not in administration or liquidation it is for the directors to propose a CVA.

- Directors prepare the proposal and send the following documents to the IP who is to act as nominee.
    - The proposal (R1.4(2))
    - Written notice of proposal (R1.4(1)) This is endorsed with acceptance and returned to the directors. It acts as the nominee's consent to act
    - Statement of Affairs, which must be made up to within 14 days of service of written notice of proposal and verified by statement of truth by at least one director
- Within 28 days of endorsing the notice of proposal with his consent to act the nominee files in court: a copy of the proposal; a copy or summary of Statement of Affairs; and his report on the proposal.

3.2 Meetings of creditors and members/shareholders

- Notice must be sent to all creditors in the Statement of Affairs or of whom the nominee is otherwise aware and to all members (to best of nominee's belief).
- Meetings must be held on 14 days' notice, between 10.00 and 16.00 and in choosing location regard must be had to convenience of creditors. Remote attendance is possible.
- Meetings of members and creditors usually take place on the same day but can take place up to five business days apart (R1.13).
- The notice must include the following documents.
    - Copy proposal
    - Statement of Affairs or summary
    - Comments on proposal
    - Proxy form and proof of debt form
    - Statement about requisite majorities
- The notice must state effect of the rules on the requisite majorities to approve the proposal.
- Meetings must be held not more than 28 days from the date of filing of the nominee's report.

Proxies

[Note that the rules mirror those that apply in other insolvency procedures.]

Rules governing the use of proxies are found in Rule 8.1 onwards. Additional guidance is given to IPs in SIP 10. A proxy is 'the authority given by one person to another to attend, speak and vote as his representative at a meeting'.

All notices convening meetings must enclose a form of proxy. No proxy form can be sent out with the name or description of any person already endorsed on it.

To be valid a proxy must comply with the following rules:

- The proxy must be received by the time and date specified in the notice
- A proxy can be signed by either the principal or on his behalf by an authorised person. The relationship of the authorised person to the principal must be stated on the proxy form eg a director of the company
- A proxy issued for a specific meeting can be used at any adjournment of that meeting (unless the proxy form removes his discretion)
- The principal may revoke a proxy at will
- A faxed proxy is valid for voting purposes *IRC Conbeer v Anor*. (Following the changes introduced by the 2010 Amendment Rules electronic delivery is also possible if the rules relating to such delivery are complied with)
- Although the chair of a meeting has discretion to admit a proof not lodged in time due to circumstances beyond the creditor's control there is no such discretion in respect of failure to lodge a proxy
- If a proxy represents a corporation (eg a company) at a meeting he must produce to the chairman of the meeting a copy of the resolution (letter of authority) from which he derives his authority.

Voting requirements

Votes at the creditors meeting are calculated according to the amount of the creditor's debt at the date of the meeting. Where a creditor has an unliquidated or unascertained claim, the creditor should be admitted to vote for £1 unless the chairman agrees a higher amount.

If in administration – votes are calculated according to the amount of the creditor's debt at the date the company went into administration.

If a Schedule 1 small company moratorium applies – votes are calculated according to the amount of the creditor's debt at the date of the beginning of the moratorium.

Secured creditors cannot vote with the secured element of their claim.

Votes at the members meeting are calculated according to the rights attaching to their shares in accordance with the company's Articles of Association.

Majorities

The rules state that at least 3/4s or more of the votes cast at the creditors' meeting are required to approve or modify the proposal (R1.19(2)).

Any other resolution taken requires a simple majority.

At the members' meeting a simple majority of the votes cast at the members' meeting is required.

Any resolution is invalid if a simple majority of notified, valid, non-connected creditors vote **against** it (R1.19(4)).

s4A – the decision of the creditors' meeting is effective, even if the members' meeting reaches a different decision, but is subject to the right of any member to apply to the court to overturn the decision (see below).

Appeals

Appeals may be made by any creditor or member, within 28 days of the filing of the chairman's report to the court – s4(6). If the member/creditor was not notified of the meeting then the appeal must be made within 28 days of hearing that the relevant meeting had been held. The court can reverse, vary or confirm the chairman's decision or order another meeting to be held, but only if the grounds of appeal reveal unfair prejudice or material irregularity.

Adjournments

The chairman may (and if the meeting resolves shall) adjourn either meeting for up to 14 days. Multiple adjournments are possible but the final meeting must still be no more than 14 days from the original meeting. Suspension of the meeting for up to an hour is possible but only after the meeting has been formally opened.

Modifications

The meetings may propose modifications to the proposal. Although it is not a statutory requirement for directors to consent to modifications, it is recommended (by SIP 3.2) that the nominee should find out and report to the meeting the directors' views on any proposed modifications which they may be required to implement if approved.

All agreed modifications should be evidenced in writing by those members present or represented.

Reporting the result of the meeting

The chairman prepares a report of the meetings and within four business days must file them in court (R1.24(3)). All those notified of the meetings must be sent notice of its result as soon as reasonably practicable after the filing of the report (R1.24(4)).

If the CVA is approved, a copy of the report must also be sent to the Registrar of Companies (R1.24(5)) as soon as reasonably practicable. This is the responsibility of the supervisor who may not necessarily be the chairman of the meeting.

The report should state:

- Whether the proposal was approved by the creditors or by the creditors and members (and whether there were any modifications)
- Details of the resolutions taken and the decision on each one
- A list of creditors and members present or represented (with their values) and how they voted on each resolution
- The supervisor's opinion as to applicability of the EC Regulation
- Any further information considered necessary

Recording the meeting

- SIP 12 ('Records of Meetings in Formal Insolvency Proceedings') provides that it is best practice that records should be kept of all meetings of creditors and members. (See Chapter 3 for the requirements of SIP 12.)

3.3 Procedure for director(s) to obtain a moratorium

Director(s) are able to apply to the court for a moratorium.

3.3.1 Eligibility

- This is restricted to 'eligible' companies ie those falling within the definition of a 'small' company for Companies Act purposes (s382 CA 06). Broadly this is a company which satisfies two of the following three criteria:
    - Turnover does not exceed £6.5m
    - Balance sheet total does not exceed £3.26m
    - Average no of employees does not exceed 50

[The balance sheet total is based upon total assets excluding liabilities.]

The company must also not be part of a larger group.

The company must not be excluded under para 4 of Sch A1. A company is excluded if at the date of filing:

- The company is in administration
- The company is being wound up
- There is an administrative receiver in office
- There is a already in place CVA
- There is a provisional liquidator in office

- There has been either an administrator in office or a moratorium in force in the previous 12 months and either no CVA had effect or there was a CVA but it came to a premature end

3.3.2 Required action

- Directors provide the nominee with:
    - Documents setting out terms of proposed CVA
    - Statements of Affairs (made up to within two weeks of the date of delivery) and verified by statement of truth by at least one director
    - Any other information requested by the nominee
- Before obtaining a moratorium, the directors need to obtain from the nominee a statement in prescribed form to the effect that in the nominee's opinion the:
    - CVA has a reasonable prospect of approval and implementation
    - Company has adequate funding to continue trading during the moratorium
    - Meetings of creditors and shareholders should be called to consider the proposal.

Nominee's comments on the proposal and consent to act should be annexed to the statement.

Within three business days of receiving the nominee's statement the directors file the following documents in court (R1.39).

- The document setting out the terms of the proposed CVA and the statement of affairs
- A statement that the company is eligible for a moratorium
- The nominee's statement with attachments
- If the nominee allowed an extension to the two week period for the Statement of Affairs under R1.37(3) he must submit a statement of his reasons for doing so.

The moratorium comes into effect on the date of filing and is initially for 28 days.

3.4 Effect of the moratorium

The protection provided by the moratorium will be extensive.

- Landlords are not able to exercise CRAR or forfeit by peaceful re-entry or otherwise.
- No petition can be presented for winding up nor a winding up order made.
- No meeting of members can be called and no resolution passed for winding up.
- No petition for an administration order can be presented.
- No administrative receiver can be appointed.
- No enforcement of security or repossession of HP goods.
- No other proceedings, execution or legal process.

During the moratorium, the company's notepaper must state that the moratorium is in force and the company may not obtain credit of £250 or more without disclosing that a moratorium is in force.

Having filed the documents in court the directors give notice to the nominee.

The nominee will now take the following steps.

- Advertise the moratorium in the *Gazette* and advertise it in such other manner as he thinks fit (if any). The advert must confirm the nature of the business of the company, confirm that the moratorium is in place and the date upon which it came into force
- Give notice to the company
- Give notice to the Registrar of Companies
- Give notice to any creditors who have exercised CRAR, any creditor(s) petitioning for winding up and the court enforcement officer(s)

Safeguards

The nominee must consider the directors' proposals and although he can rely on information provided by the directors, he is giving his opinion when he makes a statement that there is a reasonable prospect of implementation and can be held liable on it.

The nominee must monitor the company during the moratorium and must report to the meetings on this.

The nominee must withdraw his consent to act (and the moratorium will then come to an end) if the following apply:

- It emerges that the company was not eligible or was excluded
- The directors fail to comply with their duties
- The nominee no longer believes that there is a reasonable prospect of implementation or that the CVA can be funded

Credit of £250 or more may not be obtained without disclosing that the company is subject to a moratorium. As with bankruptcy there is a broad definition of credit including the receipt of deposits for goods/services, to be delivered or provided later.

Asset disposals outside the ordinary course of business require nominee approval. The meetings can vote to extend the moratorium and if they do so a committee can be formed which can also sanction such disposals.

Pursuant to Sch A1 para 20 floating charge assets can be disposed of, but assets subject to a fixed charge require agreement of the charge holder or court sanction.

3.5 Procedure where proposal made by liquidator or administrator

The procedure is the same as for the directors, but:

- The proposal must give names, addresses and values of preferential creditors if company in administration or liquidation.
- The Statement of Affairs in the CVA is that already obtained in the existing insolvency proceedings.
- A report to the court and comments on proposals are not required if the liquidator or administrator is to act as nominee.
- The company's assets are protected, without the need for a small company moratorium.
- Creditor votes are calculated by reference to the amount of the creditor's debt as at the date the company went into administration or liquidation.

Interactive question 2: Mayflower Limited

Jim Etherton, a director of Mayflower Limited, has contacted your office for advice.

He tells you that the company has recently been experiencing cash flow problems. This is due mainly to a number of disagreements with suppliers which have caused delays on current projects. A new supplier has been found, however the current problems are anticipated to continue for a number of months.

The finance director has recommended that the company put forward proposals for a company voluntary arrangement. Jim is uncertain what this means and whether he should be in agreement with it.

Requirement

Outline:

- The advantages and disadvantages of entering into a company voluntary arrangement for the company and its directors.
- What can be done to protect the company from creditors threatening enforcement action.
- What voting majorities are required in order for a company voluntary arrangement to be approved.

See **Answer** at the end of this section.

4 Post approval matters

> **Section overview**
> - There are a number of matters which the supervisor has to deal with after approval of the arrangement.

4.1 Effect of approval

A voluntary arrangement comes into effect under s5 when the proposal has been approved by both a meeting of the company and a meeting of its creditors.

The approved voluntary arrangement:

- Takes effect as if made by the company at the creditors' meeting
- Binds every person who was entitled to vote at that meeting (whether or not he was present or represented at the meeting or whether or not he received notice)
- If members vote against a proposal approved by the creditors the CVA takes effect but subject to the rights of members to apply to court to challenge the decision

Once approved the nominee becomes the supervisor.

4.2 Challenge of decision of the meeting

An application to the court may be made on the grounds that:

- A voluntary arrangement approved at the meetings summoned under s3 unfairly prejudices the interests of a creditor, member or contributory of the company; and/or
- There has been some material irregularity at or in relation to either of the meetings.

The persons who may apply are:

- A person entitled, in accordance with the rules, to vote at either of the meetings
- The nominee or any person who has replaced him
- If the company is being wound up or an administration order is in force, the liquidator or administrator

The application must be made within 28 days of the chairman's report to the court, or if a member/creditor was not notified of the creditors' meeting, within 28 days of him becoming aware that the relevant meeting took place.

4.3 Monies outstanding to a liquidator, administrator or OR

R1.23(2) where the company is in liquidation or administration the supervisor of the CVA on taking possession of the company's assets shall discharge any balance due to the IP by way of:

- Remuneration
- On account of fees, costs, charges and expenses
- On account of any advances made in respect of the company at the date it went into liquidation or entered administration (plus interest at the statutory rate)

As an alternative the supervisor can give a written undertaking to the IP to discharge sums due out of first realisations.

In any event the liquidator, administrator or OR has a charge on the CVA assets for the sums due until they have been discharged. However the supervisor is entitled to deduct first the costs etc of realisation.

4.4 Progress reports – R1.26A

A supervisor must at least once every twelve months prepare a report on the progress of the arrangement with an abstract of receipts and payments and send it (within two months) to the Registrar of Companies, the company, all creditors and members bound by the CVA and the company's auditors (assuming the company is not in liquidation). This must be accompanied by his comments on the progress and efficacy of the arrangement. The supervisor may apply for the court's permission not to circulate the report to the company's members but to advertise the availability of the report and then make it available only to those who request a copy.

4.5 Completion or termination of the arrangement - R1.29

Following completion or termination of the CVA the supervisor must send notice to all creditors and members that the CVA has been fully implemented or terminated together with his report summarising his receipts and payments within 28 days.

The supervisor also sends a copy of the notice and the report to the Registrar of Companies and the court within 28 days.

4.6 Failure

In circumstances of failure or default it will be necessary to consider how matters should proceed. It is essential that the proposal should set out in specific terms the circumstances in which it shall be deemed to have failed and state what action the supervisor is required to take in the event of failure.

When failure has occurred the supervisor should notify the creditors accordingly and advise them what action he has taken or proposes to take.

The supervisor has the power to present a winding up petition.

As in an IVA the CVA assets are usually held on trust for the CVA creditors and will be distributed to them accordingly. Such assets will not form part of the estate in liquidation.

4.7 Resignation and release

There are no statutory provisions dealing with the resignation and release of a supervisor. The terms of the arrangement would have to be checked to ascertain the mechanism by which the supervisor may resign and be released from office.

The agreement of 100% of the creditors may be required unless a specific majority is stated in the proposal.

In the absence of a specific clause the supervisor would have to obtain a court order to deal with his release.

In practice, the proposal would determine when the arrangement comes to an end, either on the issue of a notice of due compliance, or notice of non-compliance. At this point the supervisor would be released.

4.8 Request for statement of time spent on CVA

Within two years of the IP ceasing to act the creditors, directors or members may request a statement of how much time the IP or his staff have spend on the arrangement. The statement must be provided free of charge within 28 days of it being requested (R1.55).

Summary and Self-test

Summary

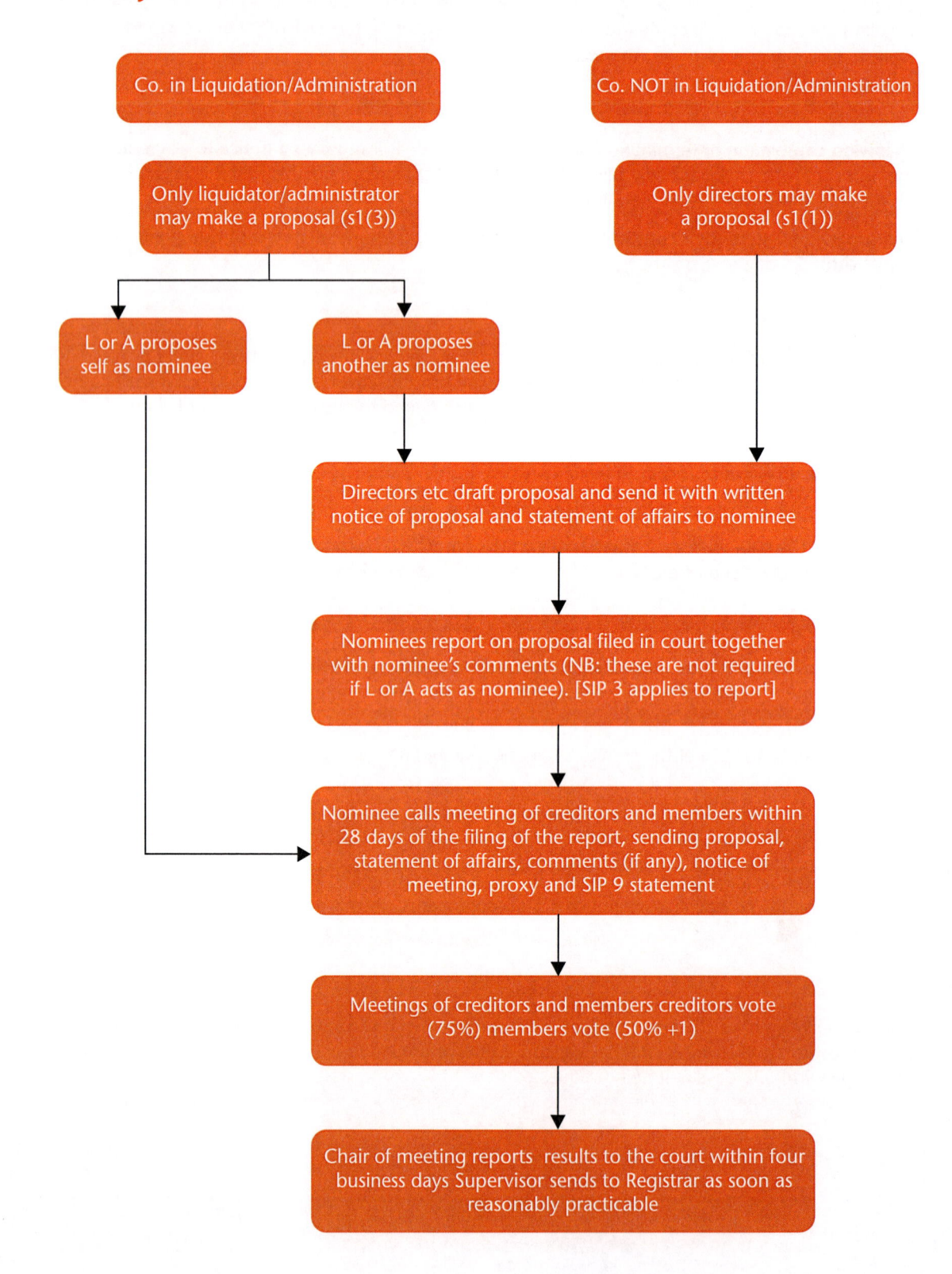

```
┌─────────────────────────────┐                    ┌─────────────────────────────┐
│ Co. in Liquidation/         │                    │ Co. NOT in Liquidation/     │
│ Administration              │                    │ Administration              │
└─────────────────────────────┘                    └─────────────────────────────┘
              │                                                   │
              ▼                                                   ▼
┌─────────────────────────────┐                    ┌─────────────────────────────┐
│ Only liquidator/administrator│                   │ Only directors may make     │
│ may make a proposal (s1(3)) │                    │ a proposal (s1(1))          │
└─────────────────────────────┘                    └─────────────────────────────┘
        │              │                                          │
        ▼              ▼                                          │
┌──────────────┐  ┌──────────────┐                                │
│ L or A       │  │ L or A       │                                │
│ proposes     │  │ proposes     │                                │
│ self as      │  │ another as   │                                │
│ nominee      │  │ nominee      │                                │
└──────────────┘  └──────────────┘                                │
        │              │                                          │
        │              ▼                                          ▼
        │        ┌────────────────────────────────────────────────────┐
        │        │ Directors etc draft proposal and send it with      │
        │        │ written notice of proposal and statement of        │
        │        │ affairs to nominee                                 │
        │        └────────────────────────────────────────────────────┘
        │                             │
        │                             ▼
        │        ┌────────────────────────────────────────────────────┐
        │        │ Nominees report on proposal filed in court together│
        │        │ with nominee's comments (NB: these are not required│
        │        │ if L or A acts as nominee). [SIP 3 applies to report]│
        │        └────────────────────────────────────────────────────┘
        │                             │
        │                             ▼
        │        ┌────────────────────────────────────────────────────┐
        └───────▶│ Nominee calls meeting of creditors and members     │
                 │ within 28 days of the filing of the report, sending│
                 │ proposal, statement of affairs, comments (if any), │
                 │ notice of meeting, proxy and SIP 9 statement       │
                 └────────────────────────────────────────────────────┘
                                      │
                                      ▼
                 ┌────────────────────────────────────────────────────┐
                 │ Meetings of creditors and members creditors vote   │
                 │ (75%) members vote (50% +1)                        │
                 └────────────────────────────────────────────────────┘
                                      │
                                      ▼
                 ┌────────────────────────────────────────────────────┐
                 │ Chair of meeting reports results to the court      │
                 │ within four business days Supervisor sends to      │
                 │ Registrar as soon as reasonably practicable        │
                 └────────────────────────────────────────────────────┘
```

Self-test

Answer the following questions.

1 Which of the following persons may not make a proposal for a CVA?

   A   Directors
   B   Contributories
   C   Liquidator where company in liquidation
   D   Administrator where company in administration

2 Which of the following matters is the nominee not required to consider when assessing a proposal for a CVA?

   A   That it is feasible
   B   That it is an acceptable alternative to liquidation or other formal insolvency process
   C   That it is fair to the debtor and creditors
   D   That the creditors will be paid in full

3 Which of the following criteria is not required to be met when applying for a small company moratorium?

   A   Turnover no greater than £6.5m
   B   No more than 50 employees
   C   Liabilities on balance sheet no greater than £1m
   D   Assets on balance sheet no greater than £3.25m

4 Which SIP deals with Company Voluntary Arrangements?

   A   SIP 12
   B   SIP 4
   C   SIP 9
   D   SIP 3.2

5 Within how many days of receiving notice of a proposal for a CVA must the nominee file his report in court?

   A   7 days
   B   14 days
   C   21 days
   D   28 days

6 The creditors' meeting to consider a CVA must be held before the members' meeting. Within how many business days of the creditors' meeting must the members' meeting be held?

   A   Up to 5
   B   Up to 14
   C   Up to 21
   D   Up to 28

Now, go back to the Learning Objectives in the Introduction. If you are satisfied that you have achieved these objectives, please tick them off.

Answers to Self-test

1 B
2 D
3 C
4 D
5 D
6 A

Answers to Interactive questions

Answer to Interactive question 1: Fine Foods Limited

ESTIMATED OUTCOME STATEMENT
FINE FOODS LIMITED

	Workings	Creditors' Voluntary Liquidation £	Company Voluntary Arrangement £
Realisations:			
Freehold property	1	204,500	–
Machinery		30,000	–
Fixtures and fittings		14,000	–
Stock		10,000	–
Vehicles		5,000	–
Debtors		95,000	120,000
Contributions from trading	2	–	240,000
Total realisations		358,500	360,000
Less: costs			
Chattel agent's fees	3	2,950	–
Debt collection fees	4	9,500	12,000
Liquidator's remuneration		30,000	–
Nominee's fees		–	4,000
Supervisor's fees	5	–	14,000
Total costs		42,450	30,000
Assets available to creditors		316,050	330,000
Creditors			
Pay in lieu of notice		51,000	–
Redundancy		47,000	–
Trade creditors		475,000	375,000
		573,000	375,000
Return to creditors		55p in £	88p in £

Workings/Assumptions

1. Freehold property:

	£
Realisations	300,000
Less agent's fees @ 1.5%	(4,500)
legal fees @ 2%	(6,000)
satby Bank plc	(85,000)
	204,500

2. Contributions from trading:

   £5,000 x 12 x 4 years = £240,000

3. Chattel agents fees:

   Realisations £59,000 @ 5% = £2,950

4. Debt collection fees:

   Realisations   95,000 @ 10% = £9,500
                     120,000 @ 10% = £12,000

5. Supervisor's fees:

   3,500 x 4 years = £14,000

Answer to Interactive question 2: Mayflower Limited

A company voluntary arrangement is an agreement between the company and the creditors in satisfaction of the company's debts.

- The advantages of a CVA are:
    - Directors retain control of the company (albeit under the supervision of the supervisor).
    - No D forms completed.
    - Possible survival of the company as a going concern.
    - Binds all creditors at the date of the meeting.
    - No notice required on letterhead, helps preserve goodwill.
    - Lower costs than liquidation, better returns to creditors.

The disadvantages of a CVA are:

- Supervisor has no power to claw back assets under s238, s239 and s244.
- If arrangement fails, liquidation is likely to be the only remaining course of action.
- Unlike an IVA, a CVA does not have moratorium as an intrinsic part of the procedure and it is only available to small companies.
- Act of notifying creditors of the CVA may precipitate a run on the assets.
- Secured and preferential creditors must consent to any modification of their rights.

The directors have two options to protect the company's assets:

- Petition for an administration order:
    - This will give the benefit of an automatic moratorium
    - Directors can appoint administrator without going to court
    - CVA could be the purpose of the administrator's proposals
    - Additional costs, directors lose control of the company

- Obtain a small company moratorium:
    - Must meet two out of the following three criteria:
        1. Turnover no greater than £6.5m
        2. Assets on balance sheet no greater than £3.26m
        3. No more than 50 employees in the relevant period
    - Also, company will be excluded if at the date of filing:
        1. Administration order is in force
        2. Company is being wound up
        3. An administrative receiver has been appointed
        4. A CVA is in force
        5. A provisional liquidator has been appointed
        6. Either an administrator or a moratorium has been in force in the previous 12 months and a CVA came to a premature end or no CVA had effect.

- The requisite majorities required to approve a CVA are:
    - Three-quarters or more of the votes cast at the creditors' meeting to approve or modify the proposal
    - Simple majority to approve any other resolution
    - A simple majority of votes cast at the members meeting
    - Any resolution is invalid if a simple majority of notified, valid, non connected creditors vote against it

CHAPTER 14

Introduction to administrations

Introduction
Topic List
   1 Introduction to administrations
Summary and Self-test
Answers to Self-test

Introduction

Learning objectives

- Explain the purpose and effects of administration
- Describe and explain the role and remuneration of the administrator

Tick off

Stop and think

What are the benefits of administration? How does it differ to a company voluntary arrangement? Why are companies entering into administration rather than administrative receivership?

Working context

Since the introduction of a new administration procedure on 15 September 2003 (which coincided with a restriction on secured creditors to appoint an AR) many more companies have entered into administration. It is likely therefore that in a work environment you will be asked to assist in an administration. An understanding of the purposes and benefits of administration is therefore important.

1 Introduction to administrations

> **Section overview**
>
> - A new administration procedure came into effect on 15 September 2003. The reforms were designed to make administration with its emphasis on rescuing companies the primary recovery procedure for floating charge holders. However, as we have mentioned in this Manual already administrative receivership remains an option for those charge holders with pre 15 September 2003 debentures/charges. Although administration is often sought by floating charge holders, other creditors and the company/directors, can also seek administration for the company. In this chapter we focus on the advantages of administration (as compared with administrative receivership) and the procedure to place a company into liquidation. We will see that there are both 'out of court' and 'court appointment' routes into administration. The statutory legislation governing administrations is found in Schedule B1 of the Act and Part 2 of the Rules (R2.1 – R2.132). If you need to review the law relating to floating charges see Chapter 5.

1.1 Role of the administrator

Administration provides an alternative to winding-up so that where possible, the company or at least its business, can be rescued.

The administrator must try to rescue the company although if this is not reasonably practicable he or she can pursue a more modest objective such as a better outcome for creditors generally than in winding-up. (See the para 3 objectives below.)

The administrator takes over the management of the company and drafts proposals for achieving the purpose of the administration. These proposals must in most circumstances be put to the creditors for their approval.

The administrator must act in the interests of creditors generally. As an 'officer of the court' the administrator owes duties of (fairness) to the creditors. The Insolvency Act requires him or her to perform his duties as quickly and efficiently as possible.

1.2 Purpose of administration (the para 3 objectives)

The purposes of administration are set out in para 3(1) of Schedule B1 to the Act. These purposes are hierarchical.

- Purpose (1)(a) is 'rescuing the company as a going concern'. The administrator must perform his functions with this objective unless he thinks either that:
    - It is not reasonably practicable to rescue the company as a going concern; or
    - The objective in sub-paragraph (1)(b) would achieve a better result for the creditors as a whole.

- Purpose (1)(b) is 'achieving a better result for the company's creditors as a whole than would be likely if the company were wound up (without first being in administration)'.

- Purpose (1)(c) 'realising property in order to make a distribution to one or more secured or preferential creditors' may only be pursued if:
    - The administrator thinks that it is **not** reasonably practicable to achieve either objective (1)(a) or (1)(b)
    - It does not unnecessarily harm the interests of the creditors of the company as a whole

- Crystallisation and/or mitigation of company debts where there is shareholder discord does not in its own right give grounds to one of the three objectives.

- Achieving the approval of a CVA or the sanctioning of a s895 CA 06 Scheme of Arrangement are not statutory purposes of administration. However, both procedures can still be used by the administrator as techniques to aid in achieving any of the three specified objectives.

- The objective in para 3(1)(c) (realisation followed by distributions to secured/preferential creditors) may prove useful to administrators appointed by QFC holders, where there are insufficient assets to pay a dividend to unsecured creditors.

The administrator must perform his functions in the interests of the company's creditors as a whole.

1.3 Who may appoint an administrator?

Out of court appointments

Out of court routes to appoint an administrator (the company will then be 'in administration') are available to the following:

- Qualifying floating charge holders (QFCH) under para 14 Schedule B1
- The directors (under para 22 but subject to para 25 Schedule B1 – see below)
- The company

Creditors (other than qualifying floating charge holders) may only put a company into administration by applying to the court.

Para 25 Schedule B1 provides that an administrator cannot be appointed out of court by the directors or the company where:

- A petition for winding up has been presented and has not yet been disposed of
- An application to court for an administration order has been made and has not yet been disposed of
- An administrative receiver (AR) of the company is in office

The company must not be in compulsory liquidation nor must a provisional liquidator have been appointed.

Court appointed administrator

Application to court for an 'administration order' may be made by the following or by any combination of them (Para12(2) Schedule B1):

- The company
- The directors
- Justices chief executive for a magistrates court (this is in relation to enforcement of fines against a company)
- One or more creditors of the company
- The supervisor of a CVA (S7(4)(b))
- A liquidator where the company is in voluntary or compulsory liquidation(Para 38 Schedule B1)
- A qualifying floating charge holder where the company is in compulsory winding up
- The Financial Services Authority (FSA) under s359 Financial Services and Markets Act 2000 (FSMA 00)

The court cannot make an administration order where an Administrative Receiver ('AR') is in office unless the:

- Appointing debenture holder consents; or
- If an administration order were made, a charge (or charges) is likely to be voidable under either the transaction at an undervalue, preference, or invalid floating charge provisions of the Act. (See Chapter 9 for further details of the law relating to antecedent transactions.) This is a judgment which must be made by the court hence the need for the directors to apply rather than relying on their para 22(1) power to appoint an administrator out of court.

[See Chapter 15 for the detailed procedure to appoint an administrator.]

1.4 Advantages/disadvantages of administration (compared with administrative receivership)

- **Ease of appointment.** An administrator can be appointed post 15 September 2003 by filing certain documentation with the court. This includes provision for filing out of court hours in cases of urgency by faxing/emailing documents to a designated fax number or email address. Consequently administration is now a relatively cheap, quick and speedy process sharing many of the initiation advantages of administrative receivership. None-the-less the filing requirements in administration are more onerous than the simple procedure to appoint an AR. Also, unlike an administrator an AR can be appointed whether or not the company is in liquidation. An AR appointment can still be made where an administration moratorium has been obtained in the previous 12 months.

- **Publicity.** There may be less reputational risk in appointing an administrator as opposed to an AR in that the administrator acts for all the creditors and may be less linked in the public eye with the appointing bank than a receiver would be. This may be important where the charge holder is seeking to avoid any perception of 'pulling the plug' on a company in which there is significant local or public interest (eg a pensions provider or football club).

- **EC Regulation.** Administrations are recognised under the EC Regulation while administrative receiverships are not. Where there are assets located in other EU jurisdictions and where the IP wishes to exercise his or her powers in those territories administration has the advantage that the regulation requires overseas courts to co-operate with the IP.

- **Collective dealing.** Where there are multiple floating charge holders it may be easier for the holder of the senior charge to appoint an administrator rather than for all the charge holders to negotiate for a single AR to represent their collective interests.

- **Moratorium.** An administrator has the benefit of a moratorium while an AR does not. In cases where the company depends on leased or HP equipment this will provide a useful breathing space in which the administrator can arrange for the continued financing of the various contracts.

- **Powers.** An administrator has the same powers to trade, manage and sell the business as a going concern as an AR. Where such a sale is likely and the charge holder's security covers the amount due, the charge holder may be content to allow the directors to appoint an administrator.

- **Liability of charge holder.** A charge holder has no potential liability to indemnify an administrator. There may be such a liability where an AR has succeeded in negotiating an indemnity with the appointing debenture holder.

- **Exit routes.** There are many flexible exit routes out of administration, however administration only lasts for 12 months (initially). There is no statutory time limit on administrative receivership.

- **Status.** An administrator is an officer of the court who owes duties to the court and to creditors generally. This is so notwithstanding that the administrator is appointed out of court, and by a qualifying charge holder. An AR on the other hand has:

    - A primary duty to realise charged assets so as to repay the principal debt with interest to the appointer
    - A duty to pay preferential creditors in priority to the floating charge holder
    - Only a duty of due diligence to unsecured creditors and guarantors of the company's debt. An AR owes no duty to unsecured creditors or to the company to delay a sale in the hope of a better price

- **Choice of IP.** The new administration procedure is designed to ensure that the floating charge holder gets their choice of IP but it is probably fair to say that it is easier for unsecured creditors to secure the removal of an administrator (and his replacement by another IP) than it would be in administrative receivership. For instance where the creditors reject the administrator's proposals the court has wide powers including replacement of the administrator. Also creditors entitled to appoint ARs can 'veto' the appointment of an administrator – Para 26 Schedule B1.

- **Influence of charge holder.** In administrative receivership the AR will discuss the strategy for the receivership with the appointing debenture holder. In administration the debenture holder clearly influences strategy but ultimately the administrator's proposals must be approved by the body of creditors (see paragraphs 49 to 58 of Schedule B1) so that the chargeholder has less control over the process in administration than in administrative receivership.

- **Impact of statutory purpose.** The AR and charge holder are not constrained by any statutory purposes. In administration the statutory objective is in the first instance to rescue the company (although this can be superseded by more modest objectives where the administrator believes this to be advantageous). The AR could adopt a strategy for instance of selling the assets and undertaking and subsequently arranging for the liquidation of the shell of the company that is left behind.

- **Tax.** Corporation tax on a capital gain is an ordinary unsecured debt in administrative receivership but will rank as an expense in administration and consequently will be paid out before any return to creditors.

- **Moratorium.** Available in administration but not administrative receivership.

- **Other considerations.**
    - Administrator can retain, appoint and remove directors from office.
    - An administrator can challenge voidable/antecedent transaction such as preferences an AR cannot.
    - Will have to submit 'D' forms on directors' conduct (as will an AR).
    - Administrator cannot be appointed once an AR is in office unless by consent.
    - Although a cheaper procedure than it used to be CVAs and administrative receivership are still generally cheaper than administration.
    - Like tax, business rates and rent (where property is occupied by the administrator) are expenses of the administration.

1.5 Status and duties of the administrator

- The administrator must be a qualified insolvency practitioner (para 6 of Schedule B1, and also see s388(1)(a)).

- The administrator is an officer of the court (para 5 of Schedule B1) and this is irrespective of whether he or she is appointed by the court or out of court. As an officer of the court the administrator owes duties to both the court and to creditors generally, and in particular is required to act fairly and impartially in dealing with creditors.
    - *Oldham v Kyrris 2003* – the administrator owes his duties to the company and to the general body of creditors and not to any individual creditor.
    - *Re Atlantic Computers* details the administrators duties as an officer of the court in dealing with applications by creditors with proprietary rights for leave to repossess goods or enforce their security (see the section on the moratorium in Chapter 15).

- Para 3(1) of Schedule B1 provides that the administrator must perform his functions with the three objectives listed in that paragraph (see para 1.2 above). The administrator must perform his functions in the interests of the creditors of the company as a whole (para 3(2)). Note however that this duty is modified where the para 3(1)(c) objective is being pursued, which envisages only secured or preferential creditors being paid.

- An administrator must perform his functions as quickly and efficiently as is reasonably practicable para 4 of Schedule B1.

- On appointment the administrator must take custody or control of all the property to which he thinks the company is entitled (para 67 of Schedule B1).

- The administrator must manage the affairs, business and property of the company in accordance with the proposals for achieving his para 3 objective (whether as originally approved or later revised).

- The administrator must comply with any court directions.

- The administrator must submit a D Return on the conduct of directors.

- The administrator must publicise his appointment (see Chapter 15 for details).
- The administrator must request a Statement of Affairs (see Chapter 15 for details).
- To make a statement setting out his proposals for achieving the purpose of administration (see Chapter 15 for details).
- The administrator must call a meeting of creditors to consider his proposals (see Chapter 15 for details).
- An administrator has a statutory power to make distributions to secured and preferential creditors.

1.6 Powers of the administrator

1 An administrator has a general power to do anything necessary or expedient for the management of the affairs, business and property of the company (para 59(1) of schedule B1).

2 The administrator has the same Schedule 1, IA 86 powers to trade and manage the business as an administrative receiver.

3 Other general powers of an administrator are to:

- Remove a director of the company and to appoint a director to the board of the company (para 61) the existing directors may be retained to conduct the day to day management of the company

  (Note. Officers can only exercise management powers with the consent of the administrator)

- Call a meeting of members or creditors
- Apply to the court for directions
- Make a distribution:
  - To secured or preferential creditors
  - Under SBEEA 2015, to an ordinary unsecured creditor. Application to Court is no longer necessary.

4 To dispose of floating charge assets as if they were not subject to the charge. The charge holder will have the same priority in respect of the 'acquired' property as he had in respect of the property disposed of. 'Acquired' property means property directly or indirectly representing the property disposed of.

5 Paragraph 71 B1 applies to security other than floating charge security. The administrator is empowered to apply to the court for an order to enable him to dispose of the (fixed) charge property. However:

- The disposal must be likely to promote the purpose of the administration
- It must be a condition of the order that the charge holder receives the net proceeds of sale, plus any additional money so as to produce the amount determined by the court as the net market value of the property.

6 The administrator has a similar power in para 72 schedule B1 to apply to the court for an order authorising disposal of 'goods' under an 'HP agreement'. Para 111 defines 'HP agreement' as including a conditional sale, chattel leasing or ROT agreement.

7 An administrator has similar powers to bring actions against directors and others as a liquidator. Administrators are **not** empowered to bring actions under s212 (Misfeasance), or s216 (Phoenix Companies), although these provisions will become available if a company in administration is subsequently liquidated. The SBEEA2015 made it possible for the administrator to pursue wrongful and fraudulent trading claims.

Administrator can challenge transactions at undervalue (s238), preferences (s239), extortionate credit transactions (s244), s245 floating charges and s423 transactions defrauding creditors. For ss238, 239 and 245 the 'relevant time' is calculated as follows.

- In appointments out of court from the date of filing of notice of intention to appoint an administrator. In addition the period between filing of this notice and the appointment of the administrator is also a relevant time.

- If there is no QFCH and therefore no need to serve notice of intention to appoint, the date of the appointment of an administrator will be taken.
- In cases where an application to court for an administration order is made, the date of application is taken. Again the period between the application and the order is also a relevant time.

Administrators may use the statutory powers contained in ss234–237 (regarding getting in the company's property and enforcing co-operation) to ensure the compliance of the directors and others.

8 An administrator has the power in s233 to require supplies from a utility company.

9 As agent of the company the administrator can bind the company to contracts with third parties.

Summary and Self-test

Summary

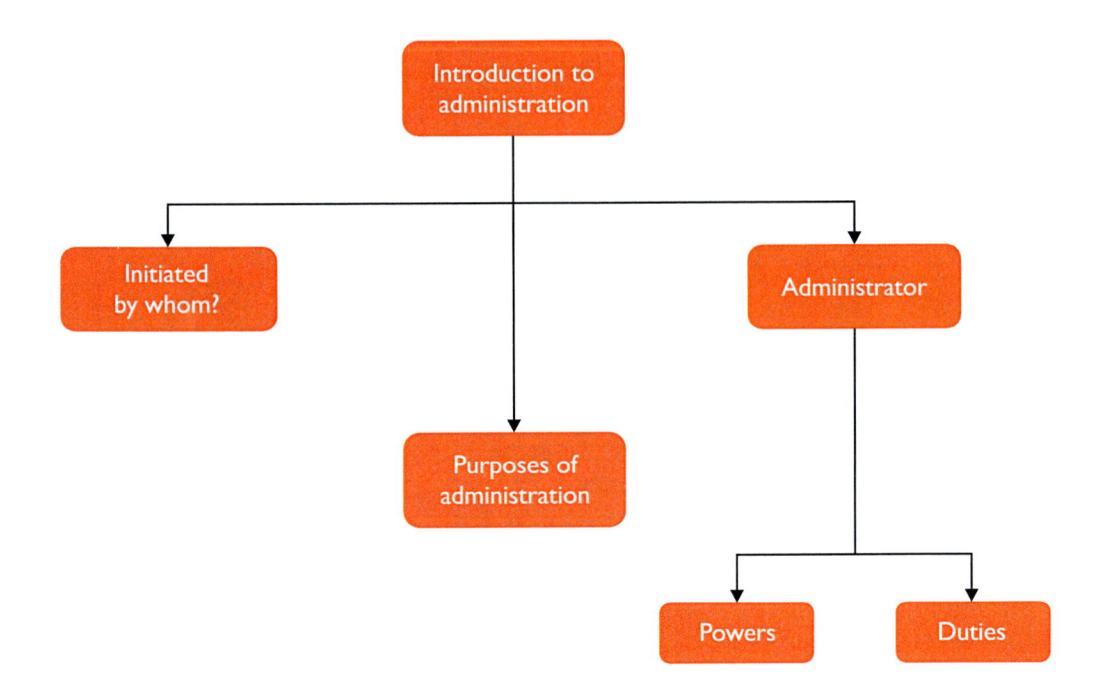

```
                    ┌─────────────────────┐
                    │   Introduction to   │
                    │    administration   │
                    └──────────┬──────────┘
          ┌────────────────────┼────────────────────┐
          ▼                    ▼                    ▼
   ┌─────────────┐     ┌─────────────┐      ┌─────────────┐
   │  Initiated  │     │ Purposes of │      │Administrator│
   │  by whom?   │     │administration│     └──────┬──────┘
   └─────────────┘     └─────────────┘            │
                                         ┌────────┴────────┐
                                         ▼                 ▼
                                   ┌──────────┐      ┌──────────┐
                                   │  Powers  │      │  Duties  │
                                   └──────────┘      └──────────┘
```

Self-test

Answer the following questions.

1. Which of the following is not a para 3(1) purpose of administration?

    A   Realise property in order to make a distribution to one or more secured or preferential creditors

    B   Rescue the company as a going concern

    C   Achieve a better result for the creditors as a whole than would be likely if the company were wound up

    D   Achieve approval of a CVA

2. Which of the following powers does the administrator not have?

    A   To make a distribution to secured or preferential creditors
    B   To trade and manage the business
    C   To bring an action for misfeasance under s212
    D   To require supplies from utilities under s233

3. Which of the following persons may not make an application for an administration order?

    A   Liquidator of the company
    B   Administrative receiver of the company
    C   The holder of a qualifying floating charge
    D   A contingent creditor of the company

4. Which Schedule of the Act deals with the powers of the administrator?

    A   Sch 5
    B   Sch 2
    C   Sch 4
    D   Sch 1

5. In what order are the purposes of administration set out in para 3(1) of Schedule B1 of the Act?

6. What is the status of the administrator in relation to the company?

Now, go back to the Learning Objectives in the Introduction. If you are satisfied that you have achieved these objectives, please tick them off.

Answers to Self-test

1. D
2. C
3. B
4. D
5. Purpose (1)(a) – rescuing the company as a going concern.

   Purpose (1)(b) – achieving a better result for the company's creditors as a whole than would be likely if the company were wound up (without first being in administration).

   Purpose (1)(c) – realising property in order to make a distribution to one or more secured or preferential creditors.

   Remember the order is important as the purposes of administration are hierarchical.

6. The company's agent.

CHAPTER 15

Procedure for administration

Introduction
Topic List
1. Out of court appointments
2. Appointments by the court (para 12)
3. The moratorium
4. Steps to be taken by an administrator after appointment

Appendix 1
Summary and Self-test
Answers to Self-test

Introduction

Learning objectives

- Explain the processes involved in the commencement of an administration
- Describe the on-going obligations upon the insolvency practitioner in an administration
- Describe and explain the following aspects of administration
    - The moratorium
    - Notice and advertising requirements
    - Proposals
    - Meetings

Stop and think

Why can administration be initiated by a number of different people? Why is the court not involved in all applications for an administration order? Who needs to be notified of an application for an administration order?

Working context

You may be asked to assist with preparing notices to creditors, putting together a Statement of Affairs, ensuring that the statutory provisions re the administration process are adhered to.

1 Out of court appointments

Section overview

- Out of court appointments may be made by qualifying floating charge holders and directors of the company. There are some restrictions on out of court appointments, they cannot for example, be made for insurance companies, although they can be made in respect of a bank. Any references to para numbers can be found in Schedule B1 IA 86 unless otherwise stated.

1.1 Out of court appointments by qualifying floating charge holders (QFCH) (Para 14)

Summary of procedure to appoint administrator under para 14 (see detail below).

Step 1	Check that floating charge is a QFC and pre-conditions in the Act are met.
Step 2	Give 2 business days' notice of intention to appoint to any prior QFCH (or obtain consent in writing) and file at court. Interim moratorium now in place.

Step 3	- Appointment of administrator can proceed.
	- File necessary documentation at court:
	  – Notice of appointment
	  – A statutory declaration
	  – The administrator's statement
	- Administrator now appointed and full moratorium in place.

1.1.1 What is a QFC and a QFCH?

The concept of whether a creditor is a qualifying floating charge holder (QFCH) is important. There are two areas of the statute to consider.

1. The charge must be a qualifying floating charge (QFC).

    Under para 14 (1) Sch B1 a floating charge is a qualifying floating charge if the legal document that created it contains a provision that:

    – Para 14 (1) applies to the floating charge; or
    – It purports to give the floating charge holder the power to appoint an administrator; or
    – It purports to give the floating charge holder the power to appoint an Administrative Receiver.

2. The holder of the qualifying floating charge will be a QFCH if the charge gives security over the whole or substantially the whole of the company's property, or the qualifying floating charge together with other charges or forms of security, give security over the whole or substantially the whole of the company's property.

1.1.2 Pre-conditions to appoint

Assuming that a charge holder is a QFCH and the pre-conditions specified in the Act are satisfied the QFCH will be able to appoint an administrator out of court. The pre-conditions are as follows:

1. The floating charge on which the appointment relies must be enforceable. On normal principles this means that there has been default under the terms of the debenture/charge. For default to be established in respect of an overdraft the charge holder must show that time to repay has been given and a demand for repayment not satisfied.

    Note. There is no requirement for the company to be unable to pay its debts, ie be insolvent, on a QFCH administration.

2. The company must not already be in administration (para 7) – subject to provisions allowing for replacement administrators.
3. The company must not be in administrative receivership (para 17(b)).
4. No provisional liquidator must have been appointed (para 17(a)).
5. The company must not be in liquidation (voluntary or compulsory) (para 8(1)).

1.1.3 Procedure to appoint an administrator

Notice of Intention to appoint

- The QFCH must give at least two business days' notice to any prior QFCH or obtain their consent in writing. On usual principles a qualifying floating charge is 'prior' either because its floating charge was created first or because a deed of priority so provides.

  The idea is to always give the most senior floating charge holder the opportunity to take the initiative and appoint its own choice of IP as administrator. The prior QFCH holder may now take one of the following steps.

    - Consent to the appointment of an administrator by the QFCH who served notice on them.
    - Do nothing in which case the serving QFCH will be entitled to appoint an administrator at the expiry of the two days.
    - Take steps to appoint their own choice of administrator.

- A copy of the notice ('notice of intention to appoint') must at the same time be filed in court.

- Filing the notice in court (form 2.5B) triggers an interim moratorium which lasts until an administrator is actually appointed (or for five business days if no administrator appointed).

Notice of appointment

- The QFCH files in court three copies of a notice of appointment. The notice of appointment must include a statutory declaration which must have been made not more than five business days before being filed in court. The statutory declaration must state that:

    - The appointer of the administrator is a QFCH
    - Each floating charge relied on in making the appointment is or was enforceable on the date of the appointment
    - The appointment is compliant with Schedule B1 IA86

- The notice of appointment must identify the administrator and must be accompanied by a (Form 2.2B) statement by the administrator that:

    - He consents to the appointment
    - In his opinion the purpose of the administration is likely to be achieved
    - Details of any prior professional relationship with the company

- The court will now seal the notices of appointment and endorse them with the date and time of filing. It will issue two sealed copies to the appointer who will give one to the administrator as soon as is reasonably practicable.

1.2 Out of hours appointments

When the court is closed a QFCH can still appoint by faxing the notice of appointment to a designated fax number that may be found on the Insolvency Service website (not the local court fax) or by emailing it to a designated email address. The appointment takes effect from the date and time of the fax transmission or email. Paper copies together with a statement providing full reasons for the out of hours filing must then be filed at court on the next day that the court is open for business. Failure to comply with the requirement of the rules (R2.19) will mean that the administrator's appointment will lapse.

1.3 Out of court appointments by directors or the company (para 22)

Summary of procedure to appoint administrator under para 22 (see detail below).

Step 1	Check that restrictions on appointing an administrator do not apply.
Step 2	Give 5 business days' notice of intention to appoint to any QFCH able to appoint either an administrative receiver or an out of court administrator. Notice must also be given to those specified in Rule 2.20. (See para 1.2.2 below).
Step 3	To obtain an interim moratorium the directors must file the necessary documentation in court: • Notice of intention to appoint • A statutory declaration • Accompanying resolutions
Step 4	Assuming that the QFCH does not intervene and the five business days have either expired or the QFCH has consented to the appointment, the directors will file the necessary documentation in court: • Notice of appointment • A statutory declaration • The administrator's statement The administrator now appointed and full moratorium now in place.

1.3.1 Restrictions on power to make an appointment

- **As with** QFCHs, directors/the company may not appoint an administrator in the following circumstances.
    - The company is already in administration (subject to the provisions re replacement administrators)
    - The company is in liquidation (either voluntary or compulsory)
    - An administrative receiver (AR) of the company is already in office
- **Unlike** QFCHs directors/the company may also not appoint an administrator where:
    - The company has been in administration in the previous 12 months
    - A CVA small company moratorium was obtained in the previous 12 months and no CVA came into force, or the CVA ended prematurely
    - A petition for winding-up has been presented and is not yet disposed of although it does not preclude an appointment where the petition is presented after the notice of intention has been issued unless the petition is presented on public interest grounds
    - An administration application has been made and is not yet disposed of

Note. In the last three cases the directors/company retain their right to apply to the court for administration order – they are simply unable to achieve the appointment out of court.

1.3.2 Procedure to appoint

Notice of Intention to appoint

- Under para 26 the directors/company must give five business days' notice of their intention to appoint a named administrator to any person entitled to appoint an administrative receiver or an administrator under para 14 (ie any QFCH). The intention here is to give the holder the opportunity to intervene at this stage and appoint their own choice of IP as administrator or to appoint an administrative receiver (where the floating charge was created pre 15 September 2003).

    Additionally notice must be given under Rule 2.20 to:
    - Any enforcement officer charged with execution or other legal process against the company
    - Any person who has exercised CRAR against the company or its directors

- Any supervisor of a CVA
- The company (assuming it is the directors and not the company which is proposing to make the appointment)

Failure to give proper notice to the company will render the appointment invalid. Rule 2.8 specifies that service can be effected by delivering the documents to the company's registered office.

- The directors/company file a copy of the notice of intention to appoint together with any documents accompanying it in court (para 27(1)). The notice of intention will be accompanied by a statutory declaration and the requisite resolution. If the appointment is by the directors, a valid board resolution authorising the appointment will be needed or if the appointment is by the company, a resolution of the members in General Meeting authorising named shareholders to appoint an administrator.

    The statutory declaration (made not more than five business days pre-filing) by the directors/company must state (para 27(2)):

    - Company is or is likely to become unable to pay its debts
    - Company is not in liquidation
    - Appointment is not prevented by any of the restrictions on the power to make an appointment see para 1.2.1

    An interim moratorium now comes into effect.

- The directors/company may not make an appointment:
    - Until the five business days' notice to QFCHs mentioned above has expired
    - Not after 10 business days beginning with the day of filing of the notice of intention to appoint in court (para 28(2)). (During this period an interim moratorium is in place.)

    If there are no QFCHs entitled to appoint an AR or administrator, no notice of intention need be filed and the directors/company can go straight to the next stage.

Notice of appointment

- Directors/company now file three copies of a notice of appointment in court (para 29(1)(a)):
    - Prescribed Form 2.9B must be used, unless no notice of intention to appoint was served in which case Form 2.10B is used (and includes the statutory declaration which normally accompanies the notice of intention to appoint). (Notice of intention to appoint is not needed where there is no QFCH)
    - The notice must identify the administrator
    - The notice includes a statutory declaration by the appointer (made not more than five business days pre filing of notice by R2.24) stating that:
        (i) Appointer entitled to make a para 22 appointment
        (ii) Appointment is in accordance with Schedule B1
        (iii) So far as the appointer is able to ascertain the statements made and information given in the statutory declaration filed with the notice of intention to appoint remain accurate

- Also filed with notice of appointment:
    - Administrators statement in Form 2.2B (consents to appointment and purpose of administration likely to be achieved)
    - Written consents of QFCHs unless the five business days' notice period has expired
    - A statement re joint administrator appointments
    - Copy board resolution/general meeting resolution authorising the appointment of an administrator (only where no notice of intention to appoint filed first)

The court will now seal the notices of appointment and endorse them with the date and time of filing. It will issue two sealed copies to the appointer who will give one to the administrator as soon as is reasonably practicable.

2 Appointments by the court (para 12)

> **Section overview**
>
> - For an order to be made by the court the company must not already be in administration and subject to certain exceptions, voluntary liquidation or compulsory liquidation. The company must be, or be unlikely to be, able to pay its debts and the administration must be likely to achieve one of the para 3 objectives.

Summary of procedure to appoint administrator under para 12 (see detail below)

Step 1	Company, directors, or creditor(s) file application to court in prescribed form accompanied by supporting documents.
Step 2	Court fixes a date and time for hearing and returns copies for service. Interim moratorium now in place.
Step 3	Copies of application and supporting documents duly served and certificate of service filed at court.
Step 4	Court hears the application and either makes the order or dismisses the application.
Step 5	Depending upon the outcome above the administration commences with a full moratorium.

2.1 Restrictions on power to make an appointment

Para 8(1) provides that a person may not be appointed as administrator of a company which is in compulsory or voluntary liquidation. However this is subject to the exceptions in paras 37-38:

Para 37 – A QFCH may make an administration application where the company is in compulsory liquidation. If the court makes the administration order, it must discharge the winding up order.

Para 38 – The liquidator of a company in liquidation may make an administration application.

2.2 Procedure to be followed

Application to the court

- The application to the court for an administration order must be supported by a proposed administrator's written statement attached to the application stating:
    - That the IP consents to the appointment
    - Details of any prior professional relationships
    - The IP's opinion that it is reasonably likely that the purpose of the administration will be achieved
- Application must be accompanied by a witness statement in support (R2.2(1)). Who swears the witness statement depends upon the particular circumstances that apply to the company.
    - Where the application is made by the company or its directors – one director or the company secretary will make the witness statement on behalf of the board or the company as appropriate.
    - Where the application is made by the creditors there is no restriction on who can make the witness statement providing that they are authorised to do so and duly state why they have knowledge of the matters stated in the witness statement.

- If a company is in liquidation the witness statement in support of the administration application must, in addition to the standard content of any witness statement (R2.4) give the information required by R2.11, namely:

    (i) Full details of the liquidation including name and address of the liquidator, date of appointment and by whom appointed

    (ii) Reasons why it has subsequently been considered appropriate that an application should be made

    (iii) Other matters which would in the opinion of the applicant assist the court in considering the need to make provision in respect of matters arising in connection with the liquidation

- The standard content of the witness statement under R2.4 includes:

    - A statement of the company's financial position

    - Details of any security known or believed to be held by creditors of the company, and whether in any case the security is such as to confer power on the holder to appoint an AR or to appoint an administrator and whether an AR has been appointed

    - Details of any insolvency proceedings in relation to the company

    - Whether the EC Regulation applies and if so whether the proceedings will be main (ie the Centre of Main Interests of the company 'COMI' is in the UK), or secondary or territorial (ie the COMI is in another member state)

The court sets the hearing date

- The application, administrator's statement and witness statement must be filed in court with sufficient copies for service. The court seals the copies, and endorses them with the date and time of filing and the venue for the hearing. These documents are returned to the applicant for service. The court keeps a copy for the court file.

- The application and supporting documents must now be served on the following:

    - Any person who has appointed an AR, any AR, and any person who is or may be entitled to appoint an AR or administrator under para 14

    - Any petitioner for winding-up and any provisional liquidator

    - The proposed administrator

    - Any supervisor of a CVA

    - If the application is by the creditors or a QFCH – the company

    - In addition, notice of filing of the application must be given to any enforcement officer charged with execution and any person who has exercised CRAR against the company or its property

- The applicant must file a certificate of service confirming that the above rules have been complied with at least one business day before the hearing.

- QFCHs, ARs, supervisors, the directors, the company, the applicant and the proposed administrator may all appear or be represented at the hearing. Assuming that the court makes an order the applicant will be sent two copy orders and will send one to the newly appointed administrator.

3 The moratorium

Section overview

- During the administration, the moratorium prevents secured and other creditors from exercising their rights to enforce their security, or repossess goods and so on without the permission of the administrator or the court. The moratorium provides a breathing space during which the administrator can put together a strategy to take the company forward.

3.1 The interim moratorium

An interim moratorium applies in two situations. First where there has been an application to the court but the application has not yet been dealt with, or it has been granted but has not yet 'taken effect'. Second where a QFCH has filed notice of intention to appoint. An interim moratorium will come into effect and will last until the earlier of the expiry of five business days or the appointment of an administrator. This also applies to out of court appointments by the company or the directors, except that 10 business days rather than five represents the maximum duration of the interim moratorium.

The interim moratorium **does not** prevent the following actions.

- Presentation of a winding-up petition by the Financial Services Authority or by the Secretary of State on public interest grounds.

- Appointment of an AR. If an AR is appointed he can carry out his functions in the usual way, including realising the charged assets. The interim moratorium will not come into effect unless and until the appointer consents to the AR stepping down.

3.2 The full moratorium

This applies when the administration takes effect. Administration takes effect either at the time specified in the Court Order or if no time is specified when the order is made.

Impact on existing administrative receivership:

- Note that where an AR has been validly appointed and does not consent to the appointment of an administrator it will not be possible for the company to be placed into administration. However an existing AR will vacate office either because the appointer consents or because the court orders it after finding that the charge or charges on which the appointment depends are potentially voidable under ss238, 239 or 245. If removed, an AR's remuneration is charged on and paid out of any property of the company which was in his custody or control immediately before he vacated office, in priority to the appointer. 'Remuneration' includes expenses properly incurred as well as the AR's indemnity out of company assets (in relation to contracts entered into and adopted employment contracts).

- Once the company is in administration no new AR can be appointed.

Impact on other receivers:

- Receivers other than ARs, must vacate office if the administrator so requires. Even if the receiver is allowed to remain in office he will be unable to enforce the appointer's security without the consent of the administrator or the permission of the court.

Impact on winding-up:

- No resolution may be passed for winding up the company or order made. This does not apply to orders made on public interest or FSA petitions. If such a petition is presented the administrator should apply to the court for directions.

Impact on creditors with proprietary rights (unless the consent of administrator or permission of the court is obtained).

- No steps may be taken to enforce any security.

- No steps may be taken to repossess goods in the company's possession under an HP agreement. By para 111(1) this includes a conditional sale of agreement, a chattel leasing agreement and a retention of title clause.

- Landlords may not:
    - Institute or continue CRAR against the property of the company
    - Exercise a right of forfeiture by peaceable re-entry
    - Apply to the court for forfeiture (because this is a 'legal process' – see para 43(6))

No legal process including legal proceedings and executions may be instituted or continued against the company without the consent of the administrator or permission of the court. [See para 1.2 of Chapter 16 for details of how the administrator will approach the giving of consent.]

4 Steps to be taken by the administrator after appointment

> **Section overview**
> - Once appointed the administrator has a number of duties, specifically advertising his appointment, calling for a Statement of Affairs, setting out proposals for achieving the purpose of administration and convening a meeting of creditors to consider his proposals.

4.1 Give notice of appointment

The administrator must advertise his or her appointment as soon as reasonably practicable (para 46(2)(a) and R2.27(1)). The advertisement must be placed in the *London Gazette* and may be also advertised in whatever other manner the administrator thinks fit. The administrator must also give notice of appointment as soon as reasonably practicable to:

- The company
- (Having obtained a list of the company's creditors) the creditors of whose claims and addresses he is aware
- Any receiver or AR who has been appointed
- Any enforcement officer who to the administrator's knowledge is charged with execution or other legal process against the company
- Any person who to the administrator's knowledge has exercised CRAR against the company or its property
- Any supervisor of a CVA
- If there is a pending winding up petition, to the petitioning creditor
- For an existing of a qualifying permission scheme PA2004, the PPF, TPR and scheme surety

The administrator shall send notice of his appointment to the Registrar of Companies within seven days.

'Seven days' and 'as soon as reasonably practicable' are calculated from when the administrator receives from the appointer the sealed copy of the notice of appointment. In cases where an application to court is necessary the date of the administration order is taken.

In addition where the appointment is 'out of court' notice must be filed in court.

4.2 Obtain a Statement of Affairs

As soon as reasonably practicable the administrator shall, by notice, require one or more 'relevant persons' to provide a Statement of Affairs. Relevant persons are persons who are or have been officers of the company or those who in the previous year have been promoters or employees of the company or officers or employees of a corporate director of the company.

The relevant person(s) have 11 days in which to submit a Statement although the administrator has power to extend this period even after its expiry or even to revoke the demand for a Statement of Affairs altogether. The administrator may also require other 'relevant persons' to make a statement of concurrence with the statement of affairs verified by a statement of truth.

R2.30 gives the administrator the power to apply to the court for an order of limited disclosure in respect of the Statement of Affairs on the grounds that disclosure would prejudice the conduct of the administration or might reasonably be expected to lead to violence against any person. The court can order that all or part of the Statement 'shall not be filed with the Registrar of Companies'. Creditors may, on three business days' notice to the administrator, apply to court for an order of disclosure. Any such order may be subject to conditions regarding confidentiality. The administrator has a duty to apply to court for an order rescinding the original order wherever there is a change of circumstances such that the limit on disclosure is no longer necessary.

The expenses of preparing a Statement of Affairs are paid as an expense of the administration. The statement of affairs shall be filed with the registrar of companies as soon as reasonably practicable.

4.3 Prepare proposals

The proposals must, where appropriate, explain why the administrator believes that the para 3(1)(a) or (b) objectives are not achievable (para 49(2)(b)).

Para 49 specifically provides that the proposals can propose a Part 26 CA 06 Scheme of Arrangement or CVA.

The required content of the proposals are set out in Rule 2.33 and a summary of the rule is in the appendix to this chapter.

Para 73 provides that an administrator's proposals may not have any negative impact on secured or preferential creditors unless they consent.

A copy of the proposals must be sent to the Registrar of Companies and to all creditors and members of whose claim and address the administrator is aware. The proposal should be sent as soon as reasonably practicable and in any event within eight weeks from the date the company entered administration. (Administrator may apply to court for extension of time.) Under para 49 the administrator can seek an order to dispense with the need to send personal copies to members but advertise its availability instead and send only to these members that request it. As with the Statement of Affairs it is possible for a limited disclosure order to be obtained (R2.33A). Electronic delivery of the proposals is possible provided Rule 12A.11 is complied with. Also the proposals can be made available by posting on a website (R12A.12).

Note. In the recent case of Re UK Coal Operations Limited [2013], the court granted the administrators permission to dispense with the requirements to make proposals and call a creditors' meeting. On the facts there was a reasonable excuse for non compliance which was avoiding the expense of making formal proposals, sending out copies of the proposals followed by consideration of the proposals at a creditors' meeting, when by the time of the meeting the company would no longer be in administration.

4.4 Convene meeting of creditors

4.4.1 Notice of meeting

This meeting is referred to in the Act and rules as the 'initial creditors' meeting' (para 51).

The administrator's proposals must be accompanied by an 'invitation' to the initial creditors' meeting. The notice specifies the purpose of the meeting, sets out the requisite majority rules and contains a proxy form.

Note. In three situations no initial meeting of creditors to approve proposals is required and therefore no notice need be included with the proposals sent to the creditors (see para 52). These are:

- Where proposals state that the company has sufficient property to enable each creditor to be paid in full

- Where proposals state that the company has insufficient property to enable a distribution to be made to unsecured creditors (except under prescribed part rules)

- Where neither of the objectives in para 3(1)(a) or (b) can be achieved. Remember this would leave only the para (c) objective which envisages a distribution only to preferential or secured creditors – so that as in the previous paragraph – ordinary, unsecured creditors would effectively have no interest in the outcome of the administration

Even in these three circumstances the creditors (10% by value) can requisition an initial meeting of creditors. They have eight business days from the sending out of the proposals to requisition the meeting. The administrator must ensure the meeting is held within 28 days of receipt of the notice requiring the meeting. If no meeting is requisitioned the proposals are deemed approved. Notice of deemed approval must be sent to the Registrar of Companies, the court and the creditors (R2.33 (5A)).

The initial meeting must be held as soon as reasonably practicable, in any event within 10 weeks of the company going into administration. The administrator can apply under para 107 for an extension of time. The rules provide for creditors' meetings to be held remotely or by correspondence.

14 days' notice of the meeting is required. Those who should be notified are:

- All creditors known to the administrator and who had claims against the company at the date it entered administration. Any creditor who has subsequently been paid in full, does not, however, have to be notified.
- Directors or officers (including past directors or officers) whose presence at the meeting is in the administrator's opinion required.

Notice of the meeting must be placed in the *Gazette*. It may also be advertised in any other manner that the administrator thinks fit.

It is possible to apply to court to seek permission to give notice of any meeting by general advertisement rather than individually. The court will consider costs, amount of assets and the interests of creditors and members when reaching a decision.

4.4.2 Purpose of the meeting

The function of the initial meeting is to approve the administrator's proposals, together with any modifications. The rules are:

- The administrator must consent to any proposed modification (para 53(1)(b))
- The proposals, whether or not modified are approved by a simple majority in value of those present and voting in person or by proxy (R2.43(1)). However, such a resolution will be invalid if those voting against include a simple majority of notified unconnected creditors
- If the administrator's proposal includes the setting up of a CVA the 'initial meeting' can also perform the function of a s3 meeting to approve the CVA proposal but s3 approval requires 75% or more by value to vote in favour
- If a resolution approving the administrator's proposal is not passed, the chairman can adjourn the meeting for up to 14 days. The administrator should then notify the creditors of the venue of the adjourned meeting as soon as reasonably practicable (R2.34(4) & R2.35(6C) & (6D))

4.4.3 Voting at the meeting

There are detailed rules on entitlement to vote (R2.38 to 2.42):

- The deadline for proofs and proxies is 12.00 noon on the business day preceding the day of the meeting, although the chair has a discretion to allow a creditor to vote where their failure to lodge a claim on time was 'due to circumstances beyond the creditors control'.
- In quantifying a claim value, the value at the date the company went into administration is taken less any:
    - Set-off
    - Amounts paid to the creditor since that date
- Secured creditors can usually only vote for the unsecured element of their claim. However where the administrator's proposals state that there is insufficient property to pay a dividend to unsecured creditors (other than under 'prescribed part rules') and creditors have requisitioned an 'initial meeting' under Rule 2.40, at that requisitioned meeting, secured creditors will be entitled to vote for the full value of their debt without deduction of the value of their security.
- HP, chattel lease and conditional sale agreement creditors are entitled to vote for the amount due and payable to them at the date the company entered administration.
- A creditor shall not vote in respect of unliquidated or unascertained claims unless the chair agrees to put upon the debt an estimated minimum value for the purpose of entitlement to vote (R2.38(5)). The wording of this rule is as in the equivalent rule in liquidation and bankruptcy and **not** as in VAs where such claims are to be valued at a minimum of £1.
- Where a chair is in doubt regarding the validity of a claim he may require the creditor to produce documents or evidence to substantiate the claim (R2.38(3)). Where doubt persists he should allow the creditor to vote but mark the claim as 'objected to' (R2.39(3)).

    Any creditor can appeal against the chair's determination on the validity or quantum of a claim but at an 'initial' meeting only has 21 days from after the date of the meeting to do so.

4.4.4 Reporting on the outcome of the meeting

Para 53(2) requires the administrator to report the decision of the initial meeting, as soon as reasonably practicable, to:

- Every creditor and every other person who received a copy of the original proposals (this might include the members)
- The court and the Registrar of Companies
- Any creditors who did not receive notice of the meeting or of whose claim the administrator has become subsequently aware

4.4.5 The creditors' committee

A creditors' meeting may establish a creditors' committee (para 57 (1) Sch B).

The committee (if established) will consist of at least three and not more than five creditors of the company (R2.50).

The creditors' committee does not come into being and may not act until the administrator has issued a certificate of its due constitution. The certificate must be sent to the Registrar of Companies 'as soon as reasonably practicable'.

The committee may, on giving not less than seven days' notice, require the administrator to attend before it at any reasonable time, and furnish it with such information relating to the carrying out of his functions as it may reasonably require.

It is possible for meetings to be attended remotely (R12A.26). Also resolutions can be passed 'otherwise then at a meeting' eg by correspondence (R2.61).

4.5 Other duties of an administrator

These include:

- Exercising his powers in the interests of the creditors as a whole
- Complying with court directions
- Submitting a D return on the conduct of the directors
- Making statutory returns
- Maintain IP case records

4.6 Progress reports

Within one month of the expiration of six months from the date of appointment, and every subsequent six month period, the administrator must submit a copy of his progress report with his accruals based receipts and payments account to the Registrar of Companies and creditors. Electronic delivery and service by posting on a website are possible if the Rules are complied with. (See Chapter 3 for more detail.)

Appendix 1

R2.33 Content of administrator's proposals

- Details of the court where the proceedings are and the relevant court reference number.
- The full name, registered address, registered number and any other trading names of the company.
- Details relating to his appointment as administrator, including the date of appointment and the person making the application or appointment and, where there are joint administrators, details of the matters set out in para 100(2).
- The names of the directors and secretary of the company and details of any shareholdings in the company they may have.
- An account of the circumstances giving rise to the appointment of the administrator.
- If a statement of the company's affairs has been submitted, a copy or summary of it, with the administrator's comments, if any.
- If an order limiting disclosure of the statement of affairs has been made, a statement of this fact, as well as:
    - Details of who provided the statement of affairs
    - The date of the order of limited disclosure
    - The details or a summary of the details that are not subject to that order
- If a full statement of affairs is not provided, the names, addresses and debts of the creditors including details of any security held.
- If no statement of affairs has been submitted, details of the financial position of the company at the latest practicable date, a list of the company's creditors including their names, addresses and details of their debts, including any security held, and an explanation as to why there is no statement of affairs.
- The basis upon which it is proposed that the administrator's remuneration should be fixed. Additional information must be provided as per IR2015 and SIP9, if the administrator wishes to seek a resolution for remuneration on a time costs basis.
- To the best of the administrator's knowledge and belief:
    - An estimate of the value of the prescribed part and an estimate of the value of the company's net property
    - Whether, and if so why, the administrator proposes to make an application to court under s176A(5)
    - How it is envisaged the purpose of the administration will be achieved and how it is proposed that the administration will end
- Where the administrator has decided not to call a meeting of creditors, his reasons.
- The manner in which the affairs and business of the company:
    - Have, since the date of the administrator's appointment, been managed and financed, including, where any assets have been disposed of, the reasons for such disposals and the terms upon which such disposals were made
    - Will, if the administrator's proposals are approved, continue to be managed and financed
- Whether the EC Regulation applies and if so whether the proceedings are main, secondary or territorial proceedings.
- Such other information as the administrator thinks necessary to enable creditors to decide whether or not to vote for the adoption of the proposals.

From 6.4.10

- Disclose any pre-appointment costs charged or incurred by the administrator (or other IP). Full breakdown must be provided.

Summary and Self-test

Summary

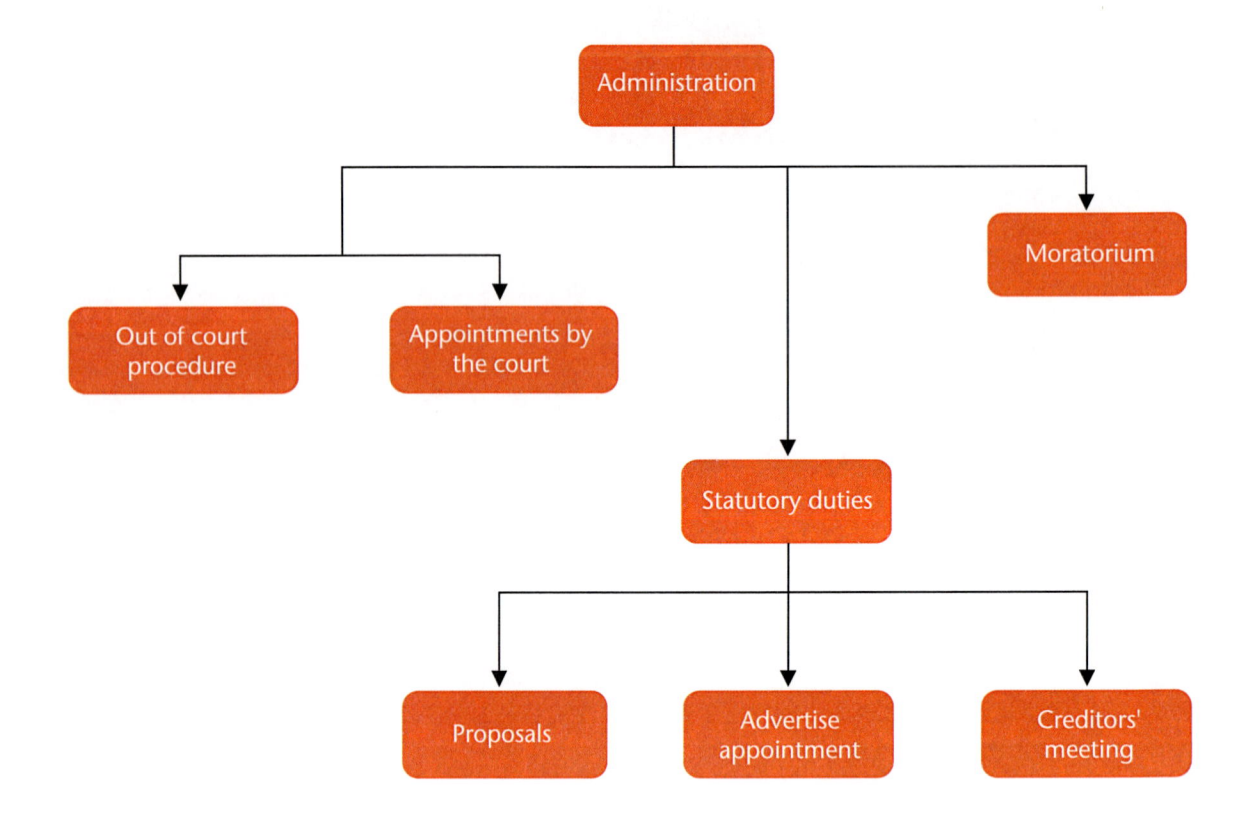

```
                    Administration
            ┌────────────┼────────────┐
            │            │            │
            ▼            ▼            ▼
       Out of court  Appointments   Moratorium
        procedure    by the court
                         │
                         ▼
                   Statutory duties
            ┌────────────┼────────────┐
            ▼            ▼            ▼
        Proposals    Advertise    Creditors'
                    appointment    meeting
```

Self-test

Answer the following questions.

1 Which of the following is not a pre-condition for a QFCH to appoint an administrator?

    A   Floating charge must be enforceable
    B   No administrative receiver must be appointed
    C   No provisional liquidator appointed
    D   Company is unable to pay its debts

2 How many business days' notice must the directors give to a QFCH of their intention to appoint a named administrator?

    A   2
    B   5
    C   7
    D   14

3 An interim moratorium is triggered by filing Form 2.5B (Notice of appointment) by a QFCH. If no administrator is appointed, for how many business days will the interim moratorium last?

    A   5
    B   7
    C   2
    D   28

4 Within how many days of his appointment must the administrator notify the Registrar of Companies?

    A   7
    B   14
    C   21
    D   28

5 Within how many weeks of the company entering administration must the administrator hold an initial meeting of the company's creditors?

    A   Within 1 week
    B   Within 2 weeks
    C   Within 5 weeks
    D   Within 10 weeks

6 Are the following statements about the appointment of an administrator true or false?

    (i)   An out of hours appointment by a QFCH is effected by faxing (or emailing) the requisite documents to the relevant court's fax (or email address).

            A   True
            B   False

    (ii)   Paper copies of the requisite documents must then be posted to the court as soon as reasonably practicable or the appointment will lapse.

            C   True
            D   False

Now, go back to the Learning Objectives in the Introduction. If you are satisfied that you have achieved these objectives, please tick them off.

Answers to Self-test

1. D
2. B
3. A
4. A
5. D
6. (i) B – documents must be sent to the designated fax number or email address, not that of the court itself.
   (ii) D – paper copies together with a statement providing full reasons for the out of hours appointment must be actually filed at the court on the next day that it is open for business.

CHAPTER 16

Implementation of administration

Introduction
Topic List
1 Implementation of administration
2 Trading on
3 Practical steps to take on appointment
4 Selling the business
5 Exiting administration

Summary and Self-test
Answers to Self-test

Introduction

Learning objectives

- Explain the processes involved in the commencement of an administration
- Describe how an individual ceases to be an administrator, through discharge, release or other exit routes
- Define 'pre-packs' and explain the relative requirements of SIP 16 and the main role of the Pre Pack Pool (PPP)

Tick off
☐
☐
☐

Stop and think

Why is there more than one way to exit an administration? Why does the administrator only have the power to pay dividends to secured and preferential creditors? How are dividends paid to unsecured creditors?

Working context

This is a very practical chapter. It is likely that in a work environment you will be asked to work on matters dealt with in this chapter, for example dealing with creditors who have made retention of title claims or putting together a sales pack.

1 Implementation of administration

Section overview

- Once the company enters administration, the administrator takes over responsibility for running the company and a proposal is put together for the agreement of the creditors. A moratorium comes into force which has the effect of preventing creditors of the company taking enforcement action against the company.

1.1 Effect of administration moratorium

- Any administrative receiver will vacate office.
- Receivers, other than administrative receivers, must vacate office if the administrator requires it.
- No resolution may be passed for the winding up of the company.
- No order may be made for the winding up of the company.
- No steps may be taken to enforce security.
- No steps may be taken to repossess goods in the company's possession under a Hire Purchase agreement, chattel leasing agreement or retention of title agreement.
- Landlords may not:
    - Institute or continue CRAR against property of the company
    - Exercise a right of forfeiture by peaceable re-entry except with the consent of the administrator or leave of the court
- No legal process, including legal proceedings and executions, may be instituted or continued against the company without the consent of the administrator or permission of the court

1.2 Application by creditors for permission to enforce security

Creditors with proprietary rights may continue with an action if the court or the administrator allows it. In dealing with such application the administrator should follow the guidelines set down in *Re: Atlantic Computers* and consider whether the court would be likely to give permission (see below). The administrator is an officer of the court, therefore when a creditor applies to him for permission he should:

- Act speedily (if necessary making an interim decision – eg retaining the goods/machinery etc but meeting current payments as an expense of administration)
- Act "responsibly"
- Not use the moratorium as a bargaining tool
- Give succinct reasons for his/her decision

How do the courts deal with applications? General matters.

- Court will not adjudicate on disputes on the existence or validity of security, unless it concerns a simple point of law which it is convenient to decide
- Onus is on the applicant for permission to make out their case
- The court considers all relevant matters including the conduct of the parties
- The court has a broad discretion unfettered by rules of rigid application

If granting permission is unlikely to impede the achievement of the para 3 purpose – permission should normally be granted.

If granting permission will impede achieving the para 3 purpose, the court must carry out a 'balancing exercise'.

- Court/administrator balance the legitimate interests of the applicant against the interests of the creditors generally.
- Great importance is attached to the proprietary interests of the applicant.
    - Administration for the benefit of unsecured creditors should not be conducted at the expense of those who have proprietary rights.
    - The purpose of the power to give permission is to enable the court to relax the moratorium where it would be inequitable for the prohibition to apply.

Consequently if **significant** loss would be caused by refusal, permission will normally be granted. If **substantially** greater loss would be caused to others by granting permission which is **out of all proportion** to the loss to the applicant – permission may be refused.

In assessing losses the court will look at the financial position of the company and specifically its capacity to pay on-going interest or rental payments under the agreement.

A likely compromise for the administrator is to retain the goods equipment etc. but subject to the condition that rental and other payments during the period for which the order is in force are paid as an expense of the administration.

2 Trading on

Section overview

- The administrator's primary duty is to save the company as a going concern. This will require the administrator to continue trading the company. The practical points in this section are equally applicable to administrative receivers (AR) who continue to trade. The administrator and the AR both have the statutory power to trade the company under Schedule 1 IA 86. However the administrator enjoys the advantage of the moratorium which the AR does not. An administrator therefore has more time in which to deal with the claims of creditors with proprietary rights.

2.1 The decision to trade

1 **In the short term**

Trade will be continued in the short term in order to:

- Complete work in progress thereby increasing its value
- Protect outstanding book debts
- Provide a breathing space in which the IP can investigate the possibility of a going concern sale and if appropriate continuing to trade until it is implemented

After his appointment, the IP should ascertain:

- Whether the finished goods would be marketable
- The costs of completion
- The difference between the sale value of the raw materials and the value of the finished goods

He will assemble a cash forecast accordingly.

2 **In the longer term**

The administrator's primary duty is to save the company as a going concern. He owes a duty to all creditors generally and must ensure that the creditors are not prejudiced by the decision to continue trading.

There are advantages to trading in the longer term:

- Continuing to trade facilitates a going concern sale which should realise more for the assets than a forced sale.
- Minimises bad publicity caused by closures and job losses.
- If the IP's trading is profitable, this will enhance floating charge realisations over and above the increase in asset realisations to be obtained from a going concern sale (para 3(1)) purpose if company cannot be saved).

The decision should be based on whether continuing to trade will achieve a better financial outcome. In order to assist in making this decision the IP should:

- Prepare inventories of assets with estimated values on going concern and break up bases
- Obtain valuations of assets on going concern and break up bases
- Evaluate preferential and prior secured claims as well as claim of the appointing debenture holder
- Produce estimated outcome statements indicating whether there is a financial advantage in continuing to trade

2.2 Practical difficulties

1 **Premises**

The company may trade from leasehold premises. If rent is in arrears the landlord may have a right of forfeiture or may exercise CRAR for unpaid rent, however the moratorium will provide protection. On-going rent and business rates will be an expense of the administration.

2 **Customers and suppliers**

Generally the IP will not be liable on existing contracts. He may repudiate (terminate) such contracts.

The IP should ensure that there will be customers for the finished products and evaluate the effect of a potential lack of after sales services.

Projected sales forecasts should be prepared.

The IP must confirm that suppliers will be willing to continue supporting the company. May have to make payment of sums due to them to ensure continued supplies.

Retention of title (ROT) claims should be identified and the value of stocks subject to ROT should be evaluated. Are other suppliers available?

3 **Production capacity issues**

Will the workforce continue to support the administrator? What wage arrears are there? Employees may have to be paid by the IP to ensure continued employee co-operation. What Transfer of Undertaking (TUPE) liabilities are attached to employee contracts? This may be relevant to achieving a going concern sale. (See post for details on the application of TUPE.)

Are there any arrears on HP or leasing agreements which may result in the repossession of machinery?

The age, reliability, safety and quality of existing plant has to be assessed. Are there any health and safety issues?

Overheads – what are they and can they be reduced?

Are any hauliers claiming liens over the company's property?

4 **Management**

IP must depend on existing management as his own staff are unlikely to be specialists.

IP must assess the capability and motivation of existing management.

5 **Product and other liabilities**

IP must assess any liabilities arising from the failure (if any) of the company's products which have arisen after sale.

Does the company have all necessary licences in place?

Is the business of the company lawful?

Are there any Environmental Protection Act problems?

Does the company have all necessary planning permissions?

6 **Funding**

The IP must ensure that adequate levels of working capital are available to support ongoing trading. Obtain the continued support of the bank.

7 **Supplies of utilities**

s233 states that utility companies (suppliers of gas, water, electricity and telecommunications services) cannot make it a condition of supplying services to a company in administration that outstanding charges from before commencement of the administration be paid. They are however, entitled to demand that the administrator personally guarantees payment of future charges.

The list of those suppliers to which this can apply s233 was increased in the 2015 update of this Act.

8 **Taxation**

Corporation tax arising on profits made will be an expense of the administration.

2.3 Position of employees

- **To what extent are employees preferential?**

The position is the same as in other insolvency procedures – the first £800 of an employee's claim for unpaid remuneration **in respect of the four month period leading up to insolvency** will be preferential debt.

'Remuneration' includes:

- Wages or salary
- Time off for ante-natal care or carrying out of trades union duties
- Sick pay and statutory maternity pay
- Holiday pay for up to a six week period within 12 months of relevant date is also preferential and this is **not** subject to the £800 cap

Payments into occupational pension schemes also have preferential status. (Employer contributions for up to 12 months, employee contributions for up to 4 months.)

Employees are ordinary unsecured creditors in respect of redundancy pay, compensation for unfair dismissal, payment in lieu of notice and wrongful dismissal. Additionally protective awards made against an administrator for failing to consult properly with employees under the Trades Union Labour Relations (Consolidation) Act 1992, are also unsecured claims. (See later for role of National Insurance Fund 'NIF'.)

[Protective awards made against the company are preferential.]

- **What is the position of directors?**

Directors who are genuine employees (regardless of any shareholding) are usually treated as employees under insolvency legislation. An executive director who has an employment contract with the company and day to day management responsibilities is likely to be an employee. Non-executive directors are likely to be self-employed. (Technical Release 6 deals with this area.)

- **Administrator's liability for on-going wages?**

    The administrator must make a decision about whether or not he wants to retain employees within the first 14 days of his appointment.

    After that period he will be deemed to have adopted the employment contracts, and ongoing wages and salary will enjoy special priority as an expense of the administration. These amounts will be paid in priority to the administrator's remuneration and general expenses.

    Para 99 states what will be treated as wages and salary in this situation ('qualifying liabilities'):

    – Sums due in respect of holiday pay or payable in lien of holiday, period of absence for sickness, or other good cause

    – Sums which would constitute earnings for the purpose of social security legislation (eg wages)

    – Contributions to occupational pension schemes

    No special status is provided to:

    – redundancy payments and unfair dismissal awards
    – protective awards made against an administrator
    – wrongful dismissal/pay in lieu of notice awards

- **Pay in lieu of notice**

    – This claim will be made where the employee has been dismissed without being given proper notice or pay in lieu of notice. 'Proper notice' is the statutory minimum notice period provided for by the Employment Rights Act 1996 (ERA 1996), unless the contract of employment provides for a longer period in which case that period applies.

    Statutory minimum notice periods are as follows:

Period of continuous employment	Minimum notice
Less than 1 month	–
1 month – 2 years	1 week
2 years – less than 3 years	2 weeks
3 years – less than 4 years	3 weeks

    And so on up to a maximum of 12 weeks.

- **Redundancy:**

    Claim for a statutory redundancy payment may be made where the employee:

    – Is employed under a contract of service (as opposed to being a subcontractor employed under a contract for services)

    – Has been continuously employed for a period of two years

    – Has been dismissed and redundancy is the reason for dismissal

    Redundancy occurs when:

    – Employer ceasing or intending to cease carrying on business; or

    – The requirements for employees to carry out work of a particular kind have ceased or diminished.

    The amount of a statutory redundancy payment depends on the length of service and age of the employee and is as follows:

Age of employee	No of weeks' pay
18–21 years old	½ week per year of employment
22–40 years old	1 week per year of employment
41+ years old	1½ weeks per year of employment

    This is subject to a maximum multiplier of 30 weeks, or £14,250 (whichever if the lower.) Maximum amount per week £475.

In reality, where an administrator needs to retain employees during the administration period they are likely to be paid.

[The position in administrative receivership is very similar except that where the receiver has adopted an employment contract he will have personal liability for sums due. He can however claim an indemnity from the assets of the company.]

Non-preferential claims will form a claim against the company. The NIF will agree to pay some monies to redundant employees in respect of their claims subject to certain limits. These claims are administered by the Redundancy Payments Office (RPO). The NIF/RPO has a subrogated claim in the administration for sums paid out to employees in advance of any distribution to creditors. The amounts employees may claim are summarised below.

Claim	Preferential	Unsecured	Against NIF
Arrears of wages/ salary	Restricted to four months pre-relevant date Maximum of £800 per employee	Any excess over the preferential limits	Restricted to the eight weeks accrued pre-'appropriate' date
Holiday Pay	All accrued holiday pay is preferential	Not applicable	Restricted to six weeks accrued in the 12 months pre-appropriate date
Pay in Lieu of Notice	Not preferential	Valid claim for greater of contractual or statutory period Employee has duty to mitigate claim	Statutory (but not contractual) notice
Redundancy	Not preferential	Valid claim for greater of contractual or statutory redundancy	Statutory (but not contractual) redundancy
Occupational Pension Scheme	Restricted to employer contributions in the 12 months prior to relevant date, and employee contributions in the four months prior to relevant date	Any excess over the preferential limits	Employer contributions lowest of – 12 months' contributions – 10% of 12 months' pay – Amount certified to meet liability to pay employees pension 12 months' employee contributions

Note. The 'appropriate date' in respect of the NIF claims for arrears of wages and holiday pay is the date of appointment of the administrator. However, none of these claims can be brought unless the employees are made redundant. In respect of the NIF claim, the weeks need not be the latest weeks of employment, nor need they be consecutive, choose the eight weeks that are most beneficial to the employee.

- **Employees and administration sales**

    The Transfer of Undertakings (Protection of Employment) Regulations 2006 (TUPE) seek to protect the position of employees when ownership of a business or undertaking changes hands. This is a very complex area on which legal advice should always be sought by an IP but generally the Regulations give the following key protections to transferring employees:

    1   Protection against dismissal in connection with a TUPE transfer

    2   The obligation to inform and consult with representatives of the affected employees

3 Automatic transfer of employment contracts to the new owners

4 Restriction on the ability of the new owners to change the terms of employment of the transferring employees

The TUPE provisions are relaxed in circumstances where a transfer is in connection with a terminal (as opposed to non-terminal) insolvency procedure. Insolvent liquidation is clearly a terminal procedure administrative receivership and voluntary arrangements are not.

With regard to the position in administration it has been settled by the courts that administration is not a terminal procedure and so the employees will transfer to the buyer and have special protection against unfair dismissal. In the case of *Crystal Palace FC Ltd v Kavanagh and others*, the Court of Appeal held that dismissals made by a company of administration can, in certain circumstances, be for an economic, technical or organisational reason and therefore liability under TUPE would not pass.

3 Practical steps to take on appointment

Section overview

- There are a number of practical matters with which the administrator should deal with on his appointment. These will apply equally to an administrative receiver who is continuing to trade.

- IP should meet with directors and management
    - Advise them of his appointment and the impact that the appointment has on the business and its officers and employees
    - Obtain information about the company in order to assess the validity of continuing the operation of the business in whole or in part
    - Prepare a schedule of matters requiring urgent attention
- Assess whether or not it will be advantageous to continue to trade
- Identify potential purchasers of the business
    - Ask directors to identify interested parties
    - Possibility of a management buyout should be considered
- Obtain inventory of all assets
    - Valuations on going concern and break-up bases
    - Identify assets subject to HP
    - Ensure adequate insurance in place in respect of all potential liabilities
- Stop movement of goods, assets or stock from the premises. Carry out stock-take and implement controls over stock movements.
- Open new bank accounts. IP should have control of company cheque books and credit cards. Ensure adequate accounting records are maintained.
- Prepare detailed profit and cash flow forecasts. Identify working capital requirements.
- Review all incoming and outgoing mail. Outgoing mail and documents should contain a statement that an administrator has been appointed and should preferably be signed by the office holder or his representative.
- ROT creditors.
    - The supplier should be invited to identify the stock which is claimed to be subject to a reservation of title claim
    - Ask suppliers to compete a ROT questionnaire and submit with copies of invoices etc
    - Take legal advice on the validity of the claim

[See Chapters 2 and 10 if you need a recap on the law relating to ROT claims.]

4 Selling the business

> **Section overview**
> - The administrator's primary purpose is to sell the business as a going concern. There are a number of practical matters to be considered when selling the business to avoid claims of breach of duty. These matters will also apply to an AR. Note that both an administrator (and AR) have a statutory power to sell (Schedule 1).

4.1 Considerations on sale

- Instruct agents to prepare written valuations on alternative bases. In the case of unusual or high value property the IP may seek a second opinion.
- Consider whether the valuation can be enhanced by obtaining planning permission.
- Decide upon the mode of sale. Consider sale by auction or private treaty. If sale by auction ensure that use qualified, competent, professional auctioneers. Ensure the catalogue fully describes assets to be sold and is sufficiently circulated. Adequate viewing arrangements must be available.
- Publicity – finding a buyer.
    - Circulate details to known interested parties
    - Consider if there may be interest from competitors
    - Are the directors interested in a management buy-out 'MBO'?
    - Advertise in:
        - The FT / other newspapers
        - Specialist press
    - Other sources of intelligence:
        - The firm's database
        - The bank's database
        - Specialist agent's contacts
- A sales pack should be prepared
- When dealing with potentially interested parties:
    - All expressions of interest need to be followed up
    - May require purchaser to sign a confidentiality letter
    - Arrange for accompanied visits to premises

4.2 Sales to directors – SIP 13

The SIP ensures that office holders are familiar with the legal obligations of directors in relation to the acquisition of assets of companies and the statutory provisions relating to such acquisitions. It sets out best practice with regard to the disposal of assets to, and their acquisition by, directors and the disclosure of such transactions. Chapter 6 considers the application of the SIP in more detail.

A sale to a director amounts to a connected party transaction and should be disclosed. In administration the administrator should include in his proposals reference to any connected party transaction undertaken in the period since his appointment. If a creditors' committee is appointed, the members of the committee should be advised of any such transaction undertaken after the meeting of creditors to consider the proposals.

4.3 Pre-pack administration sales

A pre-pack administration sale involves agreeing the sale of the business before the company enters into administration. This allows the sale of the business to be completed immediately after administration is effected and should give the best deal for creditors.

The IP should ensure that a pre-pack is the best option. The directors should be advised to obtain professional valuations of the company's assets. Any offer accepted should be in line with the professional valuation so that the sale cannot be attacked at a later date as a transaction at an undervalue.

The IP should include in his proposals to creditors details of the proposed pre-pack sale.

Note that although pre-pack sales are associated with administration they can be used to effect sales in other insolvency procedures too.

4.4 SIP 16 and pre-packaged administration sales

SIP 16 was introduced in January 2009 to counter creditor concerns that pre-pack sales were not in their best interests. A revised SIP 16 was issued on 1 November 2015 to coincide with the reporting obligations on the administrator, should the purchaser choose to make an application to the PPP to determine whether the proposed sale is to be sanctioned.

The PPP is not a body for the IP and the referral of a purchaser to PPP is discretional, rather than mandatory.

SIP 16 requires IPs involved in pre-pack sales to keep detailed records of the reasoning behind the decision to undertake a pre-pack. It also requires that the IP advises their RPB, rather than the Insolvency Service who have ceased to be involved in the matter.

An administrator has the power to sell assets without prior approval from creditors or the permission of the court. However such sales may still be challenged under paras 74 and 75 as misfeasance. The administrator should ensure the powers he exercises are fulfilling the purposes of the administration to avoid such challenges.

The practitioner should make it clear they are advising the company in the pre-appointment period and not the directors personally. The directors should be encouraged to take independent legal advice especially where they are purchasing the assets of the company in the proposed sale.

Practitioners should be mindful of the risk of liability attaching to them if the company incurs credit in this pre-appointment period where there is no good reason to believe it will be repaid.

Practitioners should consider whether they have performed their functions in the interests of the company's creditors as a whole and whether they have discharged the duty to avoid unnecessarily harming the interests of creditors as a whole.

Creditors should be provided, with a detailed explanation and justification of why a pre-pack sale was undertaken so that they can be satisfied that the administrator has acted with regard for their interests.

The following information should be sent with the first notification to creditors.

Unsecured creditors need to be provided with a detailed explanation and justification of why a pre-packaged sale was undertaken as they are not given an opportunity to consider the same. The following information should be disclosed:

- The source of the administrator's initial introduction
- The extent of the administrator's involvement pre-appointment
- The alternative courses of action that were considered by the administrator with an explanation of possible financial outcomes
- Whether efforts were made to consult with major creditors and the outcome of any consultations
- Why it was not appropriate to trade the business and offer it for sale as a going concern during the administration
- Details of requests made to potential funders to fund working capital requirements
- Details of registered charges with dates of creation
- If the business or assets have been acquired from an IP within the previous 24 months or longer if the administrator deems that relevant to creditors' understanding, disclose details of that transaction and whether the administrator, his firm or associates were involved

- Any marketing activities conducted by the company and/or administrator and the outcome of those activities, or an explanation of why no marketing was undertaken
- The names and professional qualifications of the valuers/advisors and confirmation that they have confirmed their independence
- The valuations obtained of the business or assets
- Summary of the basis of the valuation adopted by the administrator or his valuers/advisors
- Rationale for the basis of the valuations obtained and an explanation of the sale of the assets compared to those valuations
- If no valuation has been obtained, the reason for not having done so and how the administrator was satisfied as to the value of the assets
- The date of the transaction
- The identity of the purchaser
- Any connection between the purchaser and the directors, shareholders or secured creditors of the company or their associates
- The names of any directors, or former directors, of the company who are involved in the management or ownership of the purchaser, or of any other entity into which any of the assets are transferred
- In transactions impacting on more than one related company the administrator should ensure that the disclosure is sufficient to enable a transparent explanation (ie allocation of consideration paid)
- Whether any directors had given guarantees for amounts due from the company to a prior financier and whether that financier is financing the new business
- Details of the assets involved and the nature of the transaction
- The consideration for the transaction, terms of payment and any condition of the contract that could materially affect the consideration
- Sale consideration disclosed under broad asset valuation categories and split between fixed and floating charge realisations
- Any options, buy back agreements, deferred consideration or other conditions attached to the contract of sale
- If the sale is part of a wider transaction, a description of the other aspects of the transaction

The information should be provided in every case unless there are exceptional circumstances in which case the reason why the information is not being provided should be stated. If the sale is to a connected party, it is unlikely that confidentiality will outweigh the creditors' right to the information.

The information should be provided with the first notification to creditors, and in any event within 7 calendar days of the transaction. If the administrator has been unable to meet this requirement they should provide a reasonable explanation for the delay.

When a pre-packaged sale has been undertaken, the administrator should seek the requisite approval of his proposals as soon as practicable after appointment.

5 Exiting administration

Section overview

- There are a number of options for the administrator when seeking to bring an administration to an end. Which route is most appropriate will depend on the purpose of the administration and whether there are funds available to distribute to creditors.

5.1 Priority of payments

Administrators – fixed charge assets

The order of payment here is:

- Costs of preserving and realising the assets including the costs of any paragraph 71 application (see below)
- The fixed charge holder

This looks similar to the position in administrative receivership but there are two key differences:

- An administrator can only realise fixed charge assets with the consent of the charge holder or the court. An application to the court is made under paragraph 71 of Schedule B1 of the Act.
- Where the court consents to the administrator disposing of the assets it will be a condition of the court order that the charge holder receives the higher of the net proceeds of sale or open market value.

Administrators – floating charge assets

The order of payment here is:

- Costs of preserving and realising the assets
- Liabilities on two types of contract rank equally
  - Liabilities for wages and salaries etc on contracts of employment 'adopted' by the administrator. (Any employment contracts which the administrator does not terminate by the 14th day of the administration are automatically adopted by him)
  - Liabilities on other contracts entered into by the administrator
- The administrator's general remuneration costs and expenses. The order of payment of these is set out in R2.67.
- Preferential creditors. The relevant date here will be the date the company entered administration.
- Where the floating charge was created on or after 15 September 2003 a prescribed part of the net property must be paid to the unsecured creditors (see Chapter 5).
- Floating charges.
- Any surplus must be made available to the unsecured creditors.

5.2 Exit routes

Exit routes available are:

- Handing the company back to the directors
- Petitioning the court for compulsory winding up
- Filing to place the company into a creditors' voluntary liquidation
- Filing for the dissolution of the company (only possible once realisations have been distributed)
- Obtaining the creditors' approval to a CVA and ending the administration
- Allowing the administration to lapse through expiry of the 12 month fixed period
- Applying to court for the ending of the administration

The administrator will have already stated the envisaged exit route in the proposals to creditors (R2.33).

1 Handing the company back to the directors

This is an option available where the administrator has achieved a para 3(a) purpose ie rescuing the company as a going concern. Schedule B1 para 65 now provides the administrator with an express power to make distributions.

No sanction of the court is needed if the payment is to a secured or preferential creditor. However, sanction of the court is required if the payment is to ordinary unsecured creditors. Para 65 expressly states that s175 of the Act applies to administrator's distributions. In other words, as in a winding up the preferential creditors will take priority to the holders of floating charges.

2 Petitioning the court for compulsory winding up

Petitioning for compulsory winding up may be appropriate where the creditors want a thorough investigation into allegations of misconduct against the directors.

An administrator has a specific power to present a winding up petition (para 21 schedule 1). R4.7(7) provides that the petition must:

- State the name of the administrator
- State the court case number
- State the date the company entered administration
- Contain an application under para 79 schedule B1 requesting that the appointment of the administrator ceases to have effect
- Be accompanied by a progress report from the date the company entered administration or from the last progress report

The administrator must give notice to the appointing creditor(s) or the applicant(s) for the administration order of his intention to apply to court and whether he intends to seek appointment as liquidator.

The court will make the winding up order and the administrator may be appointed liquidator. If this occurs the OR will not become the liquidator and therefore will not have a duty to consider whether or not to call a meeting of creditors.

Any creditors' committee in the administration will be suspended pending the liquidator's certificate of continuance (R4.174A).

It would be inappropriate for the court to appoint the administrator as liquidator where the:

- Creditors are unhappy with the conduct of the administration and have required the administrator to apply to court for the ending of the administration
- The administrator is concerned about a potential conflict of interest

If the administrator is not appointed the OR will become the liquidator. Consequently Rule 4.174A will not apply and the committee in administration will not become the liquidation committee.

3 Filing to place the company into creditors' voluntary liquidation (CVL) (para 83 Schedule B1)

The administrator sends a notice to the Registrar of Companies that para 83 applies. A copy of the notice must also be filed with the court and sent to all creditors of whose claim and address the administrator is aware, as well as to all those who received notice of the administrator's appointment.

The registrar registers the para 83 notice and from this time the appointment of the administrator ceases to have effect, and the company is wound up as if a resolution for voluntary winding up under s84 was passed on the day on which the notice is registered.

As soon as reasonably practicable after the day on which the Registrar registers the notice the administrator must send a final progress report to the Registrar and those who received notice of the administrator's appointment. (R2.117A(1)).

There is no requirement for a board meeting, meeting of shareholders or a s98 meeting of creditors.

The committee in the administration will become the liquidation committee in the CVL.

As already mentioned the administrator should state in his proposals how it is proposed the administration should end. If a CVL is proposed he should provide details of the proposed liquidator (usually the administrator) and a statement that creditors may nominate a different person as the proposed liquidator before the proposals are approved. If no other liquidator is appointed, the administrator will become liquidator.

The para 83 CVL route may only be used where:

- The total amount which each secured creditor of the company is likely to receive has been paid or set aside

- A distribution to the unsecured creditors will be made over and above the prescribed part

There are a number of advantages to the CVL route:

- It avoids any problems in respect of completing the administration within 12 months or having to obtain an extension of time from creditors or the court (see point 6 post)

- The office holder when acting as liquidator has enforcement powers which are not available to an administrator eg to bring action against directors for misfeasance and wrongful and fraudulent trading (the relevant time will be calculated from the commencement of the administration not from the resolution to wind up)

- A liquidator has a statutory power to disclaim onerous property (an administrator does not)

- The liquidator has full powers to compromise claims with creditors and the lack of a 12 month time limit provides time to negotiate and settle complex claims

4 Dissolution of the company/striking off

Schedule B1 para 65 provides the administrator with an express power to make distributions.

No sanction of the court is needed if the payment is to a secured or preferential creditors, however sanction of the court is required if the payment is to ordinary unsecured creditors.

The preferential creditors must be paid out of floating charge realisations in priority to the holders of floating charges.

Moving from administration to dissolution is straightforward and is effected by the filing of a notice with the Registrar of Companies and sending copies to the creditors of whose name and address he is aware.

On registration the administration ceases to have effect and three months later the company is deemed dissolved.

This procedure (together with the administrator's powers of distribution) enables the administrator to bring the administration to an end and conclude the company's affairs without the need for a formal liquidation.

5 Company voluntary arrangement (CVA)

Schedule B1 para 49 expressly states that the administrator's proposals may include a proposal for a CVA. This would be consistent with the statutory purpose of rescuing the company as a going concern.

The proposals can be put to creditors at the same time as the meeting to approve the administrator's proposals for achieving this para 3 purpose.

Advantages of a CVA are:

- The proposal can contain detailed provisions on the agreement and compromising of claims against the company

- Directors will remain involved in management of the company and this may maximize the 'buy-in' of the current management team

Disadvantages of a CVA are:

- The supervisor has no power to challenge antecedent transactions and has no power to enforce the directors co-operation under ss234 – 237

- At the end of the CVA further steps may have to be taken to dissolve or liquidate the company if the CVA has not resulted in the survival of the company

- Supervisors have no powers to bring actions under the misfeasance, fraudulent and wrongful trading provisions ss212 – 214, nor can they disclaim onerous assets

6 Administration comes to an end through the passage of time

The appointment of an administrator ceases to have effect at the end of one year beginning when the administration takes effect. The court can extend this for a specified period upon the application of the administrator.

The creditors can also extend the administration for a maximum period of 12 months, which was extended from 6 in SBEEA 2015.

Where there will be a distribution to unsecured creditors consent can be given by:

- Each secured creditor
- More than 50% of the unsecured creditors (disregarding the debts of any creditor who does not respond to an invitation to give or withhold consent)

The administration can only be extended by the creditors once. The court can extend an administration indefinitely. The administrator can apply even if he has already had a six month extension by creditor consent, but pursuant to the 2014 Practice Direction he must apply not less than one month before the administration comes to an end.

7 Applying to court for the ending of the administration

Para 80 provides a procedure where an administrator appointed out of court under paras 14 or 22 has achieved the objective of the administration.

The administrator files notice with the court and the Registrar of Companies and his appointment then ceases to have effect.

This may be appropriate where the administrator has succeeded in securing the survival of the company as a going concern or the administrator's proposals for a CVA have been approved by the creditors.

5.3 Other ways in which an administration may come to an end

- Administrator applies to court under para 79(2) sch B1 IA86 if he thinks (1) the purpose of administration cannot be achieved (see earlier) (2) the company should not have entered administration or (3) a creditors' meeting requires him to apply.
- Administrator appointed by the court applies to the court under para 85 for discharge of the order.
- A creditor applies to the court under para 81 on the grounds that the appointers (appointments out of court) or applicants (appointments by the court) had an 'improper motive'. In addition under para 74 creditors can apply to the court on the basis that their interests are being or will be unfairly harmed by the administrator. One of the courts powers under para 74 is to end the administration.

5.4 Administrator's final report

Where an administrator ceases to act, he must prepare a progress report covering the period from his last report until the time he ceases to act.

This must be sent, to the creditors of whom he is aware and the Registrar of Companies.

The final progress report must include a summary of (R2.110):

- The administrator's proposals
- Any major amendments to or deviations from those proposals
- The steps taken during the administration
- The outcome

5.5 Discharge from liability

Where an IP ceases to be the administrator (however so he ceases to act) he is discharged from liability in respect of any action of his as administrator (para 98 (1)).

Discharge takes effect:

- In the case of death, on the filing with the court of notice of his death
- In the case of an administrator appointment under paras 14 or 22, at a time appointed by the resolution of the creditors' committee or creditors or in any case, at a time specified by the court

Summary and Self-test

Summary

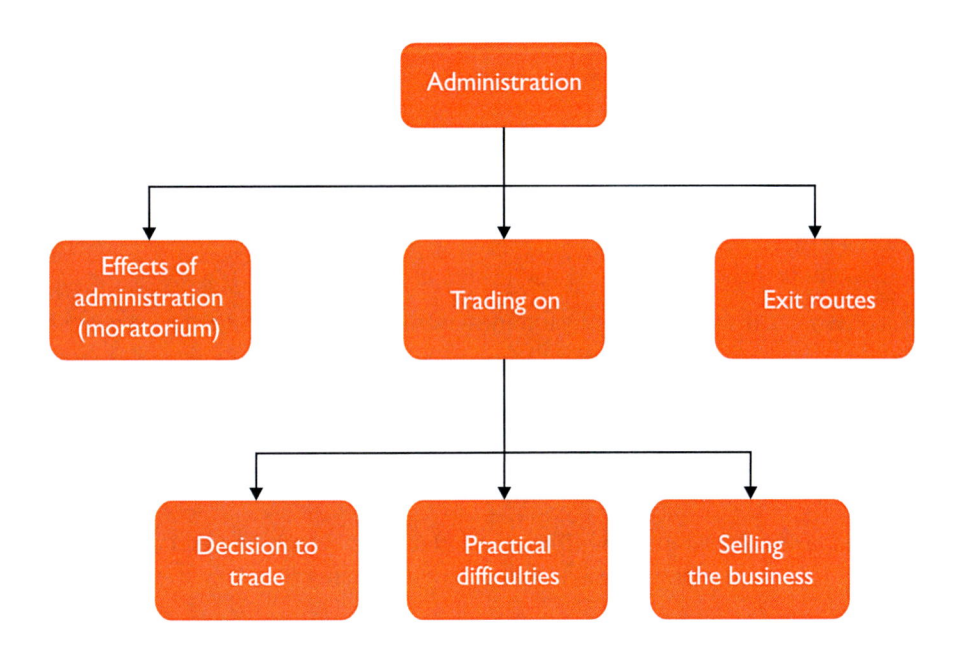

```
                        ┌──────────────────┐
                        │  Administration  │
                        └──────────────────┘
                                 │
          ┌──────────────────────┼──────────────────────┐
          ▼                      ▼                      ▼
┌──────────────────┐    ┌──────────────┐       ┌──────────────┐
│    Effects of    │    │              │       │              │
│  administration  │    │  Trading on  │       │  Exit routes │
│   (moratorium)   │    │              │       │              │
└──────────────────┘    └──────────────┘       └──────────────┘
                                │
              ┌─────────────────┼─────────────────┐
              ▼                 ▼                 ▼
       ┌────────────┐   ┌──────────────┐   ┌──────────────┐
       │ Decision to│   │   Practical  │   │    Selling   │
       │    trade   │   │ difficulties │   │ the business │
       └────────────┘   └──────────────┘   └──────────────┘
```

Self test

Answer the following questions.

1. ABC Ltd entered administration on 1 December 20X1. The company has net property, prior to the payment of any creditors of £380,000 and has the following creditors:

	£
First qualifying charge holder	270,000
Second qualifying charge holder	30,000
Employees' claims for holiday pay	20,000
Unsecured claims	390,000

    Calculate the funds available for distribution to each of the above creditors.

2. How often should the administrator send a progress report on the conduct of the administration?

    A Every 6 months
    B Every 12 months
    C At the end of administration
    D At his discretion

3. To which **two** of the following is the administrator not required to send a copy of his progress report?

    A Creditors
    B Directors
    C The court
    D Registrar of Companies

4. An administrator can exit an administration by placing the company into creditors' voluntary liquidation. This route is only available if two conditions are met. What are these conditions?

5. Which SIP deals with pre-packaged administration sales?

    A 3
    B 12
    C 15
    D 16

6. In relation to administration are the following statements true or false.

    (i) The maximum length of an administration is six months unless extended by the creditors or the court.

    A True
    B False

    (ii) Creditors can extend an administration only once for a maximum of 12 months thereafter only the court can extend the duration of any administration.

    C True
    D False

Now, go back to the Learning Objectives in the Introduction. If you are satisfied that you have achieved these, please tick them off.

Answers to Self-test

1

	£
Net property	380,000
Less: preferential creditors	(20,000)
	360,000

Prescribed part:	
50% x 10,000	5,000
20% x 350,000	70,000
	75,000

Floating charge realisations	380,000
Less: Preferential creditors	(20,000)
Prescribed part	(75,000)
Available to floating charge holders	285,000

Prescribed part available to unsecured creditors(not floating charge)	75,000

Unsecured creditors totaling £390,000 – 19.23p in £

First QFC holder receives £270,000 – 100p in £

Second QFC holder receives £15,000 – 50p in £

2   A

3   B and C

4   (a)   The total amount which each secured creditor of the company is likely to receive has been paid or set aside, and

    (b)   A distribution to the unsecured creditors will be made

5   D

6   (i)   B
    (ii) C – The maximum length of the administration is 12 months

CHAPTER 17

Introduction to receivership

Introduction
Topic List
1 Types of receivership
2 The Administrative Receiver
3 Appointment of fixed charge receivers
Summary and Self-test
Answers to Self-test

Introduction

Learning objectives

- State the classes of creditor and their rights in corporate insolvency
- Explain the effect of the Law of Property Act 1925 and its relation to fixed charge receiverships
- Explain the effect of the Enterprise Act 2002 in relation to administrative receivership
- State the different type of receiver and their roles

Tick off
☐
☐
☐
☐

Stop and think

What is a floating charge asset? Why are there different types of receivership? What does a receiver do? Why does an administrative receiver have different powers and duties to a receiver appointed under a fixed charge?

Working context

Administrative receiverships are still relevant despite the changes introduced by the Enterprise Act 2002. It is important to understand when an administrative receiver will be appointed as opposed to a different type of receiver and what the powers and duties of the receiver (administrative or otherwise) are.

1 Types of receivership

Section overview

There are three types of receiver:

- An Administrative Receiver (AR)
- A receiver appointed by a secured creditor holding a fixed charge only (either under the provisions of the Law of Property Act 1925 ('LPA 25') or the security documentation)
- A receiver appointed by the court

Receivers are appointed following a company's default under the terms of either a fixed charge or following default under the terms of a pre 15.9.2003 floating charge (administrative receivers only). If you need a reminder about the differences between fixed and floating charges, or the rights of these secured creditors on insolvency go back to Chapter 5 and review that chapter again before starting this one.

Definition

Administrative Receiver (AR): a receiver or manager of the whole (or substantially the whole) of a company's property appointed by or on behalf of the holders of any debentures of the company secured by a floating charge which was created before 15th September 2003. [Remember in respect of floating charges created on or after that date by virtue of the Enterprise Act 2002, which introduced changes into the Insolvency Act 1986, a floating charge holder may only appoint an administrator.]

1.1 Administrative receivership

Although it had been the government's intention to abolish administrative receivership and replace it entirely with administration the Insolvency Act as amended by Enterprise Act 2002 still allows a floating charge holder to appoint an AR where the floating charge was created prior to 15 September 2003 (s72A(4)). This is in addition to any right to appoint an administrator, support a CVA or seek liquidation of the company.

Although s72A(1) prohibits the holders of floating charges created on or after 15 September 2003 from appointing an AR there are exceptions including:

- Capital market arrangements exceeding £50m in value
- Large public finance projects where the provider of finance retains 'step-in rights'

As there are still many pre 15 September 2003 floating charges in existence administrative receivership is still highly relevant for assessment purposes.

1.2 Advantages of administrative receivership over administration

[Please see the Introduction to administrations Chapter 14 for a full discussion of this area.]

1.3 Fixed charge receivership

Definition

Fixed charge receiver: A person, not necessarily an IP, appointed under an express power in a security document creating fixed charges over assets. The powers of the fixed charge receiver will be those set out in the Law of Property Act 1925 as modified by the security documentation.

1.4 LPA receivership

Definition

LPA receiver: A person, not necessarily an IP, appointed under the Law of Property Act 1925 ('LPA 25') by the holder of a fixed charge over property to enforce the lender's security. An LPA receiver has the powers and duties specified in and limited by the Law of Property Act 1925. An LPA receiver is usually appointed with a view to selling the charged property or collecting the rental income from it for the lender. Most modern security documents contain an express power to appoint a receiver and it is now rare for a lender to rely on the powers implied by the Law of Property Act 1925. These can be modified by express provisions in the security document.

2 The Administrative Receiver

Section overview

- An Administrative Receiver (AR) may be appointed by the holder of a floating charge which was created prior to 15 September 2003. The statutory regulations are contained in s42–49 IA 86 and s72A–72H IA 86 and Part 3 of the Rules (Rules 3.1 – 3.40).

2.1 Who may act as AR

- Only licensed IPs may act as an AR. It is an offence to act as an IP when not qualified to do so s389. [See Chapter 3 for further details about the necessary qualifications of an IP.]
- Remember that before an IP accepts an appointment he must consider whether or not the Insolvency Code of Ethics permits him to accept the appointment and be sure that he has the correct security/bond in place.

Note. The amount of specific bond required is equal to the amount that would be available for the unsecured creditors (including the preferential creditors) if the company was in liquidation at the date of the AR's appointment.

- Receivers who are not ARs do not need to be IPs.

2.2 Validity of appointment

Before the appointment can be made, the floating charge holder must be able to make the appointment. This right will usually crystallise on the charge becoming enforceable, for example, as a result of the company going into default under the loan agreement in respect of which the floating charge was granted.

Before accepting an appointment as an AR an IP must check that the charge is valid and that the right to appoint an AR has arisen.

2.2.1 Validity of debenture

The AR may only be validly appointed if the charge under which he is appointed is itself valid and the floating charge will withstand any legal attack for example under the registration provisions of Companies Act 2006 (see below), s245 IA 86 (invalid floating charge) or the preference provisions in IA 86.

Checklist for the receiver.

- **Has the charge instrument been properly executed?**
    - It must have been executed under seal or as a deed
    - It is not possible to create a legal mortgage if executed under hand

- **Does it satisfy the provisions of Companies Act 2006 (CA06)?**
    - Was the giving of the security *intra vires* the company?

        Check the objects clause in the memorandum. (Post the implementation of CA06 any restriction in the company's memorandum will take effect as if contained within the company's articles. However note that under ss39 – 42 CA 06 third parties (eg charge holders) are protected if they enter into *ultra vires* transactions in good faith. It is probable that this provision would protect the charge holder.
    - Was the giving of the security *intra vires* the directors powers?

        Check if there is an effective board resolution authorising the issue of the debenture and the giving of security? If there is not check that the charge holder had no reason to suspect that the directors were acting outside their authority as agents of the company.
    - Was the charge registered within 21 days of its creation (s870 CA 06)?

        If the charge is not validly registered it is void as against a liquidator, administrator or creditor of the company. The charge holder thereby loses his status as a secured creditor and thereby his ability to appoint an AR.

- **Can the charge be attacked under the IA 86?**
    - Could the creation of the charge constitute a preference under s239? Remember although the appointment of receiver does **not** trigger s239 for the purpose of determining 'relevant time' the company going into liquidation or administration will.
    - Could the charge (if floating) be invalidated under s245?

        Again the section is only activated by the liquidation or administration of the company and not by the appointment of an AR. If the company does subsequently go into liquidation it is important to note that the effect of s245 is not retrospective (*Mace Builders (Glasgow) Ltd v Lunn (1986)* ie the AR's acts prior to the liquidation will be valid, despite the fact that the charge under which AR appointed has now been invalidated under s245.

- **Does the debenture authorise the appointment of an AR and has the right been triggered?**

    The following matters should be dealt with in order to confirm that the appointment itself is valid:
    - Check that the debenture does authorise appointment of an AR in the circumstances that have arisen
    - Note that an overdraft is (unless otherwise agreed) repayable on demand. However there is no liability to repay until a demand is made and no security can be enforced until a demand has been made and not complied with. Therefore check that:

        (i) A letter of demand has been sent (although the amount demanded does not need to be the exact sum due)

        (ii) Time has been given for the mechanics of repayment – although time does not necessarily have to be given to allow the company to raise capital or seek to re-finance the loan.

Note. The company must not be in administration. Once the company is in administration an AR cannot be appointed.

2.3 Procedure to appoint

The charge holder will prepare the appointment instrument and send it to the proposed AR. The Insolvency Rules contain detailed provisions as to how the appointment should be accepted, the timescale in which it will be accepted and how the AR will give notification of his acceptance.

- The appointment instrument/document must be received and accepted by the AR(s) by end of next business day.
- Acceptance can be oral or written (but if oral must be confirmed in writing within five business days).

- Acceptance must state the date and time of receipt of the appointment and the date and time of acceptance. If the appointment is duly accepted it is deemed to take effect at the time the instrument of appointment was received.

- Two or more insolvency practitioners may be appointed joint ARs of a company. The acceptance of each must be confirmed in writing and the appointment is effective only when all of them have confirmed acceptance (R3.1(1)). Their appointment is deemed to have been made at the time at which the instrument of appointment was received by or on behalf of all of them (Rule 3.1(1)). The appointment must declare whether any act required or authorised under any enactment to be done by the AR is to be done by all or any one or more of the persons for the time being holding the office (s231).

The acts of an individual as AR are deemed to be valid despite any defect in his appointment (s232). If there is an invalid appointment of an AR (purportedly appointed out of court) then the court may order the person who purported to appoint him to indemnify him against any liability arising solely by reason of the invalidity of the appointment (s34).

However s232 will not protect an AR where there was no power to appoint in the first place.

2.4 Notification of appointment

- If an AR is appointed the appointer must, under penalty, within seven days give notice in the prescribed form to the Registrar of Companies, and the Registrar will note the appointment in the register of charges, s871 CA 06. On appointment, an AR of a company must, under penalty, as soon as reasonably practicable send to the company a notice of his appointment and must publish an advertisement in the *Gazette* and it may also be advertised in such other manner as the AR thinks fit (s46(1)(a) and (4) and Sch10; R3.2(3)).

- Unless the court otherwise directs, the AR must also send a notice to all creditors of the company of whose addresses he is aware within 28 days of his appointment (s46(1)(b) and (4) and Sch10). The contents of the advertisement and the notice to the company and the creditors are specified in Rule 3.2(2) and (4).

- The notice must contain the information specified in Rule 3.2(2) including:
    - The registered name of the company as at the date of the appointment, and its registered number
    - The name and address of the AR and the date of his appointment
    - The name of the appointer
    - Nature of the business of the company
    - The date of the instrument conferring the power under which the appointment was made, together with a brief description of the instrument
    - A brief description of the assets of the company (if any) in respect of which the person appointed is not made a receiver

3 Appointment of fixed charge receivers

Section overview

- Such a receiver may be appointed:
    - Under the provisions of the Law of Property Act 1925 (LPA)
    - Under a power contained in an instrument
    - By the court

3.1 Validity of appointment

Before any appointment can be made, the fixed charge holder must be able to make the appointment and so will need to check that the conditions for making the appointment are properly satisfied. If the receiver is appointed under the provisions of a charge/agreement rather than the LPA 25, then as with an Administrative Receivership the IP must check that the charge is valid, properly registered under CA06 and not subject to attack as a preference etc. Where an appointment is made under the provisions of the LPA 25 care must be taken to ascertain that the statutory provisions permitting appointment are duly satisfied. In addition to those considerations s110 LPA 25 provides that if the mortgagor (ie the debtor) is in liquidation then the permission of the court is required before a receiver can be appointed.

3.2 Receivers appointed under an agreement

It is most common that receivers are appointed under the terms of an agreement rather than the provisions of the LPA 25. The reason why the LPA 25 route is unpopular is that a mortgagee's power to appoint a receiver is restricted and once appointed the powers of a receiver are limited to collecting rents.

It is common therefore to make express provision in the mortgage concerning the circumstances in which a receiver can be appointed and the powers that the receiver once appointed will have.

The mortgage deed commonly gives the receiver:

- Power to take possession and sell the property
- Power to borrow money to carry out the statutory duties in s109 LPA 25 (to insure and repair)

The mortgage deed may also give the receiver:

- Extensive powers to manage the company's business – however trading on may prove difficult in practice as the receiver only has access to the charged assets and would be a trespasser if, for instance, he used stock not covered by his appointer's charges

3.3 Receiver appointed under LPA 1925

A mortgagee under a legal mortgage (ie created by deed) has the right to appoint a receiver (s101).

However this power only arises after:

- The mortgage money has become due (s101 LPA 25)
- The mortgagee has become entitled to exercise the statutory power of sale (s109 LPA 25)

By s103 LPA 25 the power of sale arises:

- Where there has been a default in repayment of a loan for three months after a notice requiring it; or
- Interest remains unpaid for two months after becoming due; or
- There is some other breach of the deed or Act.

The receiver's powers are limited to collecting rents and income.

Chatsworth Properties Ltd v Effiom – receiver should make it clear that he is acting as the mortgagors' agent when collecting rents, this will prevent any tenancy arising between himself and the tenants.

Note. A receiver has no statutory power to recover possession against the mortgagor (the Act does give that power to the mortgagee).

Receiver also has a duty to keep the property in repair and to insure.

Summary and Self-test

Summary

Below is a table which sets out and compares the ways in which the different types of receiver are appointed.

	Administrative Receiver	Fixed Charge Receiver	LPA Receiver
Status	Must be IP (ss230(2), 388(1)(a)) IA 86.	Need not be IP.	Need not be IP.
Appointment	By charge holder in circumstances set out in security documentation. Appointment must be permitted under terms of ss72 A to H IA 86	By charge holder in circumstances set out in security documentation.	By charge holder in the limited circumstances set out in the LPA 1925.
Charges	To qualify as AR must be appointed over the whole or substantially the whole of company's property. By holders of floating charges (s29(2) IA 86).	Charge holder will hold fixed charge(s) and possibly floating charge(s) also.	As for fixed charge receiver.

Self-test

1. Which of the following assets will not usually be covered by a fixed charge?

    A   Goodwill
    B   Unfactored book debts
    C   Intellectual property rights
    D   Fixed plant

2. Within how many days of creation should a charge be registered at Companies House?

    A   7 days
    B   14 days
    C   21 days
    D   28 days

3. A floating charge granted to an unconnected party may be challenged under s245 if created within what period of the onset of insolvency?

    A   6 months
    B   1 year
    C   2 years
    D   3 years

4. When an IP gives oral acceptance of an appointment as AR within how many business days must he confirm his appointment in writing?

    A   5
    B   7
    C   10
    D   14

5. Within how many days of his appointment must an AR send notice to creditors?

    A   7
    B   14
    C   21
    D   28

Now, go back to the Learning Objectives in the Introduction. If you are satisfied that you have achieved these objectives, please tick them off.

Answers to Self-test

1 B
2 C
3 B
4 A
5 D

CHAPTER 18

Effect of administrative receivership and duties of receivers

Introduction
Topic List
1 Effect of administrative receivership
2 Powers of an Administrative Receiver
3 Agency
4 Duties of Administrative Receiver

Summary and Self-test
Answers to Self-test
Answer to Interactive question

Introduction

Learning objectives

- Explain the purpose and effects of administrative receivership
- Describe the on-going obligations upon the insolvency practitioner in an administrative receivership with regard to
    - Meetings
    - Record keeping
    - Reporting
    - Time limits

Tick off

Stop and think

What powers does an Administrative receiver have? Where do these come from? What qualifications must an individual have before he can accept appointment as an administrative receiver? To whom does the administrative receiver owe his duties?

Working context

When dealing with an administrative receivership in a work environment it is important to understand what powers the administrative receiver has and what liabilities he will incur in respect of ongoing trading. You may also be asked to assist in convening the s48 meeting of creditors or with preparing the Statement of Affairs.

1 Effect of administrative receivership

> **Section overview**
> - From the time of his appointment the AR of a company has sole authority to deal with the charged property. The directors of the company no longer have authority to deal with the charged property. The directors do retain custody and control of any assets which are not covered by the appointers charge.

1.1 Effect on directors

1.1.1 The director's office

- The appointment of an AR does not terminate the directors' office.
- It follows that the directors retain statutory duties such as the duty to make returns and submit documents to the Registrar of Companies. To facilitate compliance with these residual duties the AR should be prepared to provide necessary information to directors and access to relevant documentation.
- It also follows that the directors retain their power to institute proceedings in the company's name. Directors may therefore:
    - Challenge the validity of the AR's appointment; or
    - Oppose a petition to wind-up the company; or
    - Cause the company to sue the AR for breach of duty.

1.1.2 The director's contract of employment

The appointment of an AR does not automatically terminate contracts of employment. Directors therefore retain their employment unless and until the AR terminates those contracts, or the company is liquidated.

In practice the AR may wish to retain the services of the directors (at least in the short term) to run the day to day operations of the company whilst the AR looks into the viability of trading on and effecting a going concern sale.

In such a situation the AR will, at an early meeting with the directors, explain that the:

- Co-operation of the directors will assist the AR's attempts to trade on and sell
- Directors retain their employment for the time being (although no absolute guarantees for the future can be given)
- AR will, however, make funds available to pay the directors

1.1.3 The director's potential liabilities

One or more directors will be required to submit a Statement of Affairs.

The AR is required to report on the conduct of directors to the Secretary of State under the Company Directors Disqualification Act (ie submit a 'D' form).

1.1.4 The director's duties to AR

- Under s235 past and present officers of the company have a duty:
    - To give the AR such information as the AR shall require concerning the company and its promotion, formation, business, dealings, affairs or property, and attend on the AR at such times as the AR shall reasonably require. This also extends to sub-contractors eg consultants s235(3)(c) and auditors who are officers of the company.

    Those failing to comply (without reasonable excuse) are liable to a fine.

- Under s234 ARs can obtain a court order to force directors and other to hand over charged property and relevant documentation.

- An AR can (under s236) apply to the court for an order that any office holder of the company appear before the court. In addition the court can require such a person to submit a witness statement containing an account of his dealings with the company, or produce any document relating to the company or to its property or business.

    If an officer is likely to be un-cooperative the court can issue a warrant for his arrest, and seizure of relevant documentation or goods.

- The directors must submit a Statement of Affairs within 21 days of the AR's request. (s47).

Interactive question: Foale Limited

Your principal has just been appointed Administrative Receiver of Foale Limited under the terms of a floating charge held by Satby Bank plc and she has requested that you arrange an urgent meeting with the directors of the company.

Requirement

What effect will the administrative receivership have on the directors of the company.

See **Answer** at the end of this chapter.

1.2 Other effects

1.2.1 Contracts of employment

The appointment of an AR does **not** automatically terminate the company's contracts of employment. AR is free to repudiate (terminate) or adopt such contracts.

By s44(1)(b) the AR is personally liable on any contracts of employment adopted by him.

The AR will be taken to have 'adopted' merely by **not** repudiating such pre-existing contracts.

s44(2) however, provides that the AR shall not be taken to have adopted a contract of employment by reason of anything done or omitted to be done within 14 days after his appointment.

1.2.2 Effect on other proceedings

The appointment of an AR will prevent any person appointing an administrator out of court.

The court will only be able to appoint an administrator if either the AR's appointer consents or the charge under which the AR has been appointed is deemed invalid.

[Note. The position is different with a fixed charge receiver who can be forced from office by the administrator.]

1.2.3 Effect on company contracts (other than employment contracts)

The appointment of an AR will not automatically terminate company contracts but may trigger a right for the other party to terminate. Such a right must be contained in the terms and conditions of the contract. If the continuance of the contract is important to the company and the receivership, the receiver will take such steps as are necessary to avoid its termination.

If the contract is of no importance and the receiver makes it clear that the company in receivership will not now comply with its contractual obligations that will amount to a breach of contract by the company enabling the other party to choose to terminate the contract and sue for a remedy.

1.2.4 Effect on company's documentation

Every document of the company in receivership eg invoices, letter headed notepaper, purchase orders must state that the company is in receivership. This requirement applies equally to hard and electronic documents. Additionally the company's website, if any, must contain a statement to this effect. Any breach of this requirement constitutes an offence (s39).

2 Powers of an Administrative Receiver

Section overview

- A professionally drafted contract of floating charge will confer on an AR appointed under the contract a wide range of powers, s42(1) and Sch 1 confer upon every AR a standardised list of powers. A person dealing with an AR of a company in good faith and for value is entitled to assume that the receiver is acting within his powers s42(3). References to the property of the company are to the property of which he is or, but for the appointment of some other person as the receiver of part of the company's property, would be, the receiver or manager.

- For assessment purposes the powers of the AR are more important than fixed charge receivers, however the summary table at the end of this chapter sets out their position also.

The AR has the power to do the following:

- Take possession of, collect and take in the property of the company and, for that purpose, take such proceedings as may seem to him expedient
- Sell or otherwise dispose of the property of the company by public auction or private contract
- Raise or borrow money and thereby grant security over the property of the company
- Appoint a solicitor, accountant or other professionally qualified person to assist him in the performance of his functions
- Bring or defend any actions or other legal proceedings in the name of and on behalf of the company
- Refer to arbitration any question affecting the company
- Effect and maintain insurances in respect of the business and property of the company
- Use the company's seal
- Do all acts and to execute in the name of and on behalf of the company any deed, receipt or other document
- Draw, accept, make or endorse any bill of exchange or promissory note in the name of, and on behalf of, the company
- Appoint any agent to do any business which he is unable to do himself, or which can more conveniently be done by an agent
- Do all such things (including the carrying out of works) as may be necessary for the realisation of the property of the company
- Make any payment which is necessary or incidental to the performance of his functions
- Carry on the business of the company, establish subsidiaries and transfer to subsidiaries the whole or any part of the business and property of the company
- Make any arrangement or compromise on behalf of the company
- Grant or accept a surrender of a lease or tenancy of any property of the company, and take a lease or tenancy of any property required or convenient for the business of the company
- Call up any uncalled share capital of the company
- Rank and claim in the bankruptcy, insolvency, sequestration or liquidation of any person indebted to the company and to receive dividends, or to accede to trust deeds for the creditors of any such person
- Present or defend a petition for the winding up of the company
- Change the situation of the company's registered office
- Employ and dismiss employees
- Power to do all other things incidental to the exercise of the foregoing powers

2.1 Application to court for directions

An AR appointed out of court may apply to the court for directions in relation to any particular matter arising in connection with the carrying out of his functions (s35(1)).

The person by whom, or on whose behalf, he was appointed may also apply for such directions.

On any application the court has the option to give directions or make a declaratory order.

2.2 s43 power to apply to court for an order sanctioning disposal of property subject to prior charges

In many situations the most effective way of progressing the administrative receivership will be to dispose of the entire undertaking of the company as a going concern. Clearly the existence of prior charges may impede such a sale.

The AR will seek to negotiate a settlement with any prior charge holder.

Where an agreement cannot be reached the AR has the power to apply to the court.

The court must be satisfied that the disposal (with or without other assets) of the property subject to security would be likely to promote a more advantageous realisation of the company's assets than would otherwise be effected.

It must be a condition of the order that the greater of the proceeds of sale or the open market value of the property as determined by the court is paid to the prior charge holder.

The court will send two copies of the order sanctioning the disposal to the AR (Rule 3.31(4)) who will then serve one on the prior chargee and send one within 14 days to the Registrar of Companies.

2.3 Powers the AR does *not* have

- Disclaim a lease
- Pay a dividend to unsecured creditors
- Also act as liquidator of a company
- Bring court actions for:
    - Director's wrongful trading/fraudulent trading
    - Preferences
    - Transactions at undervalue
    - The AR can bring an action in respect of a transaction defrauding creditors but only on behalf of the appointer as a victim of the transaction
- Remove directors from office (only shareholders can)

3 Agency

> **Section overview**
> - By s44 (1)(a) IA 86, the AR is deemed to be the company's agent unless and until the company goes into liquidation.
> - For assessment purposes the agency of the AR is more important than that of fixed charge receivers, however the summary table at the end of this chapter sets out key points about their position also.

3.1 Implications of s44 (1)(a) IA 86

In the law of agency the principal (the company) is liable on contracts entered into by the agent (the AR). The agent will only be personally liable if he acts outside his authority. Consequently whilst the company will be liable on contracts entered into by the AR, the debenture holder will not be (it is **not** the principal).

3.2 Personal liability of the AR

By s44(1)(b) the AR is personally liable on any contract entered into by him in the carrying out of his functions.

- The rule in s44(1)(b) is that the AR is personally liable on contracts **entered into** by him. The rule does **not** say that he is liable on pre-appointment contracts.
- Pre-appointment contracts are contracts with the company not with the AR. The AR can either:
  - Repudiate (terminate) such contracts (in which case the third party can sue the company for breach and will be an unsecured creditor) note that the AR does not have personal liability; or
  - Allow the contract to continue. The AR does **not** become a party to the contract nor is he personally liable on it.
- An AR who re-negotiates a contract does risk that the contract will be treated as a post appointment one and therefore one under which he is personally liable.

This has implications for a trading receivership where the AR may be entering into new contracts. The IA 86 therefore provides:

- The AR may contractually exclude his liability in the contract. s44(1)(b) provides for personal liability 'except in so far as the contract otherwise provides'
- The AR 'is entitled in respect of that liability to an indemnity out of the assets of the company' (s44 (1) (c)).

Note that the AR can still demand an indemnity from the charge holder as a term of accepting the appointment.

3.3 Nature of agency

Cases such as *Gomba Holdings UK Ltd v Homan (1986)* and *Ratford Northavon District Council (1987)* point out that it is an unusual agency.

- Company (principal) cannot dismiss AR (agent)
- Company cannot instruct AR as to how duties should be performed
- AR's prime duty owed to charge holder not to the company

4 Duties of Administrative Receiver

Section overview

The duties of the Administrative Receiver arise from:

- Common law – to take reasonable care to obtain a true market value of assets. This duty is owed primarily to the appointer, but also to preferential creditors, the company and other interested parties such as guarantors.

- Equitable fiduciary duties – not to sell assets to himself and only to sell to associated parties if in good faith and for value.

- Statutory duties – submit receipts and payments accounts, conduct s48 meeting, obtain statement of affairs etc.

The Administrative Receiver has a general duty to assume control of the property comprised in the charge and to safeguard such property.

For assessment purposes the duties of the AR are more important than fixed charge receivers, however the summary table at the end of this chapter sets out key points about their position also.

4.1 Case law duties

The AR has a duty of care to obtain the best price reasonably obtainable in any sale of charged assets. The duty is primarily owed to the appointing charge holder.

An AR owes a duty to preferential creditors not to dissipate the assets out of which those creditors are paid.

The AR has no duty to postpone exercising the power of sale pending the further pursuit or outcome of an application for planning permission, or to take any steps to improve or increase the value of property.

The AR has no duty to the company to preserve its goodwill and business.

Examples of lack of care:

- Failure to advertise the sale in appropriate publications
- Failure to seek specialist advice *Amex Bank*
- Failure to inform potential purchasers of factors rendering assets more valuable

4.2 Equitable fiduciary duties

These derive from the AR's status as agent of the company. The duties are owed to the company which may sue for breach of duty. The company will act through its directors or majority shareholders.

The AR should avoid conflicts of interest and should not therefore sell charged assets to himself.

4.3 Statutory duties

1 **Obtain Statement of Affairs**

   'Nominated persons'

   An AR must require some or all of the persons listed below to make out and submit to him a Statement of Affairs of the company (s47). Such persons are referred to as the 'nominated persons' (Rule 3.3(2)). They are:

   - Persons who are or have been (at any time) officers of the company

   - If the company was formed within one year before the date of appointment of the AR, persons who took part in its formation

   - Persons who are in the company's employment, or who have been in its employment within the year preceding the date of appointment of the AR, and are, in the AR's opinion, capable of giving the information required

   - If another company is an officer of the company or has been within the year preceding the date of appointment of the AR, persons who are, or have been within that year, officers of that other company

   Statement of concurrence

   A person making a Statement of Affairs must verify it by statement of truth. The AR may require other persons listed in s47 to submit a statement of concurrence stating that he concurs in the Statement of Affairs. Such statements of concurrence must be kept with the receivership records (Rule 3.4(6)) and copies must be sent to the Registrar of Companies when the Statement of Affairs is filed (Rule 3.8(3) and (4)).

   Procedure to obtain Statement of Affairs

   An AR who wishes to make persons responsible for a Statement of Affairs must serve notice in the prescribed form on every such person (s47(4); Rule 3.3). Nominated persons have 21 days in which to prepare the Statement (s47(4)), though the notice may specify a longer time or the time may be subsequently extended by the AR. If the AR refuses to extend the time limit, the nominated person may appeal to the court (s47(5)). The notice must state the names and addresses of all the deponents to whom it has been sent (Rule 3.3(3)(a)). On request, the Administrative Receiver must furnish each nominated person with the forms required for preparing the Statement (R3.3(4)).

The expenses of a nominated person making a Statement of Affairs are payable by the AR from his receipts. The amount payable is what the receiver considers reasonable subject to a right of appeal to the court (Rule 3.7).

[Failure by a director to comply with an obligation to make out and submit a Statement of Affairs is a matter to which the court may pay particular regard when deciding whether to make a disqualification order (CDDA 1986, Sch 1, para 10(a)).]

A Statement of Affairs must be in the prescribed form (s47(1)) and must be verified by statement of truth by the persons required to submit it (s47(2)). The principle information given by a Statement of Affairs is (s47(2)):

- Particulars of the company's assets, debts and liabilities
- The names and addresses of its creditors
- The securities held by creditors
- The dates when securities were given

The affairs of the company must be shown as at the date of appointment of the AR.

Publication of the Statement of Affairs

A sworn copy of the Statement of Affairs must be retained by the AR as part of the records of the receivership (Rule 3.4(6)). A copy of the Statement of Affairs must be sent to the Registrar of Companies, either with the AR's report to the creditors (if the Statement has been submitted by the time that the report is filed) or later (Rule 3.8(3)).

The AR's report to creditors must include a summary of the Statement of Affairs (s48(5)).

A Statement of Affairs must be filed at Companies House (Rule 3.8(3) and (4)) where it may be inspected by anyone (CA 2006, s1085(1)). If the AR thinks that it would prejudice the conduct of the receivership or may lead to violence against any person for the whole or part of the Statement of Affairs to be disclosed, he may apply to the court, under Rule 3.5, for an order of limited disclosure in respect of the Statement or any part of it. This is an order that the Statement, or part of it, is not to be open to inspection otherwise than with the permission of the court. The court may also include directions as to the delivery of documents to the Registrar and the disclosure of relevant information to any other persons.

When submitting his report to creditors an AR may omit from his summary of the Statement of Affairs any information which, if disclosed, would seriously prejudice the carrying out of the receiver's functions (s48(6)).

2   **s48 duty**

Within three months of his appointment the AR of a company must, under penalty, prepare a report for the company's creditors in accordance with s48. The court may extend the time limit. Once prepared the report must be served on the secured creditors and filed with the Registrar of Companies. With regard to service on the unsecured creditors it is usual for the AR to publish (in the *Gazette* and other publications thought appropriate) an address to which those unsecured creditors can write to obtain a copy. Copies will then be sent free of charge. Publication and service may also be achieved by posting on a website or electronic service (see Chapter 3).

The main matters on which the receiver must report are:

- The events leading up to his appointment, so far as he is aware of them
- The disposal or proposed disposal by him of any property of the company and the carrying on or proposed carrying on by him of any business of the company
- The amounts payable to the charge holder by whom he was appointed and the amount of any preferential debts
- The amount, if any, likely to be available to pay other creditors

The report must also include a summary of the Statement of Affairs submitted to the AR and a summary of the AR's comments (if any) on the statement (s48(5)). The report may omit any information which, if disclosed, would seriously prejudice the carrying out of the AR's functions (s48(6)).

3 Meeting of unsecured creditors

Convening the meeting

An AR of a company that is not in liquidation must either (s48(2) and (3)):

- Summon a meeting of unsecured creditors, giving not less than 14 days' notice, before which he will lay a copy of the report; or
- State in the report that he intends to apply to the court for a direction that no meeting be held.

The report must be sent to all unsecured creditors whose addresses are known to the AR or he must advertise in the *Gazette* and in such other manner as he thinks fit, that the report is available to be sent free of charge (Rule 3.8(1)). If the AR decides to apply to the court for a direction that no unsecured creditors' meeting need be held, then the application cannot be heard until 14 days have elapsed since the report was published or advertised to the unsecured creditors (s48(3)(b)). The venue of the court hearing must be stated in the report or the advertisement (Rule 3.8(2)).

The meeting must be held within three months after the date of appointment of the AR, unless the court allows an extension of time. The AR is liable to be fined for failing to meet the time limit (s48(2) and (8) and Sch 10).

In deciding the venue for the meeting the AR must have regard to the convenience of the unsecured creditors (Rule 3.9(1)) and it must in any case start between 10.00 and 16.00 hours on a business day unless the court directs otherwise (R3.9(2)). Not less than 14 days' notice must be given of the meeting (s48(2);R3.9(2)). Notice must be given to all the creditors of the company who are identified in the Statement of Affairs, or are known to the AR and have claims against the company at the date of his appointment (R3.9(3)). Proxy forms must be sent with the notice (R3.9(4)).

Notice must also be Gazetted and advertised in such other manner as the AR thinks fit. (R3.9(6)).

The notice must include a statement of the effect of Rule 3.11(1) (entitlement to vote) and a statement that creditors whose claims are wholly secured are not entitled to attend or be represented at the meeting – it is a meeting of unsecured creditors (R3.9(5) and (7)).

Conduct at the meeting

The AR must chair the meeting or he must nominate someone in writing to chair it (R3.10(1)). A nominated substitute must either be a qualified insolvency practitioner or an employee of the AR (or the AR's firm) who is experienced in insolvency matters (R3.10(2)).

The quorum for the unsecured creditors' meeting is one creditor entitled to vote present in person or by proxy. If there is no quorum the meeting is not adjourned unless the chairman thinks it appropriate to do so. If there is no quorum and the meeting is not adjourned it is deemed to have been duly summoned and held (R3.14(3)).

Decisions at the meeting of unsecured creditors are taken by a simple majority, **in value**, of the unsecured creditors who are present and vote in person or by proxy (R3.15(1)).

In order to establish an entitlement to vote a creditor must give to the AR, not later than 12.00 hours on the business day before the day fixed for the meeting, details in writing of the debt claimed to be due (Rule 3.11(1)). A creditor who has failed to comply with this requirement may be allowed by the chairman of the meeting to vote if the chairman is satisfied the failure was due to circumstances beyond the creditor's control (R3.11(2)).

The AR (or the chairman) may call for documents or other evidence that he thinks necessary for substantiating a claim (Rule 3.11(3)). The following rules apply on valuation of claims:

- A debt is valued as at the date of the AR's appointment but any amount paid in respect of the debt since that date must be deducted (R3.11(4))
- A creditor with an unliquidated or unascertained debt is not entitled to vote unless the chairman agrees to assign a value to the debt for the purposes of voting (R3.11(5))
- A secured creditor is entitled to vote only in respect of the balance (if any) of his debt after deducting the value of his security as estimated by him (R3.11(6))

The chairman of the unsecured creditors' meeting has the power to admit or reject a creditor's claim for the purpose of his entitlement to vote, and may exercise that right over all or part of the claim (Rule 3.12(1)). A decision by the chairman is subject to appeal to the court (Rule 3.12(2)). If the chairman doubts whether a claim should be admitted or rejected he may leave the question for later determination (by himself or the court) and permit the creditor to vote, subject to the vote being disallowed if the claim is subsequently rejected (R3.12(3)).

If on appeal the chairman's decision is reversed or varied, or a creditor's vote is declared invalid, the court may order that another meeting be summoned or make such other order as it thinks just (R3.12(4)).

Neither the AR nor the chairman is to be personally liable for the costs of an appeal unless the court orders otherwise (R3.12(5)).

The chair of the meeting shall cause a record to be made of the proceedings and kept as part of the records of the receivership (R3.15(2)). This shall include a list of attendees and if a committee has been established the names and addresses of those elected to be members.

Minutes of the meeting should be kept with the company records.

SIP 12 provides best practice in maintaining records of meeting of creditors.

4 Creditors' committee

The rules concerning creditors' committees in administrative receivership are those concerning creditors' committees in administration (Rule 3.16 to 3.30A). [See Chapter 15.]

5 Duty to account

AR has a duty to account to the company *(Gomba Holdings UK Ltd v Homan 1986)*.

- Directors must be supplied with accounts to enable them to fulfil their statutory duty to prepare annual accounts.
- Any liquidator of the company may require the AR to 'render proper accounts of his receipts and payments and to vouch them and pay over to the liquidator the amount properly payable to him' s41(1)(b).
- Further information may be required from the AR by the directors where they demonstrate a 'need to know' for the purpose of exercising their duties.

R 3.32 requires the AR to send the requisite accounts of his receipts and payments on Form 3.6 to:

- The appointer
- The Registrar of Companies
- The company
- Each member of the creditors committee

Receipts and payments can be summarised under the following headings:

Accounts should be submitted in Form 3.6 within two months after the end of 12 months from the date of appointment and every subsequent 12 month period, and within two months of ceasing to act.

Receipts:

- Pre-appointment debtors
- Post-appointment debtors
- Sale of assets (land and buildings, plant and machinery, vehicles and other shown separately)

Payments:

- Wages and salaries (gross)
- Suppliers of goods and services (post appointment)
- Receiver's disbursements
- Receiver's fees
- Sundry payments

- Pre-appointment creditors (HP, preferential, secured and unsecured shown separately)
- Balance paid by the receiver to those entitled to it

6 **IP Regs 2005**

IP Regs 2005 require the AR to maintain a record of the appointment, however this was updated in the IP Regs 2015 to state it no longer needed to be in a prescribed form and that the IP should extended matters of a material nature to the contents of the form.

7 **CDDA**

The AR must submit a D return on the conduct of directors.

4.4 Duties of receivers appointed under fixed charge only

The fixed charge receiver has a number of duties.

He must deliver to the Registrar his account of his receipts and payments. These must be sent within one month of the expiration of 12 months from the date of appointment and thereafter, within one month of every subsequent period of six months. A receipts and payment account must also be sent within one month of him ceasing to act as receiver and manager, covering the period from the date on which the last abstract was made up, to the present (s38).

Contravention – receiver liable to a fine.

A statement must appear on all letters, invoices etc that a receiver has been appointed (s39).

Where appointed under a fixed and floating charge the receiver must pay preferential creditors in priority to holders of floating charges (s40). Such a receiver would normally be an Administrative Receiver, but can be a 'fixed charge' receiver where the charges do not extend to the 'whole or substantially the whole', of the company's assets.

4.5 Summary

Below is a table which sets out the main differences and similarities between an AR, a fixed charge receiver and a LPA receiver. For the position in respect of status, appointment and charges see preceding chapter.

	AR	Fixed Charge	LPA
Agency	Agent of the company (s44(1)(a)).	Security documentation will state agent of company.	(s109(2) LPA) agent of the company.
Liability on contracts	Personally liable on contracts entered into in performance of his functions (s44(1)(b)). Subject to indemnity out of assets of company (s44(1)(c)).	Personally liable on contracts entered into in performance of functions (s37(1)(a)). Subject to indemnity out of assets of company (s37(1)(b)).	s29 includes LPA receiver in definition of receiver generally therefore s37 applies.
Liability on adopted contracts of employment	Personally liable on adopted contracts of employment (s44(1)(b)). Restricted to qualifying liabilities. Entitled to indemnity out of company's assets. 14 day liability free period.	Personally liable on adopted contracts of employment. **not** restricted to qualifying liabilities (s37(1)(a)). Entitled to indemnity out of company's assets. 14 day liability free period.	As for fixed charge receiver.

	AR	Fixed Charge	LPA
Powers	Statutory powers to manage the company (Schedule 1).	Powers set out in the security documentation.	Statutory powers in LPA limited to (s109(3)) demanding and recovering income and giving receipts.
	Debenture may limit or extend these powers.	Will normally empower receiver to take possession and sell charged assets.	No power to take possession and sell.
	s233 power to demand supply of utilities.	No such statutory powers to enforce co-operation.	No such statutory powers to enforce co-operation.
	Has statutory powers to enforce co-operation of directors.	s43 does **not** apply.	s43 does **not** apply.
	s43 power to apply to the court for sanction to dispose of property subject to prior charges.		
Duties	s40 to pay prefs in priority to holders of floating charges.	s40 applies only if receiver also appointed under floating charge.	As fixed charge receiver no duty to report s48 does not apply.
	s7(3)(d) CDDA to report to Secretary of State on conduct of directors.	No duty to report.	N/A.
	s48 to report to and call meeting of unsecured creditors.	s48 does not apply. N/A.	
	To deal with ERA claims by employees.		
Receipts and Payments	Rule 3.32 Accounts to be delivered to Co's House within two months of:	s38 Accounts to be delivered to Co's House within one month of:	As for fixed charge receiver.
	12 months from appointment;	12 months from appointment;	
	Every subsequent 12 months;	Every subsequent six months;	
	Ceasing to act as AR.	Ceasing to act as receiver.	
Publicity	s39 statement to appear on all letters invoices etc. that a AR appointed.	As for AR.	As for AR.

Summary and Self-test

Summary

```
Pre appointment checks
├── Personal
│   ├── IP
│   ├── Sufficient
│   │   ├── Staff
│   │   └── Experience
│   ├── Ethics
│   │   ├── Significant professional relationship
│   │   └── e.g. auditors
│   └── Bonding under IP regs & "bordereau"
├── Validity of debenture & charges
│   ├── General matters
│   │   Memo/Arts – Co's power
│   │   Board minutes
│   │   Original
│   │   Registered (s.395)
│   │   Executed validly
│   │   Directors resolutions
│   └── Voidability of security
│       ├── s245 invalid floating charge
│       ├── s238 transaction at a undervalue
│       └── s239 preference
└── Validity of appointment [see later]
```

```
Validity of appointment
├── Does debenture permit appointment
│   └── Default
│       ├── Demad for payment
│       └── Time for "mechanics" of £ to be transferred e.g. 1 hour? 1 day? depends on circumstances
├── Letter from directors requesting appointment (Good to stop them from criticising you later)
└── Procedural steps
    └── Appointor sends document of appointment to IP
        ├── Appointment commences upon receipt if IP accepts
        ├── If oral acceptance – IP must confirm it in writing within 5 business days stating time & date of receipt in the prescribed form
        └── IP must accept by end of next working day
```

Certificate in Insolvency

Self-test

Answer the following questions.

1 Answer true or false to the following statements:

 The AR owes a duty to all creditors to obtain the best price reasonably obtainable in any sale of charged assets.

 A True
 B False

 An AR's duty to preferential creditors is to ensure that the assets out of which they will be paid are not dissipated.

 A True
 B False

2 What is the AR's status in relation to the company?

3 A 'nominated person' must submit a Statement of Affairs within how many days if receiving a request?

 A 7 days
 B 14 days
 C 21 days
 D 28 days

4 Within how many months of his appointment must an AR prepare a report for the company's creditors in accordance with s48?

5 If a meeting of the unsecured creditors is to be held under s48 the unsecured creditors must receive how many days' notice?

6 What majority of unsecured creditors must vote in favour for a decision to be passed at the s48 meeting?

Answers to Self-test

1. B – false. The duty is owned to the appointing charge holder.
   A – true.
2. He is the company's agent.
3. C (unless extended).
4. 3 months.
5. 14 days.
6. A majority by value.

Answer to Interactive question

Answer to Interactive question: Foale Limited

1. Director's power over charged assets cease.

    - The AR has sole authority to deal with charged property
    - Directors do however retain custody and control of any assets which are not covered by the appointer's charge

2. Directors should be advised to seek independent professional advice on their position.

3. Appointment of AR does not terminate the director's office.

4. Directors retain statutory duties, to make returns and submit documents to the Registrar of Companies.

5. Directors retain powers to institute proceedings in the company's name.

    - May challenge the validity of the AR's appointment
    - Oppose a petition to wind up the company
    - Cause the company to sue the AR for breach of duty

6. The appointment of the AR does not automatically terminate the director's contract of employment. Director's retain employment unless and until the AR terminates those contracts or the company is liquidated.

7. AR is likely to require the co-operation and assistance of the directors to continue the running of the company whilst a going concern sale is effected.

8. One or more of the directors will be required to submit a statement of affairs.

9. The AR is under a duty to report on the conduct of the directors under the CDDA.

10. The directors have a duty to give to the AR such information as the AR shall require concerning the company and its promotion, formation, business, dealings, affairs or property.

11. The directors are under a duty to attend on the AR at such times as the receiver shall reasonably require.

12. The AR can obtain court orders to force directors to hand over charged property and relevant documentation (under s234).

13. Under s236 the AR can apply to court for an order that any office holder of the company appear before the court.

CHAPTER 19

Administrative receivership: practical aspects and closure

Introduction

Topic List
1. Trading on
2. Claims by employees
3. Selling the business
4. Progress reports
5. AR's responsibility for the company's records
6. AR's responsibility to preferential creditors SIP 14
7. Effect of liquidation
8. Completion

Summary and Self-test

Answers to Self-test

Answers to Interactive questions

Introduction

Learning objectives

- Explain the actions to be taken by an insolvency practitioner in a given scenario
- Describe the impact of an insolvency on employees, creditors and other affected parties
- Describe the on-going obligations upon the insolvency practitioner in an administrative receivership
- State the criteria for completion of an administrative receivership and describe the process of completion

Stop and think

Why would the AR not wish to trade on? What responsibilities does the AR have towards the employees of the company? How does an AR sell the business? How is an administrative receivership ended?

Working context

This chapter deals with very practical matters with which an AR has to deal. For example, if you are asked to assist on a trading receivership you may be required to deal with employee claims, ROT creditors or putting together the AR's statutory returns.

1 Trading on

> **Section overview**
>
> - The AR's prime duty is to realise assets to meet the appointing charge holder's claim. The best way of doing this may be to trade on with a view to selling all or part of the business as a going concern. However unlike an administrator the AR does not have the benefit of the moratorium to protect the company's assets.

1.1 AR's decision to trade on

At the initial meeting with the debenture holder on appointment the AR should agree:

- That the AR will trade on in the short term pending preparation of a report by the AR on the advisability of trading in the longer term
- An overdraft facility to finance the trading
- A suitable indemnity from the debenture holder

The benefits of trading on in the short term should be highlighted. These are:

- By completing work in progress (WIP) the realisable asset value will usually be increased
- Protects outstanding book debts
- Low risk – generally the AR is completing existing contracts not entering new ones
- Provides a breathing space in which the AR can investigate the possibility of a going concern sale and continuing to trade until it is implemented

The AR must be aware of his duty not to worsen the position of preferential creditors

There is no moratorium protecting the assets from creditors seeking to recover their debts.

1.2 Rights of creditors in administrative receivership and the effect on AR's ability to trade

As the AR does not have the benefit of a moratorium the claims of creditors with proprietary rights such as ROT creditors, execution creditors and landlords will be particularly pressing and duress payments may need to be made to secure the availability of essential assets. A recap on the rights of these creditors follows with an emphasis on the position in administrative receivership.

1.2.1 Retention of title (ROT) creditors

Trade suppliers to companies often include in their standard conditions of sale a clause stating that goods supplied to the company will remain the supplier's property until all monies owing to the supplier have been paid. [Refer back to Chapter 10 if you need to refresh your memory about ROT clauses and their validity generally.]

A ROT supplier may, following appointment of an AR seek to recover such goods from the company.

- If the AR wrongfully prevents the supplier from removing the goods he may be liable to pay damages to the supplier.
- However if the AR allows the supplier to remove the goods and the ROT later turns out to be invalid the AR will have dissipated assets which should have been available for the prefs and appointing debenture holder.

It is important therefore to ascertain the validity of the ROT claim by:

- Examining the contract
- Ascertaining whether or not the ROT has been validly incorporated into the contract. If it has the AR should require a representative of the suppliers to attend and identify the goods supplied
- Obtaining legal advice

In practice, while validity is being ascertained the AR may agree to pay supplier for goods actually used.

1.2.2 Execution creditors

Creditors with the benefit of a court judgment may seek to enforce that judgment against the company despite the administrative receivership. There is no moratorium or statutory protection afforded to the company. Consequently, the AR may have to negotiate terms with the creditor to settle the matter on the best possible terms.

1.2.3 Landlords

Where premises are essential to the receivership and a landlord's right to exercise CRAR or forfeit has been triggered, the AR will have to come to some arrangement with the landlord as his rights are unaffected by the administrative receivership.

1.3 Disposal of charged property

If the property of a company in administrative receivership is subject to a charge that ranks before that of the AR, he may apply to the court for an order authorising him to dispose of the property free from that charge, provided the proceeds of disposal go first to paying the obligation owed to the prior chargee (s43). If the proceeds are less than the market value of the property then the court may order that the deficiency be paid to the prior chargee (and presumably no receiver would seek an order unless he knew that the other assets of the company could be used to pay the deficiency).

Before making an order under s43 the court must be satisfied that it will enable the company's assets to be realised more advantageously then if the order were not made (s43 (1)). The procedure would, for example, be appropriate where the AR wanted to sell a group of assets together, some of which were subject to fixed charges.

The AR must give the chargee notice of the court hearing (R3.31 (1) and (2)). If the court makes an order the AR must, under penalty, send an office copy of the order to the Registrar of Companies within 14 days of the making of the order (s43(5) and (6)). The AR must also send an office copy to the owner (R3.31 (3) and (4)).

1.4 Supplies by utilities

s233 states that utility companies (suppliers of gas, water, electricity and telecommunications services) cannot make it a condition of supplying services to a company in receivership that outstanding charges from before commencement of the receivership be paid. They are however entitled to demand that the AR personally guarantees payment of future charges.

The number of business bound by s233 was increased in the 2015 update of the regulations.

1.5 Taxation

Corporation taxes arising on profits made in the period of the receivership are assessable on the company and not the receiver. Where the profits are related to a pre winding up period the tax will rank as an unsecured claim. When the profit relates to a period post liquidation, the tax will be treated as a liquidation expense.

2 Claims by employees

> **Section overview**
>
> - A vital aspect of the conduct of administrative receivership is dealing with claims by employees and limiting the AR's personal exposure in relation to those claims.

The position of an AR in respect of employee liabilities is shown in the table below with a comparison with the position of an administrator.

	Administrative receiver	**Administrator**
Agency	(s44(1)(a)) Deemed to be the company's agent unless and until liquidation.	In exercising his powers deemed to act as the company's agent.

Contractual Liability	(s44(1)(b)) Personally liable on:
	• Adopted contracts of employment to extent of qualifying liabilities, and contracts entered into in performance of functions.
	AR entitled to:
	• Contract out of liability (but not adopted employment contracts)
	• The benefit of any indemnity negotiated with the appointer
	• An indemnity out of the company's assets
		Not personally liable. However:
		• Liabilities on adopted contracts of employment for wages and salary and liabilities on contracts entered into in performance of functions are:
		  – Payable out of floating charge assets;
		  – In priority to administrator's remuneration and expenses
		  – But ranking equally between each other

Liability Free Period	s44(2) Not to be taken to have adopted a contract of employment by reason of anything done/not done within 14 days after his appointment.	As for AR.

Definition

Adopt: Defined in case law as 'conduct amounting to an election to treat the contract as giving rise to a separate liability in the administrative receivership or administration'.

An IP accepts the continuance of an employment contract by not repudiating (terminating) it within 14 days of appointment.

2.1 Qualifying liabilities

An AR's liability is limited to the extent of 'qualifying liabilities'. These are post adoption liabilities for:

- Wages/salaries
- Contributions to an occupational pension scheme
- Wages/salary payable in respect of a period of holiday or absence from work for sickness or other good cause

(Note. An administrator's liability is similarly restricted to qualifying liabilities.)

2.2 Claims by employees

Technical Release 5 deals with non-preferential claims by employees dismissed without proper notice by insolvent employers.

Employees may have claims for:

- Arrears of pay
- Holiday pay
- Pay in lieu of notice
- Redundancy
- Contributions to occupational pension schemes
- Contractual expenses

These will form a claim against the company. The National Insurance Fund (NIF) will agree to pay some monies to employees in respect of their claims subject to certain limits. The amounts employees can claim are summarised below.

[Note that this is the same as the position in administration, see Chapter 16, but the detail is reproduced here for ease of reference.]

Claim	Preferential	Unsecured	Against NIF
Arrears of wages/salary	Restricted to four months pre-relevant date Maximum of £800 per employee	Any excess over the preferential limits	Restricted to the eight weeks accrued pre-appropriate date*
Holiday Pay	All accrued holiday pay is preferential	Not applicable	Restricted to six weeks accrued in the 12 months pre-appropriate date*
Pay in Lieu of Notice	Not preferential	Valid claim for greater of contractual or statutory period Employee has duty to mitigate claim	Statutory (but not contractual) notice
Redundancy	Not preferential	Valid claim for greater of contractual or statutory redundancy	Statutory (but not contractual) redundancy capped at 30 weeks or £14,250, whichever is the lower.
Occupational Pension Scheme	Restricted to employer contributions in the 12 months prior to relevant date, and Employee contributions in the four months prior to relevant date	Any excess over the preferential limits	Employer contributions lowest of – 12 months contributions – 10% of 12 months pay – Amount certified to meet liability to pay employees pension 12 months employee contributions

*Note. The 'appropriate date' in respect of the NIF claims for arrears of wages and holiday pay is the date of appointment of the AR. However, none of these claims can be brought unless the employees are made redundant. In respect of the NIF claim, the weeks need not be the latest weeks of employment, nor need they be consecutive, choose the eight weeks that are most beneficial to the employee.

- Arrears of pay:
    - AR may have to provide funds for payment of arrears to maintain employee loyalty
    - Included as employee's remuneration will be statutory sick pay and contractual bonuses and overtime
    - In respect of the NIF claim, the weeks need not be the latest weeks of employment, nor need they be consecutive. They should be the eight weeks that are financially most beneficial to the employee
- Pay in lieu of notice
    - This claim will be made where the employee has been dismissed without being given proper notice or pay in lieu of notice
    - 'Proper notice' is the statutory minimum notice period provided for by the Employment Rights Act 1996 (ERA 1996), unless the contract of employment provides for a longer period in which case that period applies

Statutory minimum notice periods are as follows:

Period of continuous employment	Minimum notice
Less than 1 month	–
1 month – 2 years	1 week
2 years – less than 3 years	2 weeks
3 years – less than 4 years	3 weeks

And so on up to a maximum of 12 weeks.

- Redundancy:

    Claim for a statutory redundancy payment may be made where the employee:

    - Is employed under a contract of service (as opposed to being self employed and employed under a contract for services)
    - Has been continuously employed for a period of two years
    - Has been dismissed
    - Redundancy is the reason for dismissal

    Redundancy means the dismissal is attributable wholly or mainly to:

    - Employer ceasing or intending to cease carrying on a business; or
    - The requirements for employees to carry out work of a particular kind have been ceased or diminished.

    The amount of a statutory redundancy payment depends on the length of service and age of the employee and is as follows:

Age of employee	No of weeks pay
18–21 years old	½ week per year of employment
22–40 years old	1 week per year of employment
41+ years old	1½ weeks per year of employment

    Subject to a maximum multiplier of 30 weeks, or £14,250, whichever is the lower

2.3 Claims by directors as employees

Technical Release 6 deals with claims by directors as employees in insolvencies.

Directors who are genuine employees (regardless of any shareholding) are usually treated as employees under insolvency legislation. An executive director who has an employment contract with the company and day to day management responsibilities is likely to be an employee. Non-executive directors are likely to be self-employed.

Interactive question 1: Jane Jones

Jane Jones was made redundant upon the administrative receivership of Building Bricks Limited on 1 November 20X9. At that date she was owed five weeks holiday pay at £1,500 per week and nine weeks wage arrears in the sum of £1,500 per week. Redundancy pay has been calculated at £14,562.

Requirement

What amount may be claimed by Jane Jones and what are the status of those claims?

See **Answer** at the end of the chapter.

3 Selling the business

Section overview

- The AR has statutory powers to sell (Schedule 1) and the debenture should also state that the AR has full power to sell the company's business. The same approach to selling the business will apply as in administrations so please refer back to Chapter 16. SIP 13 also applies where the assets are to be purchased by the directors of the company.

4 Progress reports

Section overview

- An AR must, once a year, prepare an abstract of receipts and payments – R3.32. [For a reminder of best practice regarding the preparation of the receipts and payments account please refer back to Chapter 5.]

- **In administrative receivership** the receiver must:
    - Within three months of his appointment send out an initial report (s48 report) on the company to the creditors
    - Thereafter he must send an account of his receipts and payments to each member of the creditor's committee, the Registrar of Companies, the company and his appointer within 2 months after the end of 12 months from the date of appointment and every subsequent period of 12 months. If he ceases to act the account must be sent within two months (Rule 3.32)
    - Documents can be delivered electronically and posting on a website is permissible – see Chapter 3 for further details

If the AR fails to file statutory returns then any member, creditor, the Registrar of Companies or the liquidator may apply to court for an order requiring the AR to make good his default – s41 IA 86.

SIP 7 provides guidance to IP's on the preparation of receipts and payments accounts.

Within two months of ceasing to act the AR must send a copy of his final receipts and payments account to:

- The Registrar of Companies
- The company
- The appointer
- The creditors committee

5 AR's responsibility for the company's records

Section overview

- SIP 17 summarises best practice when ARs are approached by liquidators or directors seeking access to or custody of a company's books and records.

5.1 Classification of records

Company records are classified in SIP 17 as follows:

- Company records maintained prior to appointment of an AR

These are further subdivided:

    - 'Statutory Records'. These are the non-accounting records which the directors are required to maintain by the Companies Act. Examples include:

(i) The statutory registers (eg of members and directors)
(ii) Minute books (eg of board meetings)
(iii) Charges

- 'Statutory accounting and other non-statutory records'

- Company records maintained post appointment of an AR.

    These consist of:

    - 'Statutory Accounting Records' which are in turn further subdivided into – those 'relating to the period after the appointment of a liquidator'

    - 'Other Records' which consist of the company records, the charge holders' records, and the ARs personal records.

    The notes follow the above classification.

5.2 Pre-appointment records

Statutory records

- As the SIP points out the directors' responsibility to maintain, and their power to make entries in these records is unaffected by the AR's appointment (because that appointment does not terminate a director's office).

- It follows that it is not the AR's obligation to maintain these records and indeed the AR should not normally do so.

- On appointment the AR can either leave the statutory records in the custody of the directors, or take possession of them for safe keeping.

- If the AR leaves these records in the custody of the directors they should be located at the company's registered office (this is a Companies Act requirement). This option facilitates the directors in the performance of their duty to maintain the records. The AR has a power to inspect these at any time.

- If the AR takes possession (he has a statutory power to do so in Schedule 1) the AR:

    - Should remind directors of the statutory responsibility to maintain the records

    - Allow the directors free access for this purpose

    - Prepare a detailed receipt of all the records taken into his or her possession which should be signed by a director or other responsible official of the company in receivership

    'Taking possession' does not conflict with the CA 2006 requirement for records to be held at the registered office providing the AR arranges for the registered office to be changed to his own firm and for the registers to be transferred accordingly.

    When the AR vacates office the registers etc should be returned to the directors or to the liquidator if applicable. (An AR has no statutory authority to destroy any pre-appointment records.)

5.3 Statutory and other non-statutory records

- A distinction is made between those records which are necessary for the purposes of the receivership and those which are not.

- Those which are required should be taken into the AR's possession and/or control. The AR has statutory powers in ss234-236 to enforce co-operation and obtain possession.

- Those which are definitely not required may be left with the directors. It is advisable for the AR to list these and note their whereabouts.

- The AR is under no statutory duty to bring records up to date although for practical purposes (eg where necessary to give potential purchasers an indication of the financial state of the business) the AR may have to do so.

- As a separate matter the AR may have to hand over company records to purchasers of company assets (the SIP gives the example of the debtors' ledger or plant registers where there are sales of book debts or plant and machinery).
    - Preferably the AR should retain the originals and either provide copies or allow the purchaser to retain the originals long enough to make own copies.
    - If not the asset sale agreement should provide for the purchaser to make original documents available to the AR on demand.
- If the AR transfers the business of a company to a third party as a going concern s49 VAT Act 1994 place the obligation of preserving records relating to the business on the transferee (ie the purchaser). Note that:
    - The Transferor (AR) can request HMRC to direct otherwise
    - The rule applies even if VAT registration is not transferred and whether or not the transfer itself is treated as one of goods or services
    - Documents covered by the rule include orders, delivery notes, purchase and sales records, annual accounts, VAT accounts and credit and debit notes

5.4 Post appointment records

- **Statutory accounting records**

    Relating to the period prior to appointment of a liquidator
    - The directors retain their statutory duty to prepare accounts.
    - The AR should establish proper accounting records and render full and proper records to the company so that the directors can comply with these obligations.
    - An AR has a duty to make returns of receipts and payments under Rule 3.32.
    - As with pre-appointment records the AR has no authority to destroy them and should be prepared to hand them over to the directors or liquidator on vacating office.

    Relating to the period after the appointment of a liquidator
    - AR must still maintain accounting records.
    - AR must still comply with Rule 3.32.
    - s41 allows any member, creditor, liquidator or the Registrar of Companies to enforce these duties.

- **Other records**

    Company records
    - The SIP citing *Gomba Holdings UK Ltd v Minories Finance Ltd (1989)* makes it clear that only documents generated or received pursuant to the AR's duty to manage the company's business or dispose of its assets fall within this category.
    - These records belong to the company and should be returned to the directors or liquidator on vacation of office.
    - These records should be treated in the same way as the pre-appointment of AR Statutory Accounting and Non-Statutory Records dealt with earlier.

    Charge holders' records
    - These records do **not** belong to the company. They do not therefore need to be handed over to the directors or liquidator on the AR's vacation.
    - They include documents containing advice and information to the appointer and notes, calculations and memoranda prepared to enable the AR to discharge his professional duty to his appointer.

AR's personal records

- These are those records prepared by the AR for the purpose of better enabling the AR to discharge his or her professional duties.
- They include records which must be maintained under the IP Regs 2005 (as amended.)
- Disclosure of these records is a matter for the AR's discretion. The SIP points out, however, that in any legal action against the AR these records may have to be disclosed through the process of disclosure of documents.

Best practice

Reference has already been made to the obligation to provide directors with the information necessary for them to fulfil their statutory duties.

The SIP states that it is best practice to make the above records available to the company (acting through its directors or liquidator) at their request, except for:

- The charge holder and AR's personal records
- Where disclosure would be contrary to the interests of the appointer (eg documents in respect of current negotiations for the sale of assets)

Any records an AR is required to keep by the IP Regs must be preserved for 6 years from the later of the:

- AR's resignation; or
- Time when any security or caution maintained in respect of the company ceases to have effect.

6 AR's responsibility to preferential creditors SIP 14

Section overview

- SIP 14 is concerned with the receiver's responsibility to preferential creditors. The company's preferential debts shall be paid out of floating charge assets in priority to any claims a floating charge holder has under that floating charge. No deduction of preferential debts is made from any fixed charge assets.

6.1 Categorisation of assets and allocation of proceeds

It is not sufficient for the AR to rely upon a statement in the security documentation specifying that the charge is fixed or floating as the courts have struck down charges that purport to be fixed when they are floating.

The receiver has a duty to allocate assets and proceeds correctly and should seek legal advice where necessary.

6.2 Apportionment of costs

The costs of realising floating charge assets should be deducted from the floating charge proceeds before deducting preferential claims. It is important that those costs are allocated correctly. They fall into three categories:

- Liabilities incurred by the company
- Costs of the receiver in discharging his statutory duties
- Remuneration and disbursements of the receiver

In allocating costs the AR should uphold the statutory rights of the preferential creditors, the provisions of the security document and maintain a proper balance between the classes of creditors.

6.3 Determination of preferential debts

The receiver should provide adequate information to the creditors for them to calculate their claims. Where the claim is from an employee, the receiver should obtain all information from the employee and company records and calculate the claim. The employee should then be provided with the calculation and an explanation of how it is arrived at.

Where any payment has been made out of the National Insurance Fund, the Secretary of State is entitled to any preferential debt payment from the receiver.

6.4 Payment of preferential debts

As soon as practicable after funds become available the AR should take steps to pay them. Section 40 makes it clear that payment to preferential creditors is in priority to payments to debenture holders (floating charge holders).

6.5 Disclosure to creditors with preferential debts

Where there are insufficient funds to pay the preferential creditors in full, a statement showing asset categorisation and costs allocated should be sent to those creditors.

7 Effect of liquidation

Section overview

- The appointment of an administrative receiver does not prevent a creditor presenting a petition to wind up the company compulsorily.

7.1 Effect of winding up order

The effects of a winding up order being made are summarised below:

1 **Agency**

   By s44 (1) (a) the AR's agency relationship with the company is terminated by the winding up order. The significance of this is that the AR will now enter post-winding up order contracts as principal and in relation to such contracts the AR will **not** have any indemnity out of the company's assets in respect of his or her personal liability. However, in theory the AR could still seek to exclude liability in the contract itself, and remains entitled to the benefit of the indemnity negotiated with the bank.

   The winding up order has no effect on the AR's position in regard to contracts he had already entered into prior to the winding up order ie the AR retains an indemnity out of the company's assets in relation to these.

2 **Employees**

   Contracts of employment will be automatically terminated by a compulsory winding up order.

   The practical problem for the AR is that the employees may be required to trade the business with a view to a going concern sale.

   The AR can re-employ the employees as principal but:

   - Will be personally liable on their contracts of employment
   - That liability will not be limited to 'qualifying liabilities'
   - The AR will not have an indemnity against the company but will retain any indemnity negotiated with the bank

3 **Charges**

   The AR retains custody and control of the charged assets and retains power to realise and sell company property subject to the charges. He may continue to carry on the company's business and retains his general powers of management in Schedule 1.

   s245 will be triggered by the winding up order, so that a floating charge created within 12 months of the petition, at a time when the company is insolvent, will be invalid except to the extent that fresh consideration is provided.

In practice the turnover of the company's bank account often provides the new money which validates the appointer's charge.

Note that the effect of s245 is not retrospective so that realisations and distributions (eg to the prefs or the appointer) made prior to the winding up order remain valid.

The problem which s245 creates for the AR therefore is that if the floating charge is invalidated, the AR will be a trespasser if he deals with those assets *after* the date of the winding up order. This may give rise to a liability to pay damages.

4 'Statutory effects'

By s41 (1) (b) the AR has a duty to the liquidator (if he so requires) to:

- Render proper accounts of receipts and payments
- Pay over any amounts properly payable

This duty can be enforced by the court.

The AR retains his duty to make returns of receipts and payments to the Registrar of Companies and others under Rule 3.32.

SIP 17 advises members to provide all post appointment company documentation (as opposed to the AR's or appointer's papers) to the liquidator unless disclosure would be contrary to the interests of the appointer.

By s48 (4) (a) the AR shall provide the liquidator with a copy of the s48 report within seven days of the later of:

- The appointment of the liquidator; or
- The AR's compliance with his duty to send the s48 report to the Registrar of Companies.

In any event if no s48 meeting has been held to date none now needs to be held.

s48 (5) a copy of the Statement of Affairs must be sent to the liquidator.

s235 (3) (c) the AR has a general duty to co-operate with the liquidator.

5 Potential actions which may be brought by a liquidator against an AR

s36 (1) the liquidator may apply to the court for an order fixing the AR's remuneration. This procedure should not however be used as a means of routinely checking an AR's costs but should only be applied where costs are clearly excessive.

s212 misfeasance – where there is evidence that the AR is in breach of his duties or has been guilty of a misapplication of company property.

An action against the AR for trespass/conversion (for the benefit of unsecured creditors).

Application to court under s45 (1) for the removal of the AR.

Examination.

6 The preferential creditors

The AR retains his duty to pay preferential creditors under s40. The relevant date from which the AR calculates preferential creditors remains the date of appointment of the AR and this is not affected by a subsequent winding up.

The liquidator also has a quite separate duty to pay preferential creditors under s175. The liquidator takes the date of the order as the relevant date. In practice, the preferential debts may all have been met by the AR or the liquidator may not have sufficient funds to pay the preferential creditors.

7 Discussions with the bank

The bank will have to weigh up whether or not trading on in liquidation, with the potential liabilities that may arise, outweigh the potential benefit of achieving a going concern sale.

7.2 Administrative receivership commencing after date of the winding up order

The notes so far have been concerned with the more common situation where administrative receivership is followed by winding up.

It is possible however for an AR to be appointed where a company is already in liquidation. The law seems to accept that a charge holder has a right to protect its interests in this way even though a liquidator must generally respect the existing property rights of secured creditors and even though two office holders in a company will increase costs.

Here the AR will never be agent of the company and will act as principal from the outset.

Although the provisions of the Act are far from clear it seems that the AR will acquire a duty to pay preferential creditors in priority to the appointer under the floating charge (see s175). The relevant date used will be the date of the liquidation not the date of appointment of the AR.

Interactive question 2: Redwood Limited

Your principal was appointed AR of Redwood Limited five months ago. He has continued to trade the company for this period but to date no sale as a going concern has been achieved.

The directors of the company have today notified you that a creditor has presented a petition for the compulsory winding up of the company to the court.

They are concerned about the impact of liquidation on the AR and have asked you to write to them with all of the necessary information.

Requirement

Outline the effects of the liquidation on the administrative receivership and the AR personally if the winding up order is made.

You should cover details of the following matters:

(a) Effect on the administrative receiver
(b) Effect on the continued trading of the company
(c) Effect on the directors.

See **Answer** at the end of this chapter.

8 Completion

Section overview

- Completion of the receivership will occur if all debts secured by the charge under which the receiver was appointed are paid, or if all property covered by the charge is realised by the receiver and the proceeds paid to the persons entitled to them.

8.1 Vacation of office

An AR of a company vacates office in the following circumstances.

- Death
- The making of an administration order in relation to the company (para 41 (1) Sch B1)
- Removal from office by order of the court (s45 (1)) – note that a charge holder who appointed a receiver out of court cannot remove him from office
- Resignation on a minimum of five business days' notice to the person by whom he was appointed, to the company (or, if it is then in liquidation, to its liquidator) and to the members of the creditors committee (if any) (s45 (1); R3.33 (1)). The notice must state the date from which the resignation is to be effective (R3.33 (2))

- Ceasing to be qualified to act as an insolvency practitioner (s45 (2))
- Completion of the receivership, which will occur if all debts secured by the charge under which the receiver was appointed are paid, or if all property covered by the charge is realised by the receiver and the proceeds paid to the persons entitled to them
- Dissolution of the company

8.2 Notice of vacation of office

- s45 (4) provides that the AR gives notice of his vacation to the Registrar of Companies within 14 days. (This provision does not extend to an AR vacating due to death for obvious reasons.)
- R3.35 provides that AR should give notice to the company (or liquidator if in liquidation) and creditors committee (if any).
- Within two months of ceasing to act the AR must send a copy of his final receipts and payments account to:
    - The Registrar of Companies
    - The company
    - The appointer
    - The creditors' committee

Summary and Self-test

Summary

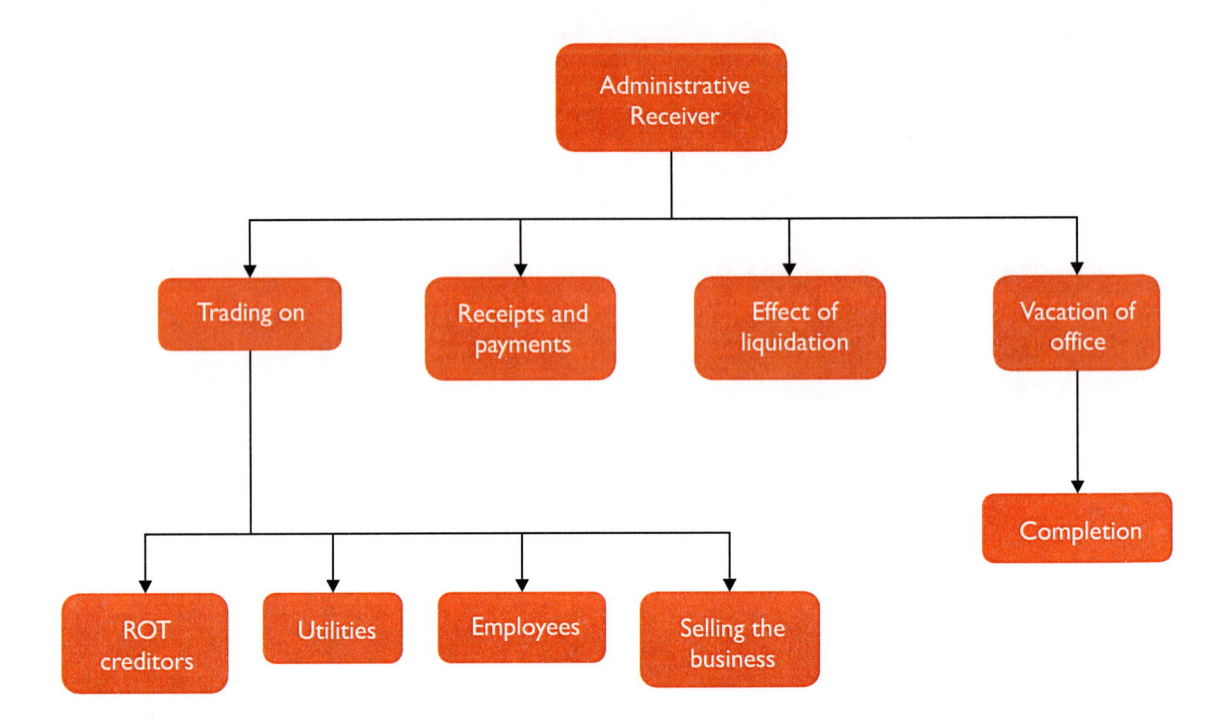

```
                    Administrative
                      Receiver
                          │
    ┌─────────────┬───────┴───────┬─────────────┐
    ▼             ▼               ▼             ▼
 Trading on   Receipts and    Effect of     Vacation of
              payments        liquidation    office
    │                                           │
    │                                           ▼
    │                                       Completion
    │
 ┌──────┬──────┬──────┬──────┐
 ▼      ▼      ▼      ▼
ROT   Utilities Employees Selling the
creditors                 business
```

Self-test

Answer the following questions.

1. You have been trading the company as administrative receiver and have made a profit on trading. What best describes the taxable position on any such profits earned?

    A   Tax is treated as a liquidation expense in a subsequent liquidation
    B   Tax will be a preferential claim in a subsequent liquidation
    C   Tax will be assessable on the company
    D   There will be no tax charge

2. What amounts due to an employee may be claimed preferentially?

3. Which SIP gives guidance to the administrative receiver on the preparation of receipts and payments accounts?

    A   SIP 3
    B   SIP 11
    C   SIP 9
    D   SIP 7

4. Within how many days of vacating office must the administrative receiver give notice to the Registrar of Companies?

    A   7 days
    B   14 days
    C   21 days
    D   28 days

5. Under what section of the Act does an administrative receiver have a duty to pay preferential creditors?

    A   s14
    B   s40
    C   s99
    D   s178

6. What is the effect of any winding-up order on the agency of the AR?

Now, go back to the Learning Objectives in the Introduction. If you are satisfied that you have achieved these objectives, please tick them off.

Answers to Self-test

1. C

2. (i) All holiday pay without limit
   (ii) Up to four months' wage arrears subject to a maximum preferential claim of £800
   (iii) Payments into occupational pension scheme

3. D

4. B

5. B

6. The agency relationship is terminated, the AR now enters into contracts as principal and the AR's indemnity from the company's assets will cease. The AR will therefore seek to rely on the indemnity from the appointer direct. The effect of winding up is not retrospective.

Answers to Interactive questions

Answer to Interactive question 1: Jane Jones

Holiday pay:

- May be claimed in full as a preferential debt as within the maximum of 6 weeks entitlement for 12 months prior to relevant date.
- Five weeks x £1,500 = £7,500

Wage arrears:

- Up to four months arrears may be claimed preferentially up to a maximum preferential claim of £800
- Balance of claim is unsecured

Therefore total claim is nine weeks x £1,500 = £13,500, of which £800 preferential, £12,700 unsecured.

Redundancy:

- Unsecured claim in full.

Answer to Interactive question 2: Redwood Limited

(a) **Effect on the AR**

  (i) s44 (1) (a) AR's agency relationship with the company is terminated.

  (ii) AR will enter into post-winding up contracts as principal.

  (iii) Will not be entitled to an indemnity out of the company's assets in relation to such contracts.

  (iv) AR remains entitled to the benefit of the indemnity negotiated with the charge holder.

  (v) Winding up has no effect on the AR's position in regard to contracts entered into prior to the winding up.

(b) **Effect on the continued trading of the company**

  (i) AR may continue to carry on the company's business.

  (ii) s245 will be triggered by the winding up order. This will not be retrospective in respect of realisations and distributions made prior to the winding up order.

  (iii) AR will be a trespasser if he deals with assets not subject to the floating charge after the date of the winding up order.

  (iv) Contracts of employment will be terminated on the making of the winding up order.

  (v) May cause a problem if employees are required for continued trading.

  (vi) AR can re-employ the employees but as principal and will therefore be personally liable on their contracts.

  (vii) Trading will be riskier for the AR because of personal liability for contracts entered into.

  (viii) Winding up order may affect the ability to sell the business as a going concern.

(c) **Effect on directors (see Chapter 18 for detail)**

  (i) Directors will have to comply with any reasonable requests from the liquidator as well as the AR.

  (ii) Directors will have to attend on the OR for interview regarding the company's affairs following the making of the winding up order.

  (iii) OR has a duty to investigate the affairs of the company and the causes of its insolvency.

(iv) May be required to submit a further Statement of Affairs if any one prepared previously is too old.

(v) Liquidator has a duty to report the conduct of the directors to the Secretary of State under CDDA.

(vi) Any proceedings that may be taken under the CDDA would have to be commenced within two years of the appointment of the AR rather than from the commencement of liquidation.

Section C:

Personal insolvency

CHAPTER 20

Bankruptcy

Introduction
Topic List
1 Informal options for the debtor
2 Formal options for the debtor
3 Options for creditors
4 Introduction to bankruptcy procedures
5 Creditor's petition
6 Debtor's petition
7 Supervisor's petition
8 Investigation into possible IVA
9 Interim receiver
10 Special manager

Summary and Self-test
Answers to Self-test
Answers to Interactive questions

Introduction

Learning objectives

- Compare the characteristics of the different types of personal insolvency, including statutory and non-statutory types and their characteristics
- Explain the processes involved in the creation of a bankruptcy order including the grounds for debtor and creditor bankruptcy petitions
- State the effect of the bankruptcy

Stop and think

How is an individual affected by being in debt, what are the options available, what are the advantages and disadvantages of bankruptcy?

Working context

The topics covered in this chapter are very practical and deal with matters that anyone involved in bankruptcy cases in a work environment will have to be familiar with including the options open to both the debtor and creditors and the consequences for the debtor of being made bankrupt.

1 Informal options for the debtor

> **Section overview**
>
> - Personal insolvency is defined as an inability to pay debts as they fall due (known as the cash flow test). The cash flow test is failed if a debtor owes a creditor £5,000 or more and the creditor issues a statutory demand which is neither complied with or set aside in accordance with the rules within 21 days, or an execution or other process in respect of a judgment debt has been returned unsatisfied (s268). There are a number of options (both informal and formal) for a debtor who has become insolvent. Consider the advantages and disadvantages of each option from both the debtor's and creditor's point of view.

1.1 Do nothing

Many debtors may well choose to take this option but it should never be advised. Invariably this option will result in lots of stress and almost inevitably bankruptcy as creditors may sue and obtain judgment and/or serve a statutory demand upon which a bankruptcy petition may be based.

1.2 Mortgage/Re-mortgaging

Where a debtor is a home owner, another option is to mortgage or re-mortgage the property to release any equity. The equity can then be used to settle the debts. A mortgage has lower interest than other debts and is stretched over a much longer term. The effect is that monthly repayments may be substantially reduced.

The key problem with this option however is that it converts an unsecured debt into a secured debt. Once a debt is secured it will not be affected by a future bankruptcy and hence there will be no debt forgiveness.

1.3 Refinance/consolidation of debts

Where a debtor has an income refinancing may be an option. It is most appropriate where a debtor has a number of loans eg high interest rate credit card debts. In the most successful cases it can leave the debtor with a smaller monthly repayment and a lower overall interest charge. It will of course also avoid the stigma, obligations and disabilities of bankruptcy.

It should always be remembered however that refinancing does not get the debtor out of debt and he may have to carry the burden of that debt for a significant period of time. It will not be an appropriate option where the debtor has such a bad credit record that he cannot obtain refinancing.

1.4 Informal settlement of debts

This can be appropriate in circumstances where the debtor has only a small number of creditors who are supportive of the debtor. The informal settlement will re-schedule the repayment of debts.

There are many advantages including the fact that:

- It is inexpensive
- There is no court involvement
- Avoids formal insolvency
- The restrictions of an IVA are avoided
- It avoids the disabilities, obligations and stigma of bankruptcy

The main disadvantage however is that it requires the approval of all creditors and despite that approval will not necessarily be legally binding on creditors. Even if a creditor initially consents to an informal arrangement he may be at liberty to change his mind even after the arrangement has been in place for some time. Legal advice should be sought to ensure that any compromise reached between the debtor and his creditors is legally binding.

1.5 Debt management plan

Where a debtor wishes to avoid the stigma of bankruptcy, a debt management plan may be another option.

In this case, a debt management company will assess the debtor's financial situation to establish an affordable monthly repayment amount. The debt management company will then contact all of the debtor's creditors to negotiate a reduced monthly repayment. Interest on the debt will often be frozen

The debtor will thereafter pay the debt management company one sum and they in turn will pay the creditors a pro-rata amount.

As with all other pre-insolvency options however, there are the main disadvantages that: there is no debt forgiveness; it is not necessarily legally binding; there is no legal protection from creditors; and the debtor must pay the debt in full over time.

Because of these serious disadvantages a debt management plan should be approached with caution and considered solely as a short term solution.

2 Formal options for the debtor

> **Section overview**
>
> There are a number of formal options available to a debtor. These include:
>
> - Debt relief orders
> - County Court administration orders
> - Individual voluntary arrangements
> - Deed of arrangement
> - Bankruptcy

2.1 Debt relief orders

Debt Relief Orders (DRO) are applied for online to the Official Receiver with an approved intermediary helping to complete the application. They are intended to give debt relief to people who owe relatively little money, have little or no disposable income and no assets to repay what they owe and cannot afford to make themselves bankrupt. They offer an alternative to bankruptcy at a reduced cost. If successful a DRO has the effect of writing off all the debtor's unsecured debt.

In order to be eligible for a DRO the applicant must meet the following criteria:

- Must be unable to pay his debts

- Have unsecured debts of less than £20,000

- Have assets of less than £1,000 (additionally a motor vehicle worth less than £1,000 will be exempt)

- Have surplus income of less than £50 per month

- Be domiciled in England or Wales, or for the last three years have been resident or carrying on a business there

- Not be involved in any other formal insolvency procedure at the time of the application for a DRO eg current IVA or bankruptcy or be subject to a bankruptcy restrictions order or undertaking

- Must be no pending bankruptcy petition

During the period of the DRO the debtor will be subject to a number of restrictions which are similar to the restrictions imposed on a bankrupt regarding obtaining credit, acting as a director and carrying on a business. During the period of the DRO the debtor:

- Must notify a lender that he is subject to a DRO before obtaining credit of £500 or more, either alone or jointly with another person

- If carrying on a business in a name that is different from the name under which the DRO was granted, the debtor must notify all those with whom he does business of the name under which the DRO was granted

- May not be involved (directly or indirectly) with the promotion, formation or management of a limited company and may not act as a company director

- Will not be eligible to apply for a DRO again for a period of six years

Whilst subject to the DRO the debtor will also have a number of obligations:

- Must comply with the official receiver's requests for further information
- Inform the official receiver of any assets obtained or increases in income whilst subject to the DRO
- Must not obtain credit of £500 or more without disclosing the DRO
- Not make payments direct to creditors included in the DRO

The DRO will last for 12 months and during this time the debtor will be protected from enforcement action by the creditors included in the DRO. The debtor will be free from those debts at the end of the period.

2.2 County Court administration orders

This is a little used procedure available only to those debtors who have been unable to satisfy a County Court judgment and have combined debts totalling no more than £5,000. When invoked it is an alternative to bankruptcy. If made the administration order will provide for payment of the total debt in instalments. Any creditor owed in excess of £1,500 can seek to defeat the order by petitioning for the debtor's bankruptcy, but such action must be taken within 28 days of the order being made.

2.3 Individual voluntary arrangement

Individual voluntary arrangements were first introduced by the Insolvency Act 1986. The purpose was to enable debtors to obtain relief from their debts outside bankruptcy. An IVA is an agreement between the debtor and his creditors that is legally binding and enables an insolvent debtor to secure a moratorium on his debts. Once an arrangement is in place the creditors' outstanding indebtedness will be settled wholly through the terms of the arrangement.

One advantage of voluntary arrangements is that not all the creditors have to support it to be bound by it. Provided that 75% or more of creditors by value are in favour all unsecured creditors will be bound by the arrangement.

An insolvency practitioner may have two roles to play in a voluntary arrangement, that of nominee and provided that he is appointed to act as such by the creditors, that of supervisor. We will look at the differences between these roles in greater detail later.

2.4 Deed of arrangement

A deed of arrangement is a formal agreement governed by the Deeds of Arrangement Act 1914. It is probable that an IVA will prove more attractive to debtors. The main reason for this is that a dissenting creditor (unlike in an IVA) cannot be bound into the arrangement, leaving him free to pursue all of his remedies against the debtor.

There are however some advantages, namely:

- Long established mechanism with good precedents
- Simple and speedy procedures
- It requires only a simple majority of the creditors in number and value to bring it into effect
- It will not be necessary to call a meeting of creditors
- No need to appoint an insolvency practitioner to act as nominee

As a consequence the costs of a Deed of Arrangement are likely to be lower.

Deeds or arrangement were repealed under the Deregulation Act 2015.

2.5 Bankruptcy

The final option for a debtor is bankruptcy. A court will order that the debtor's assets and liabilities be delivered to the official receiver, who then investigates the debtor's financial position and reports back to the creditors.

There are many disadvantages (not least the stigma attached to bankruptcy) which explains why so many debtors try so hard to avoid bankruptcy although there are some advantages too.

2.5.1 Advantages of bankruptcy

- Automatic discharge after a maximum of one year.
- Vast majority of debts will not survive bankruptcy so the bankrupt is given a clean slate.
- Bankrupt will have no further contact with creditors which should lead to less stress.

2.5.2 Disadvantages of bankruptcy

- All assets vest in the trustee, so the debtor loses control of his assets (including his home).
- The debtor becomes subject to the disabilities, obligations and stigma that arise in bankruptcy. For example, there are restrictions on running a business and obtaining credit which may make it difficult for a debtor to continue to trade.
- In certain circumstances a bankrupt's behaviour, either before or after the bankruptcy, may constitute a criminal offence for which he may now be prosecuted.
- The trustee can investigate transactions that the debtor entered into before or after his bankruptcy and challenge their validity. For example a trustee could seek to recover gifts that the debtor made before becoming bankrupt.
- Even after discharge, the debtor will have a poor credit rating.

3 Options for creditors

> **Section overview**
>
> There are a number of options available to a creditor to recover his debt from the debtor. These include:
>
> - Compromise the debt
> - Sue and obtain judgment
> - Support a voluntary arrangement
> - Petition for bankruptcy

3.1 Compromise

If at all possible (assuming that the debtor cannot genuinely afford repayment) compromise is the best option. However being able to establish the exact state of the debtor's financing and establishing liability may not be possible without court proceedings. If a compromise is achieved the terms of that compromise should be properly recorded (with the aid of legal advice if necessary). The creditor should also be aware that the compromise could (assuming that bankruptcy does follow at some stage) be challenged on the ground that it amounts to a preference (s340).

3.2 Sue and obtain judgment

The main advantage of such action is that it indicates to the debtor that the creditor is serious about recovery of the debt and it will put liability and quantum beyond doubt.

Taking court proceedings may however prove to be expensive and even if judgment is obtained recovery will only be possible if the debtor is good for payment.

3.3 Support a voluntary arrangement

Creditors are concerned primarily about the amount that they are likely to receive from the estate in bankruptcy. Most creditors will support a voluntary arrangement that appears to offer a better return than bankruptcy and looks likely to be successful.

Clearly a creditor will have to be satisfied that the proposal is feasible and that all assets that would be available in bankruptcy will be in the arrangement. It may be possible to exclude such assets but creditors are likely to demand compensation for such exclusion, which is normally provided by way of third party funds.

One reason that creditors may choose not to support an arrangement which, on paper at least, appears to offer a better return than bankruptcy, would be if there was a lack of trust in the debtor's integrity.

It should always be remembered when advising a creditor that a supervisor of a voluntary arrangement only has the power to investigate transactions defrauding creditors pursuant to s423. A trustee in bankruptcy can however investigate the whole range of antecedent transactions.

3.4 Serve a statutory demand and petition for bankruptcy

This option is often referred to as the 'nuclear deterrent' of debt collection. If it results in full payment prior to the petition being issued it will have achieved its objective quickly and cheaply.

Once a petition is issued however it is likely that other creditors may support the petition making bankruptcy much more likely. It should be remembered that there are disadvantages in bankruptcy for the creditor as well as the debtor, not least the likelihood of a low or zero dividend.

Bankruptcy is looked at in more detail in the next section of this chapter.

4 Introduction to bankruptcy procedures

Section overview

- Before a debtor can become bankrupt a bankruptcy petition must be presented to the court and a bankruptcy commences when the court makes a bankruptcy order. A petition for a bankruptcy order may be presented to court by either:
    - A creditor
    - The debtor
    - The supervisor (or bound creditor) of a voluntary arrangement
- The legislation governing bankruptcies may be found in Part IX IA 86 (s264 – s385) and Part 6 of the Rules (R6.1 – R6.251).

4.1 Commencement

A bankruptcy is deemed to commence on the date of the bankruptcy order (note – it is not backdated to the date of the petition as in liquidations).

5 Creditor's petition

Section overview

- In order for a creditor to present a petition the debt must be:
    - Owed to the creditor
    - Must be equal to or exceed the bankruptcy level (currently £5,000)
    - Must be for a liquidated sum
    - Must be unsecured
- The debt can be for a present or future debt.

5.1 Secured debts

A secured creditor is one who has taken a charge over an asset(s) of the debtor to secure any lending. Most commonly a secured creditor will have taken a charge over land either to secure funding made available to secure its purchase or to secure subsequent loans/debts. Other assets may also be charged for example shares or intellectual property rights. The terms of the charge will determine the lender's rights on default. Usually a charge holder is entitled to take possession of the asset and sell it. Note however that in relation to residential property legislation grants some protection to occupiers and so a court order is usually required before a lender can repossess residential property. Bankruptcy will not affect the rights of a secured creditor to enforce his security.

Usually a secured creditor will seek to enforce his security rather than looking to make a debtor bankrupt however it is still possible to petition on a secured debt, s269, if:

- The petition contains a statement by the person having the right to enforce the security that he is willing, in the event of a bankruptcy order being made, to give up his security for the benefit of the bankrupt's creditors, or
- The petition is expressed not to be made in respect of the secured part of the debt and contains a statement by that person of the estimated value at the date of the petition of the security for the secured part of the debt.

5.2 Grounds of the petition

The grounds of a creditor's petition will be the debtor's inability to pay his debts. The creditor must be able to prove to the court that the debtor is unable to pay his debts or has no reasonable prospect of paying them.

This will be shown by:

- **Service of a statutory demand** (s268(1)(a)). The petitioning creditor must prove that he:
    - Has served on the debtor a demand in the prescribed form requiring him to pay the debt (of £5,000 or more) or to secure or compound for it to the satisfaction of the creditor
    - At least 21 days have elapsed since the demand was served
    - The demand has neither been complied with nor set aside in accordance with the Rules
- **Unsatisfied judgment execution** (s268(1)(b)). The petitioning creditor must prove that an execution, issued in respect of a debt due to the petitioning creditor under a judgment, has been returned unsatisfied in whole or in part. For example the petitioning creditor instructed the Court Enforcement Officer (CEO) to seize goods of the debtor to the value of the judgment debt and the CEO has reported that there are no goods available to satisfy the debt.

5.3 Statutory demand

A statutory demand is a document prepared by a creditor in the prescribed form requiring the debtor to pay the debt referred to within 21 days. Alternatively, the debtor can provide some security for the debt or come to some other arrangement for the payment of the debt with the creditor.

A demand is deemed to be necessary as the creditor must prove that the debtor owed a debt of at least £5,000. The debt of £5,000 must be due at the date of presentation of the petition. Even if the debt is satisfied post presentation, the court still retains discretion to make a bankruptcy order on the petition.

There are three forms of statutory demand for a debt:

- Presently due but not based on a judgment
- Presently due based on a judgment or order of the court
- Due at a future time

The creditor must do all that is reasonable to bring the demand to the debtor's attention and personal service is clearly preferable (R6.3(2)).

A debtor is deemed to be unable to pay his debts if at least 21 days have elapsed since a demand was served on him and he has not complied with it. Provided no application to set aside a statutory demand is made, at the expiration of the 21 day period the creditor can proceed to present a petition for bankruptcy.

An application to set aside a demand must be made within 18 days after service of the demand (R6.4(1)). The debtor must show sufficient cause for the setting aside.

- Debt is disputed in whole or part
- Debt is secured
- Debtor has a counter claim which is at least equal to the demand

If the court is not satisfied that the demand should be set aside, it may make an order authorising the creditor to present a bankruptcy petition at a specified time (R6.5).

As an alternative, a petition can be based on an unsatisfied execution and a debt at least equal to the minimum level of £5,000.

5.4 Petition

The form of the petition is prescribed in the Rules:

- Form 6.7 Failure to comply with a Statutory Demand (present debt)
- Form 6.8 Failure to comply with a Statutory Demand (future debt)
- Form 6.9 where execution or other process on a judgment has been returned in whole or part

The petition must contain the following information:

- **Details of debtor** (so far as within petitioner's knowledge) (R6.7)
  - Name
  - Names, other than his true names in which he carries on or carried on business at the date of the debt or since and names of any others with whom he has carried on business
  - Place of residence
  - Occupation
  - Nature of business and address(es) which he carries on or was carrying on at the date of the debt or since
  - Whether the debtor has his centre of main interests or an establishment in another member state
  - If to the petitioner's personal knowledge the debtor has used any name other than his true name that fact shall be stated in the petition

- **Details of debt (R6.8)**
  - Amount of debt and fact it is owed to the petitioner
  - Consideration for the debt (or if none the way in which the debt arose)
  - When the debt was incurred or became due
  - Amount, rate and grounds of claim for any interest or other charge on the debt
  - Either the debt is for a liquidated sum payable immediately and the debtor appears unable to pay it or the debt is for a liquidated payable at some certain, future time and the debtor has no reasonable prospect of being able to pay it
  - If petition is based on a statutory demand the amount claimed cannot exceed that in the demand

- **Grounds of petition**
  - Petition on a present debt – that the debt is for a liquidated sum payable immediately, and the debtor appears unable to pay it
  - Petition on a future debt – that the debt is for a liquidated sum payable at some certain, future time (that time to be specified) and the debtor appears to have no reasonable prospect of being able to pay it

- Petition on a judgment debt – court from which the execution or other process was issued and particulars of the (unsatisfied) return must be given
- **Details of statutory demand** (where appropriate)
  - Date of demand
  - Manner of service [If personal service was effected then the date of service should be as set out in the certificate of service together with confirmation whether service was effected before/after 16.00 hours on Monday to Friday or before/after 12.00 hours on a Saturday.]
  - Statement that to best of creditor's knowledge and belief: the demand neither set aside nor complied with; and there is no outstanding application to set aside

5.5 Presentation and filing of the petition

- Before presenting a petition, the creditor must conduct an Official Search with the Chief Land Registrar in the register of pending actions for pending petitions presented against the debtor. The creditor should then include a certificate at the end of the petition certifying that a search has been done and, either there are no prior petitions or prior petitions have been presented and are pending. [2014 Practice Direction]
- Rule 6.9A governs which court the petition should be presented in.

  Generally this will be the hearing centre for the district in which the debtor has resided or carried on business for the longest period in the last six months.

- In these situations the petition must be presented in the High Court:
  - The petition is presented by the Crown; or
  - The debtor resided or carried on business within the London insolvency district for a greater part of the 6 months preceding the petition and it is not a lower value bankruptcy matter; or
  - The residence or place of business of the debtor within England and Wales is unknown.

[A lower value bankruptcy matter will be dealt with in the Central London County Court. On a creditor's petition lower value is less than £50,000 on a debtor's petition less than £100,000.]

The procedure to follow is as follows:

- The creditor must deliver to the court:
  1. The petition and copies for service.
  2. Statement of truth verifying the petition.
  3. Certificate of service of statutory demand.
  4. Receipt for the deposit payable on presentation of the petition.
  5. The court fee plus a deposit on account of costs.
- The court will then:
  1. Endorse date and time of filing on petition and copies.
  2. Fix venue for hearing and again endorse on petition.
  3. Send to the Chief Land Registrar notice of the petition together with a request that it may be registered in the register of pending actions (R6.13).

A sealed copy of the petition must now be served personally on the debtor by the petitioning creditor or his solicitor, or by a person instructed by either of them, or an officer of the court.

The court can however order substituted service eg by advertisement.

5.6 Effect of presentation of the petition

Once a petition is presented the court may:

- Stay any action, execution or other legal processes against the property or person of the debtor.
- Appoint an interim receiver at any time after the presentation of a bankruptcy petition and before the making of the bankruptcy order. Generally the official receiver will be appointed as interim

receiver, however an insolvency practitioner may be appointed provided that he consents to act as such.

- Appoint a special manager of the bankrupt's estate or business under s370. It may do so where an interim receiver has been installed and it appears that it is in the interests of creditors that such an appointment be made or where the official receiver so requests (usually because the bankrupt is in business and the official receiver wants the business to continue trading).

5.7 Responses to the petition

The debtor can do the following once a petition is served upon him:

- Nothing – order likely to be made.
- Pay the debt.
- Offer to secure or compound the debt.
- Apply for an interim order under s252 (and make a proposal for a voluntary arrangement to a nominee). Once an interim order is made no bankruptcy petition may be presented or proceeded with (s252(2)(a)). Even at the application stage the court has the discretion to stay any legal process (s254(1) and (3))
- If the relevant conditions are satisfied apply for a debt relief order.
- Oppose the petition. Under Rule 6.21 where the debtor intends to oppose the petition he must file in court, at least five business days pre-hearing, notice of grounds of objection and serve a copy on the petitioning creditor or his solicitor.

Note. Failure to comply with Rule 6.21 does not prevent the debtor from defending himself at the hearing.

5.8 Pre hearing steps

Where the petition is on a future debt then under R6.17 the debtor may apply to court for an order that the creditor gives security for the debtor's costs.

Any creditors intending to attend the hearing must give the petitioner notice in Form 6.20 by 16.00 hours on the business day before the hearing date.

- A creditor failing to comply may only attend hearing with permission of court.
- Notice states identity of creditor, amount and nature of debt, contact telephone number and whether creditor intends to oppose or support petition.
- By R6.24 the petitioner must on the date of the hearing, hand in a list of the creditors who have given notice.

Note. The petition is **not** advertised, unlike in compulsory winding up proceedings.

5.9 The hearing

The following persons may appear at the hearing R6.18(3).

- Petitioning creditor
- Debtor
- Creditor (who has given notice)
- Supervisor of any voluntary arrangement in force for the debtor

Note. If petitioning creditor fails to appear he is then barred from presenting a petition in respect of the same debt again (although the court can grant permission).

The petition shall not be heard until at least 14 days have elapsed since it was served on the debtor, unless:

- The debtor has absconded
- There is a proper case for an expedited hearing
- The debtor consents

- The court must be satisfied that the debt is payable and has neither been paid nor secured or compounded for (or on a future debt that the debtor has no reasonable prospect of paying) s271(1).
    - A witness statement verifying the petition is evidence that debt was owing at the date of the petition
    - A certificate that the debt is still outstanding should be handed in on the date of the hearing

The court may:

- Dismiss the petition. Under s271(3) it may do this if satisfied:
    - Debtor able to pay all his debts (taking into account contingent or prospective liabilities); or
    - Creditor has unreasonably refused debtors offer to secure or compound.
- Stay the petition, eg petition based on judgment debt and the debtor intends to appeal.
- Permit the petitioner to withdraw petition.
- Replace a petitioner with another creditor who is present at the hearing (this is a substitution of petitioner or 'Change of Carriage' of petition).
- Adjourn the petition hearing.
- Make a bankruptcy order. This will require the bankrupt to attend on the official receiver as soon as reasonably practicable and may include a provision staying any action or proceeding against bankrupt.

5.10 Formalities on the making of the order

Court sends two sealed copies of the bankruptcy order to the Official Receiver (OR).

The OR keeps one copy and forwards the other to the bankrupt as soon as reasonably practicable.

The OR will send notice of the making of the order to the Chief Land Registrar so it can be registered in the register of writs and order affecting land.

The OR will also advertise the order in the *Gazette* and may cause notice of it to be advertised in such other manner as he thinks fit.

The order itself will require the bankrupt to attend on the OR at such time as the OR shall reasonably require.

Interactive question 1: Grounds for bankruptcy petition

What are the grounds upon which a creditor can present a bankruptcy petition and how are these grounds shown?

See **Answer** at the end of this chapter.

6 Debtor's petition

Section overview

- A debtor's petition may only be presented on one ground – that the debtor is unable to pay his debts s272 (1). This is shown by the debtor filing with the petition a statement of his affairs.

6.1 The petition

The petition must be in the prescribed form – Form 6.27 and contain the following information (Rule 6.38 – Rule 6.39):

- Name (and any other name he has at any time used), place of residence, occupation (if any)
- The name or names in which he carries on business, if other than his true name, and whether, in the case of any business of a specified nature, he carries it on alone or with others

- Nature and address(es) of his business(es)
- Any name or names, other than his true name in which he has carried on business in the period in which any of his bankruptcy debts were incurred and in the case of any such business whether he carried it on alone or with others
- Any address or addresses at which he has resided or carried on business during that period
- Statement that petitioner is unable to pay his debts
- Request that bankruptcy order be made
- Particulars of any insolvency proceedings in respect of debtor in the last five years
- Name and address of supervisor of existing voluntary arrangement (where appropriate).

6.2 Filing of the petition

The debtor will file the following documents in court:

- The petition and three copies
- A Statement of Affairs (sent to the official receiver) and a copy
- Statement of truth verifying the statement of affairs
- Receipt for deposit payable on presentation of petition
- Court Fee

Court will now:

- Hear the petition as soon as reasonably practicable or fix a venue and endorse on the petitions

    Note. If an existing voluntary arrangement is in place, court will fix a venue and give the supervisor at least 14 days' notice of it.

- Send as soon as reasonably practicable to the Chief Land Registrar, notice of the petition for registration in the register of pending actions R6.43.

6.3 Effect of filing of the petition

The court may stay proceedings and appoint an interim receiver (see later in this chapter) as on a creditor's petition.

6.4 Statement of Affairs

The statement of affairs must be submitted in Form 6.28 and verified by a statement of truth.

It requires details of the following:

- List of secured creditors (name, address of creditor, amount owed, nature and value of assets subject to security).
- List of unsecured creditors (name, address of creditor, amount claimed by creditor, amount debtor 'thinks' he owes).
- Inventory of assets (including bank and building society accounts (personal, joint and business), savings, motor vehicles, other assets).
- Name, age (if under 18) and relationship to debtor of any dependants. Also details of any distress levied against debtor.
- Details of any attempt made to come to any agreement with creditors. Debtor's opinion as to whether it is likely a voluntary arrangement will be acceptable to creditors.
- Statement of means (income and expenditure).

6.5 Pre-hearing steps

If there is an existing voluntary arrangement and the petition requests the supervisor to become trustee, that IP must, not less than two business days before the hearing file a report in court R6.42.

The report will give particulars of a date on which he gave written notification to the creditors bound by the arrangement of the intention to seek his appointment as trustee.

This date must be at least seven business days before the of filing of the report.

Details of any response from the creditors must also be given.

6.6 Hearing

At the hearing the court may:

- Appoint an IP to enquire and report into the feasibility of a voluntary arrangement. In order to do this the following conditions must be met:
    - The aggregate of unsecured bankruptcy debts are less than the small bankruptcies level (£40,000)
    - The value of the estate is equal to or exceeds the minimum amount (£4,000)
    - The debtor has not been adjudged bankrupt or entered into a composition or scheme in the last five years from the date of presentation of the petition.

    The report once finalised will be filed at court and if appropriate a creditors' meeting to approve a voluntary arrangement will be arranged

- Refer to an intermediary for a debt relief order (s274A(2))
- Make a bankruptcy order
- Dismiss the petition – this would happen if the debtor fails to satisfy the court that a ground for the making of an order exists

6.7 Formalities upon making of the order

Court sends two sealed copies of the bankruptcy order to the Official Receiver (OR).

The OR keeps one copy and forwards the other to the bankrupt as soon as reasonably practicable.

The OR will send notice of the making of the order to the Chief Land Registrar for registration in the register of writs and order affecting land.

The OR will advertise the order in the *Gazette* and it may also be advertised in such other manner as he thinks fit.

Interactive question 2: Nora Bones

You have an appointment with Nora Bones who has approached your office for some insolvency advice. Six months ago Nora left her employment with the local authority to set up her own business. Unfortunately, due to a series of unforeseen events the business has not been a success and Nora has reluctantly ceased trading. She has incurred business debts of £80,000 during the period of trading and coupled with personal debts in excess of £38,000 she is unable to meet her liabilities as they fall due.

Requirement

What is the procedure to be followed by Nora in order to declare herself bankrupt.

See **Answer** at the end of this chapter.

7 Supervisor's petition

Section overview
- The supervisor or any creditor bound by a voluntary arrangement may present a default petition pursuant to s264(1)(c).

7.1 Grounds

There are three grounds for presenting a default petition:

- Failure to comply with obligations under the IVA
- Giving false or misleading material information or making a material omission in any statement at the creditors' meeting
- Failure to comply with the supervisor's reasonable requests

(See Chapter 31 for more details.)

8 Investigation into possible IVA

Section overview
- The court may appoint an IP to enquire and report into the feasibility of a voluntary arrangement.
- The conditions are:
  - The aggregate of unsecured bankruptcy debts are less than the small bankruptcies level (£40,000)
  - The value of the estate is equal to or exceeds the minimum amount (£4,000)
  - The debtor has not been adjudged bankrupt or entered into a composition or scheme in the last five years from the date of presentation of the petition
  - It would be appropriate to appoint a person to prepare a s274 report

8.1 Appointment

The court will appoint an IP to prepare the report and ultimately to act as supervisor. A fee is payable to the IP by the court on submission of the report.

Once the IP has been appointed, the court will fix the venue for a hearing to consider the IP's report. The debtor will also be notified of the hearing.

8.2 IP's report

s274 – the IP will state the following in his report:

- Whether the debtor is willing to make a proposal for an IVA
- Whether, in his opinion, a meeting of creditors should be held to consider the proposal
- Date, time and place of the proposed meeting

9 Interim receiver

> **Section overview**
> - Where there is a risk that the debtor's assets may be dissipated application may be made for the appointment of an interim receiver. An interim receiver may be appointed at any time after the presentation of a bankruptcy petition and before the making of the bankruptcy order. Generally the official receiver will be appointed as interim receiver, however an IP may be appointed provided that he consents to act as such.

9.1 Procedure for appointment

A creditor of the debtor, the debtor, an Insolvency Practitioner appointed under s273(2) a temporary administrator or a member state liquidator appointed in main proceedings, may apply to the court for the appointment of an interim receiver.

The application is made by way of a witness statement giving the grounds of the application, the estimated value of the estate, whether a voluntary arrangement is in force and whether the OR has been given a copy of the application.

The grounds for an application are 'it is necessary for the protection of the debtor's property'.

The applicant sends the application and statement to the person proposed to be the interim receiver.

Before the court will make an order the applicant must deposit or secure such sum as the court directs to cover the remuneration and expenses of the interim receiver. The interim receiver can come back to the court for more funds if this initial amount proves insufficient.

The court will draw up the order appointing the interim receiver and two sealed copies will be sent to them. The interim receiver will send one copy to the debtor.

9.2 Functions and powers of interim receiver

The function of an interim receiver is to take immediate possession of the debtor's property or part of it if the court has limited the scope of his powers.

The interim receiver has all the rights, powers, duties and indemnities of a receiver and manager.

The court however, can direct that an interim receiver's powers are restricted in any respect.

If the OR is acting as interim receiver he may apply to the court under s370 for the appointment of a special manager.

9.3 Effect of appointment

The debtor must give the interim receiver an inventory of his property and provide such additional information and attend on the interim receiver at such times as he shall reasonably require s286(5).

Creditors may not commence any action or legal proceedings against the debtor without the permission of the court s285 (3).

9.4 Termination of appointment

The appointment of an interim receiver may be terminated by: the court following an application by the official receiver, the debtor or a creditor; or following the making of a bankruptcy order or the dismissal of the petition.

10 Special manager

Section overview

The court may appoint a special manager of the bankrupt's estate or business under s370 where an interim receiver has been installed and it appears that it is in the interests of creditors that such an appointment be made or where the official receiver has been made receiver of the bankrupt's estate on the making of a bankruptcy order.

10.1 Procedure

Application for appointment may be made by the official receiver or trustee of the bankrupt's estate where it appears that the nature of the estate, property or business, or the interests of the creditors generally, require the appointment of another person to manage the estate, property or business.

The application is accompanied by a report setting out:

- The reasons for the application
- An estimate of the value of the estate, property or business which the special manager is to manage

The court will make an order specifying the duration of the appointment (for a specified time or until the occurrence of a specified event) (R6.167(2)).

The powers of the special manager will be set out in the court order (and may include any of the powers exercisable by the trustee).

The remuneration of the special manager will be fixed from time to time by the court (R6.167(4)).

10.2 Duties of the special manager

The special manager has a number of duties.

- Give security: The appointment of the special manager does not take effect until the person appointed has given security to the person who applied for his appointment (R6.168). The amount of the security shall be not less than the value of the estate, property or business in respect of which the special manager is to be appointed. The appointer must file a certificate of adequacy of security in court.

- Prepare and keep accounts: The special manager must, every three months, prepare accounts containing details of his receipts and payments, for the approval of the trustee. When approved the special manager's accounts shall be added to those of the trustee.

- Produce accounts in accordance with the rules to the Secretary of State or to such other persons as may be prescribed.

10.3 Termination of appointment

The appointment will automatically terminate if the bankruptcy petition is dismissed.

If the official receiver/trustee are of the opinion that the employment of a special manager is no longer necessary or profitable for the estate, he may apply to the court for the appointment to be terminated.

The official receiver/trustee must apply to court if creditors pass a resolution requiring that the appointment of the special manager be terminated.

Summary and Self-test

Summary

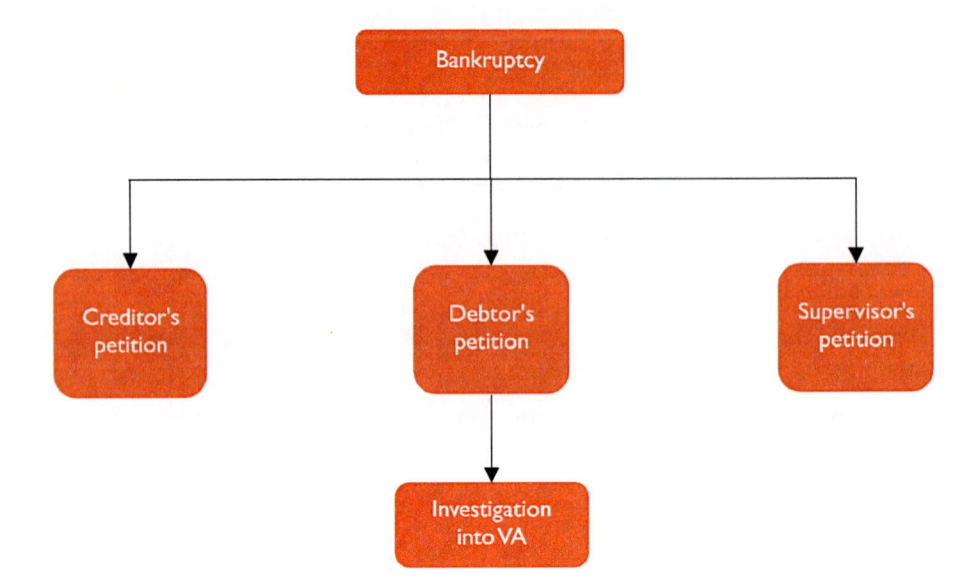

```
                    Bankruptcy
                        │
        ┌───────────────┼───────────────┐
        ▼               ▼               ▼
    Creditor's      Debtor's        Supervisor's
     petition       petition          petition
                        │
                        ▼
                  Investigation
                     into VA
```

Self-test

Answer the following questions:

1   On what grounds may the supervisor of an IVA present a default petition?

2   When is the bankruptcy of an individual deemed to commence?

    A   The date of the appointment of a trustee
    B   The date of the making of a bankruptcy order
    C   The date of the presentation of the petition upon which the bankruptcy order is made
    D   The date on which the statutory demand was served

3   John owes Charles £15,500. Charles has decided to petition for John's bankruptcy. John has lived in Birmingham for 10 years but moved to London two months ago. In what court should Charles present his petition?

    A   The High Court in Birmingham
    B   The High Court in London
    C   Birmingham County Court
    D   Central London County Court

4   The prescribed limit on a debtor's petition is:

    A   £750 or more
    B   In excess of £750
    C   £1,000
    D   There is no limit

5   What are the advantages and disadvantages of bankruptcy to a debtor?

Now, go back to the Learning Objectives in the Introduction. If you are satisfied that you have achieved these objectives please tick them off.

Answers to Self-test

1. Failure to comply with obligations under an IVA.

    Giving false or misleading material information or making a material omission in any document at the creditors meeting.

    Failure to comply with the supervisor's reasonable requests.

2. B

3. C

4. D The debtor proves his inability to pay debts by a statement of affairs.

5. The advantages of bankruptcy to a debtor are:

    (i) Automatic discharge after one year.
    (ii) Vast majority of debts will not survive bankruptcy.
    (iii) Bankrupt will have no further contact with creditors which should lead to less stress.

    The disadvantages of bankruptcy to a debtor are:

    (i) All assets vest in the trustee, so debtor loses control of his assets (includes the debtor's home).

    (ii) The debtor becomes subject to the disabilities (restrictions on obtaining credit), obligations and stigma that arises in bankruptcy. This may make it difficult for a debtor to continue to trade.

    (iii) Potential liability for bankruptcy offences.

    (iv) The trustee can challenge the validity of transactions if they appear to have been at an undervalue or a preference.

    (v) Even after discharge, the debtor will have a poor credit rating.

Answers to Interactive questions

Answer to Interactive question 1: Grounds for bankruptcy petition

A creditor can present a bankruptcy petition on the grounds of the debtor's inability to pay his debts. The creditor must be able to prove to the court that the debtor is unable to pay his debts or has no reasonable prospect of paying them.

This will be shown by:

- Serving a statutory demand

    - The creditor serves on the debtor a demand in the prescribed form requiring him to pay the debt or to secure or compound for it to the satisfaction of the creditor.

    - The debtor is deemed unable to pay his debts if at least three weeks have elapsed since the demand was served on him and he has not complied with it.

- Obtaining judgment on a debt and levying execution or other enforcement process which is not satisfied.

    The creditor can obtain a judgment on a debt and then issue a statutory demand which is not complied with.

In all cases, the debt must be for at least £5,000.

Answer to Interactive question 2: Nora Bones

Nora can present a bankruptcy petition on the grounds that she is unable to pay her debts. The procedure to be followed is:

- Prepare the petition in Form 6.27 and the statement of affairs in Form 6.28

- File in court:

    - Three copies of the petition
    - One copy of her statement of affairs
    - Statement of truth verifying the statement of affairs
    - Receipt for deposit payable on presentation of the petition
    - Court fee

The court will hear the petition as soon as reasonably practicable or fix a venue and endorse on the petitions.

If the court is satisfied that Nora cannot pay her debts then a bankruptcy order will be made, or the court will appoint an IP to enquire and report into the feasibility of an IVA.

On the making of the order the official receiver is appointed receiver and manager of Nora's estate.

CHAPTER 21

Post bankruptcy order procedure

Introduction
Topic List
1 The bankruptcy order
2 Checklist of matters to be dealt with immediately by trustee on appointment

Summary and Self-test
Answers to Self-test
Answers to Interactive questions

Introduction

Learning objectives

- Describe the consequences of bankruptcy for the bankrupt including the impact on employment or business and bankruptcy offences
- State the roles of the trustee in bankruptcy and the official receiver
- Explain the actions to be taken by an IP acting as a trustee immediately and in a given scenario
- Explain the powers rights and obligations of an IP when acting as a trustee

Stop and think

How is an individual affected by being declared bankrupt? Why is an IP not appointed trustee in every bankruptcy case? What is the role of a trustee?

Working context

The topics covered in this chapter are very practical and deal with matters that anyone involved in bankruptcy cases in a work environment will have to be familiar with. It includes how a trustee is appointed, his powers duties and obligations, formalities to be dealt with upon appointment, the consequences for the bankrupt of being made bankrupt and identifying bankruptcy offences committed by the bankrupt.

1 The bankruptcy order

Section overview

- Assuming that the court makes a bankruptcy order the debtor's bankruptcy will commence on that date and continue until discharge (usually automatic within a period of not more than 12 months). During this period the bankrupt will be subject to various restrictions and become subject to new obligations.

- The Official Receiver ('OR') is appointed receiver and manager of the bankrupt's estate unless:

    – The order is based on a failed voluntary arrangement, then the supervisor is usually appointed as trustee; or

    – The order is made on a debtor's petition and the court ordered an enquiry into the debtor's affairs which concluded that a voluntary arrangement would not be appropriate. The insolvency practitioner who undertook the enquiry is usually appointed trustee.

- By Rule 6.121(2) the trustee must have filed in court a statement to the effect that he is an IP and consents to act.

- By s297(7) the trustee gives notice of his appointment to creditors (the court can allow this to be done by advertisement). By s297(8) the trustee's notice will state whether he intends to summon a creditors' meeting to appoint a creditors' committee and will inform creditors of their right to requisition a meeting.

- The OR will continue as receiver and manager until a trustee is appointed. He may become the trustee or he may call a creditors' meeting to ask the creditors to appoint a private insolvency practitioner as trustee. Although control of the bankrupt's estate passes to the OR on the making of the order the bankrupt remains the legal owner until such time as a trustee is appointed. Once a trustee is appointed ownership of the estate assets vest in the trustee and the duties that the debtor previously owed to the OR pass to the trustee.

- On the making of a bankruptcy order the creditors rights to pursue the debtor for payment cease. The creditors new right is to claim a dividend from the estate of the bankrupt. The process of claiming a dividend is referred to as 'proving for a debt'.

In this section we will look at the consequences of the making of the bankruptcy order for the bankrupt, the OR and the creditors.

1.1 Consequences of a bankruptcy order being made

Consequences of bankruptcy on		
Bankrupt	**Creditors**	**Official Receiver 'OR' (or trustee if immediately appointed)**
Loses control of the estate.	Cannot accept payment from bankrupt. All dispositions from bankrupt's estate now void.	Has duty to take all steps he thinks fit for protecting the estate. May appoint a special manager.
Legal proceedings usually stayed. Threat of new legal proceedings and debt recovery generally lifted.	Can only sue bankrupt with permission of court. Existing proceedings likely to be stayed by the court.	
	Cannot continue with execution to recover debts unless court gives permission.	

Consequences of bankruptcy on		
Bankrupt	**Creditors**	**Official Receiver 'OR' (or trustee if immediately appointed)**
	A landlord's right to exercise CRAR limited to 6 months rent arrears accrued before the bankruptcy order made.	
Must prepare a statement of affairs (if not a debtor's petition), provide accounts for previous three years (if requested) and tell a trustee of any increase in income or after acquired property within 21 days. Must attend on OR and deliver up all books, papers, records, and deliver up possession of the estate.		If necessary must investigate the affairs and conduct of the bankrupt.
Must attend creditors meetings if requested.	Can prove in bankruptcy and attend a creditors' meeting if called by the OR. Can vote on the appointment of a trustee and the creation of a creditors' committee. Can force the trustee to call a general creditors' meeting if have support of 10% (in value) of the creditors. (25% for calling first meeting and meeting to remove trustee.)	Must decide whether to call a creditors' meeting within 12 weeks of the order and **must** call one if 25% (in value) of the creditors so request. (Not if trustee already acting.)
Must comply with any court orders and submit to a private or public examination if necessary. Failure will be contempt of court.	Can apply to court for directions if unhappy with the conduct of the bankruptcy.	May apply to court for directions and apply for examination of the bankrupt.

Consequences of bankruptcy on		
Bankrupt	Creditors	Official Receiver 'OR' (or trustee if immediately appointed)
The bankrupt becomes subject to the following obligations and restrictions. • Must not obtain credit in excess of £500 without disclosing bankruptcy status. • May only trade in his bankruptcy name or he must disclose the name in which he was adjudged bankrupt. • May be precluded from certain professional appointments, eg solicitor. • Simple partnerships will automatically dissolve unless the deed provides otherwise. • Will be disqualified as acting as a director under s11 CDDA 86. • May be subject to a bankruptcy restrictions order.		

1.2 Post petition dispositions

Under s284 dispositions by the bankrupt from the presentation of the petition to the vesting of the estate in a trustee are void except to the extent that the court consents to or subsequently ratifies the disposition.

A disposition includes a payment in cash or otherwise or disposition of property, and this rule applies even if the assets would not have formed part of the estate.

Third parties receiving payments from the bankrupt hold those payments as part of the bankrupt's estate.

Payees suffering a loss as a result of this section are treated as a pre-bankruptcy creditor, unless they had notice of the petition at the date the debt to them was incurred.

Persons acquiring interests through innocent third parties, or payments received prior to the commencement of bankruptcy by a *bona fide* third party, for value, without notice, are protected.

1.3 The Statement of Affairs

s288 provides that where a bankruptcy order has been made (other than on a debtor's petition) the bankrupt must submit a statement of affairs to the OR within 21 days of the bankruptcy order being made.

The time limit may be extended by the OR or he may release the bankrupt from the duty to submit.

The bankrupt may apply to court to be released from this duty.

The statement must include the following details.

- List of secured creditors – name, address of creditor, amount owed, nature and value of assets subject to security
- List of unsecured creditors – name, address of creditor, amount claimed by creditor, amount the bankrupt 'thinks' he owes
- Inventory of assets – including cash at bank or building society, household furniture and belongings, life policies, debtors, stocks in trade, motor vehicles, and other property, and in each case the value of the asset.

The debtor must verify the form by statement of truth and deliver a copy to the OR.

The OR will provide the debtor with the form of statement of affairs and written guidance on how to complete it. The OR may employ someone to assist the bankrupt preparing the statement at the expense of the estate. The OR may, at the bankrupt's request, authorise an allowance so that the bankrupt can employ someone to assist him.

The OR may demand further written particulars from the bankrupt expanding on his statement of affairs and may require this information to be verified by witness statement.

The OR must send a report to the creditors containing a summary of the statement of affairs, a summary of any further particulars of it given by the debtor and any observations by the OR.

1.4 Provision of accounts Rules 6.64 and 6.66

On request of the OR the bankrupt has a duty to furnish him with accounts relating to his affairs of such nature, as at such date and for such period as the OR may specify.

This can be for up to three years before presentation of petition or longer with the permission of the court.

Again persons may be employed to assist in the preparation as for the Statement of Affairs.

The accounts should be delivered within 21 days of request or longer if the OR allows. They should be verified by statement of truth if the OR requires it.

1.5 Private and public examinations

At any time before discharge the OR may apply to court for the public examination of the bankrupt (s290(1)). This is often done at the request of the trustee. The OR must apply for a public examination if requisitioned by half or more of the creditors in value.

A simple majority of creditors by value may requisition a public examination by sending a written request to the OR together with:

- List of requisitioning creditors and the value of their claims
- Written confirmation from each creditor concurring with the request
- Statement of reasons why examination requested

OR must now apply to court within 28 days, unless he can show the court that the request is unreasonable.

Before an application to court is made, the OR will demand the requisitionists deposit a sum as security for the costs of the examination.

- Steps to be taken before the hearing (R6.172)
    - OR applies to court for an order that the bankrupt be publicly examined
    - Court makes order and sets venue
    - OR sends copy order to bankrupt
    - OR gives 14 days' notice of examination to any trustee, special manager or creditor
    - OR may advertise (at least 14 days pre-hearing)

- Procedure at the hearing (R6.175)
    - Examination is on oath
    - The OR, trustee, special manager and creditors may ask questions in person or (with court approval) through their lawyers or representatives appointed in writing
    - The bankrupt can at his own expense employ a solicitor, with or without counsel, who may put to him such questions as the court may allow for the purpose of enabling him to explain or qualify any answers given by him and may make representations on his behalf
    - A record of the hearing is made which the bankrupt must sign and verify by statement of truth
    - This record is admissible as evidence in legal proceedings (R6.175 (5) + (6))
    - Expenses of the hearing will be taken from the creditor's deposit (if a requisitioned examination) otherwise by the estate
- Non-attendance without reasonable excuse is contempt of court and may lead to a warrant being issued for the arrest of the bankrupt.
- The trustee or the OR may apply to court for the private examination under s366 of:
    - Bankrupt
    - Bankrupt's spouse or former spouse or civil partner or former civil partner
    - Any person, known or believed to have any property comprised in the bankrupt's estate in his possession
    - Bankrupt's debtors
    - Any person appearing to the court to be able to give information concerning the bankrupt or the bankrupt's dealings, affairs or property

The court may require persons in possession of the bankrupts' property or relevant information, or the bankrupt's debtors to:

- Submit witness statements accounting for their dealings with the bankrupt
- Produce any documents in their control/possession relating to the bankrupt's dealings, affairs or property

The court may issue a warrant for the:

- Arrest of any persons summoned
- Seizure of any books, papers, records, money or goods, in that persons possession

1.6 Stay of bankruptcy proceedings

Application may be made to the court for the bankruptcy order to be stayed (for an order to stop the bankruptcy from proceeding further or to stop further advertisement of the bankruptcy). This may occur where:

- An application for annulment has been made; or
- An application for an interim order is pending (where the bankrupt intends to make a proposal for an IVA).

1.7 Bankruptcy offences

There are a number of bankruptcy offences that can be committed by the bankrupt, some of them retrospective.

The following table provides a summary of the main offences and defences.

Bankruptcy Offence	Defence	Penalty Schedule
s353. Non-disclosure of property/failure to inform of a disposal which might be set aside	Innocent intent s352	Seven years imprisonment, a fine or both
s354. Concealment of property. If the Bankrupt fails to deliver up to OR or his trustee all his assets or if he conceals any debt due to or from him or any property with value £1,000+ commits an offence. Applies retrospectively to concealment within 12 months pre-petition	As above	As above
s354(3). Offence if fails to account without reasonable excuse for loss of any substantial part of his property incurred in the 12 months before the petition was presented against him	No defence under s352	Two years imprisonment, a fine or both
s355. Failure to deliver up books, papers, and other records or prevent production or conceal or destroy them constitutes an offence (retrospective liability if carried out 12 months before presentation of petition)	Innocent intent s352	Seven years imprisonment, a fine or both
s356(1). Offence if bankrupt makes any material omission	Innocent intent s352	As above
s356(2). Offence if bankrupt makes false statement or fails to inform the trustee when a false debt is proved (retrospective liability if false statement made 12 months before presentation of petition)	No defence under s352	As above
s357. Offence committed if bankrupt makes any gift or transfer of property within five years of commencement. Further, concealment or removal of property within two months before or after judgment constitutes an offence	Innocent intent s352	Two years imprisonment, a fine or both
s358. Offence if bankrupt leaves or attempts to leave or makes any preparation to leave England or Wales with property £1,000+ in value in six months prior to presentation of petition	Innocent intent s352	As above

Bankruptcy Offence	Defence	Penalty Schedule
s359. Offence if within 12 months pre-petition dispose of any property obtained on credit in respect of which money still owing	Innocent intent s352	Seven years imprisonment, a fine or both
s360. Obtaining credit and engaging in business in name other than made bankrupt without disclosing bankruptcy or BRO status	No defence under s352	Two years imprisonment, a fine or both
s11 CDDA 1986 Offence to be directly or indirectly involved in the management of a limited company without court permission whilst an undischarged bankrupt or whilst BRO/BRU is in force		Two years imprisonment, a fine or both

1.8 Rights of the bankrupt

The bankrupt also has rights.

- To challenge trustee's decisions.
    - If a bankrupt (or any creditor) is dissatisfied by any act, omission or decision of a trustee he may make an application to the court. The court will have the power to confirm, reverse or modify any such decision or act. The court may also give the trustee any direction as it thinks fit (s303).
    - The court is only likely to interfere where the trustee has acted in bad faith or been fraudulent. It is unlikely to interfere with day to day administrative matters.
- To complain to the relevant professional body of which the trustee is a member:

    The bankrupt may do this if he considers that the trustee is not complying with his ethical guidelines.

- To receive information.

    The bankrupt has a right to request that the trustee provide him with a statement of receipts and payments. The trustee must comply within 14 days of the receipt of any request. The statement should cover the period of one year, up to the last anniversary of the trustee's appointment which preceded the request.

- Right to apply to vary or discharge an income payments order or agreement (R6.193).
- Right to challenge the trustee's remuneration as excessive where an annulment application is sought on ground of discharge of bankruptcy debts.

Interactive question 1: Bankruptcy order

(a) What are the consequences for the debtor if a bankruptcy order is made?

(b) Following the making of a bankruptcy order, what are the obligations of a bankrupt?

See **Answer** at the end of this chapter.

1.9 First meeting of creditors

As soon as practicable in the period of 12 weeks from the date of the bankruptcy order the OR must decide whether to call a meeting of the bankrupt's creditors.

The function of this meeting is to:

- Appoint a trustee s293(1)
- To establish a creditors committee s301(1)

If the OR decides not to call a meeting, he must give notice of his decision to the court and to all creditors known to him or appearing in the bankrupt's statement of affairs.

The OR becomes trustee from the date of this notice.

If the OR has decided not to call a meeting or hasn't yet decided, the creditors may request the OR to summon a meeting. If the request is backed by 25% by value of the creditors the OR must summon a meeting (R294(2)).

Procedure on creditor's requisition (R6.83(1)):

- Creditors' apply on Form 6.34 accompanied by:
    - List of concurring creditors and details of their claims
    - Written confirmation of concurrence from each creditor
    - Statement of purpose of the proposed meeting
- The OR will fix a venue for the meeting to take place not more than 28 days from receipt of the request and give creditors' 14 days' notice.

If the OR decides to call a meeting he must fix a venue (not later than four months from the date of the bankruptcy order) for the first meeting of creditors.

The business of the first meeting is restricted by R6.80.

At the first meeting of creditors, no resolutions shall be taken other than the following.

- A resolution to appoint a named insolvency practitioner to be trustee in bankruptcy or two or more named insolvency practitioners as joint trustees
- A resolution to establish a creditors committee
- (Unless it has been resolved to establish a creditors committee) a resolution specifying the terms on which the trustee is to be remunerated, or to defer consideration of that matter
- (If, and only if, two or more persons are appointed to act jointly as trustee) a resolution specifying whether acts are to be done by both or all of them, or by only one
- (Where the meeting has been requisitioned under s294) a resolution authorising payment out of the estate, as an expense of the bankruptcy, of the cost of summoning and holding the meeting
- A resolution to adjourn the meeting for not more than 14 days
- Any other resolution which the chairman thinks it right to allow for special reasons

By Rule 6.120(A) the OR shall not be appointed trustee by a resolution of the creditors.

If the meeting fails to appoint a trustee the OR now has a duty to decide whether to refer the need for appointment to the Secretary of State.

If the OR decides not to refer he will become trustee (s295(4)) and must notify the court accordingly.

If he decides to refer, the Secretary of State will either:

- Decline to make an appointment (OR now becomes trustee and notifies court); or
- Make an appointment (under s296) and give two copies of the certificate of appointment to OR who sends one to the IP and one to court.

If the meeting appoints a trustee, R6.120:

- The potential trustee provides the chairman with written statement that he:
    - Is a qualified IP
    - Consents to act

- The chairman of meeting certifies the appointment. The appointment takes effect from date endorsed on certificate of appointment.

- The trustee now advertises appointment in the *Gazette* and it may be advertised in such other manner as the trustee thinks fit (R6.124). The cost of advertising is borne by trustee, but he is entitled to reimbursement out of the estate.

Note. Where the trustee has been appointed by the Secretary of State the trustee gives notice to the creditors of his appointment or, if the court allows, advertises his appointment in accordance with the court's directions (s296(4)).

If more than one IP is nominated at the meeting a vote will be required. If a nominee gets a simple majority of those attending and voting he will be appointed. If no nominee gets a simple majority the nominee with fewest votes drops out and vote is taken again.

The process is repeated until clear winner emerges.

The chairman may put a resolution to the meeting at any time that joint nominees be appointed.

The IP and his associates may not exercise either their votes or their proxies' votes on matters in which they are interested.

Interactive question 2: Simon Flatt

Jane Long is a creditor of Simon Flatt. She has received notification from the OR that a meeting of creditors is to be held.

Requirement

Advise Jane what matters will be dealt with at the first meeting of creditors in bankruptcy.

See **Answer** at the end of this chapter.

2 Checklist of matters to be dealt with immediately by trustee on appointment

Section overview

- The trustee has to comply with a number of practical and regulatory matters on his appointment.

2.1 Checklist

A summary checklist is provided below.

- **Formalities and documentation**
    - Trustee ensures has office copy of document of appointment in his possession and obtains office copy of bankruptcy order (see below)
    - Trustee takes steps to advertise appointment. He must comply with Rule 6.124 which requires him to advertise in the *Gazette* as soon as reasonably practicable. He may also advertise in such other manner as he thinks fit
    - Notify HMRC
    - Deal with OR's debit balance
    - Open file

- **Professional**
    - Inform insurers in respect of bordereau – general penalty bond of £250,000 and specific penalty bond sum of not less than the estimated value of the bankrupt's assets (minimum value £5,000 and maximum value £5,000,000)

- Seek to recover premium out of first realisations
- Establish information to put into the case administration record (formally the IP record)

- **Assets – protection of estate**
    - Check that significant assets in the estate are insured, that the policies have not lapsed and cover is adequate and index linked
    - Notify any mortgagees (building society etc) of the trustee's interest
    - If any property forming part of the estate is vacant check physical security, instruct agents with a view to sale and so on
    - Notify any parties holding assets of the bankrupt of the trustee's interest (eg banks, pension providers)
    - Consider disclaiming any onerous assets

- **Legal**
    - Notify solicitors
    - Trustee has power to search Land Register
    - Trustee to arrange to register restrictions over land where appropriate

- **Bankrupt**
    - Arrange for bankrupt to attend at office as soon as possible
    - If no statement of affairs has been obtained from the bankrupt – call for one
    - Write to those owing money to the bankrupt requesting them to forward monies to the trustee direct

- **Statutory duties triggered by appointment**
    - The trustee must 'get in' the estate (s305)

    It will be the trustee's duty in due course to:
    - Realise assets for a proper price, distribute in accordance with the statutory order of priority and (if appropriate) account to the bankrupt for any surplus
    - Pay cash receipts into the ISA once every 14 days or immediately if £5,000 or more
    - Prepare and send progress reports as required by the Rules, maintain receipts and payments account and IP record
    - Take possession of books, papers and other records (s311)
    - Call meeting of creditors if required to do so (on a 10% requisition)
    - Prepare and keep a separate financial record on each bankrupt. Such records must be retained for a period of six years following his vacation of office unless permission to destroy them is received from the OR
    - Upon request of the Secretary of State, send to him an account of his receipts and payments

2.2 IP Record

Prior to the IP Regs 2015, the trustee is required to maintain an IP case record in a prescribed form (Schedule 3 IP Regs 2005). Changes in the 2015 regs state that this information must no longer be in a prescribed form and that the IP must add matters of materiality to the document.

[See Chapter 3 for details.]

Summary and Self-test

Summary

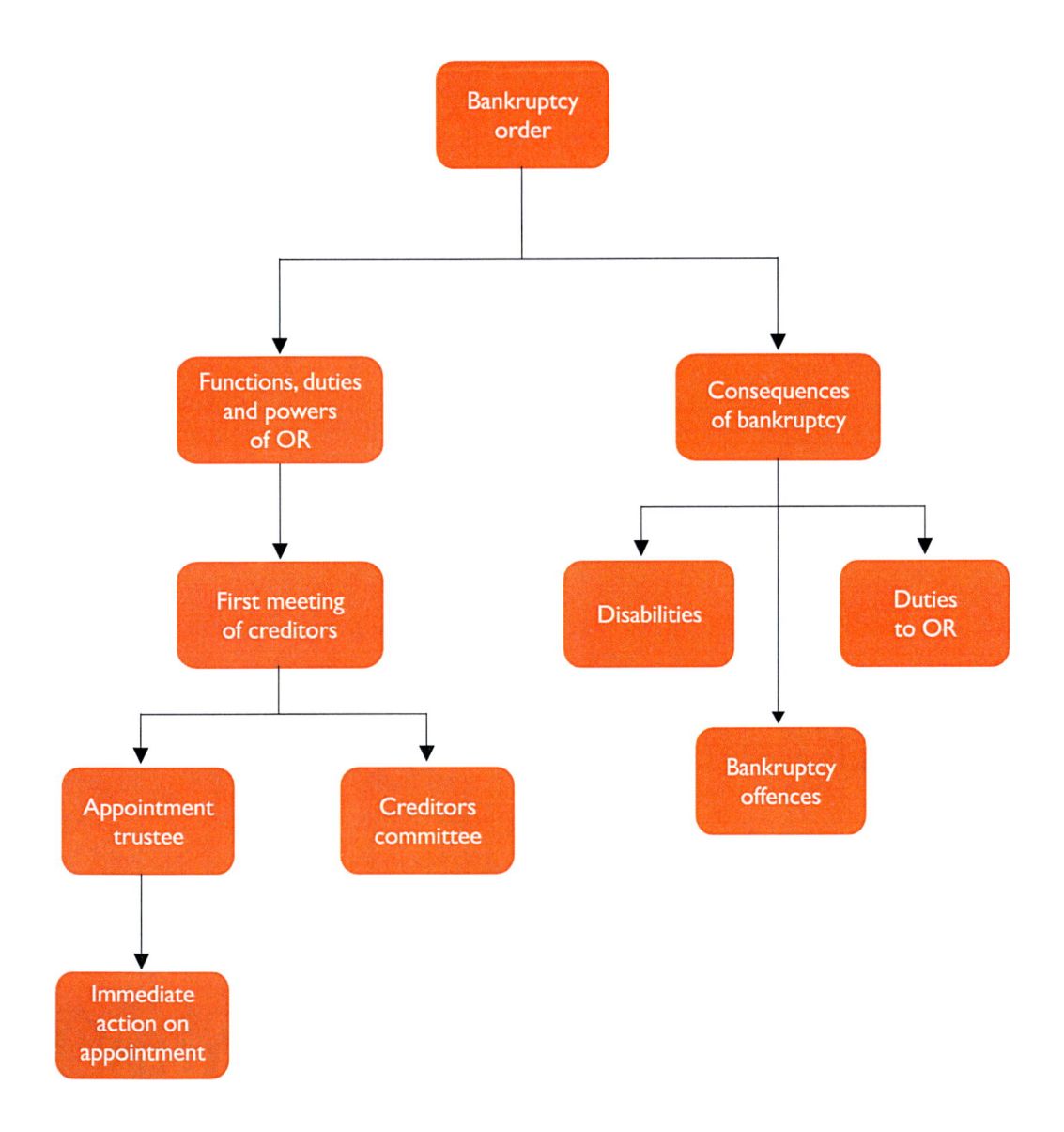

```
                        Bankruptcy
                          order
                    _____|_____
                   |                 |
         Functions, duties    Consequences
         and powers           of bankruptcy
         of OR                    |
            |              _____|_____
            |             |       |       |
         First meeting  Disabilities    Duties
         of creditors                    to OR
            |                    |
       _____|_____         Bankruptcy
      |           |         offences
   Appointment  Creditors
   trustee      committee
      |
   Immediate
   action on
   appointment
```

Post bankruptcy order procedure 349

Self-test

Answer the following questions.

1. Under which section of the IA 86 are post petition dispositions by the debtor void?

    A   s320
    B   s42
    C   s284
    D   s196

2. A bankrupt is unable to obtain credit in excess of a certain level without disclosing the name under which they were adjudged bankrupt. What is this level?

    A   £350
    B   £400
    C   £150
    D   £500

3. Within how many days of the bankruptcy order being made (on a creditor's petition) must the debtor submit a statement of affairs to the OR?

    A   7 days
    B   14 days
    C   21 days
    D   28 days

4. What value of creditors may request the OR to requisition a public examination of the bankrupt?

    A   ½ in number
    B   ½ in value
    C   ¾ in number
    D   ¾ in value

5. To which of the following offences does the defence of innocent intent not apply?

    A   Making a material omission s356(1)
    B   Obtaining credit in excess of £500 without disclosing bankruptcy status s360
    C   Concealing property s354
    D   Failing to deliver up books and records s355

6. Within how many weeks of the bankruptcy order must the OR decide whether to call a meeting of the bankrupt's creditors?

    A   2 weeks
    B   4 weeks
    C   8 weeks
    D   12 weeks

Now, go back to the Learning Objectives in the Introduction. If you are satisfied that you have achieved these objectives, please tick them off.

Answers to Self-test

1 C
2 D
3 C
4 B
5 B
6 D

Answers to Interactive questions

Answer to Interactive question 1: Bankruptcy order

(a) Consequences of bankruptcy:

   (i)   OR will be appointed as receiver and manager of the bankrupt's estate.

   (ii)   Ownership of the estate assets vests in the trustee upon his appointment.

   (iii)   Professional disqualification ie solicitor, accountant, IP.

   (iv)   Cannot obtain credit of £500 without disclosing bankruptcy status.

   (v)   Automatically disqualified from acting as a director.

   (vi)   Partnerships will automatically dissolve.

   (vii)   Cannot engage in a business under a name other than that in which he was adjudged bankrupt without disclosing bankruptcy status.

   (viii) Post petition dispositions are void.

   (ix)   May be liable for bankruptcy offences.

   (x)   Owes a number of duties to the OR.

(b) Obligations of the bankrupt:

   (i)   s291

   – Must deliver up to the OR (or trustee) all books, papers and other records of which he has possession or control.

   – Give to the OR such inventory of the estate, further information and personal attendance as the OR shall require.

   – Duty to deliver possession of his estate to the OR.

   (ii)   Provide accounts for the previous three years (when involved in running a business).

   (iii)   Provide a Statement of Affairs within 21 days of the bankruptcy order.

   (iv)   Notify the OR within 21 days of any after acquired property or changes in income.

   (v)   Attend public or private examination if requested to do so.

   (vi)   Attend creditor meetings if required.

   (vii)   At least six monthly, provide the trustee with information in respect of his business, showing details of goods/services sold, goods/services purchased and any profit/loss arising from the business.

Answer to Interactive question 2: Simon Flatt

The business at the first meeting is restricted by R6.80 to:

(a) A resolution to appoint a named insolvency practitioner to be trustee in bankruptcy or two or more named insolvency practitioners as joint trustees.

(b) A resolution to consider the establishment of a creditors committee.

(c) (Unless it has been resolved to establish a creditors committee) a resolution specifying the terms on which the trustee is to be remunerated, or to defer consideration of that matter.

(d) (If, and only if, two or more persons are appointed to act jointly as trustees) a resolution specifying whether acts are to be done by both or all of them, or by only one.

(e) (Where the meeting has been requisitioned under s294) a resolution authorising payment out of the estate, as an expense of the bankruptcy, the cost of summoning and holding the meeting.

(f) A resolution to adjourn the meeting for not more than 14 days.

(g) Any other resolution which the chairman thinks it right to allow for special reasons.

The OR may not be appointed trustee by a resolution of the creditors Rule 6.120A.

CHAPTER 22

Meetings of creditors

Introduction
Topic List
1 General meetings of creditors
2 Final meeting of creditors
3 Meetings of the creditors' committee
4 Best practice – keeping minutes – SIP 12

Summary and Self-test
Answers to Self-test
Answers to Interactive questions

Introduction

Learning objectives

Tick off

- State the position of creditors in bankruptcy and the role of the creditors' committee ☐
- Describe the ongoing obligations upon the insolvency practitioner in a bankruptcy with regard to
    - Meetings
    - Record keeping
    - Reporting ☐

Stop and think

Why is legislation required to cover meetings of creditors? Why are creditor meetings important? Why should a creditors' committee be established, what is its purpose?

Working context

It is important for an IP to be aware of the statutory requirements when convening meetings of creditors. If a meeting is not validly convened any resolutions passed at the meeting may be challenged.

1 General meetings of creditors

Section overview

- Meetings of creditors may be convened by the Official Receiver (OR) or the trustee for the purposes of ascertaining the wishes of the creditors in any matter relating to the bankruptcy (Rule 6.81).
- Creditors may also requisition a meeting by making a request to the OR or to the trustee R6.83. The statutory provisions relating to creditors' meetings are contained in R6.79 – R6.95. In this section we look at general meetings, the final creditors' meeting and meetings of the creditors' committee.
- Note that the first meeting was covered in the preceding chapter.

1.1 Procedure for calling meetings

The convener, in fixing a venue, date and time for the meeting must have regard to the convenience of the creditors.

Definition

Convener: the person calling the meeting.

The meeting must commence between 10.00 – 16.00 hours on a business day unless the court otherwise directs.

14 days' notice must be given to all creditors known to the convener.

The notice must state:

- Purpose of the meeting
- Date and time by which proxies and outstanding proofs must be lodged (by 12.00 on the business day before the creditors meeting)

Proxy forms must be included with the notice.

As soon as reasonably practicable after sending notice to creditors the convener must give additional notice of the meeting. Such notice shall be Gazetted and advertised in such other manner as the convener thinks fit. In addition to the requirements specified above, the notice must also state who summoned the meeting and, if summoned by a creditor, the fact that it was so summoned and the applicable section of the Act under which it was requested.

Under R6.85 the court may order that notice be given by advertisement only and not to individual creditors.

Under s314(7) creditors can force the trustee to requisition a meeting provided that the request is supported by 10% in value of the bankrupt's creditors (including the creditor(s) making the request).

1.1.1 Electronic delivery of documents

Subject to a particular form of delivery being required by the Act, Rules or court order, notices and documents can be given, delivered or sent electronically provided that the intended recipient has consented and provided an electronic address for delivery, R12A.10.

Any notice or document sent by an office holder must either contain or be accompanied by a statement that the recipient may request a hard copy of the notice or document and give details of how the hard copy can be requested. Where so requested, the hard copy must be sent within 5 business days of receipt of the request by the office holder. No fee can be charged R12A.11.

1.1.2 Use of websites

Except where personal service is required the trustee (and other office holders) may give deliver or send a document to any person by sending notice that it is available for viewing on a website.

Information about the right to request a hard copy must also be given and it must be sent within five business days of any request.

1.2 Procedure at the meeting

1 **Chairman**

- If the OR has convened the meeting, the OR or a person nominated by him will act as chairman.

- If the convener is not the OR, the convener or a person nominated by him in writing to so act, will be chair. Such a nominated person must be an IP, or an employee of the trustee or of his firm, who is experienced in insolvency matters. Where the Chair is not the IP, authority to chair the meeting must be provided by the IP.

2 **Attendance**

The chairman has discretion to admit the bankrupt or any other person who has given reasonable notice of his wish to be present.

3 **Quorum**

R12A.21 – a quorum is at least one creditor entitled to vote, present in person or by proxy.

4 **Entitlement to vote**

A creditor will establish his right to vote by submitting a proof of debt form. [This proof will also be important for establishing the value of the creditor's debt for dividend purposes.]

A creditor can vote if:

- He has lodged a proof of debt by the deadline in the notice calling the meeting
- The trustee accepts the proof (or part of it) for voting purposes. If a creditor wants to vote by proxy it must have been filed before the deadline (if appropriate)

If the creditor has not submitted a proof of debt form in compliance with the Rules the chairman may still allow the creditor to vote if he is satisfied that his failure to comply with the Rules was for reasons out of his control. A creditor can appeal any decision of the chairman at the meeting provided that the appeal is lodged within 21 days of the meeting.

What creditors cannot vote?

- Creditors with unliquidated or unascertained debts eg a damages claim. Exception – where chairman agrees an estimated minimum value for the debt and admits the proof for purpose of voting
- Secured creditors can only vote with any unsecured element of the debt
- Debts on or secured on bills of exchange or promissory notes

5 **Attendance of the bankrupt**

The trustee has the power to ask the bankrupt to attend and the chairman may allow the creditors to ask the bankrupt questions.

6 **Resolutions**

Resolutions are passed by a majority in value of those present and voting in person or by proxy.

7 **Adjournments**

Meetings may be adjourned for a maximum of 14 days to such time and place as the chairman thinks fit. The same meeting may be adjourned more than once, but all adjourned meetings must take place within 14 days of the date of the first meeting unless the court directs otherwise.

8 Suspension of the meeting

R6.90 the chairman may, only once in the course of any meeting, declare the meeting suspended for any period up to one hour.

9 Minutes

R6.95(1) the chairman at any creditors' meeting shall ensure that signed minutes of the proceedings are retained by him as part of the records of the bankruptcy.

R6.95(2) he shall also keep a list of all the creditors who attended the meeting.

R6.95(3) the minutes of the meeting must include a record of every resolution passed.

SIP 12 gives guidance on record taking at meetings.

10 Proxies

Rules governing the use of proxies are found in rule 8.1 onwards. Additional guidance is given to IPs in SIP 10.

'A proxy is the authority given by one person to another to attend, speak and vote as his representative at a meeting.'

All notices convening meetings must enclose a form of proxy. No proxy form can be sent out with the name or description of any person already endorsed on it.

To be valid a proxy must comply with the following rules.

- The proxy must be received by the time and date specified in the notice
- A proxy can be signed by either the principal or on his behalf by an authorised person. The relationship of the authorised person to the principal must be stated on the proxy form eg director of the company
- A proxy issued for a specific meeting can be used at any adjournment of that meeting
- The principal may revoke a proxy at will
- A faxed proxy is valid for voting purposes *IRC Conbeer v Anor*
- Although the chairman of a meeting has discretion to allow a creditor to vote if his failure to lodge a proof was due to circumstances beyond his control there is no such discretion in respect of failure to lodge a proxy
- If a proxy represents a corporation eg a company at a meeting he must produce to the chair of the meeting a copy of the resolution from which he derives his authority

1.3 Written resolutions

A trustee in bankruptcy can obtain a resolution of creditors by correspondence without holding a meeting (R6.88A). The procedure for so doing is:

- The trustee sends notice of the resolution that he wants to put to the creditors to all creditors who would be entitled to attend a creditors' meeting
- The notice must specify a closing date for the responses (not less than 14 days from the date on which the trustee gave notice)
- If no responses are received the trustee must convene a meeting
- A single vote is sufficient to pass the resolution
- 10% of creditors by value can (within five business days of the trustee giving notice) require the trustee to call a meeting to consider the proposed resolution

1.4 Remote attendance at meetings

Pursuant to s379A meetings of creditors may be held remotely. Creditors have the right to request a place for a meeting to be held Rule12A.22.

2 Final meeting of creditors

Section overview
- A final meeting of creditors will be called to receive the trustee's report and for the trustee to seek his release.

R6.137 – the trustee gives 28 days' notice of the final meeting to all creditors of which he is aware and the bankrupt.

As soon as reasonably practicable after giving notice the trustee must *Gazette* a notice of the meeting and advertise it in whatever other manner he thinks fit. The meeting cannot be held until Rule 6.78B, which requires the trustee to send the draft final report to creditors, has been complied with.

The trustee lays a report before the meeting under s331 which includes a summary of his receipts and payments, and a statement that he has reconciled his account with the Insolvency Service Account ('ISA').

At the final meeting the creditors may question the trustee with regard to any matter contained in his report and can resolve against him having his release.

The trustee gives notice to the court that the final meeting has been held and gives the court a copy of his report. A copy of the notice is also sent by the trustee to the OR.

The trustee is released when the notice in filed in court, unless the creditors' committee have resolved that the trustee shall not have his release, in which case he must obtain his release from the Secretary of State.

Interactive question 1: Bob Frampton

Giles has approached you for some advice. He is a creditor of Bob Frampton who was declared bankrupt 18 months ago owing Giles £2,500.

He has received a dividend of 20p in the £ and has just received notification that a final meeting of creditors is to be held.

Requirement

Consider

(a) What matters will be dealt with at the final meeting
(b) Whether he is required to attend or not
(c) What happens after the final meeting

See **Answer** at the end of this chapter.

3 Meetings of the creditors' committee

Section overview
- A creditors' committee of between three and five members may be established at the first or subsequent meetings of creditors. If no committee is appointed its functions vest in the Secretary of State.

3.1 Who may be appointed?

Rule 6.150 states that in order for a creditor to be eligible to sit on the committee he must:

- Have proved a debt or have lodged a proof which has not been wholly refused for dividend or voting purposes

- Be owed a debt which is not fully secured
- Have consented to act on the committee

Company creditors can only act through a representative. A person cannot appear as a representative for more than one committee member, or as a committee member and as a representative for another member. A person acting as a committee member's representative must hold a letter of authority entitling him to act. The creditor's committee must consist of at least 3 and not more than 5 members.

No member may be represented by: a body corporate; a person who is an undischarged bankrupt; a disqualified director; or a person who is subject to a bankruptcy restrictions order or bankruptcy restrictions undertaking or interim bankruptcy restrictions order.

The acts of the committee are valid notwithstanding any defect in the appointment or qualification of any committee member's representative.

3.2 Formalities of establishment

The committee does not come into being, and accordingly cannot act, until the trustee has issued a certificate of its due constitution (Rule 6.151(1)).

The trustee cannot issue the certificate until at least three persons elected to the committee have agreed to act. As and when other members (if any) agree, the trustee will issue an amended certificate.

The trustee shall file the certificate in court.

3.3 Vacation of office

A member will vacate office if he:

- Resigns by written notice to trustee
- Becomes bankrupt (his trustee takes his place on the committee)
- Fails to attend (personally or through a representative) at three consecutive meetings. However the committee can resolve that this rule is not to apply
- Ceases to be, or is found never to have been, a creditor

A member can be removed by a general meeting of creditors held on 14 days' notice.

Vacancies can be filled either by the trustee (with the committee's agreement) or by a meeting of creditors. The creditor must consent to act in either case.

3.4 Creditors' committee meetings

Meetings of the committee shall be held when and where determined by the trustee (Rule 6.153).

Notice: five business days' notice must be given. (Remote attendance 7 business days).

3.4.1 First meeting

Must be held within six weeks of the appointment of the trustee or the establishment of committee (if later).

Subsequent meetings may be held if:

- Called by the trustee of own motion
- Called by the trustee within 21 days of any member's request
- The committee so resolves

3.4.2 Remote attendance/resolutions otherwise than at a meeting

Provided that the procedure specified in Rule 12A.26 is complied with meetings of the committee may be held remotely.

Further in accordance with Rule 6.162 meetings may be avoided if resolutions are sent to members for approval eg by post or email. Any member may request a meeting to consider matters raised by the resolution within seven business days of the resolution being sent.

3.4.3 Chairman of meeting

Trustee or person nominated by trustee who must be either a qualified IP or an employee of the trustee or his firm who is experienced in insolvency matters.

3.4.4 Quorum

A meeting of the committee will be quorate if notice of it has been given to all members and two members are present in person or by representative (Rule 6.155).

3.4.5 Voting

Each member has one vote and resolutions are passed by simple majority. Members/representatives votes where they are interested in a transaction must be disallowed. Postal resolutions may be passed.

3.4.6 Minutes

Chairman must keep minutes of each meeting which are authenticated by him and retained as part of the records of the bankruptcy.

Every resolution passed must be recorded in writing (either separately or as part of the minutes) authenticated by the chairman and kept with the records of the bankruptcy.

3.5 Functions of the creditors' committee

To receive notice from the trustee of the employment of a solicitor and/or the disposal of any assets to an associate of the bankrupt.

To fix the trustee's remuneration if the creditors' meeting has not reserved this matter to itself.

s314(2) – to consent to the trustee appointing the bankrupt to:

- Superintend the management of his estate
- Carry on the business for the creditors' benefit
- Assist in the administration of the estate

[Consent should be obtained at the outset, however the trustee may, without undue delay, seek later ratification in cases of urgency. Under Rule 6.166 where the committee's functions are vested in the Secretary of State they may be exercised by the OR.]

To review the trustee's security for his office.

Historically the committee would give sanction for the exercise of the powers listed in Schedule 5. This is now no longer required.

To sanction, in its existing form, the division among the creditors of any property which cannot be readily sold (s326).

[Note that SIP 15 now provides guidance notes for members of creditors' committees in bankruptcy, insolvent liquidations, administration and administrative receivership.]

3.6 Dealings between the creditors' committee and the trustee

Committee members may not receive out of the estate payment for services given or goods supplied in connection with the estate administration, obtain profit from the administration or acquire an asset forming part of the estate without either the sanction of the court (can be retrospective in urgent situations) or sanction of the committee. Full value must be given. The court has the power to set aside any transaction entered into in contravention of Rule 6.165.

3.7 Expenses

Committee members can recover reasonable travelling expenses (directly incurred in attending meetings or on committee business) as an expense of the administration of the estate.

3.8 Reports

Under Rule 6.152 the trustee must report on matters which the trustee considers are of concern to the committee, or which the committee have indicated are of concern to it. The trustee must report unless:

- The estate is without funds sufficient to enable him to comply
- Costs of compliance would be too great having regard to the importance of the matter
- The request is frivolous

If the committee is established more than 28 days after the trustee came to office the committee is entitled to receive a report from the trustee (in summary form) detailing the actions he has taken since his appointment. If requested the trustee must answer such questions as maybe put to him about the conduct of the bankruptcy so far.

Under Rule 6.163 the committee are entitled to receive six monthly reports from the trustee (or up to two monthly on the committee's request) and to call for production of the trustee's accounts and records (and to consider whether to ask for an audit of the trustee's records).

4 Best practice – keeping minutes – SIP 12

Section overview

- Records should be kept of all meetings of creditors and committees of creditors held under the Act or Rules or under provisions contained in a voluntary arrangement approved by the creditors.

The record should include, as a minimum, the following information.

- The title of the proceedings
- The date, time and venue of the meeting
- The name and description of the chairman and any other person involved in the conduct of the meeting
- A list, either incorporated into the report or appended to it, of the creditors, members or contributories attending or represented at the meeting
- The name of any officer or former officer of the company attending the meeting if not attending in one of the above capacities
- The exercise of any discretion by the chairman in relation to the admissibility or value of any claim for voting purposes
- The resolutions taken and the decision on each one and, in the event of a poll being taken, the value or number (as appropriate) of votes for and against each resolution
- Where a committee is established, the names and addresses of the members
- Such other matters as are required by the statutory provisions applicable to the relevant insolvency procedure or, in the case of a voluntary arrangement, by the terms of the proposal
- When the meeting ended

Where a meeting has been asked to approve an office holder's remuneration, the information provided to the meeting in support of that request should form part of, or be retained with, the record of the proceedings.

The record should be authenticated by the chairman and be either:

- Retained with the record of the proceedings or
- Entered in the company's minute book, with a copy retained with the record of the proceedings, whichever is appropriate.

In the case of committee meetings a copy of the record should be sent to every person who attended, or was entitled to attend, the meeting.

Forms of proxy retained under Rule 8.4 and, where a poll is taken, the poll cards, should be kept with the record of the proceedings.

Where a member is the office holder or is appointed office holder as a result of the proceedings at the meeting and has not himself acted as chairman of the meeting, he should endeavour to ensure that the record is signed by the chairman and complies with the above principles. If the member is not satisfied that the record signed by the chairman is an accurate record of the proceedings, he should either prepare his own record for his files or prepare a note for his files explaining in what respects he disagrees with the chairman's record.

Interactive question 2: Peter May

Murtwell Kitchens Limited are owed £12,500 by Peter May who was declared bankrupt on 25 January 20X1.

They want to sit on a creditors' committee and have approached you for some advice about what it is that the creditors' committee does.

Requirement

What are the functions of the creditors' committee?

See **Answer** at the end of this chapter.

Summary and Self-test

Summary

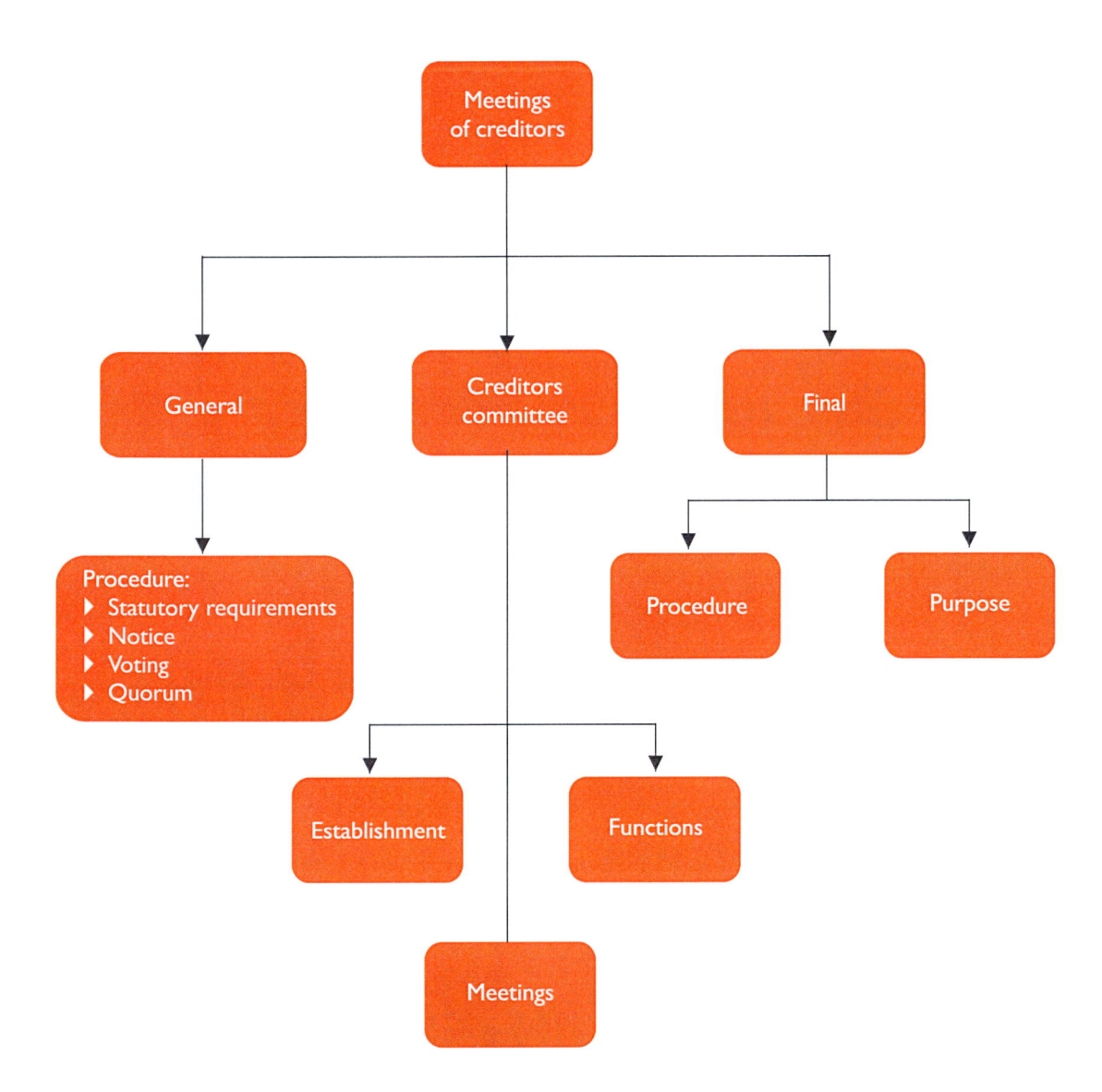

```
                    Meetings
                   of creditors
                         │
        ┌────────────────┼────────────────┐
        ▼                ▼                ▼
     General         Creditors          Final
                     committee            │
        │                │          ┌─────┴─────┐
        ▼                │          ▼           ▼
  Procedure:             │      Procedure    Purpose
  ▸ Statutory            │
    requirements         │
  ▸ Notice               │
  ▸ Voting               │
  ▸ Quorum               │
                ┌────────┼────────┐
                ▼        ▼        
          Establishment  Functions
                │
                ▼
             Meetings
```

Self-test

Answer the following questions.

1 How many days' notice must be given to creditors of a general meeting of creditors?

    A   7 days
    B   14 days
    C   21 days
    D   28 days

2 Which SIP gives guidance to IPs when recording meetings?

    A   SIP 4
    B   SIP 11
    C   SIP 2
    D   SIP 12

3 How many days' notice must creditors be given of a final meeting of creditors?

    A   7 days
    B   14 days
    C   21 days
    D   28 days

4 What majority is required to pass a resolution at a meeting of creditors?

5 When must the first meeting of the creditors' committee be held?

Now, go back to the Learning Objectives in the Introduction. If you are satisfied that you have achieved those objectives, please tick them off.

Answers to Self-test

1. B
2. D
3. D
4. A resolution is passed by a majority in value of those present and voting in person or by proxy.
5. Within six weeks of the establishment of the committee.

Answers to Interactive questions

Answer to Interactive question 1: Bob Frampton

The trustee must give all creditors 28 days' notice of the final meeting – Giles has received this notice.

The final meeting is held when the trustee has realised all of the assets of the bankrupt, made all possible dividend payments to creditors and considers that the administration of the bankruptcy estate is complete.

At the meeting the trustee will lay his report on the conduct of the bankruptcy, together with his receipts and payments account and a statement that he has reconciled his account with the ISA.

The creditors will have an opportunity to question the trustee with regard to any matters contained in the report and will be asked to resolve that the trustee obtains his release. (As a creditor, Giles could resolve against the trustee's release, in which case the trustee would have to apply to the Secretary of State).

The trustee must give notice to the court that the final meeting has been held together with a copy of his report. A copy of the notice must also be sent to the OR.

The case is then closed.

Giles has received a dividend of 20p in the £ in full satisfaction of his debt. He will not be able to pursue the bankrupt for the shortfall.

Answer to Interactive question 2: Peter May

The functions of the committee are:

1 To receive notice from the trustee of the employment of a solicitor or the disposal of any assets to an associate of the bankrupt.

2 To fix the trustee's remuneration.

3 To receive reports on matters which the trustee considers are of concern to the committee, or which the committee have indicated are of concern to it.

4 To consent to the trustee appointing the bankrupt to:

- Superintend the management of his estate
- Carry on the business for the creditor's benefit
- Assist in the administration of the estate

5 To attend committee meetings and to receive reasonable travelling expenses.

6 To receive six monthly reports from the trustee.

7 Review the security for the office given by the office holder.

8 To give sanction for the exercise of powers listed in Schedule 5 Part 1 IA 86.

CHAPTER 23

Bankruptcy estate

Introduction
Topic List
1 The estate
2 Powers of trustee to augment the estate
3 Antecedent transactions
Summary and Self-test
Answers to Self-test
Answer to Interactive question

Introduction

Learning objectives

- Describe the consequences of bankruptcy for the bankrupt, including income payment orders and agreements, the bankruptcy estate, antecedent transactions. State the classes of assets that arise in bankruptcies and the characteristics of each

- Calculate the value of assets or a group of assets in an insolvency using information given and explain how the value is arrived at

- Explain the antecedent transaction rules and identify such transactions from information given

- Explain the powers, rights and on-going obligations of an insolvency practitioner acting as an IP in bankruptcy

Stop and think

Why are some assets excluded from the bankrupt's estate? Should the trustee be able to claim assets acquired by the debtor after the date of the bankruptcy order?

Working context

A trustee's main duty is to realise the assets of the debtor for the benefit of the bankruptcy creditors. In order to do this the trustee must know what assets form part of the bankruptcy estate and what powers he has to augment the estate.

1 The estate

Section overview

- A bankrupt's estate comprises all property belonging to or vested in the bankrupt at the commencement of bankruptcy – s283(1).

Definitions

Property: includes money, goods, **things in action**, land and every description of property wherever situated and also obligations and every description of interest, whether present or future, vested or contingent, arising out of or incidental to property (s436).

Commencement: a bankruptcy is deemed to commence on the date of the bankruptcy order.

Things in action: a 'thing in action' is a property right the value of which derives from the right to sue in respect of it eg the right to enforce a contract.

1.1 Vesting of the estate

The bankrupt's estate vests in the trustee immediately upon his appointment taking effect, or in the case of the OR, on his becoming trustee. (s306(1)). The estate vests automatically by operation of law ie there is no need for any conveyance, assignment or transfer.

When the appointment takes effect depends on the manner of the trustee's appointment:

- **Trustee appointed by a creditors' meeting**

    Date of chairman's certificate.

- **Trustee appointed by the court**

    The appointment takes effect at the time specified in the order.

    There are two situations where a trustee may be appointed by the court.

    - On a debtor's petition where the court has ordered an IP to 'inquire and report' into the feasibility of an IVA but no IVA is entered into, the court may on making a bankruptcy order appoint that IP as trustee.

    - Where the debtor was subject to an IVA but has been made bankrupt the court may appoint the supervisor of the IVA to act as trustee.

- **Trustee appointed by Secretary of State**

    The time specified in the Secretary of State's certificate (R6.122(2)).

1.2 Assets excluded from the estate

The following assets do not form part of the bankrupt's estate:

- Such tools, books, vehicles and other items of equipment as are necessary to the bankrupt for use personally by him in his employment, business or vocation

- Such clothing, bedding, furniture, household equipment and provisions as are necessary for satisfying the basic domestic needs of the bankrupt and his family

- Property held by the bankrupt on trust for any other person

- Income for reasonable domestic needs

- After acquired property

- Assets forfeited on the making of the order (for example, a commercial lease usually provides for forfeiture on bankruptcy)

- Peerages and titles of honour

- Liens on books, papers or records of the bankrupt are unenforceable to the extent they would deny possession to the trustee (s349)

- Rights under an approved pension scheme

2 Powers of the trustee to augment the estate

> **Section overview**
> - The trustee has a number of powers which enable him to bring assets into the estate which would otherwise be excluded.

2.1 Items of excess value

The general provision is that household effects and tools/equipment necessary for the bankrupt's trade are excluded from the bankruptcy estate (s283(2)).

However, where it appears to the trustee that the realisable value of the whole or any part of the excluded property exceeds the cost of a **reasonable** replacement, the trustee may give written notice to claim the property.

> **Definition**
>
> **Reasonable**: defined in s308(4) as being 'reasonably adequate for meeting the needs met by the other property'.

By s309 the trustee must serve the notice within 42 days from date on which the property in question first came to his 'knowledge'. Note that successor trustees are deemed to have the knowledge of their predecessors in title, but any pre-appointment knowledge of a trustee is not deemed to come to his knowledge until appointment.

The effect of serving of the notice is that:

- The property vests in trustee and forms part of the bankrupt's estate.

- The trustee's title relates back to commencement of the bankruptcy (subject to the rights of any *bona fide* purchaser for value without notice).

- The trustee now has a duty to apply estate funds to purchase a reasonable replacement for the property recovered under s309. However the duty to fund a replacement only applies once there are sufficient funds in the estate. The replacement item can be purchased before or after the realisation of the property it replaces. A third party can' buy off' the trustee by paying a sum of money sufficient to leave the bankrupt in possession of the item(s) being claimed.

    Note. The duty to replace has priority over the obligation of the trustee to distribute the estate.

- A dissatisfied bankrupt may apply to the court under s303 which can do as it thinks just.

2.2 Income payment orders

Income generally does not form part of the bankrupt's estate. However, s310(1) allows the trustee to apply to the court for an order that part of the bankrupt's income is paid over. Such income will then form part of the estate. When assessing the bankrupt's income for the purpose of an IPO the assessment will include all income available to meet household expenses such as: the salary of the bankrupt and others who might be expected to contribute towards household expenses for example the bankrupt's partner; monies paid by a lodger or adult children; state benefits including tax credits and child benefit; income from a pension (excluding any GMP or PR element – see 2.7 post); income from savings; trust income; and student loans.

The bankrupt must be left with sufficient monies for meeting the reasonable domestic needs of himself and his family. Expenditure which is likely to be considered excessive and will usually be disallowed will include: private health insurance premiums/payments; monies used for gambling, alcohol and tobacco;

subscriptions to TV services; excessive mortgage payments; charitable donations and voluntary payments into a pension scheme. This guidance is given by the Insolvency Service. Although it must be remembered that there can always be specific circumstances in which this guidance will not be followed for assessment purposes it should be assumed that these expenses will be disallowed.

In practice the trustee will only apply for an IPO if unable to negotiate a figure with the bankrupt. The bankrupt has the option of consenting to an income payments agreement (IPA).

The application may be made in respect of any income including the proceeds of any office, employment or business.

The procedure for the trustee to follow to claim the income is as follows:

1. The trustee applies to the court and a venue is fixed. (The application must be made pre-discharge of the bankrupt.)

2. The trustee must give 28 days' notice to the bankrupt together with a copy of the application and a short statement of the grounds for the application.

3. The bankrupt can now:

    - Consent in writing to the application (to the court and the trustee) at least five business days before the hearing; or

    - Attend the hearing and show cause why the order should be other than that applied for.

4. The order must leave the bankrupt with sufficient income for meeting the reasonable domestic needs of him and his family.

5. At the hearing two types of order can be made.

    - Bankrupt to pay the trustee:

        – Bankrupt will be sent copy of court order by trustee (R6.190(1)).

        – If the bankrupt fails to comply the trustee can apply to court to vary the terms of the order so that payor pays the trustee direct.

    - Person who pays the bankrupt (the '**payor**') to pay the trustee direct:

        – The payor will be sent copy of court order by trustee (bankrupt also gets copy).

        – The payor must now 'make arrangements requisite for immediate compliance with the order' (R6.192(1)). The payor may deduct clerical and administrative costs from the amount to be paid and must give the bankrupt a written statement of those deductions (currently fixed at £0.50p).

        – The payor notifies the trustee if no longer liable to make payments.

Definition

Payor: A person who pays a debt or is obliged to pay a debt by a written instrument.

- Duration is usually three years from the order or agreement and therefore will usually continue beyond discharge.

- s310(4) where the court makes an IPO it may vary or discharge any attachment of earnings order currently in force.

- The court may vary or discharge an IPO.

    – Either the trustee or bankrupt may apply.

    – If the trustee applies the procedure is the same as when a trustee applies for an order in the first place (R6.193(2)).

    – If the bankrupt applies he must provide a short statement of the grounds of the application.

- The court cannot dismiss the application without giving the applicant a chance to make representation. The hearing will be without notice to any other party but the applicant will receive at least five business days' notice. At that hearing the court will either dismiss the application or set a date for a full hearing.

2.3 Income payments agreements

An IPA is a written agreement made between the bankrupt and his trustee by which the bankrupt voluntarily agrees to pay a specified sum to his estate for a specified period of time. It comes into force on the date on which the OR, or the trustee, dates it.

As with an IPO an IPA must be entered into prior to discharge. An IPA can be enforced in the same way as an IPO.

The bankrupt, or the trustee, can vary an IPO/IPA on application to the court. The application can be made before or after discharge. The procedure is contained in Rule 6.193C.

The period of the IPO is a maximum period of three years from the making of the order (or agreement) (s310). This means that the bankrupt may have to continue to pay into the estate notwithstanding his discharge from bankruptcy.

In *Thomas v Edmondson (2014)*, the undischarged bankrupt had entered into an IPA with the official receiver in relation to additional income he expected to receive from HMRC. The trustee took over the appointment and sought to agree a new IPA for any surplus income over and above the tax receipts. The bankrupt refused on the grounds that he had a pre existing IPA. The trustee applied to court for an IPO.

The Court decided that IPOs and IPAs are not mutually exclusive regimes so that an IPO and an IPA could co-exist.

2.4 After acquired property

The trustee has the power under s307 to claim property acquired by the debtor after the date of the bankruptcy order.

The debtor must advise the trustee within 21 days of receipt. The trustee must therefore serve written notice on the bankrupt claiming the asset within 42 days of becoming aware of the property.

s307(4) provides protection for:

- *Bona fide* purchasers for value without notice ie those purchasing an asset from the bankrupt in good faith, at market value and without knowledge of his bankruptcy
- Banks entering into a transaction in good faith and without notice

The effect of giving notice under s307 is that the property vests in the trustee as part of the bankrupt's estate and the trustee's title relates back to the moment of acquisition.

2.5 Execution

Under s346, a creditor cannot retain the benefit of an execution or any sum paid to avoid execution unless it was **completed** or the sums were paid before bankruptcy commenced.

Definition

Completion:

- Execution against goods – on seizure and sale or in the making of a final charging order under s1 Charging Orders Act 1979.
- Execution against land – by seizure, appointment of a receiver or making of a charging order.
- Attachment of debts – on receipt by the judgment creditor of the debt.

The effect of this rule is that if the court enforcement officer is notified of the making of a bankruptcy order he must, at the OR/trustee's request, deliver up goods or money seized or recovered in part satisfaction of the execution.

The court enforcement officer's costs are a first charge on the proceeds or property.

- If execution is levied for a sum of £1,000 or more (including costs) the court enforcement officer must retain the balance (including money paid to avoid seizure and sale) for 14 days and if during that time he is notified of a bankruptcy petition – he must hand over that balance to the trustee after deduction of his costs.

- Third parties acquiring goods from a court enforcement officer or other officer, in good faith, take a good title.

- Court can set aside the rights of the OR/trustee under these rules.

2.6 Commercial Rent Arrears Recovery

The 'self-help' remedy of distress has been abolished by the coming into force of Part 3 of the Tribunals, Courts and Enforcement Act 2007 and the Taking Control of Goods Regulations 2013. It has been replaced by the new process of CRAR which applies (i) only in respect of commercial premises (ii) where the lease is evidenced in writing and (iii) for the recovery of rent only – the sum payable for possession and use of the premises.

CRAR applies even after the trustee has been appointed and the bankrupt's assets have vested in the trustee.

There are three restrictions, on the right to exercise CRAR:

1. Where a creditor uses CRAR in the three months before the bankruptcy order
2. Where a landlord uses CRAR post-order (in respect of pre-order rent arrears)
3. Where a landlord uses CRAR between the petition and the order

1. **Where a creditor exercises CRAR in the three months before the bankruptcy order (s347(3) and (4)):**

    - The rule provides that the goods or effects seized under CRAR, or the proceeds of their sale shall be charged with payment of the preferential debts of the bankrupt's estate, where the estate is for the time being insufficient for meeting those debts.

    - The distress creditor will now rank as preferential for an amount equal to the value which was surrendered to the trustee by complying with this rule. In effect, the CRAR creditor forms his own separate class of creditor ranking behind the other prefs but ahead of ordinary unsecured creditors.

2. **Where a landlord exercises CRAR post-order in respect of pre-order rent arrears (s347(1)):**

    - Here although the landlord can exercise CRAR he is limited to six months' rent accrued pre-order.

    - The six months do not need to be consecutive.

    - The landlord can exercise CRAR post-order in relation to new arrears (ie generated post order) without restriction.

    - If a landlord exercises CRAR for more than six months' worth of pre order arrears – the balance will have to be surrendered to the trustee.

3. **Where a landlord exercises CRAR between the petition and the order:**

    - Here the six month rule in s347(1) should be applied first (see s347(2)). If the landlord has exercised CRAR for more than six months' rent accrued due the balance will have to be surrendered to the trustee.

    - Now the three month rule in s347(3) should be applied to the proceeds of CRAR still held in the landlord's hand after the application of s347(1). Again the landlord will rank as preferential in relation to the amount of any clawback by the trustee pursuant to s347(3).

    - The landlord would then be entitled to retain any balance remaining after the application of the two rules.

2.7 Pensions

It is important to understand the various different types of pensions referred to in the legislation.

A personal pension policy is a contractual agreement with a pension provider (eg Standard Life), which is a form of investment agreement.

An occupational scheme is a pension trust set up by an individual's employer. The employer will usually be 'principal employer' under the scheme and trustees will be appointed to administer it. The employer will make contributions to the scheme as well as the employee.

An approved scheme is defined in s11 of the Welfare Reform and Pensions Act 1999 ('WRPA') and includes personal pension policies and occupational pension schemes approved by HMRC.

With both a personal pension and an occupational pension scheme an employee may 'contract out' of the State Second Pension 'SSP'. The element of the personal pension representing the SSP is known as a 'guaranteed minimum pension' (GMP) or 'protected rights', depending on the type of pension and the time the pension was taken out.

The protected rights or GMP element are protected from an individual's insolvency by virtue of the s159(5) Pension Schemes Act 1993 ie they do not vest in the trustee. Consequently, it is the other constituents of the fund that a trustee may be interested in.

s11 of the WRPA provides that where a bankruptcy order is made against a petition presented after 29 May 2000, any rights of his under an approved pension arrangement are excluded from his estate. Both personal and occupational approved pension arrangements are protected.

However, a trustee will be able to apply for an income payments order in respect of any pension payments made to the bankrupt.

s342A to C Insolvency Act 1986 provides that a trustee can apply to court for an order that excessive contributions previously made by a bankrupt into his pension, that have unfairly prejudiced his creditors, be paid back to the estate. The trustee can attack contributions made by the bankrupt, or on his behalf by someone else, made at any time ie there is no set relevant time limit. The court will consider whether:

- Any of the contributions were made for the purpose of putting assets beyond the reach of creditors
- The total amount of any contributions are excessive in view of the individual's circumstances when those contributions were made

The court may make such order as it thinks fit for restoring the position to what it would have been had the excessive contributions not been made. This might include:

- Requiring the person responsible for the pension arrangement to pay an amount to the estate
- Adjusting the liabilities of the arrangement in respect of the bankrupt or any other beneficiary
- Payment of the costs of the person responsible complying with the court order

s12 WRPA, provides that the court may exclude pension rights in unapproved arrangements from a bankrupt's estate. The court will take into consideration the future likely needs of the bankrupt and his family and whether any benefits under the pension appear likely to be adequate for meeting those needs.

A bankrupt's rights under a personal pension policy cannot be forfeited by reason of his bankruptcy (s14 WRPA).

3 Antecedent transactions

Section overview

- The trustee has the power to take action to recover assets for the estate in respect of:
  - Transactions at an undervalue s339
  - Preferences s340
  - Extortionate credit transactions s343
  - Post petition dispositions s284
  - Excessive pension contributions s342A.

- It is of importance for this syllabus area to understand who is/is not an associate of the bankrupt as different rules apply when a transaction takes place with an associate.

3.1 Transactions at an undervalue s339

An individual enters into a transaction with a person at an undervalue if he:

- Makes a gift to that person or he otherwise enters into a transaction with that person on terms that provide for him to receive no consideration

- Enters into a transaction with that person in consideration of marriage

- Enters into a transaction with that person for a consideration the value of which, in money or money's worth, is significantly less than the value, in money or money's worth, of the consideration provided by the individual

The trustee can only apply to the court to clawback a transaction at an undervalue if it was given at a relevant time ie:

- In the five years prior to the presentation of the petition

- The donor was insolvent at the time. This rule only applies where the gift was two to five years from the petition date. Insolvency does not need to be shown if the transaction was less than two years from the petition date. Insolvency is presumed where the recipient is an associate (see para 3.8)

3.2 Preferences s340

An individual gives a preference to a person if:

- That person is one of the individual's creditors or a surety or guarantor for any of his debts or other liabilities

- The individual does anything or suffers anything to be done which (in either case) has the effect of putting that person into a position which, in the event of the individual's bankruptcy, will be better than the position he would have been in if that thing had not been done

Examples would include paying off a creditor early or granting them security over the debtor's assets.

The court will not make an order under s340 in respect of a preference given to any person unless the individual who gave the preference was influenced in deciding to give it by a desire to produce in relation to that person the effect mentioned above.

The relevant time for a preference is six months in the case of unconnected creditors, and two years in the case of associates.

Once again the donor must be insolvent at the time. The desire to prefer will be presumed where the preference was given to an associate. Insolvency will never be presumed.

3.3 Extortionate credit transactions s343

s343 applies where a person is adjudged bankrupt who is or has been party to a transaction for, or involving, the provision to him of credit.

The court may, on the application of the trustee of the bankrupt's estate, make an order with respect to the transaction if the transaction is or was extortionate and was not entered into more than three years before the commencement of the bankruptcy.

A transaction is extortionate if, having regard to the risk accepted by the person providing the credit:

- The terms of it are or were such as to require grossly exorbitant payments to be made in respect of the provision of the credit
- It otherwise grossly contravened ordinary principles of fair dealing

It shall be presumed, unless the contrary is proved, that a transaction with respect to which an application is made under this section is, or as the case may be was, extortionate.

An order under this section may contain one or more of the following as the court thinks fit:

- A provision setting aside the whole or part of any obligation created by the transaction
- A provision otherwise varying the terms of the transaction or varying the terms on which any security for the purposes of the transaction is held
- A provision requiring any person who is or was party to the transaction to pay to the trustee any sums paid to that person, by virtue of the transaction, by the bankrupt
- A provision requiring any person to surrender to the trustee any property held by him as security for the purposes of the transaction
- A provision directing accounts to be taken between any persons

3.4 Post petition dispositions s284

s284 applies from presentation of the petition to the vesting of the estate in the trustee. It applies to any disposition including payments in cash or otherwise.

Any dispositions by the bankrupt are void except to the extent that the court consents or subsequently ratifies the position.

Third parties having received payments from the bankrupt hold those payments as part of the bankrupt's estate. There is protection for those who receive payments or assets in good faith, for market value without notice of the bankruptcy (a '*bona fide* purchaser for value without notice').

3.5 Excessive pension contributions s342

By s342A the trustee can apply to court for an order that excessive contributions previously made by a bankrupt into his pension (that have unfairly prejudiced his creditors) be paid back to the estate. The trustee can attack contributions made at any time.

The court will consider:

- Whether any of the contributions were made for the purpose of putting assets beyond the reach of creditors
- Whether the total amount of any contributions are excessive in view of the individual's circumstances when those contributions were made

The court may make such order as it thinks fit for restoring the position to what it would have been had the excessive contributions not been made.

3.6 Transactions defrauding creditors s423

Actions under s423 can be brought by a trustee, supervisor and creditors. The aim of the provision is to prevent debtors from disposing of assets to the detriment of creditors. Unlike a transaction at an undervalue the legislation does not specify a relevant time limit, therefore it is a useful tool where a transaction at an undervalue claim would fail because it took place outside of the relevant time period. Such actions are however still subject to the usual rules on limitation and may be statute barred after 6 or 12 years depending upon the type of claim. To be successful any applicant for an order under s423 must establish that a transaction at an undervalue has occurred. He must further show that the intent of the debtor in entering into that transaction was to put assets beyond the reach of creditors or to prejudice their interests.

The purpose of any court order will be, as far as possible, to restore the position to what it would have been had the transaction not taken place.

3.7 Protection for third parties

Although the court has wide powers to restore assets to the estate where there has been either a transaction at an undervalue, transaction defrauding creditors, or void disposition, those third parties who have dealt with the debtor in good faith (ie for value and without notice of the insolvency/petition/order) are generally protected. They will not be ordered to restore assets to the estate. When considering value in this context the courts look for valuable consideration which is not necessarily the same as market value. Such third parties are referred to as '*bona fide* purchasers for value without notice'.

3.8 Associates

The term associate is defined in s435 IA 86 and includes a wide range of relationships. Generally the section includes spouses and civil partners and former spouses and civil partners, other relatives, partners in a partnership, companies controlled by the debtor/bankrupt and some trust relationships.

Relatives are brothers, sisters, uncles, aunts, nephews, nieces, lineal ancestors eg parents, and lineal descendents eg children.

3.9 Funding litigation

The trustee will need to garner support from the creditors – either through the committee or the general body of creditors. If the creditors are satisfied that the estate is likely to benefit from the action they may be willing to provide a fighting fund.

3.10 Summary of antecedent transactions in bankruptcy

Type of Transaction	Relevant time?	Need to show insolvent?	Anything presumed?
Transaction at an undervalue (s339)	Five years pre-petition	0–2 years No	
		2–5 years Yes	If to an associate it is presumed that the donor was insolvent
Preference (s340)	To non-associate six months	Yes	
	To associate two years pre-petition	Yes	If to an associate – 'desire to prefer' is presumed
Extortionate credit transaction (s343)	Three years pre-bankruptcy order	No	Presumed to be 'extortionate'

Type of Transaction	Relevant time?	Need to show insolvent?	Anything presumed?
Transactions defrauding creditors (s423)	Any time	No	No
Post petition dispositions (s284)	Between petition and appointment of trustee	No	No
Excessive pension contributions (s342A to C)	Anytime	No	No

Interactive question 1: James Welland

Your principal has recently been appointed trustee in bankruptcy of James Welland. He has asked you to review the files to ensure that all assets are identified. You obtain the following information:

1 James lives in a rented two bed roomed flat in Bolton. He is employed as a shop manager and has submitted an income and expenses form to the Official Receiver.

2 He has no valuable household effects apart from a 32" plasma TV which he bought new six months ago at a cost of £2,000.

3 He holds premium bonds in the sum of £500. Eight months ago he received a win in the sum of £30,000. He used this to purchase the TV and went on a luxury holiday with his girlfriend.

4 He drives a BMW, valued at £15,000 which he also purchased with his winnings.

5 James' aunt recently passed away and under the terms of her will James is to inherit her jewellery valued at £5,000. He has not yet received the inheritance.

Requirement

What assets are available to the trustee in bankruptcy?

See **Answer** at the end of this chapter.

Summary and Self-test

Summary

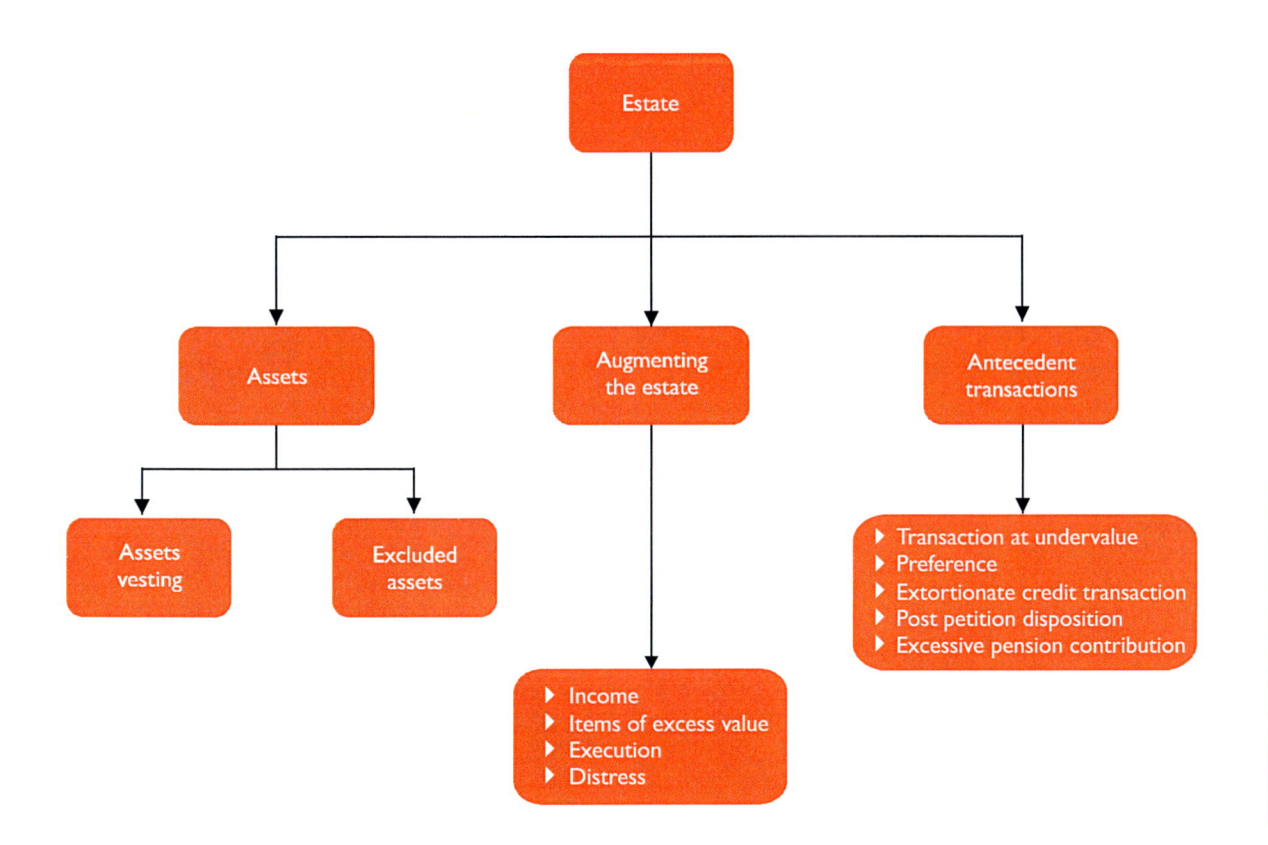

```
                          ┌─────────┐
                          │ Estate  │
                          └────┬────┘
          ┌────────────────────┼────────────────────┐
          ▼                    ▼                    ▼
      ┌────────┐        ┌──────────────┐     ┌──────────────┐
      │ Assets │        │  Augmenting  │     │  Antecedent  │
      │        │        │  the estate  │     │ transactions │
      └───┬────┘        └──────┬───────┘     └──────┬───────┘
     ┌────┴────┐                │                    │
     ▼         ▼                ▼                    ▼
```

- Assets vesting
- Excluded assets

Augmenting the estate:
- Income
- Items of excess value
- Execution
- Distress

Antecedent transactions:
- Transaction at undervalue
- Preference
- Extortionate credit transaction
- Post petition disposition
- Excessive pension contribution

CHAPTER 23

Bankruptcy estate 381

Self-test

Answer the following questions.

1   What assets are excluded from the bankruptcy estate?

2   What is the maximum period for which an Income Payments Agreement Order may last?

    A   12 months after the date of the agreement
    B   Until discharge
    C   Three years from the date of the agreement
    D   Three years from the date of the bankruptcy order

3   Within how many days of the trustee becoming aware may he claim after acquired property under s307?

    A   7 days
    B   14 days
    C   28 days
    D   42 days

4   A court enforcement officer is obliged to retain the proceeds of execution for 14 days if it exceeds a certain level.

    What is this level?

    A   £750
    B   £500
    C   £250
    D   £1,000

5   What are the main criteria that are required to exist for a transaction which took place before a bankruptcy order to amount to an extortionate credit transaction?

Now, go back to the Learning Objectives in the Introduction. If you are satisfied that you have achieved these objectives, please tick them off.

Answers to Self-test

1
- Such tools, books, vehicles and other items of equipment as are necessary to the bankrupt for use personally by him in his employment, business or vocation.
- Such clothing, bedding, furniture, household equipment and provisions as are necessary for satisfying the basic domestic needs of the bankrupt and his family.
- Property held by the bankrupt on trust for any other person.
- Income for reasonable domestic needs.
- After acquired property.
- Assets subject to forfeiture clauses (for example, a commercial lease usually provides for forfeiture and re-entry on non-payment of rent or on bankruptcy).
- Peerages and titles of honour.
- Liens on books, papers or records of the bankrupt are unenforceable to the extent they would deny possession to the trustee (s349).
- Rights under an approved pension scheme.

2   C

3   D

4   D

5   Transaction entered into within three years of commencement of bankruptcy.

The terms of the transaction were such as to require grossly exorbitant payments to be made in respect of the provision of credit.

The terms otherwise contravene the ordinary principles of fair dealing.

Answer to Interactive question

Answer to Interactive question 1: James Welland

A bankrupt's estate comprises all property belonging to or vested in the bankrupt at the commencement of bankruptcy – s283(1) IA 86.

Commencement is the date of the bankruptcy order.

Some items are excluded from the estate however, these include:

(a) Such tools, books, vehicles and other items of equipment as are necessary to the bankrupt for use personally by him in his employment, business or vocation.

(b) Such clothing, bedding, furniture, household equipment and provisions as are necessary for satisfying the basic domestic needs of the bankrupt and his family.

(c) Income for reasonable needs.

(d) After acquired property.

(e) Approved pension schemes.

Here, James' estate will consist of:

1   £500 premium bonds.

2   Income from employment – whilst income does not form part of the estate the trustee has the power to claim income in excess of that required to meet his basic needs – s310.

   Not aware if James has excess income, would need to review his income and expenditure form in more detail.

3   32" TV – basic household items are excluded from the estate, however, where it appears to the trustee that the realisable value exceeds the cost of a reasonable replacement, he may claim that asset for the benefit of the estate – s309.

   The trustee must serve written notice on James within 42 days of becoming aware of the TV. The TV will now vest in the trustee. He has a duty to apply estate funds to the purchase of a reasonable replacement for the property claimed.

4   BMW – whether James can keep a vehicle depends on whether he requires one for his job or not. If he doesn't and James has easy access to public transport the vehicle will vest in the trustee and will be realised.

   If James can demonstrate that it is necessary for him to have a vehicle, the trustee will claim the vehicle as an item of excess value under s309 and provide James with a cheaper alternative.

5   Inheritance from aunt:

   If the jewellery were inherited prior to the bankruptcy order being made these items would vest in the trustee and form part of the estate.

   If the items were received after the bankruptcy order, the trustee must claim them as an after acquired asset – s307 IA 86.

   The trustee must serve written notice on the bankrupt claiming the jewellery within 42 days of becoming aware of its existence.

   James is under a duty to notify the trustee of any property acquired after the bankruptcy order within 21 days of its receipt.

CHAPTER 24

Bankrupt's home

Introduction
Topic List
1 Bankrupt's home
2 Realising the equity
3 Steps if equity cannot be realised
4 Three-year rule

Summary and Self-test
Answers to Self-test
Answers to Interactive questions

Introduction

Learning objectives

- Describe the consequences of bankruptcy for the bankrupt in relation to the bankrupt's home which forms part of the bankruptcy estate
- Calculate the value of the bankrupt's home using information given and explain how the value is arrived at
- Explain what impact the antecedent transaction rules may have in relation to the bankrupt's home
- Explain the powers, rights and on-going obligations of an insolvency practitioner acting as an IP in relation to his dealings with the bankrupt's home

Tick off

☐
☐
☐
☐

Stop and think

Why is it often difficult for a trustee to realise equity in a bankrupt's home? Why aren't properties owned jointly always held in 50:50 shares? Why should shares in a house sometimes be adjusted and what for?

Working context

A share in the bankrupt's home is often the bankrupt's most significant asset. It is therefore important to understand the legislation regarding the realisation of this asset and the practical difficulties faced by a trustee when seeking to realise this asset.

1 Bankrupt's home

> **Section overview**
>
> - In many bankruptcies the most significant asset is likely to be the bankrupt's home. In dealing with the bankrupt's home the trustee will need to consider the following points:
>   - What equity is available
>   - How much of the equity vests in the trustee
>   - Whether the share of the equity has been affected by equitable accounting/exoneration
>   - How the trustee can realise the property
>   - What steps should be taken if the equity cannot be realised
>
> Note. References to 'spouse' in this chapter should be interpreted to include 'civil partners'.

1.1 Available equity

The trustee will have to make enquiries to establish what equity is available in the property. This will involve obtaining an up to date valuation and mortgage redemption statement. What vests in the trustee will depend upon whether the property is held in joint names or the sole name of the bankrupt.

House in joint names

In practice, building societies will normally require that couples (married or otherwise) hold the property jointly. There are two types of joint ownership or 'tenancy' – a tenancy in common and a joint tenancy. Regardless of the type of joint tenancy the mortgage will state that the couple are jointly liable for monies owed to the lender. The essential difference for the purpose of the assessment is that where the property is held as joint tenants, on the death of one co-owner that co-owner's share of the property will automatically pass to the surviving owner, this is known as the right of survivorship. By contrast where the property is held as tenants in common the right of survivorship does not apply and the deceased co-owner's share of the property will vest in his or her estate to be distributed in accordance with that person's will or the laws of intestacy.

The appointment of a trustee in bankruptcy will have the effect of severing the joint tenancy, converting it into a tenancy in common. From this point the right of survivorship will no longer apply, however the couple are still jointly liable for monies owed to the lender.

For further detail on the administration of the estates of deceased insolvents see Chapter 33.

The trustee will need to ascertain how much of the equity vests in the estate. Two situations may arise when valuing the bankrupt's share.

- **The co-owners may have expressly declared in what shares they will hold the equitable interest.**
    - 50:50 shares would be likely.
    - These declared shares are usually decisive *(Godwin v Bedwell 1982)*. Although the trustee may be able to attack the declaration as a transaction at an undervalue if it provides for non-bankrupt co-owner to receive an 'over generous' share.
    - s53 (1)(b) Law of Property Act 1925 (LPA) provides that such a declaration must be evidenced by some writing, through the court will be able to enforce an oral declaration as a constructive trust (and no formalities will be required – s53 (2).
    - Where there is an express declaration by the parties (written or oral) as to the proportion in which equity will be shared there is no need for the courts to look for evidence of what was intended. The declaration is decisive.
    - Shares are ascertained at the date of declaration, but valued at the date of sale.

- **The co-owners may not have expressly declared in what shares they will hold the equitable interest.**

    There may have been no express declaration of trust as to the proportion in which the equity is shared (written or oral). In this case the court will assume that the equity is held 50:50 *(Pettitt V Pettitt)*.

    - Should one party claim a higher than 50% share of the property, the burden will be on that party to prove an intention to split the equity in unequal shares *(Stack v Dowden 2007)*.
    - Shares are to be ascertained at date of acquisition *(Pettit v Pettit)* although the court looks at all the evidence post acquisition to infer the parties intention at that earlier date, but valued at the date of sale.

Stack v Dowden 2007 sets out the approach to take to determine equity shares.

- Is there a Deed of Trust setting out how the parties intend to split the equity?
- If not, is there an actual agreement between the couple as to how the equity should be split?
- If not, assume 50:50.
- The burden will be on the party claiming more than 50% to prove that the beneficial shares are different from the legal interests.

The following factors will be taken into account in ascertaining equity shares where the court does depart from the normal assumption that joint owners intended to hold the equity 50:50:

- Advice or discussions at the date of transfer
- Purpose for which the home was acquired
- Nature of the parties' relationship
- Whether they had any children for whom they both had a responsibility to provide a home
- How the purchase was originally funded and subsequently
- How the parties arranged their finances, separately or together
- Parties individual characters and personalities

Having taken these factors into consideration, cases where beneficial interests are different from the legal interests will be unusual.

Jones v Kernott 2011

This was a case where property had been purchased by an unmarried couple as joint tenants, they separated, and 12 years **after** that separation one party severed the joint tenancy and sought to claim 50% of the available equity in the property. The court stated that in joint ownership cases where there is no express declaration of trust the starting point is that there is a presumption that both parties have an equal share in the property. However that presumption can be displaced by evidence that their common intention was different either at the date of purchase or that it **later** became so. Common intention is to be deduced objectively from the conduct of the parties. Where the intention changes and there is no direct evidence of what the new intention is, the court will determine the shares on the basis of what it considers to be fair.

House in sole name of bankrupt

Prima facie all of the equity will vest in the trustee. However, a non-owning spouse/civil partner may be able to claim a share even though the property is in the sole name of the bankrupt and there is no express declaration of trust as to how the equity should be held. This is possible through the mechanism of resulting or constructive trusts.

The court may make a declaration that a proportion of the equity is held by the legal owner on trust for the non-owning spouse or civil partner. The court will make a decision based on the evidence as to the proportion of each parties share. The court will be looking for evidence that:

1 The legal owner promised/intended the non-legal owner to have a share of the equity

2 The non-legal owner acted in reliance of the promise/intention for example by making a financial contribution to the deposit or purchase price or mortgage or by making some other substantial contribution referable to the acquisition of the property

House in sole name of non-bankrupt co-owner

Prima facie none of the equity will vest in the trustee. However, the trustee may be able to claim a share through the same process detailed above.

The trustee should also consider whether the co-owner acquired the property for value for 'transaction at an undervalue' purposes.

1.2 Equitable accounting

This is necessary where the couple have separated and only the co-owner in occupation is now responsible for mortgage payments and outgoings.

It is necessary both where the property is held as joint tenants (with or without declaration of trusts) and where it is held as tenants in common.

The following proforma should be used to calculate the adjusted equity split:

EQUITABLE ACCOUNTING PROFORMA (non-bankrupt co-owner in occupation)

		Bankrupt	Non bankrupt co-owner
	Proceeds of Sale	X	
	Less required to redeem mortgage	(X)	
	Equity	X	
1	Apportion (assume 50:50)	X	X
2	Credit improvements of non-bankrupt co-owner	(X)	X
3	Credit capital element of non-bankrupt co-owner mortgage payments	(X)	X
4	Debit an 'occupation rent' to non-bankrupt co-owner	X	(X)
5	…but net of non-bankrupt co-owner's interest payments under the mortgage	(X)	X
6	Net occupation rent	X	(X)
7	Totals	X	X

Notes

1. Apportion according to the co-owner respective shares of the beneficial interest in the property (probably 50:50) **Accordingly all adjustments should then be split in the same shares.**

2. In practice should only credit the non-bankrupt co-owner lower of:

    (a) The cost of the improvements; **or**
    (b) The increase in the value of the home resulting from those improvements.

3. Likewise in practice the non-bankrupt co-owner would only be credited with the lower of the capital payments or the increase in value of the house.

4. 'Occupation rent' should be debited to the non-bankrupt co-owner. This is based on the idea that now that only the non-bankrupt co-owner is residing in the property, only they have the benefit of the former family home and therefore should 'pay' the bankrupt a rent. Occupation rent should only be charged from the date that the bankrupt is **excluded** from the property *(Re Pavlou)* **not** from the date of **separation**. Exclusion might be:

    (a) Where the bankrupt has been excluded by court order
    (b) Where the non-bankrupt co-owner/spouse has presented a petition for divorce *(Re Pavlou)*
    (c) Other evidence that the bankrupt is 'no longer welcome' *(Re Pavlou)*

5. Mortgage interest paid by the non-bankrupt co-owner since separation can be netted off against occupation rent. This can only go to reduce the occupation rent to zero and not to provide the non bankrupt co-owner with a further credit.

1.3 Equitable exoneration

This only applies where one party has charged their share of the bankrupt's home for the benefit of the other co-owner eg spouse/civil partner.

As the charge has to be for the benefit of the other spouse/civil partner the court will be concerned to ascertain what the monies provided were used for.

For example, in *Re Pittortou 1985*, a second mortgage was taken over the bankrupt's home. The monies raised were used for a number of purposes including funding the husband's business and the husband setting up home with another woman. The wife argued that she did not benefit from either of these expenditures. Her husband's business was loss making, she did not participate in it and she had her own independent source of income. The effect of exoneration is that the wife's position becomes that of a surety. In other words, recourse will only be had from the wife's share to the extent that her husband's share is insufficient to repay the mortgage in full.

2 Realising the equity

Section overview

- The trustee has a number of options to realise any equity available.

2.1 Without court proceedings

- The trustee should approach the non-bankrupt co-owner with a view to buying out the bankrupt's share of the equity. A lower value would probably be acceptable since the costs of sale and/or proceedings are being avoided.
- The non-bankrupt co-owner could agree to put the property up for sale on the open market. Following the sale the trustee would receive the bankrupt's share of the equity in the property.
- The trustee could come to an agreement with the bankrupt whereby the bankrupt incurs a specified liability to the estate in consideration for which the interest in the property would cease to form part of the estate. The legislation is quite vague on this area and no length for the agreement is specified, neither is any interest rate. Trustees will need to be cautious if choosing this course of action to prevent any agreement being caught under the Consumer Credit Act 1974.

2.2 Order for possession and sale

- If the non–bankrupt co-owner cannot or will not co–operate the trustee will apply to the court for an order of sale under:
    - Trust of Land and Appointment of Trustees Act 1996 (TLATA) (where property held as joint tenants). This will be an order to enforce the trust for sale; or
    - Family Law Act 1996 (FLA) (where property in sole name of bankrupt but non–bankrupt spouse/civil partner is in occupation).
- In either case the application should be made to the bankruptcy court (ss336 (2)(b) and 335A (1)).
- By s336 (4) on such an application the court shall make such order as it thinks just and reasonable having regard to:
    - Interest of bankrupt's creditors
    - Conduct of spouse/former spouse/civil partner so far as contributing to the bankruptcy and needs and resources of spouse/former spouse/civil partner
    - Needs of any children
    - All circumstances of the case (but not the bankrupt's needs)

- Note that under Schedule 5 Part 1 of the Act the power to institute legal proceedings relating to property comprised in the bankrupt's estate requires sanction by:
  - s314(1) the trustee may obtain sanction from the committee
  - Where the equity of the property is below the low equity home value which is currently £1,000, the court must dismiss applications for possession.
  - s302(1) where there is no committee its functions are vested in the Secretary of State. These functions may be exercised by the OR (R 6.166(2)).

2.3 Rights of occupation – 12 month delay

In two situations there will be rights of occupation which may delay the trustee in obtaining the order of possession under:

- FLA the non–bankrupt spouse/civil partner has a right of occupation (irrespective of whether they have a share in the property)

- s337 IA 86 the bankrupt has a right of occupation where:
  - He has a beneficial interest in the property
  - Any person under 18 has their home (at the time of presentation of petition) with the bankrupt

- By ss336 (5) and 337 (6) where either (or both) of these two situations apply, after a period of one year from the date of appointment and vesting of the estate in the trustee, the court shall assume that the interests of the bankrupt's creditors outweigh all other considerations unless the circumstances of the case are exceptional.

Case law helps to give guidance as to what may be considered exceptional.

Re Citro 1991

Hardship to wives and young children is **not** exceptional (also *Re Lowrie 1981).*

The non-bankrupt spouse (the wife) argued that if the house were sold she would not have enough equity to buy a house in the same area and therefore she would have to buy a house in a cheaper area and would have to move the children out of their present schools where they were settled. The court said that this was the normal and 'melancholy effect of debt and improvidence' and was not exceptional.

Re Holliday 1981

The court held the facts of this bankruptcy case were exceptional. Essentially Holliday (the bankrupt) would eventually be able to pay his creditors 100p in the £ plus statutory interest. Therefore the court felt able to postpone a sale of the house despite the fact that this would result in the creditors having to wait to receive their money.

Judd v Brown 1998

The sudden grave and unforeseen illness of the bankrupt's wife was held to be exceptional.

Jones v Ravel 1998

An occupier suffering from paranoid schizophrenia who would be unduly affected by having to move would be exceptional.

Re Mott 1987

Exceptional circumstances were found where the bankrupt's unwell and elderly mother was living with him. The sale was postponed until after the mother's death.

If the trustee makes an application for either an order for possession and/or sale and the application is dismissed by the court, then the property will also vest back in the bankrupt unless the court orders otherwise. Therefore if the court orders that possession be refused because of an 'exceptional circumstance' eg grave and unforeseen illness, it will be important to ensure that the proceedings are merely adjourned **not** dismissed.

[By s313A the court must dismiss applications for possession or for a s313 charge where the value of the bankrupt's interest is below £1,000, see para 3.4.]

Interactive question 1: John Smith

John Smith was declared bankrupt nine months ago in August 20X0. His trustee has realised all of the bankruptcy assets except for his share in the bankrupt's home, details of which are as follows:

- The property is a five bed roomed, detached house with a double garage. It has recently been professionally valued in the sum of £385,000.

- The property is subject to a mortgage owed to Barwest Bank plc in the sum of £184,000.

- John owns the property jointly with his wife. He lived there with her and their three children until November 20X9 (19 months ago) when they separated. John moved out of the property and his wife continued to pay the mortgage and interest payments as they fell due as follows:

	November 20X9 to August 20Y0 £	September 20Y0 to May 20Y1 £
Mortgage capital – per month	600	600
Interest – per month	400	400

- Six months ago Mrs Smith added a conservatory to the house at a cost of £25,000.

- The property would command a rent of £6,000 per annum.

- John obtained a business loan shortly after the property was purchased in the sum of £30,000 secured against the equity in the property. Despite her name appearing on the loan documents, Mrs Smith denies any knowledge of agreeing to such a loan being secured against the property.

Requirement

Prepare a schedule showing the equitable accounting in the property for both Mr and Mrs Smith as at May 20Y1. Support your calculations with any relevant narrative.

See **Answer** at the end of this chapter.

3 Steps if equity cannot be realised

Section overview

- If the property cannot be realised the trustee has the option of applying for a s313 charging order.

3.1 Purpose of charging orders

The trustee has power to apply to court under s313 for the imposition of a charge where he is unable to realise (for any reason) an interest in a dwelling house occupied by the bankrupt, spouse, civil partner or former spouse, civil partner.

The effects of a s313 charging order are that the:

- Benefit of the charge is now comprised in the bankrupt's estate (ie it vests in the trustee).

- The property ceases to be comprised in the estate and re–vests in the bankrupt. The practical effect is that the trustee has now lost control of how and when the property will be sold.

3.2 Procedure for obtaining a charge R6.237D

The trustee will:

- Make non–bankrupt spouse/civil partner a respondent to the action

- Seek to agree the terms of the charge (ie how much it is for) with the bankrupt (if this can't be agreed the court will settle terms)

- File a report on the:
  - Extent of the bankrupt's interest in the property
  - Amount remaining owing to unsecured creditors
  - An estimate of the cost of realising the interest

3.3 Advantages to obtaining a charging order

s332 (1) provides that a trustee cannot call a final meeting to obtain his release if he has been unable to realise an interest in a dwelling, unless he has applied to court for a charge (whether or not the court makes a charging order).

If a s313 charging order is an unsuitable option, the trustee may apply to the Secretary of State for certification that it is inappropriate or inexpedient to apply for a charge.

It may be inappropriate where there are no funds in the estate to make a s313 application and the creditors are unwilling to fund further litigation.

3.4 Low value homes

If the trustee makes an application for an order for sale and possession, or a charging order and the level of the bankrupt's interest is below the prescribed amount then the court will dismiss the application.

The prescribed amount has been set at £1,000 pursuant to Insolvency Proceedings (Monetary Limits) (Amendment) Order 2004.

3.5 Land Registration Rules

If a bankrupt is the sole owner of a property the trustee will protect his interest by way of a Bankruptcy Restriction Notice.

If a bankrupt owns property jointly the trustee will protect his interest by way of a Form J Restriction.

4 Three-year rule

Section overview

- Where property in the estate consists of an interest in a dwelling house which at the date of bankruptcy was the sole or principal residence of the bankrupt or the bankrupt's spouse/civil partner or former spouse/civil partner, at the end of three years from the date of the bankruptcy, the house will re-vest in the bankrupt and will therefore no longer form part of the estate.

  The rule was introduced to prevent trustees from taking no decisive action in relation to the property, waiting for the value of the house to rise and then many years later applying for repossession.

4.1 Options for the trustee

To prevent automatic re-vesting the trustee must within three year either:

- Realise the interest in the property
- Apply for an order for sale or possession
- Apply for a s313 charge
- Enter into an agreement with the bankrupt whereby the bankrupt gets the property back in return for a promise to pay money into the estate in the future

4.2 Notice under s283A/Rule 6.237

The trustee is required to serve notice to state that the dwelling house of the bankrupt is one to which the three-year rule applies. Notice should be given in Form 6.83 as soon as reasonably practicable and contain details of:

- The name of the bankrupt
- The address of the dwelling house
- If the dwelling house is registered land, the title number

Notice is served on:

- The bankrupt
- Bankrupt's spouse or civil partner
- Former spouse or civil partner

Notice cannot be served any later than 14 days prior to the expiration of the 3 year period.

4.3 Early re-vesting Rule 6.237CA

Where the trustee considers that the continued vesting of the property in the bankrupt's estate to be of no benefit to the creditors, or that the re-vesting will facilitate a more efficient administration of the estate, he must send a notice to the bankrupt to that effect. The property will re-vest in the bankrupt after the period of one month from the date of that notice.

Interactive question 2: Amy Chapple

You have recently been appointed trustee of Amy Chapple. She lives with her husband and three children, aged three, six and eight in a four bedroomed house. The property was purchased jointly with her husband when they married 11 years ago.

Requirement

What are your options, as trustee, when dealing with the bankrupt's home?

See **Answer** at the end of this chapter.

Summary and Self-test

Summary

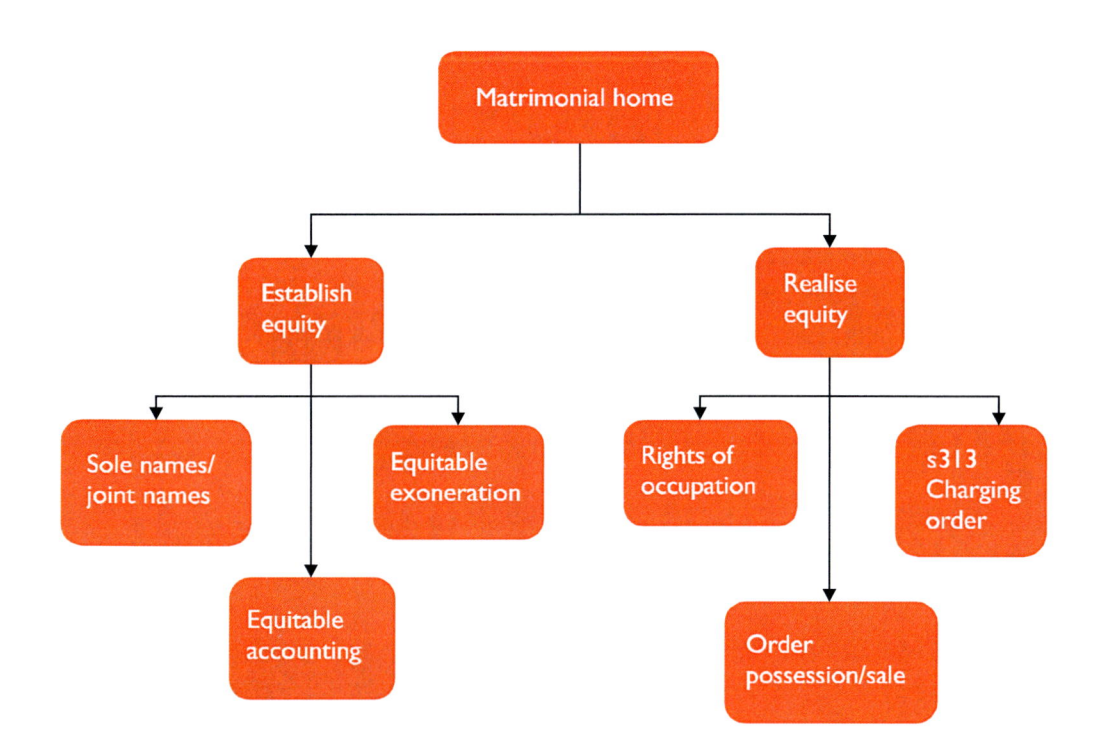

```
                    Matrimonial home
                    /              \
          Establish equity    Realise equity
           /        \          /      |       \
    Sole names/  Equitable  Rights of  Order      s313
    joint names  exoneration occupation possession/ Charging
                     |                  sale       order
                Equitable
                accounting
```

Self-test

Answer the following questions.

1. When looking at rights of occupation, in the absence of any exceptional circumstances, after what period will the court assume that the interests of the bankrupt's creditors outweigh all other considerations?

    A   6 months
    B   12 months
    C   18 months
    D   24 months

2. Within what period of time must the trustee deal with the bankrupt's interest in a dwelling house in order to prevent it re-vesting in the bankrupt?

    A   Must deal with it prior to discharge
    B   Within 12 months of the date of the bankruptcy order
    C   Within three years of the appointment of the trustee
    D   Within three years of the date of the bankruptcy order

3. The court will not grant a charging order if the value of the bankrupt's equity is below the 'prescribed amount'. What is this amount?

    A   £500
    B   £1,000
    C   £2,500
    D   £5,000

4. Under which section of the Act may a trustee apply for a charging order on the debtor's bankrupt's home?

    A   s24
    B   s313
    C   s72
    D   s198
    E   s243

5. Which of the following matters will the court not take into account when looking at an application for an order for possession and sale made by a trustee?

    A   Interests of the bankrupt's creditors
    B   Conduct of spouse/civil partner as contributing to the bankruptcy
    C   Bankrupt's interests
    D   Needs of any children
    E   All circumstances of the case

Now, go back to the Learning Objectives in the Introduction. If you are satisfied that you have achieved these objectives, please tick them off.

Answers to Self-test

1 B
2 D
3 B
4 B
5 C s336(4)

Answers to Interactive questions

Answer to Interactive question 1: John Smith

MR AND MRS SMITH EQUITABLE ACCOUNTING SCHEDULE AS AT MAY 20Y1

		Mr Smith £	Mrs Smith £
Proceeds of sale	385,000		
Less Barwest Bank plc	(184,000)		
Equity	201,000		
Apportion equity 50:50		100,500	100,500
Conservatory		(12,500)	12,500
Mortgage Payments:			
Capital November 20X9 to August 20Y0		(3,000)	3,000
September 20Y0 to May 20Y1		(2,700)	2,700
Occupational rent (Nov X9 to May Y1)		4,750	(4,750)
Mortgage Payments;			
Interest November 20X9 to August 20Y0		(2,000)	2,000
September 20Y0 to May 20Y1		(1,800)	1,800
Share of equity		83,250	117,750
Less Business Loan		(30,000)	
Final equity		53,250	

Workings

1. Equity

    In the absence of other information, assume equity is to be split 50:50. Shares are ascertained at the date of acquisition but valued at the date of sale.

2. Conservatory

    Should credit Mrs Smith with the lower of the:

    - Cost of improvements
    - Increase in the value of the property resulting from those improvements

    Assume the value of the property has increased by £25,000 as a result of the new conservatory.

3. Mortgage payments

    The period to take into account is from November 20X9, when Mr Smith left the property, to May 20Y1, the date of sale (19 months).

    Assume the capital value of the equity in the property is increased proportionately to the capital payments made by Mrs Smith.

    Capital
    November 20X9 to August 20Y0 (10 months)   600 × 10 = 6,000
    September 20Y0 to May 20Y1   (9 months)   600 × 9 = 5,400

    Interest
    November 20X9 to August 20Y0 (10 months)   400 × 10 = 4,000
    September 20Y0 to May 20Y1   (9 months)   400 × 9 = 3,600

    The interest payments are credited to Mrs Smith, to be netted off against occupational rent (can only reduce occupational rent to zero).

4. Occupational rent

    This should be charged from the date Mr Smith is excluded from the property. In the absence of other information, assume John is no longer welcome from the date of separation.

Certificate in Insolvency

5   Business loan

    There are two possible treatments:

    - Treat both parties as party to the transaction and therefore loan should be deducted equally from both parties, leaving equity of:

	£
Mr Smith	68,250
Mrs Smith	102,750

    - Assume Mrs Smith was not party to the loan and as she did not receive any benefit from it, it should be repaid from Mr Smith's equity only.

Answer to Interactive question 2: Amy Chapple

1   Must first establish whether there is any equity in the property:

    Obtain up to date valuation and mortgage redemption statement

2   Determine how much of that equity vests in the trustee:

    - Is the property in sole names/joint names?
    - Is there an express trust determining in what shares the property is held?
    - The trustee may be able to attack the declaration as a transaction at an undervalue if it provides for the non-bankrupt spouse/civil partner to receive an over generous share
    - In the absence of other information, assume held 50:50
    - May be able to refute this, need to consider who provided the deposit, who makes ongoing mortgage payments etc

3   Ensure equity is protected:

    - Ensure that ongoing mortgage payments continue to be made to prevent repossession proceedings by the mortgagee
    - Confirm property is covered by insurance
    - Notify building society/bank of trustee's interest in the property

4   Trustee has a number of informal options when realising the property:

    - Approach non-bankrupt spouse/civil partner with a view to buying out the bankrupt's share of the property (trustee may be willing to accept a lower value due to not incurring costs of sale/ possession).
    - Could put house up for sale on the open market with the agreement of spouse/civil partner.
    - Come to an agreement with the debtor whereby the debtor incurs a specified liability to the estate in consideration for which the interest in the property will cease to be part of the estate.

5   If non-bankrupt spouse/civil partner is unable or unwilling to purchase the equity, the trustee may apply to the court for an order for possession and sale (s14 Trust of Land and Appointment of Trustee's Act 1996)

    The court shall make such order as it thinks just and reasonable having regard to:

    - Interests of the bankrupt's creditors
    - Conduct of spouse/former spouse as contributing to the bankruptcy
    - Needs and resources of spouse/former spouse/civil partner
    - Needs of any children
    - All circumstances of the case (but not the bankrupt's interests)

The non-bankrupt spouse/civil partner will have a right of occupation under FLA and the bankrupt will have a right of occupation under s337 here:

- They have a beneficial interest in the property
- Any person under 18 has their home (at the time of presentation of the petition) with the bankrupt

After a period of one year from the date of appointment of the trustee:

- The court shall assume that the interests of the bankrupt's creditors outweigh all other considerations
- Unless the circumstances of the case are exceptional
- Hardship to wives and children is not exceptional, sudden grave and unforeseen illness would be exceptional

The trustee must obtain sanction from the creditors committee (or Secretary of State) before taking action.

6 If, for any reason, the trustee is unable to realise the interest in a dwelling house, under s313 he may apply to court for an imposition of a charge.

The benefit of the charge is comprised in the bankrupt's estate and the property re-vests in the bankrupt. The trustee loses control of how and when the property is sold.

If equity is low, ie less than £1,000, the court will not grant a charging order.

The trustee has three years from the date of the bankruptcy order to deal with the equity in the property. After this time the property will re-vest in the bankrupt.

CHAPTER 25

Powers of the trustee

Introduction
Topic List
1   Investigative powers
2   Powers for getting in assets
3   Administrative powers of the trustee
4   Trustee's powers of realisation
5   Trustee's powers to make payments out

Summary and Self-test
Answers to Self-test
Answer to Interactive question

Introduction

Learning objectives

- State the effect of the bankruptcy order
- State the role of the trustee in bankruptcy
- Describe the consequences of bankruptcy for the bankrupt. Describe the on-going obligations of an IP when acting as a trustee in bankruptcy

Tick off ☐ ☐ ☐

Stop and think

Why does the trustee need investigative powers when it is the duty of the OR to investigate the bankrupt's affairs? Why should the trustee need to obtain sanction before exercising certain of his powers?

Working context

The trustee has a duty to get in and realise the bankrupt's estate. It is fundamental that the trustee knows the powers that he has to aid him in administering the bankrupt's estate.

1 Investigative powers

> **Section overview**
> - The trustee's powers are contained in s314 and Schedule 5. They are investigative, enabling him to ascertain and realise assets, and administrative, to enable him to deal effectively with the bankruptcy.
> - The trustee has a number of powers to obtain information regarding the bankrupt's estate.

1.1 Powers to summon meetings of creditors R6.81

Such meetings can be requisitioned by creditors holding 10% or more in value of the bankruptcy debts (s314(7)).

The trustee must give the bankrupt 14 days' notice of the meeting (R6.84(1)) and may require him to attend (R6.84(3)).

If the trustee doesn't require his attendance the bankrupt may still be admitted at the discretion of the chairman whose decision will be final as to what (if any) intervention may be made by the bankrupt.

Where the bankrupt is present questions may be put to him by creditors, but again, this is at the chairman's discretion (R6.84(6)).

1.2 Power to summon meetings of the creditors' committee

Members of the committee may seek explanation of any matter from the trustee. The trustee may in turn request information from the bankrupt.

1.3 Public examination s290

The official receiver ('OR') may, at any time pre-discharge, apply to the court for the public examination of the bankrupt.

A simple majority of creditors by value may also requisition a public examination (s290(2)).

The trustee may attend and ask questions of the bankrupt, who will be examined as to 'his affairs, dealings and property and the causes of his failure'.

1.4 Private examination s366

The trustee or the OR may apply to court for an order that any of the following persons be summoned before it.

- Bankrupt
- Bankrupt's spouse or former spouse or civil partner or former civil partner
- Any person known or believed to have any property comprised in the bankrupt's estate in his possession (who can be ordered by the court to deliver it to the trustee or OR (s367(1))
- Bankrupt's debtors (who may be ordered to pay all/part of the debt to the trustee or OR)
- Any person appearing to the court to be able to give information concerning the bankrupt's dealings, affairs or property

The court may require persons in possession of the bankrupt's property or relevant information, and the bankrupt's debtors to:

- Submit a witness statement verified by a statement of truth accounting for their dealings with the bankrupt; and/or
- Produce any documents in their control/possession relating to the bankrupt or the bankrupt's dealings, affairs or property.

Where the person summoned fails to appear without a reasonable excuse or has absconded or is about to abscond with a view to avoiding private examination, the court may issue a warrant for the arrest of that person (who may be kept in custody) and order the seizure of any books, papers, records, money or goods in that person's possession s366(3).

The court will fix a venue for the examination which can also be heard outside the UK.

Persons summoned may be examined on oath either orally or by written questions.

Note. Private examination also available to an interim receiver (s368).

1.5 Power of arrest s364

The court has a general power to issue a warrant for the arrest of a debtor (against whom a bankruptcy petition has been issued) or a bankrupt, and a general power to issue a warrant for the seizure of books, papers, records, money, goods of such a person.

The power arises in five circumstances, if he:

- Has absconded or is about to abscond
- **Is about to** remove goods with a view to avoiding or delaying possession being taken by OR/trustee
- Has concealed or destroyed (or is about to conceal or destroy) any goods, books, papers or records which might be of use to creditors
- He has (without permission of OR or trustee) removed any goods in his possession exceeding £1,000 in value
- Has failed to attend any examination ordered by the court (without reasonable excuse)

Note. This is really a power of the court rather than the trustee though the trustee would make the application.

1.6 Seizure of bankrupt's property s365

The trustee/OR may apply to the court to issue a warrant for the seizure of any property comprised in the bankrupt's estate and/or books, papers or records relating to the bankrupt's affairs or property

s365(2) makes it clear that the person executing the warrant may break into premises and any 'receptacle of the bankrupt'.

The court has the power to issue warrants to enter third party premises but only where satisfied that the bankrupt's property is concealed there.

1.7 Power to demand production of documents by HM Revenue and Customs s369

The OR/trustee may apply to court for an order that for the purposes of public or private examination a Revenue and Customs official produce to court any:

- Return and or account(s) submitted by the bankrupt (pre or post commencement of bankruptcy)
- Assessment or determination made (pre or post commencement)
- Correspondence (pre or post commencement)

The Court can authorise disclosure of such documentation to OR/trustee/creditors.

If the document is not in the hands of the Revenue and Customs official to which the order is addressed, that official must take reasonable steps to secure possession and, if he fails to secure, to report the reasons for that failure to the court.

Note. This power is not available to an interim receiver.

1.8 Re-direction of mail s371

The OR/trustee may apply to the court for an order that the post office re-direct the bankrupt's mail to OR/trustee. Such an order may last up to three months, however the, OR/trustee may apply for subsequent orders.

1.9 Obtaining copies of entries in Land Registry

The trustee can apply for and obtain office copies and other copy documents kept by the Registrar. Office copies can be produced in court as evidence of the title in land and would for example be required to support a hearing for possession of the bankrupt's home or an application for a charging order against land that is registered in the bankrupt's name.

The trustee must provide a certificate stating that he has reasons to believe the register may contain information, which will assist in the discharge of the trustee's functions and that the enquiries relate to the land described in the trustee's certificate.

1.10 Duty of the bankrupt to provide information

He must:

- Give the OR such inventory of his estate and other information and attend on the OR at such times as the OR shall reasonably require.
- Give the trustee such information, attend on the trustee at such times and do all such other things as the trustee shall reasonably require.

In either case, breach of duty is a contempt of court. The duty persists beyond discharge (s291(5)).

1.11 Duties of bankrupt to provide documentation

The bankrupt has duty to deliver to OR:

- Possession of his estate (if not capable of delivery the bankrupt must take such steps as are reasonably required by OR to protect that property).
- All books, papers, records of which he has possession or control which relate to his estate and affairs.

Note. This includes privileged documents.

Once a trustee is appointed, the OR in turn has a duty to deliver up these things to that trustee.

The bankrupt has a duty to deliver to the trustee all books, papers and records which he has in his possession or control, of which the trustee is required to take possession.

Note. Third parties holding such documentation must deliver it up to the trustee (unless entitled by law to retain it).

Any breach of this duty is a contempt of court.

s349 makes it clear that liens (or other rights of retention) over books, papers or records of a bankrupt are unenforceable to the extent that enforcement would deny the OR or the trustee possession, however the rule does not apply to documents of title held as such.

Interactive question 1: Gillian Long

Andrew Honey was appointed trustee in bankruptcy of Gillian Long four months ago. Despite repeated requests she has refused to answer any of the letters sent by the trustee asking for information regarding her affairs.

Requirement

What powers does the trustee have to obtain information regarding Gillian's estate?

See **Answer** at the end of this chapter.

1.12 Power of Disclaimer

The trustee can disclaim any onerous property.

Definition

Onerous property: s315 – any unprofitable contract or any other property comprised in the debtor's estate which is unsaleable, or not readily saleable, or such that it may give rise to a liability to pay money or perform any onerous act.

The trustee can disclaim property even if he has:

- Taken possession of the property
- Endeavoured to sell the property
- Exercised rights of ownership in relation to it

However, the trustee cannot disclaim, except with the permission of the court:

- After acquired property that has been claimed under s30
- Household effects which exceed reasonable replacement value claimed under s308

Effect of disclaimer

- A disclaimer determines the rights, interests and liabilities of the bankrupt and his estate in respect of the disclaimed property. The disclaimer is effective from the date of the trustee's authentication of the disclaimer notice.
- It also discharges the trustee from all personal liability in respect of the property disclaimed as from the date of his appointment as trustee.

Procedure for disclaimer

Trustee prepares a notice of disclaimer, authenticates and dates it. The notice is effective from that date.

- Within seven business days of the notice the trustee must send a copy to the following people:
  - Where the property is leasehold – every person who to his knowledge claims under the bankrupt as underlessee or mortgagee.
  - Where the property is a dwelling – every person who to his knowledge is in occupation or claims a right to occupy (but minors validly served by service on a parent or a guardian).
  - Anyone who claims an interest in the property.
  - Anyone who is under any liability in respect of the property (unless it will be discharged by the disclaimer).
  - Where the property is an unprofitable contract – all parties to the contract or all those who have interests under it.

- The trustee must file a copy at court and, in the case of land, send a copy to the Chief Land Registrar as soon as reasonably practicable.

  If trustee subsequently discovers anyone who should have received notice he must then serve notice on them unless, he is satisfied that that person is already aware of the disclaimer (and its date), or the court so orders on the trustee's application.

- The trustee may also serve a disclaimer on anyone else if it is in the public interest or otherwise.

- If the trustee is unsure whether a person is interested in the property to be disclaimed he can serve a notice on him under R6.184 requiring him to declare an interest within 14 days and, if so, its nature and extent.

  If the person fails to respond the trustee can treat him as having no interest.

- In relation to leaseholds s317(2) allows the court to make orders in regard to fixtures, tenants, improvements and other matters arising out of the lease.

Rights of third parties

Disclaimers only affect third parties to the extent necessary to release the bankrupt and trustee from their obligations.

A third party suffering a loss as a result of a disclaimer can claim in the bankruptcy.

s316 allows any person interested in the property of the bankrupt to apply in writing to the trustee requiring him to decide whether or not to disclaim.

- They must serve the trustee with a notice (notice to elect) or a substantially similar form (R6.183(2)) and deliver the application to the trustee personally or by recorded delivery (or some other method that requires a signature to verify receipt).

- The trustee now has 28 days in which to disclaim the property. If he fails to disclaim, he can no longer do so (s316(1)) and is deemed to have adopted any contract.

s320 allows interested parties to apply to the court for an order vesting the disclaimed property in them eg tenants under a sub-lease where the head lease is disclaimed.

Court orders vesting disclaimed property (s320)

The following people may make an application to the court for a vesting order.

- Any person who claims an interest in the disclaimed property.

- Any person under a liability in respect of the disclaimed property eg a guarantor under a lease (unless the disclaimer will discharge it).

- Where the disclaimed property is property in a dwelling house any person in occupation or entitled to occupy at date of the petition.

The application must be made within three months of either the applicant becoming aware of the disclaimer, or service of the notice of disclaimer, whichever is earlier.

The application to court must give specific information.

- The category of applicant under s320(2).
- The date the applicant became aware/received notice of the disclaimer.
- The grounds of his application.
- The order the applicant wants the court to make.

The court will fix the venue. The applicant must give five business days notice and a copy of the application and witness statement to the trustee (R6.186(4)).

On hearing the application, the court may make an order on such terms as it thinks fit including vesting or delivering the disclaimed property to any person within the three categories of potential applicant (s320(3)). However it can only do this where 'it would be just to do so for the purpose of compensating' that person (s320(4)).

2 Powers for getting in assets

Section overview

- The trustee has a number of powers for getting in assets in the bankrupt's estate.

2.1 General power of trustee s311

s311(2) in relation to, and for the purpose of acquiring or retaining possession of the bankrupt's estate the trustee is in the same position as if he were a receiver of property appointed by the High Court.

The trustee can apply to the court which may enforce the acquisition or retention accordingly.

2.2 Private examination s366

Following a private examination the court may make an order for the seizure of books, papers or goods in the person's possession s366(3).

2.3 Power of arrest s364

The court has a general power under s364 to issue a warrant for the arrest of a debtor (against whom a bankruptcy petition has been presented) and the power to issue a warrant for the seizure of books, papers and goods of such a person.

2.4 Seizure of bankrupt's property s365

The trustee/OR may apply to court to issue a warrant for seizure of any property comprised in the bankrupt's estate.

2.5 Power to redeem assets subject to security R6.117

The trustee can redeem at the value given in the secured creditor's proof (costs of transfer will be born by estate).

The trustee must give the secured creditor 28 days' notice and creditor then has 21 days' in which to revalue the security. If the creditor does revalue the trustee can only redeem at the new price.

2.6 Power to demand delivery of estate, books, papers, records s312

The bankrupt has a duty to deliver these to the OR or trustee.

OR in turn has a duty to deliver to trustee.

Supervisors of a previous IVA, and third parties such as bankers and agents also have a duty to deliver to the trustee.

2.7 Power to redeem pledged goods s311(5)

The trustee can serve notice on any third party holding estate goods by way of pledge, pawn or other security. The effect of this is that:

- The trustee can inspect goods (unless the OR has already done so under the parallel provision in s285(5))
- A third party may not realise security until the trustee has had reasonable opportunity to inspect

The trustee can exercise the bankrupt's right of redemption.

2.8 Powers in Schedule 5 IA 86

Historically these powers would required sanction but now this is no longer required. Sanction would be given by the creditors' committee or the court. If there was no creditors' committee the power of sanction was vested in the Secretary of State. Sanction could be given retrospectively and should not be unreasonably withheld. If a trustee acted without sanction he would risk losing his indemnity.

- Powers exercisable with sanction of creditors' committee *now no longer required*

    Power, where any right, option, or other power forms part of the bankrupt's estate, to make payments or incur liabilities with a view to obtaining for the benefit of the creditors, any property which is the subject of the right or option or power.

- Powers exercisable without sanction
    - Power to deal with property to same extent as the bankrupt
    - Power to prove rank, claim and draw a dividend in respect of debts due to the bankrupt

3 Administrative powers of the trustee

Section overview

- The trustee has a number of administrative powers.

3.1 Powers in Schedule 5 IA 86 (ancillary)

- Part III of the Schedule provides that for the purposes of any of his powers under Parts viii to xi of the IA 1986 the trustee may, by his official name:
    - Hold property of every description

- Make contracts
- Sue and be sued
- Enter into any engagements binding on himself and in respect of the bankrupt's estate, on his successors in office
- Employ an agent
- Execute any power of attorney, deed or other instrument

- He may do any other act which is necessary or expedient for the purposes of or in connection with the exercise of those powers.

3.2 Powers in Schedule 5 Part I IA 86 (historically exercisable with sanction)

- Carry on the bankrupt's business (so far as lawful under any enactment) with a view to beneficial winding-up.
- Institute or defend legal actions relating to property forming part of the bankrupt's estate.
- Power to bring legal proceedings under ss339, 340, or 423.
- Power to accept as the consideration for the sale of any property comprised in the bankrupt's estate a sum of money payable at a future time subject to such stipulations as to security as the committee or court thinks fit.
- Power to mortgage or pledge any part of the bankrupt's estate for purpose of raising money to pay debts.
- Power, where any right, option or other power forms part of the bankrupt's estate, to make payments or incur liabilities with a view to obtaining, for the benefit of creditors, any property which is the subject of the right, option or power.
- Power to make such compromise or other arrangement as may be thought expedient with creditors, or other persons claiming to be creditors, in respect of bankruptcy debts.
- Power to make such compromise or other arrangement as may be thought expedient with respect to any claim arising out of or incidental to the bankrupt's estate made or capable of being made on the trustee by any person.

3.3 General Powers in Schedule 5 Part II IA 86 (exercisable without sanction)

These include the power:

- To give receipts for any money received by him, being receipts which effectually discharge the person paying the money from all responsibility in respect of its application
- Refer to arbitration or compromise on such terms as may be agreed any debts, claims or liabilities subsisting or supposed to subsist between the bankrupt and any person who may have incurred any liability to the bankrupt

3.4 Powers in relations to public utilities

The trustee can demand supplies of:

- Gas
- Electricity
- Water
- Telecommunication services

However this list was extended by the 2015 update of this Act.

The supplier may:

- Make it a condition of the giving of the supply that the trustee personally guarantees the payment of charges but **not** make it a condition that any outstanding charges for pre-commencement supplies are paid.

3.5 Power to appoint bankrupt s314

Under s314 (2) the trustee may appoint the bankrupt to:

- Superintend the management of the whole or part of the estate
- Carry on the business for the creditors' benefit
- Assist in the administration of the estate

Either the creditors' committee or the court must give permission. The permission must be specific not general and must be obtained by the trustee in advance of the exercise of the power. If it isn't the committee or court may ratify (for the purpose of enabling the trustee to meet his expenses out of the bankrupt's estate) but only if satisfied that the trustee acted in a case of urgency and has sought ratification without undue delay.

Persons dealing with the trustee in good faith and for value do not have to enquire whether permission has been given.

3.6 Power to transfer shares s311(3)

The trustee has the same right to transfer:

- Stock or shares in a company
- Shares in a ship
- Any other property transferable in the books of a company, office or person, as the bankrupt would have had but for the bankruptcy

3.7 Power to apply to court for directions s303

A trustee is entitled to use his own discretion in administering the estate.

A trustee cannot transfer the exercise of those discretions to the court by applying for directions.

Directions should only be applied for in cases of genuine difficulty.

3.8 Power to apply to the court for an order directing the bankrupt s363(3)

The court has the power to direct the bankrupt to do anything for the purposes of the bankruptcy.

Non compliance is a contempt of court.

3.9 Power to appoint a solicitor

The trustee must give notice of the appointment of a solicitor to the committee.

4 Trustee's powers of realisation

Section overview

- The trustee has a number of powers in schedule 5 which are designed to assist him in realising the bankrupt's estate.

4.1 Powers in Schedule 5 Part II IA 1986 (exercisable without sanction)

Power to sell any part of the estate including book debts and goodwill.

Power to prove rank, claim and draw a dividend in respect of debts due to the bankrupt.

4.2 Power in Schedule 5 Part I IA 1986 (exercisable with sanction)

Power to accept as consideration for the sale of any part of the estate a sum of money payable at a future time, subject to such stipulations as to security or otherwise as the committee or court thinks fit.

4.3 Power to dispose of property to the bankrupt's associates (s314(6))

The permission of the committee is not required but the committee must be notified.

Associates of the bankrupt are defined in s435 as:

- Spouse or civil partner (including former and reputed spouses/civil partners)
- Relatives of the bankrupt
- The spouses of those relatives or civil partner
- Business partners (and their spouses/civil partners or other relative)
- Employers/employees of the bankrupt
- Trustees
- Companies controlled by the bankrupt and/or his associates

[The legislation defines relatives as including brothers, sisters, uncles, aunts, nephews, nieces, children, parents, grandparents, grandchildren. If does not include cousins.]

5 Trustee's powers to make payments out

Section overview

- The trustee has a number of powers in schedule 5 and other parts of the Insolvency Act designed to assist him in compromising claims and making payments out of the estate.

5.1 Powers in Schedule 5 Part I IA 1986 (exercisable with sanction)

- Compromise or make arrangements with creditors in respect of their bankruptcy debts.
- Mortgage or pledge assets to raise money for the payment of debts.
- Enter into any compromise or arrangement in respect of claims against the estate.

5.2 Estimate the value of any debt (s322(3))

If a debt which, by reason of it being subject to any contingency or contingencies or for any other reason, does not bear a certain value then the trustee can estimate its value.

If the value of a debt is estimated by the trustee the amount provable in the bankruptcy is the amount of the estimate.

5.3 Distribute property in specie under s326(1)

Property that is not readily saleable can be distributed in specie. The permission of the committee must be sought. The terms for obtaining the permission are the same as for s314 (see para 3.5).

Definition

In specie distribution – An in specie distribution occurs where assets are distributed in their present form rather than being realised and the cash proceeds then being distributed.

Summary and Self-test

Summary

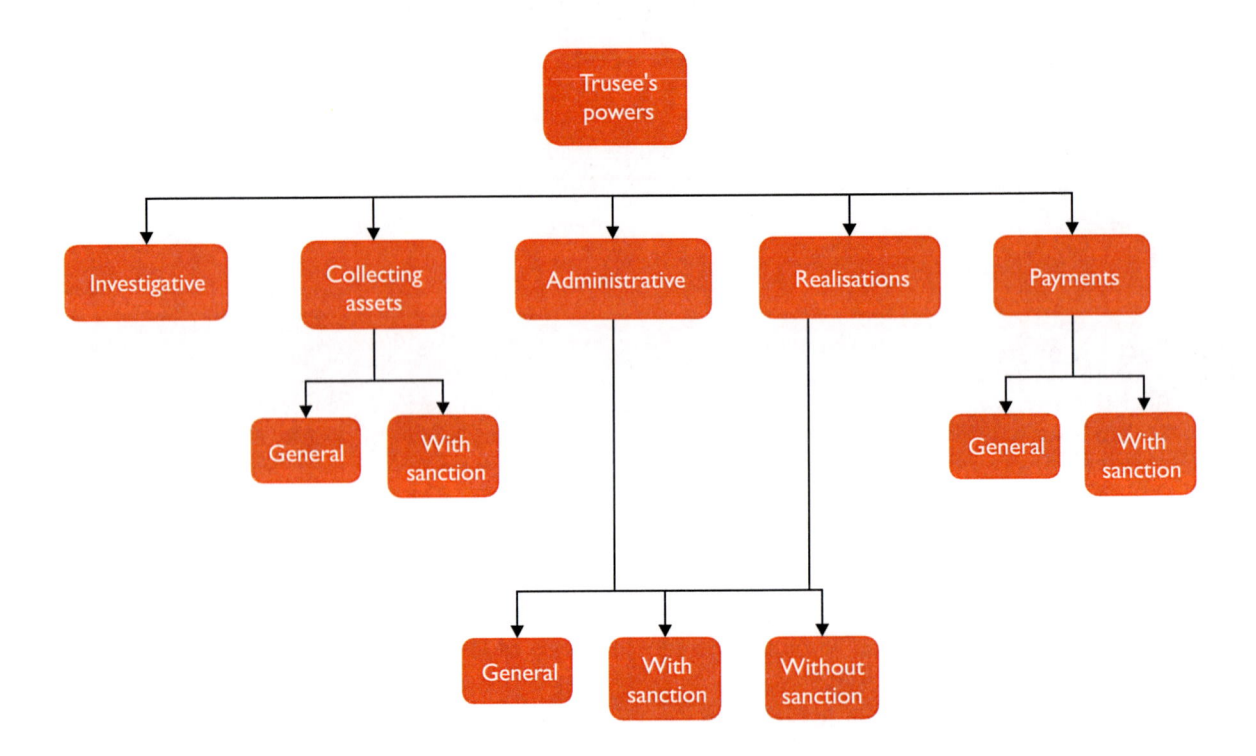

```
                        Trusee's
                        powers
    ┌──────────┬──────────┼──────────┬──────────┐
Investigative  Collecting  Administrative  Realisations  Payments
               assets
              ┌────┴────┐              │         ┌────┴────┐
           General    With                    General    With
                    sanction                           sanction
                        ┌──────────┼──────────┐
                     General     With      Without
                               sanction    sanction
```

Self-test

Now try the following questions.

1. From what date is a disclaimer of onerous property effective?

2. Who may be required to attend a private examination under s366?

3. Under what section of the IA 86 may a trustee apply to the court for an order for the production of documents by HM Revenue and Customs?

    A   s54
    B   s112
    C   s268
    D   s369
    E   s412

4. Under what section of the IA 86 may a trustee seek to re-direct a bankrupt's mail?

    A   s370
    B   s371
    C   s372
    D   s373
    E   s374

5. What duties are owed to the OR by the debtor under s291?

Now, go back to the Learning Objectives in the Introduction. If you are satisfied that you have achieved these objectives, please tick them off.

Answers to Self-test

1. The trustee will prepare the notice of disclaimer, authenticate and date it. The disclaimer is effective from that date.

2. Bankrupt

    Bankrupt's spouse or former spouse or civil partner or former civil partner

    Any person known or believed to have any property comprised in the bankrupt's estate in his possession

    Bankrupt's debtors

    Any person appearing to the court to be able to give information concerning the bankrupt's dealings, affairs or property

3. D   s369

4. B   s371

5. Duty to deliver possession of his estate.

    Deliver up all books, papers and other records of which he has possession or control.

    Give OR such inventory of his estate.

    Attend on the OR at such times as the OR may reasonably require.

Answer to Interactive question

Answer to Interactive question 1: Gillian Long

- s290 The OR can apply to court for the public examination of the bankrupt. The trustee can attend the examination and question the bankrupt as to her affairs, dealings and property.
- s366 trustee may apply to court for the private examination of:
    - Bankrupt
    - Bankrupt's spouse or former spouse or civil partner or former civil partner
    - Any person known or believed to have property comprised in the bankrupt's estate in his possession
- Can apply for the re-direction of the bankrupt's mail s371.
- Can apply under s369 for the production of documents from HM Revenue and Customs.
- Can apply for copies of entries in Land Registry.
- Can write to all known creditors requesting information regarding the bankrupt.

CHAPTER 26

Proofs of debt

Introduction
Topic List
1 Proofs of debt
2 Special cases
3 Distributions
4 Order of payment
Summary and Self-test
Answers to Self-test
Answer to Interactive question

Introduction

Learning objectives

- State the classes of creditors and their rights

Tick off ☐

Stop and think

How do creditors prove their debts in bankruptcy? What does this mean? Why are there rules concerning the order of payments and the distribution of funds by the trustee?

Working context

In a working environment it is likely that you will be asked to assist the trustee in determining the creditors' claims received in a bankruptcy. It is therefore important to know the rules relating to what debts are provable and those that aren't.

1 Proofs of debt

> **Section overview**
> - A creditor of the bankrupt will establish his right to vote at meetings and his right to a dividend by submitting a proof of debt form. It is for the trustee to decide whether or not the creditor has established his right to be treated as a bankruptcy creditor within the provisions of the Act and the Rules.

1.1 Proving for dividend and voting purposes

These must be distinguished for two reasons:

1 **Future debts**

   These need to be discounted in accordance with Rule 11.13 for dividend but not voting purposes (see 2.6).

2 **Unspecified debts**

   - For voting purposes Rule 6.93(3) provides that a creditor shall not vote in respect of such debts unless the chair agrees to put upon the debt an estimated minimum value.

   - For dividend purposes s322(3) provides that the trustee shall estimate the value of any unspecified debt ie one which by reason of it being subject to a contingency, or for any other reason, does not bear a certain value.

At any creditors' meeting the chairman has the power to admit or reject a creditor's proof for the purpose of his entitlement to vote.

If the chairman is in doubt whether a proof should be admitted or rejected, he shall mark it as objected to and allow the creditor to vote, subject to his vote being subsequently declared invalid if the objection to the proof is sustained.

1.2 Contents of a proof of debt

Proof of debt forms shall be sent out by the OR or the trustee to every creditor of the bankrupt who is known to the sender, or is identified in the bankrupt's Statement of Affairs.

R6.98 provides for the contents of a proof of debt. The contents are:

- The creditor's name and address and, if a company, its company registration number
- The total amount of his claim as at the date of the bankruptcy order
- Whether or not the amount includes outstanding un-capitalised interest
- Whether or not the claim includes VAT
- Particulars of how and when the debt was incurred by the debtor
- Particulars of any security held, the date when it was given and the value which the creditor puts upon it, including details of any reservation (retention) of title in respect of goods to which the debt refers
- The name, address and authority of the person authenticating the proof if other than the creditor himself

The trustee must examine every proof and consider its validity and if a claim is rejected by the trustee the creditor affected can apply to the court (within 21 days) to vary the trustee's decision.

The trustee shall, so long as proofs lodged with him are in his hands, allow them to be inspected by:

- A creditor who has submitted his proof of debt and it has not been rejected for the purposes of a dividend or otherwise
- The bankrupt
- Any person acting on behalf of either of the above

1.3 Provable debts

Creditors may prove for a bankruptcy debt. Bankruptcy debts are defined in s382.

- A debt or liability to which the bankrupt is subject at the commencement of the bankruptcy
- A debt or liability to which he may become subject after the commencement of the bankruptcy (including after his discharge from bankruptcy) by reason of any obligation incurred before commencement
- Interest on the above provable under s322. The trustee must estimate the value of any debts which do not have a certain value (s322)

s382(2) makes it clear that liabilities in tort are provable providing the cause of action accrued prior to commencement.

s382(3) states that it is immaterial whether the debt or liability is:

- Present or future
- Certain or contingent
- Fixed or liquidated or is capable of being ascertained by fixed rules or as a matter of opinion

1.4 Debts which are not provable

R12.3(2) the following debts are not provable.

- Any fine imposed for an offence
- Any obligation arising under an order for periodic payments made in family or domestic proceedings. (Lump sum and cost orders made in family or domestic proceedings are provable but unlike other provable debts are not discharged by the bankruptcy. Such debts survive the bankruptcy and can be enforced against the bankrupt after discharge)
- Any obligation arising under an assessment by the Child Support Agency
- Any obligation arising under a confiscation order made under s1 of the Drug Trafficking Offences Act 1986 or s71 of the Criminal Justice Act 1988 or Parts 2-4 of Proceeds of Crime Act 2002

If a claim is not provable it follows that although the creditor will not be able to receive a dividend in respect of it, the debt will at least survive the discharge of the bankruptcy.

Certain claims under the Financial Services Act 1986 and the 1987 Banking Acts are only provable once all other creditors have been paid in full.

R12.3 specifically states that it is without prejudice to other rules of law under which particular types of debt are **not** provable. For example non EU tax is not provable (see 2.8). Also student loans are not provable, nor are debts which are statute barred (see 2.12).

1.5 Interest

- **Pre-commencement interest**
    - s322(2) states that where a bankruptcy debt bears interest, that interest is provable as part of the debt except in so far as it is payable in respect of any period after the commencement of bankruptcy.

        If the contract itself provides for payment of interest the contractual rate of interest will apply unless it is extortionate.

    - On a debt due by virtue of a written instrument and payable at a certain time, for example, a debt due by virtue of a bill of exchange, the rate of interest will be that specified in s17 of the Judgments Act 1838 on the date of bankruptcy order (currently 8%).
    - In all other cases interest will only be payable if the creditor, prior to the date of presentation of the petition, serves written demand for payment of interest stating that interest would be payable from the date of service of the demand to the date of the bankruptcy order.

        The rate of interest charged is that in the Judgments Act unless the demanded rate of interest is lower in which case that will apply.

Note. Interest rates can be challenged under s343 (extortionate credit transactions).

- **Post-commencement interest**
    - s322(2) states that interest in respect of any period after the commencement of the bankruptcy is not provable.
    - s328(4) provides that if all preferential or unsecured creditors (except for deferred debts) are paid in full then any remaining funds are to be used for the payment of interest on those debts.
    - The interest is paid in respect of the period that the debts have been outstanding since the commencement of the bankruptcy.
    - The interest payable under s328(4) ranks equally even if the debts themselves do not rank equally.
    - The rate of interest payable is the greater of the rate specified in s17 of the Judgments Act 1838 on the date of commencement, and the rate applicable to that debt apart from the bankruptcy.

- **Late payment of commercial debts**
    - The Late Payment of Commercial Debts (Interest) Act 1988 (LPCD) gives businesses a statutory right to claim interest on the late payment of commercial debts by making an entitlement to interest an implied contractual term.
    - The LPCD applies to contracts for the supply of goods and services where both parties are acting in the course of business. It does not apply to consumer credit agreements, mortgages and charges.
    - Interest under the LCPD runs from the day following the agreed date of payment, or if no agreed date, from 30 days after the supplier performs his obligation under the contract.
    - The rate of interest is 8% over the base rate in force on either the 30 June or 31 December immediately before the day on which the interest starts to run. So for example if interest starts to run on 1 August 20X0 the base rate applicable on the 30 June 20X0 will be used to calculate the interest due.
    - Parties cannot contract out of the LPCD unless there is a substantial contractual remedy for late payment of the debt.

2 Special cases

Section overview

- A number of claims in bankruptcy require special treatment. These are summarised below.

2.1 Foreign currency debts

R6.111 states that the debt must be converted into sterling at the official rate as at the close of business on the date of the bankruptcy order.

The official rate is the Bank of England mid-market rate. If there is no rate then the court will determine a rate.

2.2 Discounts

R6.110 states that all discounts available to the bankrupt must be deducted (eg trade discounts) but not early settlement discounts.

2.3 Payments of a periodical nature

R6.112 states that a creditor owed a debt of a periodical nature (eg rent) can prove for amounts due and unpaid up to the date of the bankruptcy order. This will include all amounts payable in advance.

Where on the date of the order, any payment was accruing, the creditor claims for the amount that would have fallen due on that date, if accruing from day to day.

2.4 Secured creditors

R6.109 states that if a secured creditor realises his security he may prove for the balance owing.

If a secured creditor voluntarily surrenders his security he may prove for the whole debt.

Alternatively a secured creditor can estimate the value of his security and prove for any balance as an unsecured creditor.

The creditor can revalue the security in the proof with either the court's or office holder's permission.

2.5 Negotiable instruments

R6.108 states the proofs in relation to money owed on a negotiable instrument (eg cheque) must be accompanied by the original instrument or a certified copy.

2.6 Future debts

R6.114 refers to debts which are payable at a future time.

These debts can be proved for but are subject to R11.13 in relation to discounting the amount due for the purposes of paying a dividend.

R11.13 provides a formula to calculate the percentage discount.

The formula to apply is: $\dfrac{x}{1.05^n}$

Where

- x = amount of the admitted proof
- n = amount of time from the date of the bankruptcy order to the date on which the payment of the creditors' debt would otherwise be due expressed in years and months in a decimalised form.

2.7 Double proof

Where a debt has been guaranteed the general rule is that the primary creditor should prove in the proceedings not the guarantor.

2.8 Foreign tax

Government of India v Taylor provided that foreign tax claims are not enforceable in the UK courts.

Therefore they are not provable in a bankruptcy.

Article 39 of the EC Regulation on Insolvency Proceedings 2000 provides that any creditor who has a habitual residence, domicile or registered office in a Member State other than the state opening the proceedings, including the tax authorities, shall have the right to lodge claims in insolvency proceedings.

As a result any EU tax is provable in the bankruptcy. (Except in relation to Denmark which is not subject to the EC Regulation.)

2.9 Gambling debts

Generally these are not provable.

However, s16 Gaming Act provides that a debt due on a cheque drawn to enable a person to take part in gaming on licensed premises is enforceable providing:

- The cheque is not post-dated
- That it was exchanged for cash or chips at par
- That it was presented to a bank for payment within two banking days

As a result, if this can be shown and the cheque remains unpaid, the debt due upon it will be provable in the bankruptcy.

2.10 Set-off

s323 applies where, before the commencement of the bankruptcy, there have been mutual credits, debits or other dealings between the bankrupt and a creditor.

s323(2) states that an account should be taken of what is due from each party to the other in mutual dealings and the sums due from one party shall be set-off against the sums due from the other.

s323(3) states that set-off should not occur if one of the parties was aware that a petition for bankruptcy was pending at the time the sum became due.

Only the balance is provable in the bankruptcy. If the effect of set-off is that the third party owes money to the bankrupt then this amount must be paid to the trustee.

2.11 Landlords

A landlord may have claims for arrears of rent and service charge, future rent and dilapidations.

Claims for arrears of rent and/or service charge may be admitted in full.

A claim for rent payable in advance which straddles the date of the bankruptcy order should be admitted in full.

Claims for future rent are subject to mitigation as the landlord has a duty to mitigate his loss eg by re-letting the premises. A discount for early payment will apply.

Claims for dilapidations at the premises will either be liquidated or unliquidated. This will depend upon whether or not the landlord has carried out the work. If the work has been carried out and the claim liquidated, then assuming that the trustee is satisfied that the sums claimed were due under the terms of the lease, the claim will be admitted.

If the works have not been carried out and the claim is unliquidated it will be for the trustee to determine the amount due.

If the trustee disclaims the lease the landlord will be entitled to claim statutory compensation. In *Re Park Air Services plc* it was held that the landlord's compensation is measured by reference to the difference between the rents and other payments which the landlord would have received in the future but for any disclaimer, and the rents and other sums which the disclaimer would enable the landlord to receive by re-letting. Allowance should be made for early receipt using the yield on gilt-edged securities for an equivalent term from the date of disclaimer. The court held that this should be used rather than the discount specified in Rule 11.13 as the landlord's entitlement to compensation is a present right to immediate payment rather than a future payment.

2.12 Statute-barred debts

The effect of the Limitation Act is that after a set period debts and legal claims become statute barred meaning that they cannot be sued upon. The law in this area can be very complex but generally speaking claims arising from contractual disputes are statute barred after 6 years (unless the contract was made under seal/by deed in which case the period is extended to 12 years). Mortgages are made under seal so a 12 year limitation period applies for any shortfall due to a mortgage lender. Personal injury claims are statute barred after 3 years. Consequentially if a debt can not be enforced in court it cannot be proved for in bankruptcy either.

It is complicated to rely upon the Limitations Act in its own right unless the trustee is content with full knowledge of communication between debtor and creditor in the qualifying period.

Interactive question 1: Tim Bendman

Your principal is trustee of Tim Bendman. He presents you with a bundle of proofs which have been received in relation to the bankruptcy, details of which are as follows:

1. A claim by HM Revenue and Customs for unpaid VAT of £1,200 per month for the 14 months before the date of the bankruptcy order.
2. A claim by the bankrupt's brother for £8,000 which he lent to the bankrupt eight years ago.
3. A claim by the bankrupt's wife for £5,000 lent to the bankrupt two years ago before they married.

4   A claim by Satby Bank plc for sums due by way of an overdraft. The bankrupt's overdraft increased by £3,000 *after* the date of the bankruptcy order. The £3,000 increase represents a cheque which was written and presented before the date of the bankruptcy order, but which was only cleared and credited to the payee's account after the bank had been informed of the commencement of bankruptcy.

Requirement

How you would deal with each proof?

See **Answer** at the end of this chapter.

3 Distributions

> **Section overview**
>
> - Whenever the trustee has sufficient funds in hand for the purpose of making a distribution he shall, subject to the retention of such sums as may be necessary for the expenses of the bankruptcy, declare and distribute dividends among the creditors in respect of the bankruptcy debts which they have respectively proved (s324).

3.1 Notice of intention to declare dividend

The trustee must give notice of his intention to declare a dividend to all creditors whose addresses are known to him and who have not proved their debts.

Unless he has previously by public advertisement invited creditors to prove their debts, he must give notice of the intended dividend by public advertisement. The notice must be Gazetted and may be advertised in such other manner as the trustee thinks fit (R11.2(1A)).

The notice must state a last date for proving, which must be not less than 21 days from that of the notice.

The dividend must be declared within two months from the last date for proving.

The trustee must, within five business days from the last date of proving, deal with every creditor's proof.

Where a creditor's proof has been rejected, the trustee must send his reasons for rejecting the proof, in writing to the creditor, who then has 21 days to appeal to court for the decision to be reversed or varied (R6.105).

3.2 Calculation of dividend

In the calculation and distribution of a dividend the trustee shall make provision for:

- Any bankruptcy debts which appear to him to be due to persons who, by reason of the distance of their place of residence, may not have had sufficient time to tender and establish their proofs
- Any bankruptcy debts which are the subject of claims which have not yet been determined
- Disputed proofs and claims

The trustee may distribute property in *specie* (s326).

- This is where it cannot be readily or advantageously sold
- Specific sanction of the creditors' committee is required. (If not obtained the committee can ratify but only if no undue delay and trustee acted in a case of urgency)
- Innocent third parties who purchase property so distributed need not be concerned whether sanction was properly obtained their ownership will not be affected by the lack of sanction (see Chapter 25 also)

3.3 Declaration of dividend

The trustee must give notice of the dividend and of how it is proposed to distribute it to all creditors who have proved their debts.

The notice must include the following details:

- Amounts realised from the sale of assets
- Payments made by the trustee
- Provision made for unsettled claims and funds retained for that particular purpose
- The total amount to be distributed and the rate of dividend
- Whether, and if so when, any further dividend is expected to be declared

The dividend may be distributed simultaneously with the notice declaring it.

3.4 Rights of creditors

A creditor who has not proved his debt before the declaration of any dividend is not entitled to disturb, by reason that he has not participated in it, the distribution of that dividend or any other dividend declared before his debt was proved. Best practice states that if a claim is made prior to the calculation and issue of a dividend, then the trustee should include the debt for the amount he would ordinarily be entitled to prior to lapsing of the notice period.

Unless formally excluded under Rule 11.3 IR96, once the creditor has proved their debt, they are entitled to be paid. Payment for the unreceived dividend will come out of any money available for the payment of a further dividend. This payment must be made before any further dividend is distributed to creditors.

No action lies against the trustee for a dividend. However if the trustee refuses to pay a dividend the court may, if it thinks fit, order him to pay it out of his own money, together with interest from the time it was withheld, and the associated legal costs.

The SBEEA 2015 allowed the trustee to make a discretional provision to admit claims below the prescribed threshold of £1,000 for distribution purposes. This does not preclude the trustee's right to reject or exclude a claim.

4 Order of payment

Section overview

- The Act and the Rules specify the order in which the expenses of the bankruptcy and the bankruptcy debts should be paid.
- The required order is as follows:
    - Costs of the bankruptcy (see 4.1)
    - Any debts specially preferred (by virtue of s328(6))
    - Preferential debts (ss328(1), 386 and Sch 6)
    - Ordinary debts (s328(3))
    - Interest on debts above outstanding for the period **after** the bankruptcy order;
    - Debts in respect of credit supplied by a person who is the spouse or civil partner of the bankrupt at the date of the bankruptcy order (s329)
    - Debts specially postponed (s328(6))
    - If any surplus remains after payment of the above debts it must be paid to the bankrupt (s330(5)).

4.1 Costs of the bankruptcy

The order of priority of these is set out in R6.224 as follows:

- Expenses properly chargeable or incurred by the OR or the trustee in preserving, realising or getting in any of the assets of the bankrupt, including those incurred in acquiring title to after-acquired property

- Any other expenses incurred or disbursements made by the OR or under his authority, including those incurred or made in carrying on the business of a debtor or bankrupt
- Any other fees payable under any order made under s415, including those payable to the OR, and any remuneration payable to him under general regulations:
    - The fee payable under any order made under s415 for the performance by the official receiver of his general duties as OR
    - Any repayable deposit lodged by the petitioner under any such order as security for the fee mentioned (except where the deposit is applied to the payment of the remuneration of an insolvency practitioner appointed under s273 - debtor's petition)
- The cost of any security provided by an interim receiver, trustee or special manager in accordance with the Act or the Rules
- The remuneration of the interim receiver
- Any deposit lodged on an application for the appointment of an interim receiver
- The costs of the petitioner, and of any person appearing on the petition whose costs are allowed by the court
- The remuneration of the special manager
- Any amount payable to a person employed or authorised to assist in the preparation of a statement of affairs or of accounts
- Any allowance made, by order of the court, towards costs on an application for release from the obligation to submit a statement of affairs, or for an extension of time for submitting such a statement
- Any necessary disbursements by the trustee in the course of his administration (including any expenses incurred by members of the creditors' committee or their representatives and allowed by the trustee under R6.164)
- The remuneration or emoluments of any person (including the bankrupt) who has been employed by the trustee to perform any services for the estate, as required or authorised by or under the Act or the Rules
- The remuneration of the trustee, up to any amount not exceeding that which is payable to the OR under general regulations (or that laid down by creditors when seeking fees on a time cost basis which exceed the initial estimate)
- The amount of any capital gains tax on chargeable gains accruing on the realisation of any asset of the bankrupt (without regard to whether the realisation is effected by a trustee, a secured creditor, or a receiver or manager appointed to deal with a security)
- The balance of any remuneration due to the trustee

Summary and Self-test

Summary

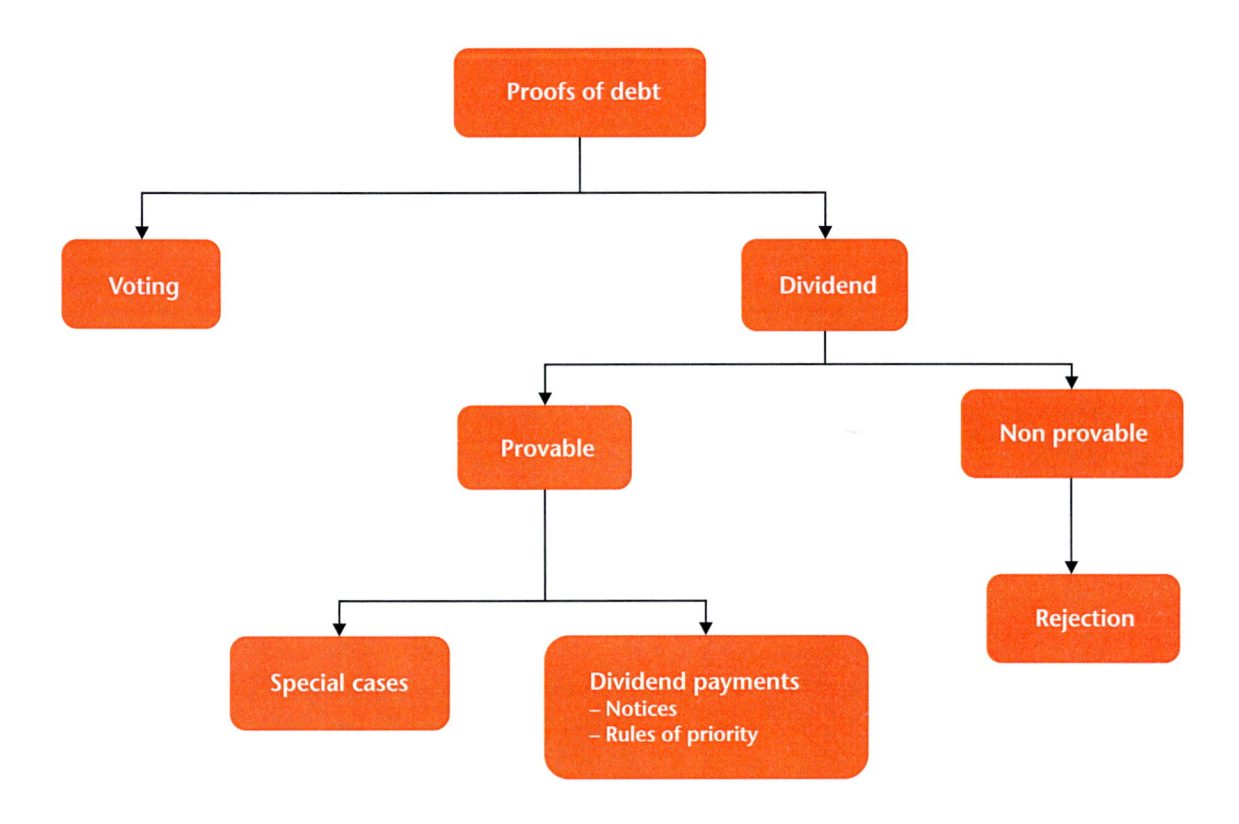

```
                    ┌──────────────────┐
                    │  Proofs of debt  │
                    └──────────────────┘
                       │            │
              ┌────────┘            └────────┐
              ▼                              ▼
        ┌──────────┐                   ┌──────────┐
        │  Voting  │                   │ Dividend │
        └──────────┘                   └──────────┘
                                    │              │
                           ┌────────┘              └────────┐
                           ▼                                ▼
                     ┌──────────┐                    ┌──────────────┐
                     │ Provable │                    │ Non provable │
                     └──────────┘                    └──────────────┘
                      │        │                            │
              ┌───────┘        └──────────┐                 ▼
              ▼                           ▼          ┌───────────┐
        ┌───────────────┐       ┌─────────────────┐  │ Rejection │
        │ Special cases │       │Dividend payments│  └───────────┘
        └───────────────┘       │ – Notices       │
                                │ – Rules of priority│
                                └─────────────────┘
```

Self-test

Answer the following questions.

1   The trustee must declare a dividend within what period of time from the last date for proving?

    A   28 days
    B   1 month
    C   2 months
    D   7 days

2   Which of the following is not required to be included in the notice of dividend?

    A   Amounts realised from the sale of assets
    B   Details of unrealised assets
    C   Payments made by the trustee
    D   Whether and if so when, any further dividend is expected to be declared

3   The trustee must deal with every creditor's proof within how many business days of the last date for proving?

    A   5
    B   10
    C   15
    D   20

4   Mr Smith, a bankrupt, has liabilities to HM Revenue and Customs of £7,000, together with trade creditors of £15,000. He has one employee who is claiming holiday pay of £450 and wage arrears of £150. The OR's costs total £900 and trustee's fees will total £5,000 with a further £300 worth of disbursements.

    What dividend will the unsecured creditors receive from realisations of £18,000?

    Ignore VAT but include the Secretary of State's administration fee in your calculations. (This is a post 6 April 2015 order.)

    A   40.18p in £
    B   53.64p in £
    C   29.34 in £
    D   41.27p in £

5   Which of the following debts is not provable in bankruptcy?

    A   Pre-commencement interest
    B   Debt in a foreign currency
    C   Future debt
    D   Claim for dilapidations
    E   Any fine imposed for an offence

Now, go back to the Learning Objectives in the Introduction. If you are satisfied that you have achieved these objectives, please tick them off.

Answers to Self-test

1. C
2. B
3. A
4. C

		£
Realisations		18,000
Less: Costs		
OR's costs		(900)
Trustee's fees		(5,000)
Disbursements		(300)
Secretary of State Administration fee		
18,000 – 2,000 = 16,000		
1,700 @ 100%	1,700	
1,500 @ 75%	1,125	
12,800 @ 15%	1,920	
16,000	4,745	(4,745)
Available to preferential creditors		7,055
Less preferential creditors		(600)
Available to unsecured creditors		6,455
Less unsecured creditors		(7,000)
		(15,000)
Deficit to unsecured creditors		15,545

Dividend: 6,455/22,000 = 29.34p in £

5. E   R12.3(2)

Answer to Interactive question

Answer to Interactive question 1: Tim Bendman

1 Admit £16,800 as an unsecured claim.

2 It has been held in cases such as *Re General Rolling Stock Company 1872* that if a debt, although at one time valid and enforceable, has become statute barred through lapse of time, the creditor will be unable to lodge a proof in the insolvency and the trustee will be under duty not to pay out any dividend in respect of that claim.

The limitation period for contract debts is six years and therefore the claim by the bankrupt's brother is statute barred, the loan having been made some eight years previously.

3 Under s329 any bankruptcy debt owed in respect of credit provided by a person who (whether or not the bankrupt's spouse at the time the credit was provided) was the bankrupt's spouse at the commencement of the bankruptcy, ranks in priority after the preferential and ordinary unsecured debts and also ranks after any interest payable on such debts pursuant to s328(4).

Under s329 the debt to the spouse is payable with interest in respect of the period during which it has been outstanding since the commencement of the bankruptcy and that interest has the same priority as the debt on which it is payable.

4 Under s284 a disposition of property made by the bankrupt in the period beginning with the day of the presentation of the bankruptcy petition and ending with the vesting of the bankrupt's estate in a trustee is void except to the extent that it is or was made with the consent of the court or is or was subsequently ratified by the court.

Where after the commencement of the bankruptcy the bankrupt has incurred a debt to a banker or other person by reason of the making of a payment which is void under s284, that debt is deemed to have been incurred before the commencement of bankruptcy unless:

- That banker or person had notice of the bankruptcy before the debt was incurred
- It is not reasonably practicable for the amount of the payment to be recovered from the person to whom it was made

In the present case, the disposition is deemed to take place, not when the cheque is written and presented but instead on the date it is cleared and credited to the payee's account.

Since the bank was aware of the making of the bankruptcy order when the cheque was cleared, the disposition cannot therefore be treated as one made before the commencement of the bankruptcy and accordingly the claim is not provable against the bankrupt's estate.

CHAPTER 27

Discharge and annulment

Introduction
Topic List
1 Discharge
2 Bankruptcy Restrictions Order
3 Annulment of bankruptcy

Summary and Self-test
Answers to Self-test

Introduction

Learning objectives

- Describe the grounds for annulment of the bankruptcy order and the processes involved in annulment
- Describe the processes involved in discharge from bankruptcy
- Describe the reasons for suspension of discharge and the process involved in suspension
- Describe the consequences of bankruptcy for the bankrupt including Bankruptcy Restrictions Orders

Stop and think

What is the difference between discharge and annulment? What does discharge mean to a debtor and the bankruptcy creditors?

Working context

You may be asked by a bankrupt to explain to them how they are discharged from bankruptcy and what it means for them in practical terms. You may also be asked by your principal to identify any conduct of the debtor which may make an application for a Bankruptcy Restrictions Order desirable.

1 Discharge

Section overview

- Bankruptcy commences on the date a bankruptcy order is made and continues until the bankrupt is discharged under IA 86.
- On discharge, the liabilities that the bankrupt has been subject to will be lifted and he will be released from most civil bankruptcy debts. The discharge does not mark the end of the administration of his estate. The trustee will not be released until he has finished administering the estate and consequently the duty of the bankrupt to assist the trustee continues after discharge.
- Assets that have vested in the trustee will not re-vest in the bankrupt following discharge.

1.1 Effects of discharge

1   The bankrupt will be released from all bankruptcy debts and interest thereon.

Bankruptcy debts are defined in s382 as any debt or liability to which:

- The bankrupt is subject at the commencement of the bankruptcy
- He became subject after the commencement of the bankruptcy (including after his discharge from bankruptcy) by reason of any obligation incurred before commencement

There are some debts that the bankrupt will not be released from. Consequently the creditors concerned will be free to sue the bankrupt and will not require permission.

The debts the bankrupt will not be released from are:

- Secured debts
- Debts arising from fraud or fraudulent breach of trust
- Fines and recognisances (exception: revenue penalties where bankrupt can be released with treasury consent)
- Lump sum orders and costs awarded in family proceedings
- Damages for personal injury awarded in tort or contract

Remember that by Rule 12.3 some debts are not provable and hence the bankrupt will not be released from them:

- Criminal confiscation orders
- Obligations arising under a periodic payments order made in family or domestic proceedings (eg arrears of maintenance)

Student loans are also not discharged.

2   The disabilities of the bankruptcy will no longer apply.

s11 CDDA (disqualification of undischarged bankrupt) no longer applies.

Disqualification under other sections is unaffected.

Duty to notify persons offering credit of £500 or more comes to an end.

3   The estate will not re-vest in the bankrupt. Assets not yet realised and distributed remain vested in the trustee. The powers and duties of the trustee in relation to the estate are unaffected by discharge. The Act and Rules continue to apply. Also an income payments order or agreement is likely to continue but cannot be applied for after discharge.

4   Discharge does not mark the end of the administration of the estate. The trustee will not be released until he has finished administering the estate.

5   Duty of the bankrupt to assist the trustee continues.

6   Discharge has no effect on the rights of creditors to prove in the bankruptcy.

7   If the bankrupt is subject to either a Bankruptcy Restrictions Order or Undertaking some of the disabilities/obligations that arise on bankruptcy will continue beyond discharge.

1.2 When is a bankrupt discharged?

Discharge will be automatic one year from the date of the bankruptcy order (s279).

However discharge can be more than one year from the order if either the OR or the trustee apply to the court for time to cease to run on the basis that the bankrupt is not complying with his obligations. The procedure to be followed on such an application is set out in Rule 6.215.

s279(2) provides that discharge can occur in less than one year where the OR files notice in court to the effect that an investigation is unnecessary unless the discharge had been suspended, or has been concluded. However this provision has now been repealed. The current position is that for any bankruptcy orders made on or after 1 October 2013, a bankrupt will be automatically discharged one year from the date of the bankruptcy order (providing they are not subject to any restrictions or their discharge has not been suspended).

As the repeal does not operate retrospectively, all bankruptcy orders made up to and on 30 September 2013 may still be subject to the early discharge provisions after 1 October 2013.

1.3 Second or subsequent bankruptcies

There is no longer a separate rule for discharge in the case of second or subsequent bankruptcies. Where after 1 April 2004 a person is made bankrupt for the second (or subsequent) time they will be automatically discharged after one year in the usual way. However where the bankruptcy is within six years of discharge of an earlier bankruptcy this is potentially grounds for a Bankruptcy Restrictions Order (see para 2).

1.4 Certificate of discharge

Under Rule 6.220 the former bankrupt may apply, on payment of a fee, for a certificate of discharge. This applies to both automatic discharge and discharge by court order. Application can also be made to the Secretary of State to advertise notice of the discharge although the Secretary of State need not proceed until he has received payment to cover the advertising costs.

1.5 Suspension of discharge

If a bankrupt does not comply with his obligations as a bankrupt or if the OR or trustee have grounds to be suspicious that the bankrupt is concealing information or property, either the OR or trustee may apply to court to seek a suspension of the automatic discharge. Application will have to be made to the Court and the Court may:

- Reject the application
- Suspend for a set period
- Suspend until the bankrupt complies with an obligation eg the obligation to deliver up property or submit to a public examination

2 Bankruptcy Restrictions Order

Section overview

- The Secretary of State or Official Receiver can apply for a Bankruptcy Restrictions Order (BRO) with regard to the conduct of the bankrupt. The effect of a BRO is to extend the period during which the disabilities resulting from bankruptcy apply. The BRO was introduced by the EA 2002 to protect the public from those bankrupts whose conduct has been either reckless or irresponsible. The provisions are set out in s281A and Schedule 4A 1A 1986.

2.1 Mechanics of a BRO

Only the Secretary of State or the OR can apply to the court for a BRO (ie not the trustee).

Only the court can make a BRO. However the Insolvency Service can accept a Bankruptcy Restrictions Undertaking (BRU) to avoid the cost of applying to the court for an order. A BRU will have the same legal effect as a BRO.

The application must be made within one year of the date of the bankruptcy order. The court has the power to extend the time period. If the court has ordered time to cease to run for the purposes of automatic discharge then an application to court for a BRO can be made up to the date of discharge.

2.2 Effect of a BRO

A BRO lasts between 2 to 15 years.

During this period the disabilities resulting from bankruptcy (eg disqualification as a director, restrictions on credit, etc) continue to apply. However note that the bankrupt is discharged from bankruptcy debts in the usual way and as a consequence it will not be possible to call a public examination or to seek an income payments order. Additionally, the former bankrupt will be able to acquire property without the application of the after acquired property provisions.

2.3 Grounds for a Bankruptcy Restrictions Order (Sch 4A)

Pursuant to Sch 4A Para 2(2) IA 86, the matters that should be taken into consideration when deciding whether an application for a BRO should be made include:

- Failing to keep records that account for the loss of property by the bankrupt or by a business carried on by him. The loss must be in the two years prior to the petition and ending by the date of the application
- Failure to produce records on the demand of the OR/trustee
- Entering into a transaction at an undervalue
- Giving a preference
- Making excessive pension contributions
- Failure to supply goods/services which were wholly or partly paid for which gave rise to a provable claim in the bankruptcy
- Trading at a time before commencement of the bankruptcy when the bankrupt knew or ought to have known that he was unable to pay his debts
- Incurring a debt before commencement with no reasonable expectation of being able to repay it
- Failure to account to the OR/trustee/court for the loss of property or for an insufficiency of property to meet bankruptcy debts
- Gambling or rash and hazardous speculation or unreasonable extravagance between the petition and the commencement of bankruptcy which materially contributed to the extent of the bankruptcy
- Neglect of business affairs
- Fraud or fraudulent breach of trust
- Failing to co-operate with the OR/trustee
- Have been bankrupt in the previous six years

2.4 Bankruptcy restrictions register

The Secretary of State maintains a register of any BRO, interim BRO or BRU which is in place. This register (as with the Individual Insolvency Register) is open for public inspection on any business day between 9am and 5pm and available online at the insolvency service website.

3 Annulment of bankruptcy

> **Section overview**
> - Annulment restores the bankrupt to his pre-bankruptcy status and he remains liable in full for all of his bankruptcy debts. Annulment does not release the trustee who remains liable to account for all his functions in respect of the estate. He obtains his release at the court's discretion (Rule 6.214).

3.1 Power of the court to annul s282(1)

The court has the power to annul a bankruptcy order where:

- On any grounds existing at the time the order was made, the order ought not to have been made (s282(1)(a)); or
- That, to the extent required by the rules, the bankruptcy debts and the expenses of the bankruptcy have all, since the making of the order, been either paid in full or secured to the satisfaction of the court (s282(1)(b)); or
- Where an IVA is approved in regard to an undischarged bankrupt (s261(2)).

The court has power to annul whether or not the bankrupt has been discharged (s282(3)).

3.2 Effect of annulment

The court can order that the property of the bankrupt vested in the trustee now vests in such a person as it shall appoint. In default of such appointment the property will re-vest in the bankrupt.

The annulled bankruptcy is disregarded for the purpose of working out whether any future bankruptcy is a 'second or subsequent' bankruptcy.

The annulment will have no effect on the pre-annulment acts of the OR, trustee or the court.

Annulment under s282 (1) (a) or (2) will result in the discharge of any BRO/BRU (Sch 4A S10 IA86).

Annulment under s261, 263D or 282 (1)(b) shall not affect any BRO/BRU either made or applied for pre-annulment.

3.3 Application for annulment Rule 6.206

- Application is made supported by a witness statement, copies of which are filed in court.
- The court issues the application and sets a date for the hearing.
- The applicant gives notice to the OR and the trustee of the hearing.
- Where the application is made under s282(1)(b) (debts all paid) the trustee must file a report on the bankruptcy in court at least 21 days pre hearing.

No report is required where the application is under s282(1)(a).

The trustee's report must comply with Rule 6.207 and deal with the following:

- The circumstances leading to the bankruptcy
- Summary of the debtor's assets and liabilities
- Details of creditors known to him but which have not proved
- Such other matters as necessary for the information of the court
- Particulars to which expenses have been paid or secured and if secured the extent to which that security is satisfactory

[Trustees (but not the OR) must also provide particulars of remuneration and expenses.]

At the hearing the court will require proof of payment of debts in full (which includes interest) and that some provision has been made in the case of disputed debts or untraced creditors.

The trustee is required to attend the hearing.

The trustee's costs must also be provided for. The bankrupt may challenge the trustee's remuneration as excessive under R6.207A and the court has the power to order that:

- The trustee's remuneration be reduced; and/or
- Some or all of the liabilities claimed as expenses of the bankruptcy estate are not payable as expenses; and/or
- The trustee in bankruptcy must re-pay to the bankruptcy estate the amount of excessive remuneration that he has received.

If the court makes the order, copies are sent to the applicant, the OR and the trustee, and the court. The OR notifies creditors as soon as reasonably practicable of the annulment (and expenses are a charge on the property of the former bankrupt).

The OR has no obligation to advertise the annulment although the ex-bankrupt can require the Secretary of State to advertise on payment of the requisite costs.

3.4 Bankruptcy register

The Secretary of State maintains a register of bankruptcy orders, to contain specified information entered into it by the OR. Provision is made for the deletion of information contained in the register in the following circumstances.

- Receipt by the Secretary of State of notice of an annulment under s282(1)(a) of the Insolvency Act (that the bankruptcy order ought not have been made)
- The expiry of five years after the date of the bankruptcy order
- The expiry of two years after the date of an annulment under s261(1)(a) (approval of a voluntary arrangement) or s282(1)(b) (payment in full)

3.5 Appeals

s375(1) provides for the court to review, rescind or vary any order made by it. This provides a 'safety valve'. This section is not to be used as an excuse for late appeals but gives courts flexibility. See *Fitch v Official Receiver (1996)*.

Summary and Self-test

Summary

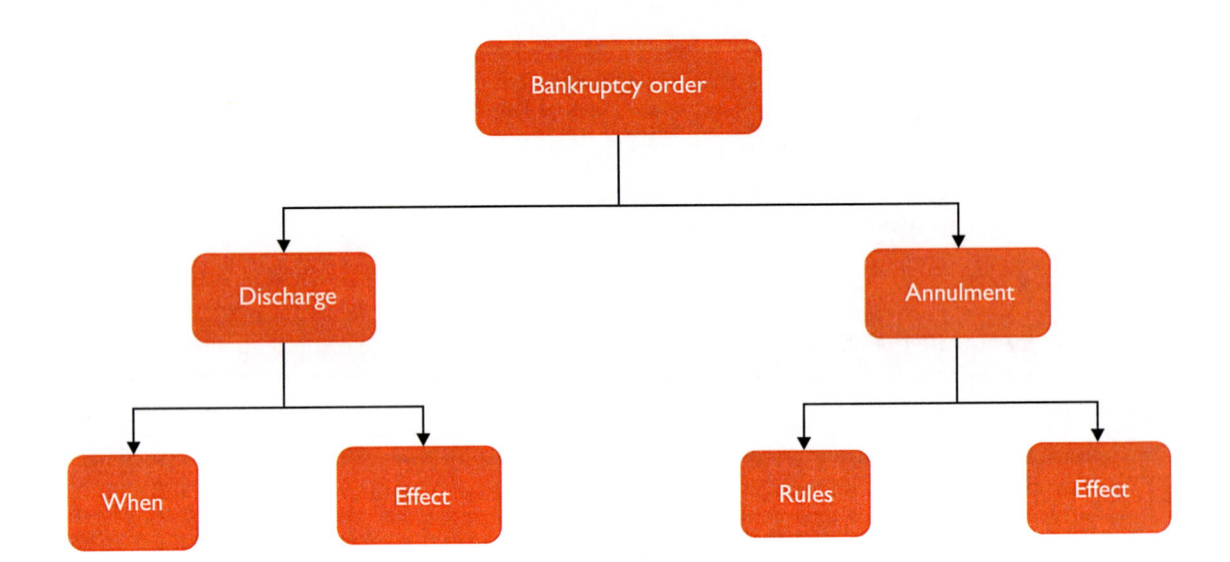

```
                    Bankruptcy order
                    /              \
              Discharge          Annulment
              /      \           /       \
           When    Effect     Rules    Effect
```

Self-test

Answer the following questions.

1 For how long does a bankruptcy order last?

    A   Twelve months
    B   Until the bankrupt is discharged
    C   Until the trustee obtains his release
    D   Three years

2 Which of the following is not an effect of the bankrupt being discharged?

    A   The disabilities of bankruptcy no longer apply
    B   The bankrupt is released from all bankruptcy debts
    C   The trustee is released
    D   The bankrupt retains his duty to assist the trustee

3 Within what period from the date of the bankruptcy order must an application for a BRO be made?

    A   Within one year
    B   Within two years
    C   Within six months
    D   There is no time limit

4 On what grounds may a bankruptcy order be annulled?

5 A BRO may last for how long?

    A   Between 2 and 15 years
    B   Between 1 and 6 years
    C   Between 2 and 6 years
    D   Between 1 and 15 years

Now, go back to the Learning Objectives in the Introduction. If you are satisfied that you have achieved these objectives, please tick them off.

Answers to Self-test

1. B (Which will usually be a maximum of 12 months.)
2. C
3. A
4.
   - On any grounds existing at the time the order was made, the order ought not to have been made.
   - That, to the extent required by the Rules, the bankruptcy debts and expenses of the bankruptcy have all, since the making of the order, been either paid in full or secured to the satisfaction of the court.
   - Where an IVA is approved in regard to an undischarged bankrupt.
5. A

CHAPTER 28

Vacation of office

Introduction
Topic List
1   Vacation of office
2   Closure checklist
Summary and Self-test
Answers to Self-test
Answer to Interactive question

Introduction

Learning objectives

- Describe the processes involved for a trustee in concluding a bankruptcy

Tick off

Stop and think

How does a trustee cease to act in relation to a debtor? Should creditors have the power to remove a trustee?

Working context

It is very probable that in a working environment you will be asked to review cases ready for closure. It is important therefore to understand what matters are required to be dealt with by the trustee before he can obtain his release.

1 Vacation of office

> **Section overview**
>
> - A trustee can vacate office in a number of ways:
>   - Resignation
>   - By operation of law
>   - On annulment of the bankruptcy order
>   - Removal by the court or the creditors
>
> - Each of these will be looked at in turn.

1.1 Resignation

A trustee can resign in the circumstances set out in R6.126.

- Ill health
- Intends ceasing to be an IP
- There are joint trustees in bankruptcy and it is no longer expedient to have more than one trustee
- A conflict of interest/change in personal circumstances precludes or makes continuation impractical

The trustee must call a meeting of creditors to receive his resignation. The notice of the meeting is accompanied by a progress report which must include a summary of his receipts and payments; details of his remuneration and expenses; and a statement that creditors can request further information from the trustee and challenge his remuneration (within seven business days of receipt of the report).

Notice of the meeting must be sent to the OR at the same time as the creditors are notified. The trustee cannot obtain his release if there is an outstanding challenge to his remuneration.

If a new trustee is appointed, he must advertise his appointment and state that the previous incumbent has resigned and been released.

The resigning trustee must deliver up assets, books, records etc to the new trustee.

1.2 Vacation by operation of law

Vacation of office by operation of law happens automatically rather than by resigning or being removed.

The circumstances when this will happen:

- On the death of the trustee
- On the trustee ceasing to be an IP (s298(6))
- Following an annulment (s298(9))

1.3 On annulment of the bankruptcy order

A trustee vacates office on annulment of the bankruptcy order (s298(9)). This is an effect of annulment, the trustee is neither resigning nor being removed.

However, annulment does not of itself release the trustee and in particular as with resignation and removal the rules require that the trustee account for all his transactions in connection with the former bankrupt's estate by submitting a copy of his final account, as soon as practicable, after the court's order annulling the bankruptcy (R 6.214).

The final account must include:

- A summary of the trustee's receipts and payments
- A statement of reconciliation with the Secretary of State's account

It is sent to the Secretary of State as soon as practicable after the annulment and filed with the court.

The court determines the time of release taking into account compliance with the above rule and whether any security under Rule 6.211(3) has been or will be released (re disputed or untraceable creditors).

1.4 On removal by the creditors or the court

- **Removal by the creditors**

    The trustee can be removed by a creditors' meeting where:
    - The trustee was appointed by a meeting of creditors
    - The trustee was previously the supervisor of the bankrupt's IVA

    If the trustee was appointed by the Secretary of State, or the court, or where the trustee is the OR, the trustee can only be removed if:
    - The court directs; or
    - The trustee consents; or
    - The meeting resolving to remove the trustee has been called on a 25% requisition (by value) from the creditors (s298).

- **Removal by the court**

    Application can be made either to remove the trustee or for an order directing the trustee to summon a meeting of creditors for that purpose.

2 Closure checklist

> **Section overview**
> - There are a number of practical and statutory matters which must be dealt with by the trustee prior to and upon closure of the bankruptcy estate to ensure that all aspects of the administration have been dealt with and that his conduct cannot be the subject of criticism.

2.1 Closure checklist

Below is a checklist of matters to be dealt with by the trustee. This list is not exhaustive.

- Review statement of affairs to ensure all available assets have been realised including the bankrupt's home, income and so on
- Reconcile receipts and payments account with the ISA, obtain a certificate of balance from the insolvency service
- Ensure received all proofs initially sent to OR
- Ensure all creditors' claims have been dealt with
- Ensure all agents and solicitor's fees have been paid
- If dividend to be paid ensure dealt with properly:
    - Given notice of intention to declare a dividend
    - Declare dividend within two months of last date for proving
    - Request cheques from ISA
    - Give notice of dividend to all creditors who have proved their debts
- Give notice of no further dividend
- Call final meeting of creditors – 28 days' notice to creditors
- Prepare trustee's final report to present to final meeting
- Report to court re outcome of final meeting
- Close bordereau

- File the final VAT returns
- File the final PAYE returns
- Close bank accounts
- Ensure remuneration is agreed and drawn
- Update PPF and issue appropriate s122 notice as required
- Close ISA account
- Complete case record (formerly IP Record)

2.2 Final meeting

Before a trustee can close a bankruptcy he must send to creditors a final progress report which will be laid before creditors at the final meeting.

The final meeting shall be called in accordance with s331.

The trustee must give notice under Rules 11.2 and 11.7 of his intention to (or not to) declare a dividend. Under Rule 6.78B at least eight weeks before the final meeting of creditors the trustee sends his final draft report to all creditors known to him and to the bankrupt. The draft report must be accompanied by a statement of the creditors' right to request information under Rule 6.78C and their right to challenge the trustee's remuneration and expenses under Rule 6.142. Secured creditors, creditors owed 5% or more of the bankrupt's total debt, or any creditor with the court's permission can request further information in respect of the report (within 21 days of receipt) and unless there are exceptional reasons why he should not, the trustee must respond within 14 days of receipt (R6.78C).

The purpose of the meeting is to provide the creditors with the trustee's report of his administration of the bankrupt's estate and to ask the creditors whether or not the trustee shall have his release.

If there is no quorum present at the final meeting, the trustee must report to court that a final meeting was summoned in accordance with the rules, but that there was no quorum present. The final meeting is then deemed to have been held and the creditors deemed not to have resolved against the trustee having his release.

It should be remembered that the final meeting cannot take place unless the bankrupt's home has been dealt with. Either the trustee will have realised his interest or obtained a s313 charge or the property will have re-vested in the bankrupt.

As soon as practicable after the final meeting the trustee must file a copy of his final account in court and submit a copy to the Secretary of State. The account must contain a summary of the receipts and payments in the administration, it must also state that the trustee has reconciled his account with that held by the Secretary of State.

Once the trustee has dealt with the account he will be in a position to seek his release.

Interactive question 1: Mr James

Your principal was appointed trustee in bankruptcy of Mr James 21 months ago. All available assets have been realised and preferential creditors have been paid in full. The creditors' committee is insisting that the trustee make an early distribution to unsecured creditors. It is clear that unsecured claims will not be met in full and once a dividend has been paid you will be in a position to close the administration.

Requirement

What steps would you take to declare and pay a dividend and to bring the administration to a close?

See **Answer** at the end of the chapter.

Summary and Self-test

Summary

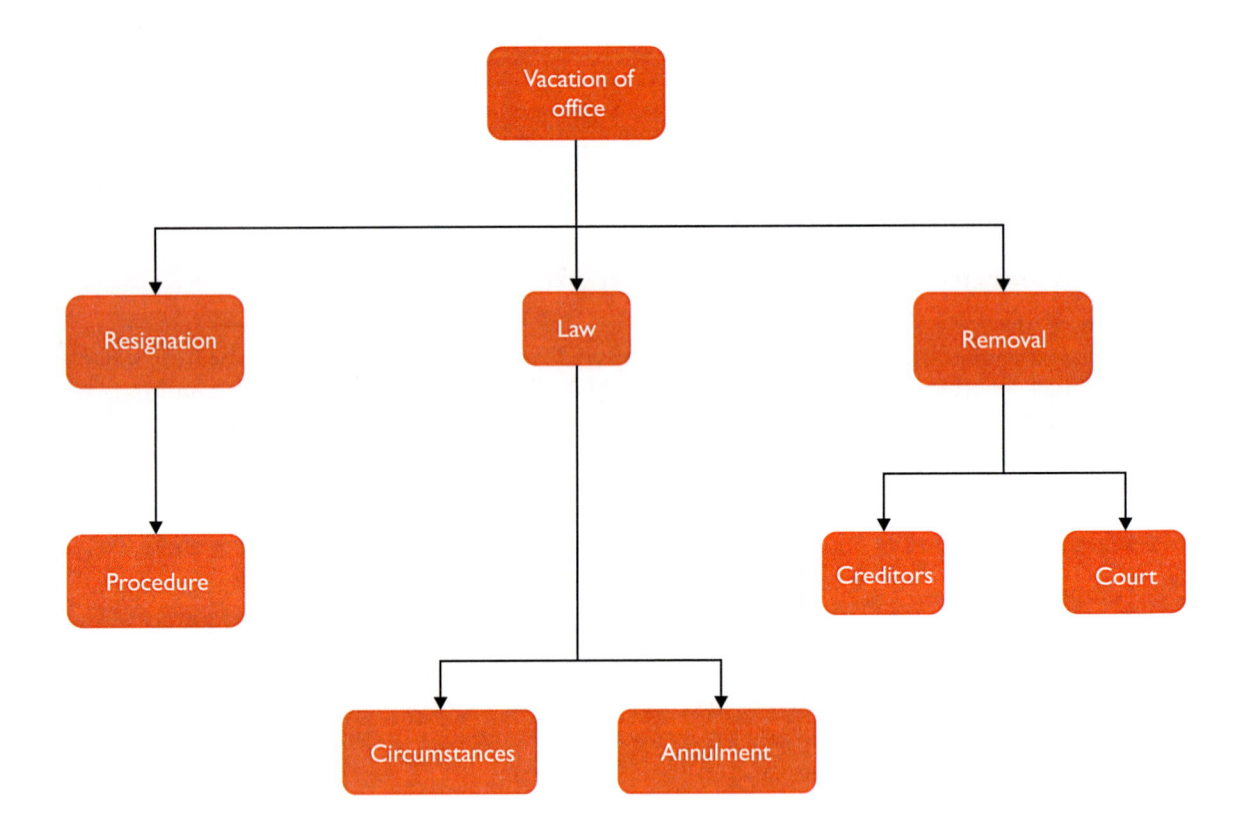

```
                    Vacation of office
                   /       |        \
            Resignation   Law      Removal
                |        /   \      /    \
            Procedure Circumstances Annulment  Creditors  Court
```

Self-test

Now answer the following questions.

1 What information must be contained in the trustee's final progress report?
2 What are the grounds on which a trustee may resign under R6.126?
3 There are three circumstances in which a trustee will automatically vacate office. What are these?
4 What value of creditors is required to convene a meeting to resolve to remove the trustee?
5 When a bankruptcy order is annulled, when does the trustee obtain his release?

Now, go back to the Learning Objectives in the Introduction. If you are satisfied that you have achieved these objectives, please tick them off.

Answers to Self-test

1.
   - A summary of the trustee's receipts and payments including comparable SofA amounts
   - Details of the trustee's remuneration and expenses, taking into consideration additional obligations under SIP9 where fees were sanctioned on a time costs basis
   - A statement about the creditors' right to request further information/challenge the trustee's remuneration

2.
   - Ill health
   - Intends ceasing to be an IP
   - Joint trustees in bankruptcy and no longer expedient to have more than one trustee
   - Conflicts of interest or change in personal circumstances which precludes or makes continuing to act impractical etc

3.
   - Death
   - On ceasing to be an IP
   - On annulment

4. 25% in value of creditors may requisition such a meeting.

5. Must submit a copy of his final account to the Secretary of State and the court. The court will then determine the date and time of release.

Answer to Interactive question

Answer to Interactive question 1: Mr James

Steps to take to declare dividend and close the case.

- Obtain clearance from OR that no further sums due to him and that he is not holding any additional proofs unknown to you
- Obtain certificate of balance from Insolvency Service and reconcile your records
- Send notice to creditors of trustee's intention to declare a dividend to include any person who may have a claim giving at least 21 days to lodge proofs
- Advertise Notice of Intended Dividend except if Notice to Prove Debt has already been given by public advertisement (usually in the appointment notice)
- Calculate dividend. A dividend must be declared within two months of the notice date
- Request cheques from Insolvency Services Account
- Within five business days of expiry of Notice of Intended Dividend adjudicate on all claims. Before paying a dividend, consider further adjudication of late proofs
- Send Notice of Dividend to all proved creditors to include receipts and payments and distribution statement
- Trustee must be able to report that the administration is complete for practical purposes
- Return out of date unclaimed dividends to Insolvency Service
- Trustee to deal with unrealised interest in any dwelling house
- Obtain OR's authority for destruction of debtor's books and records
- Call final meeting (s331) to include notice to be sent to the debtor
- Prepare and dispatch final committee report
- Advise surety of cancellation of cover
- Complete case record (formerly IP Record)
- Give notice after final meeting to the court and a copy to the OR

CHAPTER 29

Individual voluntary arrangements

Introduction
Topic List
1   Introduction to voluntary arrangements
2   Initial meeting with debtor
3   The proposal
4   IVA protocol – for use in straightforward consumer IVAs

Appendix
Summary and Self-test
Answers to Self-test
Answer to Interactive question

Introduction

Learning objectives

- Compare the characteristics of the different types of personal insolvency including the statutory and non-statutory types
- Describe the characteristics of a trading IVA and a consumer IVA and compare the two types of arrangement
- Explain the role of the Insolvency Practitioner as nominee and supervisor in an IVA
- Describe the obligations of debtors in an IVA and explain the effects of the default of a debtor
- Describe the processes undergone in the creation of an IVA
- State the contents of an IVA proposal and explain how the contents are prepared

Stop and think

Why is the proposal such an important document? Why was an alternative to bankruptcy introduced? Why isn't a voluntary arrangement suitable for everyone?

Working context

You may be asked to assist in putting together a proposal for a voluntary arrangement. It is important therefore to understand the statutory requirements regarding content of a proposal and matters to be considered by a debtor when considering a voluntary arrangement.

1 Introduction to voluntary arrangements

> **Section overview**
> - The IA 86 sets out a procedure which enables a debtor to make a proposal for a voluntary arrangement (IVA) with his creditors as an alternative to bankruptcy. The arrangement must take the form of either a composition in satisfaction of his debts or a scheme of arrangement. The legislation concerning voluntary arrangements is found in ss252 – 263 and Rules 5.1 – 5.34. SIP 3.1 also provides guidance to office holders. The Enterprise Act 2002 introduced a 'fast track' IVA for undischarged bankrupts. Following the introduction of voluntary arrangements demand grew for the introduction of a voluntary arrangement procedure more suited to 'consumer' debtors whose financial position is likely to be more straightforward than say a sole trader. A 'protocol' for consumer debtors has been introduced.

1.1 Advantages of a voluntary arrangement

- Avoids bankruptcy and its associated disabilities, obligations and stigma
- Assets don't vest in the supervisor (in bankruptcy they automatically vest in the trustee)
- Debtor retains control over his assets
- Can exclude assets from the arrangement (though creditors will seek to be compensated)
- Binds all creditors even those that did not receive notice of the creditors' meeting
- Lower costs than bankruptcy (no Secretary of State administration fee), therefore returns to creditors should be higher
- Supervisor has no power to challenge antecedent transactions (must be disclosed in the proposal)
- If obtained, an interim order prevents creditors taking action to recover their debts
- Less likely to affect employment status than bankruptcy

1.2 Disadvantages of voluntary arrangement

- Debtor will have to pay proposed nominee's costs and court fees.
- If IVA not approved, likely that the debtor will be made bankrupt.
- Requires the support of at least 75% (in value) of creditors.
- Duration is likely to be for longer than one year, particularly if making contributions from income. (Normally IVAs have a five year duration.)
- Must provide a better return than bankruptcy or creditors will not support it.
- Unlike a trustee in bankruptcy a supervisor cannot pursue antecedent transactions such as transactions at an undervalue and preferences (see Chapter 23 for details). Note however that there must be disclosure of such transactions in the proposal.

1.3 Role of IP

The role of the IP will change during the process of obtaining approval for the IVA. The IP has three roles, albeit SIP 3.1 separate the role of adviser into two, emphasising the separation of role as preparing the proposal.

- **Adviser** – the IP's role as an adviser is to consider the best course of action for the debtor in the light of his particular circumstances and expressly discuss other options including the advantages, disadvantages and costs of each. The advisor shall also create the proposal on behalf of the debtor.

- **Nominee** – the IP has a duty to perform an independent, objective review and assessment of the proposal for the purposes of reporting his opinion on the proposal. The duty of the nominee is owed to the creditors and the court.

- **Supervisor** – his responsibilities will be governed by the terms of the arrangement.

The over-riding duty of the IP is to ensure a fair balance between the interests of the debtor, the creditors and any other parties involved.

2 Initial meeting with debtor

> **Section overview**
>
> The purpose of the first meeting with the debtor is to give and obtain information to enable:
>
> - A proposal and statement of affairs to be drafted
> - Approaches to be made to strategic creditors
> - Information to be given to the debtor to explain:
>   - The procedure to obtain a voluntary arrangement
>   - His duties pursuant to legislation
>   - The role of the nominee/supervisor and his duties

2.1 Matters to be dealt with at the first meeting

1. The IP should explain to the debtor the different roles he will perform during the conduct of the case and the different duties and responsibilities that they entail. He should point out the need for the nominee and supervisor to maintain independence.

2. Establish that a voluntary arrangement is the most appropriate way of dealing with the debtor's affairs.

    The IP should explain to the debtor the alternative options available other than an IVA and advise of the relative advantages and disadvantages of an IVA and other available options.

    The debtor must be provided with a copy of the booklet 'Is a voluntary arrangement right for me?' and he should be asked to confirm in writing that he has read and understood it.

    Must ensure that the debtor is in a position to propose an IVA:

    - Debtor must be either an undischarged bankrupt or able to petition for his own bankruptcy
    - Practitioner must be willing to act as nominee
    - Debtor must intend to propose a VA

    If the debtor intends to request an interim order, it is also necessary to ensure that the debtor has not applied for an interim order in the last 12 months.

3. Should consider whether the protection of an Interim Order is required or not.

4. The IP must take all necessary steps to familiarise himself with the debtor's financial circumstances.

    It is important to ascertain how the voluntary arrangement is going to fund both the debtor and creditors.

    If income is to be provided, the creditors will want to be satisfied that any offer is reasonable. It is likely that creditors will want to see details of the debtor's expenditure.

    If assets are to be provided, the creditors will be concerned to ascertain what is available and what is excluded. Details should be obtained, ready for drafting the proposal.

    If assets are to be excluded, it is highly likely that creditors will not accept such exclusion unless such assets would have also been excluded in bankruptcy. Consequently, the extent to which compensation can be provided must be investigated at this stage.

    Such compensation is frequently made available through funds provided by a third party, often a family member.

    If third party funds are available, details and evidence of the funds will have to be provided in the proposal. As much information as possible should be obtained at this stage so that an initial approach can be made.

The IP should consider the need for separate representation of any third parties who intend to inject funds or who are otherwise affected by the IVA.

5   The debtor should be asked to provide a Statement of Affairs detailing the nature and amount of all of the debtor's assets and liabilities. The debtor should be advised that a misstatement in the Statement of Affairs could amount to a 'material irregularity', being a ground on which an approved voluntary arrangement may be challenged by a creditor.

6   The IP should require the debtor to provide details of all known or possible liabilities.

It will be necessary to ascertain the status of the creditors and their attitude to any arrangement so that they can be dealt with adequately within the proposal and approached to ascertain whether they are willing to support an IVA.

The supervisor must give notice to all the creditors of whom he is aware.

A creditor who was not notified of the meeting is none-the-less bound by the IVA (providing that creditor would have been entitled to vote had he been notified of it).

He should also seek to identify creditors who have commenced execution or other legal processes or who have special rights which may require special consideration in the proposal eg landlords, secured creditors, preferential creditors, HP creditors and those with the benefit of retention of title claims.

7   The IP should take steps to satisfy himself that the value of the assets is appropriately reflected in the Statement of Affairs.

8   If the debtor is to carry on a business, a business plan should be produced to justify the decision.

Ultimately, the debtor will have to convince both the proposed nominee and the creditors that the business can generate sufficient income to support both the debtor and IVA creditors.

9   The IP should enquire as to:

- Possible transactions at an undervalue
- Payments which may be preferences
- Liabilities which may be extortionate credit transactions

(These need to be disclosed in the proposal.)

10   The debtor must be made aware of his duties pursuant to s262A. The Act states that the debtor commits an offence if he makes any false representation or commits any other fraud for the purpose of obtaining the approval of his creditors to a proposal for an arrangement.

Any agreement between a debtor and a creditor, which is not disclosed in the arrangement and seeks to pay sums to the creditor in addition to those payable under the arrangement, is fraudulent and unenforceable by the creditor. This must be brought to the debtor's attention as a matter of course.

The proposed nominee must also impress upon the debtor the importance of ensuring that the information provided is correct in material facts and that such an obligation continues up to the date of the creditors' meeting and the meeting itself *Cadbury Schweppes plc v Somji*.

11   The IP must consider:

- The credibility of the debtor
- History of previous failures
- The need for asset protection

He should remember that there is an overriding duty to ensure a fair balance between the interests of the debtor, creditors and third parties.

12   In considering the proposal, the IP should bear in mind the following questions:

- Is it feasible?
- Is it fair to debtors and creditors?
- Is it fit to be put to creditors?
- Does it provide an acceptable alternative to bankruptcy?

In addition, case law provides *(Greystoke v Hamilton-Smith)* that where the fullness and candour of the debtor's information comes into question, the IP should check:

- That the true position re: the debtor's assets and liabilities does not differ substantially from what has been represented to the creditors
- The proposal in broad terms has a real prospect of implementation
- That there is no unavoidable and already manifest unfairness in the proposal

13 The IP should ask the debtor if he is aware of any negotiations or offers which have been made to the debtor's creditors. This is because if the general body of creditors knew of such offers it might materially affect their attitude to the proposal. In *Cadburys Schweppes v Somji*, for instance, an associate of the debtor offered to buy some of the creditors' debts at a valuation far exceeding their likely IVA dividend value. If offers like this have been made, the proposal should say so, and the IP should draw the creditors' attention to them.

A failure to make full disclosure of such offers/negotiations could constitute grounds for a default petition on the basis that there has been a material omission, and also an appeal probably on the basis of material irregularity.

14 IP should form an opinion of the appropriate method of dealing with the debtor's affairs, taking into account:

- The debtor's attitude
- The likelihood of the debtor adhering to the terms of the proposal
- The extent of control over the assets exercised by the debtor as opposed to the supervisor of the proposal
- The removal/absence of the restrictions otherwise imposed by formal bankruptcy

15 The IP should ensure that the proposal addresses all of the matters prescribed by the Rules (R5.3).

16 Emphasise that the proposal is the debtor's proposal and that it is essential that full and accurate disclosure of all relevant matters be made.

If full disclosure is not made, the following potential consequences should be borne in mind.

- Creditors may find out the true position, demand adjournments, further and better particulars, modifications or simply reject the proposals altogether.
- A petition for bankruptcy may be presented by any creditor or creditors owed £5,000 or more.
- The IP may present a bankruptcy petition.
- If full disclosure of all liabilities is not made, the nominee will not be able to notify all creditors. Non-notified creditors will be bound but may later challenge a VA under s262.
- Inducing agreement to an IVA through fraud is a criminal offence.

Continuing obligations in the proposal must be compiled with or again this will be a ground for presentation of a default petition by creditors/IP.

Valuations in the proposal are the debtors, it is essential these should be as accurate as possible (in the absence of professional valuations).

17 Outline the procedure to be followed.

If an application to court for an interim order is to be made give a brief explanation of the effect of the order and whether or not the debtor will be required to attend any hearing.

Explain that a creditors' meeting will be held at which the nominee will preside and the debtor will be required to attend and answer questions.

18 Explain to the debtor about the consequences of rejection and failure of the arrangement

19 Issue an engagement letter to the debtor setting out the matters discussed and agreed upon.

Details of the staff who will be dealing with the matter should be provided so that the debtor can contact them if there are any problems.

Request that the debtor sign a copy of the engagement letter and return it to confirm that he has read and understood the content.

3 The proposal

Section overview

- The proposal is a contractual arrangement between the parties who are free to make whatever provision they see fit within the general law and the statutory framework set out within the Act and the Rules. The terms of the arrangement are contained in the proposal which is approved by the creditors. A comprehensive and accurately drafted proposal is therefore fundamental to the arrangement. The required content of the proposal is set out in Rule 5.3 and SIP 3. Additionally standard terms and conditions have been produced for inclusion in the proposal. These are different depending upon whether or not the proposal is protocol compliant or not. Although the standard conditions may not always be used you will be expected to have some knowledge of the main provisions for the purpose of the assessment.

3.1 Contents of proposal

1. A short explanation of desirability of the IVA and reasons why the creditors may be expected to concur with it.

    - Some background and explanation of present insolvency.
    - If trading, extracts from trading accounts for previous years. This is so that:
        - If it is proposed the debtor is to continue in business (and that the revenue from that business is to assist in paying creditors) some assessment can be made of how realistic this part of the proposal is
        - The debtor can demonstrate the deteriorating situation which culminated in insolvency

2. The Statement of Affairs, which should include full details of assets and liabilities (including both business and personal assets and liabilities).

    - Should include all assets including assets outside the jurisdiction
    - Should include prospective or contingent assets with statement of the likelihood of realisation
    - Ideally professional valuations of assets should be included (but remember time and cost constraints)
    - The value of any dwelling house should reflect a realistic selling NOT asking price and should include an estimate of the debtor's equity
    - The nominee should ensure that values given are prudent especially in relation to book debts, work in progress and leases where valuation can be particularly problematic
    - The costs of realisation should be shown

    Note. The proposal may contain a disclaimer that failure to achieve stated values will not give rise to a default (debtor) or liability (nominee).

3. Details of the extent to which assets are charged.

    Look for full details of mortgages, charges, HP, liens and reservation of title clauses in favour of creditors.

4. Any assets to be excluded from the IVA.

    - The proposal may suggest the same exclusions as for bankruptcy (ie tools of trade and domestic equipment).

- If the proposal also excludes the main residence it should explain in what way creditors will be compensated eg by a third party contribution or a buy-out of the debtor's share.
- If excluded assets are used in a business there should be provision for realisation in the event of the business ceasing to trade.
- If an asset is to be excluded because realisation will be too expensive/difficult/impossible the proposal should say so.

5 Give particulars of any assets (other than the debtors) which are to be included, sources of such property and terms on which made available.

For example, cash contributions from spouse, family trust, parent, business partner or other wealthy philanthropist.

- Desirable for letter of confirmation from the third party contributor to be annexed to proposal and for funds to be already held by the supervisor in an account pending approval of the arrangement.
- Proposal may state that failure by third party contributor will constitute a default by the debtor for s276 purposes.
- Nominee will wish to be satisfied that the third party has had an opportunity to take independent advice.

6 Nature and amount of the debtor's liabilities, and the manner in which they are to be met/postponed/otherwise dealt with.

- Reasonable enquiries should be made.
- Ideally the nominee should contact each creditor with a view to obtaining an up to date statement of liability. However this is slow and increases costs and may precipitate enforcement action by creditors.
- Where a liability (eg mortgage arrears) is increasing, the proposal should state the rate of increase.
- A liability (eg on a credit card which the debtor finds convenient for use in his business) can be excluded from the IVA but the proposal must say so and the IP should draw attention to the exclusion in his comments. The credit card company is likely to withdraw the card and demand immediate repayment in full unless a deal can be arranged.

7 Treatment of preferential and secured creditors, and associates.

- Rights of preferential creditors may not be modified or excluded without their consent.
- The proposal should deal with the position regarding VAT during the period between the date of the interim order and the date of approval of the proposal (sometimes called 'the hiatus period'). This is because HM Revenue and Customs take the view that if the proposal does not deal with hiatus period VAT such VAT does not fall within the arrangement and HM Revenue and Customs are therefore entitled to take the normal enforcement measures to collect it. However if the proposal does cover hiatus period VAT, HM Revenue and Customs are bound by the proposal (assuming the creditors approve it) and therefore will not be able to take enforcement action.
- If a secured creditor has agreed to postpone enforcing his security this should be explained in the proposal. Note however that a secured creditor's right to enforce its security cannot be postponed without his consent.

8 Claims or potential claims under ss339, 340 and 343 should be detailed in the proposal.

- A supervisor has no power to challenge such transactions in an IVA and so where grounds to challenge would be available creditors may prefer bankruptcy. Alternatively the recipient of any transaction at an undervalue or preference (commonly the spouse) may offer to compromise the claim.

9 Proposed duration.

- *Re A Debtor (No 222 of 1990)* – a certain period of time should be stated.

- May be short (eg two years) where the proposal is for rapid sale of assets and distribution to creditors. Even here it may be longer before a final dividend can be paid for example if litigation or depressed market conditions make the immediate realisation of assets difficult.

- Provision may be made for an extension of proposed duration in certain circumstances. Extension is always possible if the variation route is taken.

- Protocol compliant proposals will specify a duration of five years.

10 Detail the proposed dates of distributions to creditors with estimates of their amounts.
   - Interim and final?
   - Final only?

The nominee should calculate the percentage due on the assumed periods of distribution, rather than simply stating a collective amount of distribution. For example year 1: 5%, year 2 9.2% and so on.

11 Specify the amount proposed to be paid to the nominee by way of remuneration and expenses.
   - Expenses should be quantified and described.
   - The remuneration of the nominee does not include any future remuneration once he becomes supervisor.
   - The proposal should state whether the nominee's remuneration includes or excludes sums to be paid to the debtor's solicitor for legal work.

12 Specify the manner in which it is proposed that the supervisor should be remunerated and his expenses defrayed.

   As a minimum the proposal should provide for:
   - A means of calculating and agreeing the supervisor's remuneration (eg by resolution of creditors or a creditors' committee)
   - Payment of solicitors, estate agents and other expenses
   - Payment of remuneration and expenses in priority to all other claims

13 Whether any third parties are to provide any guarantees.

   The third party (if any) should be advised to take independent advice.

14 The manner in which funds held for purposes of IVA are to be banked/invested/dealt with pending distribution.
   - All funds realised should be paid to supervisor (not to debtor).
   - Supervisor should be empowered to open bank accounts and invest (usually short term).

15 The manner in which funds held for the purpose of payment to creditors, and not so paid on the termination of the arrangement are to be dealt with.

   For example if a creditor disappears prior to receiving a final dividend the proposal could provide for this sum to be re-distributed amongst the other creditors.

16 Manner in which the debtor's business (if any) is to be conducted.
   - Any proposal that such business will generate funds for creditors is superficially attractive but it should be remembered that failure of the business is often the reason why the debtor is insolvent in the first place and the business will need to service ongoing liabilities **and** the debtor's living expenses before any surplus can go to creditors under the IVA.
   - Some measure of supervision by IP should be included eg an obligation on the debtor to provide the IP with information and to maintain proper accounts, records and banking arrangements.
   - Past trading accounts, realistic forecasts, cash flow statements and projections should be attached to the proposal.
   - Any problems in maintaining suppliers, staff etc should be explained.

- If any accounts or returns are outstanding (eg in relation to VAT) when these will be completed.

17 Give details of any further credit facilities which it is intended to arrange for the debtor and how the debts arising are to be paid.

Creditors may be reluctant to sanction further credit but credit facilities may be necessary eg to complete work-in-progress.

18 The functions and details of the supervisor and fact that he is an IP should be stated.

Specifically the proposal should:

- Give the supervisor a general power to call meetings of creditors
- Set out the supervisor's powers
- Set out rules re proofs, set-off, distribution in *specie* (perhaps by incorporating bankruptcy rules)
- Incorporate provisions re: income payments eg
    - £x per month to be paid into the IVA by direct debit
    - Obligation on debtor to inform supervisor of any change in personal circumstances or income
    - Incorporate bankruptcy provisions re windfalls
- State how it is proposed to deal with the claims of any person who is bound by the arrangement by virtue of s260 (2)(b) – non-notified creditor.

19 Bankruptcy and trust clause.

- Although not mentioned specifically in R5.3 the proposal should deal with the possibility of the debtor being subsequently made bankrupt.
- The debtor should create a trust where the 'assets' are held on trust for the purposes of the IVA/for the creditors. Trust assets will not vest in the trustee in bankruptcy but will remain available to the supervisor for payment of costs and distributions to the IVA creditors.

20 Default.

- The proposal should make the following provision:
    - Details of what will constitute a 'default' by the debtor justifying the presentation of a bankruptcy petition by the supervisor
    - Provide some mechanism for ascertaining the wishes of the creditors. This may involve circularising a statement to the creditors or holding a meeting
    - State whether the supervisor is to retain sufficient funds to present a petition under s276
- The proposal should also set out whether there are any circumstances falling short of 'default' which might result in 'failure' of the IVA. This might be a failure to realise a major asset for the stated value or the failure of a third party to make a promised contribution. The effect of failure (in absence of any s276 wrongdoing) will be the termination of the IVA although no s276 petition can be presented the debtor could be bankrupted on the ground that he is unable to pay his debts.

21 Leases.

Although not specifically mentioned in Rule 5.3 leases are an asset which will require specific provision in the proposal. The provision made will depend on what is being proposed in relation to the lease. Broadly there are three possibilities.

- The lease has premium value and the debtor proposes it should be sold, the proceeds being made available for dividend purposes.
- The lease has no or insignificant premium value and the debtor proposes that the lease should not be retained.
- The debtor proposes retaining the lease for the purposes of his or her business.

(i) Lease has premium value and the debtor proposes selling the lease.

- The proposal should state the premium value of the lease. Any professional valuation can be appended to the proposal.
- The nominee should have obtained a copy of the lease to ascertain whether license to assign is required (it usually will be).
- If license to assign is required the nominee will need to negotiate with the landlord.

It is particularly important to obtain the landlord's consent to the terms of the proposal if there are rent arrears. This is because rent arrears give rise to the following problems.

(a) Generally landlords must not unreasonably refuse the licence to assign, but a landlord is acting reasonably if he refuses licence to assign until arrears are paid.

(b) Non-payment of rent will entitle a landlord to distrain against the goods of the debtor. Although following the interim order (if obtained) the permission of the court will be needed, distraint reduces the value of assets in the estate.

(c) The landlord will be entitled to forfeit under the terms of the lease – again, this is subject to the courts consent following the interim order.

(d) Ultimately, it may be necessary to agree to pay the arrears to obtain the landlord's consent to the proposal. Although application for relief from forfeiture can be made, the court will require the payment of arrears in any event, as a condition of granting relief. In this situation it would be better to pay the arrears at the outset and avoid the costs and risks of litigation.

(ii) The debtor proposes retaining the leased premises for use in the business.

- As above, if there are arrears of rent, the potential problems of distress and forfeiture will arise. Again, the nominee will need to reach some agreement with the landlord or there is a risk that without equipment and premises, a proposal to trade on will simply not be viable.
- The proposal will need to provide for the payment of future rent during the use of the premises, as an expense of trading to prevent new arrears arising.
- Note that payment of 'strategic creditors' such as landlords is not unfairly prejudicial to other creditors of the same class *(Cazaly Irving Holdings v Cancol)*.

(iii) The debtor does not wish to retain use of leased premises.

- Nominee will wish to ascertain whether the landlord will accept a surrender.
- The landlord has two potential claims in the IVA.

    (a) Liquidated, unsecured claim for arrears of rent

    (b) Unliquidated claim for future rent (and possibly dilapidations). The proposal should deal with how this will be quantified. For voting purposes the nominee will estimate the value of the claim. For dividend purposes the proposal could state that the supervisor shall estimate the value of the claim (the landlord having a duty to mitigate).

22 Post-acceptance amendments/variation.

- *Thompson and Horrocks v John Lawson Broome 1998*, held that a properly drawn clause giving a power of variation in a voluntary arrangement is valid.

- In the absence of express provision allowing variation of the proposal, 100% of creditors affected by a proposed variation will be required for any change to be valid. Usually the proposal will allow variation provided that at least 75% in value of the creditors are in favour.

- Protocol compliant IVAs provide for some variation by the supervisor without the need to obtain the consent of creditors (see post).

23 EC Regulation.

- Whether the EC Regulation applies to the IVA and if it does, whether the proceedings are main or territorial.

23 Other points.

- The nature of the arrangement ie whether it is a composition in full and final settlement of the debts or a scheme of arrangement varying creditor rights.
- A realistic comparison of the estimated outcome of the arrangement and bankruptcy including comparative costs.
- Proposals regarding after acquired assets and windfall gains.
- Whether a committee of creditors is to be appointed and if so, what will be its powers, duties and responsibilities.
- Provision for the supervisor to be granted a charge over assets or some other suitable form of security.
- The situation with regard to contingent creditors and overseas creditors.
- The situation with regard to tax liabilities arising on disposal of the debtor's assets.
- How to deal with creditors who haven't made claims and inadvertently omitted creditors (who are now bound by the IVA).
- Confirmation that when the terms of the arrangement have been successfully completed, the creditors will no longer be entitled to pursue the debtor for the balance of their claim, that the arrangement is in full and final settlement of their liabilities.
- Requisite majorities required to pass resolutions at the meeting of creditors.
- The following information should also be provided, either in the proposal or in the nominee's comments:
    - The source of any referrals to the nominee or his firm in relation to the proposed voluntary arrangement
    - Any payments made, or proposed to be made, to the source of such referrals (proposal only)
    - Any payments made, or proposed to be made, to the nominee or his firm by the debtor whether in connection with the proposed arrangement or otherwise
    - An estimate of the total fee to be paid to the supervisor together with a statement of the assumptions made in producing the estimate
- A statement should also be made detailing whether within the 24 months preceding the date on which the proposal was delivered to the nominee, the debtor has submitted a proposal for a voluntary arrangement and applied for an interim order, and if so what the outcome was.
- The proposal must deal with maintenance orders in favour of the debtor's wife and any fines.

The case of *Re M (a debtor) 1996* held that a wife who had received a lump sum under matrimonial proceedings was bound to accept a dividend under the VA.

Interactive question 1: Barry Scott

A client in Manchester seeks your advice with regards to documents he has received concerning a proposal by Barry Scott, who trades in the same area, to his creditors for a composition in satisfaction of his debts. Barry Scott has given written notice to the nominee accompanied by a copy of the proposal and the nominee has summoned a meeting of creditors. The notice is accompanied by a summary of the statement of affairs, a list of creditors showing amounts due and the nominee's comments which state:

'I have interrogated the debtor and I am satisfied that he has submitted a satisfactory proposal. I recommend a meeting of creditors to approve the proposal'.

A summary of the proposal reads as follows:

My assets comprise stock of £45,000, work in progress of £2,500 and very good book debts of £2,500. Cash at bank is £2,000 and the house in which I reside is worth £180,000. A building society is owed £160,000 being the balance of money advanced for the purchase of the house and a bank is owed £20,000 on money advanced for my business. The business was landscape design which in November 20X5 I closed down as it was not successful and diversified into garden machinery which I believe to be successful. I propose to continue to trade in garden machinery and pay profits to the supervisor to be distributed over the next three years. All sums distributed in that time will be accepted by creditors in full and final settlement of their claims. My other creditors include £12,900 owed for PAYE/NIC, £6,890 for VAT and 25 other creditors are owed £94,000. I shall retain assets. I point out that the house in which I reside is owned by my wife and she will retain the liabilities to the building society and the bank.

Your client is owed £40,000 of which £38,000 arises from a loan made five years ago as a deposit on a house in Swindon, not mentioned on the list of creditors and £2,000 shown in the creditors' list which is for supplies of materials made during 20X6. Your client plans to attend the creditors' meeting and asks whether he should approve or reject the proposals, and whether he should bring up any matters.

Requirement

Advise Barry you should comment on the proposal and upon any other matter arising from your perusal of the documents and the information given.

See **Answer** at the end of this chapter.

4 IVA Protocol – for use in straightforward consumer IVAs

Section overview

Insolvency practitioners, bankers, the insolvency service and other interested parties have produced an IVA protocol for use in straight forward consumer debt cases. The protocol provides for agreed methods of dealing with IVAs rendered necessary because of consumer rather than business debts and liabilities. Whilst the protocol is not mandatory it has the backing and support of creditor groups particularly members of the British Bankers Association. This group have agreed to support the protocol. However note that BBA members and other supporters are not contractually bound to give support to protocol compliant IVAs – they may reject and seek modification of compliant proposals in the same way as with standard IVA proposals *(Mond v MBNA Europe Bank Ltd)*. The 2014 protocol has been reproduced at Appendix 1 to this chapter.

An updated version of the IVA Protocol is now available for use and should be used for all protocol compliant IVAs entered into on or after 2 January 2014. No 2015 version has been produced.

The 2013 version applies to all compliant IVAs from 1 March 2013. The 2010 version of the Protocol is for all protocol compliant IVAs entered into after 30 April 2010. For compliant IVAs entered into before 1 February 2010 the 2008 Protocol applies and for any period between the February and April 2010 either version of the Protocol may have been used.

The standard terms have also been revised and apply from 2 January 2014. The 2012 standard terms apply to proposals issued on or after 1 July 2012. For proposals issued before that date, the standard terms of January 2008 (as updated in July 2008) are still in use.

If the protocol is not followed fully but parts of it apply this should be highlighted in the proposal.

4.1 Who is suitable for a consumer IVA?

A person suitable for a Protocol compliant IVA or 'consumer IVA' is likely to be:

- In receipt of a regular income either from employment or from a regular pension
- Have three or more lines of credit from two or more creditors

A consumer IVA is unlikely to be suitable if the following circumstances apply to the person making the proposal:

- Insufficient income. Income should be verified by means of three months of pay slips, or a suitable equivalent for the self-employed, and bank statements (in the case of weekly pay slips, it is sufficient to check a selection to cover the three month period). In the absence of pay slips (eg if they have been lost), then bank statements should be checked.

    Where income is uneven/unpredictable, (eg people with more than 20% of their income coming from bonuses or commission), this should be highlighted in the proposal and the accompanying summary sheet.

- Where the debtor has investment properties.

- Where there is a possibility of settlement of more than 65% of the total debt within the first year of the arrangement.

4.2 Duration

It is anticipated that protocol compliant IVAs will last for 5 years (60 months), though this shall be extended where the terms of valuation and remortgage entitle the debtor to exclude the property and include further contributions in lieu of the equity as detailed at point 4.3.

4.3 The debtor's home

Where there is equity available in the debtor's home creditors who support the protocol will not seek realisation by way of sale, instead they will support realisation of funds by way of equity release. Under the protocol there should be an attempt to release home equity six months prior to the conclusion of the IVA. If equity at that time is less than the de minimis level of £5,000 it does not have to be realised and the VA term will not be extended. Where equity exceeds £5,000 but a remortgage is not possible it is envisaged that the term should be extended by 12 months.

The protocol places restriction on what funds the creditors can expect by way of re-mortgage. The amount of equity to be released will be based on affordability and it is envisaged that the debtor will be left with at least 15% of the equity in the property.

4.4 Impact on insolvency practitioners

The protocol also imposes obligations on insolvency practitioners who act in relation to protocol compliant IVAs these include:

- Accepted standards in relation to the advertisement of the IPs services
- Provisions in relation to the advice that should be given to debtors
- The required standard expected of IPs in relation to the verification of information contained in the proposal
- The use of agreed standard terms and summary sheet

Appendix

The Straightforward Consumer IVA Protocol 2014 version
Effective from January 2014

IVA PROTOCOL

Straightforward consumer individual voluntary arrangement hereinafter referred to as a Protocol Compliant Individual Voluntary Arrangement (PCIVA)

Purpose of the protocol

1.1 The purpose of the protocol is to facilitate the efficient handling of straightforward consumer individual voluntary arrangements (IVAs) (as described below). The protocol recognises that the IVA supports a valid public policy objective by providing debt relief for individuals in financial distress. It also recognises that at the centre of this process there is a person, who needs to understand the process and the associated paperwork and the impact that the IVA will have on their lives.

Scope of the protocol

2.1 The protocol is a voluntary agreement, which provides an agreed standard framework for dealing with straightforward consumer IVAs and applies to both IVA providers and creditors. By accepting the content of the protocol, IVA providers and creditors agree to follow the processes and agreed documentation that forms part of the protocol. IVA providers indicate their acceptance of the content of the protocol by drawing up a proposal based on the standard documentation, and which states that it follows the protocol. Creditors are expected to abide by the terms of the protocol in relation to proposals drawn up on that basis.

2.2 Creditors who are members of the British Bankers' Association have indicated their support for the protocol process in a letter attached at Annex 1. A list of BBA members can be found at www.bba.org.uk

2.3 It is accepted that an IVA is a regulated process under statute, which requires certain work to be undertaken, which may have a cost unconnected with the size of the IVA.

2.4 The protocol does not override the regulatory framework relevant to each party (Annex 2).

2.5 For the avoidance of doubt, IVA provider means both insolvency practitioners and IVA provider firms employing insolvency practitioners. References to creditor in this protocol refer to both creditors and the agents who vote on their behalf and act in accordance with their instructions in relation to an IVA.

2.6 The efficient operation of the protocol will be monitored and reviewed by a standing committee. The standing committee is a representative group, its membership reflecting the participants in the IVA process (debtor, creditor, IP, regulatory bodies and government). The terms of reference of the standing committee and details of its current membership are attached at (Annex 3). The committee's role will include communication and consultation, where necessary, on future developments on the IVA protocol.

The straightforward consumer IVA

3.1 Not all cases can be classified as a straightforward consumer IVA. A person suitable for a straightforward consumer IVA is likely to be :

- In receipt of a regular income either from employment or from a regular pension.
- Have 3 or more lines of credit from 2 or more creditors.

3.2 Age is not a consideration, nor is the debt level, though both factors will impact on the overall viability of the IVA.

3.3 The protocol is suitable for both home owners and non home owners. There should be no circumstances where the individual would be forced to sell their property instead of releasing equity. The only exceptions would be where this was proactively proposed by the individual.

3.4 For individuals whose circumstances do not meet the above criteria an IVA may still be the most appropriate means of dealing with their financial problems but their case is unlikely to be suitable for the full application of the protocol procedures. The following are indicators that a person's circumstances are unsuitable for the application of the protocol.

- Disputed debts – there should be no known material disputes in relation to the debt.
- Investment properties – those with investment properties would not be suitable for a straightforward consumer IVA.
- Possibility of full and final settlement – where a full and final settlement is possible in the first year.

3.5 A reasonably steady income stream is necessary in order to be suitable for the application of the protocol. There is nothing to prevent this protocol being applied to individuals who are self-employed, when that self-employment produces regular income. Where income is uneven/unpredictable, (eg people with more than 20% of their income coming from bonuses or commission), this should be highlighted in the proposal and the accompanying summary sheet.

3.6 The protocol does not require that the debtor has to follow the protocol process, even though his or her situation may fit within the definition of a straightforward consumer IVA. Where this occurs, but elements of the protocol are still used, this should be highlighted in the proposal and the accompanying summary sheet.

Transparency and co-operation

Transparency

4.1 All parties should act openly and disclose all relevant matters.

4.2 The proposal should disclose any previous attempts to deal with the debtor's financial problems (eg informal payment plans, refinancing, debt management plan, previous IVA or bankruptcy) together with a disclosure by the debtor if there were any dealings with the nominee or businesses connected with the nominee and an explanation of why these attempts were unsuccessful. There should also be disclosed any payments made by the debtor in relation thereto.

Specific attention is drawn to Statement of Insolvency Practice 3 (SIP 3) and the nominee is reminded as to the information that is required to be disclosed either in the debtor's proposal or the nominee's report.

4.3 The nominee will enquire of the debtor as to whether he/she has made any payments in connection with the matters set out in clause 4.2 to any party prior to contacting the nominee's organisation. Unless separately disclosed in accordance with SIP 3, the nominee shall record within his/her report the amount, date and nature of any such payments made by the debtor in the last 12 months prior to proposing the IVA.

4.4 All parties to this protocol must publish their processes for dealing with complaints and details of relevant regulatory authorities, in accordance with current requirements. Any complaints should be dealt with in accordance with existing processes.

Cooperation with the standing committee

4.5 Only when provided with all relevant information will the standing committee be able to monitor and review the efficient operation or otherwise of the protocol. Information required for this purpose will be determined by the standing committee. Such information, other than that which is commercially sensitive or which needs to be withheld for reasons of confidentiality, will be provided by IVA providers and creditors at the request of the standing committee.

4.6 All parties may provide information to the standing committee which will enable it to determine the effectiveness or otherwise of the protocol. Similarly, behaviour which does not comply with the terms of the protocol may be reported to the standing committee. However, the standing committee does not override existing regulatory procedures.

Obligations on insolvency practitioners

Advertising

5.1 Advertisements and other forms of marketing should be clearly distinguishable as such and have regard to the OFT Debt Management Guidance and all relevant codes of practice, in particular to the principles of legality, decency, honesty and truthfulness. Any telemarketing should comply with the codes relevant to that activity.

5.2 The IVA provider should not promote or seek to promote their services, in such a way (eg by 'cold calling') or to such an extent as to amount to harassment or in a way that causes fear or distress.

5.3 Where an IVA provider advertises for work via a third party, the IVA provider is responsible for ensuring that the third party observes all applicable advertising codes and OFT guidance. Similarly, where an IVA provider accepts from or makes referrals to others, they should also comply with the advertising codes. Third party advertisements should declare any links to IVA providers.

Advice

6.1 When approached by an individual in financial difficulty, the IVA provider will ensure the individual receives appropriate advice in the light of their particular circumstances, leading to a proposed course of action to resolve their debt problem. Full information on the advantages and disadvantages of all available debt resolution processes should be provided (eg by use of the guide entitled 'In Debt? Dealing With Your Creditors' which may be made available by the provider or can be found on the Insolvency Service website at www.bis.gov.uk/insolvency/Publications/publications-by-theme/dealing-with-debt-publications). Non-financial considerations should be taken into account.

6.2 It is accepted that for some, bankruptcy is not a preferred option as it could lead to loss of employment or membership of a professional body, which then has other financial consequences. Others may wish to avoid the perceived stigma of bankruptcy.

Verification of information contained in the proposal

Assets

7.1 As required in any IVA, steps should be taken to ensure that the value of all realisable assets is appropriately reflected in the statement of affairs. This may require independent evidence of valuation to be obtained in the case of material assets.

Liabilities

7.2 Full details should be obtained from the debtor of all known and potential creditors. The IVA provider should use their best endeavours to verify the outstanding balances by obtaining statements, letters or copies of agreements from each creditor dated within 6 weeks of the debtor's first approach to the IVA provider, and updated as necessary to reflect any changes prior to the issue of the IVA proposal. If for whatever reason the IVA provider is unable to verify any material creditor balances, this should be identified in the Nominee's report.

Income

7.3 Income should be verified by means of 3 months of pay slips, or a suitable equivalent for the self-employed, and bank statements (in the case of weekly pay slips, it is sufficient to check a selection to cover the 3 month period). In the absence of pay slips (eg if they have been lost), then bank statements should be checked.

7.4 If the debtor lives with any person aged 18 or over, and there is reasonable expectation that this person will pay board and lodging to the debtor, this payment must be added to the debtor's income in full.

Expenditure

7.5 The expenditure statement should be forward-looking and in line with StepChange Debt Charity guidelines (formerly CCCS) or the Common Financial Statement (CFS). Generally, there should be no deviation from the expenditure guidelines. However, where additional expenditure is necessary, for example due to special dietary requirements or increased heating bills due to caring for elderly relatives or above average work-related travel costs, this should be clearly explained.

7.6 (a) If the debtor wishes to continue to pay for health insurance or payment protection insurance, the proposal should contain a note stating why this is considered to be essential expenditure.

(b) Where the debtor is below the age of 55 at date of entry into the IVA, only minimum contributions to the pension scheme should be allowed. Where the debtor is aged 55 or above at the date of entry into the IVA, an average of the last 6 months' pension contributions should be allowed, subject to a contribution limit of £75 above the minimum pension contribution allowed by the scheme per month. If no minimum contribution is stated by the scheme, debtor contributions will be restricted to 4% of the debtor's gross salary. Where the debtor is a member of multiple schemes, these limits should be applied to the aggregate amount of the debtor's contributions.

7.7 The expenditure elements that require formal verification are:

- Secured loan payments - verification by sight of relevant mortgage or bank statements.
- Rent – verification by sight of rent agreement or relevant bank statement entries.
- Council tax – verification by sight of council tax bill or relevant bank statement entries.
- Vehicle Finance – verification by means of relevant HP/Finance agreement.
- Pension – verification by sight of pension scheme documentation and/or wage slip/pension contribution statement.
- Other financial commitments such as endowment policies, life policies, health insurance and payment protection insurance – verification by reference to appropriate documentation.

7.8 Where information for verification purposes, which is readily available and is not excessive, is sought from creditors, this information will be provided free of charge whether the request is made by the IVA provider or the individual.

7.9 The nominee's report will include a statement that the income and expenditure have been verified by the nominee in accordance with the protocol and provide details of the means used where the individual is self-employed.

Use of standard documentation

8.1 The use of standard documentation will streamline the IVA process and enable creditors to quickly identify those cases which are protocol compliant and also the key information contained therein.

8.2 For protocol compliant IVAs, IPs should use the agreed standard conditions (Annex 4) and the summary sheet (Annex 5). There is no standard format for the IVA proposal.

8.3 All documentation should state clearly that the IVA follows the protocol and that the agreed format IVA documentation has been used, and which version of the protocol or Standard Conditions is being used. There is no requirement to send out the protocol Standard Conditions to creditors, but the provider must make clear how a copy of these can be obtained. A hard copy must be made available on request without charge. Similarly, any variation from the protocol (for example special dietary requirements, see paragraph 7.5) should be clearly identified in all relevant paperwork.

During the IVA

Home equity (Net worth)

9.1 Six months prior to the expiry of the IVA (hereinafter referred to as the review date), there should be an attempt to release the debtor's net worth in the property. The review date would normally be after month 54, unless the IVA has been extended for any reason. However, subject to 9.3 below, where the debtor is unable to obtain a remortgage, the supervisor will have the discretion to consider accepting one of the following alternative proposals:

- A third party sum equivalent to 85% of the value of the debtor's interest in the property; or
- 12 additional monthly contributions (with the aggregate sum paid to the supervisor being limited to 85% of the value of the debtor's interest in the property).

9.2 The amount of the net worth to be released will be based upon affordability from income and will leave the debtor with at least 15% of his/her net worth in the property. Remortgage includes other secured lending such as a secured loan. Where it is appropriate to remortgage the property, the specific limits will be:

- Remortgages would be a maximum of 85% Loan To Value (LTV).
- The incremental cost of the remortgage, including cost of any new repayment vehicle, will not exceed 50% of the monthly contribution at the review date.

- The net worth released will not exceed 100p in the £ excluding statutory interest.
- The remortgage term does not extend beyond the later of the debtor's State retirement age or the existing mortgage term.
- The amount of money introduced into the arrangement will be the mortgage proceeds less the costs of the remortgage, including any costs to redeem any existing mortgage and/or secured loan

Examples illustrating the calculation of available net worth are in Annex 7

9.3 If the amount of the debtor's net worth net of remortgage costs in the home at the review date is under £5k, it is considered de minimis, and does not have to be released, and there would be no adjustment to the IVA term.

9.4 The monthly payments arising from the remortgage will be deducted from the contribution. If the increased cost of the mortgage means that monthly contributions fall below £50 per month, such monthly contributions are stopped, and the IVA is concluded.

9.5 A clause detailing the above as set out in Annex 6 is to be included, where appropriate, in the individual's proposal and the summary sheet (Annex 5) will identify that this clause is included.

9.6 The debtor should be provided with a clear written explanation illustrating the possible net worth to be released, taking into account:

(a) No increase in property value as stated in the proposal
(b) The current value inflated by 4% pa (simple interest) at the review date
(c) The estimated outstanding mortgage at the review date

9.7 At the time the debtor is asked to release the net worth in his/her property, the supervisor, or a suitable member of his/her staff, must advise him/her that he/she should seek advice from an independent financial adviser, such advice to include the most appropriate mortgage vehicle and the length of the proposed repayment term.

9.8 For the purpose of the release of net worth the property shall be subject to an independent professional valuation on an open market basis.

Use of discretion, variation and failure

10.1 The supervisor has the discretion to admit claims of £1,000 or less, or claims submitted that do not exceed 110% of the amount stated by the debtor in the proposal, without the need for additional verification.

10.2 The supervisor should ensure that he/she is provided with copies of payslips (or other supporting evidence) every 12 months. The supervisor is required to review the debtor's income and expenditure once in every 12 months, using the StepChange Debt Charity guidelines or the CFS. Where appropriate, and at the request of the supervisor, the debtor must verify increases in outgoings by providing documentary evidence. The debtor will be required to increase his/her monthly contribution by 50% of any increase in the net surplus as shown in the original proposal one month following such review.

10.3 The supervisor will be able to reduce the contribution by up to 15% in total (relative to the original proposal or last agreed variation) without referring back to creditors, to reflect changes in income and expenditure, such change to be reported in the next annual review.

10.4 Where the individual is employed, the debtor must report any overtime, bonus, commission or similar to the supervisor if not included in the original surplus calculation, where the sum exceeds 10% of the debtor's normal take home pay. Disclosure to the supervisor will be made within 14 days of receipt and 50% of the amount (over and above the 10%) shall be paid to the supervisor within 14 days of the disclosure. Failure to disclose any such overtime, bonus, commission or similar by the debtor will be considered a breach of the IVA and the supervisor shall notify the creditors in the next annual report with proposals for how the breach is to be rectified.

10.5 (a) A debtor who is subject to redundancy whilst in an IVA must:

- Inform his/her supervisor within 14 days of notice of redundancy, regardless of whether he/she has received or is to receive any redundancy payment

- Inform his/her supervisor of the amount of any redundancy payment within 14 days
- Pay to the supervisor within 14 days of receipt of any redundancy payment any amount in excess of 6 months net take home pay (as set out at the last annual review date). If there is no amount in excess of 6 months net take home pay no payment is required
- Where possible, continue to make monthly contributions into the IVA as set out at the last annual review date
- Keep the supervisor informed of any changes in employment status

Where the debtor is unable to make contributions this will be reviewed by the supervisor.

At the point new employment is obtained the supervisor will review the debtor's IVA contributions and at that point there will be an expectation that any remaining redundancy funds will be paid into the IVA, and the debtor's performance in this regard will be reported to creditors.

(b) Failure to disclose any such entitlement to redundancy payment will be considered a breach of the IVA.

10.6 A debtor will be allowed a payment break of up to 6 months once during the term of the IVA without any modification being required at the discretion of the supervisor. The term of the IVA will be extended by the length of the payment break so that the debtor will make the same number of contributions as agreed in the original proposal. An agreed payment break will not constitute a breach. Where the supervisor agrees a payment break, the creditors should be notified within 3 months from the date of agreement. At the conclusion of an agreed payment break the supervisor shall if necessary review the position and consult with creditors where appropriate.

10.7 Where the individual has failed to disclose exceptional income, the term of the IVA may be extended by up to a maximum of 6 months to recover any sums due (to correct the breach), without any modification being required.

10.8 Where the individual is unable to remedy any breach of the arrangement, the supervisor must report within 28 days to the creditors and either issue a Certificate of Termination or if the Supervisor feels it appropriate seek creditor views to do one of the following:

- Vary the terms of the arrangement; or
- Issue a certificate ('Certificate of Termination') terminating the arrangement by reason of the breach; and/or
- Present a petition for the individual's bankruptcy.

Reporting to creditors

11.1 The annual report to creditors prepared by the IVA provider should include details of the individual's income and expenditure, based on information obtained including payslips and P60s. The individual should also be asked to provide verified details of their expenditure and any material changes to it. Where the supervisor has used his or her discretion to vary the contribution, in accordance with 10.3, that should also be recorded in the annual report.

Obligations on creditors

Treatment of customers

12.1 In all dealings with a customer proposing an IVA under this protocol, creditors will continue to treat the customer in accordance with the regulatory standards and codes of practice to which they are subject, as set out in Annex 2.

12.2 Throughout the duration of a protocol compliant IVA, creditors will treat their customer as referred in 12.1. Furthermore, creditors will co-operate with the duly appointed nominee and supervisor in relation to the efficient operation of this protocol.

12.3 Lenders should take reasonable measures to avoid offering further credit to individuals known to have an IVA in place, unless this is in justifiable circumstances (eg for re-mortgage purposes). However, it should be recognised that relevant information is not always readily available to creditors and may sometimes be withheld by debtors.

Acceptance of protocol compliant IVAs

13.1 It is understood that one of the aims of the protocol is to improve efficiency in the IVA process and to this extent creditors and IVA providers will avoid the need for modifications of an IVA proposal wherever possible. This does not affect the right of creditors to vote for or against an IVA proposal.

13.2 Where a creditor or their agent on their behalf votes against a protocol compliant IVA proposal, their reason for so doing should be disclosed to the IVA provider.

13.3 By voting in favour of a protocol compliant IVA, creditors accept that the supervisor has discretion as referred to in section 10 above and in the standard terms, and should not challenge the use of that discretion.

13.4 Creditors should make reasonable endeavours to provide a proof of debt (in the form required by the IVA provider) and proxy form within 14 days of receipt of an IVA proposal and if possible at least 7 days before the date of the meeting called to approve the proposal.

13.5 Creditors not submitting claims within four months of the meeting to approve the proposal or by the date of the first dividend (whichever is the later) will be entitled to participate and receive their full share of dividends (subject to the requirement for the supervisor to adjudicate the authenticity and value of the claim), but are not entitled to disturb a distribution made prior to the submission of their claim.

Income and expenditure

14.1 Creditors will normally accept income and expenditure statements drawn up on the basis of generally accepted standard financial statements and verified in accordance with this protocol, as the basis of a protocol compliant IVA proposal. For this purpose standard financial statements includes the StepChange Debt Charity guidelines and the CFS (and any revisions in respect thereof).

14.2 Creditors will follow the guidance in the Banking/Lending Code (or any Code that replaces it)

Use of agents

15.1 It will be the responsibility of creditors to ensure that any agents carrying out instructions or acting on their behalf in relation to a protocol compliant IVA, do so in accordance with this protocol and in accordance with applicable regulatory requirements.

15.2 Where a creditor requires communication regarding the debt due or the IVA proposal to be sent via its agent, the creditor should ensure that details of the appropriate contact are provided to relevant IVA providers.

Sale of debt

16.1 Where debt is sold when an IVA is proposed but before it has been approved, creditors should ensure that the debt buyer is a signatory to the Banking/Lending Code or follows the principles contained in the Banking/Lending Code and complies with the Office of Fair Trading (OFT) Debt Collection Guidance.

Summary and Self-test

Summary

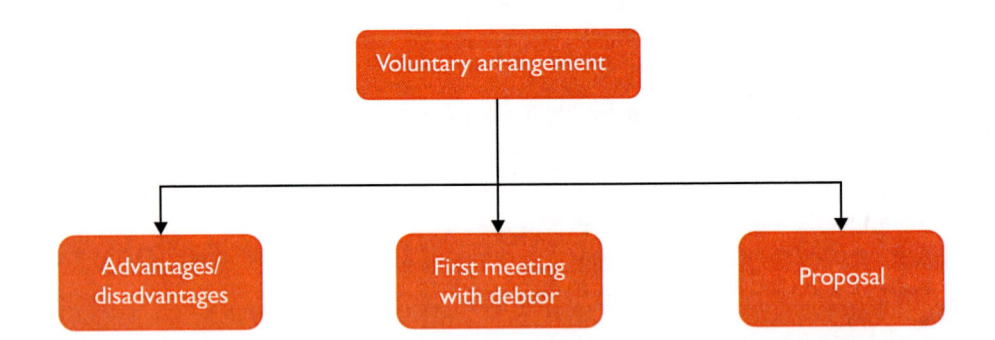

```
                    Voluntary arrangement
                             |
        ┌────────────────────┼────────────────────┐
        ▼                    ▼                    ▼
   Advantages/         First meeting           Proposal
   disadvantages        with debtor
```

Self-test

Answer the following questions.

1. What is the position of a creditor who is not notified of a meeting of creditors to consider proposals for a voluntary arrangement?

2. Which SIP deals with Voluntary Arrangements?

    A   SIPs 3
    B   SIP 6
    C   SIP 9
    D   SIP 12

3. List the advantages and disadvantages of a voluntary arrangement.

4. To be suitable for a consumer IVA a debtor should be in receipt of regular income?

    A   Yes
    B   No

5. Janice is proposing a consumer IVA to her creditors. There is a possibility that she might be able to pay off 70% of the total debt in the first year of the arrangement. Is a consumer IVA suitable for Janice?

    A   Yes
    B   No

Now, go back to the Learning Objectives in the Introduction. If you are satisfied that you have achieved these objectives, please tick them off.

Answers to Self-test

1. A creditor who is not notified of the meeting is none the less bound by the voluntary arrangement (providing they would have been entitled to vote had they been notified of it) but they may challenge the VA under s262.

2. A

3. Advantages of voluntary arrangement:

    - Avoids bankruptcy and its associated disabilities, obligations and stigma.
    - Assets don't vest in the supervisor (in bankruptcy they automatically vest in the trustee).
    - Debtor retains control over his assets.
    - Can exclude assets from the arrangement (though creditors will seek to be compensated).
    - Binds all creditors.
    - Lower costs than bankruptcy (no Secretary of State administration fees), therefore returns to creditors should be higher.
    - Supervisor has no power to challenge antecedent transactions (must be disclosed in the proposal).
    - Interim order prevents creditors taking action to recover their debts.
    - Less likely to affect employment status than bankruptcy.

    Disadvantages of voluntary arrangement:

    - Debtor will have to pay proposed nominee's costs and court fees.
    - If IVA not approved, likely that the debtor will be made bankrupt.
    - Requires the support of 75% or more (in value) of creditors.
    - Duration is likely to be for longer than one year, particularly if making contributions from income.
    - Must provide a better return than bankruptcy or creditors will not support it.
    - Creditors will not receive benefit that trustee in bankruptcy would have to pursue antecedent transactions.

4. A

5. B

Answer to Interactive question

Answer to Interactive question 1: Barry Scott

Letter format.

A proposal for a voluntary arrangement is required to state or deal with a number of matters (Rule 5.3, SIP 3.1, R3).

The proposal as it stands lacks sufficient information in key areas and the Nominee's comments on the proposal are of a general and limited nature:

- Barry Scott's proposal should give an estimate of the amount to be distributed to creditors and when the distribution will be made.

- How the business is to be conducted during the course of the arrangement should be detailed.

- Barry states that he intends to retain his realisable assets and pay creditors out of profits generated by the business over the next three years. An estimate of the profits is not given. Creditors should be provided with information to assess past trading and future prospects, for example, management accounts, budgets, sales and cash forecasts.

- The proposal does not outline any arrangement for monitoring business trading and does not state how monies generated are to be banked or distributed.

- The proposal does not state the functions to be undertaken by the supervisor.

- The proposal does not state how the supervisor is to be remunerated or his expenses defrayed.

- The proposal does not state whether there are any circumstances which would give rise to the possibility of claims under the IA covering transactions at an undervalue, preferences or extortionate credit transactions should he be adjudicated bankrupt.

- Barry Scott's proposal does not give sufficient detail with regard to his wife's ownership of the house in which he resides. His wife's acquisition of the house may be a transaction at an undervalue. There is no evidence of the house being professionally valued nor that the bank and building society advances are secured on the property. There is also no evidence that these advances are not the liability of Mr Scott and therefore competing with the claims of other creditors in the arrangement.

- There is no mention of the loan or property in relation to the £38,000 loan made by the client. The fact that neither are disclosed is a material irregularity.

- There are no details of any guarantees being given of Barry's debts.

- The proposal makes no mention of how creditor's claims are to be dealt with and in particular how it is proposed to deal with creditors who are not notified of the proposal.

- The proposal does not state whether EC Regs are to apply

- The proposal does not give sufficient information re the supervisor – name, address and qualification to act.

Barry Scott's proposal, as it stands, is incomplete and fails to comply with statutory requirements. In particular it is not possible to assess whether a better return would be achieved by his bankruptcy and immediate realisation of his assets rather than continued trading. The status of the matrimonial home and the other house needs to be established.

Suggest that creditors resolve to adjourn the meeting so that full explanations and information may be subsequently presented. The next and final meeting should be held no later than fourteen days after the date of the first meeting. If further information is not satisfactory – client should reject proposals and take necessary steps to have Barry Scott adjudicated bankrupt.

CHAPTER 30

Voluntary arrangement procedures

Introduction
Topic List
1 Interim order
2 Procedure with interim order
3 Procedure without interim order
4 Limited disclosure
5 Fast track VAs
6 Effect of approval

Summary and Self-test
Answers to Self-test
Answers to Interactive questions

Introduction

Learning objectives

- Describe the processes undergone in the creation of an IVA
- Describe the processes undergone in order to obtain an interim order
- Describe the on-going obligations on an IP in a voluntary arrangement
- Effect of approval of a voluntary arrangement

Tick off

☐
☐
☐
☐

Stop and think

Why is an interim order required? Why should creditors be prevented from taking enforcement action? Why does an interim order not last for the entire duration of the arrangement?

Working context

In a work environment you may be asked to advise a debtor on the process of obtaining approval for a voluntary arrangement, or to assist your principal in putting together proposals for a voluntary arrangement, calling a meeting of creditors etc. It is therefore appropriate that you are familiar with the statutory requirements and procedures to be followed to obtain approval for a voluntary arrangement.

1 Interim order

> **Section overview**
>
> - The voluntary arrangement procedure envisages a debtor, with the assistance of his nominee, putting a proposal to his creditors for the satisfaction of his debts. The IA 86 made the application for an interim order compulsory, however since amendments introduced by the IA 2000, a debtor may make a proposal to his creditors without first seeking an interim order (s256A). The relevant procedure for IVAs can be found in Part 5 of the Insolvency Rules 1986.

1.1 Effect of an interim order

An interim order protects the debtor from all proceedings and enforcement action whilst his proposal is being prepared and put before his creditors.

Where the debtor has only a few creditors who are willing to support a voluntary arrangement, it is likely that the debtor will save time and money and not apply for an interim order. Pursuant to s252(2), an interim order has the effect that, during the period in which it is in force, no:

- Bankruptcy petition in respect of the debtor may be presented or proceeded with
- Landlord or other person to whom rent is payable may exercise any right of forfeiture by peaceable re-entry in relation to premises let to the debtor in respect of a failure by the debtor to comply with any term or condition of his tenancy, except with leave of the court
- Other proceedings, and no other execution or other legal process, may be commenced or continued against the debtor or his property except with the leave of the court

This means that judgment creditors for example will need leave to enforce their security. However, no leave is required to take action that does not involve court proceedings for example a secured creditor can appoint a receiver under the terms of a charge.

Exceptions to the rule are:

- Enforcement action pursuant to Proceeds of Crime Act 2002 is not prevented (Re: M 1992) nor is enforcement of fines or compensation orders made in connection with criminal offences
- If a landlord wants to exercise his self help remedies of distress and forfeiture leave of the court will be required even though no court proceedings are usually required to exercise these remedies s252 (2)(aa) and s252 (2)(b) (as amended by IA 2000)

1.2 Who may apply for an interim order?

s253(3) provides that application may be made by an undischarged bankrupt, his trustee, the OR and the debtor.

s253(5) provides that an application can't be made if the debtor has petitioned for his own bankruptcy and the court has appointed an IP to inquire and report.

1.3 Grounds for granting an interim order

An interim order will be made, provided that the application is in order and the four conditions for the court to make an interim order are satisfied (s255):

- Willing nominee
- Debtor has not applied for interim order in the last 12 months
- Debtor could petition for his own bankruptcy
- Debtor intends to make a proposal for a IVA

The court is also required to take account of any representation made by any person entitled to notice of the hearing.

1.4 Duration of the interim order

Unless an application for an extension is made, an interim order will cease to have an effect at the end of 14 days from the date it is made (s255 (6)).

Provided that the nominee's report recommends that a creditors meeting be summoned, the court will further extend the interim order to enable the proposal to be considered (s256 (3A)). Otherwise, the court may discharge the interim order in force (s256 (6)).

If a concertina order is requested, (see 2.2) the interim order will be made for such period as to enable the proposal to be considered.

It is not unusual for extensions to the interim order to be requested. Often, the initial 14 day period is insufficient to enable the proposal to be put together and the report made. In addition, it is possible that the creditors' meeting may have to be adjourned.

When hearing an application to extend the interim order, the court will consider whether there is support from the creditors. If there is strong opposition from 25% of the creditors, the court should not continue the interim order *Re: Cove (a debtor) 1990*.

There is no need for a formal court order to discharge the interim order. It will automatically be discharged 28 days from the date that the decision of the creditors meeting was reported to court (s260). If the meeting rejects the arrangement, the court can make an order to discharge the interim order before the expiration of the 28 day period (s259 (2)).

2 Procedure with interim order

Section overview

- It is not possible for a debtor to act on his own to implement a voluntary arrangement. He must engage the services of an authorised insolvency practitioner who will usually act as his nominee and later his supervisor.

2.1 Summary of the procedure

- Debtor prepares proposals for a VA and sends them with a statement of affairs to the nominee who accepts the appointment.

  The Statement of Affairs should be verified by Statement of Truth. On application by the nominee, debtor or other interested person eg a creditor, the court may allow a debtor to omit information from his Statement of Affairs if satisfied that disclosure of that information would prejudice:

    - The conduct of the IVA
    - The interests of the debtor
    - The interests of the debtor's creditor(s)

- Debtor applies to court for an interim order (to obtain the Moratorium). At least two days' notice of the hearing must be given to the nominee and any creditors petitioning for bankruptcy. Court makes the order (lasting 14 days).

- At least two days before the expiry of the interim order nominee submits a report on the debtor's proposal to the court (see 2.3 for details).

- Nominee summons a creditors' meeting.

- The creditors' meeting is held which may approve the proposal, or approve with agreed modifications, or reject the proposal. A resolution to this effect is passed by 75% in value of those attending and voting subject to the right of dissidents to apply to the court on the basis of unfair prejudice or material irregularity.

- If approved the nominee becomes the supervisor and all the creditors entitled to vote at the meeting are bound by terms of the VA.

- IVA implemented.

2.2 Concertina orders

Although the Act and Rules envisage that two hearings will need to be held, a Court Practice Direction permits the court to make an interim order at the first hearing and an order that the creditors' meeting will be summoned. This is referred to a 'concertina order'. The interim order will continue until after the creditors' meeting. The practice direction also provides for an order to be made without attendance. It is not appropriate to seek a concertina order where the proposal is likely to require amendment and/or the support of creditors has not been ascertained. To take advantage of the Practice Direction the nominee must file his report with the application for the Interim Order.

2.3 Nominee's report

The nominee's report must be delivered to court before the expiration of the interim order. It is possible, however, for the nominee to apply to court for an extension of time (s256 (4)).

If the nominee fails to submit a report, the debtor can apply to court requesting the replacement of the nominee and/or an extension of the interim order. The purpose of the report is to state (s256 (1)):

- Whether the proposed arrangement has a reasonable prospect of being approved and implemented

- Whether in the opinion of the nominee a meeting of the debtor's creditors should be summoned to consider the debtor's proposal. If the report:
  - Recommends a meeting, the nominee will annexe to the report his comments on the debtor's proposal
  - Does not recommend a meeting, the nominee is obliged to give reasons for his opinion (R5.11(3))

- If a meeting of creditors is recommended, the date/time/place at which it is proposed the meeting should be held

The nominee should take care to ensure that his report is as comprehensive and accurate as it can be.

In *Greystoke v Hamilton-Smith and others*, the court set out three tests which the nominee should apply before concluding that a meeting of creditors should or should not be summoned. They are:

- That the debtor's true position as to assets and liabilities is not materially different from that which it is represented to the creditors to be

- That the debtor's proposal as represented has a real prospect of success

- That on the basis of the information before (the nominee), no already manifest yet unavoidable prospective unfairness in relation to the function of admitting or rejecting claims, is present

The Insolvency Service provided guidance to IP's in Dear IP (Millennium Edition) stating they are instructed to consider whether an arrangement is:

- Feasible
- Fair to creditors
- Fair to debtor
- Provides an acceptable alternative to bankruptcy
- Fit to be considered by the creditors

SIP 3.1 provides that an IP should comment, in their report to court, on the following matters.

- whether or not the debtor's financial position is materially different from that contained in the proposal, explaining the extent to which the information has been verified

- whether or no the IVA is manifestly unfair

- whether or not the IVA has a reasonable prospect of being approved and implemented

Pursuant to s256A the nominee must also explain whether he considers that the arrangement has a reasonable prospect of approval and implementation.

2.4 Creditors' meeting

Once the interim order has been granted, the creditors' meeting must be convened by the nominee (s257(1)).

The purpose of the meeting is to decide whether or not the proposed voluntary arrangement should be approved.

Modifications to the proposals are permitted but with certain restrictions. All modifications must be consented to by the debtor and no modifications can be made that would affect the rights of secured or preferential creditors without their consent. Care must be taken to ensure that the modifications are not such that would result in the proposal ceasing to be a composition or scheme of arrangement. It is possible to propose a modification that will result in the appointment of a new nominee.

1 **Calling the meeting**

If an interim order has been obtained on receipt of the nominee's report the court will decide whether or not a meeting of creditors should be summoned to consider the debtor's proposal. Provided the court is satisfied with the nominee's report it is likely to follow the nominee's recommendation. The interim order (if sought) will then be extended until after the creditors' meeting has taken place.

2 **Notice of the meeting**

Pursuant to s257(2) – every creditor of the debtor of whose claim and addresses the nominee is aware must be summoned.

Where an interim order is in force the meeting shall be held not less than 14 days from the date that the nominee's report was filed in court and not more than 28 days from the date on which the court considered that report.

Where there is no interim order the meeting must be held no later than 28 days from the date that the nominee received the debtor's proposal and statement of affairs under s256A.

Each creditor is entitled to 14 days' notice (R5.17), which must include a copy of the proposal, the statement of affairs or summary of it, a proxy form and the nominee's report with comments on the proposal annexed to it.

The creditors must also be given information about the requisite majorities required pursuant to R5.23.

It is possible for the creditors' meeting to take place remotely. Participation may be by telephone, video conference or on-line meeting. (See Chapter 3.)

3 **Agreement of creditors' claims**

- In an ideal situation the nominee will normally seek to agree creditors' claims prior to the creditors' meeting however this is not always possible. Consequently where documentary proof of claims has not been provided this should be obtained as soon as possible.
- Claims should also be discussed and agreed with the debtor.
- In circumstances where the nominee decides not to admit a claim for the amount claimed, notice should be given in writing to both the debtor and creditor. If either is unhappy with the decision they can apply to court to have the decision modified or reversed.
- Proxies and statements of claim to be used at the meeting may be lodged at any time, even during the course of the meeting.

4 **Role of the chairman**

- The chairman of the meeting will normally be the nominee but if for some reason the nominee is unable to attend it is possible to delegate his duties but delegation must be to a member of staff experienced in insolvency matters.
- The chair will conduct the meeting and decide whether the creditors have the right to vote and the amount they may vote for. The chair of the meeting will usually cast proxy votes but R5.20 provides that without specific directions from the proxy the chair shall not use proxy votes held by him to increase or reduce the amount of remuneration or expenses of the nominee or supervisor.

5 Who is entitled to vote?

- R5.21 provides that every creditor who was given notice of the creditors' meeting is entitled to vote. Despite the fact that R5.21 envisages notice being given by the nominee, if a creditor who was not given notice by the nominee can establish a debt due and owing, he will also be entitled to attend and vote *Re a Debtor (No 400 of 1996)*. Written notice of the creditors' claim must be given and R5.23 envisages this being given before or at the meeting.

- The chairman may admit or reject a claim in whole or in part.

- If there is any doubt about the validity of a claim the creditor should be admitted to vote but his vote is marked as objected to. This is subject to such votes being subsequently declared invalid if the objection to the claim is sustained.

- The entitlement of a creditor to vote is limited to those claims where the value can be ascertained. In other words if the debt is not of a certain value for the purposes of voting (but not otherwise) the debt shall be valued at £1 unless the chairman agrees to put a higher value on it.

6 Majority required to approve VA

- At the creditors' meeting, in order to pass any resolution or approve any proposal or modification, there must be a majority of at least three quarters in value of the creditors present, in person or by proxy, who do in fact vote on the resolution (R5.23).

- It should be noted however that when calculating the value of a creditor's debt (at the date of the meeting) some claims (or part thereof) will be left out of account. These are as follows (R5.23):

    - Written notice of the claim not given either at the meeting or before it to the chairman or the nominee. Note that *IRC V Conbeer 1996* has established that faxed proxies are valid for the purposes of insolvency legislation

    - Part or all of claim secured. A part secured creditor can vote with the unsecured balance *(Calor Gas v Piercy 1994)*

    - It is in respect of a debt wholly or partly secured on a current bill of exchange or promissory note. Exception – where creditor willing to treat the liability to him of persons liable antecedently to the debtor on the bill or note as a security. The value of that security will then be estimated and deducted from the creditor's claim for voting purposes

- The legislation is drafted so as to ensure that a VA cannot be forced through by a majority of creditors who are associated with the debtor. In order to secure approval the vote must in effect be counted twice. First all of the votes will be counted. Assuming that a majority of at least 75% is in favour a second count will then take place but this time counting only those:

    - To whom notice was sent

    - Whose votes are not to be left out under R5.23 (3) (ie as secured on a bill of exchange or as having failed to give written notice of the claim)

    - Who are not to the best of the chairman's belief, associates of the debtor

- On this second count any resolution is invalid if those voting against it include more than half in value of the creditors. The practical effect of the rule is that simple majority of valid, notified, independent creditors can veto an arrangement which would otherwise be approved by the votes of associates.

7 Procedure at meeting

The chairman presents his report to the creditors' meeting. He should then allow creditors an opportunity to make comments, ask questions or propose modifications.

All modifications must be consented to by the debtor and no modifications can be made that would affect the rights of secured or preferential creditors, without their consent.

The meeting can be suspended for any period up to one hour, R5.24.

The meeting may be adjourned if there is a failure to reach the requisite majority, however adjournment cannot be for more than 14 days. If a series of adjourned meetings are held the last meeting may not be more than 14 days from the original meeting.

If following the final meeting the proposal is not agreed to it is deemed rejected.

8 Considerations re proxy votes

If a nominee obtains proxy votes in favour of a proposal he must be careful when deciding how to deal with these proxies if new information becomes available at the meeting. He should not cast these votes without further reference to the creditors unless he is sure that it would be right to do so. If the new information is significant the nominee will have to adjourn the meeting for the purpose of relaying this information back to the creditors. This may give rise to a need to seek an extension of the interim order.

3 Procedure without interim order

Section overview

- The Insolvency Act 2000 introduced s256A which made it possible for a debtor to propose an IVA without an interim order being in place first.

3.1 Summary of procedure

The debtor prepares a proposal and sends it to the nominee who accepts the appointment.

At the same time the proposal is delivered the debtor sends to the nominee a Statement of Affairs (unless one has already been delivered in bankruptcy proceedings)

If the nominee is satisfied that the debtor is able to apply for VA, a creditors' meeting is held to approve or reject the arrangement. The voting rules are the same as those where an interim order is in place.

3.2 Nominee's report

The nominee will not file a report at court unless an application for an interim order is made.

Rule 5.14A states that provided the nominee is satisfied that the debtor's proposal has reasonable prospect of being approved and implemented and a creditor's meeting should be summoned to consider the proposal he must within 14 days of receiving the debtor's proposal deliver to each of the debtor's creditors of whom he is aware; the OR and any trustee (if applicable) and any petitioning creditor, the following documents:

- A copy of his report with his and the nominee's comments attached thereon
- A copy of the debtor's proposals and statement of affairs
- A copy of the notice to the nominee (under Rule 5.4)
- A statement that no interim order application is to be made

[In the event that the nominee considers approval unlikely or that a creditors' meeting should not be summoned he should deliver a copy of his report only to those creditors of whose addresses he is aware and give reasons to the debtor for his opinion.]

In the event that any court application is made in relation to a IVA or a proposal for an IVA where there is no interim order and there has been no report filed at court (see previous paragraph) the relevant court to file an application is either the court in which the bankruptcy order was made or the court in which the debtor could petition for his own bankruptcy depending on whether the debtor is an undischarged bankrupt or not. Any further application to the court in connection with the VA will be made to this relevant court and the report must contain sufficient detail to identify that court.

4 Limited disclosure

> **Section overview**
>
> - Changes introduced into the Insolvency Rules now permit the court to restrict the publication of information in certain circumstances.

4.1 Persons at risk of violence

The court can prevent the address of a debtor or his place of business being made public if it is reasonable to expect that publication could lead to violence against either him or his family. Under R5.67 the application supported by a witness statement detailing the risks that the debtor faces may be made by the debtor, the VA supervisor or the OR. If satisfied that there is a risk the court may order:

- Removal of the debtor's address, or business address, from the publicly available court file and have it held in a separate file not open to inspection by the public

- That the addresses (above) are not placed on the personal insolvency register

- That any notice stating that the entry of the debtor on the personal insolvency register has been removed shall not contain the debtor's address or that of his place of business

- That any alternative address of the debtor be used instead of the debtor's present address

5 Fast track VAs

> **Section overview**
>
> - This procedure was abolished by SBEEA 2015 and should therefore not be examinable.

5.1 Procedure

The former procedure was commenced by the bankrupt submitting his 'fast track proposal' and statement of affairs to the OR who, following receipt, must consider whether it has a reasonable prospect of being approved.

The OR must consider whether or not he is willing to act as nominee and whether or not the proposal should bind all creditors and not just bankruptcy creditors.

If the OR takes the view that the proposal has a reasonable prospect of success he will send the proposal to creditors and ask them to decide whether or not to accept it. The Rules envisage that this will be done by correspondence. There is no provision for modification as in a creditors meeting under s258.

The percentage in value to approve the VA is 75% as in the normal VA procedure (R5.43).

Subject to approval the VA takes effect and binds the creditors and debtor from the date on which the OR reports the outcome to court.

R5.51 to R5.59 provide for a 28 day period in which an application for annulment of the bankruptcy order can be made by either the OR or the bankrupt. During this period appeals against the decision under s263 can also be made.

6 Effect of approval of IVA

> **Section overview**
> - Once approved, the voluntary arrangement will bind all creditors entitled to vote at the creditors meeting, whether or not they voted in favour (s260(2)(b)).
>
>   The approved arrangement:
>   - Binds every person who in accordance with the Rules was entitled to vote at the meeting (whether or not he was present or represented) or,
>   - Would have been so entitled had he had notice of it, as if he were a party to the arrangement.
>   - Pursuant to IA 2000 a creditor is bound to a VA even if he did not receive notice of it
> - It is however still important that those entitled to notice receive it as a creditor who was not notified will be entitled to challenge the decision pursuant to s262. The fact that notice was not given will support such an application.

6.1 Chairman's report of the creditors' meeting

Where an interim order was applied for and the nominee's report on the proposal filed in court the report of the creditors' meeting must be filed in court within four business days of that meeting and sent to creditors as soon as reasonably practicable thereafter.

Where there was no interim order application and no report to court by the nominee the report of the creditors' meeting must be sent to creditors within four business days. R5.27. SIP 12 reminds IPs of this statutory obligation.

The report must state:

- Whether proposal approved or rejected. If approved with modification the report must state what these modifications were
- Resolutions taken at the meeting and the decision on each one
- List the creditors (with their respective values) who were present or represented at the meeting and how they voted on each resolution
- Whether the EC Regulation applies to the VA and, if so, whether the proceedings are main proceedings or territorial proceedings
- Any further information as chair thinks appropriate

6.2 Report to Secretary of State

The Secretary of State maintains a register of VAs, which is open to public inspection. R5.29 provides that as soon as practicable and in any event within the period of 14 days after the chairman has filed in court a report that the meeting has approved the voluntary arrangement (or sent to creditors as the case may be) he shall report to the Secretary of State the following details of the arrangement:

- Name and address of debtor together with gender and date of birth
- Date of creditors' approval
- Name and address of supervisor
- Any name by which the debtor was or is known if it is not the name by which he entered the IVA

The supervisor (or a later replacement supervisor) must give Secretary of State written notice of appointment or vacation of office.

6.3 Appeals

1   **Against chairman's decision at the meeting: Rule 5.22**

    Creditors of the debtor can appeal to the court against decisions of the chair on

- Entitlement to vote
- Leaving out of account all or part of a claim on the basis of lack of written notice/security/debt on or secured on a bill or note
- Identifying a person as an associate of the debtor

Application to the court must be within 28 days of the chairman's report to the court where no IO is in place, or 28 days of the meeting where an IO was in place.

If the decision on entitlement to vote gives rise to unfair prejudice or a material irregularity the court can

- Make such order as it thinks fit
- Including ordering another meeting to be summoned

Chairman will not be personally liable for costs of appeal

2   **Against the decision of the meeting: s262**

The grounds are that the VA unfairly prejudices the interests of a creditor or that there has been a material irregularity at or in relation to the s257 creditors' meeting (s262(1)).

Unfair prejudice appeals will only succeed where the prejudice arises from the unfairness of the proposal itself *(Re A Debtor No: 259 of 1990)* eg treating different types of ordinary creditor differently in regard to payment of dividend. For there to be prejudice it also must affect the rights of the creditor in some way. Material irregularity on the other hand involves procedural matters eg a complaint that the chair rejected a valid claim for voting purposes. As to whether the irregularity is material the court will take a practical approach ie it must have affected the outcome of the meeting.

Pursuant to s262 (2) applicants may be either:

- The debtor
- A person entitled to vote at the creditors' meeting
- The nominee or his replacement

The time limit for applications is within 28 days of the filing of chair's report on the meeting with the court (s262 (3)).

If the court is satisfied the ground is made out it can revoke or suspend approval or direct that a further meeting of creditors be held to consider revised proposals or reconsider original proposals.

The court can extend the interim order accordingly and give supplemental directions.

6.4 Protection for creditors not given notice

A creditor who was not given notice of the meeting is still bound by its decision however the IA 86 provides that such a creditor be protected by s262. This permits a creditor to apply to court to challenge the approval within 28 days from when he became aware of the creditors' meeting. Challenge is by court application.

It should be noted that a creditor without notice of the meeting is still entitled to receive a dividend.

Interactive question 1: Ian Edwards

Ian Edwards has come to you for some advice. He is currently working as a manager of an electrical retail shop, earning £16,500 a year.

He lives with his wife and two children, aged three and six, in a four bedroomed property on the outskirts of Exeter. The house was purchased jointly with his wife when they got married. The property has recently been valued at £178,000 and is subject to an outstanding mortgage in the sum of £135,000.

Ian is an avid stamp collector, having been introduced to stamps at the age of eight by his grandfather. He estimates that his collection is currently worth £6,000. He doesn't want to lose his collection.

He drives a VW Golf valued at £6,000 and his wife drives a VW Polo, valued at £4,000. Neither vehicle is subject to finance.

The couple hold premium bonds in the sum of £4,000 having been given them as a wedding present.

When Ian and his wife first purchased the property his wife worked as a bank manager, however she has not worked since having the children. Ian has struggled to maintain their standard of living on his wage alone, however rising interest rates have forced him to rely heavily on the use of credit cards as a way of meeting the demands of his family. He has now found himself in a position where he is unable to meet the monthly repayments on his debts.

He owes a total of £58,000 to six credit card companies. In addition, he took out a personal loan of £10,000 eight months ago which he secured on the property. His wife is not aware of the loan.

He knows that bankruptcy is an option, however his terms of employment are such that he will lose his job immediately if he is declared bankrupt. His father has suggested a voluntary arrangement and has offered to pay a lump sum of £30,000 into the arrangement if it is accepted by creditors. The money would not be forthcoming in a bankruptcy scenario and will only be made available if the family home and any equity in it is completely excluded from the arrangement.

Ian advises that his wife is now actively seeking employment. He anticipates that if his wife is successful, he would be able to pay £250 per month into an arrangement.

Nominee's and supervisor's fees are anticipated to be £4,000.

The trustee's remuneration will be calculated using the Schedule 6 scale.

Assume that the distribution fee is £1,225.

Requirement

Prepare an Estimated Outcome Statement for Ian comparing the outcomes for creditors under both voluntary arrangement and bankruptcy scenarios.

Show all workings and assumptions made.

See **Answer** at the end of this chapter.

Interactive question 2: Mrs Pantry

Mrs Pantry has put together proposals for a voluntary arrangement which she will put to her creditors at a forthcoming meeting.

Requirement

Explain to Mrs Pantry what the requisite majorities are in order for a voluntary arrangement to be approved by her creditors.

See **Answer** at the end of this chapter.

Summary and Self-test

Summary

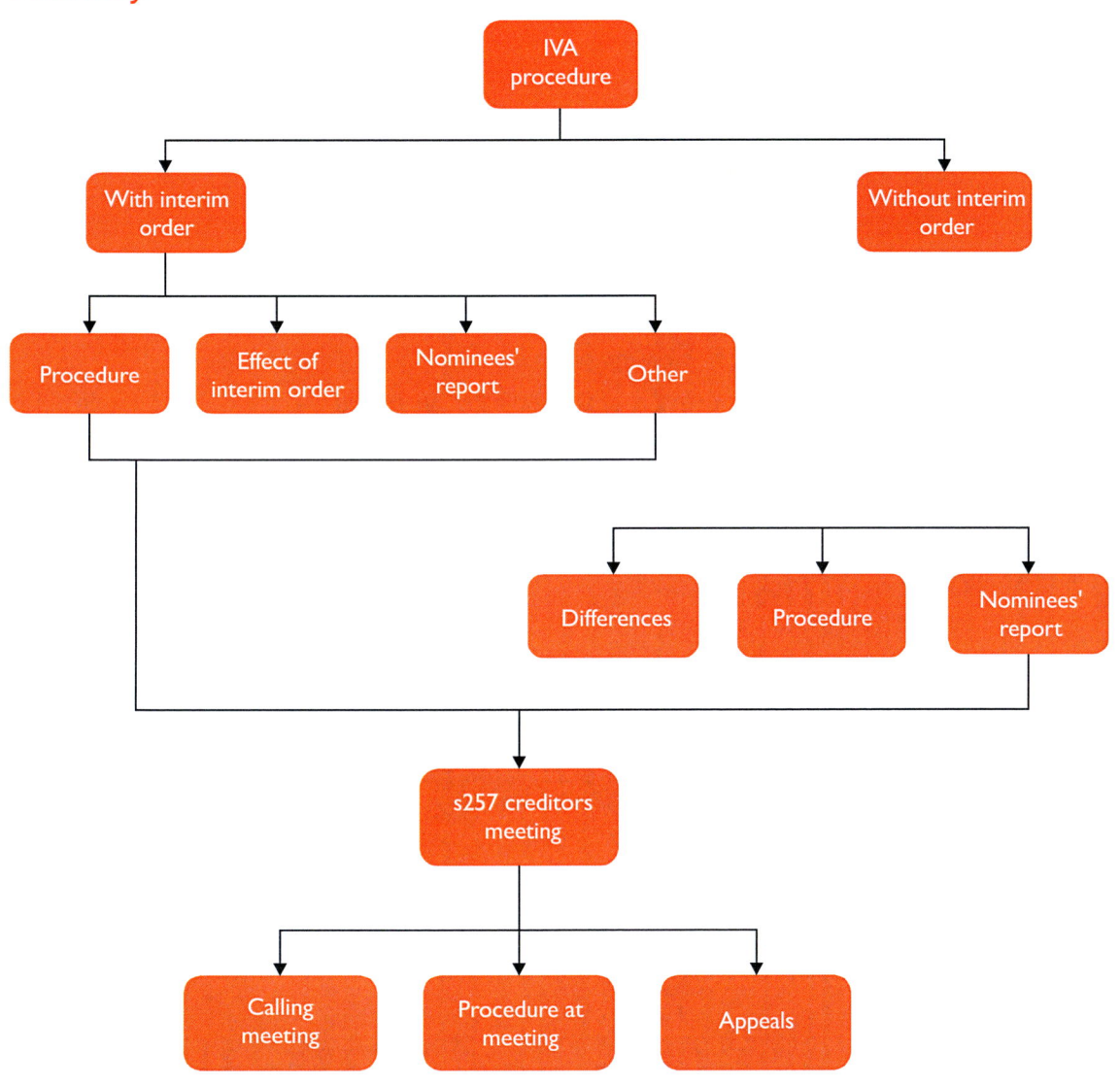

```
                            IVA procedure
                           /            \
              With interim order    Without interim order
             /    |       |    \
      Procedure  Effect of  Nominees'  Other
                 interim    report
                 order
          |
          |                    Differences  Procedure  Nominees'
          |                                             report
          |_____|
                        |
                 s257 creditors meeting
                /       |         \
        Calling    Procedure at   Appeals
        meeting      meeting
```

Voluntary arrangements procedures   489

Self-test

Answer the following questions.

1 Where no application for an extension is made, after what period will an interim order cease to have effect?

   A   7 days
   B   14 days
   C   21 days
   D   28 days

2 Within how many days before the expiration of the interim order must the nominee deliver his report to court?

   A   2 days
   B   5 days
   C   14 days
   D   21 days

3 What is the purpose of the nominee's report to court?

4 What are the three tests set out in *Greystoke v Hamilton-Smith and Others* which the nominee should apply before concluding that a meeting of creditors should or should not be summoned?

5 How many days' notice must be given to creditors of the meeting to consider the voluntary arrangement proposal?

   A   7 days
   B   14 days
   C   21 days
   D   28 days

Now, go back to the Learning Objectives in the Introduction. If you are satisfied that you have achieved these objectives, please tick them off.

Answers to Self-test

1. B
2. A
3.
   - State whether the proposed arrangement has a reasonable prospect of being approved and implemented
   - Whether, in the opinion of the nominee, a meeting of the debtor's creditors should be summoned to consider the proposal
   - The date, time and place at which it is proposed the creditors' meeting should take place
4.
   - That the debtor's true position as to assets and liabilities is not materially different from that which it is represented to the creditors to be
   - That the debtor's proposal has a real prospect of being implemented in the way it is represented to be
   - That there is no already manifest yet avoidable prospective unfairness
5. B

Answers to Interactive questions

Answer to Interactive question 1: Ian Edwards

IAN EDWARDS ESTIMATED OUTCOME STATEMENT

	Workings	Bankruptcy £	Voluntary Arrangement £
Receipts			
Matrimonial home	1	11,500	–
Father's payment	2	–	30,000
Voluntary contributions	3	–	9,000
Stamp collection	4	6,000	–
Vehicle	5	6,000	6,000
Premium bonds	6	2,000	2,000
		25,500	47,000
Less costs			
supervisor's fees		–	4,000
secretary of State fees	7	5,870	–
trustee's fees	8	4,525	–
assets available for creditors		15,105	43,000
Creditors		(58,000)	(58,000)
Dividend		26p in £	74p in £

Workings/Assumptions

1. Matrimonial home.

    - Excluded in IVA, creditors compensated by father's payment
    - Realised by trustee in bankruptcy

		£
Proceeds sale		178,000
Less mortgage		(135,000)
		43,000
Assume 50:50 split		21,500	21,500
Less secured loan (against Ian only)		(10,000)
Equity		11,500

2. Father's payment – only available under voluntary arrangement

3. Income

    - Not available in bankruptcy since Ian will lose his job
    - Assume arrangement will last for three years, 3 × 250 × 12 = £9,000

4. Stamp collection

    - Realised in bankruptcy
    - Ian will seek to exclude from a voluntary arrangement

5. VW Golf

    - Could argue that necessary for getting to work therefore may be excluded in bankruptcy. If public transport available then trustee would sell the vehicle as wife has a vehicle for family use
    - Seek to realise in voluntary arrangement

Certificate in Insolvency

6   Premium bonds

Given to both Ian and his wife so ½ share will form part of his estate to be realised.

7   Secretary of State fees

Only applicable to bankruptcy

Realisations			25,500
Less			(2,000)
			23,500

1,700	@ 100%	1,700
1,500	@ 75%	1,125
20,300	@ 15%	3,045
23,500		5,870

8   Trustee's remuneration

Only applicable to bankruptcy

Realisations:

5,000 × 20%	1,000
5,000 × 15%	750
15,500 × 10%	1,550
25,500	3,300

On sums distributed:
[Figure given in question]   1,225

Total remuneration 3,300 + 1,225 = £4,525

Answer to Interactive question 2: Mrs Pantry

For any resolution to approve any proposal or modification, there must be a majority of three-quarters in value of the creditors present, in person or by proxy, who vote in favour.

The value of the creditors debts are ascertained as follows:

- Where an interim order is in force – as at the date of the interim order
- Where there is no interim order in force – the date of the meeting
- Where the debtor is an undischarged bankrupt – the date of the bankruptcy order

When calculating the value of a creditor's claim, the following should be left out of account where:

- Written notice of the claim was not given either at the meeting or before it
- Part or all of the claim is secured
- It is in respect of a debt wholly or partly secured on a current bill of exchange or promissory note

If a 75% majority in value votes in favour, a second vote is taken, this time only counting those:

- To whom notice was sent
- Whose votes are not to be left out of account as above
- Who are not, to the best of the chair's belief, associates of the debtor

On this vote the resolution is invalid if those voting against it include more than half in value of the creditors.

So a simple majority of valid, notified, independent creditors can veto an arrangement which would otherwise be approved by the use of associates.

CHAPTER 31

Post approval matters

Introduction
Topic List
1   Duties, powers and liabilities of the supervisor
2   Post approval variation
3   Default/failure of the arrangement
4   Completion of the arrangement

Summary and Self-test
Answers to Self-test
Answers to Interactive questions

Introduction

Learning objectives

- Describe the obligations of debtors in an IVA and explain the effects of the default of a debtor
- Describe the circumstances that might bring about the failure of the arrangement, the impact that that failure has upon the parties related to the arrangement and the procedures that should be followed by the IP on failure of the arrangement

Tick off

Stop and think

What does failure of a voluntary arrangement mean for the debtor and creditors? What powers should the supervisor of a voluntary arrangement have?

Working context

You may be involved in the ongoing administration of a voluntary arrangement. Part of your duties may be to ensure that the arrangement is progressing as anticipated in the proposals. You should be aware therefore of what the implications are of an arrangement not progressing as planned and what should happen if the arrangement fails.

1 Duties, powers and liabilities of the supervisor

Section overview

- The supervisor's main duty is to ensure that the arrangement proceeds in accordance with the terms of the agreed proposal. In order to do this he should maintain regular contact with the debtor.

1.1 Statutory duties

There is little in the Act and Rules regarding the supervisor's duties given that the proposal document essentially forms the basis of the relationship between the debtor, supervisor and creditors. In addition to the proposal and statutory provisions the supervisor should also be aware of the professional guidance given by the SIPs and 'Dear IP' notices.

s263 contains the general provisions relating to the implementation and supervision of an approved arrangement. It is supplemented by the Rules.

R5.31A imposes a duty on the supervisor to keep all those interested in the arrangement informed as to its progress.

Where the supervisor is required in the arrangement to:

- Carry on the debtor's business or trade
- Realise assets of the debtor
- Otherwise administer and dispose of any of the debtor's funds

He must, keep accounts and records of his acts and dealings in connection with the arrangement including records of all receipts and payments of money.

A progress report must be sent within two months of the end of each period of 12 months (starting with the commencement of the arrangement) to:

- The debtor and
- All bound creditors of whose address he is aware

The obligation to send an annual report does not apply if the obligation to send a final report under R5.34 arises in the two month period. The report must annex an abstract of receipts and payments or a statement to the effect that there have been no receipts and payments.

1.2 Powers of the supervisor

The supervisor obtains his powers from the arrangement. He can protect his interest in land by way of notice where land is registered.

The Act gives very limited powers namely:

- s424(1)(b) – power to apply to court for an order in respect of transactions defrauding creditors
- s264(1)(c) – power to present a bankruptcy petition
- s263(4) – power to apply to court for directions

It is very important therefore that when drafting the proposal that the supervisor ensures he has sufficient powers to put the arrangement into effect. As a guide, the supervisor should be given similar powers as a trustee in bankruptcy.

If the supervisor finds that he has insufficient powers to deal with any issue post approval of the arrangement, there are steps that can be taken to rectify the situation. He should first call a meeting of creditors. Pursuant to the decision in *Raja v Rubin and Goodman 1999* provided that all the creditors agree it will be possible to amend the arrangement. Alternatively, if there is a variation procedure provided and this is followed, amendment will be possible.

1.3 Removal of the supervisor

It is envisaged that the proposal itself will make provision for the removal of a supervisor and his/her replacement. There is, however a fallback provision in IA 1986 if so required. s263(5) provides for the court to have a general power to appoint a supervisor.

1.4 Liability of the supervisor

The supervisor must be careful because he does not enjoy statutory protection. If he trades on behalf of the debtor he will be liable under general law in respect of any contracts and will need to be careful to avoid liability for tax, trade and business rate debts. The supervisor is also under a duty to exercise reasonable care and skill in the conduct of the voluntary arrangement.

s263(3) makes it clear that in circumstances where the debtor, creditors or any other person is dissatisfied by any act, omission or decision of the supervisor he has the power to apply to court. The court has the power to:

- Confirm, reverse or modify any act or decision of the supervisor
- Give directions
- Make such other order as it think fit

Given that s263 gives an effective method of enforcing the duty of a supervisor, no private action can be brought against the supervisor for breach of duty (*King v Anthony*). It should, however, be noted that the Human Rights Act 1998 may give rights of action as the supervisor in complying with the directions of the court is arguably a public authority.

As already stated, it is reasonably rare for a supervisor to run a debtor's business, but if a supervisor does get involved it should be noted that he will incur personal liability. If there are employees the arrangement will not terminate the employer/employee relationship unless there is express provision to that effect either in the proposal (or possibly the employment contract).

1.5 Time statements

Any creditor or the debtor may request a nominee or supervisor to provide a statement setting out how much time either he or his members of staff have spent on work in connection with his appointment. It must be provided free of charge and within 28 days of any request, but not after two years following the date the office holder ceased to act, R5.66.

2 Post approval variation

Section overview

- If the supervisor or the debtor consider that the terms of the arrangement may not be achieved the supervisor should take steps to discuss the situation with the debtor. It may be possible that by varying the terms of the proposal the arrangement may still be successfully completed.

2.1 Procedure when proposal provides for variation

The proposal may expressly provide for post–acceptance amendments and this situation was considered in the case of *Thompson and Horrocks v John Lawson Broome*. The court held that a properly drawn clause giving a power of variation in a voluntary arrangement is valid.

Doubts had previously been expressed as to whether it would be necessary for all of the creditors to vote in favour of such variation, or whether a majority of three–quarters in value of the creditors present in person or by proxy and voting on the resolution would suffice (the proportion necessary to approve a proposal).

The requirements of the proposal should be followed, for example, calling a creditors' meeting where a vote may take place.

If the proposal follows the IVA protocol the proposal will permit for variation of up to a 15% reduction in dividends without having to hold a further creditors' meeting.

2.2 Procedure when proposal makes no provision

If the proposal does not contain any provision for amendment and an application is made by the debtor or supervisor under s263, it is likely that the court will direct that a creditors' meeting be held. The case of *Raja v Rubin & Goodman 1999* held that, in the absence of a variation clause, 100% of the affected creditors must be in favour of a proposed amendment.

The question also arises as to the remedy available to an aggrieved minority creditor. The creditor could apply under s263(3) on the basis that he is dissatisfied by the decision of the supervisor (and not s262 which only applies to the original s257 meeting). The court would be likely to treat the application as it would if it were under s262.

Alternatively the existing arrangement could be brought to an end and a new proposal put before creditors (remember, only one interim order can be applied for in each 12 month period).

In practice, the proposal and standard terms should detail the basis upon which variation is upheld.

Interactive question 1: Mrs Packard

Mr Brown is a creditor of Amy Packard and eight months ago voted in favour of a voluntary arrangement proposed by Mrs Packard.

He has recently received a letter from Mrs Packard's supervisor advising him that Mrs Packard now wishes to vary the terms of her voluntary arrangement due to a change in her personal circumstances. Mr Brown's claim in the arrangement represents 18% of the total creditor claims.

Requirement

Can Mrs Packard vary the terms of her arrangement?

What can Mr Brown do if he doesn't agree to the variation?

See **Answer** at the end of this chapter.

3 Default/failure of the arrangement

Section overview

- The terms of the arrangement should set out clearly a definition of what constitutes default or failure of the arrangement and what the supervisor should do if these circumstances should arise. It is usual for a bankruptcy petition to be presented. The supplier or any bound creditor can present such a petition.

3.1 Grounds for presenting a bankruptcy petition

There are three grounds set out in s276(1):

- Failure to comply with obligations under the voluntary arrangement

- Giving false or misleading material information or making a material omission in any document at the creditors meeting

- Failure to comply with the supervisor's reasonable requests

3.2 Effects of bankruptcy on the voluntary arrangement

It is usual for the voluntary arrangement assets and proceeds of sale to be held on trust for the arrangement creditors. This will either be express or by implication *NT Gallagher & Son Ltd 2002*.

The proposal will detail the effect that bankruptcy will have on that trust. It would be usual for provisions to be made that the trust survives. If the proposal is silent on this point then pursuant to *NT Gallagher* by default the trust will survive.

Consequently, the voluntary arrangement assets and proceeds of sale will continue to be held exclusively for arrangement creditors.

The trustee in bankruptcy will take possession of non-arrangement assets, realise such assets and distribute on behalf of all creditors.

The arrangement creditors can prove in the bankruptcy for so much of their debt which remains after payment of what has been or will be recovered under the trust.

Where failure has occurred, the supervisor should notify the creditors accordingly and advise them what action he has taken or proposes to take.

When a bankruptcy order is made against the debtor, the supervisor should advise the OR of the circumstances. If the voluntary arrangement is terminated as an effect of the order, the supervisor should arrange for the prompt handover of assets, funds, books and records to the OR.

Interactive question 2: Katy Jones

Katy Jones' individual voluntary arrangement was approved on 2 February 20X9. A summary of her Statement of Affairs revealed the following:

K JONES STATEMENT OF AFFAIRS

	£
Matrimonial home	75,000
Mortgage	(50,000)
Husband's half share	(12,500)
	12,500
Other assets	4,500
Total assets	17,000
Liabilities	(48,000)
Shortfall	(31,000)

Significant points in her proposal were:

- That she would re-mortgage the property within ten months in order to release her share of the equity
- That she would continue to trade as a self-employed hairdresser and beautician to allow contributions from profits to be made each month of £1,000
- Contributions would be made for 36 months to enable all her creditors to be paid in full
- Her husband was to provide sufficient funds to cover all costs and expenses incurred during the arrangement

It is now 2 November 20X9 and a review of the files has taken place which has shown the following:

- The funds from the re-mortgage have not been forthcoming to date
- The debtor is four months in arrears of her contributions. A clause in the proposal states that the Supervisor must fail the arrangement should the debtor fall three months in arrears
- The debtor has failed to answer any correspondence sent to her over the past six weeks

Requirements

(a) What steps should the Supervisor take regarding the debtor's non co-operation?

(b) What steps should the Supervisor take to fail the arrangement and what considerations must be taken regarding the funds currently held?

See **Answer** at the end of the chapter.

4 Completion of the arrangement

Section overview

- When the arrangement has been fully implemented the supervisor should conclude his administration as expeditiously as possible.

4.1 Final report

The supervisor must send to all creditors the following information within 28 days of completion R5.34.

- Notice of completion or notice of non completion.

- Report to summarise all receipts and payments. It should explain any difference between the actual position and the voluntary arrangement projection.

Supervisor must send a copy of the notice and the report to the Secretary of State within the same timeframe. The supervisor will not be discharged until he has done so.

Dissatisfied creditors or the debtor can apply for directions under s263.

Summary and Self-test

Summary

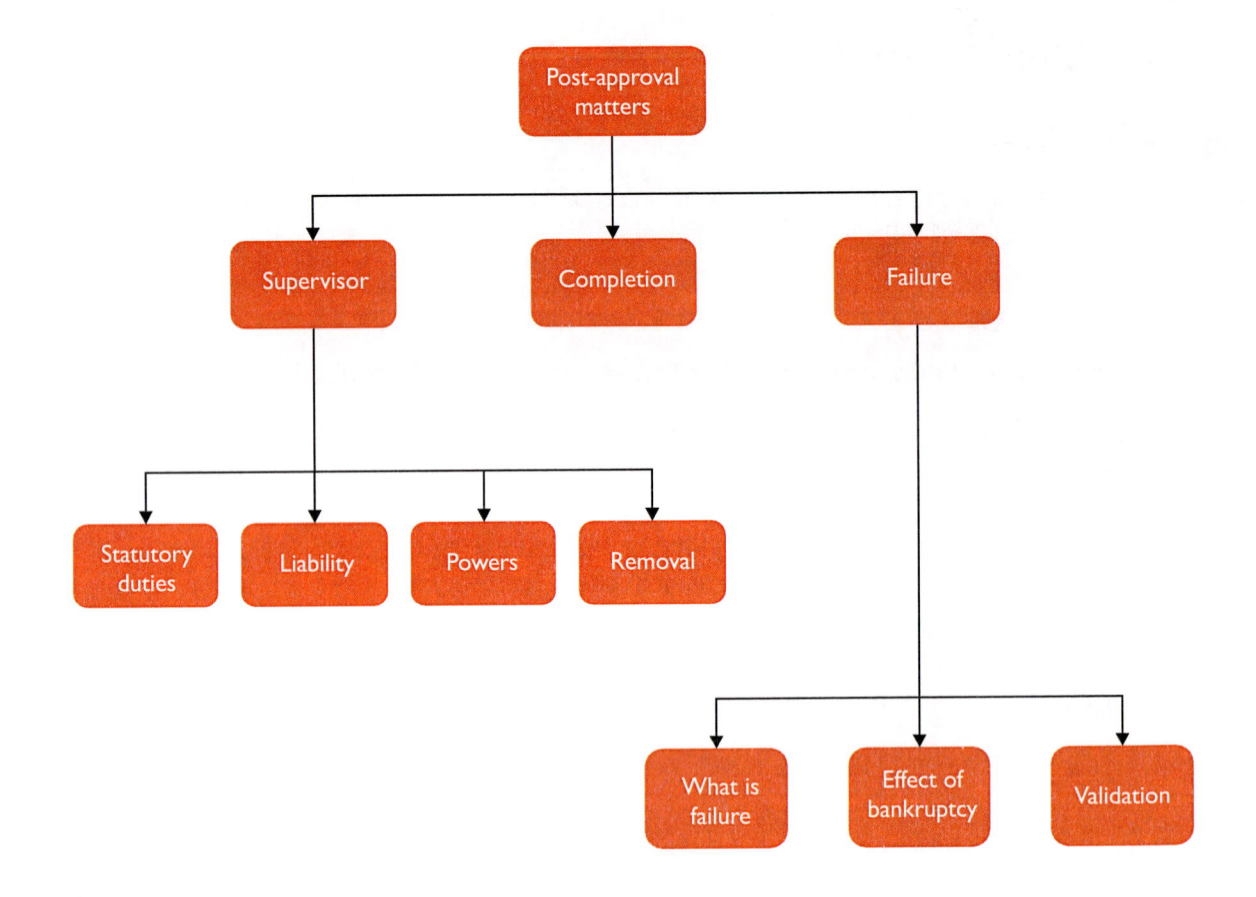

- Post-approval matters
  - Supervisor
    - Statutory duties
    - Liability
    - Powers
    - Removal
  - Completion
  - Failure
    - What is failure
    - Effect of bankruptcy
    - Validation

Self-test

Now answer the following questions.

1   How often must the supervisor send a report on the progress of the VA to creditors?

　　A   Once in every period of 6 months (from appointment)

　　B   Once in every 12 month period (from appointment)

　　C   Within one month of the end of the first 12 month period (from appointment) and six monthly thereafter

　　D   Whenever the supervisor thinks it appropriate to do so

2   The supervisor has the power to take action for which of the following?

　　A   Preference s340

　　B   Transaction at an undervalue s339

　　C   Excessive pension contributions s343

　　D   Transaction defrauding creditors s423

3   Within how many days of completion must the supervisor send to creditors a notice of completion?

　　A   7 days

　　B   14 days

　　C   21 days

　　D   28 days

4   If there is no variation clause in a proposal what percentage of creditors by value will have to approve any modification to it?

5   What are the grounds for presenting a default petition?

Now, go back to the Learning Objectives in the Introduction. If you are satisfied that you have achieved these objectives, please tick them off.

Answers to Self-test

1. B
2. D
3. D
4. 100%
5. Failure to comply with obligations under VA.

    Giving false or misleading material information or making a material omission in any document at the creditors' meeting.

    Failure to comply with the supervisor's reasonable requests.

Answers to Interactive questions

Answer to Interactive question 1: Mrs Packard

Letter format

Question doesn't make it clear whether the proposal expressly provides for post acceptance amendments or not.

1 Proposal contains a variation clause:

Thompson and Horrocks v John Lawson Broome – court held that a properly drawn clause giving a power of variation in a voluntary arrangement is valid.

Providing the terms of such a clause are followed, any variation of Mrs Packard's arrangement would be valid.

Any such clause should incorporate provisions to allow for minority creditors to appeal against an amendment.

This would allow Mr Brown to make his views regarding the variation known.

It is likely that 75% of creditors would be required to agree to the variation. Since Mr Brown only holds 18% of the votes, he would not be able to stop any variation on his own.

If the proposal followed the IVA protocol then provision for variation of up to 15% reduction in dividend may be made without holding a further meeting of creditors.

2 Proposal doesn't contain a variation clause:

The supervisor can apply to court for directions under s263.

It is likely that the court will direct that a creditors' meeting be held to consider the variation.

Raja v Rubun & Goodman 1999 – it was held that in the absence of a variation clause, 100% of the affected creditors must be in favour of a proposed amendment.

At the creditors' meeting Mr Brown could make his feelings known. If he votes against the resolution, the variation would not be able to go ahead.

If Mr Brown is aggrieved he may:

Apply to court under s263(3) on the basis that he is dissatisfied by the decision of the supervisor.

s262 would not be appropriate since it only applies to the original s257 meeting.

The court would be likely however to treat the application as though it were under s262.

Answer to Interactive question 2: Katy Jones

1. The Supervisor should make attempts to contact the debtor regarding her non co-operation – by post, telephone or attending in person at her house.

   He should remind her of her duty to comply with her obligations under the arrangement.

   He should also remind her that she must do all things that may be reasonably required by her Supervisor.

   Failure to comply with these duties will result in a petition for her bankruptcy being presented to the court on the grounds that she has failed to comply with the:

   - Obligations under the voluntary arrangement
   - Supervisor's reasonable requests

2. The debtor has failed to comply with her obligations under the voluntary arrangement.

   Contributions are in arrears and it would appear that there is no prospect of further contributions being received.

   The equity from the house has not been forthcoming.

   In addition, the debtor has failed to respond to any correspondence.

   The proposal states that the Supervisor must fail the arrangement if contributions are three months in arrears.

   The supervisor could call a meeting of creditors to seek their views, regarding the continuance of the arrangement.

   s264 (1)(c) – where the debtor has failed to comply with obligations under the arrangement the supervisor, or any creditor bound by the arrangement, can present a petition for the bankruptcy of the debtor.

   The effect of presenting a bankruptcy petition is that s284 is triggered – as such dispositions by the debtor of her assets will be void unless court sanction is obtained.

   The supervisor should ensure that IVA funds are distributed to IVA creditors before presenting default petition. (Trust clause should protect IVA assets.)

   Within 28 days of termination of the arrangement the Supervisor must report to creditors, debtor and the Secretary of State.

   The report must include an explanation of why the arrangement has not been implemented in accordance with the proposal as approved by the creditors' meeting.

CHAPTER 32

Insolvent partnerships

Introduction
Topic List
1 Partnership law
2 Options for creditors of insolvent partnerships
3 Options for insolvent partners
4 Partnership voluntary arrangements
5 Priority rules

Summary and Self-test
Answers to Self-test
Answer to Interactive question

Introduction

Learning objectives

- Describe briefly the characteristics of a partnership voluntary arrangement
- Describe the processes undergone in the creation of a partnership voluntary arrangement and compare these with the processes followed in the creation of an IVA
- State the other types of partnership insolvency

Stop and think

Why, when dealing with a partnership, is it necessary to look at the individual partner's assets and liabilities as well as the partnership assets and liabilities? How does the bankruptcy of one partner affect the partnership as a whole?

Working context

Many individuals work in partnership with others and it is likely therefore in a work environment that you will be asked to assist with an insolvent partnership or an insolvent individual who is in partnership with another. It is important therefore to have an understanding of the main issues regarding insolvent partnerships and the provisions of the Insolvent Partnership Order 1994.

1 Partnership law

Section overview

Unlike a company a partnership is not a separate legal entity from the members who make it up. If a simple partnership becomes insolvent it will have far reaching implications for the partners involved as they all share joint and several liability for the debts of the creditors. This may result in the personal insolvency of individual members. Also, the personal insolvency of an individual member may have consequences for the partnership as a whole. The partners may be companies or individuals (these notes will assume they are individuals).

Definition

Partnership (a firm): the relationship between persons carrying on business in common with a view to profit (s1 Partnership Act 1890).

1.1 Nature of a partnership

Unlike a company a partnership is not a separate legal entity from the members who make it up. Consequently a partnership has no legal personality.

- It cannot enter into a contract with a partner
- 'Partnership property' belongs collectively to all the partners not to the firm
- The name of the firm is merely a convenient collective noun for the aggregate of the partners

As a partnership is a relationship rather than a legal person any change in membership (eg by retirement or expulsion or inviting a person to join the firm) strictly speaking dissolves the old partnership and gives rise to a new one between the remaining partners. This is sometimes called a 'technical dissolution'.

Despite the above, it is often convenient to treat a firm as if it were a separate legal person. Examples of when it is treated as such include:

- VAT registration
- Partnership accounts and bank accounts in the name of the partnership
- Where the partnership is insolvent where as we will see, it can be wound up as if it were an (unregistered) company

For taxation purposes however HM Revenue and Customs assesses each partner on his or her share of the profits as if that partner were a sole trader.

1.2 The relationship between the partners

In a company the relationship between the company and its directors and shareholders is governed primarily by the Articles of Association. In a partnership the relationship between the partners is governed by the partnership contract (often in practice executed as a deed).

If there is no deed or the deed is silent the terms of the Partnership Act 1890 (PA 1890) will apply. Key provisions of the 1890 Act are set out below.

1.3 Powers of management

The PA 1890 gives all partners a right to participate in management.

Ordinary matters are decided by majority.

Unanimity is required however, for:

- The introduction of a new partner

- A change in the nature of the partnership business. This would probably include the partners initiating an insolvency procedure

Expulsion of a partner is only possible if the partnership contract/(deed) allows it.

1.4 Power to bind the firm to a contract (agency)

s5 PA 1890 provides that partners are agents of the firm and the other partners.

On ordinary agency principles a partner will therefore bind the firm/the other partners to a contract providing he acts within his:

- Express authority
- Usual (implied) authority (ie doing any act 'for carrying on in the usual way business of the kind carried on by the firm'). There are two exceptions:
  - Where the third party knows that the partner they are dealing with is acting outside their actual authority
  - The third party does not believe or know that the person they are dealing with is a partner
- Ostensible or apparent authority. This applies where a person may not have express or implied authority to enter a contract – but they are held out by the principal as if they did. The third party is entitled to rely on such a representation and the firm/partners will be bound

1.5 Duties of partners

The relationship between partners is fiduciary (of the 'utmost good faith').

This has the following implications.

- Partners have a duty to make full disclosure to other partners. s28 PA 1890 requires partners to render full accounts and information on all matters affecting the partnership.
- They must account to the firm for any benefits received personally (s29 PA 1890).

If they compete with the firm (ie make a secret profit) they must hand over any profits to the firm (s30 PA 1890).

1.6 Liability

The liability of partners for the firms debts is unlimited (although limited liability partnerships are possible under the Limited Liability Partnership Act 2000 (LLP 2000). [Note that the LLP 2000 is outside the syllabus.]

By s9 PA 1890 every partner is liable jointly with the other partners for all debts of the firm incurred while a partner.

A partner who settles a debt due from the firm personally is entitled to a contribution from the other partners.

The basic principle of the PA 1890 in the absence of contrary agreement is equality. All partners:

- Share equally in capital and profits
- Contribute equally to losses

Liability in tort (eg for negligence) is 'joint and several'. The distinction between joint (one obligation of all the partners) and joint and several (each partner separately liable) is of much less practical significance since the Civil Liability (Contribution) Act 1978.

1.7 Dissolution

The PA 1890 lists circumstances where a partnership is dissolved.

The rules on dissolution are particularly important where a partnership is solvent. Here the 1890 Act and not the IPO 1994 will tend to apply.

1.8 When will a partnership be dissolved?

There are three circumstances:

- By notice
- By operation of law
- By court order

1.9 Dissolution by notice

This is where any partner gives written notice to all other partners (s26(1) PA 1890). The date of dissolution will be the date specified in the notice – or if none the date of communication.

This right to dissolve the firm at will is often modified in the partnership deed.

1.10 Dissolution by operation of law

(s33(1) PA 1890) bankruptcy of any partner (see later).

(s33(1) PA 1890) death of any partner.

(s32(a) PA 1890) expiration of fixed term partnership or termination of single undertaking/adventure (s32(b) PA 1890).

(s34 PA 1890) occurrence of an event which renders business unlawful (eg loss of necessary licence).

(s33(2) PA 1890) at a partner's option where a partner charges his or her share of the partnership property with personal debts.

1.11 Dissolution by order of the court on application by any partner

This would be particularly relevant where the partnership agreement does not permit dissolution by notice and the partnership is solvent.

The grounds are:

- Insanity or other permanent incapacity to perform obligations under the partnership agreement (s35 PA 1890) on the part of any partner
- A partner's conduct is prejudicial to the firm's business
- A partner is wilfully or persistently in breach of the agreement, or his conduct is such that it is not reasonably practicable for the firm to continue
- The business can only be carried on at a loss
- It is just and equitable to dissolve the firm

1.12 The effect of dissolution on the partnership relationship

The rights, duties and agency of the partners only continues so far as necessary to:

- Wind up the affairs of a partnership
- Complete transactions (s38 PA 1890)

1.13 Distribution of assets

The general position (s39 PA 1890) is that property of the partnership is applied in payment of debts and liabilities of the firm, with any surplus going to the partners, deducting any sums owed to them by the firm.

Losses according to s44(a) PA 1890 are to be paid:

- Out of profits of the firm; then
- Out of capital of the firm; then
- By the partners individually in the proportions of their respective profit shares.

Assets are distributed in the following order when settling accounts between partners (s44(b)):

- To pay debts and liabilities of the firm
- To re-pay advances made by partners to the firm (ie partners are deferred)
- To pay partners back their capital advances
- Any surplus distributed as per profit share

Remember that these rules will apply only where the insolvency legislation is not invoked. The partners may well be able to distribute assets as above by agreement between themselves. If the matter cannot be settled amicably the court has powers to wind up the partnership and appoint a receiver if necessary.

2 Options for creditors of insolvent partnerships

Section overview

There are a number of options available to creditors of insolvent partnerships. These are dealt with below.

2.1 Sue and obtain judgment on the debt

The creditor has a choice either to sue the firm or individual partner(s):

Sue the firm. (Remember that, although for convenience the creditor will sue the firm in the firm's name, this is really an action against all the partners collectively.)

It is the partners at the date the cause of action accrued (eg date the debt was incurred) who are defendants to the action.

This will include partners who since this date have retired, died or been expelled.

Under the terms of a professionally drafted partnership agreement ex-partners of this type will normally have an indemnity against the firm.

Once judgment has been obtained against the firm execution can be levied:

- Against partnership property
- Against the personal property of one or more partners (but formal proof of partner status will be required eg the person has acknowledged service of the papers as a partner)

Sue an individual partner or partners. (This might be appropriate where an individual partner has substantial assets whilst the firm itself appears to be insolvent.)

If the partner sued pays up he will have a right to claim a contribution from the other partners.

The disadvantage of obtaining judgment against an individual partner is that execution can only be levied against that partner's personal estate. However, s23(2) of the 1890 Act gives judgment creditors the right to apply to court for a charging order over that partner's share of the partnership property.

2.2 Bankrupt one or more partners in the usual way without seeking to wind up the firm

This is specifically provided for by Insolvent Partnership Order 1994.

The apparent advantages of this route are:

- Relatively simple procedure (effectively we are ignoring the IPO)
- The chance of 'queue-jumping' the creditors of the firm

However, where it comes to the attention of the court that the bankrupt is a member of an insolvent firm the court may apply the terms of the IPO 1994 to the future conduct of the bankruptcy of that partner.

This might result in the creditors of the firm generally ranking *pari passu* with all other creditors of the bankrupt (including the petitioning creditor). This would negate the apparent advantage of this route.

Possible outcomes where a creditor seeks to bankrupt individual partners, the partner may:

Certificate in Insolvency

- Pay the outstanding debt to stave off bankruptcy (this partner will now have a right of contribution against the other partners)
- Apply for an interim order (IVA)
- Be made bankrupt

Effect of bankruptcy of a partner:

- The partnership is automatically dissolved in the absence of contrary intention in the deed.
- The bankrupt's estate, including his or her share in the partnership, vests in the trustee on appointment.
- The deed often provides for expulsion of the bankrupt partner, continuation of the firm between the remaining partners and some mechanism for valuing and buying out the bankrupt's share. If this buy-out is for full value it is valid.
- If there is no such buy-out of the partner's share the trustee may have to bring proceedings against the firm to realise the bankrupt's interest in the partnership business. Ultimately this may involve winding-up the firm.

2.3 Petition the court for a Partnership Administration Order

As in corporate insolvency, creditors have the power to do this but may find difficulty in compiling sufficient information about the business to draft an independent report. It is unlikely that creditors would consider this an attractive option.

3 Options for insolvent partners

Section overview

There are many options for insolvent partners which are detailed below.

3.1 To propose an IVA or IVAs

A partner can always seek to put a proposal for an IVA to his or her own creditors. This might be where:

- A creditor of the firm is seeking to 'pick-off' this partner's assets by petitioning for bankruptcy
- The other partners cannot or will not agree to trying to set up a PVA

All the partners intend proposing IVAs, which will be drafted in similar terms (interlocking IVAs).

The major advantage of the partners proposing interlocking IVAs is that the interim order should prevent:

- Legal processes against individual and partnership property
- Winding-up orders being made against the firm or bankruptcy orders against the partners

One IP will be instructed to act as nominee in relation to interlocking IVAs. The IP should:

- Ensure that the partners understand that they are each responsible for a separate retainer to the IP
- That if there is any risk of conflict that the partner concerned is advised in writing to seek independent advice

Interlocking IVAs will be more commercially attractive to the firm's creditors if the proposals provide for:

- Partnership creditors to be paid out of the firm's assets
- Any deficit to rank equally with individual creditors of the partners against the separate estates
- Any claims of partners to be deferred

Interlocking IVAs are not appropriate where there are large number of partners, material conflicts of interests or the position regarding the firm's debts is a complex one. The IA should demonstrate that no material prejudice affects debtor(s) and creditor(s).

3.2 To propose a Partnership Voluntary Arrangement (PVA)

It is for the partners of the firm to propose a PVA. The partnership deed may make express provision for the majority required to decide to propose a PVA. If it does not (as a PVA will require changes in the nature of the partnership business) to approve a PVA will require unanimous approval.

PVAs can also be proposed by an administrator of a Partnership Administration Order, or a liquidator of the firm.

It is important to remember that PVAs are modelled on CVAs. Consequently following the amendments to the Insolvency Act 1986 and the Insolvent Partnerships (Amendment) Order 2002 it is possible to apply for a small company moratorium. However note that although approval of the PVA will protect the partners' individual estates from partnership creditors there will be no protection for the partners from their individual creditors. Such creditors will not be notified of the PVA meeting because they are not creditors of the firm. They cannot therefore be bound by the terms of the PVA proposal. In practice, it may be necessary to consider setting up IVAs for partners at risk from individual creditors. The PVA procedure is very similar to that in CVA (see para 4 for more detail).

3.3 To petition to wind-up the firm as an unregistered company under Article 9 IPO 1994 (s220 to s229 IA 86)

Any partner can petition although if there are less than eight partners in the firm court leave is required (and will only be given where the petitioning partner has unsuccessfully served a statutory demand or levied execution).

Where the firm has eight or more partners the permissible grounds are as for creditor's petitions (ie inability to pay debts/just and equitable/or dissolution/cessation of business).

3.4 To petition to wind up the firm as an unregistered company and present concurrent petitions against ALL partners (under Article 10 IPO 1994)

This procedure is subject to strict conditions:

- The only available ground is the firm's inability to pay debts
- The petitions must be for orders against all partners including the petitioning partners
- Each partner must be willing to have an order made against him or her
- All petitions must be presented to the same court on the same day. The petition against the firm is advertised
- Each petition must refer to all the other petitions
- The hearing of the petition against the firm comes first and against the partners immediately after

3.5 Joint bankruptcy petition presented by individual partners

One petition is presented by all the partners (known as a Form 16 petition under Article 11 IPO 1994). The only ground is inability to pay debts. This is the partnership equivalent of the debtor's petition. It can only be presented where all the partners are individuals.

The court will order that each partner is made bankrupt and that the trustee winds-up the partnership business and administers the partnership property.

One trustee of both the estates of the individual bankrupt partners and of the firm will be appointed by a combined meeting of all creditors (whether of individual partners or the firm) failing which Secretary of State appointments can be made in the usual way, or the OR will become the joint trustee.

3.6 Petition for a Partnership Administration Order

Any partner (or creditor) can petition the court. In practice administration orders were usually sought to obtain the protection of the moratorium before seeking a PVA. Now that the moratorium is available in a PVA, PAO are of little importance.

4 Partnership voluntary arrangements

Section overview

The Insolvent Partnerships Order 1994 (IPO 1994) introduced (amongst other things) a partnership voluntary arrangement (PVA). The legislation for partnership voluntary arrangements is contained in the IPO 1994 as amended by the Insolvent Partnership (Amendment) Order 2002 and IA 1986.

4.1 Advantages of PVAs

Provides breathing space to enable the reorganisation and restructuring of the partnership.

One proposal – one creditors' meeting.

Limited disclosure – deals with partnership assets and liabilities only, not personal ones.

Partner's claims may be deferred.

Simple and cheap – costs are less than other insolvency options such as winding up as an unregistered company.

No court involvement necessary (but can apply for interim order).

Interim order provides protection from pressing creditors.

Partners remain in control of day-to-day partnership affairs.

Should provide a better return for creditors than other insolvency options.

4.2 Disadvantages of PVAs

No automatic moratorium.

Unanimity is required unless the deed provides otherwise.

Doesn't deal with personal liabilities, an IVA may be required to protect an individual's assets.

Need to be careful when considering voting rights of partners as conflicts may arise.

May also be unfair prejudice in relation to junior/salaried/retired or newly admitted partners.

Proposal must deal with the effect of any subsequent liquidation of the partnership or bankruptcy of individual partners.

Time period involved usually three-five years.

4.3 Who may propose a PVA?

A PVA may be proposed by:

- The partners (but not if partnership is in administration, or being wound up as an unregistered company, or if an order has been made under Article 11 IPO 1994)
- The administrator (if partnership is subject to a Partnership Administration Order)
- The liquidator (if partnership being wound up as an unregistered company)
- Trustee of the partnership (where an order has been made by virtue of Article 11 IPO 1994)

4.4 Role of nominee/supervisor

Nominee supervises its implementation.

The nominee must be a person who is qualified to act as an IP or authorised to act as nominee.

Upon acceptance of the arrangement by the creditors the IP will become supervisor of the arrangement.

4.5 Moratorium

Members of the partnership are able to apply for a moratorium under Sch 1A(1) IPO 1994 if certain criteria are met. To be eligible the partnership must satisfy two of the following conditions:

- Turnover not more than £6.5m
- Assets of not more than £3.26m
- No more than 50 employees

The partners cannot apply for a moratorium if:

- Partnership is in administration
- Partnership is being wound up as an unregistered company
- There is appointed an agricultural receiver
- A voluntary arrangement has effect in relation to the insolvent partnership
- A provisional liquidator has been appointed
- An order has been made by virtue of Article 11 of IPO 1994
- A moratorium has been in force for the insolvent partnership at any time during the period of 12 months ending with the date of filing and no PVA came into effect

4.6 Procedure – no application for moratorium

The procedure to be followed by members of the partnership is as follows.

- The members give notice of the proposal to the nominee to include:
    - Document setting out terms of the proposed PVA
    - Statement of the partnership affairs (particulars of partnership creditors, debts and other liabilities, details of partnership property and such other information as may be prescribed)
- Within 28 days after receiving notice, the nominee must submit a report to court (s2(2) Sch 1 IPO 1994) stating:
    - Whether, in his opinion, the proposed voluntary arrangement has a reasonable prospect of being approved and implemented
    - Whether, in his opinion, meetings of the members of the partnership and of the partnership's creditors should be summoned to consider the proposal
    - If in his opinion such meetings should be summoned, the date on which, and time and place at which, he proposes such meetings should be held
    - Whether there are in existence any insolvency proceedings in respect of the insolvent partnership or any of its members
- Convening meetings of members and creditors:

    Nominee must summon creditors' meeting for the time, date and place stated in his report to court.

    All creditors of the partnership of whose claim and address the nominee is aware must be given notice.

- Creditors' meeting:

    The purpose of the meeting is to decide whether or not to approve the PVA (with or without modifications).

    Any modifications cannot affect the rights of secured or preferential creditors without their consent.

    A modification may be agreed which nominates another person to act as nominee/supervisor.

- After meeting:

  The chair must report the result to the court and give notice of the result of the meeting to all creditors who were sent notice of the meeting.

  If the decision taken by the creditors' meeting differs from that taken by the meeting of the members of the partnership, a member may, within 28 days of the meeting, apply to the court.

  The court may order the decision of the meeting of the members of the partnership to have effect instead of the decision of the creditors' meeting, or make such other order as it sees fit.

- Appeals:

  Under s6(1) Sch 1 IPO 1994 an appeal may be made by:

  - A person entitled to vote at either of the meetings
  - A person who would have been entitled to vote at the creditors' meeting if he had had notice of it
  - The nominee

  Any appeal must be made within 28 days of the reports being made to court.

  An appeal may be made on the grounds of:

  - That the interests of a creditor, member or contributory of the partnership are unfairly prejudiced
  - That there was some material irregularity at or in relation to either of the meetings

- Effect of approval:

  The approved VA takes effect as if made by the members of the partnership at the creditors' meeting and binds every person who was entitled to vote at the meeting (whether or not he was present or represented at it) or would have been so entitled if he had had notice of it.

4.7 Powers of supervisor

The supervisor has few statutory powers, his powers will be derived from the proposal which must be detailed enough to include any powers he may need.

The following statutory powers are available:

- May apply to court for directions (s7(4) Sch 1 IPO 1994)
- May apply to court for the winding-up of the partnership as an unregistered company or for an administration order to be made in relation to the partnership
- May dispose of charged property as though it were not subject to the charge (s20 Sch 1 IPO 1994)
- Power to obtain supplies from utilities (s233)
- Power to take action in respect of transactions defrauding creditors (s423)

4.8 Duties of supervisor

If it appears to the nominee/supervisor that any past or present officer of the insolvent partnership has been guilty of any offence in connection with the moratorium or voluntary arrangement, for which the officer is criminally liable, the nominee/supervisor must (s7A(2) Sch 1 IPO 1994).

- Report the matter to the Secretary of State
- Provide the Secretary of State with such information and give him access to and facilities for inspecting and taking copies of documents

The supervisor is not required to report on the conduct of the partners under CDDA.

Records should be kept of all meetings of members and creditors.

4.9 Resignation and release

There are no statutory provisions dealing with the resignation and release of a supervisor of a PVA. The terms of the arrangement would have to be checked to ascertain the mechanism by which the supervisor may resign or be released from office. In the absence of a specific clause the supervisor would need to obtain a court order to deal with his release.

4.10 Procedure when made by liquidator or administrator

The procedure is the same as for the members however, the statement of affairs will be that already obtained in the existing proceedings and a report to court and nominee's comments are not required.

5 Priority rules

Section overview

Technically a firm cannot own property. Partnership property is simply the collective property of the partners. Each partner's estate includes their share of the firm's assets.

However, for practical reasons the IPO does distinguish between:

- The joint estate – the partnership property of an insolvent partnership
- The separate estate – the personal property of an insolvent member
- Joint debts – the debts of an insolvent partnership
- Separate debts – the debts for which a member of a partnership is liable other than the joint debts

The basic principle is that (as far as possible) joint expenses and debts are payable out of the joint estate and separate expenses and debts out of the separate estate.

5.1 Priority of debts and expenses

Step 1
Paying the expenses of winding-up the partnership and bankrupting the members

As far as possible, pay the joint expenses of winding-up out of the joint estate.

If there is a deficit apportion this unpaid balance between the separate estates of the bankrupt partners equally.

These joint expenses will rank behind the separate estate expenses but ahead of the separate estate creditors.

If any of these separate estates is unable to meet the burden of its share of the joint expenses deficit you take the unpaid balance and re-apportion it amongst the remaining partners.

Not surprisingly, the rules are the same for separate expenses. Try and pay them out of the separate estate. If there is a deficit this is now payable out of the joint estate ranking behind joint expenses but ahead of joint creditors.

Worked example: A13 Joiners

Darren, Carly and Wayne are partners in the firm of 'A13 Joiners'. The firm is being wound-up and the partners are bankrupt. After payment of winding-up expenses out of the joint estate there is a deficit of £600.

A13 Joiners

	£'000
Assets	500
Less winding-up expenses	(1,100)
	(600)

	Darren	Carly	Wayne
	£'000	£'000	£'000
Assets	850	1,000	400
Less bankruptcy expenses	(300)	(300)	(300)
Less deficit re winding-up expenses	(200)	(200)	(200)
	350	500	(100)

The deficit of £100 on Wayne's estate in respect of the balance of joint expenses will now be apportioned between Darren and Carly's estate leaving £300 and £450 respectively to meet the claims of creditors.

Note. The responsible IP can with sanction of the committee or the court pay joint and separate expenses *pari passu*.

Step 2
Paying debts of the partnership

This assumes that there is a surplus after payment of expenses.

The usual order of priority applies:

- Preferential creditors
- Ordinary unsecured creditors
- Interest on preferential and unsecured creditors
- Postponed debts
- Interest on postponed debts

If there is a surplus after payment of all debts including interest this will be distributed amongst the partners in accordance with the partnership agreement. This will increase the amount available to distribute to the separate estate creditors.

If there is a deficit the IP acting as liquidator of the firm proves for that deficit in each of the bankrupt partners' estates.

That deficit will rank equally with the separate creditors of each bankrupt partner. Notice that the whole deficit is proved for in each of the separate estates. This is NOT a breach of the rule against double proof. The liquidator is proving for the deficit in a number of estates. Double proof prevents more than one creditor from proving for the same debt in the same estate.

Worked example: Harlow New Town 'Blondes' Fitness Club'

Kylie, Shelley and Dean are partners in the Harlow New Town 'Blondes' Fitness Club – a partnership. The firm is being wound-up and the partners are bankrupt.

'Blondes' Fitness Club

	£'000
Assets	20,000
Total liabilities	(120,000)
Deficit	(100,000)

The liquidator will now prove for the £100,000 in each of the individual partner's separate estates

	Kylie	Shelly	Dean
	£'000	£'000	£'000
Assets	50,000	100,000	50,000
Liabilities			
Separate	120,000	180,000	300,000
Joint (deficit)	100,000	100,000	100,000
Total liabilities	(220,000)	(280,000)	(400,000)
Deficit	(170,000)	(180,000)	(350,000)

The outcome

Kylie pays	22.73p in the pound
Shelley pays	35.71p in the pound
Dean pays	12.50p in the pound

Note that separate and joint debts rank *pari passu*.

This much improves the position of the partnership creditors (compared to IPO 1986). Here they will receive:

	£
Partnership assets	20,000
Dividend from Kylie	22,730
Dividend from Shelley	35,710
Dividend from Dean	12,500
	90,940

ie a dividend of 75.78% (total of dividend of £90,940 divided by the total liabilities of £120,000).

Interactive question 1: Archers Limited

Sarah, Brian and Harry were partners in a clothing business which traded under the name of Archers Limited. Insolvency orders were made on the same day against the partners and against the partnership on 11 March. Jim was appointed trustee of the partners and liquidator of the partnership. All realisations have now been made and Jim wishes to distribute the estate.

Before doing so however, he shows you the following proofs of debt:

(1) A claim by Blue Jeans Ltd for £10,000 in respect of pairs of jeans sold and delivered.

(2) A claim by Surfsup Ltd for £92,000 in respect of the price of a boat sold to Harry. (Note: this sum has been jointly and severally guaranteed by Sarah and Brian).

(3) A claim by HM Revenue and Customs for £15,000 unpaid VAT on clothes sold in the 10 months before the making of the insolvency orders (representing £1,500 VAT per month).

(4) A claim by Satby Bank plc for £18,000 on a promissory note signed by Sarah, which is not due and payable for a further six months.

(5) A claim by Sarah's husband for £15,000 which he lent to her to clear her personal overdraft.

Requirement

Advise Jim how he should adjudicate on each of these proofs and also advise him in which estate they will rank for dividend.

See **Answer** at the end of this chapter.

Summary and Self-test

Summary

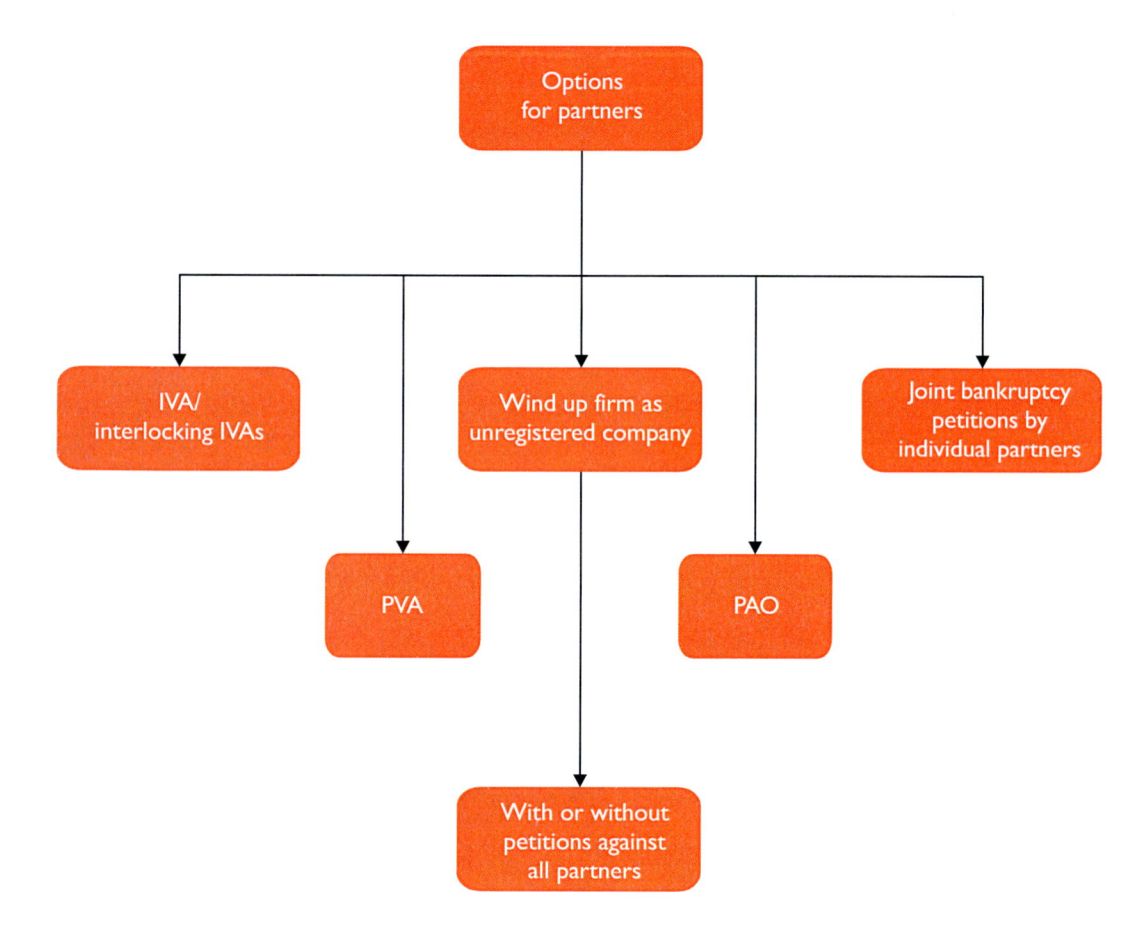

```
                    ┌─────────────────┐
                    │    Options      │
                    │   for partners  │
                    └────────┬────────┘
         ┌───────────────────┼───────────────────┐
         ▼                   ▼                   ▼
   ┌───────────┐      ┌──────────────┐    ┌──────────────┐
   │   IVA/    │      │ Wind up firm │    │   Joint      │
   │interlocking│     │ as unregistered│  │  bankruptcy  │
   │   IVAs    │      │   company    │    │ petitions by │
   └─────┬─────┘      └──────┬───────┘    │ individual   │
         │                   │            │  partners    │
         ▼                   ▼            └──────────────┘
      ┌─────┐             ┌─────┐
      │ PVA │             │ PAO │
      └─────┘             └─────┘
                             │
                             ▼
                   ┌──────────────────┐
                   │  With or without │
                   │  petitions against│
                   │   all partners   │
                   └──────────────────┘
```

Self-test

Answer the following questions.

1 What document governs the relationship between partners?
2 List the options available to a creditor of an insolvent partnership.
3 On what grounds may a partnership be wound up as an unregistered company?
4 What are the main advantages of partners presenting interlocking rather than individual IVAs?
5 Who may propose a PVA?

Now, go back to the Learning Objectives in the Introduction. If you are satisfied that you have achieved these, please tick them off.

Answers to Self-test

1   The partnership contract/(deed) or if none, the terms of the Partnership Act 1890 will apply.

2   Sue (either the firm or an individual partner) and obtain judgment on the debt.

Bankrupt one or more partners without seeking to wind up the firm.

Wind up the firm as an unregistered company without seeking to bankrupt individual partners.

Wind up firm as an unregistered company and bring concurrent petitions against one or more partners.

Petition court for a Partnership Administration Order.

3
- Inability to pay debts.
- Partnership dissolved, ceased to carry on business or is carrying on business only for the purpose of winding-up its affairs.
- Just and equitable.

4   Deals with partnership and individual assets and liabilities.

Flexible, can exclude assets.

Moratorium which should prevent legal processes against individual or partnership property.

One IP appointed, reduces costs.

More attractive to creditors as proposal could provide for:

- Partnership creditors to be paid out of firm's assets.
- Any deficit to rank equally with creditors of individual partners against separate estates.
- Claims of partners to be deferred.

Allows for continued trading of the partnership.

5
- The partners
- Administrator of a PAO
- Any liquidator of the firm

Answer to Interactive question

Interactive question 1: Archers Limited

(1) **Blue Jeans Ltd**

This would appear to be an ordinary unsecured business debt and is accordingly provable as against the estate of Archers Ltd.

(2) **Surfsup Ltd**

There is no evidence that the guarantee is secured by way of charge or mortgage and accordingly it ranks as an ordinary unsecured claim.

The primary debtor is Harry, but since there was a joint and several guarantee from Sarah and Brian, the debt is provable in the separate estates of all three partners, subject only to the proviso that the creditor is not to receive more than 100% of the amount due.

(3) **Revenue and Customs**

VAT no longer ranks as a preferential debt. Since the VAT appears to have arisen out of the carrying on of the business, it is provable as an unsecured claim against the estate of Archers Ltd.

(4) **Satby Bank plc**

This is a debt payable at a future time and Rule 11.13 provides that the debt may be proved for subject to an adjustment where the payment of the dividend is made prior to the due date for payment of the debt.

The debt should be reduced using the following formula:

$$\frac{X}{1.05^n}$$

Where x = amount of the debt due

n = decimalised amount of time from the date of the bankruptcy order to the date the debt is due.

This debt would rank in Sarah's estate (as signatory) unless it is shown that the debt incurred was in the ordinary course of the partnership's business in which case it would rank in the estate of Archers Ltd.

(5) **Sarah's husband**

Under s329 debts owed by the bankrupt to a person who (whether or not the bankrupt's spouse at the time the credit was provided) was the bankrupt's spouse at the commencement of bankruptcy, are admissible to rank for dividend after preferential and ordinary and unsecured debts and after interest has been paid on such debts under s328 out of any surplus funds. Interest will be payable on the husband's claim equally with the amount of the principal sum due.

The claim will rank in the separate estate of Sarah.

CHAPTER 33

Administration of the estates of deceased insolvents

Introduction
Topic List
1 Administration of the estates of insolvent deceased individuals
2 Death of existing bankrupt
Self-test
Answers to Self-test

Introduction

Learning objectives

- Understand how to deal with the estate of an insolvent deceased individual
- Understand how the death of a debtor affects an existing bankruptcy or IVA

Tick off

Stop and think

Why are the debts of an individual not cancelled upon their death? How does the death of a debtor affect a voluntary arrangement?

Working context

You may be asked to deal with the estate of an insolvent deceased individual it is important therefore to have an understanding of how such an estate should be dealt with.

1 Administration of the estates of insolvent deceased individuals

Section overview

It is a common misconception that when a person dies his debts are automatically discharged. Debts are not discharged upon death unless specific provision has been made for them to be discharged eg by an insurance policy. All debts that are not provided for must be met from the assets of the deceased debtor. Where the assets are insufficient to meet all the debts, the estate is insolvent.

This area is governed by the Administration of Insolvent Estates of Deceased Persons Order 1986 – referred to here as 'DPO 1986' for ease of reference.

The purpose of DPO 1986 is to modify the IA 1986 in respect of insolvent estates. In the event of any conflict between the two the DPO 1986 prevails.

The DPO 1986 applies whether an existing bankrupt dies or where following the death of a person it is revealed that his estate is insolvent. Either way the estate must be administered for the benefit of the estate creditors and not the beneficiaries of any will or intestacy.

1.1 Insolvent estate

Where a person dies before the presentation of a bankruptcy petition and it is found that the estate is insolvent the provisions of any will made relating to beneficiaries do not apply. The estate should be administered under the provisions of the DPO 1986 and s421 IA 86. The following table sets out the difference in terminology between the IA 86 and DPO 86.

IA 86 references	DPO 1986 modifications
The bankrupt, the debtor	The deceased debtor or his personal representatives
The bankrupt's estate	The deceased debtor's estate
The commencement of bankruptcy	The date of the insolvency administration
A bankruptcy order	An insolvency administration order
An individual being adjudged bankrupt	An insolvency administration order being made
A debtor's petition	A petition by the personal representatives of a deceased debtor for an insolvency administration

1.2 Insolvency administration order (IAO)

Although it is possible to deal with an insolvent estate without an IAO it is usual for a petition to be lodged in all but the simplest of cases.

Definitions

Insolvency administration order: an order for the administration in bankruptcy of the insolvent estate of a deceased debtor.

Insolvency administration petition: a petition for an IAO.

The following persons may apply for an IPO:

- Personal representatives (PR) on the grounds that the deceased is insolvent. This will be shown by a statement of affairs. If the court is satisfied as to the deceased's insolvency it must make the order.

- Creditors (or supervisor of an IVA) in relation to the deceased on the ground that the estate is insolvent. Conditions for presentation are that:

- The debtor must have owed the petitioning creditor a debt/debts of at least £750
- The debt must be for a liquidated amount
- The debt must be unsecured

The court may make the order if it is satisfied that the debt is due and owing or there is no reasonable prospects of it being paid when it falls due AND there is a 'reasonable probability' that the estate will be insolvent. The petition must be served on the PR.

1.3 Interim receiver

If necessary for the protection of the deceased's property the court can appoint the OR as interim receiver prior to the appointment of the trustee.

The OR's duties may be restricted by the order appointing him. The OR, as interim receiver, will have all the powers and duties of a receiver and manager. The PR has a duty to co-operate with the interim receiver and to provide details of the assets which should be taken into immediate possession pending the hearing of the petition.

1.4 Effect of the administration order

The OR is appointed receiver and manager of the deceased's estate. Control of the estate passes from the PR to the OR.

On receipt of the IAO the OR should contact the deceased debtor's PR as soon as possible. The PR is either:

- The person(s) named as executor in the deceased debtor's will with the responsibility of administering the estate of the deceased; or
- Where the deceased debtor dies without making a will (intestate), a person who is known as the administrator, who is granted letters of administration by a court of probate.

Where there is no PR or administrator, the OR should contact the closest surviving relative of the deceased debtor.

The PR (or other such person as the court may direct) is required to submit to the OR, within 56 days of the IAO being made, a statement of affairs. The statement of affairs should contain both the position at the date of death and at the making of the IAO and should be completed on Form SADI.

The PR owes a number of duties to the OR.

- Notify the OR of any assets which may be claimed for the estate by the trustee
- Provide an inventory of the estate to the OR
- Attend on the OR as reasonably required
- Provide information regarding the assets, liabilities and affairs of the deceased debtor

Failure to comply may be a contempt of court. The OR may apply to the court for the PR to be privately examined if he does not comply with his obligations.

The PR may not dispose of estate assets once they have received notice of the petition without leave of the court (s284 IA as modified by DPO 1986 Sch 1). A *bona fide* purchaser for value, without notice, is however protected.

If there are sufficient assets a trustee may subsequently be appointed in much the same way as if the bankrupt was not deceased. The OR should call a meeting of creditors, however the notices and forms sent out should be amended to make it clear that the meeting relates to the IAO and not to a bankruptcy order. The proof of debt forms should show the date of death as being the date to which claims should be made.

1.5 Items excluded from the estate

s283(2) IA 86 is modified by DPO 1986 Article 3 so that the only personal and household effects that are excluded from the estate are those belonging to the family of the deceased. The trustee can claim items of excess value and after acquired property (from death) as per bankruptcy.

1.6 Deceased persons home

When dealing with the home similar considerations apply as in normal bankruptcy. As mentioned in Chapter 24 where property is held as joint tenants (as opposed to tenants in common) on the death of one joint tenant that persons share of the property passes automatically to the surviving joint tenant by **the right of survivorship**. Hence where a IAO is made after death that asset is no longer part of the deceased bankrupt's estate. However although the deceased's share of the home is no longer vested in him at death, s421A IA 86 enables a trustee to apply to court for an order that a surviving joint tenant pay an amount equivalent to the deceased's share of the property to the trustee for the benefit of the estate.

The court is not compelled to make the order and must have regard to all the circumstances of the case including the interests of the creditors and surviving tenant(s) (co-owners). The court may therefore make such order as it thinks fit.

1.7 Investigation of the deceased's affairs/conduct

The OR is not under any duty to investigate the conduct or affairs of the deceased debtor but may if he thinks fit report to the court on the activities of the deceased debtor (s289 IA 86 as amended by DPO 1986 Article 3).

1.8 Antecedent transactions

The trustee can investigate antecedent transactions. The only way in which the rules on antecedents different in respect of a deceased bankrupt is that the relevant time (as per s341 IA 86) is now assessed up to the date of death of the deceased debtor rather than the date of the presentation of the petition (Article 3 DPO 1986).

1.9 Potential criminal offence under DPO 1986

Pursuant to Article 3 DPO 1986 a third party is guilty of an offence if, in the 12 months before the date of the death of the deceased he acquired or received property from the deceased knowing or believing that the deceased debtor owed money in respect of the property and did not intend, or was unlikely to be able, to repay it (s359(2)).

It is a defence to such a charge that the acquisition or receipt of property was in the ordinary course of business.

The price paid for the property will be taken into account.

1.10 Control of trustee

As in bankruptcy the creditors may form a committee for the control of the trustee. In addition, s303 (as modified) applies, hence the trustee is subject to the general control of the court.

1.11 Creditors' claims

The same rules apply as in bankruptcy.

1.12 Order of priority

As per bankruptcy – the relevant date for preferential creditors and interest is the date of death.

The trustee must however have regard to any claim by the PR for reasonable funeral, testamentary and administrative expenses in dealing with the estate. If the trustee is in funds these claims will be paid out in priority to the remaining debts.

Any surplus is returned to the PR.

1.13 Rules re distribution of the estate

As per bankruptcy.

2 Effect of Death on insolvency process

> **Section overview**
> - Section 5 of DPO governs the position where the debtor dies following the making of a bankruptcy order or after presentation of a bankruptcy petition.
> - We also consider what happens to an individual voluntary arrangement when the the debtor dies.

2.1 Death of existing bankrupt

The administration of the estate continues as if the bankrupt were alive (s5(1) DPO 1986). The reasonable funeral and testamentary expenses of the PR have priority to preferential debts.

2.2 Death of debtor after presentation of bankruptcy petition

Although the court can order otherwise the proceedings continue as if the debtor were still alive (s5(3) DPO 1986).

If an order is made by the court it is a bankruptcy order and is administered accordingly with some necessary modifications. The deceased debtor's PR (or other appropriate person) is required to complete the statement of affairs.

Where a deceased debtor owned property under a joint tenancy and died after a bankruptcy petition was presented but before a bankruptcy order was made, the deceased debtor's interest in the property passes to the surviving tenant and does not form part of the estate. s421A IA does not apply in this case and the value lost to the estate cannot be recovered.

The reasonable funeral and testamentary expenses relating to the deceased debtor have priority over preferential debts but notice of these expenses must be communicated to the trustee.

2.3 Effect of death on voluntary arrangements

As the debtor will be insolvent at the time of death DPO 1986 will apply with the estate being administered for the benefit of the deceased creditors.

If a debtor dies pre-approval by the creditors' meeting, the proposed arrangement is brought to an end. The nominee must notify the court of the death and any interim order will be cancelled (as will any creditor's meeting already scheduled).

If a debtor dies post approval of an IVA:

- **Post creditors' meeting, pre report to court**

    Although IVAs normally take effect as at the date of the creditors' meeting (and not the date of the chair's report to court) the DPO 1986 brings the IVA to an end where death occurs post meeting but pre report to court.

- **Post report to court**

    Whether or not the IVA continues depends upon the terms of the arrangement and whether or not death will result in failure. The proposal should also deal with the effect of such failure (see *NT Gallgher*).

Self-test

Answer the following questions.

1. Under the Administration of Insolvent Estates of Deceased Persons Order 1986, who may present a petition for an Insolvency Administration Order?

2. Under what grounds may an Insolvency Administration Order be applied for by a personal representative?

3. What is the effect of an Insolvency Administration Order being made?

4. What duty does the OR have to investigate the conduct or affairs of the deceased debtor?

5. How is the bankruptcy of a debtor affected if they die prior to discharge?

Now, go back to the Learning Objectives in the Introduction. If you are satisfied that you have achieved these, please tick them off.

Answers to Self-test

1. The personal representatives of the deceased.
   His creditors.
   Supervisor/creditor of an IVA.

2. Only on grounds of inability to pay debts.

3. OR is appointed receiver and manager of the deceased's estate.

   An interim receiver may be appointed if necessary.

   Personal representatives must submit a statement of affairs to the OR.

   Personal representatives must deliver up all books, papers and records in relation to the insolvent estate that are within their control.

   All dispositions of property following the death of the debtor are void unless permitted by the court.

4. OR has no duty to investigate but he may, if he thinks fit, report to the court on the activities of the deceased debtor.

5. The administration of the estate continues as if the bankrupt were alive. Reasonable funeral expenses incurred by the personal representatives may be paid in priority to the preferential creditors.

Index

A

Administration, 217
Administrative receiver, 267, 272
Administrator, 217
Adopt, 297
Appendix D of SIP 9, 41
Associate, 143
Atlantic Computers, 247
Avoidance of floating charges, 144

B

Balance sheet test, 126
Bodies involved in the administration of the insolvency regime, 9
Book value, 72
Business turnaround and restructuring, 17

C

Certificate of due constitution, 117
Commencement, 157, 371
Commercial insolvency test, 126
Companies House, 10
Company Directors Disqualification Act 1986, 96
Company Voluntary Arrangements, 197
Completion, 374
Compulsory liquidation, 125
Connected party transactions, 99
Connected person, 143
Contributory, 110
Convener, 357
Creditors committee, 116, 285
Creditors' voluntary liquidation, 113

D

D1 report, 97
D2 return, 97
Debt, 169
Declaration of dividend, 176
Declaration of solvency, 111
Deficiency account, 75
Director's general duties to the company, 94
Discounts, 172
Disqualification order, 97
Disqualification undertakings, 98
Dissolution, 510
Distinction between legal and non-legal rules, 5
Double proof, 173
Duties on vacating office, 188

E

Electronic delivery of documents, 34
Entity, 52
Estimated Outcome Statements, 77

Estimated realisable value, 72
Execution, 156
Exit routes, 257
Extortionate credit transaction, 144

F

Factoring, 21
Final meetings, 188
Financial restructuring, 21
Fixed charge receiver, 267, 272
Foreign tax, 173
Fraudulent trading, 144
Future debts, 173

G

General penalty bond, 56

I

In specie distribution, 411
Inability to pay debts, 125
Insolvency administration order, 527
Insolvency administration petition, 527
Insolvency Practitioners (IP), 10
Insolvency Service, 9
Intention to declare, 176
Interest, 171
Interim receiver, 528
Interlocking IVAs, 513
IP Record, 32, 348

J

Joint Insolvency Committee, 10
Just and equitable, 125

L

Liability, 169
Liquidation committee, 116
Liquidators' investigations, 141
London Rules/Approach, 21
LPA receiver, 268, 271, 272

M

Members voluntary liquidation, 110
Moratorium, 205

N

Negotiable instruments, 173
Nominee, 198

O

Occupation rent, 389

Official Receiver, 9, 130, 141
Onerous property, 161, 406

P

Partnership, 509
Partnership Administration Order, 513
Partnership Voluntary Arrangement, 514
Payor, 373
Powers, 109
Preferences, 143
Preferential creditors, 69, 175
Priority of payments, 257
Prohibited name, 95
Proof, 169
Proof of debt, 170
Property, 371
Prove, 169
Provisional liquidator, 127
Proxy form, 171, 203
Public examination, 130

R

Reasonable, 372
Recognised professional bodies, 10
Release, 188
Relevant time periods, 145
Removal, 187
Remuneration and expenses, 36
Rent, 174
Resignation, 187
Risks to directors of insolvent companies, 94
Role of the turnaround practitioner, 18, 19

S

s313 charging order, 392
Sanction, 109

Secretary of State, 9
Secured creditors, 173
Service charge, 174
Set-off, 174
SIP 2, 141
SIP 4, 97
SIP 12, 35
SIP 13, 98
Small company moratorium, 198
Special manager, 131
Special resolution, 110, 111
Specific penalty bond, 56
Statement of Affairs, 72, 282
Statutory demand, 125
Substantial property transactions, 99
Supervisor, 198

T

The courts, 10
The London Gazette, 10
Things in action, 371
Transaction, 143
Transaction at an undervalue, 143
Transactions defrauding creditors, 379
Types of director, 67, 93

V

Voidable transactions, 142
Voluntary liquidation, 109

W

Winding up order, 128

Notes

Notes